ONE WEEK LOAN

The SAGE Handbook of
Intercultural Competence

To my father
(Rev. Harold I. Bowman, 1943-2008)

The SAGE Handbook of
Intercultural
Competence

Edited by
Darla K. Deardorff
Duke University

Foreword by
Derek Bok
Harvard University

Los Angeles | London | New Delhi
Singapore | Washington DC

For information:

SAGE Publications, Inc.
2455 Teller Road
Thousand Oaks,
  California 91320
E-mail: order@sagepub.com

SAGE Publications India Pvt. Ltd.
B 1/I 1 Mohan Cooperative
  Industrial Area
Mathura Road, New Delhi 110 044
India

SAGE Publications Ltd.
1 Oliver's Yard
55 City Road
London EC1Y 1SP
United Kingdom

SAGE Publications
  Asia-Pacific Pte. Ltd.
33 Pekin Street #02-01
Far East Square
Singapore 048763

Printed in the United States of America

Library of Congress Cataloging-in-Publication Data

The SAGE handbook of intercultural competence / edited by Darla K. Deardorff.
   p. cm.
Includes bibliographical references and index.
ISBN 978-1-4129-6045-8 (cloth)
   1. Intercultural communication. 2. Cultural pluralism. I. Deardorff, Darla K.

HM1211.S24 2009
303.48¢209051—dc22   2009006546

This book is printed on acid-free paper.

09 10 11 12 13   10 9 8 7 6 5 4 3 2 1

Acquisitions Editor:	Todd R. Armstrong
Editorial Assistant:	Aja Baker
Production Editor:	Astrid Virding
Copy Editor:	Gillian Dickens
Typesetter:	C&M Digitals (P) Ltd.
Proofreader:	Dennis W. Webb
Indexer:	Ellen Slavitz
Cover Designer:	Arup Giri
Marketing Manager:	Jennifer Reed Banando

Contents

Acknowledgments

Deep gratitude is expressed first and foremost to the contributors of this handbook. The contributors made this handbook such a pleasure to edit, and without them, this resource would not be possible. It was indeed an honor to work with them. A special thank you goes to Peggy Pusch for her guidance on the initial project and to those who enthusiastically supported the conceptualization of this project, including the late Bob Kohls, Janet Bennett, Michael Paige, and Brian Spitzberg. I also appreciate the assistance of SAGE editor Todd Armstrong and the SAGE editorial staff for answering my many questions and for providing such wonderful support throughout the process. Many thanks to initial reviewers as well as to colleagues who reviewed chapters of this handbook, including Luis Rivera, Susan Buck Sutton, and Alan Dupont. Above all, I am immensely grateful to my family and especially my husband, Duane Deardorff, for his enormous patience, perseverance, encouragement—and most of all—his unwavering support.

Dr. Darla K. Deardorff
Durham, NC, USA

Reviewer List

Lily A. Arasaratnam (Macquarie University, Sydney Australia)

Mark A. Ashwill (Institute of International Education-Vietnam)

Michael Byram (University of Durham, England)

Prue Holmes (Waikato Management School, University of Waikato)

Young Yun Kim (University of Oklahoma)

Barbara Kappler Mikk (University of Minnesota)

R. Michael Paige (University of Minnesota)

Mark V. Redmond (Iowa State University)

Melissa A. Rychener (Slippery Rock University)

Foreword

Every serious account of the major forces transforming our world today includes the word *globalization*. Of course, much of what we mean by globalization is largely a continuation of trends and practices that were evident long before the 21st century. Yet there are aspects of today's world that seem different enough, or at least accentuated enough, to make our situation seem different from what has gone before.

For one thing, modern communication has developed to a point that it is possible to collaborate more effectively than ever before with people anywhere in the world. Thanks to the Internet and teleconferencing, scientists as far away as Russia and China are being hired to do applied research with colleagues in corporate laboratories here in the United States. Polish doctors can analyze CAT scans for hospitals located in New York City. College graduates in Bangalore prepare the tax returns for hundreds of thousands of Americans every year.

High-speed travel greatly increases personal contact across national borders. Jet airplanes allow business executives to visit multiple countries in Asia during a single week to seek new orders, create joint ventures, or consult about common problems. International meetings of all kinds—for public officials, professors, doctors, and many others—have multiplied in number. Tourism has expanded tremendously, bringing ever greater numbers of foreign nationals to the United States while sending mounting numbers of Americans to other nations and cultures the world over.

More and more people, especially from poorer countries, are moving to search for jobs and success in more prosperous parts of the world. In 2002, the number of persons living in countries other than their land of birth reached 175 million, more than double the number in 1975. The United States has been experiencing a huge influx of immigrants not only from Latin America and the Caribbean but from Asia as well. As a result, the United States is fast becoming a nation of minorities in which no group, including Whites, will be able to claim a majority of the population.

These developments have created a more urgent need than ever before for Americans to develop intercultural understanding and an ability to live and work productively and harmoniously with people having very different values, backgrounds, and habits. As James Duderstadt, former president of the University of Michigan, has put it, "Understanding cultures other than our own has become necessary not only for personal enrichment and good citizenship but for our very survival as a nation."

Nowhere is this need felt more keenly than in educational institutions, which must play a central role in helping prepare younger generations for the cosmopolitan world that awaits them, a world in which they are bound to interaction with foreign nationals and different ethnic groups and feel the influence of different values and cultures on a scale unequalled in previous generations. The magnitude of this challenge is surely one reason why a seasoned observer such as Peter Scott, long-time editor of the *Times Higher Education Supplement*, would assert that "globalization is perhaps the most fundamental challenge faced by the university in its long history."

Fortunately, educators do not start from scratch in coping with this challenge. Students in many public schools and almost all colleges and universities in the United States have been highly diverse for many years. Not only do these institutions have long experience with welcoming students from abroad; they, along with many schools, have also included in their student bodies many young people from ethnic minority groups who have different values and life experiences and often speak another language at home. Such diversity, albeit among fellow Americans, presents challenges not unlike those involving immigrants and visitors from foreign lands.

Educational institutions in the United States also possess many of the ingredients that can almost certainly play a useful role in developing intercultural competence. Schools and colleges have foreign language classes and courses on world history. Colleges have highly trained faculty who specialize in teaching about the history, literature, and political institutions of other countries. Most colleges have even offered over many years a variety of programs for study abroad.

Despite these invaluable resources, educators are still far from understanding how to develop intercultural competence. Many questions remain unanswered. In our colleges, for example, how can we give students such competence amid all the other competing purposes that an undergraduate education is supposed to fulfill? What should we do about teaching foreign languages when few of our students can predict what languages they will need in later life, and precious little time is available to build even a rudimentary competence in a single language? What can we usefully teach about other cultures when students rarely know which countries they may eventually live in or which will eventually prove important to their lives and careers? How can we integrate foreign students fully into the residential and extracurricular life of our universities where they are most likely to learn how to live and work effectively with one another? Above all, how can we figure out how to impart something as subtle and intangible as "intercultural competence"? Do we even know what the term really means?

Amid these many vexing questions, one thing is clear. We will never succeed in finding answers unless those actively engaged with these questions talk seriously with one another and help others learn from the insights and wisdom accumulated during years of experience. That is the guiding purpose behind the collection of essays that fill this handbook—to start a conversation, share experience, sharpen perceptions, and thereby speed the learning process for all who have an interest in this urgent issue of intercultural competence and a stake in its solution. Nothing could be more welcome or more timely for teachers and educators everywhere.

Derek Bok
Harvard University

Preface

We must learn to live together as brothers or perish together as fools.

Martin Luther King, Jr.

Wat is intercultural competence? This was the driving question behind my dissertation research in the early part of this millennium that brought together leading intercultural experts, primarily in the United States, to reach a consensus definition of intercultural competence, from which two models were developed (Deardorff, 2006). In the course of my research, I saw a need for a comprehensive volume that would address this very question. Scholars have written on this topic for over five decades. This is the first comprehensive volume that brings together those voices from a variety of cultures and fields to discuss this complex concept of intercultural competence. As Derek Bok noted in the Foreword for this handbook, the guiding purpose of this text is to bring together this experience in an effort to further conversations and "sharpen perceptions" on this crucial topic for the 21st century.

Specifically, the goals of this volume include providing the reader with a broader context for intercultural competence, offering the reader more practical knowledge on how intercultural competence is manifested and developed in specific fields as well as to offer practical guidance on researching and assessing this elusive concept. By bringing together the leading voices on this concept and synthesizing some of the latest work on intercultural competence, this interdisciplinary book is intended to be a useful resource for many students, faculty, administrators, and professionals in a variety of fields. It is intended to be used in a range of advanced undergraduate and graduate courses in different disciplines, most specifically in advanced courses in cross-cultural communication. This volume seeks to address cutting-edge issues by providing a concrete resource for practical application and assessment of intercultural competence, broadly defined as appropriate and effective communication and behavior in intercultural situations, although many more detailed definitions and models are provided in the text itself. As such, it can be of use not only to faculty and students but also to business professionals, senior-level postsecondary administrators, study abroad advisers, second-language acquisition instructors, public school teachers, and cross-cultural trainers.

This handbook is divided into three sections. The first section is conceptual and addresses the theoretical frameworks of this concept as well as ways in which intercultural competence is viewed from a variety of different cultural perspectives, including African, Arab, Chinese, Indian, and Latin American perspectives. This section begins with a comprehensive review of over 20 definitions and models of intercultural competence, primarily from Western perspectives. This is then followed by several chapters that explore such questions as the role of identity in intercultural competence that is often considered as core to this concept (Magala, 2005), the intersection of leadership and intercultural competence, the role of trust in this concept, the process-nature of intercultural competence development, and the different approaches to resolving intercultural conflicts as part of intercultural competence. This section concludes with numerous chapters specifically written from different cultural perspectives. While it is not possible for a few scholars to speak for entire groups of people, these chapters provide insights into how this concept may be viewed from other culturally conditioned perspectives. The importance of seeing from others' perspectives is a key aspect of intercultural competence, and thus the inclusion and understanding of other cultural perspectives is fundamental as we seek to comprehend more fully what it means to relate successfully with those from other cultures. In reading the chapters in this first section of the handbook, readers are encouraged to look for common themes that emerge from these various perspectives, to explore questions that may arise from these readings, and to dialogue with colleagues in an effort to sharpen our perceptions around this complex concept.

The reality of the 21st-century workforce is that workers from many different cultures interact and work together, regardless of their location. The second section addresses the applications of intercultural competence in a variety of fields, including education, business, engineering, social work, health care, and even within religious organizations. There are, of course, many other fields that could have been included in this section, such as tourism or policing or the military. The challenge for the reader is to explore what intercultural competence means in these and other fields. What does an interculturally competent worker "look like" in a particular field? For example, the specific intercultural skills and knowledge needed for a globally competent engineer are somewhat different than those needed for a culturally competent health care worker. In diverse societies, teachers must be trained to know how to teach and work with students from many different cultural backgrounds, in order for those students to in turn become more interculturally competent in today's world. Thus, this section strives to put some of the more theoretical and abstract concepts into practical realities of the different fields. One caveat about the chapters in this second section: These chapters are written from a primarily U.S. perspective, based on the fields as they have developed within the United States.

So how do we know if someone is interculturally competent? What are the best ways to assess and research this concept in others? Assessing intercultural competence is highly complex in that it involves not only the individuals' perspective but also that of others to truly assess the *appropriateness* of the behavior and communication. The third section of this handbook provides several chapters that discuss research and assessment methodologies as well as some of the practical applications of such research and assessment. Numerous research topics related to more in-depth study of intercultural competence and its assessment are suggested for further exploration. It is hoped that readers will use the experience and knowledge found in these chapters to hone understanding of this concept.

Based on my research on this topic, here are some concluding thoughts about intercultural competence as you prepare to delve into this handbook: Derek Bok, in his book *Our Underachieving Colleges* (2006), notes the crucial need for students to "think interculturally"—that knowledge alone is not sufficient. Furthermore, language alone may be necessary but not sufficient for intercultural competence. In fact, two studies found that experts could not reach consensus on the role of language in intercultural competence (Deardorff, 2006; Hunter, White, & Godbey, 2006), implying that language by itself does not make one interculturally competent. In education, the focus naturally tends to be on knowledge—history, literature, language, music, and so on—the products of a culture, sometimes referred to as "objective culture." While such products provide valuable windows into understanding a culture, such knowledge is not sufficient in developing one's intercultural competence—in helping one to think, behave, and communicate interculturally. Thus, within education, there is an urgent need to address "subjective culture" (Triandis, 1994)—to provide learners with the foundations, frameworks, skills, and knowledge to develop an understanding of underlying cultural values, communication styles, and worldviews to better understand others' behaviors to interact effectively and appropriately with others and, ultimately, to become more interculturally competent.

Intercultural experience alone is not enough; it is not enough to send someone into another culture for study or work and expect him or her to return interculturally competent. Mere contact is not sufficient to develop intercultural competence, as Allport (1954) noted so long ago. Building authentic relationships, however, is key in this cultural learning process—through observing, listening, and asking those who are from different backgrounds to teach, to share, to enter into dialogue together about relevant needs and issues. Respect and trust become essential building blocks in developing these authentic relationships from which to learn from each other. Research (Savicki, 2008) has shown that adequate preparation is necessary to learners' intercultural competence development, especially prior to intercultural experiences such as an international work assignment or education abroad. Intercultural competence doesn't just happen; if it did, there would be far fewer cross-cultural misunderstandings. Rather, we must be intentional about developing learners' intercultural competence. Such development can occur through adequate preparation, substantive intercultural interactions, and relationship building.

Intercultural competence is a lifelong process; there is no pinnacle at which someone becomes "interculturally competent." Given the lifelong learning inherent in intercultural competence development, therefore, it is imperative that learners regularly engage in reflective practice in regard to their own development in this area (Deardorff, 2006; Yershova, DeJaeghere, & Mestenhauser, 2000). Moreover, one single workshop or course, while a possible start in framing some of the issues, is not sufficient in this development process; rather, the integration of aspects of intercultural competence must be addressed throughout one's education and professional development. For schools, this may mean revisiting the overall curriculum in an effort to determine how to incorporate aspects of intercultural competence—such as other worldviews—into the whole of the curriculum. This also necessitates instructors being adequately prepared to guide learners in this development process, meaning that instructors themselves need to understand more fully the concept of intercultural competence.

It is hoped that this handbook provides some of the foundation and frameworks for developing learners' intercultural competence and serves as a springboard for continuing vital dialogue and research on this crucial concept. Seeking to understand each other better and to interact more successfully—and peacefully—with each other are essential as we address the pressing human needs and issues across cultures—together. Our very survival depends on this. In the words of Martin Luther King, Jr., "We must learn to live together as brothers or perish together as fools."

References

Allport, G. W. (1954). *The nature of prejudice.* Cambridge, MA: Addison-Wesley.

Bok, D. (2006). *Our underachieving colleges: A candid look at how much students learn and why they should be learning more.* Princeton, NJ: Princeton University Press.

Deardorff, D. K. (2006). The identification and assessment of intercultural competence. *Journal of Studies in International Education, 10,* 241–266.

Hunter, W., White, G. P., & Godbey, G. C. (2006). What does it mean to be globally competent? *Journal of Studies in International Education, 10,* 267–285.

Magala, S. (2005). *Cross-cultural competence.* London: Routledge.

Savicki, V. (2008). *Developing intercultural competence and transformation: Theory, research, and application in international education.* Sterling, VA: Stylus.

Triandis, H. C. (1994). *Culture and social behavior.* New York: McGraw-Hill.

Yershova, Y., DeJaeghere, D., & Mestenhauser, J. (2000). Thinking not as usual: Adding the intercultural perspective. *Journal of Studies in International Education, 4,* 39–78.

PART I

Conceptualizing Intercultural Competence

CHAPTER 1

Conceptualizing Intercultural Competence

Brian H. Spitzberg and Gabrielle Changnon

The *Genesis* narrative of the Tower of Babel tells of a time when all people of the earth were of one language, or one speech. Their ambition to reach the heavens through machinations of their own design led to their scattering and confounding of languages and lands. As long ago as only 500 years, "humans spoke 14,000 languages. Today, that number is below 7,000, and 40 percent of the world's population speaks one of only eight languages. In 2008, we will lose between 20 and 30 languages" (*Seed: Science and Culture*, January/February 2008, p. 65). Whereas a world of one people and one speech is unlikely in any imminently foreseeable future, the objective of finding common purpose through mutually coordinated communication across cultures and languages continues to be a goal of many if not most people, organizations, and nations. In pursuing such objectives, scholars have been endeavoring not only to understand the nature of competence in native communication but also to extend such conceptions to the requisite adaptations across cultural contexts. If conceptualizing communication competence is difficult *within* a given culture, the challenge is clearly multiplied when extending such concepts across distinct cultural milieus. This chapter intends to review selective models of intercultural communication competence that have been proffered, with an eye toward identifying (a) common themes and distinct emphases that may assist in directing future efforts for integrative theorizing, (b) conceptual pathways that have been relatively overlooked, and (c) ideological presumptions that may need reevaluation in the formulation of future models. It is taken for granted that a single chapter cannot possibly either do justice to the models reviewed or be comprehensive in its representation of the breadth and depth of models available for analysis. Thus, this chapter should be viewed more as an attempt to provide a heuristic theoretical analysis. There are many excellent reviews of cultural (Tyler, 2001), communication (Rickheit, Strohner, &

Vorwerg, 2008; Spitzberg & Cupach, 2002), and intercultural (see, e.g., Arasaratnam, 2007; Arasaratnam & Doerfel, 2005; Dinges & Baldwin, 1996; Hammer, 1989; Lustig & Spitzberg, 1993; Luszczynska, Gutiérrez-Doña, & Martin, 1993; Rathje, 2007; Spitzberg, 1989) competence available for the interested reader. With some illustrative exceptions, models of intercultural communication competence designed for specific contexts (e.g., educational: Anderson, Lawton, Rexeisen, & Hubbard, 2006; Heyward, 2002; Kayes, Kayes, & Yamazaki, 2005; Milhouse, 1996; sales or service: Chaisrakeo & Speece, 2004; Hopkins, Hopkins, & Hoffman, 2005; conflict: Euwema & Van Emmerik, 2007; Hammer, 2005; Ting-Toomey, 1988, 2007; health care: Gibson & Zhong, 2005; counseling: Li, Kim, & O'Brien, 2007; Sue, 2001; international adjustment: Bhaskar-Shrinivas, Harrison, Shaffer, & Luk, 2005; B. K. Lee & Chen, 2000; immigrant: Bourhis, Moïse, Perreault, & Senécal, 1997; organizations/management: Fisher & Härtel, 2003; Torbiörn, 1985; Valentine & Yunxia, 2001) are excluded from this review in order to focus on some of the more foundational models in the field. Investigations directed primarily to measurement development rather than model development are also excluded (e.g., Gamst et al., 2004; Hammer, Bennett, & Wiseman, 2003; Lapinski & Orbe, 2007; Prechtl & Lund, 2007; Sheu & Lent, 2007). There is little doubt as well that some important models will be missed inadvertently in the process of review. Most of the theories and models reviewed were selected due to their importance to the field, evidenced by the existence of multiple citations referencing them, although in other instances, models were selected for purely illustrative purposes of a given type of model or set of components.

To pursue a reasonable review of conceptualizations of intercultural communication competence, several steps are undertaken. First, the rationale for conceptualizing the phenomenon at all is briefly examined. Second, several theoretical issues relevant to models and modeling are established, including the formulation of some basic terms, classifications, and selection criteria. Third, a brief history of the concept is provided. Fourth, a synoptic review of selective theories and models of intercultural communication competence is undertaken, with emphasis on the visual representation of these models, some of which are taken directly from researchers and others that have been envisioned by the authors of this chapter. It is proposed that the ability to translate theories and approaches to intercultural communication competence into a visual grammar involves its own theoretical rigor and helps identify key intersections of perspectives that are often missed in purely narrative readings. Fifth, given the catalog of models, a critical review is undertaken of the state of the art of conceptualizing intercultural communication competence. It is important to note that this discussion is provided from a Western perspective and thus highlights the development and evolution of intercultural competence primarily in Anglo cultures.

The Importance of Intercultural Competence

According to the U.S. Census Bureau, in 2006 the United States accounted for $910 billion in exports, controlling 88% of the total value of exported goods worldwide (www.census.gov). This extensive amount of exports provides an important explanation as to why, in an ever globalizing society, intercultural communication competence is necessary. To compete globally, persons must be equipped with the knowledge and skills to behave in a manner becoming to a specific culture (Committee for Economic Development, 2006). Inevitably, cultural diversity will manifest within the global marketplace, making intercultural competence an extremely important skill. The ability to manage the interconnectedness of the diversity that is created is a major skill employers seek (Bremer, 2006; Deardorff & Hunter, 2006; Hulstrand, 2008). The ability to relate to and with people from vastly different cultural and ethnic backgrounds is an increasingly important competency both domestically and abroad (Lustig, 2005). Large companies such as Nike adopt cultural diversity as part of company policy, in a sense requiring employers to be interculturally competent. One way to receive this preparation is through the further development and expansion of college students studying abroad.

Currently, there are more than 200,000 U.S. students annually traversing countries and studying abroad (http://travel.state.gov). These numbers unfortunately only equate to about 1% of all students attending colleges and universities (Ashwill, 2004). In the 1998 American Council on Education (ACE) report, it was concluded that less than 7% of students in higher education are achieving basic standards of global preparedness (cited in Hunter, White, & Godbey, 2006). However, U.S. officials want this number to increase and believe there is a great need for increased support for students to be able to study abroad (Herrin, 2004).

Not only is it important for these students to learn about other cultures, but it is also important to produce competent American citizens to teach others about our cultural views. With the current political situations around the world, it is vital that nation-states recognize what one another has to offer politically, socially, and culturally in the form of collaborative interaction (Ashwill, 2004; Herrin, 2004). In recognition of these kinds of stakes, a study published in College Learning for the New Global Century indicated that 46% of employers believe colleges should place more emphasis on proficiency in a foreign language, and 56% think more emphasis should be placed on the establishment of cultural values and traditions in the United States and other countries (National Leadership Council, 2007).

With ample opportunities for employment overseas, it becomes important for internationally competitive business to hire interculturally competent employees, if only for the future success of the business. In one study conducted in a Japanese industry, the lack of intercultural communication competence on the part of one expatriate employee led to a 98% loss of the company's market share to a different competitor (Tung, 1987). Another study of 80 U.S. multinational companies found that between 10% and 20% of the expatriates "failed," in essence being unable to perform effectively in a foreign country, leading to termination or reassignment (Tung, 1987). This failure not only damages a business financially but could also damage an employer's public face, resulting in long-term damage to the company.

Beyond the need to be competitive in a globalized society, people are traveling abroad in mass quantities. According to the U.S. Department of State, for example, over 12 million U.S. passports were issued in 2006 (http://travel.state.gov). In 2004, 61.8 million travelers went abroad, creating a 10% increase from just one year prior (www.commerce.gov). Of those traveling, 38% cited traveling for leisure and 22% traveling for business. These expatriates become an extension of the United States, leaving impressions of the United States upon other cultures. Whether for business or pleasure, it is critical to continue to pursue research in how to be an interculturally competent communicator.

A Grammar of Intercultural Competence Conceptualizations

Conceptualizations of intercultural communication competence are highly diverse in their disciplines, terminologies, and scholarly and practical objectives. It is therefore essential to establish some basic premises to both assist with selection of conceptualizations for this review and establish a working grammar for analysis. In the process, no doubt sacred theoretical presumptions of some authors will be distorted in the sake of seeking the most useful implications of existing models.

There is no need to lose the proverbial forest in the trees of terms such as *approach, perspective, paradigm, model,* and *theory.* The purpose of this chapter is to overview conceptualizations, which will be taken as either relatively well-defined models or theories. There are many bases upon which theories and models may be defined and evaluated (see, e.g., Britt, 1997; Shoemaker, Tankard, & Lasorsa, 2004; Spitzberg, 2001). To be a "conceptualization" of intercultural competence, a core concept of "competence" or "adaptation" must be *explained,* either by narrative forms that are or could be stated in propositional form (e.g., $X = f\,Y$; or "As X increases, Y increases") or represented in visual form that implies causal relationships. The visual and narrative expositional forms will need to represent an interrelated set of propositions that render the concept of competence or adaptation sensible. In essence, a reader should be able to interpret and experience the conceptualization by sensing an understanding of how competence functions, comes about, or operates in relation to a number of other concepts that systemically account for the competence. Many discussions and investigations of factors or variables are expected to influence intercultural competence, but this chapter focuses on more comprehensive models and theories.

A word is warranted on the concepts of process and causation. All explanations are at some level or another, implicitly or explicitly, causal in nature. No description of watch components, gears, or springs can hope to explain what a watch is or does. All theoretical explanations of human activity attempt to cope with the complexities of process. The concept of *process* is essentially a primitive theoretical term but broadly implies systemic aspects of ongoing or continuous change over time, functional interdependence, equifinality (different paths to the same outcome), and multifinality (one path to multiple outcomes). Process is far easier to explain in broad narrative terms than it is to depict visually or assess methodologically. Conceptualizations of intercultural competence all presuppose that they are envisioning a process, even if language and iconography are poor media for its communication.

The term *competence* is itself a contested conceptual site. For some time, the term has been too loosely bandied about in scholarly literatures (Deardorff, 2006), with surprisingly little attention to its many semantic and conceptual landmines (Spitzberg & Cupach, 1984, 2002). Competence has been variously equated with understanding (e.g., accuracy, clarity, co-orientation, overlap of meanings), relationship development (e.g., attraction, intimacy), satisfaction (e.g., communication satisfaction, relational satisfaction, relational quality), effectiveness (e.g., goal achievement, efficiency, institutional success, negotiation success), appropriateness (e.g., legitimacy, acceptance, assimilation), and adaptation. Each of these criteria of competence has been defended or criticized elsewhere (see McCroskey, 1982; Parks, 1985; Spitzberg, 1993, 1994a, 1994b, 2000, 2003; Spitzberg & Cupach, 1984, 1989, 2002). Furthermore, competence is sometimes conceptually equated with a set of abilities or skills and at other times a subjective evaluative impression. The former meaning is by far the most common approach and fits with the more normative semantic sense of the term. There are, however, numerous problems with such an approach. The same behavior or skill may be perceived as competent in one context but not another or one perceiver but not another, and thus no particular skill or ability is likely to ever be universally "competent" (Spitzberg, 2000, 2007; Spitzberg & Cupach, 1984, 2002). Despite such problems, for the purposes of this review, any competence conceptualizations are considered relevant that attempt to account for the process of managing interaction in ways that are likely to produce more appropriate and effective individual, relational, group, or institutional outcomes.

Many conceptualizations, theories, and models of intercultural competence attempt to account for adjustment, assimilation, or adaptation. These concepts often are even equated with competence and therefore require some consideration. *Assimilation* typically represents the extent to which a sojourner blends in with or becomes similar to the host culture. Whether assimilation represents attitudinal and cognitive shifts toward the indigenous culture or merely requires behavioral mimicking of the culture is not always specified, but most conceptualizations of competence seem to imply that movement occurs in all these areas. *Adjustment* is widely used in clinical psychology literatures and typically implies a normalization process, such that a person becomes "well adjusted" to an environment and no longer experiences stress or culture shock. In contrast, *adaptation* tends to be used in two senses: micro and macro. Conceptualizations of adaptation at the micro-level are concerned with the interdependence and alteration of behavior in episodes of interaction, such that the actions of one interactant influence the actions of the other interactant(s) in the context. Adaptation at the more macro-level tends to refer to notions involving the overlaps of assimilation and adjustment. Macro-level adaptation means that a communicator is adept at making adjustments to the host culture across episodes and contexts of interaction within that culture. To some extent, therefore, these could be viewed as state versus trait conceptions of adaptation.

Many views and definitions of culture have been proffered. For the purposes of this review, *culture* will be considered a primitive theoretical term, concerned with enduring yet evolving intergenerational attitudes, values, beliefs, rituals/customs, and behavioral patterns into which people are born but that is structurationally created and maintained by people's ongoing actions. Thus, *inter*cultural competence is the appropriate and effective management of interaction between people who, to some degree or another, represent different or divergent affective, cognitive, and behavioral orientations to the world. These orientations will most commonly be reflected in such normative categories as nationality, race, ethnicity, tribe, religion, or region. To a large extent, therefore, intercultural interaction is tantamount to intergroup interaction. It is important to point out, however, that groups do not interact—individuals interact (Spitzberg, 1989). The extent to which individuals *manifest* aspects of, or are influenced by, their group or cultural affiliations and characteristics is what makes an interaction an *inter*cultural process.

Most theories and models begin with the individual as the unit of analysis, although most recognize the importance of including other factors. A purely chronological review of intercultural competence theories and models would likely reveal a progression from individual-based models to more systemic and inclusive models. To provide a working grammar for this review, we elaborate several standard conceptual *topoi*. At least since the 1950s, an intuitive, if somewhat Kantian, conative approach has dominated models of human competence (Bloom, 1956; Havighurst, 1957) consisting of the following core components: *motivation* (affective, emotion), *knowledge* (cognitive), and *skills* (behavioral, actional). To incorporate the broader set of influences on human competence, Spitzberg and Cupach (1984) expanded the conceptualization to include *context* (situation, environment, culture, relationship, function) and *outcomes* (e.g., perceived appropriateness, perceived effectiveness, satisfaction, understanding, attraction, intimacy, assimilation, task achievement). To a large extent, all theories and models of intercultural competence rely extensively on these basic conceptual metaphors to guide their explanations (e.g., Gertsen, 1990; Lustig & Koester, 2006; Spitzberg, 1997; Sue, 2001). Despite decades of influence from systems-theoretic perspectives, the individual human is still the most intuitive and fundamental theoretic locus of explanation, despite attempts by many models to incorporate other interactants and contextual factors into their explanatory framework.

A Synoptic Review of Intercultural Competence Theories and Models

A Very Brief History

Ambassadors, diplomats, and emissaries throughout history have probably understood the importance of becoming schooled not only in the arts of social skills but also in the cultural milieu in which they seek audience. An important part of the selection process for such representatives for any authority seeking good diplomatic relations has probably been the persons' familiarity and competence with the cultural practices of their destinations. As nation-states increasingly developed and as the consequences of war became ever more unacceptable, the premium for intercultural competence among those seeking interactional contact and exchange across national, ethnic, and cultural boundaries has likely increased accordingly.

In parallel manner, it is likely that as the multinational interests of organizations have increased, both public and private, profit and nonprofit, so have their interests in selecting and training employees in the skills and competencies that might facilitate the productive initiation and maintenance of profitable forms of interaction, in all senses of the term *profitable.*

After World War II, the United States sought greater involvement and investment in foreign lands and businesses. The cold war increased the importance not only of strong diplomatic alliances but also of the business alliances that often undergirded such relationships. The search for international stability led also to expanded foreign aid programs to countries with humanitarian problems that might signal dangerous political instabilities. In this context, organizations such as the Peace Corps arose, providing a new and significant context in which individuals were recruited to serve in a culture very different than the one in which they were born and raised.

The need to select and train individuals to serve effectively in programs such as the Peace Corps stimulated a new government and social scientific interest in the concept of intercultural competence. For example, Smith (1966; see also Smith, Fawcett, Ezekiel, & Roth, 1963) conducted a Q-sort of characteristics of competence among young Peace Corps workers who underwent training and served 2-year terms in Ghana. The author identified "a pattern defined on its good side by qualities of warranted self-confidence, commitment, energy, responsibility, autonomy, flexibility, and hopeful realism together with other skills and attitudes more specifically appropriate to the role of Peace Corps teacher" (p. 558). The personality patterns associated with good teachers in this context included interpersonal sensitivity, maturity, interpersonal openness, nurturance, empathy, and self-involvement.

Using somewhat different methods for identifying characteristics of Peace Corps workers, Ezekiel (1968) found that more competent volunteers tended to be characterized by a wider range of interests, valuing intellectual matters, higher aspirations, cheerfulness, verbal fluency and ability to express ideas well, a generally talkative disposition, valuing of autonomy, and an ability to create and exploit dependency in people. Less competent volunteers tended to be "uncomfortable with uncertainty and complexities," "thin-skinned; sensitive to anything that can be construed as criticism or any interpersonal slight," "reluctant to commit self to any definite course of action," "basically distrustful of people in general," "self-defeating," and inclined to give up and withdraw "in the face of frustration and adversity" (p. 24).

By the mid-1970s, scholars and practitioners were both consolidating and expanding the list of characteristics expected for success in Peace Corps foreign assignments. Harris (1977) summarized 24 variables that differentiated highly successful from less successful volunteers in Tonga. Many of the characteristics were relatively specific to the teaching role (e.g., coverage of content, talents as teacher, control of classroom), but others suggest relevance to intercultural competence more generally, including facility with language, adaptability, responsibility, cultural sensitivity, interest in nationals, realism of goals, agreement and compromise, inner strength, self-reliance, patience/tolerance, perseverance, initiative, reliability, argumentativeness, courteousness, cooperativeness, friendliness, and general maturity. This list clearly presages more contemporary characterizations of traits and dispositions needed for intercultural competence. The study of Peace Corps volunteer experiences and other areas of study such as Navy personnel adjustment (Benson, 1978) illustrate that many contemporary research efforts may be reinventing wheels that were already reasonably well designed some time ago.

Terms such as *intercultural competence, intercultural effectiveness,* and *intercultural adaptation* largely trace back to the 1970s (e.g., Hammer, Gudykunst, & Wiseman, 1978; Ruben, 1976; Ruben & Kealey, 1979) and 1980s (e.g., Wiseman & Abe, 1986). By this time, the need for interculturally competent government, educational, and business representatives was well recognized, but there was (and still is) no widely accepted model for training and assessment of intercultural "readiness." As often is the case, methodological and measurement forays began to outstrip the theoretical frameworks available to guide such efforts. A number of sophisticated efforts were undertaken to develop, validate, and refine measures of intercultural competence (e.g., Abe & Wiseman, 1983; Gudykunst & Hammer, 1984; Hammer, 1987; Hammer et al., 1978; Koester & Olebe, 1988; Martin & Hammer, 1989; Wiseman & Abe, 1986). These efforts typically revealed that although the core concept of adaptability may necessarily underlie the concept of intercultural competence, any comprehensive measure would undoubtedly be multidimensional in nature. The question was *which* dimensions, and *why*.

From the 1990s to the present, measurement efforts have begun developing that are based on more elaborate conceptual models (e.g., Byram, 1997, 2003; Byram, Nichols, & Stevens, 2001; Milhouse, 1993; Prechtl & Lund, 2007) and that are more contextually (e.g., B. S. K. Kim, Cartwright, Asay, & D'Andrea, 2003; Martin, Hammer, & Bradford, 1994) or process (e.g., Hajek & Giles, 2003) focused. The majority of these studies assessed knowledge and skills (Bradford, Allen, & Beisser, 2000), largely ignoring the affective or motivational component identified by several models (i.e., Spitzberg & Cupach, 1984). At the same time, a shift in the communication and social psychology disciplines to focus more on relationship development across a variety of contexts led to more relationally focused inquiries into intercultural interactions (e.g., Chen, 2002; Collier, 1996) or interethnic (e.g., Hecht, Larkey, & Johnson, 1992; Hecht & Ribeau, 1984; Martin, Hecht, & Larkey, 1994) contexts.

Contemporary Models

At least two approaches to reviewing programs of theoretical or empirical achievements could be considered sequential or topical. A sequential approach would discuss one model and then another model, and another, and so on. A topical approach would examine concepts *across* models. The sequential approach emphasizes uniqueness of models, whereas the topical approach emphasizes commonalities of models. Both approaches are pursued in this review. Rather than merely use a chronological ordering for the sequential review, however, a typology of models is employed as a higher-order organization. There are many ways of distinguishing models at an analytic level, such as level of abstraction, generalization, synthesis, incorporation of time, or testability (e.g., Turner, 1985, 1990), but for purposes of this review, models of intercultural communication competence will be divided into the following types: compositional, co-orientational, developmental, adaptational, and causal process. These categories are purely subjective categories that emerged from the search for potential similarities among the models.

Compositional models are similar to what Turner (1985) might refer to as an analytic scheme or typology. These models identify the hypothesized components of competence without specifying the relations among those components. Such models represent "lists" of relevant or probable traits, characteristics, and skills supposed to be productive or constitutive of competent interaction. *Co-orientational models* are models that are primarily devoted to conceptualizing the interactional achievement of intercultural understanding or any of its variants (e.g., perceptual accuracy, empathy, perspective taking, clarity, overlap of meaning systems). Such models may share many of the features of other models but are focused on a particular criterion of communicative mutuality and shared meanings. *Developmental models* retain a dominant role for the time dimension of intercultural interaction, specifying stages of progression or maturity through which competence is hypothesized to evolve. Such models may share components of other models but emphasize the process of progression over time. *Adaptational models* tend to have two distinctive characteristics: First, they typically envision multiple interactants in the process, and second, they emphasize interdependence of these multiple interactants by modeling the process of mutual adjustment. The multiple interactants may be modeled as conceptual reflections of one another, and the adjustment process may be hypothesized to represent or include any number of various outcomes, but the core emphasis is that competence is manifest in mutual alteration of actions, attitudes, and understandings based on interaction with members of another culture. Thus, adaptation itself is taken as a type of criterion of competence. Finally, *causal process* models reflect fairly specified interrelationships among components and are the most easily formalized or translated from or into testable propositions. These models typically take a form similar to a path model, with an identifiable set of distal-to-proximal concepts leading to a downstream set of outcomes that mark or provide a criterion of competence. These five types of models are not mutually exclusive, and no doubt there are alternative typological systems that could be productively applied. These categories will nevertheless serve to delineate important distinctions among the models.

Compositional Models

Howard Hamilton, Richardson, and Shuford (1998) formulated a relatively typical conative listing of competence components (Figure 1.1). In the attitudes (i.e., motivation) component, interculturally competent interactants are expected to value their own group, the basic equality of groups, multicentrism, risk taking, and the role of cross-cultural interactions on quality of life. Such values will complement knowledge competencies such as understanding cultural identities, group boundaries and histories of oppression, and the influences of cultural differences on communication processes. Such motivation and knowledge would be compatible with the basic skills of self-reflection, articulation of differences, perspective-taking, assertive challenging of discriminatory actions, and communicating cross-culturally in general. Such compositional models and the measures intended to operationalize them often haphazardly represent multiple levels of abstraction (Spitzberg, 2003, 2007). Thus, "challenging discriminatory acts" represents a much more specific and narrow range of actions than engaging in self-reflection. Furthermore, compositional models and their measures also often mistake what constitutes an internal affective or cognitive factor, as opposed to a behavioral factor (i.e., skill). Thus, engaging in "self-reflection" and "taking multiple perspectives" are arguably internal information-processing activities and do not have obvious referents in the behavioral realm.

Attitudes
- **Awareness: Values . . .**
  - Own group
  - Group equality
- **Understanding: Devalues . . .**
  - Discrimination
  - Ethnocentric assumptions
- **Appreciation: Values . . .**
  - Risk taking
  - Life enhancing role of cross-cultural interactions

Skills
- **Awareness: Ability to . . .**
  - Engage in self-reflection
  - Identify and articulate cultural similarities and differences
- **Understanding: Ability to . . .**
  - Take multiple perspectives
  - Understand differences in multiple contexts
- **Appreciation: Ability to . . .**
  - Challenge discriminatory acts
  - Communicate cross-culturally

Knowledge
- **Awareness: Knowledge of . . .**
  - Self as it relates to cultural identity
  - Similarities and differences across cultures
- **Understanding: Knowledge of . . .**
  - Oppressions
  - Intersecting oppressions (race, gender, class, religion, etc.)
- **Appreciation: Knowledge of . . .**
  - Elements involved in social change
  - Effects of cultural differences on communication

Figure 1.1 Intercultural Competence Components Model

SOURCE: Adapted from Howard Hamilton et al. (1998).

Ting-Toomey and Kurogi (1998) formulated a model to represent a facework management theory of intercultural communication competence (Figure 1.2). Their model de-emphasizes motivational factors and emphasizes cognitive, behavioral, and outcome factors. A mindfulness dimension represents abilities such as mindful reflexivity, taking multiple perspectives, analytical empathy, and intentional creativity. Openness to novelty is considered a mindfulness facet but clearly also reflects a motivational orientation toward the world. The knowledge component reflects the importance of understanding differences due to individualism and collectivism, power distance, negotiating self and other face, and facework styles. The primary skills associated with competent intercultural interaction include listening, observation, trust building, dialogic collaboration, and face management. Together, these cognitive and behavioral abilities are expected to increase the likelihood of appropriate, effective, mutually satisfying, and mutually adaptive outcomes. Distinct from causal path models, this model assumes iterative relations among all the components of the model, such that changes in every component are expected to influence every other component.

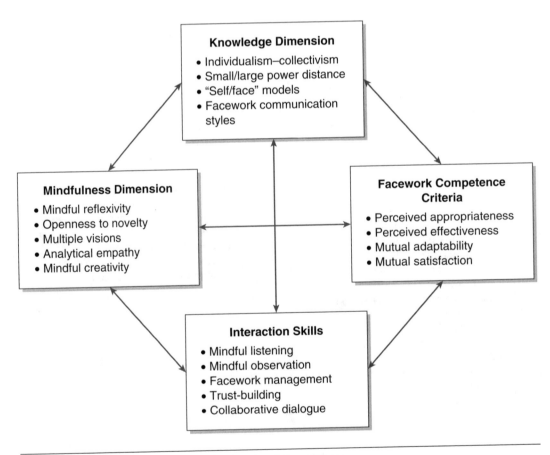

Figure 1.2   Facework-Based Model of Intercultural Competence

SOURCE: Adapted visualization from Ting-Toomey and Kurogi (1998).

In one of the relatively few efforts to identify a set of research-based components of intercultural competence that capitalizes on both deductive and inductive processes, Deardorff (2006) employed a Delphi methodology in which 23 intercultural experts participated, resulting in the first research study to document consensus among these leading intercultural experts on a definition and components of intercultural competence. This reiterative grounded-theory method relies on the experts to invoke their own conceptual perspectives and theories to inform the process in terms of raw inputs yet employs an inductive technique to build a model from those data through documented consensus. Deardorff synthesized the resulting data in two visual models, one of which is a pyramid model of intercultural competence, in which the lower levels are viewed as enhancing the higher levels (Figure 1.3) and the other of which is a process model (Figure 1.21) that is discussed later in the chapter. Similar to many cognitive approaches, this pyramid model represents motivational (requisite attitudes), cognitive

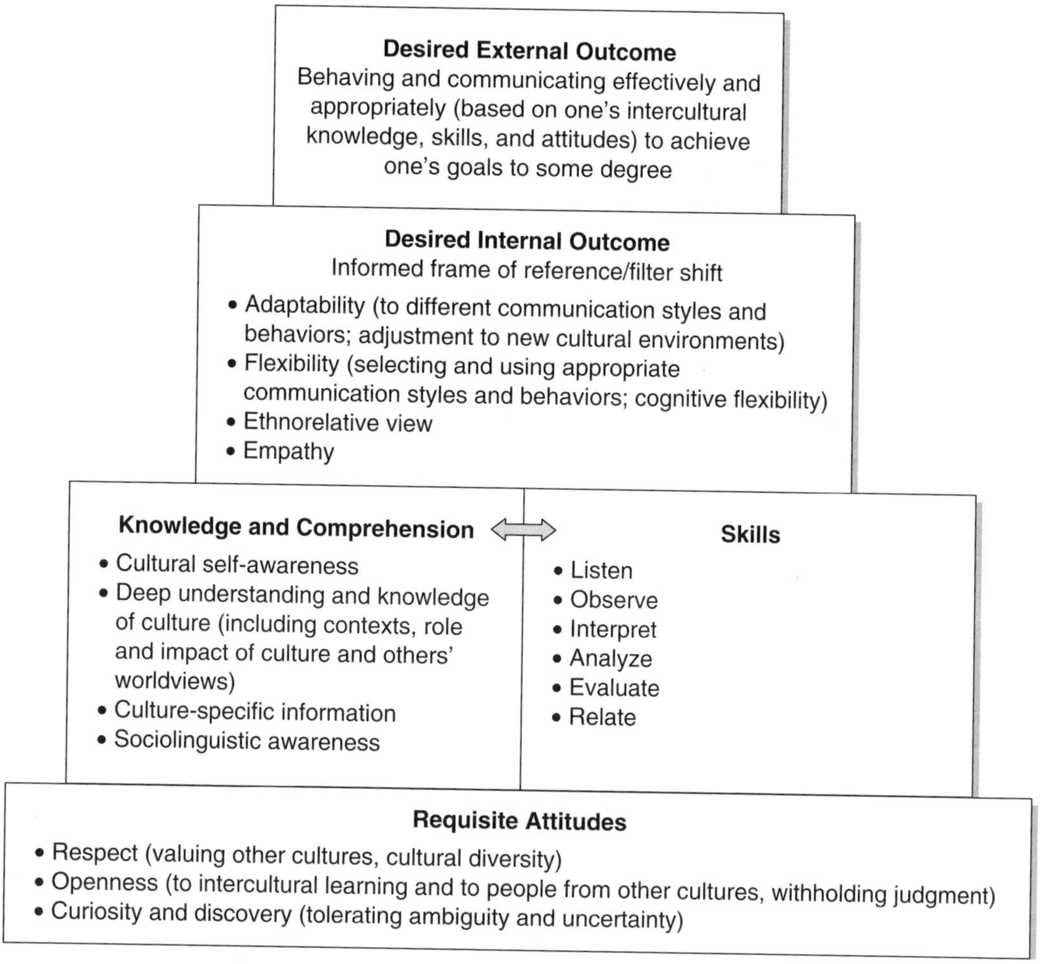

Desired External Outcome
Behaving and communicating effectively and appropriately (based on one's intercultural knowledge, skills, and attitudes) to achieve one's goals to some degree

Desired Internal Outcome
Informed frame of reference/filter shift

- Adaptability (to different communication styles and behaviors; adjustment to new cultural environments)
- Flexibility (selecting and using appropriate communication styles and behaviors; cognitive flexibility)
- Ethnorelative view
- Empathy

Knowledge and Comprehension ⟺   **Skills**

- Cultural self-awareness
- Deep understanding and knowledge of culture (including contexts, role and impact of culture and others' worldviews)
- Culture-specific information
- Sociolinguistic awareness

- Listen
- Observe
- Interpret
- Analyze
- Evaluate
- Relate

Requisite Attitudes
- Respect (valuing other cultures, cultural diversity)
- Openness (to intercultural learning and to people from other cultures, withholding judgment)
- Curiosity and discovery (tolerating ambiguity and uncertainty)

Figure 1.3 Deardorff Pyramid Model of Intercultural Competence

SOURCE: Deardorff (2006). Used by permission.

(knowledge and comprehension), and skills elements and incorporates context within these components. Unlike many of the other conative approaches, however, this model attempts to represent figuratively a conception of foundational elements and an implicit ordering of elements with the resulting external (visible) outcome being the effective and appropriate communication and behavior in intercultural situations. Knowledge and skills presuppose some attitudinal dispositions, and collectively, attitudes, knowledge, and skills are likely to produce outcomes that illustrate the recursive nature of competence—outcomes are the result of elements that produce them, in this case attitudes, knowledge, skills, and resulting behaviors. According to Deardorff, the specific attitudes, knowledge, and skills outlined in the model can be used to derive specific indicators and criteria in each of those domains (see Chapter 28 for further discussion on using this model for assessment).

In what amounts to a needs assessment for "global competencies," Hunter et al. (2006) report a Delphi analysis that engaged 17 educators, human resource managers, diplomats, trainers, and government officials in an effort to identify the components of this construct (Figure 1.4). The core competencies reflect the opinion that "a person should attempt to understand his or her own cultural box before stepping into someone else's" (p. 279). Thus, the ability to understand one's own cultural norms and expectations and to recognize cultural differences, openness to new experiences and diversity, and nonjudgmental stance are expected to provide a

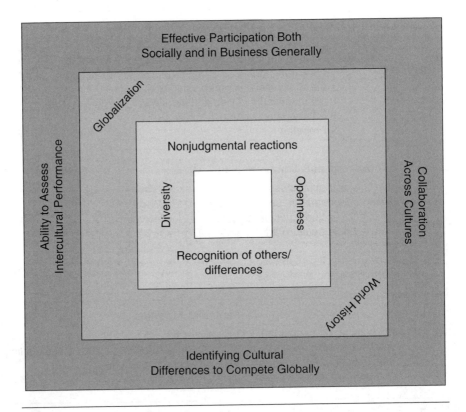

Figure 1.4 Global Competencies Model

SOURCE: Hunter, White, and Godbey (2006). Used by permission.

foundation for entering a more globalized world. In the process of engaging that globalized world, an understanding of world history will help prepare a person for (a) identifying and understanding cultural differences, (b) participating effectively in and across these cultures through (c) mutually collaborative means, and (d) evaluating his or her own performance in these contexts. The authors note the surprising relative absence of second-language learning and experience abroad in the competencies identified as most important. The implication may be that language learning is secondary to the basic motivational and cognitive orientations that permit movement in and among such cultures with or without language competence.

Compositional models have been very useful in defining the basic scope and contents that a theory of intercultural communication competence needs to incorporate. They are theoretically weak, however, in their ability to specify conditional relations among the components. They are also theoretically weak in leaving fundamentally undefined the precise criteria by which competence itself is defined. It is generally not clear, in other words, what *constitutes* competence in these models—what levels of proficiency, what specific combination of criteria or outcomes, would be determinative of competence? One approach to competence that attempts more focused criteria of competence is to view the primary objective of intercultural competence as co-orientation.

Co-orientational Models

Co-orientation is a term that summarizes several cognate concepts relevant to comprehension outcomes of interactional processes, including understanding, overlapping perspectives, accuracy, directness, and clarity. The latter characteristics are arguably more in the realm of skills, as in "speak more clearly or directly," but obviously imply the criterion of accurate understanding as the measure against which clarity would be evaluated. It is not surprising that co-orientation would occupy a relatively central focus of attempts at conceptualizing intercultural competence. People coming from divergent cultures, experiences, histories, races, and languages seem likely to face as their first predicament of interaction the problem of understanding. All subsequent progress in interaction seems logically predicated upon the achievement of some base level of co-orientation toward the common referential world.

Fantini (1995) summarized many of the elements necessarily involved in the linguistic processes involved in achieving co-orientation (Figure 1.5). In any interaction among interlocutors, systems of selective perception become "translated" into concepts and thoughts, which are "translated" into semantic clusters, which are then transformed into specific expression-based units (morphology and syntax) and overt expressed actions (phonology, graphemes, signs, etc.). Fantini (2001) concurs that the kinds of traits identified in the componential models (i.e., flexibility, humor, patience, openness, interest, curiosity, empathy, tolerance for ambiguity, suspending judgment, etc.) are likely to facilitate the process of interlocution, and these traits are likely organized along the familiar dimensions (awareness, attitudes, knowledge, and skills). If interlocutors are successful, Fantini (1995) proposes a process by which the perspectives, or worldviews, of the interactants increasingly display co-orientation (Figure 1.6). Through competent interaction, the overlap of

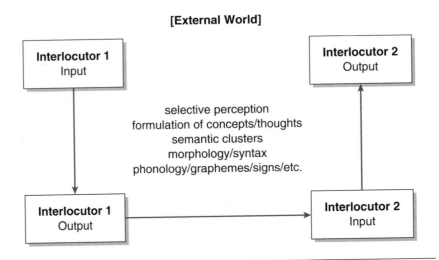

Figure 1.5   Intercultural Interlocutor Competence Model

SOURCE: Fantini (1995).

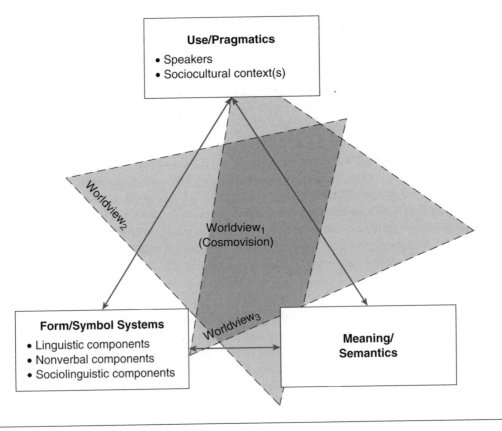

Figure 1.6   Worldviews Convergence Model

SOURCE: Fantini (1995).

respective symbol systems (languages), denotative and connotative meanings, and usage norms will display increasing amounts of correspondence.

Byram and colleagues (Byram, 1997, 2003; Byram et al., 2001) have developed an influential model that involves several commonalities with co-orientational models, although it is somewhat more concerned with negotiating identity in the "space" within and across cultures (Figure 1.7). The model identifies a distinction

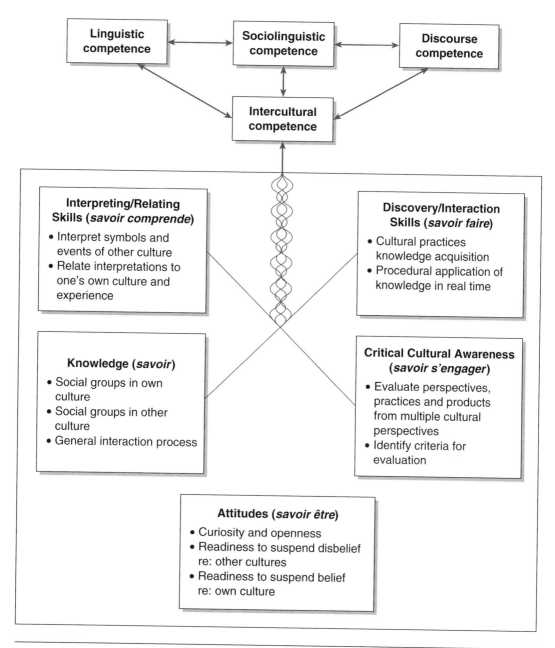

Figure 1.7 Intercultural Competence Model

SOURCE: Byram (1997).

between what it means to be "bicultural" in contrast to "intercultural." Bicultural speakers tend to have experience in two cultures and possess motivation (i.e., attitudes), knowledge, and skills that facilitate interaction competence in both, but the person's identity is conflicted. There are tensions between the person's values and identity in one culture vis-à-vis the other culture. The interactant values aspects of both cultural identities, but these identities are not always compatible, and the person's identity and cultural performances can suffer as a result. The intercultural speaker, however, is more of a mediator between cultures, able to negotiate in both, but possessing individual identity that is flexible in its ability to combine aspects of multiple cultures in performance. The most competent intercultural mediators

> are those who have an understanding of the relationship between their own language and language varieties and their own culture and cultures of different social groups in their society, on the one hand, and the language (varieties) and culture(s) of others, between (inter) which they find themselves acting as mediators. (Byram, 2003, p. 61)

In one of the more exhaustive efforts at developing a conceptual model of intercultural communication competence, Kupka (2008) defines intercultural communication competence in terms of "*impression management that allows members of different cultural systems to be aware of their cultural identity and cultural differences, and to interact effectively and appropriately with each other in diverse contexts by agreeing on the meaning of diverse symbol systems with the result of mutually satisfying relationships*" (p. 16). This definition clearly has allegiance to other models but specifies three outcome criteria (i.e., impressions of appropriateness and effectiveness, awareness and agreement on diverse meaning systems, and mutual relationship satisfaction). Thus, despite the model's relevance to componential and adaptational approaches, it is reviewed as a co-orientational model because of the extent to which all three outcomes are predicated on levels of mutuality and agreement in meaning systems (Figure 1.8). The model posits that basic human needs (i.e., motivations) are relatively common across cultures. The perceptual world of one interactant interacts with the perceptual world of another interactant through the process of communication (simultaneous action—reaction), producing levels of overlap in the interactants' shared symbol systems and thus their levels of mutual understanding. All this takes place in the context of various sources of contextual (e.g., environmental, situational) and personal (physiological, psychological, semantic) interference. The components that facilitate individual competence include many of the commonly recognized constructs, including perception of cultural distance, foreign language competence, verbal and nonverbal communication skills, self-awareness, motivation, and knowledge. Although not modeled as outcomes, appropriateness, effectiveness, and affinity represent implicit criteria by which individual competence is evaluated, even though the model clearly portrays the outcome of interaction as an overlap of meaning systems.

Co-orientation models take for granted the value of mutual understanding. Rathje (2007) attempts to point out that such presumptions oversimplify underlying

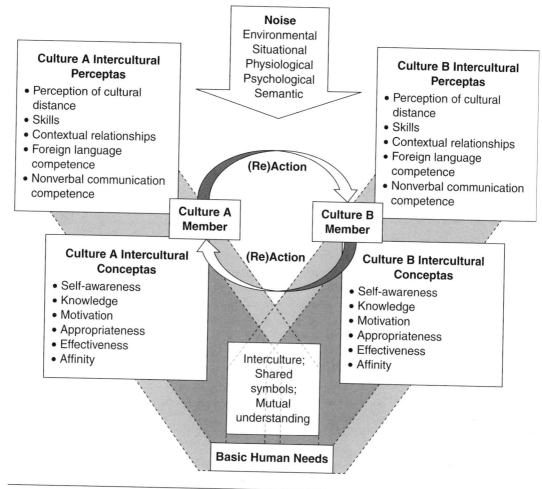

Figure 1.8 Intercultural Competence Model for Strategic Human Resource Management
SOURCE: Adapted visualization from Kupla (2008).

dialectics of cultural tension (Figure 1.9). Cultures have the effects of unifying (coherence vs. cohesion). Members of cultures understand the differences within their own cultural "multicollectivity" and understand these differences in ways that members from other cultures do not understand. The unique feature of culture is that it achieves its unity in large part by its unique amalgam of internal differences. Although ongoing interactional adaptation and integration within a culture do produce degrees of uniformity and coherence among its members (the left side of the model), this process also produces a sense of cohesion in which individual differences are sustained as a unique marker of the culture itself (the right side of the model). "Intercultural competence is best characterized therefore, by the transformation of intercultural interaction into culture itself" (p. 263). The co-orientation that occurs in competent intercultural interaction is the coproduction of a cultural milieu that does not *reflect* common cultural identities but actually produces those

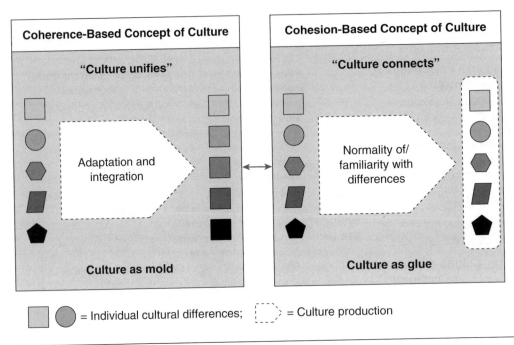

Figure 1.9 Coherence-Cohesion Model of Intercultural Competence

SOURCE: Adapted visualization from Rathje (2007).

common identities, without overly conforming the interactants to any particular hegemonic identity.

Co-orientational models are useful in drawing attention to the foundational importance of achieving some minimal level of common reference through interaction. They also emphasize one of the most fundamental issues underlying the study of communication since the earliest scholarly efforts to model it—how do we account for the fact that we are able to co-orient (i.e., adapt to one another's meanings and behaviors) given that we come from different, or even divergent, perspectives toward the world? To some extent, from this view of co-orientation, all interactions are in part intercultural (Rathje, 2007). One of the biggest problems that co-orientation models face, however, is that much of competent everyday interaction is dependent on ambiguity, uncertainty, misunderstanding, and disparity in comprehension. Politeness, for example, is considered a universal pragmatic (Brown & Levinson, 1987) and is obviously integral to competence. Politeness, however, requires considerable ambiguity, indirectness, and even legerdemain in its competent achievement. Ambiguity, uncertainty, and indirectness therefore become vital interactional resources for the ongoing maintenance of any relationships, perhaps especially intercultural relationships. It is largely for this reason that many theorists view co-orientation as a criterion subordinate to other more macro-level objectives of interaction (e.g., Spitzberg, 2000, 2003, 2007; Spitzberg & Cupach, 1984, 2002). The maintenance of intercultural relationships depends in part, therefore, on the deft management and balancing of directness and indirectness, understanding and misunderstanding, clarity and ambiguity.

If intercultural interaction competence is understood from the perspective of an ongoing relationship, rather than an episodic achievement, it illustrates the importance of an element missing from the compositional and co-orientational models: time. Not only is time an important causal consideration in terms of what follows what in the process of a given interaction, but it is also an inevitable factor to consider in any ongoing relationship among representatives of different cultures. One of the ways that models of intercultural communication competence have accounted for the role of time is to consider the process from a developmental perspective.

Developmental Models

Developmental models have in common a recognition that competence evolves over time, either individually or relationally, or both. Recognizing both rich traditions in developmental psychology and the more recent developments in understanding personal relationships, developmental models draw attention to the prospect that relationships are capable of becoming more competent through ongoing interaction that produces greater co-orientation, learning, and incorporation of respective cultural perspectives. Furthermore, just as adults are generally considered more interactionally competent than infants, due largely to the learning process that provides for stages of growth to build sequentially upon one another, developmental models often attempt to identify the stages of progression that would mark the achievement of more competent levels of interaction.

A typical representation of levels of progressive competence is provided by King and Baxter Magolda (2005). By identifying initial, intermediate, and mature levels of intercultural development, the process of maturation is emphasized (Figure 1.10). Similar to assessment rubrics for evaluating student competence, this model attempts to identify the levels of awareness of, sensitivity to, and ability to adapt to distinctions across cultures. Low levels of awareness and sensitivity represent less competent modes of intercultural interaction, and greater levels of awareness and sensitivity represent more competent modes of intercultural interaction. The presumption of the model is that individuals progress toward the more mature levels of competence only through ongoing study, observation, and interaction with representatives of another culture.

A presumption of the King and Baxter Magolda (2005) model is that over time, interactants progress from relatively *ethnocentric* understandings of other cultures to a more *ethnorelative* comprehension and appreciation. This dimension of development is emphasized by Bennett's (1986) stage model of intercultural sensitivity (Figure 1.11). "The underlying assumption of the model is that as one's *experience of cultural difference* becomes more complex and sophisticated, one's potential competence in intercultural relations increases" (Hammer et al., 2003, p. 423). Interactants progress from a monocultural worldview to more differentiated, complex, and sophisticated multicultural worldviews. The *denial* stage reflects attitudes that only one's own culture is in some sense real or legitimate. Other cultures are considered relatively irrelevant. *Defense* represents more of a recognition of the other culture but in more of an "us" versus "them" perspective. *Defense reversal* can

Initial Development Level	Intermediate Development Level	Mature Development Level

• **Cognitive**
  ○ Categorical knowledge
  ○ Naïve about cultural practices
  ○ Resists knowledge challenges
 	
• **Intrapersonal**
  ○ Lacks awareness of social role intersections (race, class, etc.)
  ○ Lacks awareness of cultures
  ○ Externally defined beliefs
  ○ Differences viewed as threats
 	
• **Interpersonal**
  ○ Identity dependent on similar others
  ○ Different views are considered wrong
  ○ Lacks awareness of social systems and norms
  ○ Views social problems egocentrically
	• **Cognitive**
	  ○ Evolving awareness and acceptance of perspectives
	  ○ Shift from authority to autonomous knowledge
	
	• **Intrapersonal**
	  ○ Evolving identity distinct from external perceptions
	  ○ Tension between internal and external prompts
	  ○ Recognizes legitimacy of other cultures
	
	• **Interpersonal**
	  ○ Willingness to interact with divergent others
	  ○ Explores how social systems affect group norms and relations
		• **Cognitive**
		  ○ Able to consciously shift perspectives
		  ○ Use multiple cultural frames
		
		• **Intrapersonal**
		  ○ Able to create internal self
		  ○ Challenges own views of social identities (class, race)
		  ○ Integrates self identity
		
		• **Interpersonal**
		  ○ Able to engage in diverse interdependent relationships
		  ○ Ground relations in appreciation of differences
		  ○ Understands intersection of social systems and practices
		  ○ Willing to work for others' rights

Figure 1.10   Intercultural Maturity Model

SOURCE: Adapted from King and Baxter Magolda (2005, p. 576).

occur when an adopted culture succeeds a person's estranged culture, reflected in the conversion experienced when a person "goes native." *Minimization* incorporates the differences discovered in other culture(s) as somehow reflected in or extended from one's own culture in various forms of universalistic thinking. As interactants cross over to more ethnorelative perspectives, they are better able to view their own culture from the perspective of another culture or cultures. The recognition of one's indigenous culture as one among the many variable cultures of the world represents a process of *acceptance*. In progressing along the continuum, an interactant is increasingly able and inclined to employ such acceptance in the process of *adapting* behavior to accord with the standards of appropriateness in the other culture. If an interactant continues to develop toward more ethnorelative communication, the process will lead to *integration* of self's and other cultural worldviews, to the point that identity is constructed in ways that recognize marginality in the overlap of multiple cultural identities and groupings. "Integration is not necessarily better than adaptation in situations demanding intercultural competence, but it is descriptive of a growing number of people, including many members of non-dominant

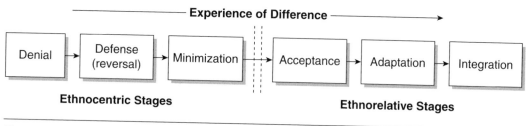

Figure 1.11 Developmental Intercultural Competence Model

SOURCE: Adapted visualization from Bennett (1986).

cultures, long-term expatriates, and 'global nomads'" (Hammer et al., 2003, p. 425). This model has been highly influential in training and research (e.g., Altshuler, Sussman, & Kachur, 2003; Klak & Martin, 2003).

Another influential developmental model adapts the concept of culture shock (for reviews, see Black & Mendenhall, 1991; Furnham & Bochner, 1986) to a stage model of cultural adjustment. Lysgaard (1955) proposed a U-curve hypothesis, later expanded by Gullahorn and Gullahorn (1962). The model proposes that there is a multistage wave response of adjustment and satisfaction in response to acculturation (Figure 1.12). Obviously tailored to people living abroad or spending substantial time in a different culture, the model hypothesizes that initial experiences in a culture may well reveal a *honeymoon* stage in which experiences are relatively positive in the context of a halo effect of novelty. A precipitous plunge in adjustment

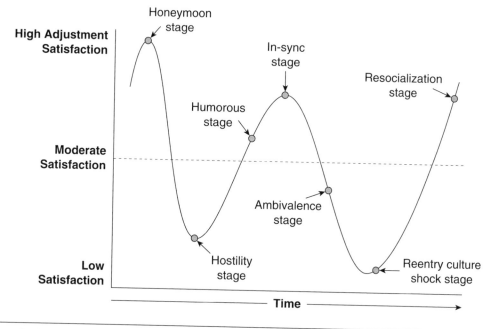

Figure 1.12 U-Curve Model of Intercultural Adjustment

SOURCE: Adapted visualization from Gullahorn and Gullahorn (1962).

is predicted in which the starkness of differences rudely confronts a person's adaptive resources, resulting in a *hostility* stage. Presuming continuous adaptive efforts, however, interactants are expected to recover and even recognize the *humorous* nature of the incongruities between the cultures. Eventually, it is expected that competent interactants will begin to feel *in sync* with the cultural milieu and its rhythms, rituals, and rules. Sojourners who spend enough time in another culture, however, are expected to experience some degree of *ambivalence* as they face the prospect of returning home and departing their newfound sense of relative comfort. Having made the adjustment, they now experience *reentry culture shock* as they find themselves attempting to reintegrate the cultural norms of their home culture, eventually experiencing *resocialization*. Some version of this model has served as rationale for many studies of sojourn experience (e.g., Forman & Zachar, 2001; Ward, Okura, Kennedy, & Kojima, 1998; Ying, 2005), and various alternate versions have been suggested (e.g., Onwumechili, Nwosu, Jackson, & James-Hughes, 2003). All tend to theorize that there is a developmental learning curve in which sense of competence and actual interactional competence in a culture vary in response to varying degrees of absorption of the host culture. Unpublished work suggests that this stage model has ambivalent support at best (Berardo, 2006).

Developmental models serve the important function of drawing attention to the evolutionary nature of interaction and relationships. Social systems, of which institutional, social, and personal relationships are types, are processual and change over time. To the extent that different social systems reflect similar types of changes over time and in certain contexts (e.g., sojourner), then theory may be able to represent such changes in a form similar to Piaget-like stages that presuppose and therefore successively build upon one another. To the extent that theoretical factors are identified that increase the likelihood of progressing through the course of the evolutionary process, such work would be of considerable value to those involved in extended sojourning experiences in other cultures. Developmental models, however, tend to be strong in modeling systemic stages of change but correspondingly weak in specifying the interpersonal and intercultural competence traits that facilitate or moderate the course of such evolution (Black & Mendenhall, 1991; Forman & Zachar, 2001).

Adaptational Models

Adaptational models extend compositional approaches from relatively *monadic* models into more *dyadic* models. Furthermore, as co-orientational models emphasize a particular outcome of competent interaction, so too adaptational models tend to emphasize the process of adaptation itself as a criterion of competence. To a large extent, the process of adaptation is prima facie evidence of competence by demonstrating the movement from an ethnocentric perspective in which adaptation is not seen as important to a more ethnorelative perspective in which adaptation is the sine qua non of intercultural interaction.

Y. Y. Kim (1988) has articulated a complex model of adaptation in which individual dispositions (e.g., cultural/ethnic background, openness, resilience) prepare an interactant to use both interactional and mass communication experiences to inform the competence of interaction with a representative of another culture (Figure 1.13). Different contextual factors, such as pressures to conform to the dominant or host culture, and the culture's tolerance for alternative cultural approaches are expected to moderate the extent to which interactants can take full advantage of the interpersonal and societal sources of informational insight into the interaction process. To the extent that these sources of information are incorporated into an adaptive process in which one interactant's behaviors are adjusted to the cultural orientation of another interactant, competence is likely to ensue.

Communication accommodation theory models a particular process of adaptation in which interactants adjust their communicative styles to the styles of the other interactants (Gallois, Franklyn-Stokes, Giles, & Coupland, 1988). Because identity is bound up in the interaction process, the goals of a given episode of interaction are translated into behaviors that are more or less focused on the other interlocutor(s). When there are cultural differences between the interlocutors, the strain of adaptation is predicted to be asymmetric, in that the more dependent, nondominant interactant is likely to engage in greater effort at adaptation than the member of the more independent and dominant culture (Figure 1.14). Such adaptations, however, are also moderated by the extent to which one's own identity is represented by the solidarity his or her speech provides with a given cultural group. Thus, if the importance of gaining compliance on a given issue outweighs interactants' sense

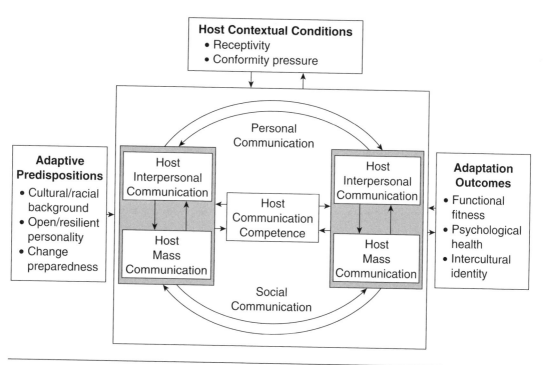

Figure 1.13 Intercultural Communicative Competence Model

SOURCE: Adapted visualization from Kim (1988).

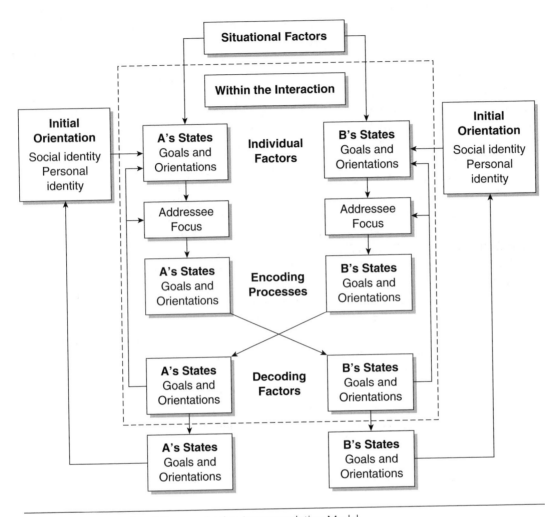

Figure 1.14   Intercultural Communicative Accommodation Model

SOURCE: Adapted visualization from Gallois, Franklyn-Stokes, Giles, and Coupland (1988).

of speech solidarity with their own cultural group, their speech is likely to be accommodated by (i.e., adapted to) the speech style of the other group, such that characteristics of the other group's communication style will be incorporated in the interaction. Generally speaking, therefore, competence is evaluated both within one's group and between groups, and depending on the affiliations and solidarity these different speech communities elicit in a person, competence may be revealed by either adaptation to the self's own group or to the other group with which interaction is engaged.

The tension of adapting to another culture versus maintaining one's own culture represents one of the fundamental dialectics of any approach to intercultural competence. Berry, Kim, Power, Young, and Bujaki (1989) explicitly recognized this tension in their model of acculturation. If the attitudes toward adapting to another society and maintaining one's own cultural identity are viewed as both orthogonal and potentially dichotomous, it presents a typology in which four potential acculturation styles are defined (Figure 1.15). *Assimilation* results when the choice is made to value the absorption of identity into the host culture. *Integration,* in contrast, accepts the possibility of multicultural groups operating in a multicollective system. Each group and its members maintain their identities but recognize the importance of sustaining the working collective in which alternative group identities need to be preserved. When there is little interest in the status of other groups, combined with interest in sustaining the identity of one's own group affiliations, an imposed *segregation* or a more voluntary *separation* may be pursued. Granted as an approach that is difficult to define, Berry et al. propose that when there is little interest in either taking on another cultural identity or the identity of one's own cultural origins, a sense of acculturative stress is anticipated, resulting in a sense of *marginalization.*

Navas et al. (2005; Navas, Rojas, García, & Pumares, 2007) extend the Berry et al. (1989) model into a more elaborate adaptational model of acculturation (Figure 1.16). In a complicated recognition of the importance of both host and immigrant or sojourner perspectives, this model posits that there are real and ideal preferences for both groups. The ideal is what each group prefers. For example, the host group may

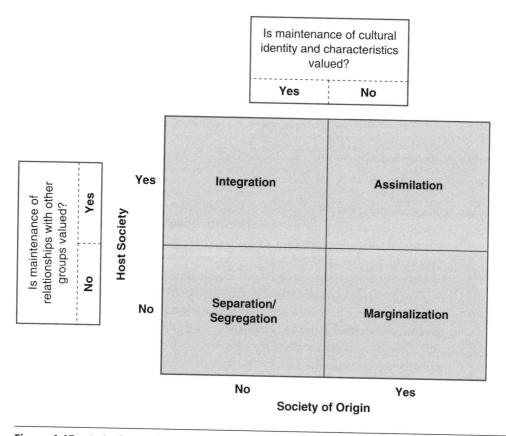

Figure 1.15 Attitude Acculturation Model

SOURCE: Adapted visualization from Berry, Kim, Power, Young, and Bujaki (1989).

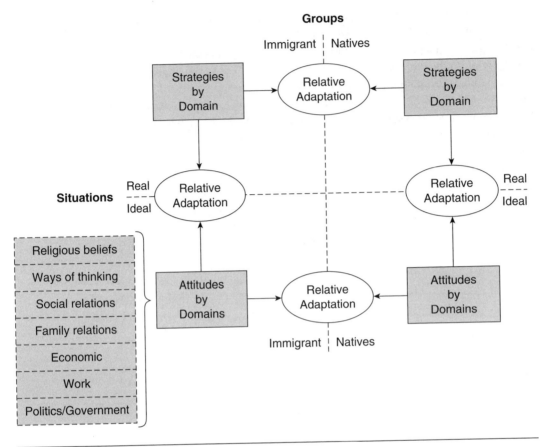

Figure 1.16   Relative Acculturation Extended Model

SOURCE: Adapted visualization from Navas et al. (2005).

prefer the immigrant group to want to separate, whereas the immigrant group may prefer the host society to desire immigrant integration. In contrast, the real attitudes reflect what each group perceives it and the other group enacts. These attitudes are expected to align themselves primarily along seven secondary domains of personal and societal functioning (practices and values surrounding religion, customs and ways of thinking, social relations, family relations, economic activity, work and labor, and politics and government). As each group interacts with its respective strategies at acculturation, at individual and group levels, the strategies may either conflict or comport with the ideal attitudes projected by the other group. Competence will be indexed largely by the extent to which the strategies employed by one group fit with the idealized aspirations of the other group.

Adaptational models point to one of the core axioms of competence models—adaptability is foundational to achieving competence (see Spitzberg & Cupach, 1989). Competence may occasionally be attributed to individuals who set the path for what the group is expected to adapt to, but in the vast majority of encounters generally, particularly in intercultural interactions, some degree of mutual adaptation is typically considered a necessary condition of competence. Adaptational models nevertheless raise theoretical problems. Adaptation in and of itself is a questionable criterion of competence (Spitzberg, 1993). Furthermore, given that adaptation is likely to be developmental, most adaptational models have yet to articulate the types of mutual adaptation necessary at various stages of development.

Causal Path Models

Most adaptational models reveal a strong debt to basic process models and general systems models common to early models of communication (e.g., Berlo, 1960). They attempt to depict highly interdependent systemic processes in which both interlocutors are simultaneously providing inputs and outputs into the system. In contrast, causal path models attempt to represent intercultural competence as a theoretical linear system, which makes it amenable to empirical tests by standard cross-sectional multivariate techniques. Causal path models tend to conceive variables at a downstream location, which successively influence and are influenced by moderating or mediating variables that in turn influence upstream variables. For example, Arasaratnam (2008) proposes that empathy both directly facilitates competence but also produces indirect effects through interaction involvement and global attitudes, which are also influenced by intercultural and interactional experiences (Figure 1.17). These collective variables are predicted to influence motivation to interact competently, which then also influences competence. Thus, there are two distinct theoretical paths to competent interaction.

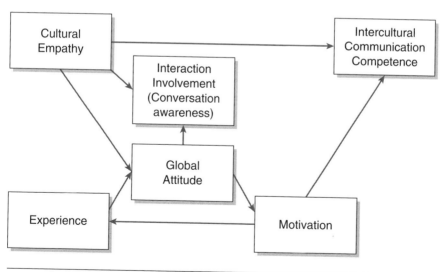

Figure 1.17 Model of Intercultural Communication Competence

SOURCE: Adapted visualization from Arasaratnam (2008).

Griffith and Harvey (2000) propose a relatively saturated theoretical model in which cultural understanding and communication competence influence each other, directly predict relationship quality, and indirectly predict it through cultural interaction and communicative interaction experiences (Figure 1.18). This model envisions communication competence as a component in a network of intercultural constructs that collectively are evaluated in their competence by the criterion of relationship quality. In an attempt to bring many of the factors identified by past models and theories together into an integrative model, Ting-Toomey (1999) hypothesizes three sets of factors: antecedent (system level, individual level, interpersonal level), managing change process (managing culture shock, managing identity change, managing new relationships, and managing environment), and outcome factors (system level, interpersonal level, personal identity). This model proposes that change processes mediate (or at least moderate) the influence of antecedent factors (Figure 1.19). The changes brought about by individual, interpersonal, and systemic influences can be managed competently or incompetently in the change process, thereby influencing the various outcomes.

In an explicit test and extension of an existing theory, Hammer, Wiseman, Rasmussen, and Bruschke (1998) posit that attributional confidence and anxiety reduction mediate the relationship between four sets of factors and the criterion of satisfaction (Figure 1.20). Interpersonal saliencies include the intimacy of the relationship and the attraction to the relationship. People attracted to and intimate with each other will experience greater confidence in understanding the other,

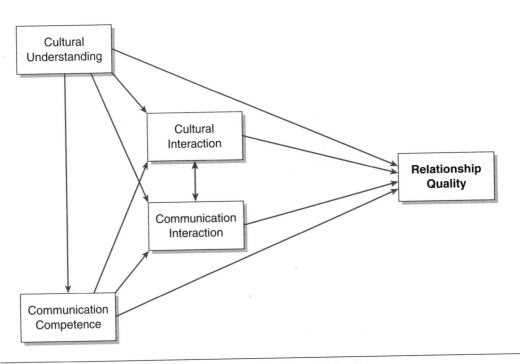

Figure 1.18   Intercultural Communication Model of Relationship Quality

SOURCE: Adapted visualization from Griffith and Harvey (2000).

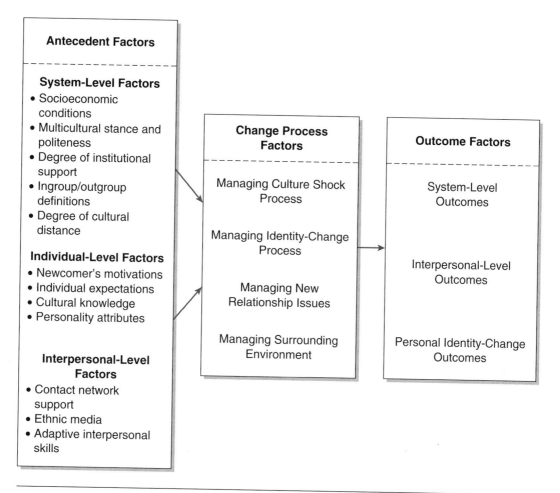

Figure 1.19   Multilevel Process Change Model of Intercultural Competence

SOURCE: Adapted visualization from Ting-Toomey (1999).

thereby reducing anxiety and enhancing satisfaction. Intergroup saliencies include cultural identity, knowledge of host culture, and degree of cultural similarity, all of which should enhance attributional confidence and diminish anxiety, thereby facilitating relationship development and satisfaction. Communication message exchange factors involve knowledge acquisition strategies (passive, interactive, self-disclosure) and language proficiency, which also facilitate attributional confidence and anxiety reduction. Finally, factors that facilitate host contact (i.e., positive host attitudes and favorable contact experiences) also facilitate greater confidence and uncertainty reduction.

The final two causal path models bear some visual structural similarities to adaptational models but posit explicit outcomes that index competent achievement. In particular, they both continue the conative approach, with central explanatory roles for motivation/attitude, knowledge/comprehension, and skills. Deardorff (2006), using a grounded-theory approach resulting in the consensual aspects of intercultural competence agreed upon by leading intercultural experts, developed a process model

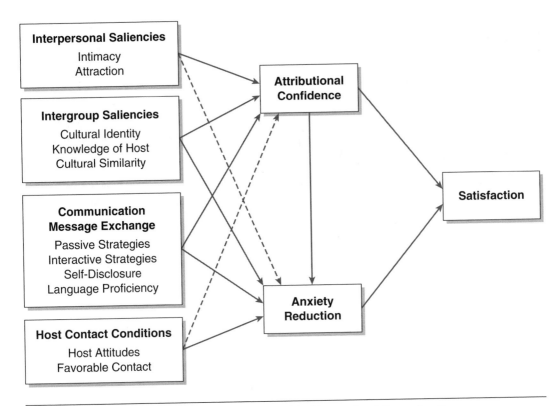

Figure 1.20 Anxiety/Uncertainty Management Model of Intercultural Competence

SOURCE: Adapted visualization from Hammer, Wiseman, Rasmussen, and Bruschke (1998).

that identifies attitudes that facilitate intercultural competence (i.e., appropriateness and effectiveness), including respect, openness, and curiosity (Figure 1.21). Motivation is enhanced by the influence of knowledge (cultural self-awareness, deep cultural knowledge, sociolinguistic awareness) and skills (listening, observing, evaluating, analyzing, interpreting, relating) components. These aspects of motivation, knowledge, and skills also follow a path to facilitating shifts of internal frames that enhance empathy, ethnorelativity, and adaptability. These shifts of internal frames then also predict appropriate and effective outcomes. The model envisions a simultaneous interactional process that feeds back into itself at almost all levels but also anticipates several specific sequential causal paths.

Imahori and Lanigan (1989) propose a model derived in part from Spitzberg and Cupach (1984). Sojourners and host-nationals are mirror-image interlocutors, and both are modeled in terms of their motivation (e.g., positive attitudes toward culture and partner), knowledge (e.g., language, interaction rules, and culture), and skills (e.g., respect, interaction posture, knowledge acquisition, empathy, role flexibility, interaction management, ambiguity tolerance, linguistics, speech accommodation, and affinity testing). The interactants' motivation, knowledge, and skills interact with their goals and experiences (Figure 1.22). To the extent either or both interlocutors are motivated, knowledgeable, skilled, and goal driven toward productive experiences, a variety of outcomes that index competent intercultural interaction are

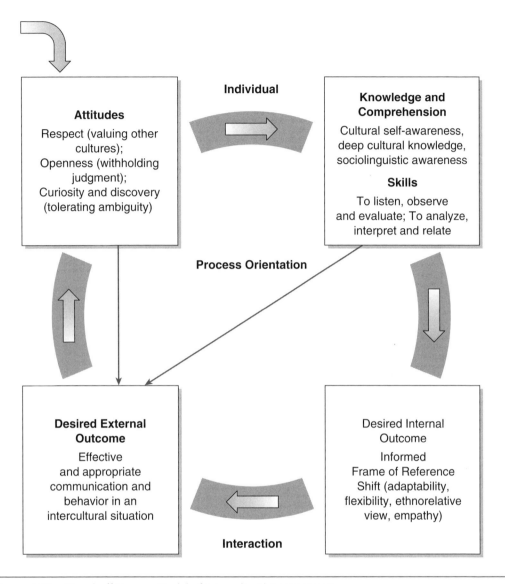

Figure 1.21   Deardorff Process Model of Intercultural Competence

SOURCE: Deardorff (2006). Used by permisssion.

likely to result (e.g., effectiveness, relational satisfaction, intimacy, commitment, and uncertainty reduction).

Causal path models have the advantage of their relatively easy adaptation to research purposes. They also comport well with the traditional notion of theoretical explanation. Causality underlies all explanation to some extent, and causal path models posit explicit hypotheses in their component connections. These very strengths also reveal one of the weaknesses of these models—to the extent they build too many feedback loops or two-way arrows (causal paths), they reduce their value as guides to explicit theory testing through hypothesis verification of falsification.

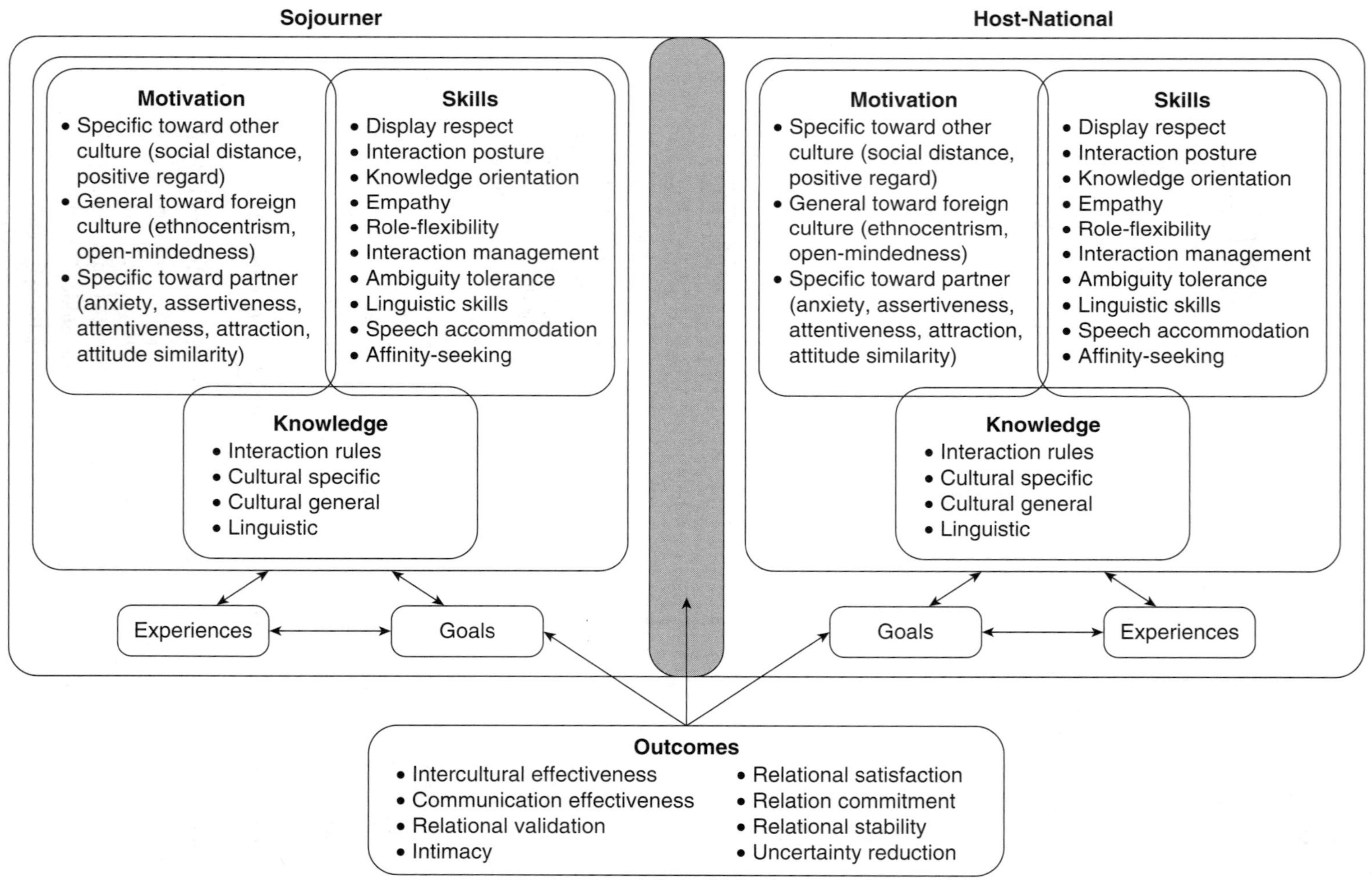

Figure 1.22 Relational Model of Intercultural Competence

SOURCE: Adapted visualization from Imahori and Lanigan (1989), after Spitzberg and Cupach (1984).

The Status of Conceptualizations
of Intercultural Communication Competence

There is obviously no shortage of feasible approaches or models for guiding conceptualizations, theories, measurements, and investigations of intercultural competence. The theories and models display both considerable similarity in their broad brushstrokes (e.g., motivation, knowledge, skills, context, outcomes) and yet extensive diversity at the level of specific conceptual subcomponents. This similarity and diversity is thoroughly illustrated in Table 1.1, in which components from across a broad range of research on intercultural communication competence research and models are organized. This list no doubt does damage to some of the individual concepts, but it suggests that there may be greater commonality across models than initially assumed.

The deeper theoretical issues involved in whether motivation, knowledge, and skills are really separable states and processes remain a concern. In addition, some potentially relevant concepts appear noticeably absent. For example, there is virtually no attention paid to physiological and emotional aspects of interactants. Aside from the traumatizing effects of culture shock or the implicit correlatives of anxiety, interactants are conceptualized as largely cognitive, rational beings. In contrast, political consultants and psycholinguists point out that the vast majority of thought and language processing occurs at a subconscious level (e.g., see *Orwell in America*, http://www.mapdigital.com/orwell/ondemand.html). It seems likely that conceptualizations of intercultural communication competence have depicted interactants as too conceptual, too rational, too conscious, and too intentional. With the exception of anxiety, even the motivation component tends to be overly cognitive in nature, and even anxiety is often viewed as a product of rational information processing. In this regard, emotion appraisal theories and affect theories may make important complements to existing models of intercultural competence (e.g., Guerrero, Andersen, & Trost, 1998).

A second set of issues regards the primitive conceptual nature of the concept of adaptability. Adaptability seems implicitly or explicitly central to virtually all models of intercultural competence. The concept of adaptability, however, has not been measured very validly, in part because it has not been conceptualized very carefully. The subcomponents of adaptability, such as sensitivity, empathy, or perspective taking, also have not been operationalized or conceptualized with much specificity or demonstrated validity. For example, adaptability is always a process of shift or change, but from what? If adaptation is a core feature of competence, and if a sojourner is supposed to adapt to the host-national culture, it is unclear to what extent both must adapt to one another. If both are adapting, it seems possible that both interactants become chameleons without a clear target pattern to which to adapt. If adaptation results in excessive compromise of personal identity, such a trade-off may exact costs on other aspects of competent performance. Finally, adaptability is by definition a process of variability, but most approaches to measurement treat it as a trait, a consistent predisposition to behave inconsistently. These and other problems and issues

Table 1.1   Listing of Concept and Factor Labels Associated With Interpersonal, Communicative, and Intercultural Competence

Motivation

- Agency (Ezekiel, 1968)
- Attraction (Gudykunst, 1993)
- Basic human needs (rainbow model)
- Collective self-esteem (Ting-Toomey, 1993)
- Demand (long-term goal orientation) (Ezekiel, 1968)
- Developing affective-cognitive congruence (Ting-Toomey, 1993)
- General toward foreign culture (ethnocentrism, open-mindedness, sojourner/host-national) (Imahori & Lanigan, 1989)
- Inclusion-differentiation dialectic (Ting-Toomey, 1993)
- Involvement in culture (Kealey, 1996)
- Managing self-esteem (Ting-Toomey, 1993)
- Needs (rainbow model)
- Needs (Gudykunst, 1993)
- Openness to others (Kealey, 1996)
- Openness to new information (Gudykunst, 1993)
- Patience (Kealey, 1996)
- Positive attitudes (Lonner & Hayes, 2004)
- Professional commitment, perseverance, initiative (Kealey, 1996)
- Regulating ego-focused and other-focused emotions (Ting-Toomey, 1993)
- Security-vulnerability dialectic (Ting-Toomey, 1993)
- Self-esteem
- Self-confidence (Kealey, 1996)
- Specific toward other culture (social distance, positive regard, sojourner/host-national) (Imahori & Lanigan, 1989)
- Specific toward partner (anxiety, assertiveness, attentiveness, attraction, attitude similarity, sojourner/host-national) (Imahori & Lanigan, 1989)
- Stress tolerance (Kealey, 1996)
- Tolerance (Kealey, 1996)

Knowledge

- Ability to create new categories (Gudykunst, 1993)
- Ability to gather appropriate information (Gudykunst, 1993)
- Ability to tolerate ambiguity (Gudykunst, 1993; Ruben in Arasaratnam, 2008; Imahori & Lanigan, 1989)
- Analytical empathy (Ting-Toomey & Kurogi, 1998)
- Analyze (Deardorff, 2006)
- Beliefs regarding ingroup-outgroup miscategorization (Cooper, Doucet, & Pratt, 2007)
- Biases of assessment (Sue, 2001)
- Categorization-particularization (Ting-Toomey, 1993)
- Cognitive complexity
- Content rules (Collier in Hammer, 1989)
- Culture-bound, class-bound, and linguistic features of support (Sue, 2001)
- Cultural general (sojourner/host-national) (Imahori & Lanigan, 1989)
- Cultural identity images (Ting-Toomey, 1993)

- Cultural intelligent (Cooper et al., 2007)
- Cultural self-awareness (Deardorff, 2006)
- Cultural sensitivity (Kealey, 1996)
- Cultural specific (sojourner/host-national) (Imahori & Lanigan, 1989)
- Cultural understanding (Griffith & Harvey, 2000)
- Culture-specific information (Deardorff, 2006)
- Decoding skills (reception, perception, interpretation skills)
- Deep understanding and knowledge of culture (including contexts, role, and impact of culture and others' worldviews) (Deardorff, 2006)
- Differentiation (Ezekiel, 1968)
- Discriminatory practices operating at community level (Sue, 2001)
- Ethnorelative view (Deardorff, 2006)
- Expectations (Gudykunst, 1993)
- Expression rules (e.g., assertiveness) (Collier in Hammer, 1989)
- General competence as teacher (task) (Harris, 1977)
- Groups with which one belongs or works (Sue, 2001)
- Human identity images (Ting-Toomey, 1993)
- Interaction rules (sojourner/host-national) (Imahori & Lanigan, 1989)
- Knowledge of more than one perspective (Gudykunst, 1993)
- Knowledge of alternative interpretations (Gudykunst, 1993)
- Knowledge of similarities and differences (Gudykunst, 1993)
- Language proficiency (Hammer, Wiseman, Rasmussen, & Bruschke, 1998)
- Linguistic (sojourner/host-national) (Imahori & Lanigan, 1989)
- Mindfullness-mindlessness (Ting-Toomey, 1993)
- Mindful creativity (Ting-Toomey & Kurogi, 1998)
- Mindful reflexivity (Ting-Toomey & Kurogi, 1998)
- Multiple vision (Ting-Toomey & Kurogi, 1998)
- Observe (Deardorff, 2006)
- Openness to novelty (Ting-Toomey & Kurogi, 1998)
- Own racial/cultural heritage and its effects (Sue, 2001)
- Personal identity images (Ting-Toomey, 1993)
- Personal self-esteem (Ting-Toomey, 1993)
- Political astuteness (Kealey, 1996)
- Problem solving (Kealey, 1996)
- Racial identity development (Sue, 2001)
- Role prescription rules (Collier in Hammer, 1989)
- Relational climate rules (Collier in Hammer, 1989)
- Realism (Kealey, 1996)
- "Self/face" models (Ting-Toomey & Kurogi, 1998)
- Seeks consultation with traditional healers (Sue, 2001)
- Seeks educational, consultative, and multicultural training (Sue, 2001)
- Seeks understanding of self as racial/cultural being (Sue, 2001)
- Self-monitoring
- Sense of identity coherence (Ting-Toomey, 1993)
- Shared networks (Gudykunst, 1993)
- Small/large power distance (Ting-Toomey & Kurogi, 1998)
- Social identity images (Ting-Toomey, 1993)
- Sociolinguistic awareness (Deardorff, 2006)

(Continued)

Table 1.1 (Continued)

- Sociopolitics, immigration, poverty, powerlessness, etc. (Sue, 2001)
- Transfer of "software" (Hwang, Chase, & Arden-Ogle, 1985)
- Unarticulated and articulated self-images (Ting-Toomey, 1993)
- World history (Hunter, White, & Godbey, 2006)

Skills: Higher-Order Skills (Ability to Use Certain Behaviors)

- Ability to accommodate behavior (Gudykunst, 1993)
- Ability to adapt communication (Gudykunst, 1993)
- Ability to adjust to different cultures (Abe & Wiseman, 1983)
- Ability to communicate interpersonally (Abe & Wiseman, 1983)
- Ability to deal with different societal systems (Abe & Wiseman, 1983)
- Ability to deal with psychological stress (Hammer, 1987; Hammer, Gudykunst, & Wiseman, 1978; Hammer, Nishida, & Jezek, 1986; Wiseman & Abe, 1986)
- Ability to effectively communicate (Hammer, 1987; Hammer et al., 1978; Hammer et al., 1986; Wiseman & Abe, 1986)
- Ability to empathize (Gudykunst, 1993)
- Ability to establish interpersonal relationships (Abe & Wiseman, 1983; Hammer, 1987; Hammer et al., 1978; Hammer et al., 1986; Wiseman & Abe, 1986)
- Ability to understand others (Abe & Wiseman, 1983)
- Collaborative dialogue (Ting-Toomey & Kurogi, 1998)
- Communication competence (Griffith & Harvey, 2000)
- Curiosity and discovery (tolerating ambiguity and uncertainty) (Deardorff, 2006)
- Displaying behavioral adaptation and flexibility (Ting-Toomey, 1993)
- Educates clients of own practice (Sue, 2001)
- Engage in variety of verbal and nonverbal helping styles (Sue, 2001)
- Evaluate (Deardorff, 2006)
- Facework management (Ting-Toomey & Kurogi, 1998)
- Flexibility (Lonner & Hayes, 2004)
- Interaction skills (Ting-Toomey & Kurogi, 1998)
- Interpret (Deardorff, 2006)
- Involved with minority groups outside of work roles (Sue, 2001)
- Listen (Deardorff, 2006)
- Mindful listening (Ting-Toomey & Kurogi, 1998)
- Mindful observation (Ting-Toomey & Kurogi, 1998)
- Monitoring mutual self-presentation behaviors (Ting-Toomey, 1993)
- Observe (Deardorff, 2006)
- Relate (Deardorff, 2006)
- Relationship building (Kealey, 1996)
- Stress tolerance (Lonner & Hayes, 2004)
- Takes responsibility to provide linguistic competence (Sue, 2001)
- Trust building (Ting-Toomey & Kurogi, 1998)
- Works to eliminate biases, prejudice, and discrimination (Sue, 2001)

Macro-Level Skills/Competencies

- Ability to communicate effectively (deal with misunderstandings, different styles)
- Ability to establish interpersonal relationships

- Ability to facilitate communication (Martin, 1986)
- Adaptability
- Adaptability (to different communication styles and behaviors; adjustment to new cultural environments)
- Awareness
- Awareness of implications and cultural differences (Martin, 1986)
- Awareness of self and culture (Martin, 1986)
- Conversational skills
- Creativity
- Cultural interaction (Harris, 1977)
- Decoding and encoding
- Decoding skills (reception, perception, interpretation skills)
- Diversity (Hunter et al., 2006)
- Facework communication styles (Ting-Toomey & Kurogi, 1998)
- Flexibility
- Flexibility (selecting and using appropriate communication styles and behaviors; cognitive flexibility)
- Individualism-collectivism (Ting-Toomey & Kurogi, 1998)
- Interpersonal flexibility (Martin, 1986)
- Mutual adaptability (Ting-Toomey & Kurogi, 1998)
- Mutual satisfaction (Ting-Toomey & Kurogi, 1998)
- Nonverbal communication competence (rainbow model)
- Perceived appropriateness (Ting-Toomey & Kurogi, 1998)
- Perceived effectiveness (Ting-Toomey & Kurogi, 1998)
- Nonverbal communication competence (rainbow model)
- Racial/ethnic effects on personality, career, etc. (Sue, 2001)
- Similarity
- Social ability/skill
- Social bonds (Gudykunst, 1993)
- Social impact and communication styles (Sue, 2001)
- Strength of personality (Harris, 1977)
- Verbal skills

Skills

Attentiveness

- Acceptance
- Adaptiveness (Hwang et al., 1985)
- Affiliation
- Affinity (rainbow model)
- Affinity seeking (sojourner/host-national) (Imahori & Lanigan, 1989)
- Aggressiveness/aggression
- Altercentrism
- Attention
- Attentiveness

(Continued)

Table 1.1 (Continued)

- Be friendly
- Be polite (Martin and Hammer in Martin, 1986)
- Boorishness
- Confirmation
- Cooperativeness (Hwang et al., 1985; Spitzberg & Cupach, 2002)
- Cultural empathy
- Decoding
- Disapproval/criticism of others
- Disdainfulness of others
- Display respect (sojourner/host-national) (Imahori & Lanigan, 1989)
- Distance
- Enhancement
- Emotional sensitivity
- Emotional support
- Empathy (Deardorfff, 2006; Hwang, Chase, & Kelly, 1980; Hwang et al., 1985; Imahori & Lanigan, 1989; Spitzberg & Cupach, 2002)
- Enmeshment
- Eye gaze (Martin & Hammer in Hammer, 1989)
- Friendliness/outgoingness
- Helping
- Hostile depression
- Hostile domination
- Interaction management (sojourner/host-national) (Imahori & Lanigan, 1989)
- Interaction posture (sojourner/host-national) (Imahori & Lanigan, 1989)
- Interpersonal diplomacy
- Intimacy (Hammer et al., 1998)
- Intimacy/warmth
- Knowledge orientation (sojourner/host-national) (Imahori & Lanigan, 1989)
- Linguistic skills (sojourner/host-national) (Imahori & Lanigan, 1989)
- Listening
- Negative assertion
- Nonjudgmental reactions (Hunter et al., 2006)
- Openness (Hunter et al., 2006)
- Other-orientation/directedness
- Perceptiveness
- Personality traits (empathy, tolerance)
- Politeness rules (e.g., behave politely) (Hammer, 1987)
- Prosocial competence/skills
- Recognition of others' differences (Hunter et al., 2006)
- Reflectiveness
- Responsiveness
- Role flexibility (sojourner/host-national) (Imahori & Lanigan, 1989)
- Self-centeredness
- Show interest
- Social interaction (display respect, appropriate behavior)
- Social offensiveness
- Social sensitivity

- Speech accommodation (sojourner/host-national) (Imahori & Lanigan, 1989)
- Understanding

Composure

- Ability to deal with psychological stress
- Anxiety (comfort, composure, confidence, nervous movements)
- Assertiveness
- Autonomy
- Avoidance/social withdrawal
- Commitment
- Coping with feelings
- Dominance
- Emotional control
- Initiation
- Instrumental skills
- Intentionality
- Interpersonal endeavors/perils
- Interpersonal skills (establish relationship, initiate talking)
- Managerial ability (motivation, creativity)
- Need for achievement
- Persuasiveness
- Pleading
- Self-efficacy
- Self-orientation
- Social control
- Social instrumental skills
- Social manipulation
- Social relaxation/ease
- Social superiority

Coordination

- Evaluation and acceptance of feedback
- Head nods (Martin & Hammer in Hammer, 1989)
- Interaction management skills
- Interruptions (Martin & Hammer in Hammer, 1989)
- Message orientation

Expressiveness

- Ability to be understood
- Activity in conversation
- Affective skills
- Animation
- Articulation
- Body nonverbal behavior
- Clarity
- Communication apprehension (Hwang et al., 1980; Hwang et al., 1985)

(Continued)

Table 1.1 (Continued)

- Confrontation/anger expression
- Emotional control
- Emotional expressivity
- Emotionality
- Encoding
- Expressiveness/expressivity
- Facial expressiveness and vocalic behavior
- Interactive strategies (Hammer et al., 1998)
- Managing reactive emotions (Ting-Toomey, 1993)
- Nonverbal behavior
- Openness/confiding
- Passive strategies (Hammer et al., 1998)
- Personal appearance/physical attraction
- Self-disclosure (Hammer et al., 1998)
- Self-disclosure/expression
- Smiling (Martin & Hammer in Hammer, 1989)
- Social expressivity
- Vocalic skills
- Wit

Contextual Competencies

- Conflict management/handling differences
- Cultural identity (Hammer et al., 1998)
- Cultural similarity (Hammer et al., 1998)
- Educates clients of own practice (Sue, 2001)
- Heterosocial contact
- Relations with authority figures
- Social activity/experience

Outcomes

- Ability to assess intercultural performance (Hunter et al., 2006)
- Appropriateness
- Attraction (Hammer et al., 1998)
- Behaving and communicating effectively and appropriately (based on one's intercultural knowledge, skills, and attitudes) to achieve one's goals to some degree (Deardorff, 2006)
- Coherence: adaptation and integration (Rathje, 2007)
- Cohesion (Cooper, Doucet, & Pratt, 2007)
- Cohesion: normality of differences (Rathje, 2007)
- Cohesion: familiarity with differences (Rathje, 2007)
- Collaboration across cultures (Hunter et al., 2006)
- Communication competence
- Communication effectiveness (Imahori & Lanigan, 1989)
- Communication satisfaction
- Effective communication (Gudykunst, 1993)
- Effectiveness
- Effective participation both socially and in business generally (Hunter et al., 2006)

Table 1.1 (Continued)

- Goal attainment (Cooper et al., 2007)
- Identifying cultural differences to compete globally (Hunter et al., 2006)
- Interactive identity attunement (Ting-Toomey, 1993)
- Interactive identity confirmation (Ting-Toomey, 1993)
- Interactive identity coordination (Ting-Toomey, 1993)
- Intercultural effectiveness (Imahori & Lanigan, 1989)
- Intercultural interaction (Hawes & Kealey, 1981)
- Interpersonal liking (Cooper et al., 2007)
- Intimacy (Imahori & Lanigan, 1989)
- Level of conflict (Cooper et al., 2007)
- Likelihood that behaviors are assessed as appropriate (Cooper et al., 2007)
- Likelihood that individuals are categorized as outgroup (Cooper et al., 2007)
- Likelihood that nation is basis for categorization (Cooper et al., 2007)
- Personal/family adjustment (Hawes & Kealey, 1981)
- Relational commitment (Imahori & Lanigan, 1989)
- Relational satisfaction (Imahori & Lanigan, 1989)
- Relational stability (Imahori & Lanigan, 1989)
- Relational validation (Imahori & Lanigan, 1989)
- Relationship quality (Griffith & Harvey, 2000)
- Rewarding impression
- Satisfaction (Hammer et al., 1998)
- Task accomplishment (Hawes & Kealey, 1981)
- Task completion
- Uncertainty reduction (Imahori & Lanigan, 1989)

Context

- Environmental situation (rainbow model)
- Exercises institutional intervention skills for clients (Sue, 2001)
- Geocentric staffing practices (vs. polycentric) (Cooper et al., 2007)
- Globalization (Hunter et al., 2006)
- Host contact conditions (Hammer et al., 1998)
- Institutional barriers effects (Sue, 2001)
- Integration (Cooper et al., 2007)
- Internationalization (Cooper et al., 2007)
- Likelihood of cross-national interactions (Cooper et al., 2007)
- Marriage/family stability (Kealey, 1996)
- Minority family structures, community, etc. (Sue, 2001)

with the concept of adaptability have been examined previously but have yet to produce convincing solutions (see Friedman & Antal, 2005; Gamst et al., 2004; Hammer
et al., 2003; Spitzberg, 1993, 1994b; Spitzberg & Cupach, 1984, 1989).

A third set of concerns is the potential ethnocentricity of the models. Most of the
models and related assessments have been developed in Western or Anglo contexts.
It is difficult to ascertain at present the extent to which such contexts may bias or
shift emphasis. For example, the Western emphasis on individuality would tend to

prioritize assertiveness skills, whereas the collectivistic tendencies of Eastern perspectives might emphasize empathy, sensitivity, and conformity (Spitzberg, 1994a, 1994b). Yet, even within U.S. social scientific approaches to social skills, assertiveness training has fallen out of favor, whereas empathy, perspective taking, and adaptability continue to serve as the hallmarks of most models of intercultural competence, regardless of the cultural origins of the authors or models. Expanding literatures in the Central and South Americas, India, South Korea, Japan, and Africa open up new possibilities for rethinking the relevance of Western concepts of competence (see other chapters in this section for non-Western perspectives on intercultural competence). Future research needs to make the cross-cultural generalizability of these models and their respective measures a priority for future research.

In rethinking the relevance of Western concepts of competence, there is an opportunity to revisit arguments made before yet largely ignored in the competence literature. Competence is still largely viewed as an *individual* and *trait* concept and is almost always measured accordingly, despite repeated calls for expanded and more *relational* perspectives toward competence (Spitzberg & Cupach, 1984, 1989). Many models assume a partner, but most define skills and knowledge as possessed by the individual, thereby locating the competence in the individual's possession or level of these competencies. Relational perspectives, such as those suggested by recent developments in the assessment and statistical analysis of dyadic processes such as empathy (e.g., Ickes & Simpson, 1997; Kenny, 1994), permit far more sophisticated modeling of competencies located in the interaction itself, in addition to the competencies located in the individuals who comprise the interaction process. From a theoretical modeling perspective, this raises fundamental questions about *where competence is located*, which largely have yet to be seriously resolved in the competence literature.

A final consideration is whether or how the "best" model or models would be identified. On one hand, it is tempting to argue that the variety of models is a sign of postmodern diversity and that cultural diversity itself may require a parallel range of models. On the other hand, it is obvious that there is a core of common theoretical metaphors running across most models. Spitzberg and Cupach (1984) argued that any comprehensive model of interpersonal competence will need to conceptualize a minimum of five components: motivation, knowledge, skills, context, and outcomes. Developmental models draw attention to integrate the time element of relationships, and relational models emphasize the importance of including all of the participants involved and their interaction process, rather than just the individual person as the unit of analysis. Thus, as a rather general criterion of quality, it is proposed that the more a model incorporates specific conceptualization of interactants' motivation, knowledge, skills, context, and outcomes, in the context of an ongoing relationship over time, the more advanced the model.

Conclusion

Conceptualizations of intercultural communication competence have seen over five decades of scholarly activity. An encouraging conclusion from this activity is that there is a rich conceptual and theoretical landscape from which many models have emerged.

Furthermore, there is extensive commonality across these models, which provides strong conceptual paths along which future theory development can and should progress. There is also, however, a strong suspicion, depicted in Table 1.1, that many conceptual wheels are being reinvented at the expense of legitimate progress. Specifically, relatively few efforts have been made to systematically test the validity and cross-cultural generality of the models posited to date. Only a few efforts have been made to produce models inductively generated by thorough surveys of existing theoretical models (e.g., Kupka, 2008; Spitzberg & Cupach, 2002) or actual interactants or experts (e.g., Deardorff, 2006; Prechtl & Lund, 2007). Identifying a hierarchical structure within which the 300-plus terms and concepts related to interpersonal and intercultural competence can fit will be a challenging task, but there is a need to provide a more parsimonious model that can successfully integrate such diversity. It is highly unlikely that there are actually more than 300 theoretically distinct constructs as displayed in Table 1.1 that need to be modeled explicitly. Social processes and systems are very complex, but it seems implausible that they need to be this complex. Models are necessarily simplified versions of the reality they seek to represent and therefore need to provide parsimonious guidance to theoretical and investigative pursuits. Theorists will be in a better position to develop more useful and conceptually integrated models (and measures) to the extent the underlying theoretical structures, dimensions, and processes examined in these models are identified and synthesized.

References

Abe, H., & Wiseman, R. L. (1983). A cross-cultural confirmation of the dimensions of intercultural effectiveness. *International Journal of Intercultural Relations, 7,* 53–67.

Altshuler, L., Sussman, N. M., & Kachur, E. (2003). Assessing changes in intercultural sensitivity among physician trainees using the intercultural development inventory. *International Journal of Intercultural Relations, 27,* 387–401.

Anderson, P. H., Lawton, L., Rexeisen, R. J., & Hubbard, A. C. (2006). Short-term study abroad and intercultural sensitivity: A pilot study. *International Journal of Intercultural Relations, 30,* 457–469.

Arasaratnam, L. A. (2007). Research in intercultural communication competence. *Journal of International Communication, 13*(2), 66–73.

Arasaratnam, L. A. (2008, May). *Further testing of a new model of intercultural communication competence.* Paper presented at the annual meeting of the International Communication Association, New York, NY.

Arasaratnam, L. A., & Doerfel, M. L. (2005). Intercultural communication competence: Identifying key components from multicultural perspectives. *International Journal of Intercultural Relations, 29,* 137–163.

Ashwill, M. A. (2004). Developing intercultural competence for the masses. *International Educator, 13*(2), 16–25.

Beamer, L. (1992). Learning intercultural communication competence. *Journal of Business Communication, 29,* 285–303.

Bennett, M. J. (1986). A developmental approach to training for intercultural sensitivity. *International Journal of Intercultural Relations, 10,* 179–196.

Benson, P. G. (1978). Measuring cross-cultural adjustment: The problem of criteria. *International Journal of Intercultural Relations, 2,* 21–37.

Berardo. (2006). *The U-curve of adjustment: A study in the evolution and evaluation of a 50-year old model.* Bedfordshire, UK: Luton Business School, University of Bedfordshire. Retrieved September 9, 2008, from http://www.pacific.edu/SIS/docs/FINAL-Berardo-Forum-Handouts.doc

Berlo, D. K. (1960). *The process of communication.* New York: Holt, Rinehart & Wilson.

Berry, J. W., Kim, U., Power, S., Young, M., & Bujaki, M. (1989). Acculturation in plural societies. *Applied Psychology: An International Review, 38,* 185–206.

Bhaskar-Shrinivas, P., Harrison, D. A., Shaffer, M. A., & Luk, D. M. (2005). Input-based and time-based models of international adjustment: Meta-analytic evidence and theoretical extensions. *Academy of Management Journal, 48,* 257–281.

Black, J. S., & Mendenhall, M. (1991). The U-curve adjustment hypothesis revisited: A review and theoretical framework. *Journal of International Business Studies, 22,* 225–247.

Bloom, B. S. (1956). *Taxonomy of educational objectives, handbook I: The cognitive domain.* New York: David McKay.

Bourhis, R. Y., Moïse, L. C., Perreault, S., & Senécal, S. (1997). Towards an interactive acculturation model: A social psychological approach. *International Journal of Psychology, 32,* 369–386.

Bradford, L., Allen, M., & Beisser, K. R. (2000). Meta-analysis of intercultural communication competence research. *World Communication, 29,* 28–51.

Bremer, D. (2006). Wanted: Global workers. *International Educator, 15*(3), 40–45.

Britt, D. W. (1997). *A conceptual introduction to modeling: Qualitative and quantitative perspectives.* Mahwah, NJ: Lawrence Erlbaum.

Brown, P., & Levinson, S. C. (1987). *Politeness: Some universals in language usage.* New York: Cambridge University Press.

Byram, M. (1997). *Teaching and assessing intercultural communication competence.* New York: Multilingual Matters.

Byram, M. (2003). On being 'bicultural' and 'intercultural.' In G. Alred, M. Byram, & M. Fleming (Eds.), *Intercultural experience and education* (pp. 50–66). Tonowanda, NY: Multilingual Matters.

Byram, M., Nichols, A., & Stevens, D. (2001). *Developing intercultural competence in practice.* New York: Multilingual Matters.

Chaisrakeo, S., & Speece, M. (2004). Culture, intercultural communication competence and sales negotiation: A qualitative research approach. *Journal of Business & Industrial Marketing, 19,* 267–282.

Chen, L. (2002). Perceptions of intercultural interaction and communication satisfaction: A study on initial encounters. *Communication Research, 15,* 133–147.

Collier, M. J. (1996). Communication competence problematic in ethnic friendships. *Communication Monographs, 63,* 314–336.

Committee for Economic Development Research and Policy Committee. (2006). *Education for global leadership: The importance of international studies and foreign language education for U.S. economic and national security.* Washington, DC: Committee for Economic Development.

Cooper, D., Doucet, L., & Pratt, M. (2007). Understanding 'appropriateness' in multinational organizations. *Journal of Organizational Behavior, 28,* 303–335.

Deardorff, D. K. (2006). Identification and assessment of intercultural competence as a student outcome of internationalization. *Journal of Studies in Intercultural Education, 10,* 241–266.

Deardorff, D. K., & Hunter, W. (2006). Educating global-ready graduates. *International Educator, 15*(3), 72–83.

Dinges, N. G., & Baldwin, K. D. (1996). Intercultural competence: A research perspective. In D. Landis & R. S. Bhagat (Eds.), *Handbook of intercultural training* (2nd ed., pp. 106–123). Thousand Oaks, CA: Sage.

Euwema, M. C., & Van Emmerik, I. J. H. (2007). Intercultural competencies and conglomerated conflict behaviors in intercultural conflicts. *International Journal of Intercultural Relations, 31,* 427–441.

Ezekiel, R. S. (1968). The personal future and Peace Corps competence. *Journal of Personality and Social Psychology, 8*(Monograph Suppl., No. 2, Pt. 2), 1–26.

Fantini, A. E. (1995). Language, culture, and world view: Exploring the nexus. *International Journal of Intercultural Relations, 19,* 143–153.

Fantini, A. E. (2001, April). *Exploring intercultural competence: A construct proposal.* Paper presented at the National Council of Less Commonly Taught Languages, Arlington, VA.

Fisher, G. B., & Härtel, C. E. (2003). Cross-cultural effectiveness of Western expatriate-Thai client interactions: Lessons learned for IHRM research and theory. *Cross Cultural Management, 10*(4), 4–28.

Forman, S., & Zachar, P. (2001). Cross-cultural adjustment of international officers during professional military education in the United States. *Military Psychology, 13,* 117–128.

Friedman, V. J., & Antal, A. B. (2005). Negotiating reality: A theory of action approach to intercultural competence. *Management Learning, 36,* 69–86.

Furnham, A., & Bochner, S. (1986). *Culture shock: Psychological reactions to unfamiliar environments.* New York: Metheun.

Gallois, C., Franklyn-Stokes, A., Giles, H., & Coupland, N. (1988). Communication accommodation in intercultural encounters. In Y. Y. Kim (Ed.), *Theories in intercultural communication* (pp. 157–185). Newbury Park, CA: Sage.

Gamst, G., Dana, R. H., Der-Karabetian, A., Aragon, M., Arellano, L., Morrow, G., et al. (2004). Cultural competency revised: The California brief multicultural competence scale. *Measurement and Evaluation in Counseling and Development, 37,* 163–183.

Gertsen, M. C. (1990). Intercultural competence and expatriates. *International Journal of Human Resource Management, 1,* 341–362.

Gibson, D., & Zhong, M. (2005). Intercultural communication competence in the healthcare context. *International Journal of Intercultural Relations, 29,* 621–634.

Griffith, D. A., & Harvey, M. G. (2000). An intercultural communication model for use in global interorganizational networks. *Journal of International Marketing, 9*(3), 87–103.

Gudykunst, W. B. (1993). Toward a theory of effective interpersonal and intergroup communication. In R. J. Wiseman & J. Koester (Eds.), *Intercultural communication competence* (International and Intercultural Communication Annual, Vol. 16, pp. 3–71). Newbury Park, CA: Sage.

Gudykunst, W. B., & Hammer, M. R. (1984). Dimensions of intercultural effectiveness: Culture specific or culture general? *International Journal of Intercultural Relations, 8,* 1–10.

Guerrero, L. K., Andersen, P. A., & Trost, M. R. (1998). Communication and emotion: Basic concepts and approaches. In P. A. Andersen & L. K. Guerrero (Eds.), *Handbook of communication and emotion: Research, theory, applications, and contexts* (pp. 3–27). San Diego: Academic.

Gullahorn, J. R., & Gullahorn, J. E. (1962). An extension of the U-curve hypothesis. *Journal of Social Issues, 3,* 33–47.

Hajek, C., & Giles, H. (2003). New directions in intercultural communication competence: The process model. In J. O. Greene & B. R. Burleson (Eds.), *Handbook of communication and social interaction skills* (pp. 935–957). Mahwah, NJ: Lawrence Erlbaum.

Howard Hamilton, M. F., Richardson, B. J., & Shuford, B. (1998). Promoting multicultural education: A holistic approach. *College Student Affairs Journal, 18,* 5–17.

Hammer, M. R. (1987). Behavioral dimensions of intercultural effectiveness: A replication and extension. *International Journal of Intercultural Relations, 11,* 65–88.

Hammer, M. R. (1989). Intercultural communication competence. In M. K. Asante & W. B. Gudykunst (Eds.), *Handbook of international and intercultural communication* (pp. 247–260). Newbury Park, CA: Sage.

Hammer, M. R. (2005). The intercultural conflict style inventory: A conceptual framework and measure of intercultural conflict resolution approaches. *International Journal of Intercultural Relations, 2,* 675–695.

Hammer, M. R., Bennett, M. J., & Wiseman, R. L. (2003). Measuring intercultural sensitivity: The intercultural development inventory. *International Journal of Intercultural Relations, 27,* 421–443.

Hammer, M. R., Gudykunst, W. B., & Wiseman, R. L. (1978). Dimensions of intercultural effectiveness: An exploratory study. *International Journal of Intercultural Relations, 2,* 382–393.

Hammer, M. R., Nishida, H., & Jezek, L. (1986, November). *A cross-cultural comparison of dimensions of interpersonal effectiveness: Japan, Mexico and the United States.* Paper presented at the Speech Communication Association Conference, Chicago.

Hammer, M. R., Wiseman, R. L., Rasmussen, J. L., & Bruschke, J. C. (1998). A test of anxiety/uncertainty management theory: The intercultural adaptation context. *Communication Quarterly, 46,* 309–326.

Harris, J. G., Jr. (1977). Identification of cross-cultural talent: The empirical approach of the Peace Corps. In R. W. Brislin (Ed.), *Culture learning: Concepts, applications, and research* (pp. 182–194). Honolulu: University of Hawaii.

Havighurst, R. J. (1957). The social competence of middle-aged people. *Genetic Psychology Monographs, 56,* 297–375.

Hawes, F., & Kealey, D. J. (1981). An empirical study of Canadian technical assistance. *International Journal of Intercultural Relations, 5,* 239–258.

Hecht, M. L., Larkey, L. K., & Johnson, J. N. (1992). African American and European American perceptions of problematic issues in interethnic communication effectiveness. *Human Communication Research, 19,* 209–236.

Hecht, M. L., & Ribeau, S. (1984). Ethnic communication: A comparative analysis of satisfying communication. *International Journal of Intercultural Relations, 8,* 135–151.

Herrin, C. (2004). It's time for advancing education abroad. *International Educator, 13*(1), 3–4.

Heyward, M. (2002). From international to intercultural: Redefining the international school for a globalized world. *Journal of Research in International Education, 1,* 9–32.

Hopkins, S. A., Hopkins, W. E., & Hoffman, K. D. (2005). Domestic inter-cultural service encounters: An integrated model. *Managing Service Quarterly, 15,* 329–343.

Hulstrand, J. (2008). Building a fluent workforce. *International Educator, 17*(5), 24–31.

Hunter, B., White, G. P., & Godbey, G. C. (2006). What does it mean to be globally competent? *Journal of Studies in Intercultural Education, 10,* 267–285.

Hwang, J. C., Chase, L. J., & Arden-Ogle, E. (1985, May). *Communication competence across three cultures: In search of similarity.* Paper presented at the International Communication Association Conference, Chicago.

Hwang, J. C., Chase, L. J., & Kelly, C. W. (1980, May). *An intercultural examination of communication competence.* Paper presented at the International Communication Association Conference, Acapulco, Mexico.

Ickes, W., & Simpson, J. A. (1997). Managing empathic accuracy in close relationships. In W. Ickes (Ed.), *Empathic accuracy* (pp. 218–250). New York: Guilford.

Imahori, T. T., & Lanigan, M. L. (1989). Relational model of intercultural communication competence. *Intercultural Communication Competence, 13,* 269–286.

Kayes, D. C., Kayes, A. B., & Yamazaki, Y. (2005). Essential competencies for cross-cultural knowledge absorption. *Journal of Managerial Psychology, 20,* 578–589.

Kealey, D. J. (1996). The challenge of international personnel selection. In D. L. Landis & R. S. Bhagat (Eds.), *Handbook of intercultural training* (pp. 81–105). Thousand Oaks, CA: Sage.

Kenny, D. A. (1994). *Interpersonal perception: A social relations analysis.* New York: Guilford.

Kim, B. S. K., Cartwright, B. Y., Asay, P. A., & D'Andrea, M. J. (2003). A revision of the multicultural awareness, knowledge, and skills survey: Counselor edition. *Measurement and Evaluation in Counseling and Development, 36,* 161–180.

Kim, Y. Y. (1988). *Communication and cross-cultural adaptation: An integrative theory.* Philadelphia: Multilingual Matters.

King, P. M., & Baxter Magolda, M. B. (2005). A developmental model of intercultural maturity. *Journal of College Student Development, 46,* 571–592.

Klak, T., & Martin, P. (2003). Do university-sponsored international cultural events help students to appreciate "difference"? *International Journal of Intercultural Relations, 27,* 445–465.

Koester, J., & Olebe, M. (1988). The behavioral assessment scale for intercultural assessment. *International Journal of Intercultural Relations, 12,* 233-246.

Kupka, B. (2008). *Creation of an instrument to assess intercultural communication competence for strategic international human resource management.* Unpublished doctoral dissertation, University of Otago, Otago, New Zealand.

Lapinski, M. K., & Orbe, M. P. (2007). Evidence for the construct validity and reliability of the co-cultural theory scales. *Communication Methods and Measures, 1,* 137–164.

Lee, B. K., & Chen, L. (2000). Cultural communication competence and psychological adjustment: A study of Chinese immigrant children's cross-cultural adaptation in Canada. *Communication Research, 27,* 764–792.

Li, L. C., Kim, B. S., & O'Brien, K. M. (2007). An analogue study of the effects of Asian cultural values and counselor multicultural competence on counseling process. *Psychotherapy: Theory, Research, Practice, Training, 44,* 90–95.

Lonner, W. J., & Hayes, S. A. (2004). Understanding the cognitive and social aspects of intercultural competence. In R. Sternberg & E. Grigorenko (Eds.), *Culture and competence: Contexts of life success* (pp. 89–110). Washington, DC: American Psychological Association.

Lustig, M. W. (2005). Toward a well-functioning intercultural nation. *Western Journal of Communication, 69,* 377–379.

Lustig, M. W., & Koester, J. (2006). *Intercultural competence: Interpersonal communication across culture* (5th ed.). Boston: Pearson.

Lustig, M. W., & Spitzberg, B. H. (1993). Methodological issues in the study of intercultural communication competence. In R. L. Wiseman & J. Koester (Eds.), *Intercultural communication competence* (pp. 153–167). Newbury Park, CA: Sage.

Luszczynska, A., Gutiérrez-Doña, B., & Martin, J. N. (1993). Intercultural communication competence. In R. L. Wiseman & J. Koester (Eds.), *Intercultural communication competence* (International and Intercultural Communication Annual, Vol. 16, pp. 16–29). Newbury Park, CA: Sage.

Lysgaard, S. (1955). Adjustment in a foreign society: Norwegian Fulbright grantees visiting the United States. *International Social Science Bulletin, 7,* 45–51.

Martin, J. N. (1986, November). *The relationship between student sojourner perceptions of intercultural competencies and previous sojourn experience.* Paper presented at the Speech Communication Association Conference, Chicago.

Martin, J. N., & Hammer, M. R. (1989). Behavioral categories of intercultural communication competence: Everyday communicators' perceptions. *International Journal of Intercultural Relations, 13,* 303–332.

Martin, J. N., Hammer, M. R., & Bradford, L. (1994). The influence of cultural and situational contexts on Hispanic and non-Hispanic communication competence behaviors. *Communication Quarterly, 42,* 160–179.

Martin, J. N., Hecht, M. L., & Larkey, L. K. (1994). Conversational improvement strategies for interethnic communication: African American and European American perspectives. *Communication Monographs, 61,* 236–255.

McCroskey, J.C. (1982).Communication competence and performance:A research and pedagogical perspective. *Communication Education,* 31, 1–8.

Milhouse, V. H. (1993). The applicability of interpersonal communication competence to the intercultural communication context. In R. L. Wiseman & J. Koester (Eds.), *Intercultural communication competence* (pp. 184–203). Newbury Park, CA: Sage.

Milhouse, V. H. (1996). Intercultural strategic competence: An effective tool collectivist and individualist students can use to better understand each other. *Journal of Instructional Psychology, 23,* 45–54.

National Leadership Council for Liberal Education and America's Promise. (2007). *College learning for the new global century.* Washington, DC: Author.

Navas, M., García, M. C., Sánchez, J., Rojas, A. J., Pumares, P., & Fernández, J. S. (2005). Relative acculturation extended model (RAEM): New contributions with regard to the study of acculturation. *International Journal of Intercultural Relations, 29,* 21–37.

Navas, M., Rojas, A. J., García, M., & Pumares, P. (2007). Acculturation strategies and attitudes according to the relative acculturation extended model (RAEM): The perspectives of natives versus immigrants. *International Journal of Intercultural Relations, 31,* 67–86.

Onwumechili, C., Nwosu, P. O., Jackson, R. L., II, & James-Hughes, J. (2003). In the deep valley with mountains to climb: Exploring identity and multiple reacculturation. *International Journal of Intercultural Relations, 27,* 41–62.

Parks, M. R. (1985). Interpersonal communication and the quest for personal competence. In M. L. Knapp & G. R. Miller (Eds.), *Handbook of interpersonal communication* (pp. 171–201). Beverly Hills, CA: Sage.

Prechtl, E., & Lund, A. D. (2007). Intercultural competence and assessment: Perspectives from the INCA project. In H. Kotthoff & H. Spencer-Oatey (Eds.), *Handbook of intercultural communication* (pp. 467–490). New York: Mouton de Gruyter.

Rathje, S. (2007). Intercultural competence: The status and future of a controversial concept. *Language and Intercultural Communication, 7,* 254–266.

Rickheit, G., Strohner, H., & Vorwerg, C. (2008). The concept of communicative competence. In G. Rickheit & H. Strohner (Eds.), *Handbook of communication competence* (pp. 15–62). New York: Mouton de Gruyter.

Ruben, B. D. (1976). Assessing communication competency for intercultural adaptation. *Group & Organization Studies, 1,* 334–354.

Ruben, B. D., & Kealey, D. J. (1979). Behavioral assessment of communication competency and the prediction of cross-cultural adaptation. *International Journal of Intercultural Relations, 3,* 15–47.

Sheu, H.-B., & Lent, R. W. (2007). Development and initial validation of the multicultural counseling self-efficacy scale-racial diversity form. *Psychotherapy: Theory, Research, Practice, Training, 44,* 30–45.

Shoemaker, P. J., Tankard, J. W., Jr., & Lasorsa, D. L. (2004). *How to build social science theories.* Thousand Oaks, CA: Sage.

Smith, M. B. (1966). Explorations in competence: A study of Peace Corps teachers in Ghana. *American Psychologist, 21,* 555–566.

Smith, M. B., Fawcett, J. T., Ezekiel, R., & Roth, S. (1963). A factorial study of morale among Peace Corps teachers in Ghana. *Journal of Social Issues, 14,* 10–32.

Spitzberg, B. H. (1989). Issues in the development of a theory of interpersonal competence in the intercultural context. *International Journal of Intercultural Relations, 13,* 241–268.

Spitzberg, B. H. (1993). The dialectics of (in)competence. *Journal of Social and Personal Relationships, 10,* 137–158.

Spitzberg, B. H. (1994a). The dark side of (in)competence. In W. R. Cupach & B. H. Spitzberg (Eds.), *The dark side of interpersonal communication* (pp. 25–49). Hillsdale, NJ: Lawrence Erlbaum.

Spitzberg, B. H. (1994b). Ideological issues in competence assessment. In S. Morreale, M. Brooks, R. Berko, & C. Cooke (Eds.), *Assessing college student competency in speech communication* (1994 SCA Summer Conference Proceedings, pp. 129–148). Annandale, VA: Speech Communication Association.

Spitzberg, B. H. (1997). Intercultural effectiveness. In L. A. Samovar & R. E. Porter (Eds.), *Intercultural communication: A reader* (8th ed., pp. 379–3391). Belmont, CA: Wadsworth.

Spitzberg, B. H. (2000). What is good communication? *Journal of the Association for Communication Administration, 29,* 103–119.

Spitzberg, B. H. (2001). The status of attribution theory *qua* theory in personal relationships. In V. Manusov & J. H. Harvey (Eds.), *Attribution, communication behavior, and close relationships* (pp. 353–371). Cambridge, UK: Cambridge University Press.

Spitzberg, B. H. (2003). Methods of skill assessment. In J. O. Greene & B. R. Burleson (Eds.), *Handbook of communication and social interaction skills* (pp. 93–134). Mahwah, NJ: Lawrence Erlbaum.

Spitzberg, B. H. (2007). *CSRS: The conversational skills rating scale: An instructional assessment of interpersonal competence* (NCA Diagnostic Series, 2nd ed.). Annandale, VA: National Communication Association.

Spitzberg, B. H., & Cupach, W. R. (1984). *Interpersonal communication competence.* Beverly Hills, CA: Sage.

Spitzberg, B. H., & Cupach, W. R. (1989). *Handbook of interpersonal competence research.* New York: Springer-Verlag.

Spitzberg, B. H., & Cupach, W. R. (2002). Interpersonal skills. In M. L. Knapp & J. R. Daly (Eds.), *Handbook of interpersonal communication* (3rd ed., pp. 564–611). Thousand Oaks, CA: Sage.

Sue, D. W. (2001). Multidimensional facets of cultural competence. *Counseling Psychologist, 29,* 790–821.

Ting-Toomey, S. (1988). Intercultural conflict styles: A face-negotiation theory. In Y. Y. Kim (Ed.), *Theories in intercultural communication* (pp. 213–235). Newbury Park, CA: Sage.

Ting-Toomey, S. (1993). Communicative resourcefulness: An identity negotiation perspective. In R. J. Wiseman & J. Koester (Eds.), *Intercultural communication competence* (International and Intercultural Communication Annual, Vol. 16, pp. 72–111). Newbury Park, CA: Sage.

Ting-Toomey, S. (1999). *Communicating across cultures.* New York: Guilford.

Ting-Toomey, S. (2007). Researching intercultural conflict competence. *Journal of International Communication, 13,* 7–30.

Ting-Toomey, S., & Kurogi, A. (1998). Facework competence in intercultural conflict: An updated face-negotiation theory. *International Journal of Intercultural Relations, 22,* 187–225.

Torbiörn, I. (1985). The structure of managerial roles in cross-cultural settings. *International Studies of Management and Organization, 25,* 52–74.

Tung, R. L. (1987). Expatriate assignments: Enhancing success and minimizing failure. *Academy of Management Executive, 1,* 341–362.

Turner, J. H. (1985). In defense of positivism. *Sociological Theory, 3,* 24–30.

Turner, J. H. (1990). The misuse and use of metatheory. *Sociological Forum, 5,* 37–53.

Tyler, F. B. (2001). *Cultures, communities, competence, and change.* New York: Kluwer Academic/Plenum.

Valentine, D., & Ynxia, Z. (2001). Using a knowledge-based approach to develop student intercultural competence in industry. *Business Communication Quarterly, 64,* 102–109.

Ward, C., Okura, Y., Kennedy, A., & Kojima, T. (1998). The U-curve on trial: A longitudinal study of psychological and sociocultural adjustment during cross-cultural transition. *International Journal of Intercultural Relations, 22,* 277–291.

Wiseman, R. L., & Abe, H. (1986). Cognitive complexity and intercultural effectiveness: Perceptions in American-Japanese dyads. In M. L. McLaughlin (Ed.), *Communication yearbook 9* (pp. 611–622). Beverly Hills, CA: Sage.

Wiseman, R. L., & Koester, J. (Eds.). (1993). *Intercultural communication competence* (International and Intercultural Communication Annual). Newbury Park, CA: Sage.

Ying, Y.-W. (2005). Variation in acculturative stressors over time: A study of Taiwanese students in the United States. *International Journal of Intercultural Relations, 29,* 59–71.

CHAPTER 2

The Identity Factor in Intercultural Competence

Young Yun Kim

The tightly knit system of communication and transportation has brought differing cultures, nationalities, races, religions, and linguistic communities closer than ever before in a web of interdependence and a common fate. The business-as-usual ways of doing things are fast losing their relevance, as individuals are challenged to face one another's various differences and search for human similarities, so as to move beyond their customary imagination in search of creative solutions to problems. Paradoxically, the very forces that diminish physical boundaries have surfaced the notion of identity as a powerful way to differentiate, diverge, and even denigrate culturally and ethnically dissimilar others. Such an identity posturing often exacerbates ethnic and national rivalries, rendering alarming daily news headlines and a deeply unsettling global political landscape. To many, the seemingly innocent banner of group identity is now a compelling sore spot galvanizing them into an us-against-them line drawing. The relatively simple civic consensus in the vision of a diverse yet cohesive society, or a peaceful world, is being seriously challenged by one that upholds a particular group identity at the exclusion of all others.

In this political turn in identity conceptions, the primacy of the individual is challenged as the attempts to elevate group distinctiveness override the particularities of an individual. Absent in the group-identity polemics are the supposed ideals behind the concept of intercultural competence itself—that people with different cultural and ethnic roots can coexist and strive for mutuality and cooperation by looking across and beyond the frontiers of traditional group boundaries with minimum prejudice or illusion. Pragmatic concerns such as these underlie the author's main aim for this theoretical chapter, that is, to put forth an argument for the significance of the identity factor in intercultural competence and to reclaim the primacy of the *individual* (vs. group) dimension of identity in affecting the quality of intercultural encounters.

With this aim, the author employs a broad definition of intercultural competence as the overall capacity of an individual to enact behaviors and activities that foster cooperative relationships with culturally (or ethnically) dissimilar others. Differentiated from "cultural (or culture-specific) competence," intercultural competence is conceived as a culture-general and context-general concept that is applicable to all encounters between individuals of differing cultural (or ethnic) backgrounds, regardless of the particularities of the cultural backgrounds and the social situations involved. Whether in the context of immigrants or temporary sojourners struggling to function in a new cultural environment, neighbors and classmates finding themselves in physical proximity, or employees of multinational companies or organizations working together on a daily basis, the author seeks to make a case that the identity orientations of the individuals involved influence their overall participation in fruitful communication activities that cultivate mutuality and cooperation in intercultural relationships.

Identity and Intercultural Engagement

Identity is, indeed, one of the most ubiquitous and extensively investigated concepts in social science research. From the early years of the 20th century (e.g., Simmel, 1908/1950; Stonequist, 1937), the notion of identity, in general, and cultural identity, in particular, has occupied a central place in social science research on intercultural relations and intergroup behavior.

Systematic investigations of identity can be traced back to psychologist Erikson's (1950) theoretical framework. Erikson described the process of identity development as one in which the two identities—of the individual (or the personal) and of the group (or the social collective)—are merged into one. Erikson thus placed cultural identity at the core of the individual and yet also in the core of his or her "common culture." Erikson's identity conception has since been echoed in subsequent academic writings but in a way that increasingly emphasizes the importance of the group dimension in an individual's identity. Increasingly, collective interests have become of concern, above and beyond their implications for personal self-interest. As Turner, Hogg, Oakes, Reicher, and Wetherell (1987) observe, there has been "a shift towards the perception of self as an interchangeable exemplar of some social category and away from the perception of self as a unique person" (p. 50). The emphasis on group-level cultural or ethnic identity has been a dominant voice in academic discourse in recent decades.

Given the inseparability of the personal and the social in these conceptions, the term *identity* is employed in this chapter as an individual's global self-identity that is constituted by both personal and social dimensions. This holistic conception of identity is viewed to serve as the general self-other orientation of an individual, that is, the routinized way or "personal schema" (Horowitz, 1991) with which individuals respond to external stimuli. As such, identity is regarded as the more or less enduring core constitution of personhood that influences the individual's intercultural behavior. The term *cultural identity* is employed throughout this chapter to refer to the group dimension of identity. It is used as a broad, inclusive concept that represents similar terms such as *national, cultural, ethnolinguistic, racial,* and *religious* identity, following the common usage of the term among social scientists.

On the basis of a close examination of many of the existing theoretical ideas and research findings pertinent to issues of identity in intercultural and interethnic contexts, Kim (2005b) identified *identity inclusivity* and *identity security* as two interrelated but conceptually distinct key communicator characteristics that are significant to understanding an individual's associative behavior in situations involving culturally or ethnically dissimilar others. The same two concepts are presented below as representing the core facets of the identity factor that underpin various specific concepts associated with intercultural competence, including cultural knowledge (e.g., Ting-Toomey, 2005), intercultural sensitivity (e.g., Bennett & Bennett, 2004), mindfulness (e.g., Gudykunst, 2005), and adaptability (Kim, 1991).

Identity Inclusivity

Various concepts have been used across social science disciplines to signify patterns of behavior that are associated with engagement or disengagement with culturally or ethnically dissimilar others. To begin with, the widely observed tendency of individuals to categorize themselves and others as "in-group" and "out-group" members has been explained as impeding constructive intercultural engagement in social identity theory and its twin theory of self-categorization (Tajfel, 1974; Tajfel & Turner, 1986; Turner, 1982). Categorical or exclusive in-group identification is explained to serve as both cognitive and motivational bases of intercultural behavior. The common psychological tendency of human beings is to simplify cognitive representations of the social world by dividing persons into discrete social categories, that is, to perceive out-group members as "undifferentiated items in a unified social category" and not as individuals (Turner, 1982, p. 28). The theory further argues that individuals identify with a group such that a positive self-identity is maintained and that this motivation is enacted in such interrelated forms as in-group bias, in-group commitment, in-group loyalty, and out-group discrimination.

Empirical studies have shown that the psychological tendencies identified in social identity theory and self-categorization theory lead to dissociative behaviors in intercultural contexts. Once such categories have been defined and labeled, processes of stereotyping (e.g., Hewstone & Giles, 1986) and ethnocentrism (e.g., Bennett & Castiglioni, 2004; Brewer, 1986) are set into motion. Distinction is made between in-groups ("us") and out-groups ("them"), leading to the tendency to accentuate differences or de-accentuate similarities (e.g., Oddou & Mendenhall, 1984) as well as the tendency of depersonalization or de-individuation (e.g., Tajfel, 1970). Such categorical cognitive behavior constrains intercultural communication as it creates self-fulfilling prophecies, prompting us to see behavior that confirms our expectations even when it is absent (e.g., Hamilton, Sherman, & Ruvolo, 1990). In addition, strong in-group identity has been linked to biased attribution, psychological distance, and communicative distance (Lukens, 1979). Such an exclusive group-based identity orientation is further linked to prejudicial talk (e.g., Gumperz & Cook-Gumperz, 1982; Van Dijk, 1987), divergent behavior (e.g., Gallois, Ogay, & Giles, 2005), and hate speeches (e.g., Kirkland, Greenberg, & Pyszczynski, 1987).

These concepts related to category-based identity orientation are counterbalanced by additional concepts related to inclusive identity orientation. Among such concepts are cognitive differentiation (Brewer & Miller, 1988), multiple categorization (e.g., Crisp, Hewstone, & Rubin, 2001), decategorization (Billig, 1987), recategorization (Brewer & Gaertner, 2001), wide categorization (Detweiler, 1986), and message complexity (Applegate & Sypher, 1988). Langer (1989) has employed a more global term, *mindfulness,* to describe the pattern of perception and thought that seeks a finer cognitive discrimination and more creative ways of interpreting messages about and from out-group members. These concepts generally refer to a degree of cognitive refinement that allows for a less stereotypical and more personalized way with which to perceive and orient oneself to culturally dissimilar others—a more sensitive way to interact interculturally and foster communicative synchrony (Kim, 1992).

Further reinforcing the positive association between identity inclusivity and associative intercultural behavior is Kim's (1988, 2001, 2005a) concept of "intercultural identity." As an extension and a counterpoint to the group-based conception of cultural identity, Kim (1988) introduced this concept to refer to an *achieved* self-other orientation that an *individual* develops over time. Intercultural identity is thus conceived as a *continuum* of adaptive changes from a monocultural to an increasingly complex and inclusive character. Kim (2001, 2005a) has explained that, through extensive and prolonged experiences of intercultural communication, an individual's identity is likely to undergo two interrelated transformative processes of *individuation* and *universalization. Individuation* involves a clear self-definition and definition of the other as a singular individual rather than a member of a conventional social category. With this capacity, one is better able to transcend conventional in-group and out-group categories and to see oneself and others on the basis of unique individual qualities. Accompanying individuation is *universalization,* a parallel development of a synergistic cognition born out of an awareness of the relative nature of values and of the universal aspect of human nature. In the process of becoming intercultural in identity orientation, according to Kim, the individual is likely to become more competent in making deliberate choices of constructive actions rather than simply being dictated by the prevailing norms of a particular culture.

By highlighting these two transformational processes of individuation and universalization in self-other orientation, Kim (1988, 2001, 2005a) differentiates intercultural identity from related concepts such as *bicultural identity* and *hybrid identity* that focus on additions and subtractions of particular cultural characteristics. At the same time, intercultural identity echoes other existing terms such as Adler's (1982) *multicultural identity,* which captures a psychological state of not "owning or being owned by a single culture" (p. 391), and Appiah's (2006) philosophical concept, *cosmopolitanism,* a kind of moral worldliness and inclusivity employed as an alternative to nationalist ideology.

A substantial body of research data is available to provide broad empirical support for the present theoretical account of identity inclusivity as a factor facilitating greater intercultural relational engagement. Kim, Lujan, and Dixon (1998), for instance, analyzed the subjective identity experience of American Indians in Oklahoma. On the basis of an analysis of both quantitative data and the verbal transcripts obtained through 182 one-on-one interviews conducted throughout the state, the authors reported a preponderance of the intercultural identity orientation that is universalized and individuated. Positive associations were observed between intercultural identity development and interpersonal engagement with non-Indians, as well as functional fitness and psychological health with respect to American society at large. Likewise, Thijs (2002), on the basis of a study of Dutch and Turkish adolescents in the Netherlands, found that, among the Turkish adolescents, their strong in-group identification was positively related to ethnic maintenance but not to adaptation in Dutch society. Agreement with cultural adaptation was lowest among those who strongly identified with Turkish ethnic background.

Among other recent studies that have provided empirical evidence for the importance of inclusive identity orientation in intercultural engagement is a three-phase experimental study conducted by Matsumoto, LeRoux, Bernhard, and Gray (2004). These investigators examined the psychological correlates of intercultural adjustment potential, and their findings provided strong evidence for the openness and flexibility, along with critical thinking, as significant personality characteristics contributing to intercultural adjustment. A similar finding was reported by Polek, Oudenhoven, and Berge (2007), who reported that, among immigrants in the Netherlands, those immigrants whose identity orientation was more "cosmopolitan" were better adapted in the host society than those with a strong attachment to their in-group identity.

Although varied in specific research questions and sociocultural contexts being addressed in these studies, the findings suggest a common empirical insight into the present assertion that identity inclusivity serves to facilitate constructive intercultural engagement and relationship development and thus works as a fundamental force underlying an individual's intercultural competence.

Identity Security

Along with identity inclusivity, the degree to which individuals feel secure in their identity adds to the overall intercultural competence that enables them to engage in associative behaviors and activities involving culturally dissimilar others. The level of identity security reflects the level of an individual's overall "ego-strength" (Lazarus, 1966), which he or she uses to react to a stressful situation with composure and clear and rational thinking. Identity security, as such, is a kind of inner resource that allows for qualities of flexibility and relaxedness in one's behavior, that is, the ability to "bend" and empathize with others without losing the ability to maintain one's integrity and to be creative and effective in responding to impending problems. As Worchel (1979) observed, "Cooperation could be induced by having each side set aside its weapons or reduce its potential to threaten or harm the other. The less the two parties fear each other, the greater should be the likelihood that they will cooperate" (p. 266).

As a broad concept, identity security serves to integrate many of the more narrowly defined terms, including *risk taking* (e.g., Fiske & Maddi, 1961), *self-confidence* (e.g., Van den Broucke, de Soete, & Bohrer, 1989), *self-esteem* (e.g., Padilla, Wagatsuma, & Lindholm, 1985), and *hardiness* (Walton, 1990). Relatedly, the strength of identity security is likely to be revealed in the generally positive attitudes toward and evaluations of oneself and others. Positive identity (Kim, 2001, 2005b), or an affirmative and optimistic outlook or general self-efficacy (Harrison, Chadwick, & Scales, 1996), is also an important element of identity security, as it is likely to work as a source of the "metamotivation" (Maslow, 1969, p. 35), a kind of self-trust that allows individuals not to cripple themselves with irrational feelings of inferiority or defensiveness and instead to seek more practical and adaptive alternatives when interacting interculturally.

Indeed, in many social psychological studies of intergroup relations, identity has been examined narrowly in terms of the insecurity that members of nondominant groups feel about their group's relative status in the symbolic sense of the group's importance, worth, and respectability, or in the practical sense of its social power and control. Among the concepts used in investigating identity security-insecurity in these studies are status anxiety (e.g., De Vos, 1990), perceived threat (e.g., Giles & Johnson, 1986), collective self-esteem (e.g., Crocker & Luthanen, 1990), marginality (e.g., Taft, 1977), and identity salience or psychological distinctiveness (e.g., Bourhis, Giles, Leyens, & Tajfel, 1979). These and related concepts have been linked to various forms of dissociative behavior, including stereotyping (e.g., Francis, 1976) and aggression (e.g., Berkowitz, 1962).

The present theoretical linkage of identity security and intercultural engagement in regard to intercultural competence is further suggested in findings from Kleg's (1993) study conducted in the United States. Kleg found that, compared to ethnic minorities, European Americans tended to derive their personal strength and self-esteem from their personal identity rather than from their group identity. Similar observations were made by Brown, McNatt, and Cooper (2003), who found that ethnic minority group members (Jewish) showed stronger in-group preferences for romantic partners than ethnic majority group members, and by David, Morrison, Johnson, and Ross (2002), who reported that Whites identified with both Black and White fashion models, whereas Blacks tended to identify more strongly with Black models. Likewise, Nesdale (2003), in a survey study in Australia of immigrant adults from Hong Kong, Vietnam, Bosnia, Sri Lanka, and New Zealand, reported that "personal self-esteem" but not "ethnic self-esteem" was a significant predictor of the immigrants' relational involvement with Australians, as well as of their individual achievements.

Also supporting the present theoretical linkage between identity security and competent intercultural relational engagement is the related finding of an experimental study conducted by Goff, Steele, and Davies (2008), who showed that the threat of appearing racist may have the ironic effect of causing Whites to distance themselves from Black conversation partners. In a four-part sequenced experimental study, the authors found that participants distanced themselves more from Black partners under conditions of threat, and this distance correlated with the activation of a "White racist" stereotype. Conversely, Thijs (2002), in the previously cited study of minority and majority adolescents in the Netherlands, reported that Turkish adolescents who strongly identified themselves as Turks tended to perceive greater discrimination from the majority group.

Theorems

The theoretical arguments and research findings presented in this chapter with respect to the two identity orientations, identity inclusivity and identity security, as two facets of the core dimension of intercultural competence are summarized in the following two theorems.

Theorem 1: The more inclusive an individual's identity orientation, the greater his or her capacity to engage in cooperative intercultural relationships.

Theorem 2: The more secure an individual's identity orientation of an individual, the greater his or her capacity to engage in cooperative intercultural relationships.

These two theorems are proposed to claim the identity factor as a core underlying dimension of intercultural competence. Together, the theorems highlight the profound role that differing identity orientations are likely to play as a deeper level dimension of an individual's overall ability to act and behave in ways that facilitate the development of mutuality in intercultural relationships.

Case Illustrations

Along with the previously cited research evidence supporting the two theorems, ample anecdotal evidence can be gleaned from publicly available firsthand accounts of individual stories that bear witness to concrete realities the theorems address. Such accounts have appeared in news stories, memoirs, and essays of self-reflection, among others. Many of these accounts, including the four presented here as exemplars, provide an insight into the nature of identity inclusivity and identity security, as well as the role that these identity orientations play interculturally.

Muneo Yoshikawa

One of the most succinct testimonials to the present conceptual formulation of identity orientations is provided by Muneo Yoshikawa, a native of Japan and a professor emeritus at Kauai Community College, University of Hawaii. In an essay of personal reflections, Yoshikawa (1978) offered the following insight into his own psychological evolution—an insight that speaks to the role of identity inclusivity and identity security as the very essence of what it means to be an interculturally competent person.

I am now able to look at both cultures with objectivity as well as subjectivity; I am able to move in both cultures, back and forth without any apparent conflict. . . . I think that something *beyond the sum of each identification* took place, and that it became something akin to the concept of "*synergy*"—when one adds 1 and 1, one gets three, or a little more. This something extra is not culture-specific but something unique of its own, probably the *emergence of a new attribute or a new self-awareness,* born out of an awareness of the relative nature of values and of the universal aspect of human nature. . . . I really am not concerned whether others take me as a Japanese or an American; I can accept myself as I am. I feel I am much *freer* than ever before, not only in the cognitive domain (perception, thoughts, etc.), but also in the affective (feeling, attitudes, etc.) and behavioral domains. (p. 220, italics added)

Yo-Yo Ma

The many-faceted career of cellist Yo-Yo Ma, his life story, and his philosophy offer yet another testament to a continual search for intercultural learning and synthesis.

Born to Chinese parents living in Paris, he began to study the cello with his father at age 4 and soon came with his family to New York, where he spent most of his formative years and received his musical education at the Juilliard School. He draws inspiration from a wide circle of collaborators and has explored music as a means of intercultural communication and as a vehicle for the migrations of ideas across a range of cultures throughout the world. In his own words recently posted on his Web site (www.yo-yoma.com), Ma explains his intercultural journey as follows:

> In my musical journey I have had the opportunity to *learn from a wealth of different musical voices*—from the immense compassion and grace of Bach's cello suites, to the ancient Celtic fiddle traditions alive in Appalachia, to the soulful strains of the bandoneon of Argentina's tango cafes. Throughout my travels I have thought about the culture, religions and ideas that have been influential for centuries along the historic land and sea routes that comprised the Silk Road, and *have wondered how these complex interconnections occurred and how new musical voices were formed from the diversity of these traditions.* . . . In 1998, I founded the Silk Road Project to study the ebb and flow of ideas among different cultures along the Silk Road, illuminating the heritages of its countries and identifying the voices that represent these traditions today. Through this journey of discovery, the *Silk Road Project* hopes to *plant the seeds of new artistic and cultural growth,* and to celebrate living traditions and musical voices throughout the world. (Italics added)

Orhan Pamuk

The creative insight into human conditions reflecting a remarkable level of intercultural competence has been the driving passion for the 2006 winner of the Nobel Prize in Literature, the Turkish novelist Orhan Pamuk, who is widely recognized for having captured in his writings new symbols for the interlacing of cultures. In an interview with the National Public Radio following the Nobel Prize announcement (National Public Radio, 2006), Pamuk was reminded by the interviewer that he had talked previously about "coming from one of those countries . . . on the periphery of the Western world where the art was developed, and being one of those writers who is grabbing that art from the center to the periphery and then *producing something new* to show the world" (italics added). Pamuk reaffirmed this intercultural focus in his work and expresses his secure sense of inclusive identity as follows:

> My whole book, my whole life, is a testimony to the fact that East and West actually *combine, come together gracefully and produce something new.* That is what I have been trying to do all my life. . . . I don't believe in clashes of civilization. I think that was a fanciful idea which, unfortunately, is sometimes coming to be true. But no, I think that East and West meet. I think that my whole work is a testimony to the fact that *we should find ways of looking, combining East and West without any clash, but with harmony, with grace, and produce something new for humanity.* (Italics added)

Shimon Waronker

Yet another compelling illustration of inclusive and secure identity comes from Shimon Waronker. Waronker is the principal of Junior High School 22, in the South Bronx. According to a recent story reported in the *New York Times* (Gootman, 2008), Waronker was named the principal after the school had had six principals in just over 2 years and was suffering from enormous academic and discipline problems. Teachers, parents, and students at the school, which is mostly Hispanic and Black, were taken aback by the sight of their new leader: Waronker is member of the Chabad-Lubavitch sect of Hasidic Judaism with a beard, a black hat, and a velvet yarmulke. Some teachers were skeptical, and some parents saw Waronker as too much of an "outsider."

Despite warnings from some in the school system that he was a cultural mismatch for a predominantly minority school, Waronker has outlasted his predecessors. According to the story, test scores have risen enough to earn his school an A on its new school report card. The school, once on the city's list of the 12 most dangerous, has since been removed from that list, and attendance among the students has increased to 93% or higher. One of Waronker's first acts as principal was to meet with all teachers individually to solicit their perspective and goals with his first question, "How can I help you?" He enlisted teachers in an effort to "take back the hallways" from students who seemed to have no fear of authority. Waronka also enlisted the students by creating a democratically elected student congress. These days, according to the story, the congress gathers in Waronker's office for leadership lessons, including lessons on etiquette. When Waronker finds himself being quizzed by some his Hasidic neighbors wondering why he is devoting himself to a Bronx public school instead of a Brooklyn yeshiva, he is quoted as saying, "We're all connected. . . . I feel the hand of the Lord here all the time."

Emanating from this story of Shimon Waronker, as well as the stories of Muneo Yoshikawa, Yo-Yo Ma, and Orhan Pamuk, is an inspiring message of dedication to intercultural engagement and relationship building. Their stories, indeed, suggest the hopeful possibility that anyone with an inclusive and secure identity can make a positive and creative difference in his or her own realm of life. Each story reveals personal strivings that are driven by an appreciation for the common humanity (identity inclusivity) and a clear sense of confidence in one's own personhood (identity security). None of their efforts appears to have been bound by a rigidly categorical outlook on culture or to suffer from a sense of confusion as to whom they are as individuals.

Conclusion

The present focus on the identity factor in intercultural competence addresses the author's concern regarding the politicization of cultural identity to work against the presumed ideal behind inquiry in intercultural competence—to bring culturally or ethnically dissimilar individuals closer together in a constructive relational engagement. Guided by this pragmatic interest, the author has sought to reclaim the presumed ideal by defining intercultural competence as an individual's overall capacity to engage in behaviors and activities that foster cooperative relationships in all types of social and cultural contexts in which culturally or ethnically dissimilar others interface.

In this approach, the primacy of the individual is emphasized by way of two interrelated identity orientations: identity inclusivity and identity security. The two theorems explicated in this chapter link an individual's identity inclusivity and identity security to his or her overall capacity to engage in cooperative intercultural relationships. Through these theorems, the author hopes to provide a way of an understanding of intercultural competence at a level that is deeper than the various specific factors of cognition, affect, and skill that are more readily observable. That is, many of the components of intercultural competence identified in the literature are likely to hinge on the extent that an individual holds an identity that is inclusive and secure enough to be open to and even embrace culturally or ethnically dissimilar others. Although some of the supporting research evidence and four case illustrations have been presented in support of this theoretical claim, the author invites interested researchers to test it in a variety of intercultural contexts.

For practitioners of intercultural contact and communication, the present theoretical account may serve as a call for recognizing that an inclusive and secure identity is a necessity for anyone striving to develop meaningful and fruitful intercultural relationships. It is also a possibility that, even in adulthood, individual identity orientations can be cultivated and transformed toward greater inclusivity and security, as has been documented in many empirical studies of long-term immigrants (see Kim, 2001, for an extensive literature review). At the same time, however, the present theoretical account suggests a potential challenge for intercultural practitioners. On one hand, cultural identity accords a profound symbolic as well as substantive significance to many people, which interculturally competent persons need to recognize and appreciate. On the other hand, as has been argued in this chapter, categorical in-group commitment and loyalty, particularly when coupled with insecurity-driven defensive identity claims, are likely to impede the chances for success in working toward mutual understanding and constructive engagement with members of certain out-groups. In striving for a satisfying intercultural engagement, active participants in intercultural interaction are challenged to reflect on and find a way to reconcile these two competing considerations.

In the end, intercultural competence at its deepest level has to be found among individuals such as Muneo Yoshikawa, Yo-Yo Ma, Orhan Pamuk, and Shimon Waronker. Through their integrative intercultural thoughts and actions, they represent many other intercultural persons around the world who defy simplistic and conventional categorizations, who are capable to transcend traditional group boundaries, who are secure in who they are, and who bear witness to the remarkable human spirit. They are the ones who can better engage and cultivate meaningful relationships with people who are different. And they are likely to do so, not as an act of "surrendering" their own personal or cultural integrity but out of genuine respect for cultural differences that leaves neither the lender nor the borrower deprived.

References

Adler, P. (1982). Beyond cultural identity: Reflections on cultural and multicultural man. In L. Samovar & R. Porter (Eds.), *Intercultural communication: A reader* (3rd ed., pp. 389–408). Belmont, CA: Wadsworth.

Appiah, K. A. (2006). *Cosmopolitanism: Ethics in a world of strangers.* New York: W. W. Norton.

Applegate, J., & Sypher, H. (1988). A constructivist theory of communication and culture. In Y. Y. Kim & W. Gudykunst (Eds.), *Theories in intercultural communication* (pp. 41–65). Newbury Park, CA: Sage.

Bennett, J., & Bennett, M. (2004). Developing intercultural sensitivity: An integrative approach to global and domestic diversity. In D. Landis, J. Bennett, & M. Bennett (Eds.), *Handbook of intercultural training* (3rd ed., pp. 147–165). Thousand Oaks, CA: Sage.

Bennett, M., & Castiglioni, I. (2004). Embodied ethnocentrism and the feeling of culture: A key to training for intercultural competence. In D. Landis, J. Bennett, & M. Bennett (Eds.), *Handbook of intercultural training* (3rd ed., pp. 249–265). Thousand Oaks, CA: Sage.

Berkowitz, L. (1962). *Aggression: A social psychological analysis.* New York: McGraw-Hill.

Billig, M. (1987). *Arguing and thinking: A rhetorical approach to social psychology.* New York: Cambridge University Press.

Bourhis, R., Giles, H., Leyens, J., & Tajfel, H. (1979). Psychological distinctiveness: Language divergence in Belgium. In H. Giles & R. St Clair (Eds.), *Language and social psychology* (pp. 158–185). Oxford, England: Blackwell.

Brewer, M. (1986). The role of ethnocentrism in intergroup conflict. In S. Worchel & W. Austin (Eds.), *Psychology of intergroup relations* (2nd ed., pp. 88–102). Chicago: Nelson-Hall.

Brewer, M., & Gaertner, S. (2001). Toward reduction of prejudice. In R. Brown & S. Gaertner (Eds.), *The Blackwell handbook of social psychology: Intergroup processes* (pp. 451–472). Oxford, UK: Blackwell.

Brewer, M., & Miller, N. (1988). Contact and cooperation: When do they work? In P. Katz & D. Taylor (Eds.), *Eliminating racism* (pp. 315–326). Newbury Park, CA: Sage.

Brown, L., McNatt, P., & Cooper, G. (2003). Ingroup romantic preferences among Jewish and non-Jewish White undergraduates. *International Journal of Intercultural Relations, 27,* 335–354.

Crisp, R., Hewstone, M., & Rubin, M. (2001). Does multiple categorization reduce intergroup bias? *Personality and Social Psychology Bulletin, 27,* 76–89.

Crocker, J., & Luthanen, R. (1990). Collective self-esteem and ingroup bias. *Journal of Personality and Social Psychology, 58,* 60–67.

David, P., Morrison, G., Johnson, M., & Ross, F. (2002, June). Body image, race, and fashion models. *Communication Research, 29,* 270–294.

De Vos, G. A. (1990). Conflict and accommodation in ethnic interaction. In G. A. De Vos & M. Suirez-Orozco (Eds.), *Status inequality: The self in culture* (pp. 204–245). Newbury Park, CA: Sage.

Detweiler, R. (1986). Categorization, attribution and intergroup communication. In W. Gudykunst (Ed.), *Intergroup communication* (pp. 62–73). London: Edward Arnold.

Erikson, E. (1950). *Childhood and society.* New York: W. W. Norton.

Fiske, D., & Maddi, S. (Eds.). (1961). *Functions of varied experience.* Homewood, IL: Dorsey.

Francis, E. (1976). *Interethnic relations.* New York: Elsevier.

Gallois, C., Ogay, T., & Giles, H. (2005). Communication accommodation theory. In W. Gudykunst (Ed.), *Theorizing about intercultural communication* (pp. 121–148). Thousand Oaks, CA: Sage.

Giles, H., & Johnson, P. (1986). Perceived threat, ethnic commitment, and interethnic language behavior. In Y. Y. Kim (Ed.), *Interethnic communication* (pp. 91–116). Newbury Park, CA: Sage.

Goff, P., Steele, C., & Davies, P. (2008). The space between us: Stereotype threat and distance in interracial contexts. *Journal of Personality and Social Psychology, 94,* 91–107.

Gootman, E. (2008, February 8). In Bronx school, culture shock, then revival. *New York Times,* pp. A1, A4.

Gudykunst, W. (2005). An anxiety/uncertainty management (AUM) theory of effective communication: Making the mesh of the net finer. In W. Gudykunst (Ed.), *Theorizing about intercultural communication* (pp. 281–322). Thousand Oaks, CA: Sage.

Gumperz, J., & Cook-Gumperz, J. (1982). Introduction: Language and the communication of social identity. In J. Gumperz (Ed.), *Language and social identity* (pp. 1–21). New York: Cambridge University Press.

Hamilton, D., Sherman, S., & Ruvolo, C. (1990). Stereotype-based expectancies: Effects on information processing and social behavior. *Journal of Social Issues, 46*(2), 35–59.

Harrison, J., Chadwick, M., & Scales, M. (1996). The relationship between cross-cultural adjustment and the personality variables of self-efficacy and self-monitoring. *International Journal of Intercultural Relations, 20,* 167–188.

Hewstone, M., & Giles, H. (1986). Social groups and social stereotypes in intergroup communication: A review and model of intergroup communication breakdown. In W. Gudykunst (Ed.), *Intergroup communication* (pp. 10–26). London: Edward Arnold.

Horowitz, M. (1991). Person schemas. In M. Horowitz (Ed.), *Person schemas and maladaptive interpersonal patterns* (pp. 13–31). Chicago: University of Chicago Press.

Kim, Y. Y. (1988). *Communication and cross-cultural adaptation: An integrative theory.* Clevedon, UK: Multilingual Matters.

Kim, Y. Y. (1991). Intercultural communication competence: A systems-theoretic view. In S. Ting-Toomey & F. Korzenny (Eds.), *International and intercultural communication annual 17: Cross-cultural interpersonal communication* (pp. 259–275). Newbury Park, CA: Sage.

Kim, Y. Y. (1992). Synchrony and intercultural communication. In D. Crookall & K. Arai (Eds.), *Global interdependence* (pp. 99–105). New York: Springer-Verlag.

Kim, Y. Y. (2001). *Becoming intercultural: An integrative theory of communication and cross-cultural adaptation.* Thousand Oaks, CA: Sage.

Kim, Y. Y. (2005a). Adapting to a new culture: An integrative communication theory. In W. Gudykunst (Ed.), *Theorizing about intercultural communication* (pp. 375–400). Thousand Oaks, CA: Sage.

Kim, Y. Y. (2005b). Association and dissociation: A contextual theory of interethnic communication. In W. Gudykunst (Ed.), *Theorizing about intercultural communication* (pp. 323–349). Thousand Oaks, CA: Sage.

Kim, Y. Y., Lujan, P., & Dixon, L. (1998). "I can walk both ways": Identity integration of American Indians in Oklahoma. *Human Communication Research, 25,* 252–274.

Kirkland, S., Greenberg, J., & Pyszczynski, T. (1987). Further evidence of the dexterous effects of overheard DELs: Derogation beyond the target. *Personality and Social Psychological Bulletin, 13,* 126–227.

Kleg, M. (1993). *Hate, prejudice, and racism.* Albany: State University of New York Press.

Langer, E. (1989). *Mindfulness.* Reading, MA: Addison-Wesley.

Lazarus, R. (1966). *Psychological stress and the coping process.* St. Louis, MO: McGraw-Hill.

Lukens, J. (1979). Interethnic conflict and communicative distance. In H. Giles & B. Saint-Jacques (Eds.), *Language and ethnic relations* (pp. 143–158). New York: Pergamon.

Maslow, A. (1969). A theory of metamotivation: The biological rooting of the value-life. In H. Chiang & A. H. Maslow (Eds.), *The healthy personality* (pp. 35–56). New York: Van Nostrand Reinhold.

Matsumoto, D., LeRoux, J., Bernhard, R., & Gray, H. (2004). Unraveling the psychological correlates of intercultural adjustment potential. *International Journal of Intercultural Relations, 28,* 281–309.

National Public Radio. (2006, October 12). Once resented, Pamuk takes solace in Nobel. Interview transcript from *All Things Considered.* Acquired from http://www.npr.org/templates/story/story.php?storyId=625630

Nesdale, D. (2003). Ethnic identification, self-esteem and immigrant psychological health. *International Journal of Intercultural Relations, 27,* 23–40.

Oddou, G., & Mendenhall, M. (1984). Person perception in cross-cultural settings. *International Journal of Intercultural Relations, 8,* 77–96.

Padilla, A., Wagatsuma, Y., & Lindholm, K. (1985). Acculturation and personality as predictors of stress in Japanese and Japanese-Americans. *Journal of Social Psychology, 125,* 295–305.

Polek, E., Oudenhoven, J. P., & Berge, J. (2007, July). *Cosmopolitan identity: The overlooked element in policies on immigrants' adaptation.* Paper presented at the biennial conference of the International Academy for Intercultural Research, Groningen, The Netherlands.

Simmel, G. (1950). The stranger. In K. H. Wolff (Ed. & Trans.), *The sociology of Georg Simmel* (pp. 402–408). New York: Free Press. (Original work published 1908)

Stonequist, E. (1937). *The marginal man.* New York: Scribner's.

Taft, R. (1977). Coping with unfamiliar culture. In N. Warren (Ed.), *Studies in cross-cultural psychology* (Vol. 1, pp. 121–153). New York: Academic Press.

Tajfel, H. (1970). Experiments in intergroup discrimination. *Scientific American, 223*(2), 96–102.

Tajfel, H. (1974). Social identity and intergroup behavior. *Social Science Information, 13,* 65–93.

Tajfel, H., & Turner, J. (1986). The social identity theory of intergroup behavior. In S. Worchel & W. Austin (Eds.), *Psychology of intergroup relations* (2nd ed., pp. 7–24). Chicago: Nelson-Hall.

Thijs, J. (2002, February). Multiculturalism among minority and majority adolescents in the Netherlands. *International Journal of Intercultural Relations, 26,* 91–108.

Ting-Toomey, S. (2005). Identity negotiation theory: Crossing cultural boundaries. In W. Gudykunst (Ed.), *Theorizing about intercultural communication* (pp. 211–233). Thousand Oaks, CA: Sage.

Turner, J. (1982). Towards a cognitive redefinition of the social group. In H. Tajfel (Ed.), *Social identity and intergroup relations* (pp. 15–40). Cambridge, England: Cambridge University Press.

Turner, J., Hogg, M., Oakes, P., Reicher, S., & Wetherell, M. (1987). *Rediscovering the social group: A self-categorization theory.* Oxford, UK: Basil Blackwell.

Van den Broucke, S., de Soete, G., & Bohrer, A. (1989). Free-response self-description as a predictor of success and failure in adolescent exchange students. *International Journal of Intercultural Relations, 13,* 73–91.

Van Dijk, T. (1987). *Communicating racism: Ethnic prejudice in thought and talk.* Newbury Park, CA: Sage.

Walton, S. (1990). Stress management training for overseas effectiveness. *International Journal of Intercultural Relations, 14,* 507–527.

Worchel, S. (1979). Cooperation and the reduction of intergroup conflict: Some determining factors. In W. Austin & S. Worchel (Eds.), *The social psychology of intergroup relations* (pp. 262–273). Monterey, CA: Brooks/Cole.

Yoshikawa, M. (1978). Some Japanese and American cultural characteristics. In M. Prosser (Ed.), *The cultural dialogue: An introduction to intercultural communication* (pp. 220–239). Boston: Houghton Mifflin.

CHAPTER 3

The Interculturally Competent Global Leader

Margaret D. Pusch

Contemplating the work that leaders do in society, in organizations, and in the world raises a number of questions about the skills that are necessary, the attitudes that are important, and the intellectual capabilities that are essential to be a global leader. Great leaders have not always been intellectually impressive (although some level of intelligence is necessary) or endowed with extraordinary skill (although some level of technical skill is important). Seemingly gifted individuals have failed, and seemingly less endowed people have soared. Especially in this time of international connections—of organizations that span the earth; of human, economic, and environmental problems that cannot be solved without crossing borders; and of the need to think in terms of the global context—it is important to identify those critical abilities that are fundamental to functioning as a leader in the global *intercultural* environment. It is equally important to determine how those abilities can be learned by the greatest number of people in all our societies. The focus of this chapter is to identify the critical elements of the interculturally competent global leader and to suggest ways to encourage the development of those competencies.

Most research about leadership is rooted in a single culture, and much of it is tied to advice on business practices in various countries as contrasted with cultures in the West. One obvious example is the long list of books devoted to doing business with the Japanese that began to emerge in the mid-1980s (Brannen & Wilen, 1993; Hall, 1993; Hall & Hall, 1987; Ishinomori, 1988; March, 1988). There has been attention to how leadership differs from one location to another, showing contrasts in the approaches to leadership in different countries and different parts of the world (Hampden-Turner & Trompenaars, 1993; House, Hanges, Javidan, Dorfman, & Gupta, 2004; Lewis, 2005), how leadership matches what motivates workers

(McGregor, 1960; Ouchi, 1981), and then increasing attention to *global* leadership and management skills in the business world as well as the public sector (Brake, 1997; Harris, Moran, & Moran, 2004; Kanter, 1995; Rosen, Digh, Singer, & Phillips, 2000). Leaders, whether they remain in their home culture or work in the global arena, must function in an environment where the population, the needs, and the values are diverse. This requires a mind-set, heart-set, and skill-set that can carry across cultural boundaries, encouraging a shift in worldview and perspective and thus achieving clarity and integrity in complex situations. While some may be born to be leaders in their own culture,[1] leaders with an ability to deal constructively in intercultural situations are made. These leaders must reach a new realization of how worldview and behavior are deeply influenced by cultural origin and how these differences can be bridged. They must learn to be interculturally competent.

Intercultural Competence: How Is It Defined?

Recent research (Deardorff, 2006) conducted to identify the components of inter-cultural competence resulted in a diagram that was a composite of the consensus reached by a panel of experienced interculturalists that included trainers, researchers, and international educational program administrators within the United States, Canada, and the United Kingdom. The resulting pyramid layers the competencies in a system that shows both internal and external outcomes of increased intercultural competency.

Most competence "lists" are just that, a lengthy listing of the many competences that are part of intercultural effectiveness. Deardorff's (2004) panel agreed on 44; she consolidated and constructed them into the pyramid pictured in Figure 3.1, suggesting that one begins with attitude and moves toward acquiring the skills and knowledge that produce both internal and external results. It could be argued that attitudes can be influenced by the need to function in a manner that allows one to navigate in an unfamiliar cultural environment or multicultural situation, which, in turn, produces a change of attitude. However, there must be the motivation to explore, to be, as Kemper (2003) puts it, an "edgewalker." Deardorff presents the acquisition of these competencies as a process that begins with attitudes of respect, openness, and curiosity, arguing that they are fundamental to the process of achieving the desired outcomes.

An exhaustive study of leaders in world-class companies in 27 countries, from Indonesia to Australia to China to Turkey and the United Kingdom, searched for those challenges faced by highly performing leaders in the global economy and the qualities that were essential to dealing effectively with those challenges (Rosen et al., 2000). One point became clear: "Leaders who leverage employees' intellectual capital, collaborative relationships, and cultures will thrive in the new millennium" (Rosen et al., 2000, p. 24). The ability to do this called for the kind of skills, attitudes, and cognitive flexibility that is represented in the Deardorff model. Earlier, Brake (1997) created the global leadership triad in which he put relationship management, personal effectiveness, and business acumen at each point in the triangle. Cross-cultural

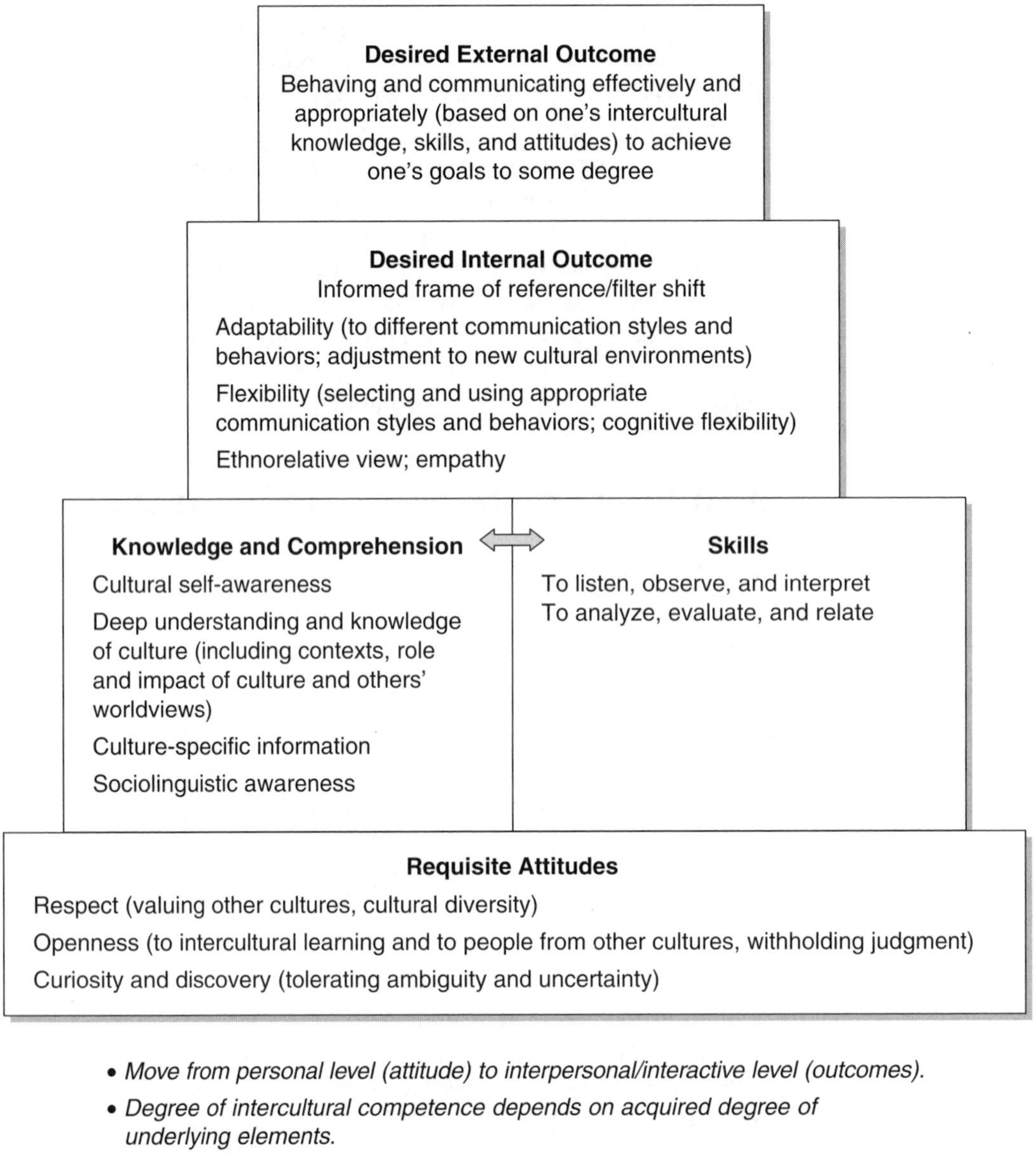

Desired External Outcome
Behaving and communicating effectively and appropriately (based on one's intercultural knowledge, skills, and attitudes) to achieve one's goals to some degree

Desired Internal Outcome
Informed frame of reference/filter shift

Adaptability (to different communication styles and behaviors; adjustment to new cultural environments)

Flexibility (selecting and using appropriate communication styles and behaviors; cognitive flexibility)

Ethnorelative view; empathy

Knowledge and Comprehension ⇐⇒ **Skills**

Cultural self-awareness

Deep understanding and knowledge of culture (including contexts, role and impact of culture and others' worldviews)

Culture-specific information

Sociolinguistic awareness

To listen, observe, and interpret
To analyze, evaluate, and relate

Requisite Attitudes

Respect (valuing other cultures, cultural diversity)

Openness (to intercultural learning and to people from other cultures, withholding judgment)

Curiosity and discovery (tolerating ambiguity and uncertainty)

- *Move from personal level (attitude) to interpersonal/interactive level (outcomes).*
- *Degree of intercultural competence depends on acquired degree of underlying elements.*

Figure 3.1   Model of Intercultural Competence

SOURCE: Deardorff (2006). Used with permission.

communication, curiosity and learning, and thinking agility, among other attributes, ranked high in the required capabilities of global leaders (Brake, 1997, p. 44). To lead in a collaborative global enterprise, it is essential that there be global competency development to produce leaders who can exhibit intercultural competencies.

There is extensive literature on intercultural competencies (see Spitzberg & Changnon in Chapter 1, this volume, for a comprehensive discussion of the literature), but the Deardorff model is a succinct visual research-based display of what has largely been discussed in other texts. A search of the literature shows that nearly all studies, no matter what the terms used in each study, identified four general behavioral capabilities or abilities that are critical to being effective and appropriate in an intercultural situation:

1. The ability to manage psychological stress

2. The ability to communicate effectively

3. The ability to take advantage of the interface between different cultures and the knowledge that comes from different cultural orientations

4. The ability to manage change in a borderless environment where culture is asserted even more, as the national borders dissolve, and where cultures encounter each other immediately through technology (Rosen et al., 2000, pp. 32–33)

The short list of skills that supports these capabilities, created by Gudykunst (1991), is appealing because those skills seem to be the most important and they can be acquired through education and experience.

1. *Mindfulness*—being cognitively aware of our own communication and the process of interaction with others. The usual pattern of being aware of our own communication: "Will they like me?" "Am I making a fool of myself?" "What can I say to make an impression?" or, in the case of leaders, "How can I maintain control?"

A more effective approach: "What is happening here? How are we reacting to each other?" "What can I say or do to help this process?" In other words, focusing on the process rather than the outcomes but being able to have a vision of the desired result. As Brake (1997, p. 205) suggests in the cultural learning cycle, it is essential that the global leader be able to recognize differences (which can be more difficult than it sounds), discover what they mean, and create new ways of relating as well as being able to reflect on and learn from the experience. Often the reflection part is neglected—the tendency is to move on rather than review and rediscover what might have been learned and the implications for the future.

2. *Cognitive flexibility*—being able to create new categories; the ability to make more rather than fewer categories and avoid the tendency to stuff new information into old, preset categories. This includes being open to new information, being aware of more than one perspective, and becoming aware of how we interpret messages and situations differently than others.

S. Black, Morrison, and Gregersen (1999) use the term *savvy* to indicate that global leaders have the ability to identify and capture resources that are needed and to make decisions, knowing when to wait for more information and when to move forward without all the information that would be useful.

3. *Tolerance for ambiguity*—the ability to be in a situation that is unclear and not become overly anxious but to determine patiently what is appropriate as the dimensions of situations and conditions become apparent.

- Low-tolerance people seek information to support their own beliefs.
- High-tolerance people seek "objective" information from others to gain an understanding of the situation and to accurately predict the behavior of others.

An important element within this skill is curiosity, emphasized by Deardorff (2006; see Figure 3.1) as well as others. S. Black et al. (1999) identify "inquisitiveness" as a component of global leadership for business, suggesting that it is the "glue" that holds everything together and breathes life into the skill set that leadership requires. Black et al. also label "embracing duality" as that ability to manage uncertainty and balance the tensions present when global and local needs and interests come into conflict. They found that global leaders actually seek out those situations or environments in which tension and uncertainty exist at a high level. This suggests that a tolerance for ambiguity not only is a critical skill but also energizes global leaders.

4. *Behavioral flexibility*—the ability to adapt and accommodate one's own behavior to people from other groups. One important aspect is to know more than one language, but language skill does not translate automatically into intercultural skill. One can be a fool in more than one language, and it is quite easy to behave foolishly in an unfamiliar culture. Language does not automatically endow one with cultural knowledge or the ability to adapt to different communicative styles or behaviors. This can be supported by the Deardorff (2004) study in which the experts did not reach consensus on the role of language in intercultural competence. Interestingly, one successful leader noted that "I used to think language skills were as important as cultural adaptability, but I now believe adaptability is far more important. . . . It can be very dangerous to pick people because they have language skills and then find out they have very little cultural adaptability *and* little interest in adapting" (Brake, 1997, p. 62). With or without language skill, the ability to engage in chameleon-like behavior remains critical to functioning interculturally (Pusch, 1994).

5. *Cross-cultural empathy*—being able to participate in another person's experience in your imagination; thinking it intellectually and feeling it emotionally. The ability to connect emotionally with people and showing compassion for others, being able to listen actively and mindfully, and viewing situations from more than one perspective is an important set of skills that demonstrate empathy.

Brake (1997) describes global leaders as capable of managing relationships, having business acumen, and having personal effectiveness. There is stress on the fundamental capacity to be entrepreneurial, to have professional expertise and know the business the leader is in (whatever it may be), and to be strategically and organizationally astute. However, this cannot be used effectively without a "global mind-set." Included in that mind-set are the competencies that Deardorff (2004, 2006), S. Black et al. (1999), and others list. Generally, it is suggested that a global leader must be able to stretch one's mind to encompass the entire world with all its complexity, while those who lead domestically need only take what is local and familiar into account.

S. Black et al. (1999) indicate several other important attributes exhibited by global leaders: "demonstrating high personal integrity" and inquisitiveness, a state of mind rather than an acquired skill (although it can be encouraged). Inquisitiveness (curiosity in Deardorff's [2004] model) produces an orientation to learning that is essential in a world that changes faster than leaders can reinvent themselves (Rosen et al., 2000, p. 25). The world is full of paradox and contradictions that must be navigated every day. A television advertisement says, "Life comes at you fast," and indeed, this is a common challenge for anyone in a leadership position. The intercultural field, especially intercultural training, has always been oriented to learning how to learn and considers that process fundamental to being effective in any cross-cultural or multicultural environment. Thomas Friedman (2005a), in a *New York Times* column, wrote of high school teachers who had inspired students and were nominated by college graduates as those teachers they especially remembered and appreciated. Four were selected to be honored over the college graduation weekend. Friedman noted that in an age when jobs are invented and become obsolete with some frequency, the "greatest survival skill is the ability to learn how to learn. The best way to learn how to learn is to love to learn, and the best way to love to learn is to have great teachers who inspire you." If a love of learning fueled by curiosity is a critical attribute for global leadership, it seems that investment in education and recognition of the influence of good teachers are essential. Moreover, developing global leaders within corporate and other organizational environments calls for similar inspirational training and mentoring.

Ethical behavior has been an equally important concern in intercultural work, and being inquisitive, as S. Black et al. (1999) suggest, may contribute to making ethical decisions, taking into account the concerns of local people as well as global goals in a given situation. Ethical decisions cannot be made from some universal code of conduct since none exists. They must be made, recognizing that there are multiple choices, drawing on the knowledge of various options, and being sensitive to the cultural issues involved.

J. Bennett (2009, p. 97) sums this up in a list that consists of a cognitive dimension (mind-set) that includes, among other qualities, culture-general frameworks that can be useful in sorting through the differences encountered, a behavioral dimension (skill set) that includes empathy, and the affective dimension (heart set) that includes attitudes and motivations mentioned above.

It should be assumed that if the competences and qualities discussed in this chapter are present in an individual and encouraged in a group, a high degree of cultural self-awareness is present. One of the first steps in becoming an interculturally competent leader is to achieve awareness not only of one's home culture but of its influence on one's behavior, values, and ways of looking at the world. Indeed, the widely stated admonition to start with oneself at home is an important one. Often, this occurs, however, when you leave home because it is hard to see your own culture when you are in the midst of it. Interestingly, nearly everyone who writes on the topic of leadership indicates that the early step in becoming globally competent is to begin to experience life in places other than your home country/culture. We can, therefore, build future leaders by having them participate in structured learning experiences abroad both during their student years as well as in a working situation. Building structured learning opportunities into business travel has been recommended most notably by Oddou, Mendenhall, and Ritchie (2000).

Finally, as mentioned earlier, the term *edgewalker* has been used to describe the "new-century leadership paradigm" essential in a complex world. Kemper (2003) states that living in a diverse world "is more than a mental construct, a memorized list of cultural differences, or a willingness to be tolerant. It's about examining how well we function at the margins and interfaces of life, where divergent ways of being and believing meet and collide."

As implied in the work devoted to identifying intercultural competencies, especially those important to global leaders, how well one functions at the point of interface calls for the competences discussed here. However, the willingness to go beyond tolerance and to be fully inclusive requires a higher level of commitment—one that involves taking responsibility for being personally connected with and learning from and caring about those who are unlike ourselves. This means a serious exploration of our beliefs and our convictions, as well as an ability to deal with the chaos that characterizes the world as we now know it. As Black and Gregersen suggest (2000), this requires a reordering of one's mental map, of stretching one's mind beyond the known to include the entire world. While no one can know everything about every country or region of the world, one can take on that "global mind-set" that recognizes that the map that was developed while growing up does not transfer to the rest of the world.

Global Leadership: Why Is Intercultural Competence Important?

Global leadership obviously requires crossing national borders and encountering many different cultures both within and among those borders. Defining the activity of "leadership" and the term *leader* is not an easy task, but attempts have been made to differentiate between the two and between being a manager and a leader. Bert Lance, President Jimmy Carter's budget director, declared "if it ain't broke, don't fix it." This defines how managers think. Leaders understand that "when it ain't broke may be the only time you can fix it" (Zaleznik, 2004). Leadership is seen as an activity, the process of mobilizing a group of people to accomplish a goal or fulfill a vision. While others, the followers, may carry out many of the tasks and be those without whom a goal could not be accomplished, the leader must articulate and inspire with vision, take responsibility for the outcome, and carry out the leadership function in collaboration with others (Golandaz, 2003). The leader is the one looking ahead, defining the path, and helping others take the walk. If this is to occur in a global setting, it necessarily involves people from different cultures with distinctly different ways of thinking, behaving, and valuing the activity and perceiving and accepting the vision or goal. The leader, therefore, must be an effective intercultural communicator.

Friedman (2005b), in his book *The World Is Flat*, states that culture matters when it comes to economic success. He explores the concept of "glocalization," which means the ability to absorb foreign ideas and the best practices from other places and meld them with indigenous traditions. He suggests that a culture that is tolerant of others, builds trust enough to allow strangers to collaborate together, and whose elites are concerned with the masses and ready to invest at home influences how well it will flourish. "When tolerance is the norm, everyone flourishes—because tolerance breeds trust, and trust is the foundation of innovation and entrepreneurship.

Increase the level of trust in any group, company, or society, and only good things happen" (p. 327). While Friedman's focus is almost exclusively on economic activities, his words ring true for leaders in every domain because while culture matters, it can also change. Culture is "nested in contexts," not hardwired into human DNA. The contexts can be altered, and leaders can change and adapt to meet the imperatives of the challenges that exist; local leaders and those who function in the global arena must be prepared to engage in glocalization (Friedman, 2005b).

Research shows that culture matters in all forms of human endeavor and certainly in how leadership is exercised. Hofstede (2001) demonstrated how cultures cluster along certain cultural patterns; similar results were demonstrated earlier by Hall (1959, 1966) and Haire, Ghiselli, and Porter (1966). Hofstede showed that corporate culture does not trump the native cultures of employees. While they may adapt to the corporate culture, their native cultural tendencies often prevail. These are resources that leaders draw on not only for insight into local cultures but as sources of learning alternative solutions to dealing with the human condition. The research of both Hofstede and Hall continues to be relevant as it provides general templates to help identify the characteristics of a culture and behavior that may be exhibited and encountered in a multinational, multicultural environment. Hofstede's research on power distance, for example, has implications for how to lead in an environment where the leader is expected to care about and assist in many aspects of the employee's or a student's life as opposed to a flat organization where power and responsibility are more evenly distributed. Hall's research on how time is viewed and used and on how relationships are more important than individual achievement provides considerable insight into what gives meaning to life and what motivates people from different cultures. These "guides" are on a continuum rather than being binary, so there is attention to the relativity of those differences rather than an "either/or" approach. Thus, they provide guidance to understanding what to watch for that might have considerable impact on exercising leadership and implications for an effective response. Both these theorists provide fundamental concepts to build the knowledge base for achieving the intercultural competency that is so critical to good leadership.

Patterned after Hofstede's seminal study, the most comprehensive study to date on examining cultural differences in leadership is known as the GLOBE research, compiled by the Global Leadership and Organizational Behavior Effectiveness Project Team (House, Hanges, Javidan, Dorfman, & Gupta, 2004). Conducted by 170 researchers who collected data from 18,000 managers in 62 countries over a period of 10 years, this team found nine distinguishing characteristics across cultures that have implications for global leadership. A third of these characteristics overlap with Hofstede's dimensions of uncertainty avoidance, power distance, and collectivism versus individualism while the rest are unique: assertiveness, future orientation, power orientation, in-group collectivism, humane orientation, and gender differentiation. One overarching finding, among many, is the increased importance of leaders' sensitivity to cultural difference. N. J. Adler (2008, p. 171) points out that Gardner (1995) made a remarkable contribution to the study of leadership when he discovered that extraordinary leaders, worldwide, consistently practice reflecting, leveraging, and framing more than most people. These leaders think deeply about what they are trying to accomplish and how they are going about it and making course corrections when things are not going well. Second, they know what their strengths are and focus on what they do well, pushing their competitive advantage hard and encouraging others to do the same. Finally, they are risk takers; when they fail, they learn from those failures and apply that learning better than others.

The Global Leader: How Can Intercultural Competence Be Identified?

The global leader is one who embraces difference and has achieved a state of ethnorelativity. Cultures teach us to be ethnocentric, to think of our own cultures as central in the universe and providing the "natural" way of doing things. The default position of people is to be ethnocentric, and yet the global leader cannot fall into the default setting but must move well beyond ethnocentricity.

The developmental model of intercultural sensitivity (DMIS) provides a way of identifying the personal change in individuals as they move from being ethnocentric to ethnorelative (M. Bennett, 1993), a shift that is essential for global leaders. The DMIS has three "states" of ethnocentrism (denial of difference, defense against difference, and minimization of difference) and three states of ethnorelativism (acceptance of difference, adaptation to difference, and integration of difference). *Ethnocentrism* can be defined as the "assumption that the worldview of one's own culture is central to reality" (M. Bennett, 1993). Signs of ethnocentrism can be seen in behavior that is dismissive of other cultures, is prejudicial toward certain groups, exhibits racist attitudes, and/or sets up clear "we/they" distinctions between their own and other groups. There may also be attempts to glorify one's own culture.

Denial is a state in which it seems impossible to comprehend cultural difference. This may be due to ignorance of, isolation from, or separation, voluntary or involuntary, from cultures different than one's own. "Others" tend to be dehumanized or identified in the most general of terms or thought of only in broad stereotypes. Cultural differences are seen as something that happens somewhere else, if it is thought of at all. *Defense* is a bit more active in that there is a recognition of difference, and it is seen as threatening. Defense may take three forms: (1) denigration in which other cultures are evaluated negatively (the greater the difference, the more negative the evaluation); (2) asserting superiority in which one's own culture is seen as better than any other and, sometimes, a propensity to enforce this perspective; and (3) reversal, a tendency to see another culture as superior to one's own, which obviously requires experience in another culture. These stages show a strong orientation to dualistic thinking.

Minimization is ethnocentric because it is still an attempt to preserve one's own worldview as central to reality. In this stage, human similarity seems more compelling than difference whether it is based on physical universalism, where we look different but everyone functions from the same script to meet fundamental human needs, or transcendent universalism, emphasizing that we come from a common source of a transcendent principle or belief system. Minimization assumes that at the core of human existence, we are all the same and can understand each other once we get past relatively superficial cultural differences. This may be a transition stage that is helping the person prepare for a greater appreciation of cultural differences. In ethnocentricity, one is in a state of unconscious incompetence, although it is possible to begin to be consciously incompetent in minimization, to recognize times of cultural insensitivity, and to attempt to learn new ways of relating to people and behaving (Howell, 1982). Certainly, there is an increased interest in learning about other cultures if only at a level of holidays, food, and celebrations.

Moving into a state of ethnorelativism usually requires a significant other-culture experience. In *acceptance,* cultural differences become something that is recognized, appreciated, and respected. Acceptance tends to begin with respect for behavioral differences and a comprehension that all behavior occurs in a cultural context. The second step in acceptance is respecting the beliefs and values of another culture. There is an acceptance of the assumptions that lie beneath behavior patterns and a recognition that values are not stationary "things"; instead, a process of valuing occurs within cultures when relative "goodness" or "rightness" is assigned to events or occurrences. One in acceptance is quite likely consciously incompetent but learning more and more effective ways of interacting across cultures.

In respecting the integrity of cultures, it is through *adaptation* that the individual more consciously and skillfully relates to and communicates with people of different cultural origins. One takes on new ways of being, though not giving up the home culture, and becomes more empathetic and able to shift worldviews. A second step is internalizing more than one worldview and shifting between them with some ease and less conscious attention. It is here that one can move beyond conscious competence to unconscious competence, but this is an uneven process. As some ways of being become more unconscious, others are just being discovered, and this process may have started long before adaptation. It appears that one is always in a state of discovery in an intercultural environment because it is impossible to learn everything about another culture, much less more than one. The unconscious competence occurs in the internalization of interculturally competent skills and of a consistent display of inclusive and adaptive attitudes.

Integration brings the person to the state of being a multicultural person as described by Peter Adler (1975). The integrated person no longer identifies solely with one culture but is able to function between and among many cultures, having mastered the skills of bridging between them and enabling members of those cultures to constructively engage with each other, often for a particular purpose. Thus, while they may become marginal in their home culture, this is not seen as a negative factor but as part of the process of adding new cultural perspectives to one's repertoire of responses to living constructively in a multifaceted, multicultural world. Having access to multiple worldviews, the integrated person is able to evaluate situations contextually, make ethical choices, and act in "the profoundly relativistic world." This person is also able to enhance intercultural interaction and is ever open to new learning and to continued development both professionally and personally. Here is a person who is in a state of *dynamic inbetweeness* (Yoshikawa, 1987).

J. Bennett (1993) addresses marginality by differentiating between constructive marginals (those who accept responsibility for choosing and constructing value sets and who are at home anywhere) from encapsulated marginals (those who lack the ability to shift between worldviews and are in danger of becoming alienated from all the cultures they know). Encapsulated marginals see themselves as so unique that it is hard for them to relate to any group, something that has been termed *terminal uniqueness*. They may seem "self-conscious and self-absorbed" and find it hard to feel at home in any environment (J. Bennett, 1993). Those who assume leadership responsibilities would tend to fall into the constructive marginal category because they exhibit an ability to be at home anywhere, to see more than one perspective rather than be captured in the ethnocentric center of their own culture, and to entertain various approaches to any situation and to exhibit good judgment in making decisions.

In applying this DMIS specifically to interculturally competent leadership, a truly competent global leader must reach the stage of adaptation to difference and, preferably, integration of difference. Since minimization is more an attitude of tolerance based on similarity, tolerance falls short of what is needed to have the requisite adaptability for effective global leadership. Minimization is a transition state in which one tends to fall back on the solutions in one's own culture as the superior or natural or correct ways of doing things. Minimization tends to be fairly benign and can be operative within one's own culture but does not hold up well in a global environment. Acceptance of difference shows a recognition and appreciation of differences in cultural behavior and values and a beginning of understanding cultural relativity. The adaptive person is able to consciously shift perspective into different cultural worldviews and behave in culturally appropriate ways. This demonstrates the use of empathy and behavioral flexibility as well as mindfulness, cognitive flexibility, and a tolerance for being in unclear situations. When the person begins to internalize different worldviews, he or she can shift unconsciously, obviously behaving in ways compatible with each worldview. The integration of multiple frames of reference allows an individual to evaluate situations from a variety of perspectives. It can lead to constructive marginality, which is useful when exercising global leadership because the constructive marginal may be seen as that edgewalker who lives and functions well at the margins between conflicting, divergent cultures and who can view situations from more than one perspective.

One might ask if it is possible to test for this kind of capacity and to predict who might have the inclination to become a global leader (see Part III of this volume for further discussion on assessment of intercultural competence). While it is possible to measure where people fall on this intercultural sensitivity continuum using an instrument such as the Intercultural Developmental Inventory (IDI; Hammer, Bennett, & Wiseman, 2003), this is not an infallible predictor of competence. People who can be expected to do well often do not, while those who seem the least likely to be successful intercultural communicators are surprisingly effective. As measures go, this has strong validity and reliability as an instrument and a considerable amount of research to support a recognized and well-established conceptual model. The proof, however, lies in how adroitly one demonstrates an ability to navigate the interfaces between contrary worldviews, make sense of them, and lead with wisdom and compassion.

The Interculturally Competent Global Leader: What Does This Leader Look Like?

The global leader is called upon to bridge the differences, to take various perspectives and life experiences into account when making decisions and interacting with others, especially when leading the work of groups of people. Achieving the more inclusive ways of thinking (intellect), feeling (emotion), and functioning (action) is critical to success for the global leader. The head, the heart, and the hands are fully engaged in whatever the global leader, as well as those with whom there is collaboration, undertakes. The total engagement is obvious when the skills are finely honed. This is, as Peter Adler (1998) described, a multicultural person. Adler began his description of the multicultural person with these words:

> A new type of person whose orientation and view of the world profoundly transcends his indigenous culture is developing from the complex of social, political, economic, and education interactions of our time. (p. 227)

The multicultural person has "psychologically and socially come to grips with a multiplicity of realities" (P. Adler, 1998) and has been able to cope well with the psychological process of adapting to a new culture and with moving from place to place. The global leader is, simultaneously, a multicultural person if one connects P. Adler's (1975) description with the capabilities needed for global leadership. Adler spans the adaptation and integration stages of the DMIS as he describes a person who is "always in the process of becoming a part of or apart from a given cultural context." Advanced adaptation and integration are marked by "attitude, emotions, and behaviors that are independent but not independent of cultural influence" (P. Adler, 1975). Yoshikawa (1987) interprets this as being "independent, yet simultaneously interdependent. This paradoxical existence can assume a new identity—the 'identity-in-unity' or 'duality-in-unity'" (pp. 142–143). This is when "one becomes capable of bringing new ways to explore the paradox of human diversity and unity" (pp. 142–143). This relates to the characteristic that S. Black et al. (1999) list as important to interculturally competent leadership, the ability to embrace duality. Coupled with being comfortable with ambiguity, the ability to embrace duality is essential when being presented with vast amounts of data and multiple ways of conducting business or making decisions, especially within a working environment. A leader must be able to sort things out, to be involved and, at the same time, objective when dealing with paradox that is inherent in the global scene.

It is important to consider how an interculturally skilled leader approaches the use of power, a topic rarely addressed when discussing intercultural competence. When we talk of leadership, we also are talking about the ability to influence events, to affect situations or environments, and, in fact, to rally support from groups of people. People in ethnocentric stages tend to be exploitative, deny others their rights, and, in minimization, fail to perceive the presence of institutional privilege. People in acceptance tend to avoid any exercise of power, feeling that it is not useful to developing good intercultural relations. Thus, it is critical for global leaders to reach the stages of adaptation and/or integration when there is greater comfort with exercising power when it is necessary. This is when people tend to "recognize and respond to power in cultural context" and are able to exert it appropriately in various cultural contexts. In integration, there is a strong orientation to consensual decision making and power sharing (M. Bennett, 1999). Global leadership calls for that kind of approach, and it takes a rather advanced level of intercultural sensitivity to exercise power in a nondominating manner and to use critical thinking to analyze structures that impede human development and, in fact, are oppressive. Value-driven leadership promotes "humane governance, socially responsible management, and multicultural cooperation" (Safty, 2003). A high level of intercultural sophistication and skill along with technical expertise contributes to that end.

There is another factor to be considered in approaches to leadership in today's world. It is becoming essential that leadership skills be widely dispersed rather than concentrated in a few at the top. Leadership happens at all levels of organizations and in society. It is essential to prepare as many people as possible to function as leaders wherever they are as they face the challenges that exist in the world today. Leaders in traditionally structured societies who understand this challenge distinguish themselves from other in their cultures and tend to become leaders because of their vision and ability to engage in changing the culture as well as functioning as leaders within it. Especially when transforming organizations, being able to bring others along and remain with the change process over a long period of time while maintaining the vision for the future is essential. It is a messy process and requires perseverance and persistence and enormous skill. In an interview about where tomorrow's leaders will be found, Hill (2008) states that decision making must be broadly distributed across institutions, and in any endeavor, collaboration is essential. No one leader can keep abreast of all that is necessary to know about the constantly changing environment, nor can innovation emerge from a single source. A distributed leadership model will draw on the abilities within groups or teams whose members have different functional abilities and varying perspectives. This model empowers people to be innovative. Hill suggests that we have to become conscious of invisible people in organizations, people who are rarely tapped for positions of authority and influence because of "gender, ethnicity, nationality or even age" ("demographic invisibles") or because they do not conveniently fit into the preconceptions of how leaders look and act ("stylistic invisibles"). Often, these invisibles have learned to lead from behind, a paradoxical statement that aptly describes how many people, unable to acquire recognized leadership positions, have learned to get things done and to be change agents. It takes extraordinary skill and hard work; many who lead from behind are perfectly capable of leading from the front. They become very adept in the competencies that are recognized as essential for global leadership and are able to exercise good judgment, set boundaries, encourage people to flourish where they are, and manage tensions that inevitably occur in a group. The issue is recognizing potential leaders by moving beyond our preconceptions about how leaders look and begin to look at how people contribute.

Jean Lipman-Blumen (1996) has studied leadership styles of more than 5,000 leaders worldwide and talks of leading in an interdependent world as requiring a fundamental shift from patterns of competitiveness, authoritarianism, and individualism to what she has labeled *connective leadership*. She quotes Vaclav Havel, who suggests that "we stand helpless" before the global challenges the world faces "because our civilization has essentially globalized only the surface of our lives" (Lipman-Blumen, 1996, p. 5). There remains a tendency to revert to our tribal ways in the midst of a demand for greater interdependence in the midst of diversity. We often feel that culture lies on the surface when indeed it is the signs of globalization that lie at a superficial level. Leaders who must deal with this new era of connectivity are those edgewalkers who must deal with the endless restructuring of organizations, of alliances, of partnerships, of the pace at which change seems to occur, all at the nexus of different expectations and needs. The connective leadership model is an important contribution because it takes into account differing styles individuals may bring to the leadership role but also includes the capacity to "identify the most effective leadership strategies" to apply in unique situations, "evaluate the leadership potential in others" and match those skills with specific challenges, and "design new types of structures" to fit tasks and "the behavioral preferences of participants" (p. 25). It requires all of the intercultural skills that we have discussed here and insight into leadership patterns, culturally based, of the past.

Rosen et al. (2000) found leaders around the world who are developing cultural literacy, who are skilled intercultural practitioners, and who are looking toward a future that has limitations as well as opportunities. There are examples of radical changes in practice to take into account the need for sustainability, to deal with global and local diversity, and to cultivate new leadership within their industries. We are not bereft of models to emulate.

The Interculturally Skilled Leader: How Does a Potential Global Leader Develop Intercultural Competence?

Moving from ethnocentrism to ethnorelativism and becoming interculturally competent requires a significant "other-culture" experience. Gregersen, Morrison, and Black (1998) suggest four strategies for creating global leadership skills: "foreign travel, with immersion in the country's way of life; the formation of teams in which individuals with diverse backgrounds and perspectives work together closely; training that involves classroom and action learning projects; and overseas assignments, which serve to broaden the outlook of future global leaders" (p. 23). One could argue that foreign travel alone, without an opportunity to become deeply involved in foreign cultures, has little merit. Being in the vicinity of another culture but failing to engage with it does little to increase intercultural skill. In-depth exposure to unfamiliar cultures with an educational emphasis on learning intercultural skills as well as the history, economic conditions, environmental issues, political realities, religion(s), and cultural practices, values, and beliefs of at least one other culture is a process that can prepare future leaders. This can occur in short stays if there is preparation for the experience, if there are encounters that challenge assumptions, and if there is guided reflection on this experience. The goal is to provide an opportunity for transformative learning. Study abroad can provide this kind of opportunity. Organizations and corporations can develop programs that provide similar experiences. It takes planning and commitment that often do not exist in our institutions.

One transformative learning model for education abroad is the international service-learning experience discussed by Brown (2005). The research conducted on the international service-learning programs of the International Partnership for Service-Learning and Leadership found, surprisingly, that students in those programs developed leadership capabilities. This finding, in fact, caused the organization to add the word *leadership* to its name and to deal with leadership skill development more consciously. Students, dealing with new methods of organizational management and leadership, must discover how to fit into the community agency to which they were assigned and assume a productive role. Many create new ways of providing service to the agency's client population and grow in self-confidence, in an ability to use scarce resources, and develop empathy for those they serve on a daily basis. Living, working, and learning in a new society with people who provide some guidance and who readily answer questions help them become the kind of skilled interculturalists that are needed in the world (Tonkin, 2004). Too many study-abroad programs are devised to imitate the systems at home, which conveniently avoids the kinds of encounters that produce the greatest learning.

Outside formal education systems, there are opportunities to devise programs for employees, volunteers, and other stakeholders that will instill a global mind-set. This does not necessarily have to be in a different country, although getting outside any semblance of a comfort zone is essential. International assignments are clearly preferable for employees, who can even take advantage of business trips by avoiding the usual cocoon of comfortable hotels, a closely managed itinerary, fine restaurants, and limited contact with those outside the corporate structure and constructing a "traveler" rather than a tourist experience (Oddou et al., 2000). Another method is to assign people to multinational teams who have a defined purpose and have been trained to function in an intercultural environment. Often these teams work virtually, which is a powerful learning experience fraught with the kinds of communication and working style differences (Brake, 2007). There are many creative solutions to the dilemma of training people to be interculturally competent without overseas assignments. Often, people working internationally do so in short spurts rather than extended stays.

Selecting potential leaders for further development could be a frustrating process fraught with the potential for serious miscalculation. Providing opportunities for "other culture" immersion to a broad range of people is a more fruitful approach. It is better to prepare everyone to be involved in the leadership activity, assuming that those who can actually "lead" will emerge from this prepared population. Leaders cannot do it alone. Creating a population that thinks more broadly, has experience with multiple cultures, and has developed a considerable set of intercultural skill provides followers, in addition to leaders, who can contribute to the future development of good relations around the globe and greater attention to the problems that we collectively face.

Safty (2004) states that leadership education is "an urgent priority." He indicates that it is important not only to establish centers of leadership education with an intercultural perspective but also to transform the many leadership programs that exist so they more consistently reflect the multicultural nature of the world in which the leaders will work.

In addition, leadership development must start early, with educational systems that begin preparing children at a young age to appreciate and understand the multicultural society in which they live and to function in an increasingly skilled manner within it. This is no small order, but it is much easier to start with the children who come with few inhibitions about exploring something new and a tendency to ask questions that an adult is reluctant to voice. Recently, I read that children coming up in the world today are more accepting of cultural differences because it has been part of their lives from birth. While greater pluralism in societies may help children learn to accept people unlike themselves "naturally," it is easy to believe that they can be diverted from this attitude by unscrupulous leaders and others who have much to gain from inciting fear, which drives those who have not fully realized the development of an ethnorelative perspective back into defense. Dedicated and interculturally competent teachers are necessary for this educational paradigm to succeed (see Cushner & Mahon in Chapter 17, this volume, for a detailed discussion on developing interculturally competent teachers). Some interculturally competent teachers exist in educational systems but need encouragement and recognition. It must be demonstrated to incoming generations of teachers that this work is valued and rewarded. Continued attention to education about differences and to training in intercultural skills throughout all the developmental stages of a child's life, through higher education, is essential to keep attitudes of openness and caring for others alive, growing, and present in the adults they become.

Conclusion

The need to develop in leaders the attitudes that go beyond tolerance toward embracing difference and living constructively and compassionately in a multicultural world is critical to the survival of humankind and the planet. How leadership qualities are exhibited, recognized, and rewarded differs from culture to culture. Leaders who can function across cultures, who can create and sustain systems that draw on the strength of those differences, and who allow innovative approaches to emerge are essential in every human endeavor. This does not come just from building a set of skills but in acquiring a new mind map. Opportunities for acquiring a global perspective, for moving from ethnocentrism to ethnorelativism, and for developing the range of competences essential for global leadership must be provided even as we look for potential leaders outside the usual leadership frame. Where will the next generation of leaders come from? Often from those who are invisible, but they must be allowed to make themselves visible, from the ranks of those who have been required to deal with challenging situations in cultures other than their own (Hill, 2008), and from the classrooms where building intercultural competencies has been taught. N. J. Adler (2008) states, "Today's challenge is . . . to become a global leader who can meet the challenges of the twenty-first century— . . . who can rise to the challenge of shaping history" (p. 171). To train leaders to play this role requires the full attention of the global society.

Note

1. Although see Lipman-Blumen (1996, p. 25), who suggests that it is impossible to learn leadership skills.

References

Adler, N.J. (1977). *International dimensions of organizational behavior.* Cincinnati, OH: South-Western College Publishing.

Adler, N. J. (with Gundersen, A.). (2008). *International dimensions of organizational behavior* (5th ed.). Canada: Thompson Southwestern.

Adler, P. (1975). *The boundary experience.* Unpublished doctoral dissertation, Union Graduate School, Yellow Spring, OH.

Adler, P. (1998). Beyond cultural identity: Reflections on multiculturalism. In M. J. Bennett (Ed.), *Basic concepts of intercultural communication: Selected readings* (pp. 225–245). Yarmouth, ME: Intercultural Press.

Bennett, J. (1993). Cultural marginality: Identity issues in intercultural training. In R. M. Paige (Ed.), *Education for the intercultural experience* (pp. 109–135). Yarmouth, ME: Intercultural Press.

Bennett, J. (2009). Transformative training designing programs for culture learning. In M. Moodian (Ed.), *Contemporary leadership and intercultural competence* (pp. 95–110). Thousand Oaks, CA: Sage.

Bennett, M. (1993). Towards a developmental model of intercultural sensitivity. In R. M. Paige (Ed.), *Education for the intercultural experience* (pp. 21–71). Yarmouth, ME: Intercultural Press.

Bennett, M. (1999). *A developmental model of intercultural sensitivity* (Handout). Portland, OR: Intercultural Communication Institute.

Black, J. S., & Gregersen, H. B. (2000). High impact training: Forging leaders for the global frontier. *Human Resource Management, 39*(2–3), 173–185.

Black, S., Morrison, A., & Gregersen, H. (1999). *Global explorers: The next generation of leaders.* New York: Routledge.

Brake, T. (1997). *The global leader: Critical factors for creating the world class organization.* Chicago: Irwin.

Brake, T. (2007). *Welcome 2 the fun house.* London: Transnational Management Associates, Ltd.

Brannen, C., & Wilen, T. (1993). *Doing business with Japanese men.* Berkeley, CA: Stonebridge Press.

Brown, N. (2005, June). *International service-learning: Uniting academic study, community service, and cultural immersion.* Paper presented at the 2005 Global Leadership Conference, Istanbul, Turkey.

Deardorff, D. K. (2004). *The identification and assessment of intercultural competence as a student outcome of internationalization at institutions of higher education in the United States.* Unpublished doctoral dissertation, North Carolina State University, Raleigh.

Deardorff, D. K. (2006). Identification and assessment of intercultural competence as a student outcome of internationalization. *Journal of Studies in Intercultural Education, 10,* 241–266.

Friedman, T. L. (2005a, June 10). "Behind every grad . . ." *New York Times.*

Friedman, T. L. (2005b). *The world is flat: A brief history of the twenty-first century.* New York: Farrar, Straus & Giroux.

Gardner, H. (1995). *Leading minds: An anatomy of leadership.* New York: Basic Books.

Golandaz, H. (2003). Leadership for capacity building. In A. Safty (Ed.), *Value leadership* (pp. 221–231). Istanbul, Turkey: School of Government and Leadership, University of Bahcesehir.

Gregersen, H., Morrison, A. J., & Black, J. S. (1998). Developing leaders for the global frontier. *Human Resource Management and Industrial Relations, 40,* 21–32.

Gudykunst, W. B. (1991). *Bridging differences: Effective intergroup interaction.* Newbury Park, CA: Sage.

Haire, M., Ghiselli, E. E., & Porter, L. W. (1966). *Managerial thinking: An international study.* New York: John Wiley.

Hall, E. T. (1959). *The silent language.* New York: Doubleday.

Hall, E. T. (1966). *The hidden dimension.* New York: Doubleday.

Hall, E. T. (1993). *Understanding cultural differences—Germans, French and Americans.* Yarmouth, ME: Intercultural Press.

Hall, E. T., & Hall, M. T. (1987). *Hidden differences: Doing business with the Japanese.* New York: Doubleday.

Hampden-Turner, C., & Trompenaars, F. (1993). *The seven cultures of capitalism.* New York: Doubleday.

Hammer, M. R., Bennett, M. J., & Wiseman, R. (2003). Measuring intercultural sensitivity: The Intercultural Development Inventory. *International Journal of Intercultural Relations, 27,* 421–443.

Harris, P. R., Moran, R. T., & Moran, S. V. (2004). *Managing cultural differences* (6th ed.). Amsterdam: Elsevier Butterworth-Heinemann.

Hill, L. A. (2008, January 1). Where will we find tomorrow's leaders? *Harvard Business Review.*

Hofstede, G. (2001). *Culture's consequences* (2nd ed.). Thousand Oaks, CA: Sage.

House, R. J., Hanges, P. J., Javidan, M., Dorfman, P., & Gupta, V. (2004). *Culture, leadership, and organizations: The GLOBE study of 62 societies.* Thousand Oaks, CA: Sage.

Howell, W. S. (1982). *The empathic communicator.* Belmont, CA: Wadsworth.

Ishinomori, S. (1988). *Japan, Inc.* Berkeley: University of California Press.

Kanter, R. M. (1995). *World class thriving locally in the global economy.* New York: Simon & Schuster.

Kemper, C. L. (2003). Edgewalking: The emerging new-century leadership paradigm. *Workforce Diversity Reader, 1*(2).

Lewis, R. D. (2005). *When cultures collide: Leading across cultures* (3rd ed.). Boston: Intercultural Press.

Lipman-Blumen, J. (1996). *The connective edge: Leading in an interdependent world.* San Francisco: Jossey-Bass.

March, R. M. (1988). *The Japanese negotiator.* Tokyo: Kondanshi, Inc.

McGregor, D. (1960). *The human side of enterprise.* New York: McGraw-Hill.

Ouchi, W. (1981). *Theory Z.* New York: HarperCollins.

Oddou, G., Mendenhall, M., & Ritchie, J. B. (2000). Leveraging travel as a tool for global leadership development. In *Human Resource Management, 39,* 159–172.

Pusch, M. (1994). The chameleon capacity. In R. D. Lambert (Ed.), *Educational exchange and global competence* (pp. 205–210). New York: Council on International Educational Exchange.

Rosen, R., Digh, P., Singer, M., & Phillips, C. (2000). *Global literacies: Lessons on business leadership and national cultures.* New York: Simon & Schuster.

Safty, A. (2003). Value leadership and governance. In A. Safty (Ed.), *Value leadership* (pp. 36–51). Istanbul, Turkey: School of Government and Leadership, University of Bahcesehir.

Safty, A. (2004). *Leadership and democracy.* New York: International Partnership for Service-Learning and Leadership.

Tonkin, H. (2004). *Service-learning across cultures: Promise and achievement.* New York: International Partnership for Service-Learning and Leadership.

Yoshikawa, M. J. (1987). Cross-cultural adaptation and perceptual development. In Y. Y. Kim & W. D. Gudykunst (Eds.), *Cross-cultural adaptation: Current approaches* (pp. 140–148). Newbury Park, CA: Sage.

Zaleznik. A. (2004, January 1). Managers and leaders: Are they different? *Harvard Business Review.*

CHAPTER 4

The Moral Circle in Intercultural Competence

Trust Across Cultures

Gert Jan Hofstede

I ntercultural competence requires the ability to participate in the social life of people who live according to different unwritten rules. This implies being a "good member" of a community other than one's own. A community, potentially ranging from a few people to all the people in the world, constitutes a "moral circle," that is, a group of which the members expect to live by a shared standard of moral rules. While these rules are usually unwritten and implicit, adhering to them is crucial.

To investigate intercultural competence, one must take a look at what it means to be "good" and "bad" in a moral circle. This is how we begin the chapter. Then we investigate trust and reputation, notions that have to do with the expectation that others will behave in moral ways. After that we turn to culture. Culture is about the unwritten rules for being an acceptable member of the moral circle, and it varies across groups. Finally, the knowledge about good and bad, trust and reputation, and culture is used to tackle practical issues of intercultural competence, whether that involves receiving outsiders, traveling abroad, or working in multicultural teams.[1]

"What do you have to do to get expelled?" This question was asked in a full conference hall by a U.S. student during the international student welcome week that is organized each year at the Dutch university at which I work. The answer disconcerted the student. He was probably expecting a list of heinous transgressions, but instead he was told, "We never expel anybody. At most we sometimes give somebody the urgent advice to leave." This anecdote shows that a university operates, among other functions, as a moral circle. The student was from a society where evil is deemed to lurk nearly everywhere, and severe punishments are often expected. He was studying in a society in which self-control rather than punishment is expected to keep people in check. The point here is not to argue which approach is best. Different explicit rules hold in both societies, based on different unwritten cultural assumptions, and thus may seem strange to those from a different culture. This example applies to any other institution in society, including institutions as varied as companies, families, teams, governments, and armies. People are moral, but culture modifies that morality.

The Biological Basis of Morality

The most quoted philosopher about morality is probably Immanuel Kant. Kant's reasoning was that any behavior that would be detrimental if everybody engaged in it was to be avoided (Johnson, 2008). This led him to formulate his categorical imperative. This categorical imperative is in fact so generic that it is found in many proverbs and religious rules. "Do to others as you would be done unto" and the religious command to "love thy neighbor as thyself" are forms of this.

We now take a big step back to consider morality from a biological point of view. It turns out that Kant's imperative has operated in evolution in all cases where between-group competition occurred. All the way from colonies of bacteria onwards, "bad" behavior benefits an individual at the detriment of the group while "good" behavior benefits the group (Wilson, 2007; Wilson & Wilson, 2007). Morality is that simple in its basics, and this is due to evolutionary logic. All along evolution, groups have competed with one another, and groups that suffered from antisocial behavior have been outcompeted by groups that did not.

At the same time, morality among human societies is incredibly complex in its ramifications. This chapter will address some of these ramifications, particularly those connected with culture. Perceptions of what benefits the group are widely different across and even within cultures given the variability in cultural perceptions of what constitutes group membership. Anybody who might be or might become a member of the moral circle deserves to be treated as a moral being, while those outside the group do not deserve such treatment. This is the logic that has made us evolve as a group-based species.

One of the foremost institutions to deal with morality in any society is religion. Other potential symbolic delimiters of moral circles are ethnic appearance, gender, caste, class, clothing style, hairstyle, education, and membership in associations or clubs. The preponderance of each of these varies greatly across and within societies. People are endlessly creative in creating group identities, and the list is not exhaustive.

Evolution of Morality

Humans have not invented morality. Many species of social mammals and birds show notions of good and bad that are very similar to our own (de Waal, 1996). Over the centuries, our ancestors took the next steps. Under selective pressures of rapid climate change and intergroup competition, they developed an ability to evolve much faster than through genetic evolution. The alternative, cultural evolution, operates by imitation and has now become a powerful force driving the evolution of human societies (Richerson & Boyd, 2005). However, a battle between levels of evolution is still raging. We are stuck with a perennial conflict of interest between our own selfish interests and the interests of the groups to which we belong. It is rare for these to not be in conflict. We reserve moral feelings for members of our groups, whatever that may be. Research in physiology and neurology confirms that the in-group/out-group distinction is basic for generating empathy and other moral feelings.

Trust

Trust and the Moral Circle

A plethora of literature about trust has appeared in the past decades in various fields of the social sciences (Doney, Cannon, & Mullen, 1998; Kramer, 1999; Nooteboom, 2002). Numerous definitions are used in psychology, management, and economics, most of which stress the single transaction between two people (e.g., "If A believes that B will act in A's best interest and accepts vulnerability to B's actions, then A trusts B"). This kind of definition captures the meaning of trust in the context of a transaction, and as such, it is useful. But most transactions take place within some kind of relationship, be it family membership, friendship, business partnership, or ownership. The wider context of trust can be defined as follows: "Trust in sociology is a relationship between people. It involves having one person thinking that the other person or idea is *benevolent, competent/good,* or *honest/true. . . .* It makes social life *predictable,* it creates a *sense of community,* and it *makes it easier for people to work together.* Trust . . . is also integral to the idea of social influence, as it is easier to influence or persuade someone who is trusting" (Wikipedia). This definition of trust restates the idea that a network of people who trust each other form a moral circle. It also implies that trust cannot be the same to people who have different ideas about benevolence, competence, or honesty. Likewise, most people have probably experienced in their lives that benevolence, competence, and honesty are not always combined in one person. What is more, they can sometimes become opposites, as, for example, when one hides a very disagreeable truth from somebody for the sake of benevolence (i.e., to spare the other's feelings). The last sentence in the Wikipedia definition points to the fact that trust is always vulnerable to exploitation by those with ill intentions. Doney et al. (1998) add two more "trust-building processes" to the three highlighted in the broader definition of trust: prediction and transference. Prediction means that A can trust B to do something in an instrumental way, as you would trust your car, regardless of B's intentions. Transference points to the practice that people rely on accounts by third persons: "Call B. You can trust him, I've known him for years." This is normally known as a reputation mechanism. The unwritten rules of reputation mechanisms vary across the world, just as do those of other social processes. For instance, what happens to a whistle-blower who exposes immoral behavior within a community? Will he become a hero or an outcast? The most likely outcome varies by culture.

The conclusion is that it is not fruitful to try and define the concept of trust in every detail since this varies by culture. A general definition would hold that one trusts others to the extent that one expects them to adhere to Kant's categorical imperative. In other words, trusting people means expecting them to behave as upstanding members of your moral circle.

Intrinsic and Enforceable Trust

A few years ago, a Japanese businessman was having pasta in a fast-food restaurant. Suddenly, he choked on something. It looked like a piece of plastic. Soon, the restaurant's staff were making profuse excuses. They in turn wrote to their Australian supplier, making it known that traces of plastic had been found in their pasta sauce and that a food safety visit was deemed necessary. Within weeks a delegation from the Japanese fast-food chain visited the Australian facilities. Not only were the ISO 9000 certificates in order, but nothing that remotely pointed to the possibility of plastic contamination was discovered. The Japanese delegation returned home, both parties feeling disappointed about the unsolved issue. Then the Japanese had another look at the offending plastic. And . . . lo and behold, it turned out to be the outer peel of an Australian onion (Storer, 2004), indicating differences in the way in which the outer peel of the onion is used in two different cultures.

This anecdote underscores an important lesson about trust. The certification system had not worked, but the visit to the factories had. After having trudged along together through the factories in a very stressful atmosphere and finding out that nothing had really happened after all, the Japanese and Australians actually had become companions in adversity. They had come to trust one another.

This story points to a general distinction into types of trust—between intrinsic and enforceable trust. In both cases, the result is that we can rely on the other. But the motivations are different.

Enforceable trust is calculative and incentive-driven. It is the trust we place in those with whom we are not necessarily on friendly terms but whom we know are better off when they live up to the trust we place in them. Contracts can create enforceable trust between two parties. ISO 9000 certificates are a case in which responsibility for trustworthy production practices is outsourced to a third party (i.e., the certifying agency). In the beginning of the pasta story, the Japanese thought they had enforceable trust, and they came to Australia to actually enforce it.

Intrinsic trust is the trust that we may feel for a person "just like that." Or more precisely, at first acquaintance, the feeling is "I think I can trust that person," and also "I would like to trust that person." This feeling relates to the basic needs of human beings to affiliate with one another, to be friends (Maslow, 1970). Then, with time, through being tested time and again and not broken, intrinsic trust can deepen. The more stringent the test, the more trust it builds: "A friend in need is a friend indeed." This is what grew between the Japanese and the Australians. Intrinsic trust is a much stronger notion than enforceable trust. Both make social life predictable, and both make it easier for people to work together. Only intrinsic trust, if it is shared in a network of friends, creates a sense of community. And only intrinsic trust makes it easier to influence others. Lenin is supposed to have said,

"Trust is good, but control is better" (see, e.g., Busch & Hantusch, 2000). This holds for enforceable trust. Intrinsic trust, however, makes control redundant. Yet the two types of trust are linked. The social environment can exert such pressure that untrustworthy behavior punishes itself. This is exactly what moral feelings of shame and guilt are for and why they evolved to such high degrees in human populations. Intrinsic trust and its attendant pleasurable emotions are the proximate mechanism by which evolution ensures the survival of well-collaborating groups at the expense of poor groups.

In any society, breaches of trust put one's reputation at risk. As Gambetta (2000) states, "It may be hard to bank on altruism, but it is much harder to avoid banking on a reputation for trustworthiness: as all bankers (and used-car dealers) know, a good reputation is their best asset." We may add that fear of losing a reputation is the best enforcer of trustworthiness. In a hypothetical environment where reputation is all-important, the distinction between intrinsic and enforceable trust becomes irrelevant to the functioning of the social network. If we have business partners we do not know well, as happens quite frequently in today's globalized business world with its volatile employment, then we better consider the incentives and punishments.

One of the basic needs of humans is what Maslow (1970) has termed *love and belonging* and what a biologist might call *affiliation*. Intrinsic trust is a consequence of feelings of affiliation. People are driven by a need for intrinsic trust.

Trust, Emotions, and Personality

In "Western" parlance about organized life, emotion is often contrasted with rationality. This chapter takes the point of view of Frijda (1986), who contends that far from being irrational, emotions are a perfectly rational mechanism that serves our interests. Emotions are the early warning system that tells us about the fulfillment of our basic needs. Some of these emotions are at the basis of intrinsic trust. Having nobody to trust is distressing. Social life is full of symbols and rituals that express the wish to trust or to be trusted. These can be as basic as the polite smile, the handshake, or the hug. They can involve rituals of sharing food and drink. Or they can be embodied in economic transactions, for example, in the modalities of contracts (Hofstede, Spaans, Schepers, Trienekens, & Beulens, 2004, p. 212). Feelings of sympathy or antipathy, attraction or repulsion guide our choice of whom to trust. For priming these feelings, perceived group membership is a quick decision aid.

In economic life, another basic need beyond affiliation is also prominent: the drive for that which Maslow calls "esteem," Nietzsche calls "Macht" (power), and a biologist would call "dominance." Political alliances, whether in the private or in the public sector, tend to be based on incentives for dominance: The partners believe that they are more powerful together. "If you can't beat them, join them" is the motive. Trust in these alliances is incentive driven rather than intrinsic, at least initially.

There is often a friction between the desire of business partners to have it their way and their need to appear trustworthy. Coercive action may not be well received because it connotes self-interest. Displays of power can generate resentfulness. Kramer (1999) gives some eloquent examples of how surveillance systems in organizations communicate to employees that they are being distrusted, making them fearful and suspicious or even inducing them to try and sabotage the surveillance system instead of doing their work.

A society is a mosaic of individuals with unique personalities. In regard to trust, the tendency to trust and the tendency to be trustworthy are both linked to personality characteristics, and this link is valid across cultures. McCrae and Costa (2003), creators of the Big Five personality model (this author's acronym is OCEAN: Openness, Conscientiousness, Extraversion, Agreeableness, Neuroticism), show that the *agreeableness* trait is linked to the benevolence component of trust as well as the honesty component. The competence component of trust is addressed by another trait, *conscientiousness.* Yet another personality trait that might affect trust is *neuroticism.* Two forms of neuroticism, *anxiety* and *angry hostility,* are the dispositional forms of two fundamental emotional states: fear and anger. Anxious persons are prone to worry, while hostile persons are prone to ill temper. Neither trait is conducive to stable, trusting relationships.

The five traits are independent, meaning for instance that an agreeable person is just as likely to be conscientious as not to be so. But the facets of one trait, such as being trusting and being trustworthy, are linked. As the proverb goes, "Ill doers are ill deemers." In conclusion, trusting and trustworthy behaviors are unequally spread across any population. Each individual is unique, and individuals with different personalities are likely to adopt different roles in society.

Culture

I was walking toward my gate in Charles de Gaulle Airport, Paris, with a few hours ahead of me, waiting for a flight to Tunis. One Tunisian-looking man was the only person in sight, so I greeted him in French. To my surprise, he replied stiffly in English, "Excuse me, I do not understand you, I am an American citizen." We started talking, and he gradually relaxed. It turned out his name was Ramadan, and he was an information technology specialist of Libyan origin living in the United States, and since U.S. authorities did not allow him to travel directly to Tripoli, he took this detour to be introduced to his intended wife, who was a distant cousin. We had a good time together. The next week, we met again at Tunis airport, and he proudly showed me pictures of his future wife, looking happy.

This episode shows the difference between *identity* and *culture.* Ramadan started the conversation rather defensively, using his identity as an American citizen to stay away from the personal sphere. But culturally, he turned out to be very much a Libyan, warm and talkative in style, arranging his marriage in a way that was accepted in his home society.

People are conscious of their identity, and to some extent they can change their identity but may not be able to change their cultural conditioning. One's culture, in many cases, is not only a source of deeply felt pride and belonging, but it is often deeply ingrained as part of an individual's worldview. This cultural conditioning denotes the most solid moral circle in which they feel included.

Any society has to come to terms with some basic issues of social life or it could not function. The unwritten rules of the social game in a society differ across the world. In other words, societies have distinct cultures. And while some societies are heterogeneous, research confirms that cultural differences between societies are generally much larger than cultural differences within societies. In many cases, countries correspond with societies. So using country data is in many cases a reasonably good way to obtain insight into the cultures of societies and the ways in which individuals have been culturally conditioned. Almost all countries themselves try to function as "moral circles." This attempt is reflected in manifold institutions. To name but one example: In the United States, many schoolchildren pledge alliance to the national flag on a daily basis.

The relations between cultural traits and processes of trust building and breaking are intricate and problematic. The same behavior that builds trust in one context can destroy it in another. Many contradicting viewpoints about trustworthiness of people and groups are held in the world. Yet patterns can be found. The chapter will now turn to such patterns by introducing a trait-based perspective on culture.

Five Basic Issues

Culture is about mutual expectations of morally acceptable behavior. Research has shown and confirmed often that a limited set of issues adequately describes the basic value orientations of societies (Hofstede, 2001; Hofstede & Hofstede, 2005). Hofstede found five independent dimensions of values related to five basic issues.[2] It is important to note that in this paradigm, "culture" is not an attribute of individuals but of societies.

Identity: Individualism Versus Collectivism

The level of interdependency that is assumed differs greatly across societies. Western travelers in Malaysia will often comment about never being left alone. On the other hand, Asians in an English-speaking country can be very lonely. Both phenomena relate to the same cultural difference. From a very early age, an Anglo child is supposed to be independent, have his or her own possessions, his or her own opinions. A Malay child is above all a small part of a harmonious group.

Hierarchy: Large Versus Small Power Distance

The asymmetry of power relations that subordinates expect varies across cultures. On Norwegian offshore platforms, leadership of the crew rotates every year, even though some members might be more able leaders than others. Leadership is distributed in an egalitarian manner in this society. On the very same kind of platform across Russia, hierarchy is absolute, and no subordinate crew member would dream of overturning it.

Gender and Aggression: Masculinity Versus Femininity

In some societies, there is a basic belief that men are intrinsically different from women: Males are fighters who defend the community, while females preserve the social fabric. By the same logic, both males and females in such societies need to be tough to survive the unforgiving conditions of societal life. In other societies, both males and females are supposed to be peace-minded. In these, there is sympathy rather than contempt for losers, and the weak can count on help.

Anxiety: Weak Versus Strong Uncertainty Avoidance

We live in an unpredictable world. Some societies take this in stride. Unexpected events and unclear rituals are welcomed. Emotional displays are avoided, and basic stress levels are low. In other societies, the reverse is the case. There is taboo and ritual everywhere, especially around bodily functions such as eating and sexuality. Often, rituals are encoded in religious practices. Deviating from these rituals or engaging in situations without clear rules causes anxiety. Strong emotional displays of internal solidarity or xenophobia are used to relieve tension.

Gratification: Short- Versus Long-Term Orientation

A set of basic drives are innate in us. They relate to food, drink, and safety in the first place, but beyond that, we are driven by the need to belong to a community, to be esteemed, to avoid boredom, and, depending on age and gender, to have sex. In some societies, seeking and giving gratification are considered morally good. This makes for happy societies, but in case of trouble, violence is not far away. Other societies hold that morality consists of keeping one's urges in check. The individual is insignificant, and there is a lot of work to do in the world. This attitude represses emotions, but it increases the power of society to respond to environmental changes.

Culture and the Moral Circle

The initial question in this chapter, "What do you do to get expelled?" touches the core of the notion of a moral circle. Knowing how a country scores on the five dimensions has predictive value for how and why people might be included or excluded. A culture instills in its members, through upbringing of infants and children, a mind-set that leads to predictable responses to events. We shall investigate this issue dimension by dimension first and then turn to the bigger picture.

Individualism/Collectivism

Western societies are at the individualistic end of the cultural spectrum. Every individual or organization is free to choose and to revoke its alliances. One hires and fires people because of their performance. In a collectivist society, on the other hand, each individual or organization is a member of a very long-lived network of relationships of interdependency. Trust in such a society is intricately linked to in-group membership. One hires people for in-group membership, and firing is difficult.

So, the degree of collectivism of a society is a measure for the solidity of the invisible wall that divides a moral group from another. In a collectivist society, each in-group is like a solid crystal that is internally very cohesive and will not mix with other crystals. In an individualistic society, each individual is like a loose molecule that can move around, make temporary alliances, and move away again.

Power Distance

In a hierarchical culture, most employees expect to be treated by their superiors as dependents at best or in an instrumental way. Their superior is of another world, so to speak. The concept of trust in such a culture is entirely different across the hierarchy than it is at one level. This has consequences for the governance of organizations. Employees from hierarchical countries tend to have problems working in network organizations. They often do not understand the concept of working partially under a line boss and partially under a project leader. How can a child have two fathers? In a hierarchical culture, fatalism is a coping strategy for life in general. Pleasing one's superior is clearly the best strategy for employees, along with hoping for mercy. In an egalitarian society, it is rather the leader who stands in danger of being ousted. The pitfall of hierarchal societies is bad leaders expelling good subordinates, while the pitfall of egalitarian societies is bad subordinates expelling good leaders.

Masculinity/Femininity

In masculine societies, people hold the implicit belief that most people can*not* be trusted. As a result, one expects that in masculine societies, people would need to exert themselves more to appear trustworthy business partners (e.g., by being certified or by drawing up contracts), and more institutions would exist to cope with distrust (e.g., lawyers, weapons). The opposite is a feminine culture, a culture in which moral rules are more forgiving, excuses are found for the weak and for failings, punishment is not so harsh, and violence is strongly condemned. This dimension is all about morality. In a culturally masculine value system, the moral world of both men and women is strongly stratified. It ranges from heroes who are widely admired and deemed without fault to losers who are despised. In a culturally feminine value system, moral qualities are more evenly allocated. Even the best of people can have shortcomings, and even the worst of criminals can have some good.

Uncertainty Avoidance

A moral circle in a culture of strong uncertainty avoidance is first and foremost a defense against the dark and dangerous world that lies beyond. Rituals that promote cohesion, including those that involve food, song, and dance, are valued and taken seriously. Anything unknown often causes anxiety, including strangers, strange food, and different religious practices. So this is a cultural trait that makes it harder for outsiders to be accepted as members of the community. Anxiety frequently leads to aggression as a way to release tension, and immigrants or foreign guests or business partners are likely scapegoats. On the other hand, uncertainty-avoiding cultures are associated with a persistent curiosity and a desire to find things out. In uncertainty-tolerant cultures, there could be a tendency to laxness as long as there is no urgency.

Long-Term/Short-Term Orientation

Long-term-oriented cultures place high value on the postponement of gratification. This is a good attitude for creating long-term commitments. In a short-term-oriented culture, business deals tend to be opportunistic. These societies will look to history to find moral certitude. Long-term-oriented cultures, on the other hand, hold that past results give no guarantees for the future, even in moral issues. They will perceive issues in pragmatic rather than moral terms because morally good behavior is that which benefits the group in a pragmatic way. When it comes to expelling members, short-term-oriented cultures tend to be inflexible and to rely on traditional rules. Long-term-oriented cultures tend to be aware of changing circumstances.

All Five Dimensions Matter

Separating the five dimensions for the sake of exposition can be useful. However, readers should not attempt to interpret real-world events using just one dimension. Cultures are holistic, and the five dimensions of culture are only meaningful in combination. Their effects all interact in actual life. There is no space here to elaborate on the combined influence of the dimensions. Hofstede and Hofstede (2005) give numerous graphs showing that the combination of scores on two of the dimensions is predictive of the social fabric of societies. To give one instance, consider the combination of power distance and uncertainty avoidance. In societies that combine large power distance with strong uncertainty avoidance, such as exist in the Latin and Orthodox world, companies are structured as pyramids in which every employee has a fixed place. Societies with a small power distance that are uncertainty tolerant, such as England and Scandinavian countries, have "adhocracies" (a term from Henry Mintzberg, adapted in Hofstede & Hofstede, 2005) in which temporary, flexible structures such as projects are important. Hierarchical, uncertainty tolerant cultures have companies that resemble families. Finally, societies that have a small power distance but are uncertainty avoiding have organizations that resemble well-oiled machines: predictable and efficient.

Toward Intercultural Competence

Understanding these five cultural dimensions leads to a greater awareness of acceptable behaviors and thus adoption of such behaviors in different moral circles. Developing intercultural competence beyond one's moral circle is a key goal (Hofstede, Pedersen, & Hofstede, 2002) and can be illustrated by the examples provided here.

Reconciling Different Life Aims

A typical international employee lives for a challenging life with adventure and success, in which doing better than one's parents or one's peers is desirable. But an employee from a collectivistic culture is much more interested in honoring his or her family or country and being a well-reputed member of the community.

Michalon (2003), after 20 years of experience in the Third World, shows vividly how this phenomenon can obstruct attempts to "develop" countries. An employee in a hierarchical country wishes above all to please those placed above him or her. And so it is for all the dimensions. Life goals vary with culture. This points to the importance of spending time building knowledge of a place, its culture, and acceptable behaviors and getting to know what constitutes the moral circle before one engages in business or other intercultural interactions. Immersion in the target culture is often very helpful in achieving this goal. The investment of time and energy will result in benefits toward a higher degree of intercultural competence.

Negotiating

Consider the following episode. A German Swiss buyer of goods is visiting a Chinese entrepreneur, trying to close a contract. The Chinese sits inscrutably while the Swiss expostulates his detailed proposal. The Swiss finishes his speech, a bit nervous at receiving so little feedback. Finally the Chinese speaks: "This is not good for us." And then "Let me take you for dinner."

If the Swiss has never been to China before, he may be in the belief that his proposal is off. According to Swiss rules, that would definitely be so: German Swiss culture is individualistic, egalitarian, masculine, and uncertainty avoiding, which leads to a performance-oriented, high-energy, no-time-to-waste work culture. In fact, the Chinese is keenly interested, and that is why, using his collectivistic, long-term-oriented mind-set, he wants to strengthen the relationship with his buyer by taking him out to dinner as a more appropriate setting for doing business. If neither is culturally savvy, it is not certain that the Swiss will come: He may consider that since the Chinese does not like his proposal, going out to eat strange Chinese food might be a disagreeable way of wasting time. So both negotiators could be letting a chance slip away, and worse, their expectations for the suitability of one another's group as business partners would be lowered, and perhaps still worse, they would never learn that culture was part of the problem here.

It is not amazing that cross-cultural negotiations are so tricky. Negotiators, by definition, have only partly coinciding interests. Their relationship hovers between friendship and enmity. Whether and how they create a common moral circle is a key issue, and in fact, explicitly creating a moral circle is precisely what the Swiss negotiator in our example did not consider necessary and what the Chinese negotiator intended to start doing in the restaurant. If the attempt to create a common moral circle fails, then negotiations break down and they will be hard to resume.

Adapting Leadership Styles

Leadership is not the same across the world (see, e.g., House, Hanges, Javidan, Dorfman, & Gupta, 2004), although some universal principles may apply to interculturally competent leadership (see Pusch [Chapter 3], Chen & An [Chapter 10], and Moran, Youngdahl, & Moran [Chapter 16], this volume). For example, autocratic behavior is imperative for leaders in hierarchical societies, or they could be ousted by a stronger leader. In egalitarian societies, such behavior will not be tolerated by followers.

Leaders in masculine societies need to appear strong, and those in feminine societies need to be forgiving. Hofstede and Dooley (2006) analyzed data from an organizational development program in a transpacific high-tech company. The combined managers from all levels in the organization had participated in focus groups, with the aim to determine leadership excellence. Statistical analysis across the focus groups revealed nine models of leadership excellence. All employees agreed that an excellent leader should be (a) optimistic and dependable, (b) approachable and have a sense of direction, and (c) focused and a developer of his or her people. Focus groups in the United States found two more factors: (d) professional at the personal level and passionate about the job and (e) a team player in implementing the organization's vision. Asian focus groups, however, came up with two very different factors: (f) a caring, authoritarian parent figure and (g) a proactive guide. The individualistic, short-term-oriented culture of the United States and the collectivistic, long-term-oriented mind-set of Southeast Asian cultures have clearly made their mark here. The lesson is that some leadership behaviors are universal, while others are local to some cultures.

International organizations are frequently populated by teams formed from members of many different cultures. To operate in such a team and especially to be able to lead it, one must create a moral circle. This means that unique rules and rituals have to be created that enable all team members to show and feel that they are good, upstanding group members. This can allow them to deviate from their own cultural conditioning (back home rules) to some extent while still feeling safe in a new moral circle.

One vignette is the story of a Dutch female manager who found herself in a meeting room in Japan with a number of Japanese males from a sister organization, all of them of lower hierarchical status than she was. Tea was waiting to be served. This created a moral deadlock for the Japanese, who have an extremely masculine and uncertainty-avoiding society in which deviating from ritual is unthinkable. Females must pour tea to males, but subordinates must do it for their bosses. What was to be done? The lady sensed this and made a speech, declaring that within the secrecy of the room, they would create their own rule: Everyone could pour his or her own tea. All were relieved and did as suggested.

Implications of Trust in Intercultural Competence

Knowing One's Biases

The essence of cross-cultural encounters is that one's own unwritten rules about proper behavior differ from those of the people one interacts with. Therefore, it is vital to know one's own cultural values. Everybody speaks with an accent (Peterson, personal communication, 2008). To realize this and to acquaint oneself with one's own culture's peculiarities is the most difficult but also the most essential ingredient for achieving intercultural competence. Means to do this include reading books about one's own culture written by foreigners or simply asking for feedback from noncompatriots. It should be noted that any such account reveals something about both the culture of the observer and the culture of the observed.

A typical case is for a visitor from a Western country of an individualistic, small power distance culture to have a work assignment in a leading position in a country with a more collectivistic and hierarchical culture. Such a visitor will routinely assume an active, self-interest motivated attitude among his or her subordinates. These subordinates will, however, be first and foremost eager to show respect. They will act with little individual initiative, avoid exposure as individuals, and expect direction. The new leader may perceive these behaviors as stupidity or disinterest. As Indian and Chinese companies emerge as major players, reverse tendencies can be observed, and confrontations can be expected between bosses who are used to an authoritarian, paternalistic style and their Western subordinates, who may be more accustomed to taking more initiative.

Adapting

"When you go Rome, do as the Romans do." If one travels and works abroad, one should adapt according to this adage. This necessitates specific knowledge of the host culture and an openness to engage in host culture rituals and behaviors when appropriate. Talking to people who have spent time in that culture, talking to expatriates from the country, and reading books by local authors can all help to prepare for such a cultural immersion experience. Adapting does not mean trying to act like somebody else. It does mean respecting the local customs and investing in learning appropriate behavior. Participate, ask questions, expect the unexpected, and be flexible. Practice in intercultural encounters is the best teacher.

Assisting

If one receives visitors in one's country, the visitors are often expected to adapt. However, visitors may not be willing or able to do so, and they may be in a position to have it their way. Serving as a cultural guide or providing orientation to one's own culture can often be helpful to visitors' adaptation process. Diplomatic qualities may be needed in such cases. The essence of diplomacy is to keep a moral circle intact: Whatever happens, we keep seeing one another as morally valuable beings. Visitors, certainly those from collectivistic cultures, can be greatly relieved if they find a cultural guide, somebody from the host culture willing to spend personal time and to explain the local rules. Finding such a person can make the difference between a successful and a failed foreign assignment. One way to do this is by finding mentors for new expatriate personnel during the first year abroad.

Leading

If one is a member or a leader of a multicultural team, certainly one that has been created by oneself, one is in a position to create a new set of unwritten rules that will enable the creation of a new moral circle. This is a crucial thing to do. In a new team, participants are likely to be anxious at first. To the extent that team members come from collectivistic, hierarchical, uncertainty-avoiding cultures, this is more likely to be so—although, obviously, members of international teams should be selected for language skills and personal qualities too.

So how can one forge team cohesion? Celebrating the team through carefully chosen shared ritual can act as a *rite de passage* to seal membership of the new moral circle. This can be a way to circumvent awkward conflicts between team members who might otherwise be prone to taking offense at one another's practices. It is the function of many meetings and conferences to build team spirit.

Another important point is to adapt leadership style to the team members. With a multicultural team, this can be especially challenging. To maintain a good working atmosphere, the leader will have to be resourceful, alert to the satisfaction of each team member, and ready to take action, based on cultural needs of the members. It is useful to work with the distinction between *cognitive* and *affective* dissonance. Cognitive dissonance occurs when people disagree about content. In a masculine, individualistic culture (e.g., Anglo cultures or work cultures of trained professionals from competitive subcultures), cognitive dissonance will be frequent. It can serve a useful purpose to clarify intellectual issues, and protagonists should be able to argue while still being loyal team members. Affective dissonance means interpersonal conflict that damages the moral circle. People who were socialized in collectivistic, hierarchical cultures have probably learned not to disagree in public, and people from feminine cultures can disagree but cannot use a confrontational style. Team members with such a background are prone to fusing cognitive dissonance with affective dissonance (i.e., bad relationship). By setting clear rules of discussion, a team leader can ensure that discussion remains intellectual and does not destroy the moral circle.

Conclusion

This chapter has introduced the notion of a moral circle as key to intercultural competence. The main argument is that people live in groups that function implicitly or explicitly as moral circles (i.e., they have mechanisms for excluding members who violate norms so that social life is facilitated by trust and by common expectations among the upstanding members). Groups can exist at all levels from dyads to humanity as a whole. Different societies have different ideas about what constitutes a moral circle. These differences can be described in basic issues of culture. Culture can thus be described as the unwritten rules of the social game that determine which behavior is accepted in which role in the moral circle.

Notes

1. A note from the author: This chapter integrates biological and organizational insights in a novel way. Where no references are given for statements, they express the author's reasoning, and nobody else is to blame for them. This chapter also includes general statements about underlying values and dimensions in different cultures that are meant to be taken as generalizations. It is recognized that persons can also operate outside of moral circles beyond the culture of origin and that intercultural competence involves finding ways to negotiate this.

2. More information about these dimensions can be found in Hofstede and Hofstede (2005). That book has data for 74 countries and regions. Some of those can also be found on the Web—for example, in graphic form at www.geert-hofstede.com (note that this Web site is not that of Geert or Gert Jan Hofstede; see www.geerthofstede.com or www.gertjanhofstede .com for those).

References

Busch, J. S., & Hantusch, N. (2000). "I don't trust you, but why don't you trust me?" *Dispute Resolution Journal, 56,* 61–64.

de Waal, F. (1996). *Good natured: The origins of right and wrong in humans and other species.* Cambridge, MA: Harvard University Press.

Doney, P. M., Cannon, J. P., & Mullen, M. R. (1998). Understanding the influence of national culture on the development of trust. *Academy of Management Review, 23,* 601–620.

Frijda, N. H. (1986). *The emotions.* Cambridge, UK: Cambridge University Press.

Gambetta, D. (2000). Can we trust trust? In D. Gambetta (Ed.), *Trust: Making and breaking cooperative relations* (pp. 213–237). Oxford, UK: Oxford University Press.

Hofstede, G. (2001). *Culture's consequences: Comparing values, behaviors, institutions, and organizations across nations* (2nd ed.). Thousand Oaks, CA: Sage.

Hofstede, G., & Hofstede, G. J. (2005). *Cultures and organizations.* New York: McGraw-Hill.

Hofstede, G. J., & Dooley, R. M. (2006). *Leadership's deep structure: A cross-national study among 400 leaders.* www.gertjanhofstede.com/my_books.htm

Hofstede, G. J., Pedersen, P. B., & Hofstede, G. (2002). *Exploring culture: Exercises, stories and synthetic cultures.* Yarmouth, ME: Intercultural Press.

Hofstede, G. J., Spaans, L., Schepers, H., Trienekens, J. H., & Beulens, A. J. M. (2004). *Hide or confide: The dilemma of transparency.* The Hague, The Netherlands: Reed Business Information.

House, R. J., Hanges, P. J., Javidan, M., Dorfman, P., & Gupta, V. (2004). *Culture, leadership, and organizations: The GLOBE study of 62 societies.* Thousand Oaks, CA: Sage.

Johnson, R. (Ed.). (2008). *Stanford encyclopedia of philosophy.* Stanford, CA: Stanford University Press.

Kramer, R. M. (1999). Trust and distrust in organizations: Emerging perspectives, enduring questions. *Annual Review of Psychology, 50,* 569–598.

Maslow, A. H. (1970). *Motivation and personality* (2nd ed.). New York: Harper & Row.

McCrae, R. R., & Costa, P. T. (2003). *Personality in adulthood.* New York: Guilford.

Michalon, C. (2003). *Différences culturelles, mode d'emploi* [Cultural differences, how to deal with them] (3rd ed.). Saint-Maur: Sépia.

Nooteboom, B. (2002). *Trust: Forms, foundations, functions, failures and figures.* Cheltenham, UK: Edward Elgar.

Peterson, M. (2008). Oral comment during masterclass in cross-cultural management, Maastricht, The Netherlands.

Richerson, P. J., & Boyd, R. (2005). *Not by genes alone—how culture transformed human evolution.* Chicago: University of Chicago Press.

Storer, C. (2004). Plastic in pasta: A Japanese-Australian food crisis. In G. J. Hofstede, L. Spaans, H. Schepers, J. M. Trienekens, & A. J. M. Beulens (Eds.), *Hide or confide? The dilemma of transparency* (pp. 67–72). The Hague, The Netherlands: Reed Business Information.

Wilson, D. S. (2007). *Evolution for everyone.* New York: Bantam Dell.

Wilson, D. S., & Wilson, E. O. (2007). Rethinking the theoretical foundation of sociobiology. *Quarterly Review of Biology, 84,* 327–348.

CHAPTER 5

Intercultural Conflict Competence as a Facet of Intercultural Competence Development

Multiple Conceptual Approaches

Stella Ting-Toomey

As the global economy becomes an everyday reality in most societies, individuals will inevitably encounter people who are culturally different in diverse workplaces and social environments. Developing intercultural conflict competence within the larger intercultural competence setting is critical because conflict creates further perceptual distortions and emotional flooding in the cultural encountering process. Sharpening the knowledge, mindfulness, and skills of intercultural conflict competence can simultaneously enhance general intercultural competence tendencies and vice versa. Under emotional anxiety and stress, even if an individual is well honed in general intercultural competence, she or he might still be overwhelmed by her or his verbal and nonverbal inaptness and awkwardness.

Thus, it is important to pay close attention to the topic of intercultural conflict competence within the broad umbrella of intercultural competence. Learning to manage antagonistic intercultural conflicts competently can bring about multiple perspectives and differentiated viewpoints in a conflicting relationship. Intercultural conflict is defined in this chapter as the perceived or actual incompatibility of cultural values, norms, face orientations, goals, scarce resources, processes, and/or outcomes in a face-to-face (or mediated) context (Ting-Toomey & Oetzel, 2001). Intercultural conflict negotiation can be about substantive, relational, and/or identity conflict goal issues.

Within intercultural competence development, it is important to consider cultural distance, which is a key contributor to intercultural conflict. The greater the cultural distance between the two conflict parties, the more likely the assessment of the conflict negotiation process would be misconstrued. The cultural membership distances can include deep-level differences such as historical grievances, cultural worldviews, and beliefs. Concurrently, they can also include the mismatch of applying different expectations in a particular conflict episode. Individuals from contrasting cultural communities often bring with them different value patterns, verbal and nonverbal habits, and interaction scripts that influence the actual conflict interaction process. Intercultural conflict often starts off with diverse expectations concerning what constitute appropriate or inappropriate verbal and nonverbal behaviors in a conflict encounter scene. Violations of expectation, in turn, often influence the attributional patterns and the communication strategies that individuals use in their conflict interaction process (Canary & Lakey, 2006).

Both the appropriateness and effectiveness features, together with the interaction adaptability feature, are part of the intercultural conflict competence criteria. If inappropriate or ineffective conflict behaviors continue, the miscommunication can very easily spiral into a complex, polarized intercultural conflict situation. More specifically, intercultural conflict competence refers to the *mindful management of emotional frustrations and conflict interaction struggles due primarily to cultural or ethnic group membership differences.*

This chapter is organized in four sections: First, the criteria and the components of intercultural conflict competence are discussed. Second, a culture-based situational conflict model is introduced to provide a "big picture" outlook in explaining the antecedent and moderating factors of intercultural conflict. Third, two identity-based theories, the integrated threat theory and the conflict face negotiation theory, are reviewed as two plausible theories that can explain more fully the intercultural conflict management process. Fourth, research directions related to intercultural conflict competence criteria are addressed.

Intercultural Conflict Competence: Criteria and Components

According to one of the assumptions of the identity negotiation theory, intercultural identity-based competence refers to the optimal integration of knowledge, mindfulness, and communication skills in managing problematic interaction scenes appropriately, effectively, and adaptively (Ting-Toomey, 1999, 2005a). An identity-based competence perspective is emphasized because knotty identity issues often spark affective-based interactional support or rejection. In any intercultural or intergroup encounter process, if repeated problematic issues arise in the same parties, it is oftentimes not the substantive or content issue at stake so much as the identity or relational issue is in jeopardy (Imahori & Cupach, 2005; Rothman, 1997).

Identity is viewed as an anchoring point in which sojourners, immigrants, and local hosts have to deal with on an everyday interaction basis (Y. Y. Kim, 2001, 2004; see Y. Y. Kim, Chapter 2, this volume). Furthermore, when it involves intercultural conflict negotiation process work, most entangled conflict situations between polarized groups or individuals have a strong identity locus. Identity is conceptualized in this chapter as reflective group membership identities and individualized self-images that are constructed, experienced, and communicated by the individuals within a culture and in a particular interaction scene (Ting-Toomey, 2005a). This section addresses the criteria and the components of becoming a competent intercultural conflict negotiator from the identity negotiation framework.

Intercultural Conflict Competence: Criteria

The criteria of communication appropriateness, effectiveness, and adaptability can serve as evaluative yardsticks of whether an intercultural conflict communicator has been perceived as behaving competently or incompetently in a conflict interaction episode (Spitzberg & Cupach, 1984; Spitzberg, Canary, & Cupach, 1994). *Appropriateness* refers to the degree to which the exchanged behaviors are regarded as proper and match the expectations generated by the insiders of the culture. To behave "properly" in any given cultural situation, competent conflict negotiators need to have the relevant value knowledge schema of the larger situational norms that guide the interaction episode (Wang, Stephen, Williams, & Kopka, 2004). They also need to acquire the specific conflict knowledge schema of what constitutes appropriate or inappropriate conflict style patterns that can promote constructive versus destructive conflict outcome. Thus, the criterion of "appropriateness" is theorized as a culture-sensitive attunement process in which individuals have mastered the deep knowledge structures of the values and norms of the conflict situation and are able to connect such knowledge structures with skillful conflict practice. This means that the conflict negotiators can meaningfully connect the various cultural value patterns and situational norms to explain a conflict interaction episode. It also means they are able to implement and perform situationally relevant, constructive conflict behaviors.

The criterion of "effectiveness" refers to the degree to which communicators achieve mutually shared meaning and integrative goal-related outcomes in the conflict episode. To engage in effective conflict communication strategies, intercultural conflict negotiators need to have a wide range of verbal and nonverbal conflict repertoires to make mindful choices and options. They need to engage in more neutrally toned attributions such as viewing the conflict trigger as unintentional or situationally induced, unstable, and particularized. In polarized blameworthy attributions, conflict parties often tend to make internally driven negative attributions and stable negative trait assumptions, and they perceive the conflict as a generalized-chronic problem (Canary & Lakey, 2006). On the intergroup conflict interpretation level, competent conflict negotiators need to mind their ESP factors (e.g., ethnocentrism, stereotypes, and prejudice identity threat factors) such as their own ethnocentric mind-set, their rigid stereotypes of out-group members, and their prejudiced tendencies (Ting-Toomey, 1999). Together with the operation of an ethnorelative mind-set (Bennett & Bennett, 2004), individuals also need to master strategic conflict negotiation skills to integrate divergent conflict goals constructively. Conflict interaction effectiveness has been achieved when multiple meanings are attended to with accuracy and in an unbiased manner and mutually desired interaction goals have been conjointly worked out in a strategic and creative manner.

More important, effectiveness and appropriateness criteria are positively interdependent. When one manages a conflict appropriately, the "good faith" behaviors can induce reciprocal interaction effectiveness. Likewise, when one promotes effective conflict and mutual goal-directed interaction paths, the effectiveness posture can induce appropriate interaction behaviors from the other conflict party. It is also possible that one can behave appropriately (following all the conflict "politeness" rituals) yet neither individual nor interpersonal conflict goal is achieved. Conversely, one can "bulldoze" his or her way to impose one's individual wish or conflict goal, but that might result in long-range conflict detriments.

To behave both appropriately and effectively in managing a diverse range of intercultural conflict situations, one needs to be mentally and behaviorally flexible and adaptive. She or he also needs to be affectively proactive rather than reactive to increase the conflict management options. *Communication adaptability* refers to our ability to change our interaction behaviors and goals to meet the specific needs of the situation. It implies mental, affective, and behavioral flexibility in dealing with the intercultural conflict situation. It signals our attunement of the other conflict party's perspectives, interests, goals, and conflict communication approach, plus our willingness to modify our own behaviors and goals to adapt to the emergent conflict situation (Rogan & Hammer, 2006). Communication adaptability connotes dynamic code-switching ability in an intercultural conflict interaction scene. Dynamic cross-cultural code switching refers to the intentional learning and moving between culturally ingrained systems of behavior (Molinsky, 2007). To behave appropriately, effectively, and adaptively, an interculturally intelligent conflict negotiator needs to pay exquisite attention to the specific components of intercultural conflict competence.

Intercultural Conflict Competence: Components

According to the conflict face negotiation theory (Ting-Toomey, 2005b), of all the components of competence, knowledge is the most important component that underscores the other components of competence. Without *culture-sensitive knowledge,* communicators cannot learn to uncover the implicit "ethnocentric lenses" they use to evaluate behaviors in an intercultural conflict interaction scene. Without knowledge, people cannot have an accurate perspective or reframe their interpretation of a problematic communication situation from the other's cultural frame of reference. Knowledge enhances cultural self-awareness and other-awareness. Knowledge here refers to developing an in-depth understanding of relevant intercultural concepts (e.g., cultural value patterns, preferred conflict mediation styles) that can help to manage culture-based conflict issues competently. To be an astute decoder of a complex intercultural conflict situation, one must develop a mindful, layered systems outlook in assessing the macro- and micro-level features of an intercultural conflict problem (Oetzel, Ting-Toomey, & Rinderle, 2006). Knowledge and an open-minded attitude are closely intertwined and reciprocally influence one another. Knowledge can enhance self-awareness and other-awareness, and awareness can lead to an incremental open-minded attitude. Alternatively, according to Deardorff (2004), attitudes of respect, openness, and curiosity can lead to the desire for more culture-sensitive knowledge. Knowledge and a discovery attitude can facilitate a mindful consciousness.

Mindfulness, in the intercultural communication competence context, means attending to one's internal communication assumptions, cognitions, and emotions and, at the same time, becoming exquisitely attuned to the other's communication assumptions, cognitions, and emotions (LeBaron, 2003; Thich, 1991, 1998; Ting-Toomey, 1999). Mindful reflexivity requires us to tune into our own cultural and personal habitual assumptions in scanning a problematic interaction scene. To be mindful of intercultural conflict differences, we have to learn to see the unfamiliar behavior from multiple cultural angles (Langer, 1989, 1997). In the context of the intercultural conflict negotiation process, for example, we have to deal with our own vulnerable emotions regarding identity and face-threatening behaviors. Concurrently, we have to be responsive to new interaction scripts awaiting us. We also need to develop multiple lenses in understanding the culture-level and situational-level factors that shape the problematic conflict episode. Mindfulness is part of the metacognition process that is a key feature in the cultural intelligence research literature (Earley & Ang, 2003; Earley & Peterson, 2004). According to Ang et al. (2007), metacognition refers to the "higher-order mental capability to think about personal thought processes, anticipate cultural preferences of others and adjust mental models during and after intercultural experiences" (p. 341). *Mindfulness of the mind* is the mediating step in linking knowledge with the intentional application of constructive conflict skill practice.

Constructive conflict communication skills refer to our operational abilities to manage a problematic interaction situation appropriately, effectively, and adaptively via skillful verbal and nonverbal communication behaviors. Many communication skills are useful in enhancing intercultural conflict interaction competencies. Of the many possible conflict management skills (see, e.g., Ting-Toomey, 2004; Ting-Toomey & Chung, 2005), skills such as deep listening, mindful reframing, de-centering, face-sensitive respectful dialogue skills, and collaborative conflict negotiation skills (e.g., the skill set of the "AEIOU" negotiation that stands for "Attack, Evade, Inform, Open, Unite," developed by Coleman & Raider, 2006) across cultural and ethnic/racial lines are critical practices. Intercultural sensitivity training strategies such as dynamic behavioral code-switching skills (Molinsky, 2007) and relativism commitment strategies can also move the conflict communicators from an ethnocentric stage to an ethnorelative stage (Bennett, 2003; Pedersen, Crethar, & Carlson, 2008). With discussion of the criteria and components of intercultural conflict competence as the backdrop, the following section will fill in the knowledge gap that is essential to becoming a competent intercultural conflict communicator.

A Culture-Based Situational Conflict Model

As cultural beings, we are socialized or "programmed" by the values and norms of our culture to think and behave in certain ways. Our family, peer groups, educational institutions, mass media system, political system, and religious institutions are some of the forces that shape and mold our cultural and personal values. Our learned values and expectancy norms are, in turn, expressed through the way we communicate. To understand differences and similarities in the value assumptions, filters, and behaviors in conflict across cultures, we need a conceptual map or framework to explain in depth why and how cultures are different or similar. This section reviews the culture-based situational conflict model (Oetzel, Dhar, & Kirschbaum, 2007; Ting-Toomey & Oetzel, 2001; Ting-Toomey & Takai, 2006; see Figure 5.1).

Cultural and Individual Socialization Value Patterns

Cultural Socialization Patterns. The cultural socialization patterns that hold a profound influence on conflict behaviors can include the study of the value patterns of individualism-collectivism and small-large power distance (Hofstede, 2001). Indeed, the most recent GLOBE ("Global Leadership and Organizational Behavior Effectiveness"—A Research Program Study of 62 Societies) research project (House, Hanges, Javidan, Dorfman, & Gupta, 2004) provided additional evidence that the foundational constructs of individualism-collectivism and small-large power distance permeate 62 countries (and with a sample size of 17,370 middle managers from three industries) at the societal, organizational, and individual levels of analysis. Basically, *individualism* refers to the broad value tendencies of a culture in emphasizing the importance of the "I" identity over the "we" identity, individual rights over group interests, and individuated-focused emotions over social-focused emotions. In comparison, *collectivism* refers to the broad value tendencies of a culture in emphasizing the importance of the "we" identity over the "I" identity, in-group interests over individual desires, and other-face concerns over self-face concerns. Individualistic and collectivistic value tendencies are manifested in everyday interpersonal, family, school, and workplace social interactions.

Beyond individualism-collectivism, another important value dimension that is critical in understanding workplace conflict interaction competence is the dimension of power distance (Carl, Gupta, & Javidan, 2004). *Power distance,* from the workplace values' analysis standpoint, refers to the way in which a corporate culture approaches and deals with status differences and social hierarchies. Individuals in *small power distance* corporate cultures tend to value equal power distributions, symmetrical relations, a mixture of positive and negative messages in feedback sessions, and equitable reward and cost distributions based on individual merits. Individuals in *large power distance* corporate cultures tend to accept unequal power distributions, asymmetrical relations, authoritative feedback from the experts or high-status individuals, and rewards and sanctions based on rank, role, status, age, and perhaps even gender identity.

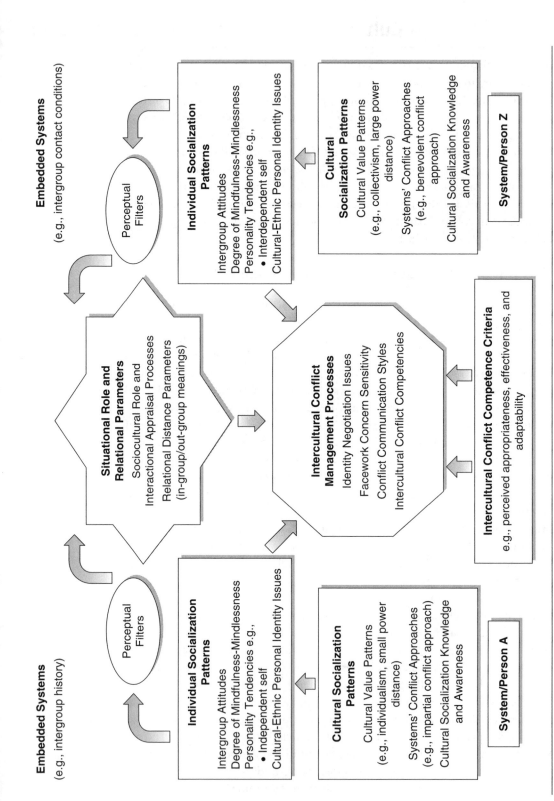

Figure 5.1 A Culture-Based Situational Conflict Model

In combining both individualism-collectivism and small-large power distance value patterns, we can discuss four predominant corporate value dimension approaches along the two grids of individualism-collectivism continuum and small-large power distance continuum: impartial, status achievement, benevolent, and communal (Ting-Toomey & Oetzel, 2001).

The *impartial approach* reflects a combination of an individualistic and small power distance value orientation, the *status-achievement approach* consists of a combination of an individualistic and large power distance value orientation, the *benevolent approach* reflects a combination of a collectivistic and large power distance value orientation, and the *communal approach* consists of a combination of collectivistic and small power distance value orientation.

Thus, managers and employees around the world have different expectations of how a workplace conflict episode should be interpreted and resolved—pending on whether the workplace culture emphasizes impartial, status achievement, benevolent, or communal interaction rituals. More specifically, for example, in the *impartial approach* to workplace conflict, the predominant values of this approach are personal freedom and equality (Smith, Dugan, Peterson, & Leung, 1998). From the impartial conflict approach lens, if an interpersonal conflict arises between a manager and an employee, the manager has a tendency to deal with the conflict in an upfront and direct manner. Specific feedback and concrete justifications are expected from the manager. Concurrently, an employee is also expected to articulate clearly his or her conflict viewpoints and defend his or her conflict concerns. In an equal-rank employee-employee conflict, the manager would generally play the "impartial" third-party role and would encourage the two employees to talk things over and find their own workable solution. Both the manager and the employees would rely on the principle of objectivity or a fact-finding approach to resolve a conflict situation. Managers in large corporations in Denmark, the Netherlands, Sweden, and Norway appear to practice the impartial communication approach (Hofstede, 2001).

Alternatively, from a *status achievement approach* to conflict, the predominant values of this approach are personal freedom and earned inequality. For example, in France, employees often feel that they have the freedom to voice directly and complain about their managers in the workplace (Storti, 2001). At the same time, they do not expect their managers to change much because they are their bosses and thus, by virtue of their titles, hold certain rights and power resources. The managers, meanwhile, also expect conflict accommodations from their subordinates. When the conflict involves two same-rank coworkers, the use of upfront conflict tactics to aggression tactics is a hallmark of the status achievement approach. Ting-Toomey and Oetzel (2001) also observed that U.S. management style often follows a conjoint impartial approach and a status achievement approach because the larger U.S. culture emphasizes that via individual hard work, personal ambition, and fierce competitiveness, status and rank can be earned and status cues can be displayed with pride and credibility. Unfortunately, while much research work has been conducted in the United States and to some extent in Western European settings, there is a scarcity of research studies concerning Eastern European, African, and Asian or Latin American management styles.

In comparison, many managers in other parts of the globe tend to see themselves as interdependent and at a different status level than others. That is, these managers think of themselves as individuals with interlocking connections with others and as members of a hierarchical network. They practice the *benevolent approach* (a combination of collectivism and large power distance value patterns) of management style (Ting-Toomey & Oetzel, 2001). The term *benevolent* implies that many managers play the authoritative parental roles in approaching or motivating their employees. Two values that pervade this approach are obligation to others and asymmetrical interaction treatment. Countries that predominantly reflect the benevolent approach include most Latin and South American nations (e.g., Mexico, Venezuela, Brazil, Chile), most Asian nations (e.g., India, Japan, China, South Korea), most Arab nations (e.g., Egypt, Saudi Arabia, Jordan), and most African nations (e.g., Nigeria, Uganda; Hofstede, 2001). For many of the large East Asian corporations, Confucian-driven hierarchical principles promote a parent-child relationship between the manager and the subordinate. However, more cross-cultural studies on international management and intercultural communication are needed to understand how the concept of "benevolence" plays out in the different types and forms of collectivistic cultural communities as many of these communities are in flux due to accelerated globalization and technological influence.

Under the benevolent conflict approach, while a manager can confront his or her employees to motivate them to work harder, it is very rare that subordinates will directly challenge the manager's authority or face during a conflict interaction process. However, they might opt for using passive aggressive or sabotage conflict strategies to deal with the workplace tensions or frustrations. In dealing with low-premium conflicts, managers would consider the "smooth-over" relational tactics or subtle face-pressuring tactics to gain employees' compliance or cooperation. However, in dealing with high-premium conflicts, benevolent managers could act in a very directive or autocratic and controlling manner. They might also practice preferential treatment or particularistic value by treating senior employees more favorably than junior employees.

Last, the *communal approach* (a combination of both collectivism and small power distance value orientation) is the least common of the four conflict approaches. The values that encompass this approach are the recognition of authentic interdependent connection to others and genuine interpersonal equality. Costa Rica is the only country found to fit this approach (Hofstede, 2001). Nonprofit mediation centers or successful start-up small businesses also appear to practice some of the communal decision-making behaviors and participatory democracy so that everyone has a say and also takes turns to rotate leadership. Similarly, feminist principles include holistic and integrative problem solving and the importance of engaging in mutual-face sensitive, collaborative dialogue (Barge, 2005).

Individual Socialization Patterns. The individual socialization patterns can include the study of the personality tendencies of independent self and interdependent self. Self-construal is one of the major individual factors that focuses on individual variation within and between cultures. *Self-construal* is one's self-image and is composed of an independent and an interdependent self (Markus & Kitayama, 1991, 1998).

The independent construal of self involves the view that an individual is a unique entity with an individuated repertoire of feelings, cognitions, and motivations. In contrast, the interdependent construal of self involves an emphasis on the importance of relational or in-group connectedness. Self-construal is the individual-level equivalent of the cultural variability dimension of individualism-collectivism. For example, Gudykunst et al. (1996) argued that independent self-construal is predominantly associated with people of individualistic cultures, while interdependent self-construal is predominantly associated with people of collectivistic cultures. However, both dimensions of self exist within each individual, regardless of cultural identity. In individualistic cultural communities, there may be more communication situations that evoke the need for independent-based decisions and behaviors. In collectivistic communities, there may be more situations that demand the sensitivity for interdependent-based decisions and actions. The manner in which individuals conceive of their self-images—independent versus interdependent selves—should have a profound influence on the expectancies of what constitutes appropriate or inappropriate communication responses in a wide variety of interactional situations across a diverse range of cultures.

For example, in a cross-national conflict study in four nations, Oetzel and Ting-Toomey (2003) found that independent self-construal is associated positively with self-face concern and the use of dominating/competing conflict strategies. Interdependent self-construal, on the other hand, is associated positively with other-face concern and the use of avoiding and integrating conflict tactics. It would appear that independent self-construal fosters the use of direct, upfront, and low-context assertive to aggressive communication responses, while interdependent self-construal emphasizes indirect, circumspective, high-context, and accommodating and nonconfrontational communication interaction patterns.

Situational Role and Relational Distance Parameters

Situational Role Parameters. The culture-based situational conflict model also emphasizes the importance of understanding the expectancy features of each communication domain such as workplace/organizational, classroom/school, community or neighborhood, and family or intimate relationship domain. For example, three of the possible factors that moderate the activation of an independent versus an interdependent self in a conflict communication episode can include a general situational appraisal process, a sociocultural role appraisal process, and an interactional appraisal process analysis (Ting-Toomey & Takai, 2006).

A *general situational appraisal process* can include an assessment of the degree of formality of the setting, the mood/climate of the situation, artifact displays, the arrangement of seating, and the room design where the conflict negotiation will take place. A *sociocultural role appraisal process* can include an assessment of the role expectancies between the conflict parties such as professional role identities, cultural/ethnic identity issues, and other salient sociocultural membership identity concerns. The appropriate role displays and enactments would greatly influence the effective development of trust, conflict goal movements, and collaborative versus competitive conflict outlook. An *interactional appraisal process* includes an analysis of anticipated rewards/costs/alternative calculations, appropriate language usage, culture-sensitive interaction channel, relevant conflict openings, convergent relational rhythms, and the necessary conflict competence skill sets needed to manage the conflict flexibly and adaptively.

Relational Distance Parameters. Many relational distance factors are important in competent intercultural conflict negotiation. However, perhaps one of the most complex factors in intercultural conflict interaction is having a good grasp of how a particular cultural community defines *in-group* and *out-group* and what constitutes appropriate in-group versus out-group conflict symbolic exchange processes. Take, for example, from the Japanese communication lens, Midooka (1990), who categorized four groups of relationships, the in-group consisting of *kino-okenai-kankei* and *nakama* and the out-group consisting of *najimi-no-tanin* and *muen-no-kankei*.

Kino-okenai-kankei ("intimate in-groups") consists of very intimate or equal-status relationships in which communication is causal, open, and direct. Examples of such relationships are best friends, family/siblings, close relatives, childhood buddies, and dating relationships. In these relationships, differences in age or seniority are superseded by intimacy, and no hierarchical rituals, especially in the "best friends" category, are heeded. Thus, in Japanese "best friends" conflict situations, the process can involve more heart-to-heart talks to direct conflict self-disclosure. *Nakama* ("familiar interactive in-groups"), on the other hand, are close-contact in-group relations, especially in terms of everyday familiarity, yet not so much as to override status differences. These typically include everyday colleagues in the same workplace, and here, maximum care must be taken to observe interpersonal rituals and preserving relational harmony even under stressful conflict condition. A certain level of decorum or formality is expected to be maintained in this particular relationship category.

On the other hand, *najimi-no-tanin* ("acquaintance interactive out-groups") refers to a less intimate, acquaintance relationship, characterized more as an out-group rather than as an in-group relationship. For example, out-group relationships in this instance could mean acquaintance colleagues in other universities or a friend of a close friend who needs a favor. While being *tanin*, communication behaviors toward this "familiar" out-group member would differ greatly depending on the perceived value or reward/cost appraisal process of the relationship. However, since Japan is an overall group-oriented society, social ties have interlocking importance and wider interdependent implications from one spectrum of the society to the next (Ting-Toomey & Takai, 2006). If the relationship poses a threat to one's public face, one is still careful to observe appropriate interaction formality and diplomatic conflict rituals. Cautious formality is exercised in the *tanin* situation more so than in the *nakama* situation—as one misstep can be costly and can ruin one's reputation or face beyond just the out-group circle. Finally, *muen-no-kankei* ("stranger out-groups") indicates a purely out-group, stranger relationship, also referred to as *aka-no-tanin*. Since strangers are way beyond the bounds of accepted social or personalized ties, oftentimes, no form of considerate behavior needs to be extended between the stranger-pair as no preexisting emotional sentiments bind the two people together. Indifference can be part of the conflict ritual in this peripheral out-group category.

In sum, the factors in the situational role and relational distance parameters have a strong impact on what appropriate and effective conflict styles and facework behaviors should be used in different types of conflict situations in different cultural communities. An interculturally competent conflict communicator would need to increase his or her awareness concerning self and other's cultural and individual socialization process and mindfully connect the value pattern orientations with situational and relational expectancy issues in adaptive intercultural conflict exchange process. The next section will turn to a discussion of perceived identity threat conditions and conflict face negotiation issues that form part of the central core processes in the culture-based situational conflict model.

Identity-Based Threats and Face-Threatening Process

Intercultural conflict interaction processes can include the study of the conflict communication styles and patterns that are used in a conflict episode. Competent conflict negotiators also need to have a firm grasp of the ESP factors that create additional anxiety and uncertainty in the conflict situation. Due to space limitations, the discussion will focus on some of the conditions that induce identity threats in intergroup conflict situations and also cite some key research findings that illustrate the conflict face negotiation theory, all of which are important to understand in developing one's intercultural conflict competence.

The Integrated Threat Theory

Throughout the years, W. Stephan, Stephan, and Gudykunst (1999) have collaborated closely together and influenced each others' ideas in their respective development of the integrated threat theory and the anxiety/uncertainty management theory (Gudykunst, 2005a, 2005b). Integrated threat theory (C. Stephan & Stephan, 2003; W. Stephan, 1999; W. Stephan & Stephan, 2001) fuses various affective theories in the social identity and intergroup prejudice literature and emphasizes one key causal factor on prejudice—namely, feelings of fear or threat. Feelings of fear or identity threat prompt intergroup animosities and conflicts. Feelings of fear or threat are closely aligned with Gudykunst's (2005a) notions on anxiety management issues and ineffective communication concepts.

The integrated threat theory can serve as a macro-level conflict theory that explains intergroup or intercultural antagonism. Macro-level theory factors refer to the "big picture" socioeconomic, institutional, and/or historical factors that frame intergroup relations in a society. According to the integrated threat theory, four antecedent conditions prime the various perceived threat types. These conditions are prior conflict history, ignorance or knowledge gap, contact, and status. According to W. Stephan (1999), *intergroup conflict history* is "the single most important seedbed of prejudice" (p. 32). More important, past intergroup conflict history serves as a backdrop to current intergroup contact relations. The more damaging and protracted the past conflict, the more perceived threats and prejudiced attitudes exist in the intergroup relations. Second, *intergroup knowledge gap or ignorance* of the out-group refers to the fact that when intergroup members know very little of each other or think they know too much (i.e., based on their overgeneralized, stereotypic lens), they are likely to perceive the other group as threatening in the context of intergroup hostility situation. Third, the *type* (positive vs. negative) *and frequency of intergroup contact* also affect feelings of security or insecurity, familiarity or unfamiliarity, and trust or mistrust between members of different identity groups (Ting-Toomey, 1993, 2005a). The more positive and personalized the contact, the more likely members of both groups can see the "human face" beyond the broad-based identity group categories. The more negative and surface level the contact, the greater the perceived negative stereotypes and prejudice justifications.

Fourth, *societal/group membership power status* refers to both institutional power dominance/resistance issues and individual power perception issues. On the institutional power level, dominant group members in a society can be perceived as controlling the key political, economic, and media functioning of a society. On the individual power level, it can refer to how high-status group members view low-status group members in a society or in a particular institutional setting and vice versa. Oftentimes, "high-status" or dominant group members may want to reinforce their own power positions and not want to give up their power resources. They might also worry about hostility or competition from the "low-status" (i.e., in the pecking order of the societal or institutional power scheme) minority group members in snatching away their precious resources in the community. Minority group members might, indeed, resent the power resources or positions amassed by the dominant group members. They might already experience the historical legacy of inequality, injustice, prejudice, and unfair treatment weighted on them. Thus, for some minority group members, they are often emotionally frustrated because of the uneven playing field. The wider the cultural relation schism and the wider the perceived power schism, the more anxiety or fear is being generated in the escalatory conflict cycles. These antecedent conditions can either escalate or de-escalate the perceived threat level in intergroup conflict.

The four basic identity threat types that lead to escalatory prejudice and conflict cycles are intergroup anxiety, negative or rigid stereotypes, tangible/realistic threats, and perceived value/symbolic threats. The theory also emphasizes *subjectively* perceived threats posed by the other, "enemy" group (W. Stephan, 1999). The first type of threat, *intergroup anxiety/anticipated consequences,* often arises in unfamiliar intergroup encounter processes (Gudykunst, 1995, 2005b). In intergroup encounters, people can be especially anxious about anticipated negative consequences such as negative psychological consequences (e.g., confusion, frustration, feeling incompetent), negative behavioral consequences (e.g., being exploited, harmed), and negative evaluations by out-group members (e.g., rejection or being identified with marginalized out-group members). Individuals have anticipated intergroup anxiety because they are concerned about potential face threats or their identities being stigmatized, embarrassed, rejected, or even excluded in intergroup contact situations (Jackson, 1999, 2002). Emotional fear or anxiety is usually heightened and intensified when there exists intergroup historical grievances, low or little prior intergroup contact, or contact that is consistently antagonistic or reinforcing existing negative stereotypes.

The second type of threats, *rigid stereotypes or negative stereotypes,* poses as threats to the in-group (especially the dominant in-group) because in-group members typically learn negative images and traits of out-groups through the mass media and secondhand sources. These negative images can generate negative self-fulfilling prophecies and expectations and thus arouse negative intergroup encountering processes and outcomes. Rigid positive stereotypes can also be considered as a potential intergroup threat because of the fear that this particular group is taking over the educational system, the technological field, or the medical health care profession. Overly positive and negative stereotypes can activate both dominant-minority and minority-minority intergroup conflicts in a multicultural society. This rigid or inflexible stereotypic mentality leads to a third type of identity threat.

The third type of threats, *tangible/realistic threats,* refers to perceived content threats from the out-groups such as the battle for territory, wealth, scarce resources, and natural resources and also the perceived threats and competitions of economics, housing, education placements, and/or political clouts. The fourth type of threats, *perceived values/symbolic threats,* is founded in cultural/ethnic membership differences in morals, beliefs, values, norms, standards, and attitudes. These are threats to the "standard way of living" and the "standard way of behaving" of the dominant in-group. Out-groups who hold worldviews and values that are different from the in-group threaten the core value systems of the in-group, which may then lead to fossilfied in-group ethnocentrism and out-group avoidance or rejection. Values or symbolic threats can be experienced by minorities, disadvantaged groups, and subordinate groups, as well as by majority groups. Research studies testing the four threat types demonstrated that three (i.e., intergroup anxiety, tangible threats, and values/symbolic threats) of the four threat types consistently predicted prejudice and attitudinal animosity from mainstream dominant group (e.g., European Americans) toward minority groups (e.g., African American, Asian American, and Mexican American groups; Plant & Devine, 2003; W. Stephan, Diaz-Loving, & Duran, 2000) and also immigrant groups (e.g., Cuban American immigrants; Spencer-Rodgers & McGovern, 2002; W. Stephan, Ybarra, & Bachman, 1999) in a multicultural society.

In sum, intergroup anxiety and fear can color our expectations and intensify our perceived identity threat levels in dealing with culturally dissimilar strangers or what we consider as our "enemies." On the macro-level of analysis, if the backdrop of the intergroup relations evokes continuous, acrimonious hostilities, it is difficult for identity group members to come together with a clean slate. With historically tainted glasses and competition for scarce resources, members from dominant and minority groups might view each other with certain mistrust, suspicions, disrespect, and face annihilation outlook (e.g., vicious verbal attacks and name-calling cycles).

The Conflict Face Negotiation Theory

Intercultural conflict often involves different face-losing and face-saving behaviors. *Face* refers to a claimed sense of desired social self-image in a relational or international setting (Ting-Toomey, 2004, 2005b). Face loss occurs when we are being treated in such a way that our identity claims are being directly or indirectly challenged or ignored. Face loss can occur on the individual level, the identity group level, or both. Repeated face loss and face threat often lead to escalatory conflict spirals or an impasse in the conflict negotiation process.

In response to the heavy reliance on the individualistic Western perspective in framing various conflict approaches, Ting-Toomey (1988) and Ting-Toomey and Kurogi (1998) developed a cross-cultural conflict theory—namely, the conflict face negotiation theory—to include a collectivistic Asian perspective to broaden the theorizing process of various conflict orientations. In sum, Ting-Toomey's (1988, 2005b) conflict face negotiation theory assumes that (a) people in all cultures try to maintain and negotiate face in all communication situations; (b) the concept of face is especially problematic in emotionally threatening or identity-vulnerable situations when the situated identities of the communicators are called into question; (c) the cultural value spectrums of individualism-collectivism (Triandis, 1995, 2002) and small-large power distance (Hofstede, 2001; House et al., 2004) shape facework concerns and styles; (d) individualism and collectivism value patterns shape members' preferences for self-oriented facework versus other-oriented facework; (e) small and large power distance value patterns shape members' preferences for horizontal-based facework versus vertical-based facework; (f) the value dimensions, in conjunction with individual, relational, and situational factors, influence the use of particular facework behaviors in particular cultural scenes; and (g) intercultural facework competence refers to the optimal integration of knowledge, mindfulness, and communication skills in managing vulnerable identity-based conflict situations appropriately, effectively, and adaptively. For a recent review of research findings in testing the conflict face negotiation theory, readers can consult Ting-Toomey (2005b) and Ting-Toomey and Takai (2006).

More specifically, for example, in a direct empirical test of the theory (Oetzel & Ting-Toomey, 2003; Oetzel et al., 2001), the research program tested the underlying assumption of the face negotiation theory that face is an explanatory mechanism for cultural membership's influence on conflict behavior. A questionnaire was administered to 768 participants in four national cultures (China, Germany, Japan, and the United States) in their respective languages asking them to recall and describe a recent interpersonal conflict. The major findings of the study are as follows: First, cultural individualism-collectivism had direct effects on conflict styles, as well as mediated effects through self-construal and face concerns. Second, *self-face concern* was associated positively with dominating style, and *other-face concern* was associated positively with avoiding and integrating styles. Third, German respondents reported the frequent use of direct-confrontive facework strategies and did not care much for avoidance facework tactics; Japanese reported the use of different pretending strategies to act as if the conflict situation does not exist; Chinese engaged in a variety of avoiding, obliging, and also passive aggressive facework tactics; and U.S. Americans reported the use of upfront expression of feelings and remaining calm as facework strategies to handle problematic conflict situations. Within the pluralistic U.S. sample, multiethnic research (Ting-Toomey et al., 2000) has also uncovered distinctive conflict interaction styles in relationship to particular ethnic identity salience issues.

While previous research studies have focused on testing the relationship between the value orientations of culture-based individualism-collectivism to conflict styles and facework strategies, recent research effort has focused more on unpacking the value spectrums of small and large power distance value dimensions in an effort to relate these value dimensions to facework expectancies and actual social practices. For example, Merkin (2006) has integrated the small-large power distance value dimension to the individualism-collectivism value dimension in explaining face-threatening response messages and conflict styles in multiple cultures. She found that high-status individuals from large power distance cultures tend to use both direct and indirect facework strategies to deal with face-threatening situations—depending on whether they were delivering positive or negative messages. Furthermore, Kaushal and Kwantes (2006) uncovered that the dominating conflict style of "high concern for self/low concern for others" was positively associated with both vertical individualism and vertical collectivism. However, the interpretation of "positive or negative messages" or the interpretation of the "dominating" conflict style as "high concern for self/low concern for others" carries strong cultural shadings—depending on whether the dominating style is viewed as a constructive motivational strategy or an oppressive de-motivational tactic. Likewise, from the Western models of interpreting the avoidance conflict style, avoidance has been consistently viewed as an indifferent or passive "flee the scene" conflict strategy that reflects the "low concern for self/low concern for others" phenomenon (Thomas, 1976; Thomas & Kilmann, 1974). The individualistic-oriented conceptualization of "avoidance" has been continuously challenged by cross-cultural conflict-style researchers (Cai & Fink, 2002; M. S. Kim & Leung, 2000; Ting-Toomey, 1988, 2005b) and their cross-national research findings. From the Asian collectivistic lens, the conflict style of avoidance can be regarded as a "high concern for self/high concern for others" tactic pending on situational and relational factors. The notion of "face" or "claimed communication identity" is considered one key domain out of the several domains of the larger intercultural or intergroup identity negotiation process.

Conclusion

While there is a systematic accumulation of cross-cultural conflict style studies, researchers need to address more fully the criteria dimensions of competent conflict management: appropriateness, effectiveness, and adaptation. For example, to understand whether appropriate conflict behaviors have been perceived, one must obtain competence evaluations from the standpoint of both conflict negotiators and interested observers. It is also critical to obtain both self-perception and other-perception data. We may think that we are acting appropriately in a conflict situation, but others may not concur with our self-assessment. Finally, post-conflict interviews or journal tracking can elicit the logic or narrative accounts that individuals use to justify their facework behaviors during and after an intercultural conflict episode. Although the knowledge component has been emphasized as the most important area for intercultural conflict competence training, we need more empirical research to test this assertion. We also need to know how we can sequence the knowledge, mindfulness, and conflict skills components in an optimal manner to train effectively and in a dynamic manner. We also need more well-designed pretest and posttest research studies to understand the rate and quality of change in the knowledge, mindfulness, and skills domains as a direct result of the intercultural conflict training program.

With the culture-based situational conflict model as a base, researchers and practitioners can locate concepts and linkage of ideas between the factors and test them in a systematic manner. The "culture-based situational conflict model" is a tentative compass or map to guide and encourage international collaborative research in the conjoint areas of intercultural and intergroup conflict communication. Creative communicators use culture-sensitive, adaptive communication skills to manage the process appropriately and integrate divergent interaction goals effectively to foster constructive productivity and team satisfaction within the system. The intricate relationship among these various communication competence process and criteria—appropriateness, effectiveness, and adaptability—especially in connection to understanding problematic intercultural interaction situations awaits to be further explored and tested from both an insider "emic" lens (see, e.g., Oetzel, Arcos, Mabizela, Weinman, & Zhang, 2006) and an outsider "etic" lens. It is hoped that by collecting meaningful data in a wide range of situational domains and in a diverse range of cultural communities, more research knowledge can transform the flat, two-dimensional plane conflict model to a multidimensional, culture-sensitive conflict framework.

In sum, this chapter has covered four key topics: a discussion of the criteria and components of intercultural conflict competence, a review of the culture-based situational conflict model, a synoptic probe of the integrated threat theory, and the conflict face negotiation theory. Last, research directions related to the intercultural conflict competence criteria are addressed. This chapter advocates the importance of understanding the multiple layers of intercultural conflict—from a macro-identity threat perspective to the micro-level of how individuals negotiate facework issues across cultures. Both international insider and outsider research collaboration efforts are urgently needed to understand the rich fabric of the different designs, patterns, and colorful threads that constitute the complex and adaptive intercultural conflict competence system. Both indigenous narrative perspective and cross-cultural comparative perspectives are needed for us to truly understand the multiple voices, stories, and dynamics of what constitutes competent versus incompetent conflict negotiation practice.

Intercultural conflict competence is one of the key facets of intercultural competence development. While the development of general intercultural competence focuses on the development of open-minded attitudes, culture-sensitive knowledge, and appropriate and effective interaction skills, intercultural conflict competence takes into account the keys of emotional and identity threats that affect the well-being of the two intercultural conflict parties or systems. Through intentional mindfulness, conflict parties can practice both general intercultural competence and specific intercultural conflict competence skills. Intercultural parties can learn to depolarize their emotional tensions and conflict positions, as well as learn to reframe the intercultural conflict from a monocultural conflict perspective to assessing it from multiple discovery perspectives. Finally, intercultural conflict intelligence demands conflict parties to use a transformational outlook in balancing focused attention with flexible behavioral repertoires in communicating appropriately, effectively, and adaptively in managing sudden conflict crises and moment-to-moment changes. Intercultural conflict competence is, in short, about the activation of a focused attunement process, behavioral flexibility, and the skillful application of the untapped human imagination between diverse identity groups, communities, and cultures.

References

Ang, S., Van Dyne, L., Koh, C., Ng, K. Y., Templer, K., Tay, C., et al. (2007). Cultural intelligence: Its measurement and effects on cultural judgment and decision making, cultural adaptation and task performance. *Management and Organization Review, 3,* 335–371.

Barge, J. K. (2005). Dialogue, conflict, and community. In J. Oetzel & S. Ting-Toomey (Eds.), *The SAGE handbook of conflict communication* (pp. 517–544). Thousand Oaks, CA: Sage.

Bennett, J. M. (2003). Turning frogs into interculturalists: A student-centered development approach to teaching intercultural communication. In R. Goodman, M. Phillips, & N. Boyacigiller (Eds.), *Crossing cultures: Insights from master teachers* (pp. 157–170). London: Routledge.

Bennett, J. M., & Bennett, M. J. (2004). Developing intercultural sensitivity: An integrative approach to global and domestic diversity. In D. Landis, J. Bennett, & M. Bennett (Eds.), *Handbook of intercultural training* (3rd ed., pp. 147–165). Thousand Oaks, CA: Sage.

Cai, D. A., & Fink, E. L. (2002). Conflict style differences between individualists and collectivists. *Communication Monographs, 69,* 67–87.

Canary, D., & Lakey, S.G. (2006). Managing conflict in a competent manner: A mindful look at events that matter. In J. Oetzel & S. Ting-Toomey (Eds.), *The SAGE handbook of conflict communication* (pp. 185–210). Thousand Oaks, CA: Sage.

Carl, D., Gupta, V., & Javidan, M. (2004). Power distance. In R. House, P. Hanges, M. Javidan, P. Dorfman, & V. Gupta (Eds.), *Culture, leadership, and organizations: The GLOBE study of 62 societies* (pp. 513–563). Thousand Oaks, CA: Sage.

Coleman, S., & Raider, E. (2006). International/intercultural conflict resolution training. In J. Oetzel & S. Ting-Toomey (Eds.), *The SAGE handbook of conflict communication* (pp. 663–690). Thousand Oaks, CA: Sage.

Deardorff, D. K. (2004). *The identification and assessment of intercultural competence as a student outcome of internationalization at institutions of higher education in the United States.* Unpublished doctoral dissertation, North Carolina State University, Raleigh.

Earley, P. C., & Ang, S. (2003). *Cultural intelligence: Individual interactions across cultures.* Palo Alto, CA: Stanford University Press.

Earley, P. C., & Peterson, R. S. (2004). The elusive cultural chameleon: Cultural intelligence as a new approach to intercultural training for the global manager. *Academy of Management Learning & Education, 3,* 100–115.

Gudykunst, W. B. (1995). Anxiety/uncertainty management (AUM) theory: Current status. In R. Wiseman (Ed.), *Intercultural communication theory* (pp. 8–58). Thousand Oaks, CA: Sage.

Gudykunst, W. B. (2005a). An anxiety/uncertainty management (AUM) theory of effective communication: Making the mesh of the net finer. In W. B. Gudykunst (Ed.), *Theorizing about intercultural communication* (pp. 281–322). Thousand Oaks, CA: Sage.

Gudykunst, W. B. (2005b). An anxiety/uncertainty management (AUM) theory of strangers' intercultural adjustment. In W. B. Gudykunst (Ed.), *Theorizing about intercultural communication* (pp. 419–458). Thousand Oaks, CA: Sage.

Gudykunst, W., Matsumoto, Y., Ting-Toomey, S., Nishida, T., Kim, K., & Heyman, S. (1996). The influence of cultural individualism-collectivism, self construals, and individual values on communication styles across cultures. *Human Communication Research, 22,* 510–543.

Hofstede, G. (2001). *Culture's consequences: Comparing values, behaviors, institutions, and organizations across cultures* (2nd ed.). Thousand Oaks, CA: Sage.

House, R., Hanges, P., Javidan, M., Dorfman, P., & Gupta, V. (Eds.). (2004). *Culture, leadership, and organizations: The GLOBE study of 62 societies.* Thousand Oaks, CA: Sage.

Imahori, T., & Cupach, W. (2005). Identity management theory: Facework in intercultural relations. In W. B. Gudykunst (Ed.), *Theorizing about intercultural communication* (pp. 195–210). Thousand Oaks, CA: Sage.

Jackson, R. (1999). *The negotiation of cultural identity.* Westport, CT: Praeger.

Jackson, R. (2002). Cultural contracts theory: Toward an understanding of identity negotiation. *Communication Quarterly, 50,* 359–367.

Kaushal, R., & Kwantes, C. (2006). The role of culture and personality in choice of conflict management strategy. *International Journal of Intercultural Relations, 30,* 579–603.

Kim, M. S., & Leung, T. (2000). A multicultural view of conflict management styles: Review and critical synthesis. In M. Roloff (Ed.), *Communication yearbook 23* (pp. 227–269). Thousand Oaks, CA: Sage.

Kim, Y. Y. (2001). *Becoming intercultural: An integrative theory of communication and cross-cultural adaptation.* Thousand Oaks, CA: Sage.

Kim, Y. Y. (2004). Long-term cross-cultural adaptation. In D. Landis, J. Bennett, & M. Bennett (Eds.), *Handbook of intercultural training* (3rd ed., pp. 337–362). Thousand Oaks, CA: Sage.

Langer, E. (1989). *Mindfulness.* Reading, MA: Addison-Wesley.

Langer, E. (1997). *The power of mindful learning.* Reading, MA: Addison-Wesley.

LeBaron, M. (2003). *Bridging cultural conflicts: A new approach for a changing world.* San Francisco: Jossey-Bass/John Wiley.

Markus, H. R., & Kitayama, S. (1991). Culture and self: Implication for cognition, emotion, and motivation. *Psychological Review, 98,* 224–253.

Markus, H. R., & Kitayama, S. (1998). The cultural psychology of personality. *Journal of Cross-Cultural Psychology 29,* 63–87.

Merkin, R. (2006). Power distance and facework strategies. *Journal of Intercultural Communication Research, 35,* 139–160.

Midooka, K. (1990). Characteristics of Japanese-style communication. *Media, Culture and Society, 12,* 477–489.

Molinsky, A. (2007). Cross-cultural code-switching: The psychological challenges of adapting behavior in foreign cultural interactions. *Academy of Management Review, 32,* 622–640.

Oetzel, J., Arcos, B., Mabizela, P., Weinman, A. M., & Zhang, Q. (2006). Historical, political, and spiritual factors of conflict: Understanding conflict perspectives and communication in the Muslim world, China, Colombia, and South Africa. In J. Oetzel & S. Ting-Toomey (Eds.), *The SAGE handbook of conflict communication* (pp. 549–574). Thousand Oaks, CA: Sage.

Oetzel, J. G., Dhar, S., & Kirschbaum, K. (2007). Intercultural conflict from a multilevel perspective: Possibilities, and future directions. *Journal of Intercultural Communication Research, 36,* 183–204.

Oetzel, J. G., & Ting-Toomey, S. (2003). Face concerns in interpersonal conflict: A cross-cultural empirical test of the face-negotiation theory. *Communication Research, 30,* 599–624.

Oetzel, J. G., Ting-Toomey, S., Masumoto, T., Yokochi, Y., Pan, X., Takai, J., et al. (2001). Face behaviors in interpersonal conflicts: A cross-cultural comparison of Germany, Japan, China, and the United States. *Communication Monographs, 68*, 235–258.

Oetzel, J. G., Ting-Toomey, S., & Rinderle, S. (2006). Conflict communication in contexts: A social ecological perspective. In J. G. Oetzel & S. Ting-Toomey (Eds.), *The SAGE handbook of conflict communication* (pp. 727–739). Thousand Oaks, CA: Sage.

Pedersen, P., Crethar, H., & Carlson, J. (2008). *Inclusive cultural empathy: Making relationships central in counseling and psychotherapy.* Washington, DC: American Psychological Association.

Plant, E., & Devine, P. (2003). The antecedents and implications of interracial anxiety. *Personality and Psychology Bulletin, 29,* 790–801.

Rogan, R. G., & Hammer, M. R. (2006). The emerging field of crisis/hostage negotiation: A communication-based perspective. In J. Oetzel & S. Ting-Toomey (Eds.), *The SAGE handbook of conflict communication* (pp. 451–478). Thousand Oaks, CA: Sage.

Rothman, J. (1997). *Resolving identity-based conflict in nations, organizations, and communities.* San Francisco: Jossey-Bass.

Smith, P. B., Dugan, S., Peterson, M. F., & Leung, K. (1998). Individualism, collectivism and the handling of disagreement: A 23 country study. *International Journal of Intercultural Relations, 22,* 351–367.

Spencer-Rodgers, J., & McGovern, T. (2002). Attitudes toward culturally different: The role of intercultural communication barriers, affective responses, consensual stereotypes, and perceived threat. *International Journal of Intercultural Relations, 26,* 609–631.

Spitzberg, B., & Cupach, W. (1984). *Interpersonal communication competence.* Beverly Hills, CA: Sage.

Spitzberg, B., Canary, D., & Cupach, W. (1994). A competence-based approach to the study of interpersonal conflict. In D. Cahn (Ed.), *Conflict in personal relationships* (pp. 183–202). Hillsdale, NJ: Lawrence Erlbaum.

Stephan, C., & Stephan, W. (2003). Cognition and affect in cross-cultural relations. In W. B. Gudykunst (Ed.), *Cross-cultural and intercultural communication* (pp. 111–126). Thousand Oaks, CA: Sage.

Stephan, W. (1999). *Reducing prejudice and stereotyping in schools.* New York: Teachers College Press/Columbia University.

Stephan, W., Diaz-Loving, R., & Duran, A. (2000). Integrated threat theory and intercultural attitudes: Mexico and the United States. *Journal of Cross-Cultural Psychology, 31,* 240–249.

Stephan, W., & Stephan, C. (2001). *Improving intergroup relations.* Thousand Oaks, CA: Sage.

Stephan, W., Stephan, C., & Gudykunst, W. B. (1999). Anxiety in intergroup relations: A Comparison of anxiety/uncertainty management theory and integrated threat theory. *International Journal of Intercultural Relations, 23,* 613–628.

Stephan, W., Ybarra, O., & Bachman, G. (1999). Prejudice toward immigrants. *Journal of Applied Social Psychology, 29,* 2221–2237.

Storti, C. (2001). *Old world/new world.* Yarmouth, ME: Intercultural Press.

Thich, N. H. (1991). *Peace is every step: The path of mindfulness in everyday life.* New York: Bantam.

Thich, N. H. (1998). *The heart of the Buddha's teaching.* Berkeley, CA: Parallex Press.

Thomas, K. W. (1976). Conflict and conflict management. In M. Dunnette (Ed.), *Handbook of industrial and social psychology* (pp. 889–935). Chicago: Rand McNally.

Thomas, K. W., & Kilmann, R. H. (1974). *Thomas-Kilmann conflict MODE instrument.* New York: Xicom.

Ting-Toomey, S. (1988). Intercultural conflicts: A face-negotiation theory. In Y. Y. Kim & W. Gudykunst (Eds.), *Theories in intercultural communication* (pp. 213–235). Newbury Park, CA: Sage.

Ting-Toomey, S. (1993). Communicative resourcefulness: An identity negotiation perspective. In R. L. Wiseman & J. Koester (Eds.), *Intercultural communication competence* (pp. 72–111). Newbury Park, CA: Sage.

Ting-Toomey, S. (1999). *Communicating across cultures.* New York: Guilford.

Ting-Toomey, S. (2004). Translating conflict face-negotiation theory into practice. In D. Landis, J. Bennett, & M. Bennett (Eds.), *Handbook of intercultural training* (3rd ed., pp. 217–248). Thousand Oaks, CA: Sage.

Ting-Toomey, S. (2005a). Identity negotiation theory: Crossing cultural boundaries. In W. B. Gudykunst (Ed.), *Theorizing about intercultural communication* (pp. 211–234). Thousand Oaks, CA: Sage.

Ting-Toomey, S. (2005b). The matrix of face: An updated face-negotiation theory. In W. B. Gudykunst (Ed.), *Theorizing about intercultural communication* (pp. 71–92). Thousand Oaks, CA: Sage.

Ting-Toomey, S., & Chung, L. C. (2005). *Understanding intercultural communication.* Los Angeles, CA: Roxbury Publications/Oxford University Press.

Ting-Toomey, S., & Kurogi, A. (1998). Facework competence in intercultural conflict: An updated face-negotiation theory. *International Journal of Intercultural Relations, 22,* 187–225.

Ting-Toomey, S., & Oetzel, J. G. (2001). *Managing intercultural conflict effectively.* Thousand Oaks, CA: Sage.

Ting-Toomey, S., & Takai, J. (2006). Explaining intercultural conflict: Promising approaches and directions. In J. Oetzel & S. Ting-Toomey (Eds.), *The SAGE handbook of conflict communication* (pp. 691–723). Thousand Oaks, CA: Sage.

Ting-Toomey, S., Yee-Jung, K., Shapiro, R., Garcia, W., Wright, T., & Oetzel, J. G. (2000). Ethnic/cultural identity salience and conflict styles in four U.S. ethnic groups. *International Journal of Intercultural Relations, 24,* 47–81.

Triandis, H. (1995). *Individualism and collectivism.* Boulder, CO: Westview.

Triandis, H. (2002). Individualism and collectivism. In M. Gannon & K. Newman (Eds.), *Handbook of cross-cultural management* (pp. 16–45). New York: Lawrence Erlbaum.

Wang, Q., Stephen, C. J., Williams, W., & Kopka, K. (2004). Culturally situated cognitive competence: A functional framework. In R. J. Sternberg & E. L. Grigorenko (Eds.), *Culture and competence: Contexts of life success* (pp. 225–249). Washington, DC: American Psychological Association.

CHAPTER 6

Cultivating Intercultural Competence

A Process Perspective

Janet M. Bennett

"And how was your flight today?"

The taxi driver in Montgomery, Alabama, greeted my colleague. Indeed, she had experienced one of those days of flying that many of us know all too well: a two-hour delay of her first flight, a mad dash to barely make the connection to her second flight, an hour and a half sitting on the tarmac while thunderstorms passed, and, of course, at the end of the day, lost luggage. She started to release her pent-up frustrations, when she took a breath and scanned her context. A driver identity card on the visor revealed a Moslem name, while prayer beads dangled from the mirror. His accent suggested Africa to her, and instead of sharing her litany of travel travails, she said it had been a fine day, and by the way, where was he from?

"I am from Africa," he responded.

"Northern Africa?" she asked.

"Why, yes," he said.

"From Sudan?" she asked.

And soon they were gently discussing the tragic events in Darfur that had led him to seek refuge in the United States. It occurred to her that she had nearly whined about lost luggage to a man whose family had been murdered before his eyes only months earlier.

A small moment in time, no doubt. But a moment that reflects the value of cultural competence during even the most transitory interactions.

Her experience illustrates an important truth: If we are to thrive in "a world lived in common with others" (Green, 1988), we must step outside of our own frame of reference and interact meaningfully with different cultural realities. In each society today, that means engaging profound cultural differences with deep cultural humility; our way is only one way of viewing the world, and perhaps we haven't a clue about what is really going on (Guskin, 1991).

This sense of identifying our own cultural patterns, acknowledging the patterns of others, and, eventually, learning to adapt across cultures is a developmental process for each of us, regardless of our place in the world (J. M. Bennett & Bennett, 2004). The call to develop the skills and abilities to live and work with culturally different others is no longer specific to a few particular disciplines and professions but rather is a call to cultural consciousness in a much wider context.

This chapter will establish a shared terminology, review relevant contexts for intercultural competence, and explore an approach to cultivating intercultural competence, either individually or in a team, a classroom, or an organization. We will examine an *intercultural positioning system* as a key part of this process and illustrate a series of steps for developing intercultural competence based on attitudes, knowledge, and skills.

Definition of Intercultural Competence

Spitzberg and Changnon (Chapter 1, this volume) synthesize earlier literature and comprehensively compare and contrast existing models and theories of intercultural competence. Whether described as a "global mind-set" (Bird & Osland, 2004), "global competence" (Hunter, White, & Godbey, 2006), "global learning" (Hovland, 2006; Musil, 2006), "culture learning" (Paige, Cohen, Kappler, Chi, & Lassegard, 2002), "intercultural effectiveness" (Vulpe, Kealey, Protheroe, & MacDonald, 2001), "cultural intelligence" (Earley & Ang, 2003; Peterson, 2004; Thomas & Inkson, 2004), "global leadership competence" (Jokinen, 2005), "intercultural communication competence" (Collier, 1989; Dinges, 1983; Dinges & Baldwin, 1996; Hammer, 1989; Y. Y. Kim, 1991; Spitzberg, 1989, 1994), or, of course, intercultural competence (Deardorff, 2005, 2006; Graf, 2004), many of the disciplinary roads lead to a similar place. There is clearly an "emerging consensus around what constitutes intercultural competence, which is most often viewed as a set of cognitive, affective, and behavioral skills and characteristics that support effective and appropriate interaction in a variety of cultural contexts" (J. M. Bennett, 2008, p. 97).

There are lengthy lists that describe precisely which knowledge, skills, and attitudes constitute intercultural competence (Bird & Osland, 2004; Jokinen, 2005; Mendenhall, 2001; Spitzberg & Changnon, Chapter 1, this volume; Yershova, DeJaeghere, & Mestenhauser, 2000). Such lists provide an excellent starting point for assessing the appropriate characteristics for the specific situation, but of course no list fits all cultures, all contexts, all conditions.

One consistent concern is that such lists do not address the application of knowledge and skills to complex interactions with culturally different others, with whom we must negotiate shared meaning (Deardorff, 2006; King & Baxter Magolda, 2005). In fact, cultural knowledge does not equal intercultural competence since a person can be an expert on a particular aspect of Chinese culture and yet be unable to negotiate well with his Chinese counterparts. This gap between knowledge and competence may be due in part to being unaware of one's own culture and therefore not fully capable of assessing the cultural position of others. Or it may reflect an overreliance on the cognitive domain, with less development of affective and behavioral capacities. This chapter will suggest approaches for putting knowledge into practice, underscoring the importance of the process inherent in intercultural competence development.

Contexts for Intercultural Competence

Professionals in every arena are recognizing the obvious need to relate effectively to those who work with them and those they serve. Whether in educational institutions, corporations, health care contexts, counseling settings, military, social services, government, or nongovernment organizations (NGOs), an increasing number of initiatives focus on developing intercultural effectiveness.

Not surprisingly, the field of education has taken a leadership role in calling for a transformation in how we approach the job of preparing learners for the 21st century. According to Musil (2006),

> The Association of American Colleges and Universities Greater Expectations Project on Accreditation and Assessment reported that global knowledge and engagement, along with intercultural knowledge and competence, have been identified as essential learning outcomes for all fields of concentration and for all majors. (p. 1)

Traditionally, campus initiatives have often focused on attracting and retaining what often is called "compositional diversity" (Milem, Chang, & Antonio, 2005), referring to having visible nondominant groups in our institutions, as if "the face of diversity, which reveals its numbers, were its only significant feature" (Beckham, 2005, p. 1). The contemporary mission of American education, however, has moved beyond this rather limited perspective (D. A. Williams, Berger, & McClendon, 2005) to focus on global competence, in a variety of forms ranging from "appreciating diversity" to "building communities that acknowledge and respect difference" to "international and global understanding"(Meacham & Gaff, 2006, p. 9).

Educators have explicitly acknowledged their role in preparing learners not only for careers but also for the complex interchange inherent in global citizenship. Referring to the work of Gurin, Dey, Hurtado, and Gurin (2002), King and Baxter Magolda (2005) observed, "In times of increased global interdependence, producing interculturally competent citizens who can engage in informed, ethical decision-making when confronted with problems that involve a diversity of perspectives is becoming an urgent educational priority" (p. 571).

Knefelkamp and Schneider (1997) "propose an even richer ambition—the goal of becoming justice-centered communities in which learning fosters new capacities for engaged citizenship and aspirational or justice-seeking democracy" (p. 340). It is a rare campus indeed that has not heeded the call to create a climate and context for learning from culturally different others, both domestically and globally.

In the corporate arena, attention to culture differences has also traditionally taken two paths, one focused on an international/global mind-set and the other on domestic diversity. From the international perspective, there has long been recognition that the human side of the enterprise affects profits. It is widely known that global joint ventures can wobble and may collapse due to intercultural conflicts, where shared goals prove elusive and cultural differences interfere (Graf, 2004). Historically, corporations have prepared transferees (often called *expatriates*) for adjustment and effective performance overseas (Adler & Gundersen, 2007; Black & Gregersen, 1999; Mendenhall & Oddou, 1986; Mendenhall et al., 2004). Mendenhall (2001) suggests "the expatriate adjustment process is one of human transformation . . . knowingly or unknowingly, for better or for worse . . . they return to their home country with new ways of seeing and thinking about the world around them" (p. 8). But until the 1990s, few organizations prepared other employees or managers for the global interface. Now, however, the organization research is focusing on global leadership and the competencies necessary for the new world of managing across cultures, whether overseas or in the home country (Bird & Osland, 2004; Boyacigiller, Beechler, Taylor, & Levy, 2004; Jokinen, 2005; Mendenhall, Kuhlmann, & Stahl, 2001; Osland, Bird, Mendenhall, & Osland, 2006).

In contrast to the global arena (where corporate transferees were the primary focus of development in the past), domestic diversity and inclusion programming has been diffused more widely in North America, where diversity programming has been instituted in a majority of all large organizations. Such training usually encompasses all employees and corporate locations and covers topics such as culture, race/ethnicity, gender, class, sexual orientation, and so on (Cox, 1994; Gardenswartz & Rowe, 1998; Hayles & Mendez Russell, 1997; O'Mara & Richter, 2006). The current perspective in the diversity field has shifted from celebrating, appreciating, or managing diversity to inclusion and intercultural competence.

Thus, in the past 20 years, there has been a growing acknowledgment that intercultural competence contributes to effectiveness in both global and domestic interaction. In fact, such competence may be a prerequisite for capably addressing issues of race, class, and gender (J. M. Bennett & Bennett, 2004). Organizations now frequently incorporate both global and domestic diversity under the umbrella of intercultural competence initiatives, where differences are recognized as contributions to the productivity of the organization, not barriers to overcome (J. M. Bennett & Bennett, 2004; Cornwell & Stoddard, 1999; Gardenswartz, Rowe, Digh, & Bennett, 2003; Gundling & Zanchettin, 2006; Wentling & Palma-Rivas, 2000). The *Workforce 2020* report sums up this new reality, noting "the rest of the world matters" (Judy & D'Amico, 1997, p. 3).

It seems that each professional context has its own call to cultural responsiveness, whether bridging the cultural gap in health care (IQ Solutions, Inc., 2001; Lewin Group, 2001), workforce development (Chicago Jobs Council, 2004), international humanitarian workers (Chang, 2007), social services (T. L. Cross, 1989;

Elliott, Adams, & Sockalingam, 1999), counseling (Sue, Arredondo, & McDavis, 1992), youth at risk (B. Williams, 2001), or hospitality (American Hospitality Academy, 2007). Essentially, on a good day, we may be served by flight attendants, hotel clerks, and salespersons who have all been prepared to work across cultures; we may avoid a speeding ticket from a police officer who has had cultural diversity training, receive health care at a clinic that cares about our culture, and arrive to work at an organization where managers are conscious of cultural competence.

While such a characterization certainly may seem overly optimistic, it is notable that literally tens of thousands of educators and trainers in the United States have been working intensively since the 1980s to ensure that most students and professionals have at least been exposed to the idea that culture matters.

From this base, acknowledging that domestic and global concerns can share the overarching perspective of intercultural competence in a variety of contexts, this chapter offers a tool for developing such competence through the metaphor of an intercultural positioning system. Modeled on the metaphor of a global positioning system, the intercultural positioning system involves the following four steps, which will be described in detail in the last section of this chapter:

1. Fostering attitudes that motivate us

2. Discovering knowledge that informs us of our own and others' cultural position

3. Assessing the challenge and support factors that affect our adaptation

4. Developing skills that enable us to interact effectively and appropriately

Intercultural Competence: Positioning Systems

As we think about the process of building intercultural competence, let us first consider the metaphor of a global positioning system (GPS). We routinely rely on this helpful technology to discover not only where we are but also where we are going.

The GPS is a global navigation system developed by the U.S. Department of Defense that uses more than 25 satellites to precisely determine our location, speed, direction, and time. The locating capacity of a single satellite is insufficient for precision, but through the use of multiple satellite messages, we can accurately assess where we are, bringing in additional satellite signals to enhance the clarity of our position.

For example, by gathering data from at least three, often four, satellites, we know exactly where we are. If someone tells us that we are 116 miles from Los Angeles, we now have a radius from which to make guesses about our location. When we add the information that we are 15 miles from Tijuana, that begins to narrow the range of where we might be. But once we add a third distance, say, we are 299 miles from Phoenix, we have triangulated our position and can conclude confidently that we are in San Diego. In fact, if we figure out a fourth dimension, it ensures even more precise information about our location: Las Vegas is 331 miles away!

If we view developing intercultural competence as a process similar to triangulation, using the contemporary metaphor of a global positioning system, Stoddard and

Cornwell (2003) suggest that this can be "a model for the way one needs to collect perspectives from differently situated knowers and citizens around the world in order to be able to make informed judgments, to have a sufficient basis for knowledge" (p. 5).

To identify our own *cultural* position in the context of others, we need to parallel the process of the global positioning system, using multiple culture maps as a tool to assess our own cultural views relative to others in what we call an intercultural positioning system.

The distinction here between *cultural* and *intercultural* is an important one. When we describe cultural generalizations about the attributes of one person with whom we are interacting or one culture group about which we are conducting research, we are often using anthropological, linguistic, or psychological frameworks as our culture maps. When we use the intercultural positioning tool, we are looking at the *interface* between two or more individuals with differing culture maps and attempting to develop a strategy for integrating their values, beliefs, and behaviors to enhance the effectiveness of their interaction.

Culture maps are simply frameworks that provide a *culture-general* (etic) perspective for comparing and contrasting cultures. Originally from linguistics, *etic* is derived from phonetics, referring "to sounds that are found across all languages," in contrast to *emic,* derived from phonemics, referring to "sounds used in a particular language" (Pike, 1967, as cited in Gelfand, Erez, & Aycan, 2007, p. 482). Based on abstract categories, such frameworks do not refer to any *specific* culture but rather provide general categories that allow us to explore cultural variables in *any* culture.

Culture maps are readily available for examining (among other topics):

1. Nonverbal behavior (Knapp & Hall, 2005; Ting-Toomey, 1999)

2. Communication styles (Gudykunst & Ting-Toomey, 1988; M. Kim, 1998; Saphiere, Mikk, & Devries, 2005; Wurzel, 2005)

3. Values (Brake & Walker, 1995; Chhokar, Brodbeck, & House, 2007; Hofstede, 2001; House, Hanges, Javidan, Dorfman, & Gupta, 2004; Lane, DiStefano, & Maznevski, 2000; Saphiere, 2007; Trompenaars & Hampden-Turner, 1997)

4. Interaction rituals (Tannen, 1994)

5. Conflict styles (Hammer, 2003; Ting-Toomey & Oetzel, 2001)

6. Cognitive and learning styles (Belenky, Clinchy, Goldberger, & Tarule, 1996; Dunn & Griggs, 1988, 1990; Edmundson, 2007; Elbow, 1973; King & Baxter Magolda, 2005; Kolb, 1984; Nisbett, 2003; Riding & Rayner, 2000; Yershova et al., 2000)

7. Identity development (W. E. Cross, 1978; Evans, Forney, & Guido-DiBrito, 1998; Helms, 1984; Parham, 1989; Phinney, 1991; Sabnani, Ponterotto, & Borodovsky, 1991; Schaetti, 2000; Sue, 2007)

For instance, the cultural map on nonverbal behavior allows us to compare and contrast our turn-taking conversational rituals with those of other cultures. In fact, it brings into awareness that we actually *have* a turn-taking ritual, an idea that may never have occurred to us!

Once we have successfully navigated several culture-general maps, then we can begin to employ *culture-specific* categories (emic), based on specific ethnographic information, for a particular culture that we want to understand. Here we may ask, "What are the turn-taking rituals in Ghana?"

Through exploration of our own position on cultural variables, we can identify similarities and differences with others and thus begin the process of building intercultural competence. Careful analysis of our position relative to the cultural position of others suggests a way of calibrating the degree of adaptation we may wish to make in our interactions. We may note that if our turn taking requires direct eye contact and rapid insertion of our opinion in the dialogue, we may have to make a substantive adaptation to a culture that relies on silence for an opening to speak, while averting eye contact.

However, the first use of an intercultural positioning system is to locate *ourselves*, to develop our own cultural self-awareness through understanding our cultural patterns. Only then can we begin exploring the gap between our values, beliefs, and behaviors and those of others. Some cultural distances will be short and readily adjusted; others, of course, may defy negotiation. And, finally, it is a joint venture to build a third culture bridge between our intercultural positions, requiring two parties willing to take the risks inevitably involved in such worthy pursuits.

Frequently, the prospect of adapting to other cultures brings up the question of whether to adapt, how much to adapt, or, perhaps of most importance, whether we have to give up ourselves if we adapt to this other person. In fact, this perspective suggests a rather reified self, as if compromising with others somehow subtracts from our personhood. Interculturalists may see it more as an additive process; not only do we remain intact, but we have added more skills to our repertoire of behaviors. We adapt when we hope to achieve shared meaning, complete an effective business transaction, teach across cultures, or accomplish anything well that involves culturally different others. We may choose not to adapt when deep culture values are substantially violated, when our safety is involved, or when the risk is higher than our tolerance.

Sometimes we interact with others who are also calibrating their cultural distance and who share our desire to adapt. We may begin to adapt, only to find the other person has already adapted to us, and rather than meeting in our bridge building, we have adapted past each other. He has modified the meeting to accommodate more North American values; we have adapted the meeting to ensure comfort for our Asian counterparts. While this usually inspires warm laughter, it is sufficiently rare to be of only slight concern; overadaptation is hardly the norm.

Fostering Attitudes That Motivate Us

Perhaps the place to begin developing intercultural competence is with motivation: What inspires us to want to learn about others? Mendenhall (2001) suggests that inquisitiveness is the critical factor, perhaps the keystone in developing intercultural effectiveness, a position supported in Deardorff's (2006) work as well.

Gregersen, Morrison, and Black (1998) define curiosity as "unbridled inquisitiveness," noting that global leaders "stated repeatedly that inquisitiveness is the fuel for increasing their global savvy, enhancing their ability to understand people and maintain integrity, and augmenting their capacity for dealing with uncertainty and managing tension" (p. 23). In defining curiosity, Opdal (2001) describes it as a sense of wonder:

> Wonder . . . always points to something beyond the accepted rules. Because of this, the feeling of being overwhelmed, or the experience of humbleness and even awe could accompany it. Wonder is the state of mind that signals we have reached the limits of our present understanding, and that things may be different from how they look. (p. 331)

When we are interacting across cultures, things are often different from how they look. We frequently encounter these teachable moments or trigger events (Osland, Bird, & Gundersen, 2007) for which we have no map, which have not yet been registered in our intercultural positioning systems, events that have no precedent in our past, that may yet inspire us to see the world in different ways. Whether we are shocked at our own negative response to a busy market in India, puzzled by an African American colleague's response to a political event, or confounded by the argument style of someone of the opposite gender—it can be a teachable moment. While this often enough inspires a flight response, there are attitudes and approaches that can turn flight into filtering ideas and flexing positions in the new context (Sergeant, 1973).

For curiosity to thrive, the first action is suspending assumptions and judgments, leaving our minds open to multiple perspectives. By asking, "What do I see here? What might it mean? What else might it mean? And yet again, what might *others* think it means?" we enhance our own perceptions and practice cultural humility (Guskin, 1991). Our way is not the only way and may not merit primacy.

The second action is to increase our tolerance of ambiguity, an essential characteristic for working effectively across cultures. Hofstede's (2001) work examined the value map of "uncertainty avoidance," suggesting that cultures have a different tolerance of the extent to which they handle ambiguity and what it takes to "allow us to sleep peacefully" (p. 146). For example, in a training context, Americans will often (not always) exhibit a relatively high tolerance for uncertainty in adjusting to vague directions or generalized case studies with few details. People from some other cultures may seek every detail of the instructor's expectations and the case study context before agreeing to proceed.

Curiosity, suspension of judgment, cognitive flexibility, cultural humility, and tolerance of ambiguity are critical core components of the affective dimension of intercultural competence.

Discovering Knowledge That Informs Us

After building on the motivation to respond appropriately to the unfamiliar cultural event, seeking knowledge is often the next step. The intercultural positioning system, with its series of culture maps, provides a tool that can move through the necessary cultural self-awareness to analysis of the other cultures with whom we are interacting. While there are many culture maps we might choose to use for illustration, let us consider the culture map of thinking styles. While the nonverbal map may be more playful and the communication styles map more readily defined, thinking styles are often a subtle barrier in our classrooms and workplaces and therefore provide an intriguing map. To use the intercultural positioning system, we might ask, "Where do I fit in the framework of thinking styles? And where does my colleague fit?"

There are no agreed-upon definitions of thinking and learning styles, and many researchers use the terms interchangeably. However, the term *cognitive styles* is used most frequently to refer to an individual's preferred patterns of interacting with the environment, through perception, gathering information, constructing meaning, and organizing and applying knowledge (Irvine & York, 1995; Jonassen & Grabowski, 1993; Oxford & Anderson, 1995). What this means in practice is that colleagues working on our intercultural team may be approaching our joint project through a completely different constructed meaning and have an entirely different sense of the application. While I was conducting a seminar on change agentry in Japan, I queried my participants on their response to change. One senior member of the group quietly offered, "The Buddha teaches us that we are all on a path that winds through life until we inevitably perish." Another responded, "Change has nothing to do with us. It can't be helped." My Western sense that we have agency, that as individuals we can make a difference, that we can apply models and anticipate outcomes felt irrelevant, as I responded to the reality that perhaps my seminar needed some rapid rethinking.

When using a culture map of thinking styles, it is essential to underscore that all members of each culture may apply a number of styles in their interactions, depending on context, but that we can benefit from mapping styles as a way to assess useful adaptations for interacting with others. We develop culture maps by consulting theory, research, and practice about the topic at hand. We then synthesize a series of dimensions that will help us to explore our own culture and that of others. While based on credible literature, we still hold our generalizations lightly (J. M. Bennett & Bennett, 2004), acknowledging that no individual can ever be expected to conform to research or precise culture maps, no matter how well developed.

We begin the thinking styles map construction with psychologist Richard Nisbett (2003), who interprets the chasm between Western and Eastern patterns of thinking, based on contrasting Greek and Confucian philosophy in his lively text *The Geography of Thought*. Nisbett was engaged one day in his own teachable moment when one of his Chinese students allowed as to how he thought on a circle, while his professor thought on a line. On the basis of his subsequent research connecting social values with thought processes, Nisbett has offered the interculturalist a series of dimensions for a culture map, suggesting that "we might expect to find differences in: patterns of attention and perception . . . preferred patterns of explanation for events . . . habits of organizing the world . . . use of formal logic rules . . . application of dialectical approaches" (pp. 44–45). Contrasting U.S. with Eastern ways of thinking, he observes,

The rhetoric of scientific papers consists of an overview of the ideas to be considered, a description of the relevant basic theories, a specific hypothesis, a statement of the methods and justification of them, a presentation of the evidence produced by the methods, an argument as to why the evidence supports the hypothesis, a refutation of possible counterarguments, a reference back to the basic theory and a comment on the larger territory of which the article is a part. For Americans, this rhetoric is constructed bit by bit from nursery school through college. (p. 74)

Compare this way of thinking to a recent presentation I attended by a researcher (Yamashita, 2007) investigating why the U.S. classroom constitutes a chilly climate for Asians. She produced a Japanese writing pattern, called *ki-sho-ten-ketsu*, undoubtedly a rhetoric constructed bit by bit from nursery school through college. The method suggests starting with the topic (ki), expanding it (sho), giving it a 180-degree turn (ten), and stating the conclusion (ketsu). She illustrated her very Western PowerPoint presentation with the following example commonly taught to young writers in Japan to help them present their thoughts:

Ki: Mr. Itoya has two daughters.

Sho: His daughters are age fourteen and sixteen.

Ten: Feudal lords kill with their bows and arrows.

Ketsu: Mr. Itoya's daughters kill with their eyes.

After she repeated it twice to her rapt Western audience, we learned that the gap between our way of thinking and hers was more intriguing than we had ever imagined. We had reached the limits of our understanding, and we were curious.

In building the thinking styles map, the traditional constructs of field independence and field dependence (now frequently called field-sensitive) styles also prove useful. Field independence refers to a style that often reflects a task orientation; abstract, analytical, digital, objective thinking; a focus on details and precision; inner direction; and autonomy. Field sensitivity refers to a style that often reflects relationship orientation; concrete, global, analogic, metaphorical thinking; and a focus on people rather than things and group consciousness (Hayashi & Jolley, 2002; Irvine & York, 1995; Oxford & Anderson, 1995). On the same theme, discussing women's ways of knowing, Belenky and her colleagues (1996) distinguished separate ways of knowing (objective, analytical, rational, concerned with validity, detached) from connected ways of knowing (subjective, metaphorical, empathic, concerned with meaning, engaged).

Finally, educator Peter Elbow (1973) contributes to our discussion with his contrast between the Doubting Game and the Believing Game, in which he suggests (similar to Belenky et al., 1996) that one approach to grasping ideas is to doubt the author, critique the ideas, and prove or disprove their validity. In contrast, the Believing Game suggests engaging the ideas, understanding them deeply, and exploring and sharing a synthesis.

While at least 20 dimensions of cognitive styles have been widely researched (Oxford & Anderson, 1995; Yershova et al., 2000), for purposes of an introductory thinking styles map, we can now synthesize a few of the questions to explore as we examine our intercultural positions:

1. To what extent is the thinking pattern based on analytical logic in contrast to holistic/global thinking? (Nisbett, 2003; Oxford & Anderson, 1995)

2. To what extent are thinking patterns verbalized abstractly in contrast to metaphorically? (Belenky et al., 1996)

3. To what extent is the thinking pattern based on objective in contrast to subjective ways of knowing? (Belenky et al., 1996; Elbow, 1973; Hayashi & Jolley, 2002)

4. To what extent is the thinking pattern dialectic in contrast to integrative? (Belenky et al., 1996; Elbow, 1973; Nisbett, 2003)

5. To what extent is the thinking pattern based on the Doubting Game in contrast to the Believing Game? (Elbow, 1973)

Intercultural positioning would allow us to compare our own perspective on these questions with the perspective of those with whom we are interacting to determine the distance from our pattern of thinking and theirs, the map gap. For instance, if a European American man was acculturated, educated, and employed in North America, he might have thinking patterns closer to the first of the two elements in each of the above questions. If he were interacting with another similar man, his adaptation distance might be negligible. However, if he were assigned to go to Vietnam to negotiate with a man who was acculturated, educated, and employed in Vietnam, he might have quite a distance between his pattern of thinking and his counterpart's, which might be more similar to the second element in each of the above questions. In that case, he would need to examine how challenging he finds this degree of compromise, adaptation, and adjustment.

While this thinking styles culture map gives us only one dimension of where we are in relationship to culturally different others, the use of multiple culture maps increases the potential for more significant knowledge about our intercultural bearings. As we gather a more precise definition of our cultural whereabouts, it is important to assess the level of challenge we face in our interactions.

Assessing the Challenge and Support Factors

Nevitt Sanford (1966) has offered an elegant guideline for educators that serves us well as we work across cultures in any profession. He has noted the essential balance required between the challenges any individual faces in a new situation and the level of support required for that person to adjust effectively.

For each person, depending on a wide variety of factors, we need to examine what aspects of the intercultural context can provide support and what aspects present challenges. If the person is overly supported, adaptation or development is less likely. If the person is overly challenged, the individual flees the intercultural context, whether psychologically, physically, or both. Each of us needs to balance challenge and support to maximize adaptation across cultures. Depending on their culture and developmental worldview, some individuals may find certain culture distances very challenging while they find others affirming.

R. Michael Paige (1993) has constructed a list of the primary intensity factors that influence the challenge of intercultural experience, including factors in the person as well as those in the environment (see also Paige & Goode, Chapter 19, this volume). For instance, the degree to which a person is ethnocentric, culturally different, and immersed in a new cultural context affects the challenge of the experience. The business professional who is confident of her culture's perspective, broadly inflexible, and immersed in an Indian corporation in Bangalore with completely different cultural values may find herself in a most intense, highly challenging context. The gap between her cultural position and that of her Indian counterparts may, in fact, be excessively challenging. Somehow, her organization needs to increase the support for her adaptation, perhaps with coaching, training, cultural mediators, and so on. Paige's intensity factors provide a barometer to assess the challenge, in order to balance that intensity with adequate support.

Developing Skills That Enable Us

Having increased our cultural self-awareness, examined the distance from our position to that of others, and assessed the level of challenge and support required, the next step in the intercultural positioning system process is to continue the lifetime task of developing the requisite skills for adaptation.

The intercultural skill set typically includes such characteristics and skills as the ability to empathize, gather appropriate information, listen, adapt, resolve conflict, and manage social interactions and anxiety.

In the past, many professionals assumed that any contact across cultures was useful contact and would reduce stereotypes and prejudice, allowing intercultural competence to synergistically evolve. Well-intentioned efforts at integration of differences quickly taught us that this was unfortunately not so, as the proposed holiday party for Africans and African Americans never occurred, and the panel of Israelis and Arabs generated more heat than light. Recent investigations have illuminated more complicated and useful perspectives on intercultural contact and how best to facilitate the development of skills.

For instance, we now know that contact does reduce prejudice among many culture groups, under many conditions. Pettigrew and Tropp's (2000) meta-analysis of 516 studies completed over 50 years on the contact hypothesis reports that 95% of these studies reflect a negative relationship between contact and prejudice of many types. And while many forms of contact reduce such bias, Pettigrew and Tropp also remind us that maintaining certain conditions, such as shared goals and equal status, can enhance the impact of contact.

But intercultural competence is more than the diminishment of prejudice. Pettigrew notes that two of the core intercultural competencies—empathy and anxiety management—contribute importantly to enhancing the impact of inter-cultural contact, even more than the acquisition of knowledge. Pettigrew's (2008) most recent research examines three variables relevant to our discussion of skill building: exploring how new knowledge about others affects attitudes, how anxi-ety reduction facilitates interactions, and how empathy with others affects our understanding. He concludes,

> Early theorists thought that intergroup contact led to learning about the outgroup, and this new knowledge in turn reduced prejudice. Recent work, however, reveals that this knowledge mediation does exist but is of minor importance. Empathy and perspective taking are far more important. (p. 190)

He also notes that friendship fosters empathy with others and often requires frame shifting that is effective in reducing prejudice, which is correlated with authoritarianism and social dominance. Finally, he underlines the importance of reducing anxiety, the "threat and uncertainty that people experience in intergroup contexts" (p. 190).

In addition to recognizing that empathy and reduced anxiety enhance prejudice reduction, we also know that positive contact requires more than being in the pres-ence of cultural difference. It must also foster engagement with that difference (D. A. Williams et al., 2005). Facilitated contact—through mentoring, coaching, train-ing, transformative learning, or reflection—often develops more intercultural compe-tence than autonomous, unguided contact (Paige, 2008; Vande Berg, 2007a, 2007b).

Thus, training is one approach, although not the only one, for developing inter-cultural skills. Exercises and methods for training and education are enumerated in handbooks designed for both global and domestic contexts (J. M. Bennett, 2003, 2008; Boyacigiller, Goodman, & Phillips, 2003; Fowler & Mumford, 1995, 1999; Gardenswartz & Rowe, 1998; Lambert, Myers, & Simons, 2000; Osland, Kolb, Rubin, & Turner, 2007; Paige et al., 2002; Saphiere, 2007; Saphiere et al., 2005; Singelis, 1998; Storti & Bennhold-Samaan, 1997; Stringer & Cassiday, 2003; Thiagarajan, 2000; Wurzel, 2005).

Anthropologists, such as Spradley (1979, 1980), can also support skill building, since they offer their well-honed disciplinary perspective on interviewing across cultures and participant observation. To satisfy curiosity, some individuals may ask questions directly, while some cultures clearly prefer the more indirect learning acquired through participant observation. Although gathering information across cultures is an essential component of intercultural competence, asking questions is not. Therefore, using credible cultural mentors can also facilitate skill building (Osland & Bird, 2000). Such bicultural, bilingual individuals may graciously offer to decode their culture for outsiders, expecting only in return that the newcomers move with equal graciousness through their communities.

Strategies for developing skills of empathy (M. J. Bennett, 1998) and resolving conflict (Hammer, 2003) are readily available in the intercultural communication and psychology literature. Each requires cognitive flexibility, the capacity to shift frames of reference, as discussed earlier. A quick three-step analysis from multiple perspectives can be used to empathically assess the mutual negative evaluation of any particular pattern, the benefits of using that pattern, and adaptive strategies for working effectively with it. This analysis offers skills practice in cognitive flexibility, empathy, listening, and, potentially, managing interactions.

Step 1. Using the thinking styles map discussed earlier in this chapter as an example, we can empathize with the perspective of others and reflect on how someone from a different culture might feel about the style of being analytically logical, abstract, objective, dialectic, and doubting. Someone not accustomed to that style might find it cold, argumentative, simplistic, critical, and downright unpleasant. In turn, the logical partner in the interaction might find the style of being holistic, metaphorical, subjective, integrative, and believing to be naive, uncritical, incoherent, illogical, and downright confusing.

Step 2. The second step involves describing the strengths of each style. We might note that one style is particularly good for creating policies, procedures, and legal contexts, while the other may be more successful with human resources management and leadership.

Step 3. The third step—perhaps the most difficult—designs adaptive processes, overtly building on the strengths of each style. For instance, this might include designing the style of meetings to take into account multiple voices or deliberately reviewing reports for diverse perspectives and, of course, eventually being able to generate those multiple perspectives individually.

If being an interculturalist is a lifetime developmental opportunity, then using the intercultural positioning system is but one of many ways we can enhance our competence. If our efforts are consistently intentional, developmental, and inclusive, we will begin to acquire the necessary knowledge, attitudes, and skills to make a small claim on intercultural competence, with a great deal of cultural humility.

Conclusion

If intercultural competence is to achieve its potential, intercultural positioning systems must become part of our daily lives. With this perspective, such a calibration holds the possibility that we can "cultivate the factual and imaginative prerequisites for recognizing humanity in the stranger and the other. . . . Ignorance and distance cramp the consciousness" (Nussbaum, 1996, p. 133). We know that contact is useful, but perhaps not useful enough if we are not transformed in important ways by our experience. And we know that to achieve that transformation, we have to intentionally and proactively seek opportunities to use our intercultural positioning system and to expose ourselves to otherness. The deeply respected former U.S. ambassador to Japan, Edwin O. Reischauer (1986), offers us a powerful goal for doing so:

We had acquired the habit of looking at things two different ways—from the Japanese angle of vision as well as from our own national viewpoint. This proved to be the key to my career and, extended worldwide, is the only hope I can see for world peace and human survival. (pp. xi–xii)

References

Adler, N. J., & Gundersen, A. (2007). *International dimensions of organizational behavior* (5th ed.). Cincinnati, OH: South-Western.

American Hospitality Academy International Hotel Management Schools. (2007). *Understanding culture: Developing tomorrow's global hospitality leaders today!* Hilton Head Island, SC: Author.

Beckham, E. (2005). Intercultural learning for inclusive excellence. *Diversity Digest, 9*(2), 1, 6.

Belenky, M. F., Clinchy, B. M., Goldberger, N. R., & Tarule, J. M. (1996). *Woman's ways of knowing: The development of self, voice, and mind* (10th ed.). New York: Basic Books (HarperCollins).

Bennett, J. M. (2003). Turning frogs into interculturalists: A student-centered development approach to teaching intercultural competence. In N. A. Boyacigiller, R. A. Goodman, & M. E. Phillips (Eds.), *Crossing cultures: Insights from master teachers* (pp. 157–170). New York: Taylor & Francis.

Bennett, J. M. (2008). Transformative training: Designing programs for culture learning. In M. A. Moodian (Ed.), *Contemporary leadership and intercultural competence: Understanding and utilizing cultural diversity to build successful organizations* (pp. 95–110). Thousand Oaks, CA: Sage.

Bennett, J. M., & Bennett, M. J. (2004). Developing intercultural sensitivity: An integrative approach to global and domestic diversity. In D. Landis, J. M. Bennett, & M. J. Bennett (Eds.), *Handbook of intercultural training* (3rd ed., pp. 147–165). Thousand Oaks, CA: Sage.

Bennett, M. J. (1998). Overcoming the golden rule: Sympathy and empathy. In M. J. Bennett (Ed.), *Basic concepts of intercultural communication: Selected readings* (pp. 191–214). Yarmouth, ME: Intercultural Press.

Bird, A., & Osland, J. S. (2004). Global competencies: An introduction. In H. W. Lane, M. L. Maznevski, M. E. Mendenhall, & J. McNett (Eds.), *The Blackwell handbook of global management: A guide to managing complexity* (pp. 57–80). Malden, MA: Blackwell.

Black, J. S., & Gregersen, H. B. (1999, March/April). The right way to manage expatriates. *Harvard Business Review,* pp. 52–62.

Boyacigiller, N., Beechler, S., Taylor, S., & Levy, O. (2004). The crucial yet illusive global mindset. In H. W. Lane, M. L. Maznevski, M. E. Mendenhall, & J. McNett (Eds.), *The Blackwell handbook of global management: A guide to managing complexity* (pp. 81–93). Malden, MA: Blackwell.

Boyacigiller, N. A., Goodman, R. A., & Phillips, M. E. (Eds.). (2003). *Crossing cultures: Insights from master teachers.* New York: Taylor & Francis.

Brake, T., & Walker, D. (1995). *Doing business internationally: The workbook for cross-cultural success.* Princeton, NJ: Princeton Training Press.

Chang, W. W. (2007, May). Cultural competence of international humanitarian workers. *Adult Education Quarterly, 57*(3), 187–204.

Chhokar, J. S., Brodbeck, F. C., & House, R. J. (Eds.). (2007). *Culture and leadership across the world: The GLOBE book of in-depth studies of 25 societies.* Mahwah, NJ: Lawrence Erlbaum.

Chicago Jobs Council. (2004). *Ready? set. grow! A starter's guide for becoming culturally competent: Cultural competency and employment initiative.* Retrieved October 29, 2008, from http://www.cjc.net/publications/5_Capacity_Building_PDFs/ReadySetGrow_Starter Guide_CultComp.pdf

Collier, M. J. (1989). Cultural and intercultural communication competence: Current approaches and directions for future research. *International Journal of Intercultural Relations, 13,* 287–302.

Cornwell, G. H., & Stoddard, E. W. (1999). *Globalizing knowledge: Connecting international and intercultural studies.* Washington, DC: Association of American Colleges and Universities.

Cox, T. (1994). *Cultural diversity in organizations: Theory, research and practice.* San Francisco: Berrett-Koehler.

Cross, T. L. (1989). *Towards a culturally competent system of care: A monograph on effective services for minority children who are severely emotionally disturbed.* Washington, DC: Georgetown University Press.

Cross, W. E., Jr. (1978). The Thomas and Cross models of psychological nigrescence: A review. *Journal of Black Psychology, 5*(1), 13–31.

Deardorff, D. K. (2005). A matter of logic? *International Educator, 14*(3), 26–31.

Deardorff, D. K. (2006). Identification and assessment of intercultural competence as a student outcome of internationalization. *Journal of Studies in International Education, 10*(3), 241–266.

Description, interpretation, and evaluation. (n.d.). Retrieved August 24, 2007, from http://www.intercultural.org/documents/resources/die.doc/

Dinges, N. (1983). Intercultural competence. In D. Landis & R. Brislin (Eds.), *Handbook of intercultural relations: Vol. 1. Theory and practice* (pp. 176–202). Elmsford, NY: Pergamon.

Dinges, N. G., & Baldwin, K D. (1996). Intercultural competence: A research perspective. In D. Landis & R. S. Bhagat (Eds.), *Handbook of intercultural training* (2nd ed., pp. 106–123). Thousand Oaks, CA: Sage.

Dunn, R., & Griggs, S. (1988). *Learning styles: Quiet revolution in American secondary schools.* Reston, VA: National Association of Secondary School Principals.

Dunn, R., & Griggs, S. (1990). Research on the learning style characteristics of selected racial and ethnic groups. *Reading, Writing, and Learning Disabilities, 6,* 261–280.

Earley, P. C., & Ang, S. (2003). *Cultural intelligence: Individual interactions across cultures.* Stanford, CA: Stanford University Press.

Edmundson, A. (2007). *Globalized e-learning cultural challenges.* Hershey, PA: Information Science Publishing (an imprint of Idea Group Inc.).

Elbow, P. (1973). *Writing without teachers.* New York: Oxford University Press.

Elliott, C., Adams, J. R., & Sockalingam, S. (1999). *Toolkit for cross-cultural collaboration.* Retrieved October 30, 2008, from http://www.awesomelibrary.org/multiculturaltoolkit.html

Evans, N. J., Forney, D. S., & Guido-DiBrito, F. (1998). Gay, lesbian, and bisexual identity development. *Student development in college: Theory, research, and practice* (pp. 89–106). San Francisco: Jossey-Bass.

Fowler, S. M., & Mumford, M. G. (Eds.). (1995). *Intercultural sourcebook: Cross-cultural training methods* (Vol. 1). Yarmouth, ME: Intercultural Press.

Fowler, S. M., & Mumford, M. G. (Eds.). (1999). *Intercultural sourcebook: Cross-cultural training methods* (Vol. 2). Yarmouth, ME: Intercultural Press.

Gardenswartz, L., & Rowe, A. (1998). *Managing diversity: A complete desk reference and planning guide* (Rev. ed.). New York: McGraw-Hill.

Gardenswartz, L., Rowe, A., Digh, P., & Bennett, M. (2003). *The global diversity desk reference: Managing an international workforce.* San Francisco: Jossey-Bass.

Gelfand, M. J., Erez, M., & Aycan, Z. (2007). Cross-cultural organizational behavior. *Annual Review of Psychology, 58,* 479–514.

Graf, A. (2004). Screening and training inter-cultural competencies: Evaluating the impact of national culture on inter-cultural competencies. *International Journal of Human Resource Management, 15,* 1124–1148.

Green, M. (1988). *The dialectic of freedom.* New York: Teachers College Press.

Gregersen, J. B., Morrison, A., & Black, J. S. (1998). Developing leaders for the global frontier. *Sloan Management Review, 40*(1), 21–33.

Gudykunst, W. B., & Ting-Toomey, S. (1988). *Culture and interpersonal communication.* Newbury Park, CA: Sage.

Gundling, E., & Zanchettin, A. (2006). *Global diversity: Winning customers and engaging employees in world markets.* Boston: Nicholas Brealey.

Gurin, P., Dey, E. L., Hurtado, S., & Gurin, G. (2002). Diversity and higher education: Theory and impact on educational outcomes. *Harvard Educational Review, 72,* 330–366.

Guskin, A. (1991). Cultural humility: A way of being in the world. *Antioch Notes, 59*(1).

Hammer, M. R. (1989). Intercultural communication competence. In M. K. Asante & W. B. Gudykunst (Eds.), *Handbook of international and intercultural communication* (pp. 247–260). Newbury Park, CA: Sage.

Hammer, M. R. (2003). *ICS interpretive guide.* Ocean Pines, MD: Hammer Consulting.

Hayashi, K., & Jolley, G. (2002). Two thoughts on analog and digital language. *Aoyama Journal of International Politics, Economics and Business, 58,* 179–196.

Hayles, R. V., & Mendez Russell, A. (1997). *The diversity directive: Why some initiatives fail and what to do about it.* Chicago: Irwin.

Helms, J. E. (1984). Toward a theoretical explanation of the effects of race on counseling: A Black and White model. *The Counseling Psychologist, 12,* 153–165.

Hofstede, G. (2001). *Culture's consequences: Comparing values, behaviors, institutions, and organizations across nations* (2nd ed.). Thousand Oaks, CA: Sage.

House, R. J., Hanges, P. J., Javidan M., Dorfman, P. W., & Gupta, V. (Eds.). (2004). *Culture, leadership, and organizations: The GLOBE study of 62 societies.* Thousand Oaks, CA: Sage.

Hovland, K. (2006). *Shared futures: Global learning and liberal education.* Washington, DC: Association of American Colleges and Universities.

Hunter, B., White, G. P., & Godbey, G. C. (2006). What does it mean to be globally competent? *Journal of Studies in International Education, 10,* 267–285.

IQ Solutions, Inc. (2001, March). *National standards for culturally and linguistically appropriate services in health care: Final report.* Retrieved September 29, 2008, from http://www.omhrc.gov/assets/pdf/checked/finalreport.pdf

Irvine, J. J., & York, D. E. (1995). Learning styles and culturally diverse students: A literature review. In J. A. Banks & C. A. M. Banks (Eds.), *Handbook of research on multicultural education* (pp. 484–497). New York: Macmillan.

Jokinen, T. (2005). Global leadership competencies: A review and discussion. *Journal of European Industrial Training, 29*(3), 199–216.

Jonassen, D. H., & Grabowski, B. L. (1993). *Handbook of individual differences, learning, and instruction.* Hillsdale, NJ: Lawrence Erlbaum.

Judy, R. W., & D'Amico, C. (1997). *Workforce 2020: Work and workers in the 21st century.* Indianapolis, IN: Hudson Institute.

Kim, M. (1998). Conversational constraints as a tool for understanding communication styles. In T. M. Singelis (Ed.), *Teaching about culture, ethnicity, and diversity* (pp. 101–109). Thousand Oaks, CA: Sage.

Kim, Y. Y. (1991). Intercultural communication competence: A systems-theoretic view. In S. Ting-Toomey & F. Korzenny (Eds.), *International and intercultural communication annual: Vol. 15. Cross-cultural interpersonal communication* (pp. 230–275). Newbury Park, CA: Sage.

King, P. M., & Baxter Magolda, M. B. (2005). A developmental model of intercultural maturity. *Journal of College Student Development, 46,* 571–592.

Knapp, M. L., & Hall, J. A. (2005). *Nonverbal communication in human interaction* (6th ed.). Belmont, CA: Wadsworth.

Knefelkamp, L., & Schneider, C. G. (1997). Education for a world lived in common with others. In R. Orrill (Ed.), *Education and democracy: Re-imagining liberal learning in America* (pp. 327–346). New York: The College Board.

Kolb, D. A. (1984). *Experiential learning: Experience as the source of learning and development.* Englewood Cliffs, NJ: Prentice Hall.

Lambert, J., Myers, S., & Simons, G. (Eds.). (2000). *Global competence: 50 training activities for succeeding in international business.* Amherst, MA: HRD Press.

Lane, H. W., DiStefano, J. J., & Maznevski, M. L. (2000). *International management behavior: Text, readings and cases* (4th ed.). Malden, MA: Blackwell Business.

Lewin Group. (2001, September). *Health resources and services administration study on measuring cultural competence in health care delivery settings: A review of the literature.* Retrieved September 29, 2008, from http://www.hrsa.gov/culturalcompetence/measures/default.htm

Meacham, J., & Gaff, J. G. (2006). Learning goals in mission statements. *Liberal Education, 92*(1), 6–13.

Mendenhall, M. E. (2001). Introduction: New perspectives on expatriate adjustment and its relationship to global leadership development. In M. E. Mendenhall, T. M. Kuhlmann, & G. K. Stahl (Eds.), *Developing global business leaders: Policies, processes, and innovations* (pp. 1–18). Westport, CT: Greenwood.

Mendenhall, M. E., Kuhlmann, T. M., & Stahl, G. K. (Eds.). (2001). *Developing global business leaders: Policies, processes, and innovations.* Westport, CT: Greenwood.

Mendenhall, M. E., & Oddou, G. R. (1986, Winter). Acculturation profiles of expatriate managers: Implications for cross-cultural training programs. *Columbia Journal of World Business,* pp. 73–79.

Mendenhall, M. E., Stahl, G. K., Ehnert, I., Oddou, G., Osland, J. S., & Kühlmann, T. M. (2004). Evaluation studies of cross-cultural training programs: A review of literature from 1988 to 2000. In D. Landis, J. M. Bennett, & M. J. Bennett (Eds.), *Handbook of intercultural training* (3rd ed., pp. 129–144). Thousand Oaks, CA: Sage.

Milem, J. F., Chang, M. J., & Antonio, A. L. (2005). *Making diversity work on campus: A research-based perspective.* Washington, DC: Association of American Colleges and Universities.

Musil, C. M. (2006). *Assessing global learning: Matching good intentions with good practice.* Washington, DC: Association of American Colleges and Universities.

Nisbett, R. E. (2003). *The geography of thought: How Asians and westerners think differently . . . and why.* New York: Free Press.

Nussbaum, M. C. (1996). *For love of country? Debating the limits of patriotism.* Boston: Beacon.

O'Mara, J., & Richter, A. (2006). *Global diversity and inclusion benchmarks.* Retrieved January 4, 2008, from www.diversityresources.com/rc42e/GDIBenchmarksOct06.pdf

Opdal, P. M. (2001). Curiosity, wonder and education seen as perspective. *Studies in Philosophy and Education, 20,* 331–344.

Osland, J. S., & Bird, A. (2000). Beyond sophisticated stereotyping: Cultural sensemaking in context. *Academy of Management Executive, 14,* 65–79.

Osland, J. S., Bird, A., & Gundersen, A. (2007, August). *Trigger events in intercultural sensemaking.* Paper presented at the meeting of the Academy of Management, Philadelphia.

Osland, J. S., Bird, A., Mendenhall, M., & Osland, A. (2006). Developing global leadership capabilities and global mindset. In G. Stahl & I. Bjorkman (Eds.), *Handbook of international human resource management research* (pp. 197–222). London: Elgar.

Osland, J. S., Kolb, D. A., Rubin, I. M., & Turner, M. E. (2007). *Organizational behavior: An experiential approach* (8th ed.). Englewood Cliffs, NJ: Prentice Hall.

Oxford, R. L., & Anderson, N. J. (1995). A crosscultural view of learning styles. *Language Teaching, 28,* 201–215.

Paige, R. M. (Ed.). (1993). *Education for the intercultural experience* (2nd ed., pp. 109–135). Yarmouth, ME: Intercultural Press.

Paige, R. M. (2008, October 3–4). *Using the IDI to guide personal and organizational development: Challenges and opportunities* (PowerPoint). Presented at the first annual Intercultural Development Inventory Conference, Minneapolis, MN.

Paige, R. M., Cohen, A. D., Kappler, B., Chi, J. C., & Lassegard, J. P. (2002). *Maximizing study abroad: A students' guide to strategies for language and culture learning and use.* Minneapolis: University of Minnesota Press.

Parham, T. A. (1989). Cycles of psychological nigrescence. *The Counseling Psychologist, 17*(2), 187–226.

Peterson, B. (2004). *Cultural intelligence: A guide to working with people from other cultures.* Yarmouth, ME: Intercultural Press.

Pettigrew, T. F. (2008). Future directions for intergroup contact theory and research. *International Journal of Intercultural Relations, 32*(3), 182–199.

Pettigrew, T. F., & Tropp, L. R. (2000). Does intergroup contact reduce prejudice? Recent meta-analytic findings. In S. Oskamp (Ed.), *Reducing prejudice and discrimination* (pp. 93–114). Mahwah, NJ: Lawrence Erlbaum.

Phinney, J. S. (1991). Ethnic identity and self-esteem: A review and integration. *Hispanic Journal of Behavioral Sciences, 13*(2), 193–208.

Reischauer, E. O. (1986). *My life between Japan and America.* New York: Harper & Row.

Riding, R., & Rayner, S. (Eds.). (2000). *Cognitive styles and learning strategies: Understanding style differences in learning and behavior.* London: David Fulton.

Sabnani, H. B., Ponterotto, J. G., & Borodovsky, L. G. (1991). White racial identity development and cross-cultural counselor training: A stage model. *The Counseling Psychologist, 19*(1), 76–102.

Sanford, N. (1966). *Self and society: Social change and individual development.* New York: Atherton.

Saphiere, D. H. (2007). *The Cultural Detective®.* http://www.culturaldetective.com

Saphiere, D. H., Mikk, B. K., & Devries, B. I. (2005). *Communication highwire: Leveraging the power of diverse communication styles.* Yarmouth, ME: Intercultural Press.

Schaetti, B. F. (2000, November). Global nomad identity: Hypothesizing a developmental model (Doctoral dissertation, The Union Institute, 2000). *Dissertation Abstracts, 6110*(A), 9992721.

Sergeant, C. (1973). *U.S. Navy overseas diplomacy guidelines for I. C. R. specialists.* Washington, DC: Bureau of Naval Personnel.

Singelis, T. M. (Ed.). (1998). *Teaching about culture, ethnicity, and diversity: Exercises and planned activities.* Thousand Oaks, CA: Sage.

Spitzberg, B. H. (1989). Theoretical issues: Issues in the development of a theory of interpersonal competence in the intercultural context. *International Journal of Intercultural Relations, 13,* 241–268.

Spitzberg, B. H. (1994). A model of intercultural communication competence. In L. A. Samovar & R. E. Porter (Eds.), *Intercultural communication: A reader* (7th ed., pp. 347–359). Belmont, CA: Wadsworth.

Spradley, J. P. (1979). *Ethnographic interview.* New York: Holt, Rinehart & Winston.

Spradley, J. P. (1980). *Participation observation.* New York: Holt, Rinehart & Winston.

Stoddard, E. W., & Cornwell, G. H. (2003). Peripheral visions: Toward a geoethics of citizenship. *Liberal Education.* Retrieved January 29, 2008, from http://www.aacu.org/liberaleducation/le-su03/le-su3fperspective.cfm

Storti, C., & Bennhold-Samaan, L. (1997). *Culture matters: The Peace Corps cross-cultural workbook.* Washington, DC: Peace Corps Information Collection and Exchange.

Stringer, D. M., & Cassiday, P. A. (2003). *52 activities for exploring values differences.* Yarmouth, ME: Intercultural Press.

Sue, D. W. (2007). *Counseling the culturally diverse: Theory and practice* (5th ed.). Hoboken, NJ: John Wiley.

Sue, D. W., Arredondo, P., & McDavis, R. J. (1992). Multicultural counseling competencies. *Journal of Multicultural Counseling & Development, 20*(2), 64–88.

Tannen, D. (1994). *Talking from 9 to 5: How women's and men's conversational styles affect who gets heard, who gets credit, and what gets done at work.* New York: William Morrow.

Thiagarajan, S. (2000). *Facilitator's toolkit.* Bloomington, IN: Workshops by Thiagi.

Thomas, D. C., & Inkson, K. (2004). *Cultural intelligence: People skills for global business.* San Francisco: Berrett-Koehler.

Ting-Toomey, S. (1999). *Communicating across cultures.* New York: Guilford.

Ting-Toomey, S., & Oetzel, J. G. (2001). *Managing intercultural conflict effectively.* Thousand Oaks, CA: Sage.

Trompenaars, F., & Hampden-Turner, C. (1997). *Riding the waves of culture: Understanding cultural diversity in business* (2nd ed.). Naperville, IL: Intercultural Management Publishers NV/Nicholas Brealey.

Vande Berg, M. (2007a, February). *It's not all about the numbers: Maximizing student learning abroad.* Paper presented at the meeting of the Association of International Education Administrators, Washington, DC.

Vande Berg, M. (2007b, July). *Intervening in student learning: The Georgetown consortium study.* Paper presented at the Summer Institute for Intercultural Communication, Portland, OR.

Vulpe, T., Kealey, D., Protheroe, D., & MacDonald, D. (2001). *A profile of the interculturally effective person* (2nd ed.). Quebec: Canadian Department of Foreign Affairs and International Trade, Centre for Intercultural Learning.

Wentling, R. M., & Palma-Rivas, N. (2000). Current status of diversity initiatives in selected multinational corporations. *Human Resource Development Quarterly, 11*(1), 35–60.

Williams, B. (2001). Accomplishing cross-cultural competence in youth development programs. *Journal of Extension, 39*(6). Retrieved October 30, 2008, from http://www.joe.org/joe/2001december/iw1.html

Williams, D. A., Berger, J. B., & McClendon, S. A. (2005). *Toward a model of inclusive excellence and change in postsecondary institutions.* Washington, DC: Association of American Colleges and Universities.

Wurzel, J. S. (2005). *Building community in the classroom: An intercultural approach.* Newton, MA: Intercultural Resource Corporation.

Yamashita, M. (2007). *Integrating East Asian international students into U.S. classrooms: An investigation of challenges and opportunities.* Presentation at doctoral dissertation meeting, School of Education, Portland State University, Portland, OR.

Yershova, Y., DeJaeghere, J., & Mestenhauser, J. (2000). Thinking not as usual: Adding the intercultural perspective. *Journal of Studies in International Education, 4*(1), 39–78.

CHAPTER 7

Developing Globally Competent Citizens

The Contrasting Cases of the United States and Vietnam

Mark A. Ashwill and Dương Thị Hoàng Oanh

Given our interdependence, any world order that elevates one nation or group of people over another will inevitably fail. So whatever we think of the past, we must not be prisoners to it.

President Barack Obama, Cairo, Egypt, 2009

The aim of this chapter is to consider global citizenship and intercultural competence, widely debated and often overlapping concepts, against the backdrop of nationalism and patriotism, "isms" that are rarely discussed in the same context. Yet they are the proverbial elephant in the room, towering issues that profoundly influence the methods and means by which global citizenship and intercultural competence are transformed from theory to practice.

This chapter explores ways in which global citizenship and intercultural competence complement and conflict with the national identity of two diametrically contrasting cultures—the United States of America and the Socialist Republic of Vietnam. What U.S. Americans and Vietnamese share, according to anecdotal evidence, the binational experience of both authors, and the results of World Values Surveys, is a deep national pride. Yet as we shall see, this national pride is radically different qualitatively for reasons that are rooted in history. Thus, we examine barriers in both cultures that may inhibit the development of globally competent citizens, as well as factors that may smooth the way.

What are the implications of global citizenship in an interconnected world in which nationalism is still very much a force to be reckoned with? To what extent is global citizenship problematic in countries in which nationalism in its more virulent incarnation forms the mind-set of the majority of citizens? We posit that the path to becoming a global or globally competent citizen may be strewn with more obstacles in some societies than in others as a result of potent historical and cultural forces that have shaped national identity and the dominant ideology, the psychic glue that holds societies together.

In this chapter, we review the concepts of global citizenship and intercultural competence, followed by a discussion of nationalism and patriotism in a U.S. and Vietnamese context. We illustrate some of the challenges associated with educating and training young people to become globally competent citizens in countries in which nationalism, as opposed to patriotism, is the dominant worldview, or ideology. Finally, we conclude with a look at the implications of global citizenship education in contrasting countries in which people hold very different views of their country and its place in the world.

Global Citizenship

Global citizenship is an orientation that universalizes the classical notion of citizenship, which entails certain rights and responsibilities and allegiance to a sovereign state. Rather than pledging allegiance to one nation-state, however, the global citizen's intellectual landscape and sense of connectedness and belonging extend to all of humanity. In this new reality, "national interests" are not paramount but rather subjugated to and measured against the interests of fellow human beings in other countries. The logically consistent global citizen supports or rejects national interests on the basis of the extent to which they complement or are damaging to those of other peoples.

Global citizenship is not just a static mind-set but a dynamic worldview imbued with a sense of commitment to issues of social and economic justice at the local, national, and international levels. In a January 2008 speech to the leadership of NAFSA: Association of International Educators, Everett Egginton (New Mexico State University) emphasized the need to prepare citizen diplomats to contribute to a more peaceful, just, and equitable world. In referring to the role that institutions of higher education around the world should play in making this a reality, he spoke of

> preparing and ensuring that their graduates know about the world in which they live, possess attitudes about others around the world that reflect appreciation of and respect for diversity, and master the skills needed both to compete and thrive in the world and to improve the quality of life worldwide. (New Mexico State University, 2008)

Citizen diplomats are equipped with the worldview and knowledge to reflect objectively and critically upon their country's strengths and shortcomings, along with its place in the world.

Intercultural Competence

Intercultural competence is generally viewed as a skill set that enables someone to function effectively in a cross-cultural setting. In a 2003 RAND Corporation report, *New Challenges for International Leadership: Lessons From Organizations With Global Missions,* the authors define cross-cultural competence simply as the ability to work well in different cultures and with people of different origins. Intercultural competence is a multifaceted state of being—which includes knowing that there are cultural differences, what they are, and how to apply that knowledge (Bikson, Treverton, Moini, & Lindstrom, 2003). Simply put, it is the ability to adapt to different cultural settings, the essence of being bicultural.

Sandra L. Russo and Leigh Ann Osborne (2008) define a globally competent student as someone who is a global citizen with some level of intercultural competence: (a) has a diverse and knowledgeable worldview, (b) comprehends international dimensions of his or her major field of study, (c) communicates effectively in another language and/or cross-culturally, (d) exhibits cross-cultural sensitivity and adaptability, and (e) carries global competencies throughout life.

In *Cultures and Organizations: Software of the Mind,* Geert Hofstede describes the three phases leading to intercultural competence—awareness, knowledge, and skills—in the following sequence:

Awareness is where it all starts. The recognition that a person carries a particular mental software because of the way that person was brought up, and that others brought up in a different environment carry a different mental software. "Without awareness, one may travel around the world feeling superior and remaining deaf and blind to all clues about the relativity of one's own mental programming. With awareness, one may become a bit like James Morier, [who was]: ' . . . gifted with a humorous sympathy that enabled him to appreciate the motives actuating persons entirely dissimilar to himself.'"

Knowledge should follow. "If we have to interact with particular other cultures, we have to learn about those cultures. We should learn about their symbols, their heroes, and their rituals; while we may never share their values, we may at least obtain an intellectual grasp of where their values differ from ours."

Skills are based on awareness and knowledge, plus practice. "We have to recognize and apply the symbols of the other culture, recognize their heroes, practice their rituals, and experience the satisfaction of getting along in the new environment, being able to resolve first the simpler, and later on some of the more complicated, problems of life among the others." (Hofstede & Hofstede, 2004, pp. 358–359)

Logically, the development of intercultural competence is accompanied by the universal values of the global citizen, who is both committed and prepared to helping build a more peaceful, just, and equitable world. Yet it is possible to decouple the two concepts. That is to say, one could conceivably become interculturally competent and place those skills at the service of a particular company or government whose interests, policies, and actions may diverge from or even conflict with those of the global community. Developing cultural awareness, acquiring cultural knowledge, and gaining and honing intercultural skills do not automatically assume a commitment to a more peaceful, just, and equitable world.

Educators must strive to create a fusion approach that unites both global citizenship and intercultural competence. As we shall see, learners in countries such as Vietnam and the United States have distinct education and training needs as they relate to the development of globally competent citizens. This is the result of history, national values, and the prevailing view of one's country and its relationship to others and its place in the world.

Nationalism and Patriotism: Similar yet Different

While all peoples are inherently ethnocentric, the extent of this ethnocentrism and the manner in which it is linked to nationalism—as distinct from patriotism—depend on each country's unique history and ideology. It is beyond the scope of this chapter to do justice to this complex and important topic, but we will touch on several key issues that are relevant to the cultivation of globally competent citizens. To use Hofstede and Hofstede's (2004) metaphor, U.S. Americans and Vietnamese each carry "a particular mental software because of the way that person was brought up, and that others brought up in a different environment carry a different mental software." As we shall see, the mental software of the former is perhaps more resistant to modification and less malleable than that of the latter.

In his developmental model of intercultural sensitivity (DMIS), Milton J. Bennett (1993) asserts that all of us are on a continuum of "increasing sophistication in dealing with cultural difference," ranging from ethnocentrism, which assumes that our worldview of our own culture is universal and synonymous with human nature, to a growing recognition and acceptance of difference, known as ethnorelativism. This continuum applies to individuals and nations with equal validity.

According to a standard dictionary definition, the distinction between patriotism and nationalism is clear. Patriotism is defined simply as "love for or devotion to one's country." This is generally thought of as a benign, sentimental, and inward-looking form of national pride. As such, it does not exclude an openness to and even embrace of other cultures, their values, and the concerns and needs of their members.

In a 2003 essay titled *A Kinder, Gentler Patriotism*, U.S. historian Howard Zinn speaks of the need to redefine patriotism and notes that "if national boundaries should not be obstacles to trade—we call it globalization—should they also not be obstacles to compassion and generosity? Should we not begin to consider all children, everywhere, as our own? In that case, war, which in our time is always an assault on children, would be unacceptable as a solution to the problems of the world. Human ingenuity would have to search for other ways." Patriotism, as defined above, does not preclude the globalization of compassion and generosity.

In contrast, nationalism is described as loyalty and devotion to a nation; especially *a sense of national consciousness exalting one nation above all others and placing primary emphasis on promotion of its culture and interests as opposed to those of other nations or supranational groups.* It is the second italicized part that distinguishes nationalism from its less strident and bellicose cousin, patriotism. Exaltation of one nation over another automatically assumes a degree of cultural superiority, a lack of openness and objectivity, and the assumption that "others" wish to be like us and, by extension, the desire to mold them in our image.

The following sections discuss how nationalism and patriotism are manifested in both the United States and Vietnam and how these two concepts contribute to or inhibit the development of interculturally competent global citizens.

U.S. Nationalism

While many U.S. Americans are patriotic in the way in which we have defined it, others possess a strong nationalistic bent as borne out in periodic surveys and opinion polls. According to the World Values Survey, which attempts to measure this phenomenon, 72% of adult Americans stated that they were proud of their country in 1999. By contrast, the figures for two of the United States' peer countries, Britain and France, were 53% and 35%, respectively (http://www.worldvaluessurvey.org, 1999).

More to the point, a Pew Research Center survey in 2003 revealed that 6 in 10 Americans believe that "our culture is superior to others" compared—in defiance of the stereotype in the United States—to only 3 in 10 French people. In their study "National Pride: A Cross-National Analysis", Tom W. Smith and Lars Jarkko measured national pride in 23 countries and found that the United States ranked number one (Smith & Jarkko, 1998).

Along the lines of wishing "others" to be more like "us" or believing that they desire the same, U.S. Americans generally consider their values to be universally applicable. According to a 2001 Pew Global Attitudes survey, 79% agreed that "it's good that American ideas and customs are spreading around the world." Unlike most countries, the United States is based on a set of shared ideals. This allows national pride to be not only particularistic, but also universal. In the United States. one can stand for both the country and more general principles (Smith & Jarkko, 1998).

Proud to Be an American?

One coauthor once taught a general education course to undergraduates at a large state university that focused on five key and intersecting areas of American experience and culture: race, gender, ethnicity, social class, and religious sectarianism. Another important curricular goal was developing an understanding of America's evolving relationship with the rest of the world.

He began one class by projecting an image of a popular U.S. bumper sticker, "Proud to be an American," on the screen as an introduction to an optional Cultural Partners program created for those students interested in further exploring the course's main themes from a cross-cultural perspective.[1] After giving the students a moment to reflect, he asked *if they were proud;* if yes, *what they were proud of* and *why.* Many of the responses he received, the vast majority of which were positive, included references to being the "best of the best," "the greatest country in the world," "America's superpower status," and "endless opportunity." These answers were offered up as unchallengeable and commonsensical assumptions—in effect, eternal truths.

As he began to probe deeper and ask for specific examples to support their general answers (the best in what respect, endless opportunity for whom, great in which ways?), it was apparent that, as with many U.S. Americans, they lacked sufficient knowledge of other societies, not to mention their own, to support their generalities.

Other responses reflected students' social class or racial bias. In sum, it was clear that the students' answers were rooted in a cultural mythology infused with a deep-seated sense of cultural superiority and an inability to critically reflect on their own society—for better and for worse. A significant percentage of U.S. Americans are ignorant not only about the rest of the world and their country's role in it but also about their own history, literature, socioeconomic trends, political institutions, and so on.

The United States and the World

U.S. Americans' reputation for lack of knowledge and disinterest in the rest of the world is well documented. Evidence of this ignorance periodically appears in the results of surveys such as those conducted by the Pew Research Center and the National Geographic Society. According to a 2006 report released by the latter, 63% of U.S. Americans ages 18 to 24 failed to correctly locate Iraq on a map of the Middle East, and 70% could not find Iran or Israel.

Here are some more results that support the understatement made by David Rutherford (2006), a specialist in geography education at the Society in Washington, D.C.:

Young Americans just don't seem to have much interest in the world outside of the United States.

Nine in 10 couldn't find Afghanistan on a map of Asia.

Fifty-four percent were unaware that Sudan is a country in Africa.

Three quarters of respondents failed to find Indonesia on a map (after the December 2004 tsunami and resulting international coverage).

Three quarters were unaware that a majority of Indonesia's population is Muslim, making it the largest Muslim country in the world.

This widespread ignorance not only represents a challenge in the quest to create globally competent citizens but has other implications in how U.S. Americans carry out their responsibilities as citizens of a democratic political system. As Mark Hertsgaard (2003) points out in *The Eagle's Shadow: Why America Fascinates and Infuriates the World*, "The embarrassing truth is that most of us know little about the outside world, and we are particularly ill-informed about what our government is doing in our name overseas" (p. 69).

One U.S. American student, who reflected upon her journey from small-town Texas to her university to London, had this to say about her perceptions of the United States, shared by many of her fellow students and citizens: "I learned to believe that America holds a global monopoly on wealth, freedom, and knowledge—so, naturally, other cultures should be more like us. Needless to say, it was a rather large step for a hick girl from Henrietta to go first to TCU in 'the big city' of Fort Worth and then to proclaim, 'I'm going to study abroad in London'" (Klein, 2001).

She added that "being away from Texas gave me a chance to be a voyeur on our own idiosyncrasies. London taught me the meaning of being an American citizen. But, as a woman who discovered strength and independence in London, I also am a citizen of the world. I refuse to be a traitor to either heritage" (Klein, 2001). This refusal "to be a traitor to either heritage" is a story of intellectual liberation and an example of one individual overcoming the solipsism that holds sway over so many U.S. Americans.

U.S. Exceptionalism

What is the dominant cultural mythology, creed, or ideology in its more generic sense that unites people from diverse religious, ethnic, and racial groups and social classes?[2] Minxin Pei, a senior associate and codirector of the China Program at the Carnegie Endowment for International Peace, wrote in 2003 that U.S. American nationalism, in contrast to other nationalisms around the world, is defined "not by notions of ethnic superiority, but by a belief in the supremacy of U.S. democratic ideals."[3]

While every country believes itself to be unique and special in some way, U.S. culture has taken this sentiment to another level. It was the U.S. writer Herman Melville who referred to Americans as "the peculiar chosen people—the Israel of our time" (Lieven, 2004, p. 33). Historically, the United States is unique in that it ascended from a humble, newly founded, and inward-looking nation to a world superpower in a stunningly short period of time.

As Stephen Kinzer (2006), a *New York Times* journalist who has reported from 50 countries, writes in *Overthrow: America's Century of Regime Change from Hawaii to Iraq,* "Filled with the exuberance and self-confidence of youth, it developed a sense of unlimited possibility. Many Americans came to believe that since they had been so successful in building their country, they not only could duplicate that success abroad but were called by Providence to do so" (pp. 321–322).

This sense of divine inspiration, protection, and mandate is confirmed by surveys, including one by the Pew Research Center survey in 2002 that asked respondents whether they thought the United States has had special protection from God for most of its history. Nearly half answered in the affirmative. This belief places the United States in a league of its own in comparison to its peer countries in Europe.

Exceptionalism, with its religious overtones and patina of cultural superiority, is a pillar of U.S. ethnocentrism. There is a belief, held by many U.S. Americans, that people in other countries want (or resent) what the United States has, including the basic features of its political and economic system.

This superiority complex is reinforced at every level in U.S. society, including political discourse. Minxin Pei (2003) notes that beliefs in the superiority of U.S. political values and institutions are omnipresent as expressed through U.S. social, cultural, and political practices. Examples include the Pledge of Allegiance, the obligatory performance of the national anthem before every sporting event, and "the ubiquitous American flags."

In the political arena, U.S. nationalism finds its clearest and most potent expression in the mission and goals of the neoconservative movement, which holds that American global leadership is good both for the United States and for the world.

This vision, whose supporters advocate an aggressive foreign policy intended to shape a world favorable to American principles and interests, falls squarely within the parameters of the denial and defense stages of the DMIS: One's own culture is experienced as the only real and good one, and the world is organized into "us" (superior) versus "them" (inferior). It is also, in some respects, a logical if proactive extension of American exceptionalism and messianism that emphasizes the United States' uniqueness, God's favor, and the obligation to spread its political and economic ideals and systems around the world.

Nationalism and the sense of cultural superiority that accompanies it naturally lead to a static and narrowly framed view of the world. The task of creating globally competent citizens cannot be accomplished without first debunking certain cultural myths, proving the "commonsensical" to be nonsensical and revealing ostensibly "eternal truths" to be falsehoods. How one feels about one's country is not merely a matter of the mind but also of the heart and soul.

Therefore, any form of global citizenship education must be approached with caution since it is a form of consciousness raising and a challenge to heartfelt beliefs and long-held assumptions that are believed to be true. Since the aim is to mold global citizens out of national citizens, to give learners the knowledge, experiences, and analytical tools to expand their consciousness and their intellectual repertoire, it involves a reorientation of their worldview.

Vietnamese Patriotism

Unlike the United States, there is a lack of survey data on what Vietnamese think of their country and its place in the world. The 2001 World Values Survey confirms what most Vietnamese and Vietnam experts already know, which is that the overwhelming majority (98%) of Vietnamese are proud of their country and willing "to fight for their country should there be a war." Perhaps nowhere in the world is the adage "past is prologue" more applicable than in Vietnam, where generations of Vietnamese have made great sacrifices for the cause of independence and national sovereignty.

Thus, Vietnamese "nationalism,"[4] which is more accurately characterized as patriotism, is based on two main factors: the extraordinary ability of its people to retain their national identity in the face of repeated invasions, occupations, war, and social dislocation and the homogeneity of its population. In contrast, the United States is not a nation-state in the same mold, and U.S. Americans' pride is based more on ideals and their perception of the United States' "special role" in the world than on the basis of a shared language or culture.

In his analysis of nationalism, Minxin Pei (2003) includes a chart that outlines prominent features of U.S. and "other nationalisms." The latter, he claims, are based on ethnicity, religion, language, and geography, fostered by government elites and promoted by various state apparatus (police, military, state-controlled media). While partially accurate (e.g., ethnicity, promoted by the state), this typology fails to capture the essence and complexity of present-day Vietnamese patriotism, which is basically forward looking and optimistic.

History. Vietnam is unique in that it defeated some of most powerful military forces ever arrayed and that its culture survived generations of foreign occupation essentially intact. In addition, with few historical exceptions, Vietnamese patriotism has maintained a defensive posture and has been directed at ridding the country of foreign invaders ranging from the Chinese and French to the Japanese and U.S. Americans. It is for this reason that Vietnamese national pride and patriotism do not translate into a national moral superiority complex.

Homogeneity. In Vietnam, there is no prospect of becoming assimilated in the U.S. sense. Foreigners who decide to make Vietnam their home and who even become fluent in Vietnamese may be accepted as fully functioning members of Vietnamese society, including getting married to a Vietnamese and being welcomed into a large extended family, but they will always be outsiders for the simple reason that they are not ethnically Vietnamese. Foreigners will forever be viewed as "the other."[5]

Ethnocentrism. Vietnamese ethnocentrism, as in other countries, expresses itself in a variety of ways, mostly benign, including intolerance, bemusement, and puzzlement, but rarely outright hostility. We assert that Vietnamese exhibit a mild form of ethnocentrism typical of countries that are ethnically and culturally homogeneous. While there may be a muted sense of regional cultural superiority among some Vietnamese vis-à-vis peoples of neighboring countries, expressed through humor and offhand remarks, Vietnamese ethnocentrism and patriotism have not been elevated to the level of cultural superiority or become driving forces behind an exaltation of Vietnam over other countries.

As in most countries, outsiders sometimes detect, if not experience directly, traces of xenophobia. This is not surprising given Vietnam's experience with mistreatment and even brutality at the hands of foreigners—even in the recent past in a history that spans thousands of years. This is merely an expression of ethnocentrism, however, and not to be confused with nationalism.

Vietnam and the World

Unlike the United States, it is only recently that Vietnam has begun to open itself up to the world and integrate itself into the global economy. Vietnam's openness to the world, including its admiration of and willingness to learn from its former enemies, is both a practical geopolitical and economic necessity, as well as an embodiment of its national psyche. The country is actively seeking solutions to a range of societal issues in the international arena.

On a political level, this is reflected by the government's pragmatic approach to foreign relations—extend the hand of friendship to all countries in the hopes of obtaining mutual benefits from as many as possible. On a personal level, it is well known, for example, that those selected members of the older generation who were educated in a French school and later fought against the French colonial forces for the cause of independence retain their affection for the language and their interest in literature and other aspects of French "high culture."

Most Vietnamese are deeply concerned about their country's development in this era of globalization and how best to develop their country. A forum titled "Is Vietnam Small or Not?" (*Nườc Việt Nam ta nhỏ hay không nhỏ?*), organized by *The Youth Newspaper* (*Báo Thanh Niên*), revealed that the majority of Vietnamese youth have serious concerns about the fate of their country (Quoc, 2006). Size is understood here in a figurative sense in reference to such qualities as strength, weakness, stature, spiritual values, and so on.

From March 27 to June 30, 2006, tens of thousands of people took part in the forum, and more than 7,000 people participated in the final review. It was a clear indication that Vietnamese from all walks of life are concerned about the status of their country, as "engaged citizens," coincidentally a core theme for institutions of higher education in the United States.

As Vietnam opens its economic and cultural doors ever wider, international perceptions of the country are more favorable than ever. Vietnam currently has trade relationships with 167 countries, including the United States, and participates in 10 multilateral relationships. In the World Trade Organization (WTO) era, there is a strong determination to integrate into the world to reap the benefits of globalization. These benefits range from economic prosperity to acceptance and a sense of legitimacy on the world stage.

The Vietnamese wish to be accepted as members of the international community and to be treated with equality and respect. In 2006, when WTO accession was being negotiated, the whole country followed the process with great interest and concern, believing that it was the first step for Vietnam to be widely acknowledged as an indispensable part of the world. Most Vietnamese are aware that decades of war and isolation, combined with poor planning and an inadequate educational and social system, are the main causes of retarded economic development.

With its integration into the global economy, Vietnam will have many opportunities to gain access to firsthand information and learn from the successes and failures of other countries. Vietnam will also face stiff competition that will test its own strengths and weaknesses. In this way, the country and its people will see with their own eyes the position Vietnam has and what it can achieve in the world. The Vietnamese people will have the opportunity to adjust and adapt themselves to be successful in a more open environment.

Relatively few Vietnamese have had a chance to visit foreign countries, especially in the past. At the same time, many Vietnamese believe that "traveling for one day can bring you tremendous knowledge" ("*Đi một ngày đàng học một sàng khôn*"). Therefore, the chance to go abroad, or even to receive international visitors at home, will provide opportunities for people to improve themselves and to share with others that which they are proud of. The prospect that other countries will begin to see Vietnam not as an image of war but rather as a vibrant and dynamic country will also be strengthened.

Increased contact with other countries will also help the Vietnamese to develop their foreign language proficiency and to use it as an effective tool to communicate with others and to make themselves more employable to the international job market. Recently, many skilled Vietnamese workers were denied employment opportunities in promising labor markets such as Singapore and Malaysia, not because they are not professionally competent but due to a lack of language proficiency.

Globalization requires major changes in infrastructure socio-psychology, a gradual and lengthy process. This is especially true in an agrarian society such as Vietnam in which manual farming labor still accounts for nearly three quarters of the workforce. Vietnamese are used to thinking on a small scale and in a localized manner. In such a situation, one possible danger is that people, especially young people, become dazzled by the perceived great and glorious achievements of other "advanced" (i.e., wealthier) countries. In other words, many tend to see these countries as guides and exemplars rather than as positive and negative role models—that is, to learn what can be adapted to a Vietnamese context and which mistakes to avoid.

Concerns about possible friction between the notion of global citizenship and conformity to the identity of a specific country have resulted in a national slogan that emphasizes integration/accommodation over assimilation/dissolution (*Hòa nhập chử không hòa tan*). According to Diana Kendall (2006) in *Sociology in Our Times: The Essentials,* accommodation means that a small, less powerful society is able to preserve a part of their culture even after prolonged contact with a larger, stronger culture and, at the same time, is able to integrate into other cultures. This is different from assimilation/dissolution, the process by which one group within the civilization adopts the norm and values of the dominant civilization to gain equal status. Many Vietnamese are eager to learn from and cooperate with other countries, but priority is given to maintaining the country's values and preserving its identity.

Proud to Be Vietnamese?

Though there is a strong belief in the values of the country, many Vietnamese have conflicting views of their culture. There are those who are fiercely patriotic and others who have an inferiority complex vis-à-vis the rest of the world. In a discussion with Vietnamese and Laotian students about national pride and globalization, a Vietnamese student asked the instructor, "How can we make people respect us?" Her reply was, "If you want people to respect you, you must first respect yourself." She then asked the students, working in groups, to discuss five reasons why people should respect them as citizens of their country.

Initially, students seemed puzzled and unsure of how to begin. After a lengthy brainstorming session, they compiled lists of reasons why other countries should respect theirs. In retrospect, the students were amazed at how many reasons they thought of as a source of pride in their country and fellow citizens. One student excitedly exclaimed, "Yes, we recognize that we have many values to uphold and be proud of." The Vietnamese lists included such items as heroism and sacrifice for the cause of national independence, identity and unification, and the desire to remain Vietnamese with Vietnam as a recognized state in the world, no matter how many more powerful countries wanted to conquer Vietnam. The other most commonly cited reasons were as follows:

preserving the nation and societal values, beliefs, and language;

a traditional eagerness to learn and respect for teachers and other educated people;

optimism and belief in a brighter future;

the spirit and determination to learn to catch up with others;

smart and hardworking people;

the national and personal pride to make others accept and recognize us so we can make rapid progress, catch up with other people, and even surpass them.

One coauthor still remembers vividly what a Laotian student said, in a shy manner: "I don't have many things to talk about my country, mine is poor and not famous, but it is beautiful and I love it merely because it is where I was born and I think people will respect my country for our love for our own country and others." This is a recognition that love and devotion for one's country are the result of randomness, an accident of birth. It is brings to mind the U.S. student's refusal not to view her home country or the United Kingdom in mutually exclusive terms. One can have multiple affiliations and possess love and devotion for more than one country.

Some of the Vietnamese students' questions revealed doubts and insecurities about their own values. One student remarked, "In many ways, I find in Vietnam we are very removed from the world. The conflict between pride and inferiority is due to our isolation from the world in many ways, meaning that we cannot make a full comparison between Vietnam and other nations." Another student added, "I think that perhaps the inferiority goes all the way back to our history of being a monarchy and then colonization." Yet another commented, "Even now, in many parts of the world, when people first hear of Vietnam, they immediately think of the war (outdated), then they think of us as a Third World country (wrong concept). This attitude reflects stereotypes and a lack of genuine understanding of Vietnam."

It is unlikely that most U.S. American students, including some who have participated in study abroad programs yet returned home essentially unchanged, would voice such concerns about their values and their country's status. Many would speak of the United States as a source of inspiration and a positive role model for other countries, while others may brand U.S. culture as inferior to a particular foreign culture, the very definition of reverse ethnocentrism. Both are black/white views that reflect a lack of intellectual rigor and introspection and perceptions that are not anchored in reality.

The fact that many Vietnamese are not sufficiently confident in their own values and beliefs leads to a phenomenon whereby they pick up many random features from other cultures. They might idealize the West too much and not try to uphold values that helped the country to exist for thousands of years. For example, one coauthor entered a university classroom naturally expecting the students to rise and greet her. When she inquired into their reasons for not standing up, they replied that it was the Western way, a sign of "professionalism," as if there is a universal definition of this concept. Sometimes, young people seem to be at a loss as to what they want, need, or have to do. The generation gaps seem wide in terms of differences in belief, practice, and thinking patterns.

The Way Forward: Strategies for Developing Interculturally Competent Global Citizens

Human history becomes more and more a race between education and catastrophe.

H. G. Wells, *Outline of History,* 1920

To me, it seems a dreadful indignity to have a soul controlled by geography.

George Santayana

Our nationality is an accident of birth. For those born in a country in which, for some of the reasons we have discussed, a heightened sense of national self-assuredness and self-confidence often spill over into nationalism, there are special challenges that can only be overcome with learner-appropriate education and training. Nationalism, whose defining features include a lack of intercultural sensitivity and a marked sense of cultural superiority, can lead to barriers such as an inability to take an objective and impartial view of one's own culture and its shortcomings. Whether of a missionary nature or not, nationalism creates significant systemic obstacles toward the development of globally competent citizens.

Given the barriers to developing interculturally competent global citizens, what are some ways to overcome such barriers? There are several strategies we would recommend, including citizenship education that helps to create "global identifications," addressing multidimensional citizenship in curriculum, and global citizenship education.

Developing Global Identifications Through Citizenship Education

In acknowledging that "nationalism and national attachments in most nations are strong and tenacious," James Banks (2003), a professor and director of the Center for Multicultural Education at the University of Washington–Seattle, highlights the need for effective citizenship education as a means of helping students develop "global identifications" and to understand better the necessity of taking action as global citizens to help solve some of the world's most vexing problems.

Many of the problems Banks (2003) identifies that require "global identifications" to solve are directly related to the UN Millennium Development Goals, including the need to (a) eradicate extreme poverty and hunger; (b) achieve universal primary education; (c) promote gender equality and empower women; (d) reduce child mortality; (e) improve maternal health; (f) combat HIV/AIDS, malaria, and other diseases; (g) ensure environmental sustainability; and (h) develop a global partnership for development.

Multidimensional Citizenship

Another way to address the development of interculturally competent global citizens is through the lens of multidimensional citizenship. In "Educating World Citizens: Toward Multinational Curriculum Development," Parker, Ninomiya, and Cogan (1999, p. 125) described how a multinational research team reached consensus on 8 of 20 competencies that citizens will need to solve global problems:

Ability to look at and approach problems as a member of a global society

Ability to work with others in a cooperative way and to take responsibility for one's roles/duties within a society

Ability to understand, accept, appreciate, and tolerate cultural differences

Capacity to think in a critical and systemic way

Willingness to resolve conflict in a nonviolent manner

Willingness and ability to participate in politics at local, national, and international levels

Willingness to change one's lifestyle and consumption habits to protect the environment

Ability to be sensitive toward and to defend human rights (e.g., rights of women, ethnic minorities)

Since these problems are international in scope, the solutions require people who are willing and able to embrace more than one identity, or "community affiliation." It is what the authors refer to as multidimensional citizenship, which encompasses personal, social, spatial, and temporal dimensions.[6] To illustrate this point, they use the example of a woman who defines herself as a Canadian citizen with attendant civic rights and responsibilities, whose culture, faith, and race are Japanese Canadian, Catholic, and Asian, respectively, and who first and foremost views herself as a mother (Parker et al., 1999, p. 127). It is this sense of multiple identities and intertwined fates that connects us to people in other communities and other countries.

Global Citizenship Education

Milton Bennett (1993) warned in the early 1990s that "intercultural sensitivity is not natural. It is not part of our primate past, nor has it characterized most of human history. Cross-cultural contact usually has been accompanied by bloodshed, oppression, or genocide. The continuation of this pattern in today's world of unimagined interdependence is not just immoral or unprofitable—it is self-destructive. . . . Education and training in intercultural communication is an approach to changing our 'natural' behavior."

In a 2003 speech, *Making Connections in Our Global Age,* J. Michael Adams, the president of Fairleigh Dickinson University and a coinstructor of a course titled

"Globalization and World Citizenship," refers to global citizenship in stark and unequivocal terms: "Quite simply, becoming a citizen of the world is an economic, practical and moral imperative. It is also an issue of our very survival." Adams points out that global citizenship "encourages you to connect the dots of your contemporary world, with attention to the global as well as the local. . . . And once those connections are made mentally, then the real connections—the personal bonds between peoples and across cultures—can blossom."

While a select group in any society should possess intercultural competence *overlaid with global citizenship,* the reality is that most will not have the opportunity to become interculturally competent, nor will they have a compelling professional or other need to do so. Global citizenship education, on the other hand, should not be the exclusive domain of the elite (i.e., college educated), an ambitious goal in and of itself that has yet to be achieved but must be extended to all citizens. While most will never develop or indeed have a practical need to develop intercultural competence, they should be able to "connect the dots" and acquire the competencies listed discussed here.

Global citizens think and feel themselves as part of something much grander and all-inclusive than one culture or nationality. They are free in the sense that they no longer unconsciously accept simple-minded slogans about their home country being "the best." Their transformation from national to global citizen liberates them from the affective and cognitive limitations of nationalism.

Application: The United States and Vietnam

The path to global or multidimensional citizenship presents a daunting challenge to citizens of the United States because of the way in which nationalism has evolved and how deeply entrenched it is in the consciousness of many U.S. Americans. Ironically, Vietnam, whose experience with "the other" has historically been one of subservience, conflict, and victimhood, may find it easier to create globally competent citizens because of the prevalence of a national identity built on patriotism.

Some Vietnam-specific barriers are related not so much to national consciousness but rather to an education system that is designed to produce conformists, a lack of resources, the power of tradition, and a tendency on the part of many young people to imitate what they see without considering the larger context or impact.

In contrast to the United States, most Vietnamese do not exalt their nation "above all others," nor is their love of country infused with a feeling of cultural superiority and a missionary spirit. As with most governments, the Vietnamese government naturally wishes to promote Vietnamese culture abroad, yet it has no desire to impose this culture on other countries. Vietnamese in general may have a deep-seated sense of national pride that permeates their identity as citizens, but it does not form the basis of a national superiority complex. While most Vietnamese may not be well informed about the outside world at the present time, it is not because of a lack of desire, interest, or curiosity but rather a lack of opportunity, contact, and access to information.

It is through global citizenship education that the United States, Vietnam, and other countries can create citizens whose loyalty and devotion to their country are not mutually exclusive with their rights and responsibilities as members of the global community. In *America Right or Wrong*, Anatol Lieven (2004) highlights the need for U.S. Americans to examine their own nationalism, which he describes as "an ability to step outside American national myths and look at the nation with detachment, not as an exceptional city on a hill, but as a mortal nation among other nations" (p. 222). This is a trenchant and timely analysis that applies in general to citizens of any country.

In a globalized world that requires cooperation, collaboration, and multilateralism, the attainment of global citizenship must become an urgent priority for any country's educational system. While it is global citizenship education that educates and empowers people to be able to "connect the dots" of their world, encompassing the global and the local, it is intercultural competence that gives them the necessary skills to make those real, interpersonal connections—to forge deep, mutually beneficial, and lasting cross-cultural personal bonds.

Notes

1. Participating students were paired with international students and required to meet on a regular basis to discuss a series of course-related issues and to share that information with their classmates in a course Web site and in class.

2. In this context, *ideology* refers to "a more or less systematic body of beliefs that explains how society works and what program of political action it should follow" (Salacuse, 2002, p. 72).

3. In *America Right or Wrong: An Anatomy of American Nationalism*, Anatol Lieven (2004) writes about the conflicting and contradictory strands of the American Creed (i.e., "the set of great democratic, legal and individualist beliefs and principles on which the American state and constitution are founded," p. 5) and what he calls American civic nationalism, as distinct from patriotism.

4. Nationalism has frequently been used by U.S. Americans who write about Vietnam to describe historical figures (e.g., Ho Chi Minh) whose beliefs and actions were motivated essentially by patriotism.

5. Eighty-seven percent are ethnic Kinh. Most members of the nation's 54 ethnic minorities live in isolated and remote regions of the country.

6. *Personal* involves commitment to nurture a citizen identity among one's other identities; *social* involves the ability and willingness to work with other citizens, including those who are different culturally or politically, on public problems; *spatial* refers to the need for citizens to view themselves as "members of multiple overlapping communities: local, regional, national, and global"; and *temporal* means that citizens have to adopt a past, present, and future orientation.

References

Adams, M. J. (2003). *Making connections in our global age: Setting the context.* Retrieved March 31, 2008, from http://www.fdu.edu/newspubs/adams/030627monaco.html

Banks, J. A. (2003). *Educating global citizens in a diverse world.* Retrieved March 31, 2008, from http://www.newhorizons.org/strategies/multicultural/banks2

Bennett, M. J. (1993). Towards ethnorelativism: A developmental model of intercultural sensitivity. In R. M. Paige (Ed.), *Education for the intercultural experience.* Yarmouth, ME: Intercultural Press.

Bikson, T. K., Treverton, G. F., Moini, J., & Lindstrom, G. (2003). *New challenges for international leadership: Lessons from organizations with global missions* (MR-1670-IP). Santa Monica, CA: RAND Corporation. Retrieved March 31, 2008, from http://www.rand.org/pubs/monograph_reports/MR1670/index.html

Hertsgaard, M. (2003). *The eagle's shadow: Why America fascinates and infuriates the world.* New York: Picador.

Hofstede, G., & Hofstede, G. J. (2004). *Cultures and organizations: Software of the mind.* New York: McGraw-Hill.

Kendall, D. (2006). *Sociology in our times: The essentials.* Belmont, CA: Wadsworth.

Kinzer, S. (2006). *Overthrow: America's century of regime change from Hawaii to Iraq.* New York: Times Books.

Klein, J. (2001). My London. *TCU Magazine.* Retrieved March 31, 2008, from http://www.magazine.tcu.edu/articles/2001–03-F01.asp?issueid=200103

Lieven, A. (2004). *America right or wrong: An anatomy of American nationalism.* Oxford, UK: Oxford University Press.

New Mexico State University. (2008, March). *News from the Dean for International and Border Programs: Citizenship diplomacy, social entrepreneurship, and international learning outcomes.* Retrieved September 14, 2008, from international.nmsu.edu/pages/news/March_2008.pdf

Parker, W. C., Ninomiya, A., & Cogan, J. (1999). Educating world citizens: Toward multinational curriculum development. *American Educational Research Journal, 36,* 117–145.

Pei, M. (2003, May/June). The paradoxes of American nationalism. *Foreign Policy,* pp. 30–37.

Quoc, D. T. (2006, March 28). Is Vietnam small or not? *Thanh Nien News.* Retrieved March 31, 2008, from http://www.thanhniennews.com/print.php?catid=13&newsid=13921

Russo, S. L., & Osborne, L. A. (2008). *The globally competent student.* The NASULGC Task Force on International Education. Retrieved March 31, 2008, from http://www.aplu.org/NetCommunity/Document.Doc?id=41

Rutherford, D. J. (2006). *Advancing geography as integrative discipline of synthesis: A view through the lens of geography education.* Unpublished dissertation synopsis, Washington, DC.

Salacuse, J. W. (2002). *Making global deals: What every executive should know about negotiating abroad.* Cambridge, MA: PON Books.

Smith, T. W., & Jarkko, L. (1998). *National pride: A cross-national analysis* (SBR-9617727). Chicago: National Opinion Research Center, University of Chicago. Retrieved June 5, 2009, from http://www2.norc.org/new/part1.pdf

Zinn, H. (2003, April). *A kinder, gentler patriotism.* Retrieved September 14, 2008, from http://www.thirdworldtraveler.com/Zinn/Kinder_Gentler_Patriotism.html

CHAPTER 8

Understanding Africans' Conceptualizations of Intercultural Competence

Peter Ogom Nwosu

The need to study and understand how Africans conceptualize intercultural competence has become increasingly paramount. Home to nearly one billion people, a population about three times the size of the United States, Africa is part of the international marketplace, exporting and importing billions of dollars worth of goods and services to markets around the globe. About 3,000 ethnic groups, each with its own cultural system, live on this continent (the second largest in the world). These groups, who speak at least 1,000 different languages (excluding dialectical variations), are distributed across the 54 countries in the continent that emerged in the aftermath of the European scramble for and partition of Africa that occurred from 1884 to 1914. Scholars have noted that in terms of distinctness, Africa is home to the world's largest language family—the Niger-Congo languages (see the works of Bleek, 1856; Koelle, 1854). The Sahara Desert (the world's largest hot desert that covers most of North Africa) divides the continent into a mostly Arab North that resides mainly along the coastal region and a mostly Black South called sub-Saharan Africa that stretches down to Southern Africa. Such groups in the North as Berbers, Beja, and Tuaregs find residence in the interior of North Africa. Below the desert (i.e., sub-Saharan Africa) reside hundreds of diverse ethnic groups such as Hausa-Fulani, Igbo, Yoruba, Zulu, Akan, Asante, Ewe, Maasai, Tutsi, Hutu, Wolof, Kikuyu, Luo, Dagomb, Amhar, Oromo, and Krio, among others. There are significant Arab populations in East and West Africa. Also, throughout East and Southern Africa, there is a thriving Asian population comprising mostly Indians, and in West Africa, there exists also a small Lebanese population. In Southern Africa, there is a significant European population, comprising mainly Afrikaners (descendants of 17th-century Dutch settlers), and the English and Portuguese.

Beyond this rich and complex diversity, Africans are participants in the evolving 21st-century knowledge economy that is fast, global, networked, and technology driven (Nwosu, 2005a, 2005b). They are also participants in the educational, health, and business contexts created by increasing migrations and population movements around the world. All participants in these contexts and in the evolving knowledge economy draw from their cultural patterns to behave in particular ways and to make judgments about culturally competent behaviors. While the African environment offers a treasure trove of opportunity for scholarly inquiry about the relationship between culture and communication, not much has been done to comprehensively study Africans' conceptualizations of intercultural competence. Such scholarly inquiry might shape better understanding of African communication and enhance the quality of human interaction processes in such areas as domestic and international relations.

The purpose of this chapter is threefold: (1) to examine the current structure of communication education in Africa and some of the impediments that affect scholarly inquiry on intercultural competence in the continent, (2) to highlight the complex cultural environment in Africa within which to understand and study intercultural competence, and (3) to develop a preliminary taxonomy of cultural orientations and discourse processes among Africans as a philosophical framework for understanding and studying Africans' conceptualizations of intercultural competence.

Communication Education in the African Public Sphere: An Overview

Perhaps an important starting point to understand the current architecture of the research on intercultural competence in Africa is to examine, first, the terrain of communication education in the continent. This examination is relevant to explaining the dominant policy perspective in higher education in Africa that has stifled the emergence of the enabling environment for scholarship on the relationship between culture and human interactions in the continent and, by implication, research on the added value for a better understanding of Africans' conceptualizations of intercultural competence in a rapidly changing global environment.

More than 50 years have passed since the American scholar Daniel Lerner posited his "magic multiplier" theory about media-audience relations in advancing national development. Lerner had argued in his 1958 landmark work, *The Passing of Traditional Society*, that the medium of mass communication was the magic driver of development: If citizens in traditional societies were informed, through the mass media, about the benefits of development, they would be psychologically disposed to seek such benefits. Soon other scholars such as Marshall McLuhan (1964) and David McClelland (1961) made similar arguments in what became ultimately the dominant paradigm for modernization and development in Africa, Asia, the

Caribbean, and Latin America. The impetus given to the so-called psychological explanations about modernization and about media-audience relations in that process propelled African universities in the dying days of colonial rule, especially in the 1960s, to establish academic programs in communication that sought measurable solutions to development problems in agriculture, health, and education, among others (for comprehensive discussion of mass media's role in national development, see Nwosu, Onwumechili, & M'bayo, 1995).

The colonial experience also produced an important dynamic in the growth and spread of journalism and mass communication education: the emergence of a print and broadcasting system that served as the ideological mouthpiece of government, a factor that continued after many African countries gained independence from the colonial powers. The resulting impact of Africa's colonial past is the conceptualization of communication education that solely promoted a media-centered superstructure, a superstructure that has undermined inquiry in those areas that examine discourse patterns and processes among Africans (i.e., how and why they communicate the way they do). Thus, inquiry on how Africans approach and conceptualize intercultural competence in the contexts of work/function, family, romance, and friendship at the domestic and international arenas has not been the real focus of communication education and scholarship in African universities.

Complicating this mass media superstructure is the urgent need for skilled personnel in areas identified by African governments for satisfying perceived specific technical and occupational needs. Indeed, as Nwosu (2005a) reports,

> The question—what will graduates do with a degree in human communication studies?—often raised by a number of communication educators and planners in Africa, underscores the limited view about the value of human communication, a view that has prevented the emergence of the enabling environment for the discipline. . . . Moreover, what has not been sufficiently established or articulated among administrators and decision makers are the benefits of developing and implementing stand-alone degree programs in human communication studies at their various universities. (p. 63)

More than 50 years since the first African country gained independence from the United Kingdom in 1957, communication education in the continent has been mostly about producing journalists and mass media practitioners (Nwosu, 2005a). The most recent effort to rethink the curricula for communication education in the continent through the work of the United Nations Educational, Scientific, and Cultural Organization (UNESCO) produced the same result (Taylor, Nwosu, & Mutua-Kombo, 2004). Thus, this narrow perspective has stifled local investments in systematic inquiry on the broad range of communication education programs and curricula (e.g., interpersonal, intercultural, organizational, and international) that can lead to improved understanding of Africans, first, with each other and, second, within the international community, in a rapidly changing global environment.

In sum, scholarly inquiry on communication processes and patterns in Africa has followed three distinct lines: a heavy focus on media studies, some focus on communication systems indigenous to the continent, and a very minimal focus on human communication forms in the continent. Media studies have generally examined mass media–audience relationships and issues of hegemony. Scholarly inquiry in this area has mostly revolved around Western-type media (print, radio, television, and related technologies) and their role in national development, as well as a critique of the philosophical underpinnings and ideological and/or hegemonic foundations of this role (for an overview of this work, see, e.g., Nwosu et al., 1995; Taylor et al., 2004). Scholarly inquiry into indigenous communication systems focuses primarily on the nature and typology of interpersonal modes of communication (both verbal and nonverbal) in African settings. Given the predominantly oral-aural nature of African society, these communication systems are largely maintained through the symbolizing codes of Africa's oral tradition. Ugboajah (1985) describes these interpersonal modes of interaction as "oramedia." Examples of these indigenous communication forms or folk media, which have been explored by scholars, include

mythology, oral literature (poetry, storytelling, proverbs), masquerades, rites of passage and other rituals expressed through oracy, music, dance, drama, use of costumes, social interplay and material symbols which accompany people from womb to tomb and much beyond. (Ugboajah, 1985, p. 166)

Subsumed under this mode of communication are indigenous technologies of communication such as talking drums and gongs and other instruments designed to convey messages. Many writers such as Doob (1961), Ugboajah (1985), and Awa (1988), among others, have focused on these media forms and symbols. In fact, most writings on this area of communication inquiry have emerged as a challenge to the dominant and pervasive influence of Western-type media on the nature of interaction and development processes in Africa and among Africans. Thus, the primary impetus for research in this area has been to document and preserve the value and utility of this media form in African social development and to situate these symbolizing codes in the context of African identity and philosophy. Frank Ugboajah's (1985) major work, titled *Mass Communication, Culture and Society in West Africa,* is informed by this impetus. Finally, scholarly inquiry on human communication in Africa, the third area of communication research in the continent, has not been expansive. The enabling environment for research in this area has not been created. Nevertheless, in this regard, attempts have been made by a number of scholars and thinkers to understand African cultural patterns and how these patterns might inform communication forms and styles among Africans (see, e.g., the works of Asante, 1989; Awa, 1988; Lassiter, 1999; Makgoba, 1997; Moemeka, 1996; Obeng-Quaido, 1986; Opubor, 2004; Taylor & Nwosu, 2001; Nwosu, 2002). Overall, these scholars offer a set of shared cultural values that help explain African communication forms and styles, some of which will be discussed in the following sections. The implications of these writings for conceptualizing intercultural competence have not yet been fully explored.

Understanding African Culture

To understand intercultural competency from the African perspective, one must first understand African culture. Lassiter (1999) has used the term *traditional African culture* to describe the shared cultural ethos that may help explain communication forms and styles in Africa and among Africans. According to him, traditional African culture represents "generally widespread sub-Saharan African core values, beliefs, cultural themes and behaviors as they existed prior to European contact; and as they still exist, especially in the rural areas and to a lesser extent in the urban areas of Africa; and upon which many, if not most, fundamental thought processes and behaviors of contemporary sub-Saharan Africans are based and continue to be derived from." Subsumed in this definition is that there is an enduring system of values, beliefs, and cultural themes that shapes behaviors. In the following paragraphs, such core values are discussed and examples provided to explain their meaning in the everyday interactions in the African setting.

The South African scholar Makgoba (1997, pp. 197–198) provides some examples of some of these core values, beliefs, and cultural themes:

- The consensus and common framework-seeking principle called *Ubuntu*

- The emphasis on community rather than the individual

- Hospitality and friendly disposition of Africans. In this regard, friendship in Africa is perceived not as a temporary affair. Friends become part of family to the extent that long-time friends are considered "cousins."

- The Ghanaian scholar Obeng-Quaido (1986) identifies four cultural themes:

Relationship of the African to the spiritual/metaphysical world. The African philosopher Mbiti (1969) notes that Africans are notoriously religious, yet one cannot draw a line in the African worldview between what is secular and what is spiritual.

Relationship to time. The Swahili proverb *Haraka haraka haina baraka* (Hurry hurry has no blessings) best reflects the relationship of Africans to time. Time is conceptualized in terms of connections, not schedules. To Africans, one must not be a slave to schedules. What is important is how much time one takes to connect with others.

Relationship to work. Notions about work can best be explained in terms of gains from work vis-à-vis its benefits to the common good, to the community. One is expected to provide and to take care of other family members if one is more privileged or blessed. The Igbo proverb *Onye ji ego ga akwa nnaya* (she or he who has money should be responsible for the father's funeral expenses) typifies this thinking.

Relationship to the individual or community. The African relationship to self and community is reflected in the African proverb "I am because we are."

The Kenyan scholar Nyasani (1997) offers three cultural traits that make up the African personhood:

- Congenital trait of sociality or sociability
- A virtuous natural endowment of patience and tolerance
- A natural disposition for mutual sympathy and acceptance

Nyasani (1997, p. 57) contends that these three cultural traits serve as important landmarks in the general description of the phenomenology of the African mind. Their significance further lies in the fact that longstanding cultural traditions and environmental conditioning have produced these cultural traits or themes.

In offering a definition of African culture, the Nigerian scholar Andrew Moemeka (1996) points to three important views of the concept in Africa: ethnocultural pluralism, cultural dualism, and Africanity.

> Ethnocultural pluralism denies the existence of purely authentic African Culture, arguing for the concept of African cultures. Cultural dualism stresses the impact of western culture in Africa, and argues that contemporary Africa stands between African tradition and western tradition. In other word, not only is the concept of African cultures no longer completely sustainable, but more important, the concept of an African Culture is no longer tenable. The existence of universal African cultural traits along side numerous unique ethnic traits is also referred to as cultural dualism. Africanity argues in favor of the existence of authentic African Culture that is easily identifiable and has a powerful impact on the behavior and worldview of the African. It does not deny the existence of ethnocultural pluralism or of cultural dualism, but gives prominence to the reality of African Culture, present all over Africa and functional over and above the unique cultures of different ethnic groups in the continent. (p. 215)

In Moemeka's (1996) view, therefore, African Culture

> refers to the fundamental characteristics of social order that are common to all Africa, even in the face of unique differences. For example, marriage in Africa is not contracted between a young man and a young woman; it is contracted between the families of the two young people. But while some ethnic groups believe in paying dowry, others believe in paying bride-price. The social drama of how marriage is contracted is an example of African Culture; the ritual of who pays for what is an example of African cultures. It is the existence of unique ethnic differences in the face of universally accepted African traits that has led to the idea of cultural dualism in Africa. But this existence does not invalidate the fact that there are irrefutable fundamental factors of social order that are uniquely African, that obtain everywhere in the continent, and that have an overwhelming impact on the communicative behavior of Africans anywhere. (pp. 198–199)

Indeed, these fundamental factors of social order, or cultural themes as other scholars have called them, are the basis by which social judgments about intercultural competence are made in African settings. The judgments are essentially about the communicative behaviors and whether they are appropriate in an African context or effective in achieving the desired objectives. In exploring the issue of appropriateness, for example, did the communication act reflect acceptable cultural rules for formality, rhetorical sensitivity, and face saving, three important elements for maintaining social order in Africa? Africans tend to be formal in their speech patterns and habits. This formality is exemplified in the use of formal titles, the use of last names, and nonverbal behaviors such as tone of voice and eye contact, among others, all calibrated effectively to demonstrate reverence for age, social status, or authority. This reverence for age, a core value orientation across many cultures within Africa, is also reflected in many African sayings. In Mali, West Africa, there is a sense that "the death of an old man/woman is like a library going on fire." The East African proverb *Asiye sikia la mkuu huvujika guu* suggests that one who does not listen to elders will not succeed in life. African children are therefore taught through a process of enculturation or informal cultural learning to show deference to individuals on the basis of age. In the Nigerian context, for example, Moemeka (1996) writes that all communities require children to show respect and obey their parents. While this requirement is a fundamental factor for maintenance of social order in African settings, the elements of the expected respect and how they should be manifested vary across communities. For example,

> Among the Ishan of the Midwest [Nigeria], while sons say, "I bow to receive your blessings," they bend down as if wanting to touch their toes, making it easy for the parents to lay their right palm on their back and bless them—daughters say the same thing but kneel down and bow; the Yoruba of the west prostrate fully in total submission, while saying so in words, and then stand up quickly to receive their parents' acknowledgment and blessings; the Hausa of the North stoop down, half raising their right hands with clenched fist, acknowledging their parents' authority and superiority, and say so in numerous praise-words; the Itshekiri of the South-West go down on one knee and say, "I adore you," and the Efik of the South-East genuflect and say something that has no direct English translation but has been taken to mean "Are you up?" or "Did you sleep well?" (p. 199)

Thus, the effectiveness of any of the above communication acts in achieving desired objectives in the Nigerian context would be judged by whether the communication acts reflected the demonstration of respect and obedience to parents, which are fundamental factors of social order in African society. Judgments about culturally competent behaviors are shaped by loyalty to this core value. Outsiders external to the environment are encouraged to show reverence to this cultural rule.

Alfred Opubor (2004), another Nigerian scholar, writes that all communication is rule governed. Consequently, cultural rules provide the basis for expectations and predictions for communication—what people would say and how they choose to say them. The cultural rules, which are learned through a process of enculturation, also provide a basis for evaluation of what is intercultural competence or "what is correct or right or good, i.e., for making ethical and moral judgments about communication practice and communication acts" (Opubor, 2004, p. 43).

In sum, understanding Africans' conceptualizations of intercultural competence would require understanding African culture. Specifically, it would require the following: suitable motivations (i.e., a willingness to learn about the African), sufficient knowledge about the African person in his or her cultural context, understanding the situational and relational contexts in Africa that produce what may be considered appropriate and effective behaviors in those contexts, and skilled actions (putting into practice what has been learned while one negotiates meaning in that specific context). Ultimately, competent intercultural communication is about the negotiation of meaning. In the next section, we discuss current trends about African communication scholarship and the importance of building a strong corpus of knowledge about intercultural competencies in uniquely African settings. This discussion is informed by literature on intercultural communication and by the writings of African scholars whose works have informed current thinking about the African cultural profile and psyche.

Understanding Africans' Conceptualizations of Intercultural Competence: Toward a Taxonomy of Intercultural Competence

In this section, we draw heavily from the works of several scholars such as Kluckohn and Strodtbeck (1961); Mbiti (1969); Moemeka (1996); Lassiter (1999); Nyasani (1997); Obeng-Quaido (1986); Taylor and Nwosu (2001); Koester, Wiseman, and Sanders (1993); and Lustig and Koester (2005), among others. General observations are made about the dimensions of cultural variability in Africa in general, with specific illustrations and examples to buttress these observations. The discussion recognizes the tremendous diversity in Africa. Consequently, the presence of within-group and between-group differences from region to region is underscored in the section. Finally, as part of this discussion, we present in Table 8.1 a preliminary taxonomy of intercultural competence in Africa and among Africans.

In reviewing extant work on the African cultural profile and its relevance for understanding intercultural competence in the African context, five dimensions of cultural variability and discourse orientations emerge as follows: approach to self and other, approach to social relations, approach to time, approach to work, and communication forms and styles. These dimensions of cultural variability are critical to understanding intercultural competence in African contexts. Specifically, what governs appropriate and effective communication in African settings? How does one communicate with Africans? Each dimension of cultural variability and discourse orientation is discussed below, and its implication for Africans' conceptualizations of intercultural competence is also discussed.

Table 8.1   Taxonomy of Intercultural Competence in Africa

Dimensions of Orientations	Characteristics	Communicative Behaviors Considered Appropriate
Self-orientation	Communalism	Deference to group, subordination of self, reverence for age and status, and value for interdependence
Relational orientation	Lineal	Deference to authority, including within-group authority; social distinctions made based on hierarchy; preference for formalized interactions; distinct gender roles; cautious approach to relational development but strong interpersonal bonds valued; focus on obligations and relational interdependence
Time orientation	Cyclical	Emphasis on the past; slow pace of life desired; time perceived as connections, ongoing, unlimited, and flexible; value for in-time polychromic orientation
Activity orientation	Being	Human events determined by fate; fatalistic; work seen as a means to an end; blurred distinction between work and play; workplace as extension of home; less mobility, extended loyalty to the organization, and longevity of service
Discourse orientation	Nonlinear	Indirect, nonlinear narrative style, oral emphasis; listener responsible, reliance on nonverbal codes; covert and implicit messages valued; greater value for face needs and a preference for reserved reactions. The purpose of communication is "to confirm, solidify, and promote communal social order" (Moemeka, 1996)

How Do Africans Manage Self?

Self-orientation describes how people form their identities and the influences on such identities. It also describes how people relate to each other and how they see themselves and their roles within a given context. Perceptions about self-orientation do tend to influence communication behaviors, as well as conceptualizations about intercultural competence. To understand how Africans manage self, some critical questions emerge: Do Africans generally view each other as equals or hierarchical?

Are they informal or formal in the way they relate to each other? Are gender roles similar or clearly defined? Do they value weak group identification or strong group identification? Do they value independence, interdependence, or dependence?

Review of relevant literature shows indisputably that notions about the self among Africans are strongly influenced by communalism, "the principle or system of social order in which the supremacy of the community is culturally and socially entrenched" (Moemeka, 1996, p. 197). Moemeka (1996) writes that the "most important characteristic (fundamental principle) of a communalistic society is the pride of place given to the Community as a supreme power over its individual members" (p. 202). In this environment,

> community welfare undergirds actions, and affectiveness (in addition to effectedness and effectiveness) underscores communication intentions. Therefore standardized coordination behavior (Cushman, 1989) prevails; and adherence to communication rules (tacit but socially sanctioned understandings about appropriate ways to interact in given situations) is a strict requirement; and noncompliance provokes strict punishment. (Moemeka, 1996, p. 198)

In general, there is, in African culture, a symbiotic relationship between the individual and the group. This relationship defines how people interact with each other and places a high value on hierarchy, formality, and distinct gender roles. The individual does not exist outside of the group. As Mbiti (1969) writes, "Whatever happens to the individual happens to the whole group, and whatever happens to the whole group happens to the individual" (p. 109). In the African context, "The individual can only say: 'I am, because we are; and since we are, therefore I am'" (Mbiti, 1969, p. 109). This conception of self in relation to the group in Africa is reflected in numerous African languages in very strong terms and in varying forms. In South Africa, for example, the Xhosa people say, "*umuntu ngumuntu ngabantu*" (a person is a person through persons). The Igbo people of Eastern Nigeria would say, "*Onye ya na Umunna ya n akwuro ga eli onwe ya*" (a person who is not with his or her extended family must bury himself). Within this identity context, hierarchical structures are in place to ensure social order and continuity. Thus, the African sense of personhood and community requires individuals to make decisions and take actions that, while personally enhancing, are socially responsive to the needs and welfare of the larger community.

Communalism, as a way of life, has been elevated to the status of a communal religion in most of traditional Africa (Taylor & Nwosu, 2001), in the same manner that individualism, as a concept, has been elevated to the status of a national religion in the West. "Whereas individualism represents commitments to independence, privacy, self, and all-important I, communalism represents commitment to interdependence, community affiliation, others, and the idea of we" (Nwosu, Taylor, & Blake, 1998, p. 237). Furthermore, in communalistic cultures, the individual is concerned with the "authenticity of community-presentation image," a concern quite different from collectivistic cultures, where the individual is concerned with "the adaptability of self-presentation image" (Moemeka, 1996, p. 198). Consequently, communication practices are informed by the effect of particular behaviors on the image of the community and not the effect the behaviors would have on the individual. Thus, what governs the African communication environment is shame rather than guilt—the shame that particular behaviors will bring to the family, the group, or the community, not the guilt of the behavior as reflected on the individual. The African believes that he or she is a part of a wheel of interacting forces, a part of the larger community of individuals, and that how he or she behaves has an impact on others and has an impact on the full functioning of the community. Therefore, what he or she chooses to do and not to do have direct bearing on preserving the community's social ethos and strengthening its fabric and fiber. To the extent that the supremacy of the community is threatened by an individual's action, social order in that community is also perceived to be under attack.

Moemeka (1996) writes that

> the community in Africa is usually like a small town where the relationships among the people are characterized as Gemeinschaft, that is intimate, familiar, sympathetic, mutually interdependent, and conspicuously manifested in a shared social consciousness. Inhabitants are usually descendants of one major common ancestor— a super-grandparent—and therefore regard themselves as close relatives, sharing their joys and sorrows. Administrative arrangements within the town are based on distinct and more closely related affinities that derive from offspring ancestors. Such finite internal groups may see themselves as communities, but because they do not have an existence independent of the town, they do not present themselves to the outside world as communities, but as units within the Community. (p. 198)

In this framework, one understands the significance of communalism as the "soul and fibre of work, activity, and social life in Africa," a vital part of the African cultural ethos, providing social security to the less fortunate members of the community (Awa, 1988, p. 136).

Communalism is manifested, for example, through the extended family system. Anyaegbunam (1995), writing on the experiences of the Igbo people of eastern Nigeria, suggests that kinship relationship (a component of the extended family structure) is a vital force in Igbo social system, in that it shapes the behaviors of the individual toward the others. The Igbo concept of *Umunna* (extended family group or kindred) typifies the emphasis on communalism or interdependence rather than individualism. In South Africa, the Zulu word *Ubuntu* also signifies the African emphasis on community or interdependence. Again, the underlying principle here is that a person can only be a person through others (Mbigi & Maree, 1995). Among the Maasai in East Africa, loyalty to the group is at the epicenter of interaction processes. This group loyalty, well grounded in the concept of interdependence, suggests a lesser emphasis on loyalty to self. Such things as personal freedom, self-assertiveness, and individual entitlements become secondary to filial piety and group identity. Among East Africans, the Swahili word *Undugu* or *ndugu,* in the most general sense, means sisterhood/brotherhood and solidarity. As a philosophy that has guided relations among nations that make up the East African community (Kenya, Tanzania, and Uganda), *Undugu* signifies community and interdependence. Because Swahili is the common language spoken among citizens in this regional community, it is not a surprise to find citizens of the different countries referring to each other as *Undugu* (my brother, my sister). To understand intercultural competence in the African context, one has to be aware of how Africans conceive of self. One must also go beyond awareness to appreciate the value of such conceptions of self to communal social order.

How Do Africans Manage Social Relations?

Social relations describe how members of the community relate to each other and how the community chooses to organize itself. In this instance, what institutional arrangements are in place to help finesse interpersonal relations in friendship, romance, family, and work/functional contexts? In the African context, the relational arrangement is one that values a lineal hierarchical superstructure in which people are unequal because of age, status, and wealth, among others. Relational obligation is also valued whereby friendship in Africa is seen as a duty that comes with certain rights and responsibilities. Questions such as "How do people address or refer to one another in these contexts?" "Do people perceive each other as superior or inferior?" "Does the language spoken reflect existing social distinctions in the culture?" "Are interaction processes formalized and organized?" and "How do people define their roles or their place in that culture?" all help to reflect the culture's relational orientation. Blake (1993) notes that

> African societies share certain fundamental values that guide the day to day life of inhabitants in traditional African settings. . . . There are, for example, certain "rules" that guide discourse in the deliberative, forensic, and epideictic genres. The "rules" are grounded in values such as respect for elders; acceptance of the supremacy of hierarchical structures; performance of certain rituals in respect of ancestors; performance of rituals for various occasions ranging from farming to death and burial ceremonies; sibling relationships, etc. (p. 8)

In the African context, for example, it is considered disrespectful to use the first names when referring to people in authority or higher in status or age. Cultural expectations require that such individuals be treated with deference, "which is displayed, in part, through one's greeting styles (handshakes, bowing, or kissing the hand or forehead)" (Nwosu, 2005b, p. 87).

A major institutional arrangement in Africa is the marriage institution. An Igbo proverb states "*nwanyi too, ajuo onye na anu ya*" (when a woman reaches of age, you ask whose wife she is). The same principle applies to the man. Marriage is therefore considered a sacred duty and responsibility in Africa. Among the Igbo people of Nigeria, marriage does not just bring man and woman together into matrimonial life. As Nwosu (2005b) writes, marriage

> also unites two families into a stronger relationship. Couples do not establish independent families; instead they enter into already existing ones. . . . family love is multidimensional. One enters into love not with one one's spouse but with all members of both families. Marriage for the Igbo people is a community affair, a joyful reality, a covenant between two *umunnas* (extended families), not merely an arrangement between a man and a woman. (p. 90)

Much has been noted about hospitality, sociability, and friendliness as important elements of the African cultural profile. Writing on the cultural grounding of personal relationships in Africa, Adams and Plaut (2003) concluded that different constructions of self and social reality influence relational experiences. Reflecting the relational interdependence of West African cultures, the authors hypothesized and observed that Ghanaian participants were significantly more likely than their counterparts in the United States to advocate caution toward friends and to emphasize practical assistance in friendship. Reflecting the atomistic independence of North American cultures, Adams and Plaut hypothesized and observed that U.S. participants were significantly more likely than their Ghanaian counterparts to indicate a large friendship network and to emphasize companionship, particularly relative to Ghanaian women. Results of their investigation suggest that there is not a universal form for friendship; instead, friendship takes different forms in different cultures.

Adams and Plaut's (2003) investigation is important for understanding how Africans might approach or construct social relations. For the African, she or he is cautious with relational constructions. While friendships are important, one must not rush into them. One must take the time to grow and to nurture such. Indeed, as the authors report, the problem with an exclusive focus on suspicious caution regarding relational constructions in African settings becomes clear when they discuss their research findings with African audiences. "Rather than ask why it is that people express so much caution about friends, people often wonder why it is that American participants express so little caution" (p. 346). This response is instructive.

These findings clearly suggest that the relative absence of caution about friends in North American settings is not the default, natural human tendency; instead, it reflects the particular realities of atomistic independence, a dominant cultural orientation, in many North American cultures. These realities therefore afford relatively open approaches to friendship that de-emphasize obligation and make it relatively easy to escape problem connections in friendship contexts (Adams & Plaut, 2003, p. 346).

On the other hand, African cultural realities regarding relational constructions afford cautious approaches, subsumed in the inherent value for strong interpersonal bonds, an understanding that genuine friendships are long lasting and enduring, and also carry certain obligations and problem connections. In the African contexts, friendship is seen as a duty, a joyful union between individuals that accords certain rights and responsibilities. This explains the seriousness with which Africans approach friendships, whether in the business, work, or functional context or in the romantic arena. What, then, does this mean for intercultural competence? It means, for example, in the business context that one must take the time to grow and nurture a business relationship. The age-old African proverb from the Democratic Republic of Congo— "Friendship is like a plant, one must nurture it, else it would die"—reflects the generally cautious attitude toward the African person's conceptualization of competent behaviors in the context of social relations. As Adams and Plaut (2003) conclude,

> The prominence of suspicious caution toward friendship is not a pathological distortion of reality . . . ; instead it reflects the particular realities of relational interdependence that are prominent in many West African worlds. These realities promote constructions of friendship that emphasize obligation and make it difficult for people to extricate themselves from connections that turn negative. Given these realities, it makes sense to be wary of friends and to limit one's friendships to a well-selected few. (p. 346)

How Do Africans Deal With Time?

A major focus of intercultural communication research deals with how cultures perceive, structure, and respond to time systems. Is there a value for individuals to be punctual at events, or is mere participation at the event more important? Is there always time, or is time limited and quantifiable? Scholarly investigation on these questions provides a framework for how a society deals with time and group members' conceptualizations about certain behaviors that are perceived as incompatible with that framework. Thus, cultural perceptions of time tend to influence the communication process, as well as what is considered appropriate behaviors. Gonzales and Zimbardo write that "there is no more powerful, pervasive influence on how individuals think and cultures interact than our different perspectives on time—the way we learn how we mentally partition time into past, present and future" (qtd. in Guerrero, DeVito, & Hecht, 1999, p. 227).

In general, cultural perceptions about time are typically framed to reflect a past, present, and future orientation. "Every child learns a time perspective that is appropriate to the values and needs of his society" (Guerrero et al., 1999, p. 227). As Burgoon, Stern, and Dillman (1995) remark, the structure, content, and urgency of communication are shaped by the dominant time orientation in that society. Individuals with a past orientation tend to place significance on history and tradition. African society tends to place salience on a past orientation. Individuals with a present orientation place significance on living for the moment and have very low risk aversion. Societies that have a future orientation tend to be goal oriented in the direction of a broad vision for the society. Cultural perceptions of time are also framed to reflect two time systems: (1) a monochromic system in which time is segmented into small units, scheduled, arranged, and managed in ways that permit the performance of specific tasks and (2) a polychronic system in which approach to time is less segmented, and there is more fluidity with schedules.

Africans conceive time as cyclical. There is a focus on history and great salience placed on polychronic orientation. In this conception of time, individuals take a more flexible approach to schedule. As a result, there is a slower pace to life. The fierce urgency to focus on tomorrow often found in cultures with a future orientation in not emphasized. There is always time in African contexts because time is not a quantifiable commodity. Conceptualization of time is not just limited to structure, where life is regimentally "scheduled" and organized. To Africans, time is about how we communicate and how we connect with each other. This explains why African greetings styles are lengthy—we are never in a hurry to ask many questions, to inquire about one's family and relatives, about the harvest, about the rain, and so on. Waving a simple hi or hello to someone is not enough. How Africans use time therefore reveals their values about respect, status, and age. Mutua-Kombo notes, "I will not say that I am in a hurry (even if I am) when I meet someone who is trying to inquire about my aging grandmother's health or well-being. How much time do I take to explain how she is doing? Seeming to be in a hurry may suggest I am disrespectful to the person inquiring about grandma as well as being disrespectful to grandma. So, in this instance, one can see how the notion of schedule conflicts with maintaining social ties, connecting with others. How one relates to others is what matters, not how much time you have, not the schedule" (personal communication, December 6, 2008).

In the countryside where most people reside, for example,

> African concepts, structure, perceptions of time are dictated by nature. People wake up to the crowing of the cock, which happens at the crack of the dawn. Dawn maybe anytime from 5:30–6:00am. If a paramount chief summons the cabinet, through a messenger, to convene at daybreak and some arrive at 5:30am and others at 6:00am; none of them will be perceived as late. Decisions by "chiefs-in-council" require full representation and participation of all section heads, and such decisions are generally preceded by a social event—the ritual breaking of kola nut, a prolonged libation ceremony, deliberately calculated to allow time for a quorum to be attained. (Awa, 1988, p. 139)

Cohen (1997) writes that the arbitrary divisions of the clock face in monochronic time systems "have little saliency in cultures grounded in the cycle of the seasons, the invariant pattern of rural life, and the calendar of religious festivities" (Cohen, 1997, p. 34). There is a focus more on using time for relational development even if such time was spent with family or friends. Clearly understanding how a culture structures time and one's role in it increases the potential for successful intercultural communication.

Subsumed in the African concept of time is the belief in reincarnation. Obeng-Quaido (1986) notes that

> death, for the African, means the death of the physical body, but the real essence of the human being lives on and would be born again into the same family or clan. Added to this is the view that the African never accepts death as a natural phenomenon. There is always a reason for death; whether it comes to the youth or to the aged, and this explains our preoccupation with necromancy and visits to the priests and shrines to find out why someone is dead. (p. 93)

Furthermore, physical death does not mean spiritual death. Africans generally believe that when an elderly person dies, the spirit of that person lives on and joins with the departed ancestors of the land. Those ancestors who have departed are believed to offer continued protection to the extended family or the clan. In offering supplications during different occasions, Africans first call upon the departed ancestors to guide and protect them. They also call upon their Supreme Deity and other lesser gods to guide and protect them as well (Nwosu et al., 1998). This connection to the ancestors and the reverence that Africans have for them explains the blurred view about what is secular and what is spiritual in African culture. The dead are referred to as the "living dead." In this sense, there is no isolation between the living and the dead. The living rely on the dead for sustenance. Communication practices such as in the pouring of libations or the kola nut rituals during all kinds of occasions, such as marriages or visits to a neighbor's home, highlight the dead and call upon them to continue to protect the community. Thus, this practice reflects the cyclical nature of time in Africa and also a reverence for the past, the living dead.

In sum, appropriate and effective interactions in uniquely African settings would require a better understanding of how Africans conceptualize and approach time in all aspects of relational construction, including work and function-based environments. Time is not about schedules. It is about the social context and how one uses that to enhance relational connections.

How Do Africans Manage Activity?

Activity orientation describes how cultural groups view expressions of self and human actions through specific activities (Lustig & Koester, 2005). Answers to questions such as how people regard and handle work and play and how people define and evaluate activity provide a window to understanding a cultural group's orientation to activity. Africans' conceptualizations of intercultural competence are also informed by this orientation. Nwosu et al. (1998) report a popular saying in parts of Africa to explain the African concept of work: When a White man is laid off from work, he may take a gun and shoot himself, but when an African is laid off, he takes his hoe and returns to the farm! This saying typifies differing conceptions of orientation to work in North America and in the African worldview. For the Westerner, work is seen as an end in itself, a duty central to one's existence, a part of one's very identity, and a loss of that work makes life meaningless and not worth living for. For the African, however, work is seen not as a duty that has some eternal reward but as a means to an end, a necessity for survival but not central to one's self identity.

Africans' conception of activity is also one that values a "being" orientation, as opposed to a "doing" or a "becoming" orientation. In this regard, there is a belief that all human events are determined by fate and are therefore inevitable. A "becoming" orientation sees individuals as evolving and capable of changing, whereas a "doing" orientation places significance on change and control. Activity in doing cultures is typically goal directed or purpose driven, and success is measured through tangible products or observable actions. An important component in the African concept of work is the blurred distinction between work and play. In the African perspective, work is not just a place to perform tasks but also a place where one establishes strong interpersonal bonds. Such interpersonal bonds are assumed to enhance the communication processes essential to good performance. The workplace is also seen as an extension of the home. Thus, it is not uncommon for employees to share their interpersonal issues with supervisors in the hope of securing support. Such cultural expectations often times are at odds with the organizational culture in a "doing" society. For individuals in a "being" culture, there is often strong loyalty to the organization, longevity of service, and less desire for job mobility. It is not uncommon for a person to stay in one job for long periods of time. The perception of disloyalty that may be created because one decides to look for another work opportunity is often at odds with the "being" orientation. A better understanding of the cultural orientation to activity shapes any understanding of how one might assess competent interactions in the work context.

Interactions in the work context reflect collective/communal expectations. For example, when a worker dies, his or her colleagues in the section or department that person was working with will contribute toward the funeral costs, attend funeral prayer meetings regularly in the evenings, travel "upcountry" to the village for the burial (which may last a few days), and have an opportunity to give a speech at the funeral. In sum, relations at work are not just business but also social. To not participate fully and actively in these events would be considered a deviance from community norms, which may threaten communal social order. Competent intercultural behaviors are judged by how one responds to these kinds of circumstances.

How Do Africans Manage Communication Both Verbally and Nonverbally?

The preceding section shows how to understand verbal and nonverbal communication issues in Africa. In examining the communication process in African settings, the elements of the communication process first should be considered. The elements include source, message, channel, receiver, feedback, and noise (i.e., forces that impede communication). How the source and the receiver of the message interact and react to each other, as well as with what channels they interact with each other, is shaped by the cultural rules in the society. Individual roles and behaviors in African contexts are therefore shaped by the prevailing cultural rules.

Individual roles would be what we do, based on what we have been taught. What we have been taught shapes cultural expectations about appropriate behaviors—for example, stopping and taking time to speak with your elder, running errands as asked without complaining, not talking back at your elders when they speak, not jumping in to participate in discussions by elders unless invited, and so on. Behaviors would reflect how we respond in and to social contexts. In the African worldview, one cannot separate the self, the individual, from the social context. For example, girls who talk "too much" would be warned that if they continued to do so, no one would marry them. The question is usually framed as follows: "Who will marry you with that mouth?" The African contexts reflect the cultural environment upon which intercultural competence is grounded as well as assessed. Thus, understanding about intercultural competence in Africa must derive from this cultural superstructure.

Other important attributes of the African communication profile that inform our understanding of intercultural competence include the Africans' preference for an indirect, nonlinear narrative style. African narrative styles include interconnecting ideas, with the story typically beginning somewhere, breaking off into another but related subject, and eventually returning to the main body of the narrative (Nwosu, 2005b). The narrative style also includes an emphasis on oral history and the importance placed on a call-response approach to communication. It allows the speaker to speak and the audience to chorus their response in support of the speaker. It is a ubiquitous pattern of communication in Africa and allows for communal participation in the culture's civic life and religious rituals. Call-response communication approach emphasizes unity, harmony, unison, agreement, and an assurance that we are all together in our thinking; an opposing view, unless by the elders, is not something that is welcome.

The African communication context is also listener responsible, as opposed to speaker responsible. In this context, the burden of communication is on the listener to decipher what the speaker is saying. Because messages tend to be covert and implicit, there is greater reliance on nonverbal symbols. Reactions to certain messages are reserved as a way to save face and to minimize conflicts. In a speaker-responsible culture, the burden of meaning in communication contexts is for the speaker to be clear and precise. The saying "one does not need to beat around the bush" reflects this perspective in the U.S. cultural setting. This penchant for directness may also create dissonance in intercultural settings where both the source and the receiver are not familiar with each other's discourse orientation. Certainly, in the African setting, the general perception is that the other person is rude and disrespectful if communicating in a direct manner. Yet, preliminary findings from the author's work for the U.S. Institute of Peace on conflict management in Nigeria (for religious and community leaders) suggest that certain sections of the Nigerian population (the Hausa-Fulani ethnic group) may have a preference for the direct approach to communication. There is therefore a very strong need to explore the potential variations in communication styles in Africa and the implications for Africans' conceptualizations of intercultural competence.

Taylor and Nwosu (2001) have cautioned that in studying African communication processes as a basis for improving intercultural competence, one cannot ignore the influence of colonialism on African history, leading, for example, to the scramble for and the partition of the continent. The emergence of Francophone, Anglophone, and Lusophone Africa, a consequence of colonialism, has had a strong impact on linguistic groupings and communication practices in the continent. In addition, the trans-Atlantic and trans-Saharan slave trades and age-old ethnic conflicts cannot be ignored in understanding communication processes and cultural patterns in Africa.

Ali Mazrui (1986), Mutua-Kombo (2008), and Karl Peltzer (2006) suggest that the complex effects of colonialism and other historical forces in Africa offer varied perspectives to understand the African cultural environment and communication forms. Mazrui's *The Africans: A Triple Heritage* identifies three main cultural influences on Africa: traditional African/indigenous culture, Islamic influence, and Western culture. Mutua-Kombo notes that understanding the African worldview today in terms of communication lies in the contention between the core values and beliefs in traditional and contemporary Africa and the historical forces imposed by contacts with Europeans. And Karl Peltzer (1995) identifies three Africa groups that have emerged from or in spite of the historical forces: (1) traditional persons, who are little affected by modernization and who are functioning within the established and seemingly timeless framework of their culture (e.g., the Maasai in East Africa and the Bushmen of the Kalahari); (2) transitional persons, often living in and shuttling between the two cultures in the course of their daily round of activities (e.g., between work and home or between the temporary urban dwelling and the ancestral village, where their extended family continues to reside); and (3) modern individuals, participating fully in the activities of the contemporary industrial or postindustrial world. This trichotomy is relevant to personal experience and functioning (Peltzer, 1995, p. 25).

Africans learn to manage these distinct spaces in their interaction styles, however long they have been gone from the traditional society. Thus, an African knows how to communicate regardless of the settings and the historical influences. As Mutua-Kombo notes, "Regardless of how long I have lived in the United Kingdom or in the United States, I know how to interact when I am in Nairobi; when I am in the village, I know how to behave; and I know how to switch codes to suit those specific contexts" (personal communication, December 6, 2008). African parents who take their American-born children on visits to Africa make sure to monitor those children's behaviors to ensure that they do not bring shame to the family. In African contexts, the burden of shame to the family or to the group is stronger than the guilt to the individual. The Kenyan proverb states, "Don't let children to grow like trees in the forests." From this saying, one can surmise that things that grow in the forest do so in different directions with no one tending to them. However, things that you grow yourself require care and nurturing. You know how to tend to it and to trim the branches when necessary. The lessons for intercultural competence are fairly obvious. To understand African communication styles, one must also be familiar with the cultural values that inform them.

Taxonomy of Intercultural Competence in Africa

This taxonomy is an attempt to provide a philosophical framework for understanding the cultural patterns that inform discourse orientation in Africa. Indeed, as the preceding sections indicate, Africa is a complex cultural environment, for both insiders and outsiders to the culture. While this philosophical framework permits broad understanding, one must not ignore within- and between-country, regional, and ethnic group differences that may affect what are considered socially appropriate behaviors. In this regard, Africa is not homogeneous. One must therefore have a reasonable amount of cultural knowledge to be able to navigate the complex cultural terrain that shapes communication practices throughout the continent and among Africans everywhere. Finally, this taxonomy also provides an important philosophical architecture for serious scholarly inquiry and theorizing about cultural patterns and discourse processes in Africa and their implications for intercultural competence in a rapidly changing global knowledge economy. The taxonomy derives from the discussions in the preceding sections. It focuses on five dominant cultural and communication themes relevant for understanding Africans' conceptualizations of intercultural competence.

Conclusion

It should be clear from this chapter that much work is needed in understanding Africans' conceptualizations of intercultural competence, especially in the area of theory building. With its diverse population and evolving engagement with the international community, Africa remains a complex but fertile cultural environment for such work. Given the value of such inquiry to promoting international understanding, enhancing business practices, and good citizenship, governments and academic institutions can provide the enabling environment to permit and promote further work in this area. In this chapter, we have merely "scratched the surface," exploring the terrain for communication education in Africa and identifying some structural impediments that continue to affect scholarly exploration about cultural orientations and discourse processes in the continent. Finally, we offered a preliminary taxonomy of cultural orientations and discourse processes among Africans as a framework for understanding and studying Africans' conceptualizations of intercultural competence. In the words of Miller (2005),

> Africa is apparently so far from the center of intercultural communication literature as to be beyond the margins. The currents of research occasionally stray briefly near the continent's northern and southern edges, but the remainder of that vast and rich cultures and people remains virtually uncontemplated. That this indicates undervaluing of African people and cultures is perhaps obvious. That it represents a weakness in the understanding of communication across the globe is less obvious but equally true. It is time for the field of intercultural communication to emulate the example of cartography and discard its distorted representations of the planet. It is time we studied Africa. (p. 227)

References

Adams, G., & Plaut, V. (2003). The cultural grounding of personal relationship: Friendship in North American and West African worlds. *Personal Relationships, 10,* 333–347.

Anyaegbunam, J. (1995). *Igbo traditional marriage and Christian marriage: Toward inculturation.* Unpublished master's thesis, University of Nigeria, Nsukka.

Asante, M. (1989). *Afrocentricity.* Trenton, NJ: African World Press.

Asante, M., & Appiah, M. (1979). The rhetoric of the Akan drum. *Western Journal of Black Studies, 3,* 8–13.

Awa, N. (1988). Communication in Africa: Implications for development planning. *Howard Journal of Communication, 1*(3), 131–144.

Blake, C. (1993). Development communication revisited: An end to Eurocentric visions. *Development, 3,* 8–11.

Bleek, W. H. (1856). *A comparative grammar of South African languages.* London: Trubner and Co.

Burgoon, J. K., Stern, L. A., & Dillman, L. (1995). *Interpersonal adaptation: Dyadic interaction patterns.* Cambridge, MA: Cambridge University Press.

Cohen, R. (1997). *Negotiating across cultures: International communication in an interdependent world* (Rev. ed.). Washington, DC: U.S. Institute of Peace.

Doob, L. (1961). *Communication in Africa: The search for boundaries.* New Haven, CT: Yale University Press.

Guerrero, L. K., DeVito, J. A., & Hecht, M. L. (1999). *The nonverbal communication reader: Classic and contemporary readings* (2nd ed.). Long Grove, IL: Waveland.

Kluckohn, F., & Strodtbeck, F. (1961). *Variations in value orientations.* Evanston, IL: Row Peterson.

Koelle, S. W. (1854). *Polyglotta Africana.* London: Church Missionary House.

Koester, J., Wiseman, R. L., & Sanders, J. A. (1993). Multiple perspectives of intercultural communication competence. In R. L. Wiseman & J. Koester (Eds.), *Intercultural communication competence* (pp. 3–15). Newbury Park, CA: Sage.

Lassiter, J. E. (1999). *African culture and personality: Bad social science, effective social activism, or a call to reinvent ethnology?* http://web.africa.ufl.edu/asq/v3/v3i2a1.htm

Lerner, D. (1958). *The passing of traditional society: Modernizing the Middle East.* New York: Free Press.

Lustig, M., & Koester, J. (2005). *Intercultural competence: Interpersonal communication across cultures.* Boston: Pearson.

Makgoba, M. W. (1997). *MOKOKO, the makgoba affair: A reflection on transformation.* Florida Hills, South Africa: Vivlia.

Mazrui, A. (1986). *The Africans: A triple heritage* [Documentary]. London: British Broadcasting Corporation.

Mbiti, J. (1969). *African religions & philosophy.* Ibadan, Nigeria: Heinemann.

Mbigi, L., & Maree, J. (1995). *Ubuntu: The spirit of African transformation and management.* Johannesburg, South Africa: Sigma Press.

McClelland, D. (1961). *The achieving society.* Princeton, NJ: Van Nostrand.

McLuhan, M. (1964). *Understanding media: The extensions of man.* Cambridge: MIT Press.

Miller, A. N. (2005). Keeping up with cartography: A call to study African communication. In W. J. Starosta & G.-M. Chen (Eds.), *International and intercultural communication annual* (Vol. 28, pp. 214–236). Washington, DC: NCA.

Moemeka, A. (1996). Interpersonal communication in communalistic societies in Africa. In W. Gudykunst, S. Ting-Toomey, & N. Tsukada (Eds.), *Personal communication across cultures* (pp. 197–216). Thousand Oaks, CA: Sage.

Mutua-Kombo, E. (2008, May). *Expanding worldviews in US classrooms: Educators' experiences from Rwanda.* Paper presented at the 5th International Conference on Intercultural Communication Competence, Wichita State University, Wichita, KS.

Nwosu, P. (2005a). *Ceteris paribus* in African social development: Rethinking communication education in Africa's universities. *CODESRIA Bulletin, 3/4,* 61–66.

Nwosu, P. (2005b). Cultural problems and intercultural growth: My American journey. In M. Lustig & J. Koester (Eds.), *Among us: Essays on identity, belonging, and intercultural competence* (pp. 118–128). Boston: Allyn & Bacon.

Nwosu, P. (2002). Negotiating with the Swazis. In J. Martin, T. Nakayama, & L. Flores (Eds.) *Readings in communication* (2nd ed.). Boston, MA: McGraw-Hill.

Nwosu, P., Onwumechili, C., & M'Bayo, R. (1995). *Communication and the transformation of society: A developing region's perspective.* Lanham, MD: University Press.

Nwosu, P., Taylor, D., & Blake, C. (1998). Communication and development: Imperatives for an Afrocentric methodology. In J. Hamlet (Ed.), *Afrocentric visions: Studies in culture and communication* (pp. 229–245). Thousand Oaks, CA: Sage.

Nyasani, J. M. (1997). *The African psyche.* Nairobi, Kenya: University of Nairobi and Theological Printing Press.

Obeng-Quaido, I. (1986). A proposal for new communication research methodologies in Africa. *Africa Media Review, 1,* 89–98.

Opubor, A. (2004). What my grandmother taught me about communication: Perspectives from African cultural values. *Africa Media Review, 12,* 43–57.

Peltzer, K. ((1995). *Psychology and health in African cultures.* Frankfurt, Germany: IKO Verlag.

Peltzer, K. (2006). Personality and person perception in Africa. In L. A. Samovar, R. E. Porter, & E. R. McDaniel (Eds.), *Intercultural communication: A reader* (pp. 135–141). Belmont, CA: Wadsworth.

Taylor, D., & Nwosu, P. (2001). Afrocentric empiricism: A model for communication research in Africa. In V. Milhouse, M. Asante, & P. Nwosu (Eds.), *Transcultural realities: Interdisciplinary perspectives on cross-cultural relations* (pp. 299–311). Thousand Oaks, CA: Sage.

Taylor, D., Nwosu, P., & Mutua-Kombo, E. (2004). Communication studies in Africa: The case for a paradigm shift for the 21st century. *Africa Media Review, 12*(2), 1–24.

Ugboajah, F. (1985). *Mass communication, culture and society in West Africa.* Toronto, Canada: World Association of Christian Communication.

CHAPTER 9

An Associative Approach to Intercultural Communication Competence in the Arab World

R. S. Zaharna

I ncreasingly, the great diversity within the Arab world is finding scholarly expression in communication research across the region. A new generation of scholars is arguing that the Arab culture should no longer be seen as singular but rather as a group of diverse social customs representing a tapestry of cultures within the Arab world. These scholars have also highlighted the importance of the Islamic influence on sociocultural beliefs and behaviors. This chapter examines how these sociocultural and religious influences combine to form a prevailing view of communication and, by extension, communication competence. Despite the diversity found among Arab and Islamic societies, a common thread running through the intricately interwoven social fabric is the premium placed on relationships and context. This emphasis is used to propose an "associative" view of communication. This associative view of communication can be seen in the interconnected patterns and associations that run throughout the Arab world.

This chapter first explores the diversity that characterizes the people and societies in the Arab world. It then discusses the associative features found in communication within the region, specifically in terms of language, religion, and social norms. Discussion proceeds by outlining the features of intracultural communication competence to attainable goals of intercultural communication competence.

The chapter concludes with special consideration for balancing tensions between individuality and individualism and the strong associative pull in the quest for intercultural communication competence in the Arab world.

A Tapestry of Cultures Within the Arab World

The complexity and diversity within the Arab world, as well as emerging contravening trends, have compounded the notion of "Arab culture." Traditionally, within the field of intercultural communication scholarship, scholars have tended to speak about the Arab culture in the singular. For example, Edward T. Hall (1958, 1966, 1976, 1990), often referred to as the "father of intercultural communication," used his training as an anthropologist to document communication behavior patterns across cultures. Hall frequently drew upon examples from the Arab culture to illustrate distinctions in intercultural concepts such as high-context and low-context cultures, as well as polychronic and monochromic cultures. In her review of intercultural scholars on the Arab culture, Feghali (1997, p. 351) found that the field "relied heavily" on Hall's work. While Hall's lucid prose and prolific writing helped give birth to the field of intercultural communication, his work relied primarily on cultural blocks such as the Americans, the Germans, the Arabs, and so forth. When contrasted against Western cultures, the Arab culture stood out as a distinctly different cultural block or undifferentiated cultural whole.

While this tendency to speak of the Arab culture as a monolithic cultural entity has been emphasized in the intercultural field and still maintains currency within contemporary intercultural writings, including introductory texts on intercultural communication, a new trend may be aloft. Increasingly, scholars within and outside the region are challenging the notion of one Arab culture (Ayish, 1998, 2003; Feghali, 1997; Iskandar, 2008). Rather than focusing on the outstanding differences between the Arab culture and other cultures, they are probing the critical distinctions among the Arab culture(s) or the array of cultures within the Arab world. In a recent discussion of Arab unity, Al-Jazeera English even used the phrase "Arab cultural systems." Understanding the distinction between Arab culture in the singular—versus Arab cultures in the plural—is a salient point of departure for developing intercultural communication competence.

The emerging distinctions between culture and cultures may stem in part from the difficulty in defining *Arab* (Feghali, 1997). As Almaney and Alwan (1982) noted, "The term 'Arab' becomes strange and baffling when you dig into just what it means . . . an Arab is not a race, religion, or nationality" (p. 30).

Arabs originated in the Arabia Peninsula (modern-day Saudi Arabia and Yemen) and were associated most closely with Bedouin tribal traditions (Ayish, 1998, 2003). The religion of Islam was also revealed in Arabia, and Arabic is the language of the Quran. With the spread of Islam, Arabs carried the religion and the language to South Asia, parts of Europe, and across North Africa (Chejne, 1965; Hitti, 1970; Hourani, 1992). A prominent early Arab scholar, Ibn Khaldun (1332–1406), who traveled from his native Tunisia to Saudi Arabia before settling in Egypt to write the earliest history on the region (*al-Muqaddima*), detailed the cultural encounters between Arabs and non-Arabs (Ibn Khaldun, 1967). The intermingling of cultures—Arabs, Assyrians, Kurds, Berbers, and Nubians—is captured in the title of historian Albert Hourani's (1992) treatise, *The History of the Arab Peoples*. In the latter half of the 20th century, Arab culture was sometimes fused with "Arab identity" and its political associations of Arab unity and Arab nationalism (Barakat, 1993; Suleiman, 2003). During this time, language became the overriding definition of Arabs as a cultural group. As Chejne (1965) observed, "Both the Arabic language and the nationalist movement have complemented each other to such a degree that they could hardly be separated" (p. 459).

Today, the League of Arab States serves as the most frequently cited reference point for defining the Arab world and, by extension, culture(s) within the Arab world. This geopolitical and economic entity, originally established in 1945, now has 22 members. The members span Mauritania, Western Sahara, Morocco, Tunisia, Algeria, Libya, and Egypt in North Africa (*el-Magrib* or "the West"); Sudan, Eritrea, Djibouti, and Somalia along the Horn of Africa; Palestine, Jordan, Lebanon, and Syria in the Fertile Crescent of the Middle East (often referred to as *bilad as-sham*, greater Syria, or the Levant); and Iraq and the Arabian peninsula, including Oman, Yemen, Saudi Arabia, Kuwait, Bahrain, Qatar, and the United Arab Emirates (often referred to as the *khaleej al-Arabi* or the Arab Gulf). When one looks at the underlying factors that shape culture—language, religion, geography, historical political, and economic experiences—the rich tapestry of cultures within the larger brushstroke of the Arab culture is not only easy to see but also hard to ignore.

Linguistically, the 22 countries share a common heritage in the Arabic language. However, for many of the ethnic groups, such as the Kurds, Berbers, and Armenians, Arabic is a second or third language. Across the region itself, one finds a wide variance as well as commonality. Classical Arabic is the written language of the Quran. The original text, compiled shortly after the death of Prophet Muhammad, has been preserved for more than 1,400 years. Modern Standard Arabic (*fusha*) is the written form of the language used in official documents and written texts such as the newspapers, books, and magazines. While people throughout the Arab world learn to read and write Modern Standard Arabic, it is not normally spoken and, when used in daily conversations, sounds stilted to the native ear (Shouby, 1951, p. 285). Each region has its own version of spoken colloquial Arabic, which can vary dramatically in terms of vocabulary, grammatical structures, idiomatic expressions, and pronunciation. Words for daily items (i.e., towel, teapot, car) and foods (tomato, cauliflower, milk, bread) tend to be particularly tied to regional dialects.

Religion, another important feature of culture, reflects another aspect of the diversity found within the Arab world. While the dominant religion is Islam, the region encompasses a host of religions. This is perhaps not surprising given that the Middle East is the birthplace of the three monotheistic religions, which at various points in history vied for dominance. During the Crusades, Christianity was the dominant religion, and large Christian population centers are found throughout Palestine, Lebanon, and Syria. Lebanon, in fact, recognizes close to 20 different religious sects.

Coptic Christians, a denomination of the early orthodox Christian church, are found in Egypt. Significant communities of Arab Jews reside in Morocco, Yemen, and Iraq. Muslim sects include Sunni, Shi'ite, as well as Druze and Alawite.

The religious diversity is perhaps more acutely reflected by the ethnic diversity. Tunisian scholar Mohsen Hamli (2005) pointed out that in 6 of the 22 countries, Arabs are a minority. Two million Assyrians live in Iraq and close to a million Assyrians in Syria. Assyrians have their own language and alphabet (a variation of Aramaic) and belong primarily to the Eastern Catholic Church (Nestorians). The Berbers in northwest Africa also have their distinct language (Afro-Asiatic linguistic classification) and traditional customs. Kurds represent another large ethnic grouping. There are more than 5 million Kurds in Iraq and up to 1.5 million in Syria. The Armenians, originating in south Caucus, number about 1 million and are spread from Egypt to Iraq.

Geographic differences also affect cultural traditions as well as the cultural pride found among the peoples in the region. The harsh environment of the Arabian desert, where one does not survive alone, spawned a nomadic Bedouin culture of fierce competition for resources and magnanimous hospitality (Hamod, 1963). The Fertile Crescent nurtured an agrarian-based society and, with it, an intense identification with the land (Zaharna, 1991). Differences are also pronounced between urban, city dwellers, and rural agricultural communities (Barakat, 1993).

Historical, political, and economic differences also play a role in distinguishing regions within the Arab world. Egypt and Iraq, for example, were home to two of the world's most prominent ancient civilizations. Syria and Iraq were home to the two major Islamic dynasties that fostered the spread of Islam from the Middle East across North Africa and into Spain. The wave of European colonialism that swept through the Arab world left a pronounced impact on language, customs, and political attitudes. Lebanon and Syria experienced the shortest period of colonial rule, about 25 years by the French, while Algeria struggled for 130 years to free itself from French control. The prevalence of English is the result of British colonialism in Egypt, Jordan, and parts of the Arab Gulf States. The continuing turmoil in Palestine has profoundly contributed to the politicization of Palestinian Arab culture. Economically, the region varies from countries such as Saudi Arabia, UAE, and Libya, which have been positively affected by the discovery and exploitation of petroleum resources to countries such as Egypt and Sudan, which struggle against mounting population pressures.

Against this admittedly brief backdrop, the great diversity found among the peoples of the Arab world stands out. Nydell (2005), a prominent writer on Arab culture, remarked, "One might wonder whether there is, in fact, such a thing as Arab culture given the diversity and spread of the Arab region" (p. 13). The notion of "Arab culture" is infinitely more complex than it is at first glance.

The Arab historian Walid Khalidi (1981) attributed the division and unity found in the Arab world to centrifugal and centripetal forces. The major centrifugal forces he cited—ethnicity and interstate conflict—are reflected in the region's diversity. Among the centripetal forces he cited that serve to unify the Arab world are shared common experiences of colonialism, Islam, Arabic, customs, and manners.

These centripetal forces provide a basis for outlining the parameters of Arab cultures. The common struggle against colonialism, albeit several decades ago, reverberates today in the writings of Arab communication scholars (Iskandar, 2008). While there is religious diversity within the region, Islam not only is the dominant religion (estimates of 83%–90% of the population) but has experienced a resurgence of prominence across the region. Communication scholars have recently turned to Islamic teachings and prescripts to suggest Islamic mass media theories (Al-Barzinji, 1998; Hamada, 2004; Mowlana, 2000, 2003) and even normative Arab-Islamic communication theory (Ayish, 1998, 2003). The Arabic language continues to serve as a powerful, defining feature of the Arab world (Suleiman, 2003; Tamari, 2008). Finally, the customs and manners are of special import to our discussion of culture and intercultural communication competence.

Among the most frequently cited customs are those that relate to relationships (Almaney & Alwan, 1982; Hall, 1976; Nydell, 2005). The importance of relationships has been observed by professionals and scholars in communication-related disciplines. Business communication scholars have spoken of establishing positive personal relationships as a prerequisite for conducting business in the Arab world (Almaney & Alwan, 1982; Harris, Moran, & Moran, 2004). Organizational scholars similarly link effective management practices in the region to one's ability to cultivate and manage relationships (A. J. Ali, 1995, 2005; Hutchings & Weir, 2006). Public relations scholars have proposed a distinctive Arab model based on relationship building, noting that the process involves "communication as a social ritual, rather than communication as transmission of information" (Vujnovic & Kruckeberg, 2005, p. 342). Similarly, in a recent collection of public diplomacy essays, former U.S. diplomats who had served extensively in the Arab world all repeatedly emphasize the centrality of relationships (Rugh, 2004). As Ambassador Kenton Keith (2004) noted, "It is hard to overestimate the importance of personal relations in the Arab world" (p. 15). Lebanese sociologist Halim Barakat (1993) perhaps best captured the central importance of relationships in a region of great diversity in his book *The Arab World: Society, Culture, and State.* In speaking of an "Arab conscious identity," Barakat discarded the notion of "cultural uniformity" and instead emphasized the "plural unity" embedded in the "networks of human relationship" (pp. xi–xii). The importance of relationships serves as the springboard for the discussion of intercultural communication competence in the Arab world.

A Common Thread: Associative View of Communication

While diversity may indeed magnify the difficulty of achieving intercultural communication competence in the Arab world, the importance of relationships and social context are pivotal communication components for navigating the region's rich cultural terrain. To capture the significance of relationships and social context, I propose an associative view of communication. From the associative perspective, the significance, meaning, and purpose of communication are derived from relationships among the parties and the social context within which it occurs. This associative view of communication underlies the observations made by Western communication scholars and scholars native to the region. Let me speak first about the Western body of literature since it may be more familiar to the readers of this text.

Association is an underlying feature of Hall's (1976) notion of "high-context" cultures. Hall distinguished between high- and low-context cultures based on how much meaning is embedded in the context versus the code. Whereas low-context communicators tend to search for meaning in the code or message, high-context communicators search for meaning in the context or setting. The connection between meaning and context is one aspect of association. Hall's description of the speaker-listener relationship is similarly revealing of the associative perspective:

> When talking about something that they have on their minds, a high-context individual will expect his interlocutor to know what's bothering him, so that he doesn't have to be specific. The result is that he will talk around and around the point, in effect putting all the pieces in place except the crucial one. Placing it properly— this keystone—is the role of his interlocutor. (p. 98)

Association is also inherent in the depiction of Arab cultures as "collectivist" cultures. In collectivist societies, group goals take priority over individual ones. Individuals pay primary attention to the needs of their group and will sacrifice personal opportunities, placing a premium on group harmony, cohesion, and stability (Ting-Toomey, 1985; Triandis, 1995). The extensive family ties and tribal groupings in Arab cultures as well as deference to group norms are cited as major factors in classifying Arab culture as collectivist (Hofstede, 1980). On the basis of his research of several Arab countries, Hofstede (2008) found these countries ranked low on individualism (38 compared to a world average ranking of 64), which, he says, "translates into a Collectivist society . . . and is manifested in a close long-term commitment to the member 'group,' that being a family, extended family, or extended relationships."

When viewed at the cultural level and in comparison to other cultural blocks, the Arab world may reflect the Western-defined criteria of "collectivist." However, there is a caveat to Arab cultures as collectivist—namely, individuality. Condon and Yousef (1975) highlighted the critical distinction between individualism and "individuality"; although individualism may suggest independence from the group, particularly group pressures toward conformity, "individuality refers to the person's freedom to act differently within the limits set by the social structure" (p. 65). The scholars suggested that individuality may be more prevalent across cultures than individualism. Indeed, this may be the case for Arab societies.

Although they usually employ the term *individualism* instead of *individuality*, both Western and regional scholars have observed the phenomenon in Arab societies. Berger (1962, for example, observed among Palestinian Arabs both a collective, group orientation and a "deep sense of individualism" (pp. 274–275). Quandt, Jabber, and Lesch (1973) noted that Palestinian individualism is not expressed in the nonconformist behavior of Western individualism but in "demands for equality and reciprocity" (p. 80). Ayish (2003) called individualism "central values in the Arab-Islamic worldview" (p. 85). He traces the "deeply ingrained individualism in Bedouin society" back to pre-Islamic traditions of honor, poetry, and courage. However, again, he notes that "unlike its conception in Western cultures, as a unifying concept that may set a limit to group involvement, individualism in Arab-Islamic cultures is composed of both individual and group identification" (p. 85).

The sense of individuality, and even speaking out against the collectivity, is evident in Islamic and cultural icons in the region. In the Quran, the idea of an individual proclaiming his or her belief in God, even at the risk of not only going against the group collective but being exiled from it, is exemplified in the related stories of the prophets (M. Y. Ali, 1934/2003). The prophet Noah is shunned and called a madman. The Prophet Abraham destroys the idols of his tribe and forsakes even his father. The prophet Lot is threatened for denouncing sin. These stories of earlier prophets give context to the Prophet Muhammad, who is persecuted by his own tribe, the powerful Quraish of Mecca, and migrates to Medina.

What is interesting about individuality is that it is rooted within the social context or group association. In the Arab world, individual dignity and honor, both critical individual attributes, are socially defined and ascribed. Thus, it may be an oversimplification to describe Arab cultures as "collectivist." Viewed from the outside at the cultural level, Arab cultures do appear to be collectivist. However, at the individual level, in terms of interpersonal communication, a more refined view would be strong individuality rooted in an associative social context. Ayish (2003), in fact, speaks of the tension created between asserting one's individuality and conforming to social pressures as the "individualism-conformity" dichotomy.

Both the Arabic language and Islamic religion are rich with examples that exemplify the associative perspective. The phenomenon of association within the Arabic language is evident on several levels. Arabic, as a Semitic language, has a three-consonant root stem. From this root stem, a whole series of associative meaning are derived. In English dictionaries, one looks up a word by the progressive sequence of the individual letters of the word—*language,* for example—l-a-n-g-u-a-g-e. The word *linguistics,* a very close associative meaning to language, has its own distinct sequential series of individual letters and is placed separately from the word *language.* For a nonnative speaker of Arabic, one cannot look up a word using the sequence of individual letters; one must first identify the three-consonant root stem, which, in turns, leads to words with associative meanings. For example, *k-t-b,* the root stem of "to write" produces associated words such as *maK-TuB* (a letter, something written), *maK-Ta-Bah* (an office or study, place where one writes), *correspondence* (exchange of something written), and so forth.

Reading written Arabic is also an associative process. In Arabic texts, vowel marks placed above and below individual letters in a word help clarify the word's meaning and function. Most children's books and primary school textbooks have these vowel marks. Part of learning to read Arabic texts is understanding the associations among the words and inserting the vowel marks. Most adult literature, including newspapers, magazines, books, and other written text, does not contain these vowel marks. The notable exception to this practice of omitting vowel marks in texts is the Quran, which has complete vowel marks so as to avoid misreading the text. The situation is much like how an English-language reader would determine whether the word *present* meant a gift, an act of offering something, or a time reference: At *present,* I cannot *present* him a *present.* One determines the meaning of a word by its context within the sentence. As G. M. Wickens (1980) explains to non-native speakers of Arabic studying the language, "The *writer* of Arabic does *not* ordinarily provide the reader with *any short vowels [i.e., vowel marks] at all:* it is the *reader's* need and duty to *supply* these" (p. 13). Wickens's observation about the writer-reader relationship parallels Hall's (1976) earlier observation about speaker-listener relationship: Communicative meaning is not isolated in the message but rather is embedded in the relationships.

Classical Arabic as illustrated in the Quran is highly associative in nature. The Quran, considered the highest literary work in the Arabic language, is replete with associative-based stylistic, linguistic, and rhetorical features. For example, the text in the Quran is not punctuated (the Quran was compiled in written form more than 1,400 years ago; punctuation is a relatively new phenomenon for Arabic text). Quranic text contains no periods, semicolons, question marks, commas, or quotation marks. One recognizes a question or statement by word cues, stylistic features, and context. The rhetorical devices in the Quran are also associatively based. The chapter on the Prophet Joseph (Sura Yusif) is illustrative of the detailed narratives with dialogue. Sura ar-Raham exemplifies the use of repetition, rhetorical questions, and juxtaposition of opposites. The most prominent devices are metaphors, analogies, similes, and parables (these terms in English refer to the Arabic word *methel* and are listed in English-language translations as *parables* in Quran indexes). As the Quran repeatedly states, it teaches by every parable. Two prominent examples are "the parable of light,"[1] which interweaves one intricate layer of metaphor upon another, and "the spider's house,"[2] which stands out for its elegant visual simplicity.

A final example of the associative strand in the Arabic language is the abundance of social greetings and ritualized responses that have been amply noted by observers of the region. Adelman and Lustig (1981) highlighted the "attention to polite interaction through elaborate and prolonged greeting rituals" (p. 352) as one of the dominant features in the region. "Handshakes can go on for minutes, while in prolix Arabic an exchange of polite questions and blessings can extend indefinitely," observed Iseman (1978, p. 51). Cohen (1987) referred to the "veneer of elaborate courtesy," calling the Arabic language a "social instrument—a device for promoting social ends as much as a means for transmitting information" (p. 31).

The strong associative strand running through the Arabic language is also mirrored in the Islamic religion or *deen al-Islam.* The Arabic word *deen* carries a different connotation than the English word *religion.* In the intercultural literature, religion or belief system is often distinguished from political system, economic system, or social system. In Arabic, the word *deen* is more holistic and encompassing than *faith* and refers to "a way of life." Writing from an Islamic perspective, Siddiqui (2000, p. 11) describes the encompassing meanings of *deen al-Islam* for believers: It is comprehensive (*deen al-kamilah*), elevates human nature to its highest potential (*deen al-fitrah*), advocates moderation and balance (*deen al-wasata*), presents a lasting upright value system (*deen al-qayyimah*), is based on a system of governance called "shura and mutual advice" (*deen an-nasihah*), and proscribes good manners and fair dealings (*deen al-adaab*).

The Quran as a manual for a way of life focuses extensively on social relations. The first pillar in Islam is *at-tawheed,* which proclaims the oneness of God. This is very much a relational statement: Nothing can be associated with God. Within the Quran, a person's most important relationship is with God. In fact, one's relationship to God is presented as a higher or more intimate level of relations than that person's relationship to himself or herself. Prominent verses within the Quran include God being closer to a person than his or her own jugular vein or knowing what is in one's heart.[3] A person's relationship to himself or herself, what might be called intrapersonal communication, is a second level of relationships. A third level of relationships discussed in the Quran deals with intimate relations such as one's parents, siblings, spouse, children, and neighbors. Social manners and knowledge of appropriate behaviors are one of the three fundamental tenets of the Islamic conception of education (Kirdar, 2006). The most expansive relationship is man's relationship within *al-Ummah,* or the community of Islam. In his commentary on the Quran, Abdullah Yusuf Ali (M. Y. Ali, 1934/2003) points out that the overwhelming focus (first 14 of 15 parts) of the Quran is on the *Ummah.*

These levels of relationship or associations within Islam discussed in the Quran are echoed throughout Islamic practices. As an illustration, Ali's (2003, N. 5461) commentary draws attention to the graduations of social contacts from the individual to international level. The proscribed five daily prayers reflect man's intimate relationship with God. The proscribed weekly prayer (Friday at midday) encompasses one's intimate relations. The proscribed two Eid prayers expand to the larger community. The prayers offered during the Hajj, or pilgrimage, which gathers Muslims from around the world in Mecca, are relations at the level of *al-Umma,* or global community of Muslims.

Communication Competence: An Associative Perspective

The associative view—which puts a premium on relationships and social context—has several important implications for intercultural communication competence. However, before discussing intercultural communication competence, it may be illuminating to highlight some of the parameters of intracultural communication competence from an associative perspective. What are some of the salient communication features or skills that distinguish competent communicators across the Arab world? A first component is linguistic ability. Throughout Arab history, eloquence has been highly prized—and this is evidenced through pre-Islamic poetry, the majesty of the Noble Quran, and public speeches of contemporary Arab leaders. Hamod (1963), who provided an historical overview of the development and changes in Arab rhetoric, highlighted the importance of eloquence:

> The linear equation was as follows: He who speaks well is well educated; he who is well educated is more qualified to render judgments and it is his advice we should follow. Eloquence and effectiveness were equated. (p. 98)

Although there has been a relative shift in the extent of embellishment, particularly with the transition from classical Arabic to Modern Standard Arabic, eloquence has remained central to communication proficiency and stature (Ayish, 1998; Chejne, 1965), and emotional resonance has remained a central component of eloquence (Hamod, 1963; Prothro, 1952). An eloquent communicator has the ability to use language to emotionally connect and stir the hearts and imagination of others.

Linguistic ability is evident on a second level in terms of social greetings and compliments. The Quran specifically addresses social greetings by admonishing believers to return a greeting with one that is better or at least equal.[4] A competent communicator stands out for his or her ability to distill the emotional mood and significance of social events into a well-crafted greeting or compliment. A relatively simple yet illustrative example can be seen in what one says after finishing a cup of coffee. Rather than offer a simple "thank you," a skilled communicator would use any news gained during the social visit to finesse his or her compliment and returns the cup to the tray, proclaiming "in celebration of your son's wedding," or "for the success of your children's exams."

Another dominant language skill exhibited by adept communicators is their sensitivity to and knowledge of dialectal differences of spoken colloquial Arabic—and ability to code-switch between their own native dialect and that being spoken. Again, whereas Modern Standard Arabic may be readily comprehensible, regional and even local dialects within a region can vary considerably. To appreciate the extent to which colloquial dialects differ and the difficulty that this linguistic skill presents even for native Arabic speakers, one can draw analogies to Latin. As Shouby (1951) explains,

> This situation [gap between literary classical Arabic and colloquial dialects] is a strong reminder of medieval Europe, when educated people wrote and read Latin but spoke the different dialects which later developed into what are now the various European languages. (p. 286)

In some respects, colloquial dialects reflect the phenomenon of expressing individuality within the larger (Arabic language) collective. One may use the vocabulary or idioms of a regional dialect to define one's self, create bonds of shared identity with those familiar with the dialect, or draw boundaries with others unfamiliar with the dialect. A skilled communicator is distinguished by his or her knowledge and familiarity with the wide array of regional dialects and ability for what might be viewed as code-switching to strengthen relational bonds.

Interestingly, but not surprisingly, many of the normative or exemplary nonverbal behaviors (manners or *adab*) of skillful communicators are specifically mentioned in the Quran and the Sunna of the Prophet Muhammad. Modesty and humility are repeatedly stressed as the guiding features of exemplary behavior. This includes modulating one's voice and even being soft spoken. In contrast, arrogance—overt displays of confidence, brash behaviors, and speech—is soundly denounced and associated with evil. The most prominent examples used in the Quran to underscore the disdain of arrogance are the stories of Iblis (the devil) and the Egyptian Pharaoh.

A final expansive category of communication skills are those associated with building and maintaining social networks. The founding Arab sociologist and historian Ibn

Khaldun linked the strength of human social organizations to the concept of *asabiyah,* or "solidarity," "group feeling," or "group consciousness." *Asabiyah* could be built within a tribal clan or politically across an entire geographic region. On an interpersonal level, a competent communicator uses the various verbal and nonverbal skills to define, enhance, and manage relations (Yousef, 1974). To extend relationships, the competent communicators demonstrate knowledge of intra- and intergroup dynamics and maintenance strategies. The skill sets used to build internal group solitary and expansive networks of alliances include mediation, negotiation, consensus building, and compliance-gaining skills.

Intercultural Communication Competence: An Associative Perspective

This rough, preliminary sketch highlights some of the distinguishing features of intracultural communication competence found within Arab societies and provides a benchmark for intercultural communication competence. The premium placed on relationships and social context has several important implications for intercultural communication competence.

First, and most immediate, is the need to adjust one's approach in terms of the level of interaction as well as analysis. There is sometimes a tendency in the study of intercultural communication to speak in broad generalities, such as "communication between cultures" or between Arabs and Americans. While this macro-level perspective may provide a vantage point for viewing larger cultural patterns, it may leave individuals seeking communication competence at a disadvantage. The premium placed on relationships and social context within Arab societies necessitates a micro- or individual perspective and a relational-level analysis. It requires what Spitzberg (1989, p. 261) identified as an interpersonal approach to intercultural communication.

At the interpersonal level, relationships are immediate and personalized to the individual with whom one is interacting. Thus, an awareness of the diversity that defines the people in the Arab world—and modifying one's expectations accordingly— is a preliminary step in developing intercultural communication competence (Almaney & Awan 1982; Nydell, 2005). Depending on one's linguistic ability, this implies sensitivity to language variations in pronunciation, vocabulary, and the idioms the speaker is using. It suggests an awareness of the other person's religious affiliation, as well as religious groupings, historical tensions, or alliances. Geography and history, while sometimes overlooked, are important avenues for connecting with the people and their past. Familiarity with local and regional politics can help one avoid misunderstandings because politics may sometimes be an unavoidable topic.

A second aspect of intercultural competence entails refining one's observation skills and attuning one's focus to social and relational cues. How well can one decipher which social cues are important? All behaviors may have meaning, but not all may imply relational significance. How well can one read, understand, and employ social cues to build relationships? For nonnative speakers of Arabic, communication competence may be better demonstrated by their social fluency rather than linguistic ability.

Intercultural scholarship often stresses language ability and encourages fluency as a determinant of communication competence (Deardorff, 2004). This focus on language is perhaps understandable, particularly if one considers the low-context focus on code as observed by Hall (1976). In addition, given the strong association between language and culture, it is sometimes suggested that if one masters the language, then one has mastered the culture. However, it is possible to be fluent in the language yet ignorant of the culture. As one international executive charged with managing relations for a major corporation advised, if given the choice between hiring someone who was fluent in the language or someone with limited language ability and high cultural awareness, choose the latter (T. McLean, personal communication, December 2006). He highlighted the danger of linguistic fluency in the absence of cultural knowledge. If someone speaks the language, there is often a corresponding expectation by the local people that the person is also familiar with the social customs and graces. Yet, as he aptly observed, people tended to be less forgiving of social gaffs from a linguistically competent individual than they are of linguistic gaffs from a culturally competent individual.

Striving for social as opposed to linguistic fluency may be particularly sage given the nature of the Arabic language. As linguistic scholars have noted and untold students have professed, Arabic is one of the most difficult languages to learn (Wickens, 1980). Even achieving a modicum of fluency can be frustrating. The written language is different from the spoken language, the spoken language varies from region to region, and within regions, it can vary from city to city. It is possible, in fact not unusual, to find individuals proficient in reading Arabic yet unable to engage others in casual conversations.

Ironically, however, it is also not unusual to find individuals with no reading ability who are adept at navigating the social terrain with only a limited linguistic ability. These individuals have gained entrée into the social arena by using language to achieve a social fluency. What this entails is learning the social grammar underlining the many greetings and expressions—what to say when and to whom, what the appropriate replies are, and the variations for particular social circumstances. Yousef (1974, p. 383) referred to the plethora of social greetings, compliments, and expressions in the Arab world as "phatic communication." Phatic (binding) communication, coined by anthropologist Malinowski (1923), is ritualistic communication that is low information content but critical to relationship building and maintenance. DeVito (1986) described phatic communication as "the small talk that precedes the big talk [that] opens up channels of communication" (p. 228). Within interpersonal communication scholarship, phatic communication is spotlighted as a preliminary level of self-disclosure (Veenendall & Feinstein, 1996, p. 140), a feed-forward message that signals a willingness to engage socially (DeVito, 2001, p. 13), and a "small but effective" measure of confirmation of the other (Patton & Giffin, 1977, p. 134).

While the importance of phatic communication is mentioned in interpersonal communication, its relevance to cultures that stress relationship building and maintenance may deserve renewed attention in intercultural communication. Developing an awareness if not appreciation of phatic communication may be particularly important for goal-oriented individuals. In their cross-cultural study of effective managers, Dean and Popp (1990) found culture-specific data illustrating how achievement-oriented individuals tend to focus more on "getting things done than developing interpersonal relationships" (p. 416). Finally, it is worth remembering that the essence of eloquence is not mastery of the language per se but rather the ability to use language to emotionally connect and move others (Hamod, 1963; Shouby, 1951). Eloquence, in Arabic, is captured by the expression, "Words from the heart fall in the heart, those from the tongue reward only the ear." One does not have to be fluent in Arabic to speak from the heart.[5]

Another aspect of intercultural competence involves modeling and employing social behaviors. This step, as well as the previous ones, parallels those within the literature. While there are many intercultural models available, a shorthand model that captures the essence of the process is Howell's (1982) interpersonal model, which has also been adapted and adopted by the U.S. Peace Corps (1999, p. 199) and has parallels with Bennett's (1998, p. 26) ethnocentric/ethnorelative model. According to Howell's model, the first stage of *unconscious incompetence* is when an individual misinterprets others' behavior but is not aware of it. The second stage, *conscious incompetence,* is when an individual is aware that he misinterprets other's behavior but does nothing about it. The third stage, *conscious competence,* is when the individual thinks about his or her communication behavior and consciously tries to modify it to increase effectiveness. The fourth stage, *unconscious competence,* is when the individual has practiced and internalized effective communication behaviors. The fifth stage, *unconscious super-competence,* represents the highest level of communication fluency. It is the second and third stages of Howell's model that reflect the aspect of modeling and employing behaviors. It is what Woodman (1973) described as "trying on behavior":

> Trying on behavior is always risky business. You may muff it, you may make a fool of yourself, and you'll almost always feel awkward, even though perhaps you don't appear that way. (p. 10)

Trying on behaviors—even if they feel awkward—can enhance an individual's effectiveness and facilitate the relationship-building process. However, the transition from conscious competence to unconscious competence can present the most difficulty for the individual in terms of intrapersonal communication in the intercultural setting. Lane (2007) adroitly identifies the hazard of this transition: "The risk is that some learners may feel like their culture and individuality is lost once they reach this advanced state" (p. 26). Grove and Torbion (1985) described individuals at this stage as "deeply involved and deeply confused" (pp. 214–215).

This reaction during this transition stage captures the phenomenon of "self-shock" (Zaharna, 1989). Whereas culture shock is an awareness of the differences of the cultural other, self-shock is an individual's awareness of the differences with and within the self. Self-shock emerges in the process of modeling and employing new behaviors. The more an individual tries to align his or her behaviors to meet cultural expectations of others to achieve intercultural communication competence, the more the individual can risk undermining his or her own identity-bound behaviors.

What is sometimes overlooked in the intercultural quest to modify one's behaviors to the new sociocultural context is that behaviors are not only culture bound (Hall, 1976) with respect to a particular cultural setting but also identity bound with respect to individuals (Zaharna, 1989). Communication behaviors carry with them not just a task function (i.e., communication to get something done) and social function (i.e., communication to facilitate relations with others) but also an identity function (i.e., communication that defines one's self to others). The identity function of communication suggests that all communication carries corresponding implicit or explicit meaning for how the individual views himself or herself and how that person wishes others to view him or her. Within the familiar confines of intracultural communication context, individuals often have a repertoire of identity-bound behaviors used to maintain a consistent and stable sense of self. The challenge of intercultural communication occurs on two levels. One is when an individual employs an identity-bound behavior that elicits unexpected or undesired responses in the other, responses that disconfirm rather than confirm the individual's identity. The other challenge is applying new and even contradictory meanings to identity-bound behaviors.

The dual challenges of identity can be particularly problematic given the delicate balance between individuality, individualism, and collectivism. As Ayish (2003) pointed out, within the Arab cultures, there is a strong sense of individuality. However, this individuality is expressed within the context of the social group. As he notes, even individuals raised in this sociocultural milieu must learn to straddle the dichotomy of individuality and collective conformity. Appreciating and developing this critical skill may be particularly challenging for persons who place a premium on individualism and/or fail to distinguish between individuality and individualism. As Condon and Yousef (1975) point out, individualism poses a strong resistance against conformity and group pressure. Confusing individuality with individualism within the collectivist context may feel like pressure to conform. The strong associative pull toward relationships can further exacerbate feelings of a pressure to conform. What is ultimately required to comfortably transition from conscious to unconscious competence is for individuals to appreciate the distinction between individualism and identity and then cultivate that personal individuality within the social relationships and contexts that define the Arab world.

Conclusion

This chapter has explored intercultural communication competence in the Arab world. Recognizing the diversity of the region as well as the importance of relationships and social context are pivotal communication components for navigating the region's rich cultural terrain. While the intense focus on the Arab world has made writing about culture and religion within the region sensitive and at times even controversial, the need for intercultural communication competence with the peoples of the Arab world has perhaps never been greater. This chapter has been a modest step in that direction and invites further exploration.

Notes

1. "Allah is the light of the heavens and the earth. The parable of His Light is as a niche and within it a lamp: the lamp is in a glass, the glass as it were a brilliant star, lit from a blessed tree, an olive, neither of the east nor of the west, whose oil would almost glow forth,

though no fire touched it. Light upon Light! Allah guides to His Light whom He wills. And Allah sets forth parables for mankind, and Allah is all-Knower of everything" (Quran 24:35).

2. "The likeness of those who take false deities as protectors other than Allah is like the spider who builds for itself a house; but truly the frailest of houses is the spider's house—if they but knew" (Quran 29:41).

3. "It was We who created man, and We know what dark suggestions his soul makes to him: for We are nearer to him than (his) jugular vein" (Quran 50:16).

4. "When you are greeted with a greeting, greet in return with what is better than it, or (at least) equal to it. Allah takes into careful account all things" (Quran 4:86).

5. Speaking from the heart tends to carry more persuasive power than intellectually rationalized arguments. This is because, as M. Y. Ali (1934/2003) noted, "[The] heart in Arabic means not only the seat of affection, piety, charity, etc., but also of understanding and intelligent appreciation of things" (p. 1698).

References

Adelman, M. B., & Lustig, M. W. (1981). Intercultural communication problems as perceived by Saudi Arabian and American managers. *International Journal of Intercultural Relations, 5,* 349–363.

Al-Barzinji, S. (1998). *Working principles for an Islamic model in mass communication* (Academic Dissertation No. 6). Herndon, VA: International Institute of Islamic Thought.

Ali, A. J. (1995). Cultural discontinuity and Arab management thought. *International Studies of Management & Organization, 25,* 7–30.

Ali, A. J. (2005). *Islamic perspectives on management and organization.* London: Edward Elgar.

Ali, M. Y. (2003). *The meaning of the Holy Qur'an* (10th ed.). Beltsville, MD: Amana. (Original work published 1934)

Almaney, A. J., & Alwan, A. J. (1982). *Communicating with the Arabs: A handbook for the business executive.* Prospect Heights, IL: Waveland.

Ayish, M. I. (1998). Communication research in the Arab world: A new perspective. *The Public, 15,* 33–57.

Ayish, M. I. (2003). Beyond Western-oriented communication theories: A normative Arab-Islamic perspective. *The Public, 10,* 79–92.

Barakat, H. (1993). *The Arab world: Society, culture, and state.* Berkeley: University of California Press.

Bennett, M. J. (1998). Intercultural communication: A current perspective. In M. J. Bennett (Ed.), *Basic concepts of intercultural communication: Selected readings* (pp. 1–34). Yarmouth, ME: Intercultural Press.

Berger, M., (1962). *The Arab world today.* Garden City, NY: Doubleday.

Chejne, A. (1965). Arabic: Its significance and place in Arab-Muslim society. *Middle East Journal, 19,* 447–470.

Cohen, R. (1987). Problems of intercultural communication in Egyptian-American diplomatic relations. *International Journal of Intercultural Relations, 11,* 29–47.

Condon, J., & Yousef, F. (1975). *An introduction to intercultural communication.* Indianapolis, IN: Bobbs-Merrill.

Dean, O., & Popp, G. (1990). Intercultural communication effectiveness as perceived by American managers in Saudi Arabia and French managers in the U.S. *International Journal of Intercultural Relations, 14,* 405–424.

Deardorff, D. K. (2004). *The identification and assessment of intercultural competence as a student outcome of internationalization at institutions of higher education in the United States.* Unpublished doctoral dissertation, North Carolina State University.

DeVito, J. A. (1986). *The communication handbook: A dictionary.* New York: Harper & Row.

DeVito, J. A. (2001). *The interpersonal communication book* (9th ed.). New York: Longman.

Feghali, E. (1997). Arab cultural communication patterns. *International Journal of Intercultural Relations, 21,* 345–378.

Grove, C. L., & Torbion, I. (1985). New conceptualization of intercultural adjustment and the goal of training. *International Journal of Intercultural Relations, 9,* 205–233.

Hall, E. T. (1958). *The hidden dimension.* New York: Anchor.

Hall, E. T. (1966). *The silent language.* New York: Anchor.

Hall, E. T. (1976). *Beyond culture.* New York: Anchor.

Hall, E. T. (with Hall, M. R.). (1990). *Understanding cultural differences.* New York: Anchor.

Hamada, B. I. (2004, Fall). Global culture or culture clash: An Islamic intercultural communication perspective. *Global Media Journal, 3.* http://lass.calumet.purdue.edu/cca/gmj/fa04/gmj-fa04-hamada.htm

Hamli, M. (2005). *Women, media and diversity in the Arab world.* Tunis: University of Manouba, Tunis, Tunisia.

Hamod, H. (1963). Arab and Moslem rhetorical theory and practice. *Central States Speech Journal, 14,* 97–104.

Harris, P. R., Moran, R. T., & Moran, S. V. (2004). *Managing cultural differences* (6th ed.). New York: Elsevier.

Hitti, P. K. (1970). *History of the Arabs* (10th ed.). New York: St. Martin's.

Hofstede, G. (1980). *Culture's consequences: International differences in work-related values.* Beverly Hills, CA: Sage.

Hofstede, G. (2008). *The Arab world.* http://www.geert-hofstede.com/hofstede_arab_world.html

Hourani, A. (1992). *A history of the Arab peoples.* New York: Time Warner.

Howell, W. (1982). *The empathetic communicator.* Belmont, CA: Wadsworth.

Hutchings, K., & Weir, D. (2006). Understanding networking in China and the Arab World: Lessons for international managers. *Journal of European Industrial Training, 30,* 272–290.

Ibn Khaldun. (1967). *The muqaddimah: An introduction to history* (F. Rosenthal, Trans., & N. J. Dawood, Ed.). Princeton, NJ: Princeton University Press.

Iseman, P. A. (1978, February). The Arabian ethos. *Harper's,* pp. 37–57.

Iskandar, A. (2008). Lines in the sand: Problematizing Arab media in the post-taxonomic era. *Arab Media & Society.* http://www.arabmediasociety.com/?article=226

Khalidi, W. (1981). Regiopolitics: Toward a U.S. policy on the Palestine problem. *Foreign Affairs, 59,* 1050–1063.

Keith, K. (2004). 'The last three feet': Making the personal connection. In W. A. Rugh (Ed.), *Engaging the Arab & Islamic worlds through public diplomacy* (pp. 11–21). Washington, DC: Public Diplomacy Council.

Kirdar, S. (2006). The development of women's education in the Arab world. In R. Griffin (Ed.), *Education in the Muslim world: Different perspectives* (pp. 191–210). Oxford, UK: Symposium Books.

Lane, H. C. (2007, July). *Metacognition and the development of intercultural competence.* Paper presented at the 13th International Conference on Artificial Intelligence in Education, Marina del Rey, CA.

Malinowski, B. (1923). The problem of meaning in primitive languages. In C. K. Ogden & I. A. Richards (Eds.), *The meaning of meaning* (Supplement I, pp. 296–336). New York: Harcourt Brace Jovanovich.

Mowlana, H. (2000). Professional ethics and sociopolitical mobilization of Muslim journalists: A study of communication, ethics and the Islamic tradition. In J. Thierstein & Y. R. Kamalipour (Eds.), *Religion, law, and freedom: A global perspective* (pp. 123–140). Westport, CT: Praeger.

Mowlana, H. (2003). Foundation of communication in Islamic societies. In J. P. Mitchell & S. Marriage (Eds.), *Mediating religion: Conversations in media, religion and culture* (pp. 305–316). New York: Continuum.

Nydell, M. K. (2005). *Understanding Arabs: A guide for Westerners.* Yarmouth, ME: Intercultural Press.

Patton, B. R., & Giffin, K. (1977). *Interpersonal communication in action: Basic text and readings* (2nd ed.). New York: Harper & Row.

Prothro, E. (1952). Arab-American differences in the judgment of written messages. *Journal of Social Psychology, 42,* 3–11.

Quandt, W. G., Jabber, F., & Lesch, A. M. (1973). *The politics of Palestinian nationalism.* Berkeley: University of California Press.

Rugh, W. A. (2004). *Engaging the Arab & Islamic worlds through public diplomacy.* Washington, DC: Public Diplomacy Council.

Shouby, E. (1951). The influence of the Arabic language on the psychology of the Arabs. *Middle East Journal, 5,* 284–302.

Siddiqui, D. A. (2000, July). *A comparative analysis of the Islamic and the Western models of news production and ethics of dissemination.* Paper presented at the annual convention of the International Association of Media and Communication Research, Nanyang Technical University, Singapore.

Spitzberg, B. H. (1989). Issues in the development of a theory of interpersonal competence in the intercultural context. *International Journal of Intercultural Relations, 13,* 241–268.

Suleiman, Y. (2003). *The Arabic language and national identity.* Washington, DC: Georgetown University Press.

Tamari, S. (2008). *Who are the Arabs?* Washington, DC: Center for Contemporary Arab Studies, Georgetown University. http://ccas.georgetown.edu/files/who_are_arabs.pdf

Ting-Toomey, S. (1985). Toward a theory of conflict and culture. In W. Gudykunst, L. Stewart, & S. Ting-Toomey (Eds.), *Communication, culture, and organizational processes* (pp. 71–86). Beverly Hills, CA: Sage.

Triandis, H. C. (1995). *Individualism and collectivism.* Boulder, CO: Westview.

U.S. Peace Corps. (1999). *Culture matters. The Peace Corps cross-cultural workbook.* Washington, DC: US Peace Corps.

Veenendall, T. L., & Feinstein, M. C. (1996). *Let's talk about relationships: Cases in study* (2nd ed.). Prospect Heights, IL: Waveland.

Vujnovic, M., & Kruckeberg, D. (2005). Imperative for an Arab model of public relations as a framework for diplomatic, corporate and nongovernmental relationships. *Public Relations Review, 31,* 338–343.

Wickens, G. M. (1980). *Arabic grammar: A first workbook.* Cambridge, UK: Cambridge University Press.

Woodman, L. (1973). *Perspectives in self-awareness: Essays on human problems.* Columbus, OH: Charles E. Merrill.

Yousef, F. S. (1974). Cross-cultural communication: Aspects of contrastive social values between North Americans and Middle Easterners. *Human Organization, 33,* 383–387.

Zaharna, R. S. (1989). Self-shock: The double-binding challenge of identity. *International Journal of Intercultural Relations, 13,* 501–525.

Zaharna, R. S. (1991). The ontological function of interpersonal communication: A cross-cultural analysis of Americans and Palestinians. *Howard Journal of Communication, 3,* 87–98.

Zaharna, R. S. (1995). Understanding cultural preferences of Arab communication patterns. *Public Relations Review, 21,* 241–255.

CHAPTER 10

A Chinese Model of Intercultural Leadership Competence

Guo-Ming Chen and Ran An

The rapid development of technology and the transformation of economy as the two major trends of globalization have affected every aspect of our lives (Chen, 2006; Chen & Starosta, 2000). Although it has been many hundreds of years since people from different cultural groups began to involve in interaction (Lubbers, 1998), no change in human society has been greater than the impact of globalization. The globalization not only changes traditional human society into a new structure but also requires a new way of thinking and lifestyle from its members. For example, from the perspective of business transaction, the old structure of the national economies and markets has been transformed into a globalized system. To survive in the new century, according to Gupta and Govindarajan (1997), a modern organization, in addition to exploring the emerging global markets and expediting the corporation's globalization process, has to equip itself with knowledgeable and skilled management in dealing with employees from diverse cultural backgrounds and in keeping pace with its globalizing customers. The trends that lift human society to a higher level of interdependence and interconnectedness between people and people, organization and organization, and government to government in different corners of the world led Friedman (2005) to conclude that "the world was no longer round but flat" (p. 11), in which the size of the world is shrunk from small to tiny.

The rapid development of technology is mainly reflected in the areas of communication and transportation. The burgeoning of the Internet is the most significant contribution among communication technologies to the global interconnectivity.

The Internet has linked every part of the world as an interwoven network and has blurred the line between mass and interpersonal communication, enabling both personal and public messages to flow across national boundaries faster by providing an opportunity for individuals from different societies to communicate on a regular basis (Flew, 2005; Manovich, 2003). Use of the Internet has become part of our daily life and has redefined the concepts of time and space by creating a global town square where members can freely express their opinions, and hundreds of thousands of nations emerging in cyberspace becomes a norm rather than an exception (Naisbitt, 1997).

The new communication and transportation technology inevitably has led to the emergence of a new economic landscape. Adler (2008) traced the development of global enterprises and found that organizations have evolved from domestic, multidomestic, and multinational to global. In the global phase, the organization becomes globally allied, hierarchically flattened, decentralized, and heavily coordinated. A successful global organization must show the ability to track its potential transnational customers and quickly transform these worldwide needs into products and services. The economic shifts to globalization obviously change the contours of the workforce and demand a new corporate culture to adapt to a new environment (O'Hara-Devereaux & Johansen, 1994).

The globalization trend also stimulates the occurrence of widespread population migrations and the development of multiculturalism (Chen & Starosta, 1996, 2005), generating a tremendous increase in intercultural interactions and togetherness across national borders. It increases the multiethnic structure in human societies, in which interaction among co-cultures becomes inevitable domestically and the demand for ethnic groups to learn to adjust to one's counterpart's identity and culture is increasing. The restructuring of the fabric of human society represents the increasing diversity of the workforce, including the diverse race, culture, age, gender, and language. Thus, the ability to learn new ways of interacting, to deal with the frictions in the process of adjusting ourselves to new cultural realities, and to reach a greater global awareness will decide the degree of our success while living in a culturally diverse society.

In sum, globalization has changed every aspect of human society through the shrinking of time and space. The new imperatives of riding the wave of globalization give human society an opportunity for new ideas and a strong demand for new leadership. In other words, the trend of globalization inevitably mirrors the problem of "leadership vacuum" in the present time (Naisbitt, 1997). The old mainstream thinkers are no longer relevant in this new globalizing society, and the new leaders are still waiting to appear. Now is the time for searching for a new approach to leadership to face the world of today, which is full of paradoxes and contradictions (Moran, Harris, & Moran, 2007; Rosen, 2000).

Hence, with its forces of dialectical dynamism, universal pervasiveness, holistic interconnectedness, cultural hybridity, and individual power, globalization calls for a never-ending quest for the leaders to deal with the inextricably linked imperatives embedded in people, relationships, and culture (Chen, 2005; Rosen, Digh, Singer, & Phillips, 2000). These imperatives include the exploration of emerging opportunities to be competitive in global society, the development of potentiality for being effective in transactions, the ability to adapt to idiosyncratic local orientations, and the ability to keep pace with others to reach global coordination and consistency (Chin, Gu, & Tubbs, 2001; Kofman & Youngs, 1996). In other words, the trend of globalization demands "global leadership competence," through which the leaders are able to search for the vision, shared understanding, and sense of multiple identities that lead to the unlocking of human potential in the development of intelligence, knowledge, and creativity for a peaceful and productive society.

The People's Republic of China (P.R. China) as a key player in this globalizing society deserves a specific look from a communication perspective, so that a mutual understanding between East and West can be reached to build a more harmonious human society. Since the economic reform in the early 1980s, hundreds of thousands of joint ventures in business and other arenas have been developed in P.R. China (*China Statistical Yearbook,* 2007). The rapid development brought about not only tremendous changes within P.R. China but also great challenges to world affairs.

Because of the way the Chinese perceive competence and the way the Chinese communicate are sharply different from Westerners (Chen & Chen, 2002; S. Liu & Chen, 2000; S. Liu, Chen, & Liu, 2006), it is crucial for people to be aware of this intercultural distinction when dealing with the Chinese. The purpose of this chapter, then, is to apply the study to the context of leadership by examining a model of leadership competence specifically from the Chinese cultural perspective. Through the model, people can better understand the Chinese, on one hand, and possibly integrate the Chinese way of thinking and behaving into a more comprehensive picture of global leadership competence, on the other.

Philosophical Foundation of Chinese Leadership

To understand leadership from the Chinese cultural perspective, one must know the philosophical assumptions that guide Chinese communication behaviors. So to the Chinese, what is the fundamental principle of the universe that dictates human interaction? The Chinese adopted the view that "change" is the only constant phenomenon of the universe that prescribes human behaviors, and change is defined by the dialectic transformation and dialogical connection of the two opposite but complementary forces (i.e., *yin* and *yang*) of the universe, and the interactional movement of the two forces can be straightforward, capacious, and cyclic (Chen, 2004; Chu, 1974; Wilhelm, 1990).

The reality or the completion of anything in the universe comes into existence through the integration of *yin* and *yang,* symbolized by the Great Ultimate or *Tai Chi,* with the dark as *yin* and the white as *yang* (see Figure 10.1). This reveals a holistic view for the Chinese to see the world, in which the Chinese assume all contradictions in the universe, including human interaction, should be resolved in the process of the dynamic movement of *yin* and *yang* (Chen & Starosta, 2003a; Cheng, 1987). According to Chen (2004), "The holistic principle unfolds the developmental feature of the cyclic movement in which individual components

are interdependent and interdetermined in a network of relations," and "The mutual dependency of
relationship reflected in the part-whole interdeter-
mination also indicates that all individual components are equally valid outcomes of *Tai Chi* or the
dialectic interaction of *yin* and *yang*" (p. 10).
Moreover, the Chinese believe that the union of *yin*
and *yang* or the *Tai Chi* is a state of equilibrium or
Great Harmony, and this is the ultimate goal human
society should aim to achieve.

The belief in change led the Chinese to consider
the universe as a great whole and is transforming in
a cyclically endless process (Chai & Chai, 1969;
C. L. Liu, 1990). Chen (2001, p. 57) applied this belief
to propose three assumptions that guide Chinese
communication behaviors:

Figure 10.1 *Tai Chi*

Assumption 1: Human communication is a changing and transforming process.

Assumption 2: Human communication is changing according to the endless but
orderly cycle of the universe.

Assumption 3: Human communication is never absolutely completed or finished.

According to Chen and Starosta (2003a), Cheng (1987), and Fang (1981), in this
continuous, cyclic, and interdependent process, human beings play a vital role, in
which mutuality, respect, and honesty are valued. Furthermore, developing and
keeping a harmonious relationship among interactants is demanded. These assumptions serve as fundamental definitions and descriptions upon which leadership competence can be assumed or inferred from the Chinese perspective. Thus, the degree
of a leader's ability to achieve harmonious relationships can be used to represent the
degree of the leader's competence (Chen, 2001).

Furthermore, to succeed in bringing harmony into the transforming process or
to regulate favorably the change of human interaction, Chinese philosophy stipu-
lates three components—that is, *shi, wei,* and *ji*—for a leader to follow (Y. Wu, 1964).
Shi refers to temporal contingencies in the process of communication, *wei* refers to
spatial contingencies, and *ji* refers to the first imperceptible beginning of movement
that shows the trace of possible consequences of the ongoing interaction.

According to Chen (2001), knowing the temporal and spatial contingencies and
the trace of any movement will increase the possibility of reaching a harmonious
state and achieving competence in communication. This ability of knowing *shi, wei,*
and *ji,* symbolizing the affairs of human, heaven and earth, is a guarantee to overcome one's counterparts in different areas of the human world, as specified in *Sun
Zi* (Li, Yang, & Tan, 1985), and this ability can only be fostered by self-nourishment
through the process of ceaseless purifying, continuous learning, sensitivity cultivation, creativity development, and empathy enhancement (Chang, 1963; Chen, 2005;

Fang, 1980). Harmony that dictates communication or leadership competence in the Chinese culture is therefore established through this ability, and in this equilibrium state, the elements of security, togetherness, joy, and benefit can be crystalized to reflect an ideal human society (Cheng, 1983, 2000; Tseng, 2005).

Finally, *zhong dao,* or the way of meaning, embedded in *cheng* (sincerity), is the guidepost for the action to achieve the equilibrium state of communication or leadership competence (Legge, 1955; Xiao, 2003). *Zhong dao* is the way of being appropriate, fitting one's communication to the situation (Tseng, 1986). It provides a principle that leads interactants to recognize the trace of movement (*ji*) and to know the right time (*shi*) to behave appropriately to fit in with environments (*wei*). As to *cheng,* it is the axis of *zhong dao,* which is sustained by three spokes: benevolence, righteousness, and propriety. *Cheng* represents the internal consistency of individuals by holding a sincere and honest mind in themselves and others, which is acquired by constant self-cultivation or purification through learning (Xiao, 2004). A sincere and honest mind is the basis of the *gan ying* (wholehearted responding), through which the interactants or the leader and the led are united as one (Wang, 1989; Y. Wu, 1976). A harmonious relationship is then established based on this symmetrical and congruent process of interaction, and a holistic system of leadership competence is therefore completed.

A Model of Chinese Leadership Competence

Based on the above Chinese philosophical assumptions, a Chinese model of leadership competence containing three interactional dimensions of self-cultivation, context profundity, and action dexterity can be proposed (see Figure 10.2). First, self-cultivation forms the affective foundation for a competent leader to foster a sincere mind, so that *zhong dao* can be put into practice to regulate the change of the dynamic world of *yin* and *yang.* Second, context profundity is the cognitive awareness of the temporal and spatial contingencies and the trace of a movement from a multicontextual or multicultural perspective, which is the bridge linking the sincere mind and the behavioral aspect of the leadership. Finally, action dexterity, representing the interactional aspect of leadership competence, brings the continuity and duration into the dynamic process of leadership. In addition to the three dimensions, two representative elements are ascribed to each dimension separately for a further explication.

Self-Cultivation

Self-cultivation is a process of transforming and moving the leader from the lower to the higher level of the developmental ladder of leadership competence. It is the process of unceasingly edifying, liberating, and purifying personal attributes of the self. These attributes are ruled under the umbrella of "great empathy," which dictates that unity is integrated with diversities, and particularity is identified with universality. This interfusion and interpenetration of human multiplicities "formulates

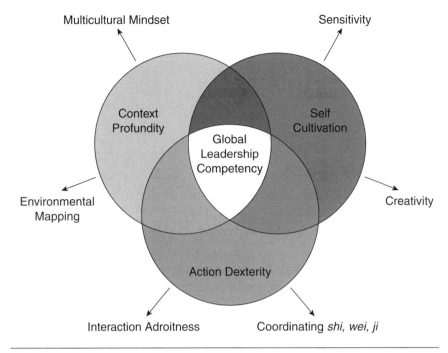

Figure 10.2 A Chinese Model of Leadership Competence

the ideal of fellow-feeling by expanding the self consciousness to the consciousness of one's fellow persons," and in the global level, "it refers to the ability to look for shared communication symbols and to project the self into another person's mind by thinking the same thoughts and feeling the same emotions as the person" (Chen & Starosta, 2004, p. 13).

From the Chinese cultural perspective, the accomplishment of the great empathy is dependent on the two human abilities of sensitivity and creativity. According to Chen and Starosta (2004),

> Sensitivity is the contraction of diversity into unity, and creativity is the expansion from unity to diversity. Working together, sensitivity supplements creativity by supporting a ground of potentiality, while creativity provides a means of actuality for great empathy to be revealed. The two move together hand in hand and their radiance is emitted through a ceaseless process of learning. (p. 13)

Context Profundity

Context profundity calls for the leaders to broaden and expand their perspectives by eliminating biases or stereotypes toward those of cultural others. This equips leaders with a mental ability to examine attentively and analyze the surrounding environment and observantly expect novel trends so that the personal and group goals can be achieved in a harmonious and productive way (Rhinesmith, 1992, 1996).

Multicultural mind-set and environmental mapping are the two elements that can be added to the dimension of context profundity from the Chinese cultural perspective.

Built on the foundation of open-mindedness and receptiveness, a multicultural mind-set prescribes the decrease or absence of ethnocentrism and parochialism (Chen & Starosta, 1998–1999). A leader with a multicultural mind-set usually possesses distinctive personal characteristics such as cultural awareness and sensitivity, flexibility, and empathetic and holistic thinking.

Environmental mapping is the ability to manifest the awareness of different contexts, in which competent leaders know how to reduce the situational ambiguity and uncertainty to create a place where they can skillfully exercise their behaviors. In the global context, it is through the cognitive process that competent leaders acquire cultural knowledge and characteristics of their own and others and further draw a picture or map of cultures to reflect the degree of their understanding through the process of bewilderment, frustration, analysis, and immersion (Chen & Starosta, 2003b; Hanvey, 1987).

Action Dexterity

Action dexterity is the leader's ability to appropriately and effectively initiate, maintain, and terminate verbal and nonverbal interaction. It is largely defined by communication performance of the leader. Two critical elements embedded in the dimension of action dexterity can be generated from the Chinese cultural perspective, including the coordination of *shi, wei,* and *ji* and interaction adroitness.

Coordinating smoothly the interplay of the components of *shi, wei,* and *ji* is to bring continuity into the process of change. In the process of human communication, *shi* as the temporal contingencies demands leaders to know the temporal relations and appropriately perform what they ought to act in the different stages of leadership communication. In this communication process, *wei* as the spatial contingencies demands leaders to determine what and where is the appropriate space for having an action, and this space is mainly dictated by the hierarchical structure of human relationship, aiming to ensure an unequal and complementary relationship in the Chinese society, based on Confucian teachings (Lin, 1988). *Ji* promotes the leader to sense what is hidden and what is evident in the process of interaction. Being able to detect the first imperceptible beginning of an interaction so that leaders behave at the right time and at right place is the sine qua non of a smooth coordination of *shi, wei,* and *ji.*

Interaction adroitness refers to the leader's ability to align the interaction with people or the led. The behavioral skills of interaction adroitness for leadership competence may include job skills, language ability, behavioral flexibility, interaction management, and identity maintenance (Chen, 2007). Interaction adroitness solidifies the ultimate goal of self-cultivation and context profundity to have the leader function effectively and appropriately at the behavioral level. In other words, the leader's mental, affective, and cognitive abilities must be integrated into a set of behavioral skills that lead to the successful and productive interaction in the globalizing society.

Evaluation of the Model

The Chinese model of leadership competence proposed in this chapter reflects an orientation toward the Chinese culture specifically and Asian cultures in general. Ontologically, the model reflects the teachings of Buddhism, Confucianism, Hinduism, Shintoism, and Taoism, decreeing a holistic, interconnected, and transitional worldview that serves as the *tao* of leadership competence. Axiologically, the model dictates that harmony, considered the lubricant of the interconnected knots of the leader and the led, is the ethical principle of leadership competence. Epistemologically, the model puts interconnectedness as the locus of leadership competence, which produces the meaning for understanding the interaction between the leader and the led. And methodologically, the model emphasizes the importance of *zhong dao*, which is a nonlinear cyclic process in favor of an intuitive, sensitive, and indirect way of communication as the appropriate way of unifying the *yin* and *yang* (Chen, 2006).

Applied to the process of interaction, these paradigmatic assumptions dictate a set of behaviors that construct the Chinese meaning of communication and leadership competence. For example, Chen (1993) identified five of the communication behaviors for being competent in Chinese interactions, including emotional control, avoidance of aggressive behaviors, avoidance of the expression of "no," face saving, and the emphasis of particularistic relationships.

These specific communication behaviors, based on the paradigmatic assumptions of Chinese leadership competence, appear to be incompatible with Western conceptions of leadership competence, which underline the atomistic, confrontational, reductionistic, and logical views. The differences were reflected in different aspects of human interaction, such as business negotiation (Chen & Chen, 2002), leadership style (M. Y. Wu, 2008), and conflict management in joint-ventured or culturally diverse companies (Knutson, Hwang, & Deng, 2000; S. Liu & Chen, 2002). Figure 10.3 further lists the contrasting paradigmatic assumptions between East and West (organized from Chen, 2006; Chen & Miike, 2006; Dissanayake, 1988; Miike, 2003; Okabe, 2007; Wei, 1981; Yum, 2007).

The contrasting beliefs on leadership competence seem to emit a pessimistic view of reaching understanding between East and West. Nevertheless, the interconnected, interdependent, and highly interactive nature of global trends strongly demands a convergent model of global leadership competence to more effectively deal with the multicultural environment of modern society. The goal for scholars and practitioners is to pursue how to change the traditional way of viewing the Eastern and Western paradigmatic assumptions as dichotomized categories and move to an integrated model of global leadership competence. In other words, while emphasizing the importance of cultural differences among diverse groups, the new model of global leadership competence should not ignore the universal values of humans, including, for example, courage, kindness, hard work, honest, integrity, love, and tolerance (Chin et al., 2001; Schwartz & Bilsky, 1987, 1990). Only through the recognition and acceptance of similarities of the interactants can the communication gap caused by differences among cultures be bridged.

Ontology	
East	West
Holistic	Atomistic
Submerged collectivistic	Discrete individualistic

Axiology		Epistemology		Methodology	
East	West	East	West	East	West
Harmonious	Confrontational	Interconnected	Reductionistic	Intuitive	Logical
indirect	direct	reciprocity	independent	subjective	objective
subtle	expressive	we	I	nonlinear	linear
adaptative	dialectical	hierarchical	equal	ambiguous	analytical
consensual	divisive	associative	free will	ritual	justificatory
agreeable	sermonic	ascribed	achieved	accommodative	manipulative

Figure 10.3   Paradigmatic Assumptions of Eastern and Western Leadership Competence

The need for a new model of global leadership competence has been advocated by scholars from different disciplines. For example, Rosen (2000) indicated that a successful global leader has to possess four distinct competencies: the personal literacy for understanding and valuing oneself, the social literacy for engaging and challenging one's counterparts, the business literacy for focusing and mobilizing one's own organization, and the cultural literacy for valuing and leveraging cultural differences. Similar competencies, identified by Adler (2008), Moran et al. (2007), and Thorn (2002), can be adopted to bridge the leadership gap between the current and future qualities of leaders.

These studies demonstrated that, although U.S. or Western leadership approaches might not be suitable for being applied to other contexts (Hofstede, 1980; Laurent, 1983), through the process of adaptation to other cultures, a working model of global leadership competence can be developed (Dorfman et al., 1997). Chin et al.'s (2001) conceptual model of global leadership competencies illustrated the possibility and potentiality of integrating Eastern and Western cultural values based on the harmonious transformational interaction of *yin* and *yang*. The authors contended that the global leadership deficiencies can be transformed into global leadership competencies through moving from the cognitive level to attitudinal level and the values level to behavioral level. In other words, this can be achieved by moving through the development processes of ignorance, awareness, understanding, appreciation, and acceptance/internalization to transformation regarding cultural differences. The Chinese model of leadership competence proposed in this chapter may hold the heuristic power for being applied to different cultural contexts through a necessary adaptation process.

Finally, a great potential of developing a new model of global leadership competence is to rely on the studies of intercultural communication competence (see Spitzberg & Changnon, Chapter 1, this volume, for a detailed discussion of this work). Many scholars from the communication discipline have been devoted to the research of intercultural communication competence for years (e.g., Byram, 1997; Chen, 2006; Chen & Starosta, 1996; Collier, 1989; Hammer, 1989; Lustig & Koester, 2005; Lustig & Spitzberg, 2002; Martin, 1993, 2002; Martin & Hammer, 1989; Ruben, 1977, 1989; Ruben & Kealey, 1979; Spitzberg, 1994), and the thoughts and research findings of these scholars can contribute to the transformation of the traditional models of leadership competence to a global context.

Conclusion

The main purpose of this chapter is to discuss a Chinese conceptualization of leadership competence and its application to intercultural context. The chapter identifies the need for a new model of intercultural leadership competence. The impact of globalization on human society has led to the demand of filling in the leadership vacuum. On the basis of the Chinese philosophical assumptions that guide Chinese behaviors, the authors outline a model of leadership competence from the Chinese cultural perspective. The model is composed of three dimensions, including self-cultivation, culture profundity, and action dexterity, with each dimension containing two elements separately. Then the model is evaluated from the perspective of an intercultural context to demonstrate the differences in the behavioral level of global leadership competence. Because the model only represents the Chinese view of leadership competence, the validity of the model applied to the global context is still subject to challenge. For future research, it is necessary to contrast and compare the model with other existing models, especially those from the Western culture, to develop further a more heuristic and integrative conceptual scheme, which can serve to advance mutual benefit of all in the global network.

References

Adler, N. J. (2008). *International dimensions of organizational behavior.* Mason, OH: Thompson.

Byram, M. (1997). *Teaching and assessing intercultural communicative competence.* Bristol, PA: Multilingual Matters.

Chai, C., & Chai, W. (1969). Introduction. In J. Legge (Trans.), *I Ching: Book of changes* (pp. xxvii–xcii). New York: University Books.

Chang, C.-Y. (1963). *Creativity and Taoism: A study of Chinese philosophy, art, and poetry.* New York: Harper & Row.

Chen, G. M. (1993, November). *A Chinese perspective of communication competence.* Paper presented at the annual meeting of the Speech Communication Association, Miami Beach, FL.

Chen, G. M. (2001). Toward transcultural understanding: A harmony theory of Chinese communication. In V. H. Milhouse, M. K. Asante, & P. O. Nwosu (Eds.), *Transcultural realities: Interdisciplinary perspectives on cross-cultural relations* (pp. 55–70). Thousand Oaks, CA: Sage.

Chen, G. M. (2004, November). *Bian (change): A perpetual discourse of I Ching.* Paper presented at the annual meeting of National Communication Association, Chicago.

Chen, G. M. (2005). A model of global communication competence. *China Media Research, 1,* 3–11.

Chen, G. M. (2006). Asian communication studies: What and where to now. *Review of Communication, 6,* 295–311.

Chen, G. M. (2007). A review of the concept of intercultural effectiveness. In M. Hinner (Ed.), *The influence of culture in the world of business* (pp. 95–116). Germany: Peter Lang.

Chen, G. M., & Chen, V. (2002). An examination of PRC business negotiations. *Communication Research Reports, 19,* 399–408.

Chen, G. M., & Miike, Y. (2006). Ferment and future of communication studies in Asia: Chinese and Japanese perspectives. *China Media Research, 2*(1), 1–12.

Chen, G. M., & Starosta, W. J. (1996). Intercultural communication competence: A synthesis. *Communication Yearbook, 19,* 353–384.

Chen, G. M., & Starosta, W. J. (1998–1999). A review of the concept of intercultural awareness. *Human Communication, 2,* 27–54.

Chen, G. M., & Starosta, W. J. (2000). Communication and global society: An introduction. In G. M. Chen & W. J. Starosta (Eds.), *Communication and global society* (pp. 1–16). New York: Peter Lang.

Chen, G. M., & Starosta, W. J. (2003a). Asian approaches to human communication: A dialogue. *Intercultural Communication Studies, 12*(4), 1–15.

Chen, G. M., & Starosta, W. J. (2003b). A review of the concept of intercultural awareness. In L. A. Samovar & R. E. Porter (Eds.), *Intercultural communication: A reader* (pp. 344–353). Belmont, CA: Wadsworth.

Chen, G. M., & Starosta, W. J. (2004). Communication among cultural diversities: A dialogue. *International and Intercultural Communication Annual, 27,* 3–16.

Chen, G. M., & Starosta, W. J. (2005). *Foundations of intercultural communication.* Lanham, MD: University Press of America.

Cheng, C.-Y. (1983). Searching for a modern model of Chinese management. *China Tribune, 16*(9), 27–31.

Cheng, C.-Y. (1987). Chinese philosophy and contemporary human communication theory. In D. L. Kincaid (Ed.), *Communication theory: Eastern and Western perspectives* (pp. 23–43). New York: Academic Press.

Cheng, C.-Y. (2000). *C Theory: Chinese management philosophy.* Shanghai: Xuelin.

Chin, C. O., Gu, J., & Tubbs, S. L. (2001). Developing global leadership competencies. *Journal of Leadership Studies, 79*(4), 20–31.

China statistical yearbook. (2007). Beijing: China Statistics Press.

Chu, S. (1974). *The interpretation of I Ching.* Taipei, Taiwan: Wen Hua.

Collier, M. J. (1989). Cultural and intercultural communication competence: Current approaches and directions for future research. *International Journal and Intercultural Relations, 13,* 287–302.

Dissanayake, W. (Ed.). (1988). *Communication theory: The Asian perspective.* Singapore: Asian Mass Communication Research and Information Center.

Dorfman, P. W., Howell, J. P., Hibino, S., Lee, J. K., Tate, U., & Bautista, A. (1997). Leadership in Western and Asian countries: Commonalities and differences in effective leadership processes across cultures. *Leadership Quarterly, 8,* 233–274.

Fang, T. H. (1980). *Creativity in man and nature.* Taipei, Taiwan: Linking.

Fang, T. H. (1981). *Chinese philosophy: Its spirit and its development.* Taipei, Taiwan: Linking.

Flew, T. (2005). *New media*. New York: Oxford University Press.

Friedman, T. L. (2005). *The world is flat: A brief history of the twenty-first century*. New York: Farrar, Straus & Giroux.

Gupta, A. K., & Govindarajan, V. (1997). *Creating a global mindset*. Retrieved December 15, 2006, from http//www.bmgt.umd.edu/cib/wplist.html

Hammer, M. R. (1989). Intercultural communication competence. In M. K. Asante & W. B. Gudykunst (Eds.), *Handbook of international and intercultural communication* (pp. 247–260). Newbury Park, CA: Sage.

Hanvey, R. G. (1987). Cross-culture awareness. In L. F. Luce & E. C. Smith (Eds.), *Toward internationalism* (pp. 13–23). Cambridge, MA: Newbury.

Hofstede, G. (1980). Motivation, leadership and organization: Do American theories apply abroad? *Organizational Dynamics, 9,* 42–63.

Knutson, T. J., Hwang, J. C., & Deng, B. C. (2000). Perception and management of conflict: A comparison of Taiwanese and US business employees. *Intercultural Communication Studies, 9*(2), 1–31.

Kofman, E., & Youngs, G. (1996). Introduction: Globalization—the second wave. In E. Kofman & G. Youngs (Eds.), *Globalization: Theory and practice* (pp. 1–8). New York: Pinter.

Laurent, A. (1983). The cultural diversity of Western conceptions of management. *International Studies of Management and Organization, 13*(1–2), 75–96.

Legge, J. (1955). *The Four Book*. Taipei, Taiwan: Wen Yo.

Li, S. J., Yang, X. J., & Tan, J. Z. (1985). *Sun Zi and management*. Hong Kong: San Lian.

Lin, Y. S. (1988). *The social philosophy of Yin Chuan's Yi Chuan*. Taipei, Taiwan: Shen Wu.

Liu, C. L. (1990). The cyclic view of I Ching and Chinese thinking. *China Yi Studies, 123,* 14–16 & *124,* 13–18.

Liu, S., & Chen, G. M. (2000). Assessing Chinese conflict management styles in joint ventures. *Intercultural Communication Studies, 9,* 71–88.

Liu, S., & Chen, G. M. (2002). Collaboration over avoidance: Conflict management strategies in state-owned enterprises in China. In G. M. Chen & Ringo Ma (Eds.), *Chinese conflict management and resolution* (pp. 163–182). Westport, CT: Ablex.

Liu, S., Chen, G. M., & Liu, Q. (2006). Through the lenses of organizational culture: A comparison of state-owned enterprises and joint ventures in China. *China Media Research, 2*(2), 15–24.

Lubbers, R. F. (1998, November). *The dynamic of globalization*. Paper presented at the Tilburg University Seminar, Tilburg, The Netherlands.

Lustig, M. W., & Koester, J. (2005). *Intercultural competence: Interpersonal communication across cultures*. Boston: Allyn & Bacon.

Lustig, M. W., & Spitzberg, B. H. (2002). Methodological issues in the study of Intercultural communication competence: A review. In R. L. Wiseman & J. Koester (Eds.), *Intercultural communication competence* (pp. 153–167). Thousand Oaks, CA: Sage.

Manovich, L. (2003). New media from Borges to HTML. In N. Wardrip-Fruin & N. Montfort (Eds.), *The new media reader* (pp. 13–25). Cambridge: MIT Press.

Martin, J. N. (1993). Intercultural communication competence: A review. In R. L. Wiseman & J. Koester (Eds.), *Intercultural communication competence* (pp. 16–32). Thousand Oaks, CA: Sage.

Martin, J. N. (2002). Intercultural communication competence: A review. In R. L. Wisemann & J. Koester (Eds.), *Intercultural communication competence* (pp. 16–29). Newbury Park, CA: Sage.

Martin, J. N., & Hammer, M. R. (1989). Behavioral categories of intercultural communication competence: Everyday communicators' perceptions. *International Journal of Intercultural Relations, 13,* 303–332.

Miike, Y. (2003). Toward an alternative metatheory of human communication: An Asiacentric vision. *Intercultural Communication Studies, 12*(4), 39–63.

Moran, R. T., Harris, P. R., & Moran, S. V. (2007). *Managing cultural differences: Global leadership strategies for the 21st century.* New York: Elsevier.

Naisbitt, J. (1997). *Global paradox.* New York: Avon.

O'Hara-Devereaux, M., & Johansen, R. (1994). *Globalwork: Bridging distance, culture, and time.* San Francisco: Jossey-Bass.

Okabe, R. (2007). The concept of rhetorical competence and sensitivity revisited: From Western and Eastern perspectives. *China Media Research, 3*(4), 74–81.

Rhinesmith, S. H. (1992, October). Global mindsets for global managers. *Training & Development,* pp. 63–68.

Rhinesmith, S. H. (1996). *A manager's guide to globalization.* Chicago: Irwin.

Rosen, R. R. (2000). What makes a globally literate leader? *Chief Executive, 154,* 46–48.

Rosen, R., Digh, P., Singer, M., & Phillips, C. (2000). *Global literacies: Lessons on business leadership and national cultures.* New York: Simon & Schuster.

Ruben, B. D. (1977). Guidelines for cross-cultural communication effectiveness. *Group & Organization Studies, 2,* 470–479.

Ruben, B. D. (1989). The study of cross-cultural competence: Traditions and contemporary issues. *International Journal of Intercultural Relations, 13,* 229–240.

Ruben, B. D., & Kealey, D. J. (1979). Behavioral assessment of communication competency and the prediction of cross-cultural adaptation. *International Journal of Intercultural Relations, 3,* 15–47.

Schwartz, S., & Bilsky, W. (1987). Toward a psychological structure of human values. *Journal of Personality and Social Psychology, 53,* 850–862.

Schwartz, S., & Bilsky, W. (1990). Toward a theory of the universal content and structure of values: Extensions and cross-cultural replications. *Journal of Personality and Social Psychology, 58,* 878–891.

Spitzberg, B. H. (1994). A model of intercultural communication competence. In L. A. Samovar & R. E. Porter (Eds.), *Intercultural communication: A reader* (pp. 347–359). Belmont, CA: Wadsworth.

Thorn, M. (2002). *Leadership in international organizations: Global leadership competencies.* Retrieved February 25, 2008, from http//www.academy.umd.edu/publications/global_leadership/marlene_thorn.htm

Tseng, S. C. (1986). *The Chinese idea of administration.* Taipei, Taiwan: Linking.

Tseng, S. C. (2005). *The way of administration.* Beijing: Peking University Press.

Wang, B. S. (1989). *Between Confucianism and Taoism.* Taipei, Taiwan: Han Kuan.

Wei, Z. T. (1981). *An introduction to Chinese culture.* Taipei, Taiwan: Shui Niu.

Wilhelm, R. (Trans.) (1990). *The I Ching.* Princeton, NY: Princeton University Press.

Wu, M. Y. (2008). Comparing expected leadership styles in Taiwan and the United States: A study of university employees. *China Media Research, 4*(1), 36–46.

Wu, Y. (1964). The concept of change in I Ching. *Chuon Kuo Yi Chou, 754,* 19–21.

Wu, Y. (1976). *The philosophy of Cheng in Chuon Yuon.* Taipei, Taiwan: Don Da.

Xiao, X. (2003). *Zhong* (Centrality): An everlasting subject of Chinese discourse. *Intercultural Communication Studies, 12*(4), 127–149.

Xiao, X. (2004). *Li* and the Chinese patterns of communication. In G. M. Chen (Ed.), *Theories and principles of Chinese communication* (pp. 379–405). Taipei, Taiwan: Wunan.

Yum, J. O. (2007). Confucianism and communication: *Jen, Li,* and *Ubuntu. China Media Research, 3*(4), 15–22.

CHAPTER 11

Intercultural Competence in German Discourse

Alois Moosmüller and Michael Schönhuth

This chapter outlines the particularities of the German intercultural competence discourse, presenting and commenting on the various lines of argumentation on this concept. A current overview of the diverse areas, theories, and applications of intercultural communication and intercultural competence is given by Straub, Weidemann, and Weidemann (2007), and a concise review of the discourse of intercultural communication in different social sciences within Germany is presented by Moosmüller (2007) and Roth and Roth (2001).

In use in Germany since the mid-1990s, the term *intercultural competence* has meanwhile become ubiquitous, playing today an important role in all realms of society. Multinational companies need intercultural competence to cope with the challenges of international business, particularly in regard to human resource management. Public institutions need intercultural competence to meet the challenges of multicultural society, particularly in regard to immigrant integration. In both realms, in international relations as well as in multicultural society, intercultural competence has come to be considered of major importance.

Intercultural communication first arose as a topic of discussion in Germany in the 1980s, starting in the area of international management, then spreading to education, psychology, linguistics, and other social sciences. The first publications explicitly concerning intercultural competence were Bernd Müller's (1993) article in applied linguistics ("German as a foreign language") and Wolfgang Hinz-Rommel's (1994) book in social work and education. Following up on U.S. publications, both went on and developed their own concepts.

The discourse on intercultural competence is multifaceted and often considered confusing. A perfect example is the discussion of the psychologist Alexander Thomas's (2003) seminal paper on intercultural competence. Its reviews neglect to deal with the paper's actual topic, a specific intercultural competence model, but rather criticize assumptions on which the model is based. Pragmatic questions on the model's validity play a subordinate role, confirming the impression that the topic of intercultural competence is murky and confusing. This chapter aims to lay out the German scene and provide more clarity on the various discourses of this complex concept.

Basically, there are two seemingly irreconcilable approaches in conceptualizing intercultural competence: the "efficiency approach" and the "growth approach." In the former, the aim of intercultural competence is to make intercultural communication more efficient, and in the latter, it is to foster the further development and growth of individuals and groups.

The following particularities were determined in the conceptualization of intercultural competence:

- intercultural competence is not conceptualized on the level of individual actors but rather on the level of organizational actors;

- there is a widespread conviction that it is impossible to discuss intercultural competence without reference to equality of power;

- the discourse on intercultural competence is dominated by theoretical questions, whereas pragmatic considerations play a subordinate role;

- intercultural competence is conceptualized completely differently in a multinational organization context than in a multicultural society context.

Thus, the conceptualization of intercultural competence in German discourses is characterized by critical reasoning, the attempt to integrate systemic aspects and the tendency to prefer the growth approach over the efficiency approach.

Terms and Synonyms

The term *competence* is polyvalent. It refers to both "authority, responsibility" and "capability, ability, skill." Competence is the individual capability that is determined by contextual and situational conditions. The terms *intercultural action competence* and *intercultural communication competence* are used synonymously for the term *intercultural competence.* Many equate intercultural competence with *key qualification,* a term coined in the 1970s by the labor and education researcher Dieter Mertens (1974). For him, *key qualifications* were qualifications that represented a "key" to acquiring new, rapidly changing expert knowledge.

Key qualification comprises four areas of competence:

- social competence (usually comprising communication skills, cooperation skills, conflict resolution skills, and empathy skills),

- method competence (analytical skills, creativity, willingness to learn, rhetorical skills),

- self-competence (productivity, capability, motivation, flexibility, reliability, independence, adaptability, stress resistance),

- action competence (yielded by the three aforementioned competencies): the ability to act in a manner appropriate to the situation while being able to realize own interests.

Due to the similarity of intercultural competence and the concept of "key qualifications," long familiar in Germany, many authors wonder what is so novel about the concept of intercultural competence. No conclusive answers have yet been found.

Areas of Application and Limitations

Is there such a thing as general intercultural competence, as many authors suggest, or is intercultural competence always context dependent? Would therefore a teacher of a multicultural class need a different form of intercultural competence than a manager of an international company? If intercultural competence is context based, it would be necessary to define empirically established area-specific typologies of intercultural competencies, which has yet to be accomplished. Furthermore, as Jürgen Straub (2007) asserts, the concept of intercultural competence should be more theory bound and better integrated into scientific discourse. He criticizes the way many authors conceptualize intercultural competence, especially that, according to them, intercultural competence

- always points out communication problems that need to be avoided or remedied;

- is based on psychological dispositions and individuals' knowledge-based abilities and skills only;

- is not related to collective subjects (authorities, organizations, groups);

- only plays a role in professional but not in private contexts like multicultural marriages and partnerships, family relations, and networks of friends;

- does not tie in enough with the fruitful discourse on the term *competence* (e.g., Habermas's discussion of communicative competence).

In conclusion, the German conceptions of intercultural competence emphasize multifaceted approaches, context boundedness, and the need to integrate more elaborate concepts.

Disciplines and Discourses

Mainly four disciplines have been engaged in the discourse on intercultural competence in Germany—applied linguistics, psychology, education, and cultural anthropology—each discipline thereby emphasizing different aspects and employing different ways of framing. Consequently, instead of one single, integrated discourse, there are several, in some ways mutually exclusive, discourses. This chapter will outline the particularities in each of them.

Foreign Language Teaching (German Language and Literature)

The question of how to acquire intercultural competence in foreign language teaching, and thus more effective and appropriate use of a foreign language, led to studying nonverbal and paraverbal aspects. As early as the 1970s, there were considerations concerning linking foreign language study with cultural studies. Impulses came particularly from textbook research (Gerighausen & Seel, 1982; Göhring, 1980). Interculturality in speech behavior was taken up in pragmalinguistics, also including affective and conative components. Approaches to the didactics of understanding the cultural other were developed, incorporating more detailed study of the history and culture of a country and the intercultural dependency of semiotics, semantics, and pragmatics (Bredella & Christ, 1995; Oksaar, 1989; Rehbein, 1985).

In the 1980s, research was conducted on culture-specific constructions of the self and the other in language and literature. The resulting intercultural studies in German literature ("Interkulturelle Germanistik"; Wierlacher, 1987) influenced the new field of study of German as a foreign language, which subsequently became an important forum for the discussion on intercultural competence. Particular attention was focused on the contextualization of foreign language teaching (Bachmann-Medick, 1987). The term *intercultural competence* emerged for the first time in an article by Müller (1993), in which he gave an overview of the various, predominantly practice-oriented approaches in U.S. intercultural communication research, favoring the opinion that contemporary foreign language teaching has to include intercultural competence. The opinion slowly prevailed that solely teaching a foreign language was not sufficient to deal with problems in international communication; rather, intercultural competence, a combination of psychological and foreign language competencies, must also be taught.

Intercultural competence in language teaching has two aspects: first, the development of competencies to promote efficacy on foreign sojourns, foreign studies, foreign assignments, in international negotiations, and so on (Bredella, 1999; Knapp-Potthoff & Liedke, 1997) and, second, how second language teaching can contribute to integrating immigrants (Hess-Lüttich, 1985). The latter was taken up by the European Union: Its "Common European Framework of Reference for Languages: Learning, Teaching, Assessment," declared in 2001, promotes intercultural competence as a mandatory goal in foreign and second language teaching. The aim is to advance the multilingualism and communication skills of Europeans and in this way their mobility. The frame of reference describes in detail what kind of knowledge and what skills need to be developed to act interculturally competent (Apfelbaum, 2007; Europarat, 2001, p. 106)—in particular, the skills

- to relate one's own culture to the foreign culture,

- to identify and apply strategies for relations with members of other cultures,

- to act as an intermediary between one's own and the other culture,

- to effectively deal with intercultural misunderstandings and conflicts,

- to overcome stereotypical attributions.

There is general consensus among applied linguists that foreign language and second language teaching and the development of intercultural competence are closely linked. However, opinions diverge greatly as to what constitutes "intercultural." One opinion is that all communication is intercultural, and intercultural competence therefore is also important in intracultural communication (Rost-Roth, 1994); another is that people with well-developed intracultural communicative skills easily acquire intercultural competence (Boeckmann, 2006). Many criticize that intercultural competence is not an actual teaching goal in German schools because Germany still does not perceive itself a multicultural society (Luchtenberg, 1999).

Psychological Approaches to Intercultural Competence

The birth of psychology as an independent experimental field of study is usually regarded as occurring in 1879, when Wilhelm Wundt founded the first laboratory for psychological research at Leipzig University. Wundt, the "father of psychology," had "two souls in his chest" since he is also considered the founder of *Völkerpsychologie* (the historical predecessor to cultural psychology). Attracted by Johann Gottfried Herder's idea of a *Volksgeist* (Herder developed this idea—each people owns a unique culture, and each culture deserves equal respect—in the treatise "On the Origin of Language" in 1772), Wundt and other early psychologists believed that psychological structures and processes are not merely determined by sensation but also by the cultures surrounding the individual.

Völkerpsychologie emerged as the complementary scientific perspective to experimental, hard fact-based psychology. Being an "ideographic science" (contrary to "nomothetic science"), *Völkerpsychologie* was not interested in providing general law-like statements but rather in highlighting the particular unique elements of the phenomenon under inquiry (Beuchelt, 1974; Chakkarath, 2003). Psychologists of the first generation, like the founding father of American psychology, Edward B. Titchener, who came to Leipzig to study with Wundt, brought the new sciences to their countries, where they continued to flourish. In Nazi Germany, they were brought to a halt. After the war, it took almost 30 years before psychologists in Germany could resume the scientific discussions and traditions of prewar Germany (Trommsdorff, 1986). But the term *Völkerpsychologie* had become contaminated, disseminating a somehow racist connotation. Hence, psychologists resorted to seemingly unencumbered English terminologies, absorbing theories and methods prevalent in American scientific discourses. Even though German psychology closely resembles American psychology, some differences can be noticed also in the field of cultural, cross-cultural, or intercultural psychology (Friedlmeier, 2007).

Unlike "cross-cultural psychology" in the United States, which can be categorized as "nomothetic science," the corresponding German term *kulturvergleichende*

Psychologie should rather be categorized as "ideographic science" since predominantly qualitative methods are applied, and researchers are more concerned with the contingencies and contextual aspects of human behavior than with the search for universals (Thomas, 1993). In the 1980s, cross-cultural research was resumed in Germany mostly in three study fields. One was developmental psychology, especially the comparison of mother-child relationships and concepts of fostering and upbringing across various cultures (Mandl, Dreher, & Kornadt, 1993; Trommsdorff, 1989). Another was organizational psychology, particularly international management and leadership styles (Kieser, 1981; von Keller, 1982), and finally the field of cultural learning and intercultural training (Dadder, 1987; Thomas, 1985).

Alexander Thomas et al. studied Youth Exchange Programs and made suggestions on how to improve those programs, thereby modifying and substantiating Allport's contact hypothesis (Danckwortt, 1985; Thomas, 1985). They tried to find out if prejudices reinforced by intercultural encounters could be reduced by strengthening the interactant's cultural sensitivity (i.e., have the interactants acquire specific knowledge about their counterpart's implicit cultural assumptions). This led to the study of the so-called *culture standards,* a term that was borrowed from cognitive anthropologist Ward Goodenough (1964). It was hypothesized that studying the culture standards of their "significant other" should make interactants inevitably realize their own implicit cultural assumptions. The culture standards approach, in combination with culture assimilator training, was found to be a useful instrument for acquiring intercultural competence (Eckensberger, 1996; Thomas, 1991).

In the 1990s, cultural psychology (*Kulturpsychologie*) or anthropological psychology emerged from the then prevalent discourses, which were, among others, informed by postcolonial study approaches. In many respects, the roots of *Kulturpsychologie* begin with Karl Bühler, the early father of Gestaltpsychology and outspoken critic of quantitative methodology. Cultural psychologists came to the conclusion that culture and mind should be regarded as two sides of the same coin (Jahoda, 1993; Shore, 1996). Intercultural psychology, having evolved from cultural psychology, takes a more dynamic view, analyzing psychological conditions, processes, and effects of individuals with different cultural backgrounds involved in intercultural interaction.

Extensive applied research in intercultural psychology has been conducted in the field of international transfers (Kühlmann, 1995). Some researchers have designed intercultural assessments to facilitate the procedure of selecting competent personnel for international assignments (Deller, 2000). Using qualitative methods, researchers developed criteria and instruments to evaluate intercultural trainings (Kinast, 1998; Podsiadlowski & Spieß, 1996), tried to improve the efficiency of training and coaching methods (Barmeyer, 2005; Kinast, 2003), and developed psychosocial on-site support for expatriates (Kühlmann & Stahl, 2001). Being the central concern in the studies mentioned, the generation of intercultural competence is best summarized in Thomas's (2003) complex learning model of intercultural competence, which is based on reflective learning and pays attention to the sociocultural framing of action and to the actor situation interdependencies.

Finally, another characteristic of the German discourse on intercultural psychology should be mentioned. The postulate of "the psychic unity of mankind," as originally promoted by Wundt and others, has become the dominant paradigm in psychology. Lucien Lévy-Bruhl (1923), the French anthropologist and contemporary of Wilhelm Wundt, had started a counterdiscourse on that subject matter. His notion of the "primitive mind" profoundly questioned the postulate of the psychic unity of mankind. The voices of those challenging the psychic unity paradigm have not ceased; they have in fact grown stronger, especially in the English-speaking world (Nisbett, 2003; Shore, 1996). By contrast, the discourse in Germany has firmly stayed within the confines of the psychic unity paradigm.

Intercultural Competence in Education and Social Work

In 2000, the Federal Republic of Germany amended its hitherto valid citizenship law based on *ius sanguinis,* bringing it in line with the laws of other Western European and North American countries. The debate on "immigration" and "integration" has intensified sharply ever since. Actually, immigration to the Federal Republic of Germany began as early as the mid-1950s, when, due to a labor shortage, workers were recruited predominantly from Southern Europe. In 1972, "guest workers" already made up 10% of the working population. Many "guest workers" did not subsequently return home but remained in Germany, bringing their families to join them. Organizations and social institutions had to adapt to this new situation. The outcome in the 1970s was "foreigner education" (*Ausländerpädagogik*), which developed into "intercultural education" in the late 1980s (Auernheimer, 1996; Nieke, 1995).

In her review of German-language research on immigration, Beck-Gernsheim (2004) critiques the immigration phenomenon in Germany as resulting in the following:

- otherness, unusualness, and exoticness are strongly emphasized;

- the dichotomization into "we" and "them" dominates the discourse;

- the image of the migrant is not differentiated, with migrants being seen as group and family minded, as well as strongly tradition and religion oriented;

- immigrants are fundamentally considered a problem accordingly, with the discussion focusing on the "foreigner problem" (*Ausländerproblem*) and the "integration problems."

Intercultural competence did not become a topic of discussion until the 1990s. One book that aroused attention was by Hinz-Rommel (1994), who examined the social practice of various welfare, political, and educational institutions and developed a concept of how to help these institutions "open up interculturally" (*Interkulturelle Öffnung*), which in particular involved hiring more staff with a "migrant background." He identified the need of intercultural competence on two levels: on the individual level as personal competence—referring here to Hammer, Gudykunst, and Wiseman (1978); Hannigan (1990); and Brislin, Cushner, Craig, and Young (1986)—and on the organizational and social level. He found it particularly important to eliminate xenophobic structures and to see migration and interculturality positively.

In intercultural education, intercultural competence—respectively, "culture" and "cultural difference"—is viewed critically. For instance, prior culture-specific knowledge can lead to "culturalisitc fallacy," which can result in stereotypical, misleading, and ultimately racist assumptions. Instead, he recommends "methodically controlled understanding of individual cases"—that is, knowledge generated by the interaction with the client (Kiesel & Volz, 2002). The concept of culture of origin is generally considered deterministic, ignoring cultural similarities between the country of origin and the immigration country, denying the heterogeneity of the own culture, and assuming a static culture uninfluenced by social and economic change.

One can differentiate between two models of intercultural communication. One is the static culture clash model: The actors are hermetically enclosed in their reference systems; misunderstandings, erroneous attributions, and stereotyping are frequent. The other is the dynamic intercultural interaction model: The actors relate to different reference systems, experimenting, improvising, and thereby creating a common culture, the "interculture." Intercultural competence must orient itself toward the dynamic model because educators and social workers must be able to deal with the following problems:

- the constant risk that intercultural interaction develops its own irritating dynamic,

- the feeling of loss of control resulting from dynamic interaction,

- simultaneous efficacy of different interpretation patterns, which may be contradictory (Leenen, Groß, & Grosch, 2002b).

Various authors draw attention to problems in the discourse on intercultural competence: first, "scientific thinking"—that is, the assumption that one can solely solve communication problems by using "instrumental rationality" (e.g., training tools such as the culture assimilator). Second, it is not taken into consideration that irritations in the communication process also may have a productive function (Auernheimer, 2002). Third, the target of education in intercultural competence is not the migrants but rather the members of the majority society, thereby consolidating asymmetrical power structures (Mecheril, 2002). Fourth, considering migrants a problem inhibits appreciation of their positive contribution to changing society, in the sense of adapting global conditions, and in particular hinders exploitation of the intercultural competence that many immigrants have already developed (BIBB, 1999).

In conclusion, it can be said that the discussion on intercultural competence in education and social work should in particular focus on

- the sensitivity to power asymmetry,

- the understanding of discriminatory practices,

- the consciousness of stereotypes and prejudices,

- the awareness of cultural divergence,

- the acceptance of otherness,

- overcoming the "false security of understanding,"

- dialogues that may lead to different norms,

- basic communicative competencies such as accepting perspectives and observing the relationship-level, meta-communication skills (Auernheimer, 2002).

A corresponding competence profile can be shown on three levels—the I, the We, and the Objective levels. These three levels can be considered to be embedded in three frame conditions—institution, society, and globality. On the I level, most important is self-reflection; on the We level, it is social competencies such as empathy, objectivity, recognizing norms, tolerating ambiguity, and mediation; and finally, on the Objective level, it is knowledge of the migration history and the ecopolitical situation of the country of sojourn, the origin of racism, and the individual migration contexts (Fischer, 2005).

Cultural Sociology and Cultural Anthropology Approaches to Intercultural Competence

Sociology as a discipline was built around the structure of modern Western societies. *Culture,* for most sociological theorists, was used only as a template or root metaphor to mark the difference between premodern communities and modern societies. Until today, there had been nothing like an established intercultural sociology or a sociology of intercultural relations in Germany, although with the new study paths of MA and BA, this is due to change.

Entry points, however, do come from cultural sociology, which looks back on a long tradition, beginning with Georg Simmel's (1971) sociology of the stranger or Max Weber's (1922/1993) comparative sociology of religions and its different cultural paths to rationalization/modernity. Simmel not only has had a strong influence on Robert Ezra Park—who had been his student for one year in Berlin—and his concept of the "marginal man." He also has seen a revival in the work of young German sociologists, who connect his concepts to those of inclusion/exclusion in stratified societies (Geenen, 2002) and "othering" (Reuter, 2002). Another strand influential for interculturality concepts is the sociology of migration (Han, 2005) and its theoretical proponents, such as Hans-Joachim Hoffmann-Nowotny (1997), who examined structural and cultural characteristics of migrant decisions in a world society, or Hartmut Esser (1980), whose migrant-assimilation model looks at personal and environmental variables that influence the assimilative decision of an actor in a migrant situation. Today, models of cultural globalization presented by theorists such as Niederbeen Pieterse (hybridization), Appadurai (ethnoscapes), or Castells (network society) do cross disciplinary borders and are influential for a cultural sociology of multiple modernities also in Germany (Reckwitz, 2007, p. 210).

Cultural anthropology from its very beginnings was meant as a scientific enterprise to describe, understand, and translate the "cultural other" for a Western audience. Therefore, it seems astonishing that the founder of the scientific paradigm of intercultural communication, anthropologist Edward T. Hall, has not been as influential within the boundaries of his own discipline as he has been in communication studies. This might be due to the fact that Hall failed to follow the mainstream anthropological concept of studying systems of single cultures holistically but instead explored the behaviors between people of different cultures in their encounter. Furthermore, his intercultural approach grew out of his applied work at the Foreign Service Institute, where he taught workshop courses on "understanding foreign people" to American diplomats (Moosmüller, 2007). Today, anthropologists have not only abandoned the concept of totalistic cultures but also have refined their fieldwork instruments, following their subjects in a world of blurring boundaries, intersections, contact zones, and traveling theories. Studies of transnationalism, transmigration, encounters at cultural cross-roads, concepts of imagined communities, and situated and fluid cultural identities build the bulk, not the exceptions, in German anthropological literature. But still there is only scarce communication between German anthropology and the so-called interculturalists (Dahlén, 1997; Hüsken, 2006), organized in societies such as SIETAR[1]—in which only a few anthropologists participate. Courses in intercultural communication are not part of standard anthropological curricula, and few universities in Germany offer postgraduate intercultural studies with the collaboration of anthropological departments. There are reasons for that, and some of them have to do with Hall's legacy. First, Hall's conception of culture, like that of other anthropologists at that time, with its fixed packages of values, languages, cultural patterns, and contrasts (high context/low context; polychron/monochron), seems to be useful only in certain contexts (i.e., in multinational companies). Empirical anthropological fieldwork in multicultural contexts shows abundantly how identities can be switched, adapted, and instrumentalized, according to circumstances and opportunities. Migrant and diaspora studies (Moosmüller, 2002; Schmidt-Lauber, 2007) in particular have shown that fixed cultural traits hamper rather than foster the examination and interpretation of intercultural issues (Nyíri & Breidenbach, 2004). Second, in Germany—at least after World War II—there has been no tradition of applied anthropology. Putting anthropology into practice may ruin academic careers, and the only legitimate way to deal scientifically with intercultural practice is to write about it. The tone is mostly sceptical and critical in regard to applied anthropology (cf. Hüsken, 2006; Soekefeld & Laviziano, 2005).

A third reason lies in the experience of any anthropological field worker—that intercultural understanding can be a hard enterprise, being more and more cumbersome and unattainable, the longer the fieldwork lasts. For those professionals, it may seem incomprehensible that intercultural competence should be attainable in nice knowledge-based workshops over the weekend. Nevertheless, a lot of German anthropologists who do not enter academic careers can be found in the intercultural field—not so much in the training and research sector but in intercultural mediation, nursing (Ettling, 2007; Uzarewicz, 2007), and migrant work (Aretmi, 2008).

Fields of Practice

In this chapter, we outline three major fields of practice where intercultural competence plays a crucial role. In the 1980s, German multinational companies began to realize that in a rapidly changing business world, successfully managing cultural differences was a major challenge. Today, even small- and medium-sized companies regard intercultural competence as an indispensable asset. The second field of practice is established by public institutions such as government authorities and offices. Due to recent changes in public opinion (most Germans nowadays accept the fact that their society has become multicultural) and in nationality law (in 2000, *ius sanguinis* was replaced by *ius soli*), intercultural competence has become a major issue. Finally, German development aid policy constitutes a third field of practice where intercultural competence—albeit less explicitly—has since long been a much discussed topic.

Business World and Organizations

Globalization has increased the complexity of the tasks facing multinational companies. Companies must deal productively with internal and external cultural diversity and come to terms with different mentalities, business practices, and scientific philosophies. In particular, they must

- gain access to new and quite strange markets;

- adapt products and processes to different local conditions as well as standardize them;

- cultivate regional stakeholder networks and contacts to political, government institutions, and decision makers;

- manage international assignments, build a transnational personnel and organizational development, and ensure knowledge transfer;

- manage international project teams and globally integrate knowledge generation.

All these tasks can be successfully accomplished only if many employees are interculturally competent on all hierarchical and function levels. Here, intercultural competence is basically understood as person-related skills and capabilities (Böning, 2000). Essential above all are toleration of ambiguity, behavioral flexibility, goal orientation, sociableness, empathy, polycentrism, and meta-communicative competence (Kühlmann, Stahl, & Mayrhofer, 2004). Other authors add to this catalog certain culture-related competencies such as the ability to be aware of one's own "cultural glasses" and cultural standards; the willingness to rethink one's own pattern of action and, if necessary, to change it; understanding the business partner's culture and culture-based practices; and basic acceptance and appreciation of cultural diversity (Moosmüller, 1997, 2004).

There seems to be consensus that to acquire intercultural competence, one must immerse oneself into another culture for a longer period of time. Foreign sojourns are therefore employed as an instrument to develop intercultural competence. Meanwhile, however, it is generally agreed that foreign sojourns alone do not suffice to develop intercultural competence but rather must be accompanied by additional intercultural measures such as intercultural trainings. Without such accompanying measures, there would be a relatively great risk that the foreign sojourn experience might reconfirm existent prejudices and reinforce ethnocentric attitudes. Although this is well known and the importance of measures for promoting intercultural competence and global management skills are emphasized, actual knowledge of these "soft topics" is relatively limited in companies, and only a minority of multinational companies in Germany actually conducts intercultural programs (Kühlmann et al., 2004).

In general, it is to be noted that German publications refer a lot to U.S. publications, especially application-oriented ones on international management and on intercultural training. For example, personnel and organizational development strategies are usually based on Perlmutter's EPRG model (ethno-, poly-, regio-, geocentric orientation of multinational companies; Deller & Kusch, 2007). And in the development of intercultural competence, many use Bennett and Hammer's Intercultural Development Inventory (Hammer, 1998). On one hand, the demand is for recipe-like "how-to knowledge" about other cultures. On the other hand, intercultural topics in general and knowledge of specific cultures in particular are viewed with skepticism. If globalization means that diversity, hybridity, and contradictions within cultures are increasing, it is no longer possible to understand foreign cultures. Therefore—this might seem paradoxical—the readiness to want *not to understand* what's happening in an intercultural situation must be fostered because it makes it possible to be able to cope better with the sense of speechlessness, insecurity, and powerlessness occurring in intercultural situations and to reduce the need of resorting to defensive measures (Graf, 2004; Hauser, 2003). It remains to be seen whether new trends in cultural trainings accomplish this.

In some multinational companies, intercultural competence is an integral part of company strategy. They practice systematic intercultural personnel development, organize intercultural knowledge management (e.g., in which repatriates pass on their implicit intercultural knowledge to new expatriates, thereby facilitating reintegration of the repatriates), promote worldwide effective collaboration in multinational teams (Moosmüller, 2001; Podsiadlowski, 2002), and implement integration programs for the increasing number of inpatriates (Moosmüller & Scheuring, 2008). These companies pursue the goal to become globally integrated. Accordingly, it is important to practice comprehensive, qualitative intercultural personnel and organizational development. Intercultural professional development and training measures still play the most important role (Bittner & Reisch, 1994; W. Weber, 1991). There are numerous books and training manuals, usually offering similar approaches (Kumbruck & Derboven, 2005). However, note that "intercultural competence and diversity" (still) play a subordinate role in German companies, and corresponding offers for further education are sparse. The antidiscrimination law (*Allgemeines Gleichbehandlungsgesetz*), effective as of 2006, may change this as it is now possible to sue an employer for ethnic or race discrimination. As the U.S. and German legal situations are quite different, a wave of litigation is not to be expected in Germany. Consequently, German companies will put less effort in conducting preventive diversity training to increase their chances of winning in court.

Public Institutions/Government Authorities and Offices

Germany is an immigration country, and people will have to learn to cope with the challenges of a multicultural society. This is especially true for those who work with migrants, such as staffs of government authorities, social institutions and welfare institutions, schools, hospitals, and so on. Despite the ample experience, in immigration countries, there is still a considerable need for social development. Parekh's (2000) conclusion still holds true:

> Multicultural societies throw up problems that have no parallel in history. They need to find ways of reconciling the legitimate demands of unity and diversity, achieving political unity without cultural uniformity, being inclusive without being assimilationist, cultivating among their citizens a common sense of belonging while respecting their legitimate cultural differences and cherishing plural cultural identities without weakening the shared and precious identity of shared citizenship. This is a formidable political task and no multicultural society so far is tackling it. (p. 343)

The challenge is to open one's own society and culture to migrants and to allow them the same access to resources and the same chances of development. To do this, we need to overcome political, economical, social, and cultural resistance. Due to its history of racist ostracism and extermination, the acceptance of otherness is basically still a sensitive issue in Germany. Suspicion of essentialist delimitation and thus racist delimitation is quick to arise. Many social workers, teachers, and other professionals working with migrants refuse to consider cultural differences as significant because they think cultural explanations only serve to mask migrants' actual social, political, and economical disadvantages.

These worries most likely express the majority's need to be politically correct and to not reject others. Members of the majority tend to neglect migrants' need also to be recognized as culturally distinct, thus ultimately denying migrants the right to be different. As a consequence, assimilation pressure increases even more. For majority members, the opportunity to reflect and reduce their own ethnocentrism and develop intercultural competence through communication with migrants is given away. Also, professionals working with migrants encounter cultural otherness on a daily basis; therefore, the attitude of not recognizing cultural differences can be particularly distressing. However, in many cases, the experience of cultural difference does not lead to acceptance of cultural otherness but rather to distrust one's own perceptions and to reproach oneself of othering. Such internal contradictions and irritations are very widespread and represent an essential motive to learn more about intercultural communication. A basic goal of such learning is to learn to differentiate, on the basis of fundamental constructive assumptions, between diverse cultural need situations, as well as to recognize differences and use this as an opportunity to reflect and reduce one's own ethnocentrism (Roth & Köck, 2004).

If one lives in a foreign culture, that person's own cultural particularities quickly become apparent. It is much more difficult to help teachers, social workers, officials, doctors, the police, and so on to become aware of their own cultural limitations, as they remain within their taken-for-granted cultural world. Thus, the methodological challenges facing cultural training designed for multicultural societies are much greater than those for multinational business organizations. To develop intercultural competence, professionals working with migrants need to be supported by the institution or organization they work for, which means that the institutions and organizations need to develop intercultural competence. Individual intercultural learning can only succeed if it is embedded in a systemic learning process, as demonstrated by specifically designed intercultural training programs for Cologne's police force (Leenen, Groß, & Grosch, 2002a) or for the City of Munich's Social Services Office (Koptelzewa, 2004).

There is a growing need for intercultural qualification measures in many areas, particularly in the field of health care, where communication between doctors, nursing staff, and patients with a migration background is made more difficult by diverse concepts of health/illness, pain, healing process, patient responsibility, and so forth. This is especially the case in schools, where teachers face problems with multicultural classes, and many migrant children are at a disadvantage. And in government and public institutions, where progress in institutional changes aimed at empowering members of minority groups (*Öffnung der Sozialdienste*) is particularly slow, there is almost no increase in the recruitment of staff with a migration background. For example, the largest German charity, the Caritasverband, has a staff of 520,000. Of these, only 5% have a migrant background, whereas they make up 20% to 30% of the German urban population. Many of the professionals working with migrants, especially if they cannot resort to their own migration experiences, feel disoriented and overwhelmed by their (seemingly) diverse and inconsistent ways of behaving and interacting. In short, the need for intercultural competence in institutions and organizations working with migrants and minorities is obvious.

Development Aid and International Cultural Policy

Four decades of development-cooperation saw a process leading from pure transfer of technology and knowledge packages to a more dialogue-oriented concept, where recipients of aid—at least on a conceptual level—are seen as partners in a common effort to develop the living conditions of the poor, as well as their capacities to plan and act for their own future. Interestingly enough, the big development theories, such as that of modernization, dependency or basic needs, have been predominantly culture blind (Faschingeder, Kolland, & Wimmer, 2003). It was only with their failure to explain modern crisis and global change (Menzel, 1992) that "sociocultural factors" and their impact on development have been up for discussion in Germany (Schönhuth, 1991). Today, two broad strands can be detected, those for whom "culture counts"—in whatever way—and those for whom the concept camouflages underlying battles for resources and power or for whom the unifying globalization process dispenses the concept of cultural diversity at all (Schönhuth, 2005, 2007).

With UNESCO activities such as the Mondiacult conferences in Mexico City (1982), Stockholm (1998), and the Universal Declaration on Cultural Diversity (UNESCO 2001), culture-oriented development policy and development-sensitive cultural policy entered common ground—best to be seen in the cultural heritage sector but also in the field of freedom of cultural expression. As for the majority of the international development community in Germany since then, the consideration of the "sociocultural dimension" is part of the concept of intercultural dialogue and sustainable development. Debated topics in the past years have been culture as a potential obstacle or motor for transformation processes, culture as social capital, culture as an investment sector (culture industries and tourism), culture as a basis for participation and empowerment of the poor, and indicators to measure cultural development (Schönhuth, 2005).

If we look at a more operational level, two opposing developments can be discerned: On one side, the consequences of ratifying the UNESCO Convention on Cultural Diversity of 2006, where Germany had a leading role, have led to tremendous momentum in the public arena and civil society bodies, leading to conferences (Auswärtiges Amt, 2006), manifestos (Kulturpolitische Gesellschaft, 2007), and activities on cultural diversity and cultural dialogue issues from the communal to national level. On the other side, the sociocultural dimension discourse in the fast-moving development arena, which in the 1990s had produced policy papers, concepts (Karkoschka & Wölte, 2003), manuals, and monographs (Schönherr, 2003), has given way to other, more fashionable debates (future of megacities, peace keeping, impact monitoring, etc.). Questions of intercultural competence are mostly confined to training packages, preparing development experts for assignments abroad, or are tied to concrete topics such as the Islam dialogue.

Other Fields of Practice

Unlike in the United States, intercultural communication in Germany has developed from quite different mother disciplines, such as applied linguistics, psychology, education, and cultural anthropology. Therefore, the fields of practice also show a tremendous variety, which we will not have space to discuss adequately here. Two recent volumes, one a handbook with a more theoretical approach (edited by Straub et al., 2007) and one with more applied focus, reflecting the results of a SIETAR symposium on intercultural fields of work (Otten, Scheitza, & Cnyrim, 2007), bear witness to this fact. While youth exchange (Thomas, 2007) may be one of the more established practice fields in Germany, the spectrum ranges from counseling in multinational teams (Köppel, 2007; Podsialowski, 2007) to international marketing (Schugk, 2007), from intercultural business communication (Bolten, 2007; Dathe, 2007) to intercultural/transcultural mediation (Azad, 2007), and from public administration (Bentner-Bechtel & Bechtel, 2007; ten Thije & Porila, 2007) to health care (Ettling, 2007; Straub & Zielke, 2007). New fields of interest to interculturalists seem to be the relationships in the nonprofessional sphere of bicultural marriages and partnerships (Nauck, 2007) and non-Western concepts of intercultural competence (Henze, 2007). Readers of German are referred to these references to learn more about trends in these fields related to intercultural competence.

German Perspectives on Intercultural Competence

One might ask what the major trends in the current discussion are and whether there are German peculiarities in the field. One point is that the discourses on intercultural competence in Germany mainly have been disciplinary. Although efforts have been made in recent years to foster multidisciplinarity in this field—as can be seen in the discussion on Thomas's (2003) seminal paper, in which authors from several disciplines were engaged, or in the handbook on intercultural competence by Straub et al. (2007), to which about 90 authors, from anthropology to theology, from economics to philosophy, contributed—fertile collaboration among different disciplines is still the exception. This applies for the handbook of Straub et al., which is rather a potpourri than a synthesis, as well as for the discussion on Thomas's paper, where the attempt to stimulate a multidisciplinary discourse failed badly, as most disputants were anxious to stay within the confines of their familiar intellectual territories. Crossing disciplines seems difficult no matter where, but as Galtung (1981) proposed in his comparative study on intellectual styles, it might be somewhat more difficult in Germany.

Another point is the often articulated need to expand the concept of intercultural competence from a solely subjective one to a more systemic one. The widely used definition of intercultural competence as the ability of a person to effectively and appropriately communicate with people of other cultures stresses the importance of an actor's dispositions and abilities, thereby disregarding the importance of situational and contextual factors. Especially authors who are concerned with organizational development (i.e., Deller & Kusch, 2007; Koptelzewa, 2004) argue that in organizations where intercultural competence is not widely accepted, an individual actor's striving to acquire intercultural competence is prone to be thwarted. Urgently needed, therefore, are theories that allow conceptualizations of intercultural competence on the level of group behavior and organizational behavior. The focus on the dependency of individual behavior on contextual factors is certainly not special to "German culture," as is widely held among interculturalists (i.e., Hall, 1989; Nees, 2000) who construct Germans as "holistic" and "system minded," but should rather be seen as the consequence of a paradigm shift in the humanities, where personality structures matter less and context-actor interaction matters much more.

A further point refers to the changing concept of intercultural competence due to changes of the culture concept. In the old understanding, culture was conceptualized as a bounded, reified entity that exerted a strong influence on individual behavior— accordingly, acquiring specific culture knowledge was considered essential for the acquisition of intercultural competence—whereas in the new understanding, culture is conceptualized as an unbounded, fluid, relational dimension. The concept of intercultural competence should have changed accordingly, which has not been realized yet. Many authors (i.e., Hüsken, 2006) suspect that the reason why the concept of intercultural competence has not changed is due to structural problems—for instance, the assumed dependency of interculturalists—who Hannerz (1992) considers as profiteers of the "culture shock prevention industry"—on international business (Dahlén, 1997). As in the point before, this is not a German peculiarity but a general problem that has still remained unsolved. A possible solution is suggested by Moosmüller (2000), who holds that it depends on the context—he differentiates between two contexts, namely between multicultural society, where the concept of culture as construct is significant, and international organization, where the concept of culture as mental model is still meaningful—whether the old or the new culture concept (respectively aspects of one or the other) can be considered significant.

The last point is related to the concept of cultural difference. Many authors in the field of intercultural communication (i.e., Auernheimer, 2002; Straub, 2007) are skeptical about cultural difference and cultural diversity. On one hand, this skepticism reflects the changes of the culture concept, especially in cultural anthropology. On the other hand, this skepticism might also be caused by the specific German situation. Compared to other European nations and to classical immigration countries such as the United States, the situation in Germany is different, namely for the legacy of the extreme racism in Nazi Germany and for the specific condition of Germany as an immigration country. First, most Germans feel a strong moral obligation to avoid anything that could be regarded as racist. Since in many debates, the construction of cultural differences has been equated with racism, many consider it very problematic to devise cultural differences. Second, the fact that until recently, Germany had been considered an ethnic nation with a citizenship law based on *ius sanguinis* (in 2000, the law was altered and is now based mainly on *ius soli*) meant a special hardship for roughly 7 million immigrants who were forced to remain foreigners, even if they had already lived for three generations in Germany—as many did. Since the end of World War II, more than 15 million ethnic German migrants (of whom about 12 millions were expelled from the eastern territories by the end of the war) have been integrated in a way that was not disturbing to majority society, and this set the benchmark for further integration (Heckmann, 2003). Against this benchmark, it has become somehow harder for foreign migrants to integrate into majority society, especially with changing conditions in the labor market in the 1990s and the discussion on "*German Leitkultur*" (dominant German cultural values to which migrants should adapt) brought up by conservative politicians.

Analyzing the debate in 2006, Rathje posits requirements that the concept of intercultural competence should comply with—but alas these requirements partly differ from their pure opposite. One of the intriguing ideas of her own concept is that *culturality* does not emerge from homogeneity of people but is associated with the recognized differences between people and groups who know and interact with each other in the same sociocultural setting (a firm, a milieu, a nation-state). *Interculturality* would be characterized by unfamiliarity or strangeness with existing differences. Intercultural competence then is the ability to familiarize difference, to endow "normality" in the process of intercultural interaction. At the end of this process is cultural cohesion, achieved through embedding cultural differences into one's own discourse of normality (Rathje, 2006). As this competence counts for every situation of unfamiliarity in personal encounters, it leads also beyond the discussion of intracultural versus intercultural differences.

Summarizing, it could be argued that the peculiarities and discrepancies of the German discourse on intercultural competence above all constitute a challenge for theorists and researchers to criticize and deconstruct the old concepts of intercultural competence and to intensify efforts to construct and refine new concepts.

Note

1. The Society for International Education, Training and Research (SIETAR) is the world's largest interdisciplinary network for professionals and students in intercultural relations.

References

Apfelbaum, B. (2007). Interkulturelle Fremdsprachendidaktik [Intercultural foreign language didactics]. In J. Straub, A. Weidenfeld, & D. Weidenfeld (Eds.), *Handbuch Interkulturelle Kommunikation und Kompetenz* (pp. 154–163). Stuttgart: J. B. Metzler.

Aretmi. (2008). *Arbeitskreis Ethnologie und Migration* [Working group anthropology and migration]. Retrieved August 8, 2008, from http://www.aretmi.de/

Auernheimer, G. (1996). *Einführung in die interkulturelle Erziehung* [Introduction into intercultural education] (2nd ed.). Darmstadt: Wissenschaftliche Buchgesellschaft.

Auernheimer, G. (2002). (Ed.). *Interkulturelle Kompetenz und Professionalität* [Intercultural competence and professionality]. Opladen: Interkulturelle Studien Bd.13.

Auswärtiges Amt. (2006). *Menschen bewegen—Kultur und Bildung in der deutschen Außenpolitik* [Moving people–culture and education in German foreign policy]. Berlin: Edition Diplomatie. Retrieved August 8, 2008, from http://www.auswaertiges-amt.de/diplo/de/Infoservice/Broschueren/AKBPMenschenBewegen.pdf

Azad, S. (2007). Zur Praxis der Mediation im interkulturellen Kontext in Berlin [Towards a practice of mediation in the intercultural context of Berlin]. In M. Otten, A. Scheitza, & A. Cnyrim (Eds.), *Interkulturelle Kompetenz im Wandel* (Vol. 2, pp. 147–176). Frankfurt am Main: IKO–Verl.f. Interkult. Kommunikation.

Bachmann-Medick, D. (1987). Verstehen und Missverstehen zwischen den Kulturen. Interpretation im Schnittpunkt von Literaturwissenschaft und Kulturanthropologie [Understanding and misunderstanding between cultures: Interpretation at the intersection between literary studies and cultural anthropology]. *Jahrbuch Deutsch als Fremdsprache, 13,* 65–77.

Barmeyer, C. (2005). Interkulturelles Coaching [Intercultural coaching]. In C. Rauen (Ed.), *Handbuch Coaching* (pp. 241–272). Göttingen: Hogrefe.

Beck-Gernsheim, E. (2004). *Wir und die Anderen. Vom Blick der Deutschen auf Migranten und Minderheiten* [We and the others: The Germans' view on migrants and minorities]. Frankfurt: Suhrkamp.

Bentner-Bechtel, A., & Bechtel, F. (2007). Interkulturelle Personalentwicklung in der öffentlichen Verwaltung—das Beispiel Kreisverwaltung Germersheim [Intercultural human resources management in public administration]. In M. Otten, A. Scheitza, & A. Cnyrim (Eds.), *Interkulturelle Kompetenz im Wandel* (Vol. 2, pp. 111–128). Frankfurt am Main: IKO–Verl.f. Interkult. Kommunikation.

Beuchelt, E. (1974). *Ideengeschichte der Völkerpsychologie* [History of ideas of the Völkerpsychologie]. Meisenheim: Hain.

BIBB. (Ed.). (1999). *Interkulturelle Kompetenz—Schlüsselqualifikation von Immigrantinnen. Dokumentation der internationalen Fachtagung vom 20. April in Berlin* [Intercultural competence–A key qualification of migrants: Documentation of the international conference in Berlin]. Berlin: Author.

Bittner, A., & Reisch, B. (1994). *Interkulturelles Personalmanagement. Internationale Personalentwicklung, Auslandsentsendungen, interkulturelles Training* [Intercultural human resource management. International human resource development, foreign assignment, intercultural training]. Wiesbaden: Gabler.

Boeckmann, K.-B. (Ed.). (2006). Themenheft Interkulturalität und Fremdsprachenunterricht. Kritische Anmerkungen und neue Perspektiven [Special edition: Interculturality and foreign language teaching: Critical comments and new perspectives]. *Zeitschrift für Interkulturellen Fremdsprachenunterricht, 11,* 3. http://zif.spz.tu-darmstadt.de/jg-11–3/jorna131.htm

Bolten, J. (2007). *Einführung in die Interkulturelle Wirtschaftskommunikation* [Introduction into intercultural business communication]. Göttingen: UTB.

Böning, U. (Ed.). (2000). *Interkulturelle Business-Kompetenz: Geheime Regeln beachten und unsichtbare Barrieren überwinden* [Intercultural business competence: Noticing hidden rules and overcoming hidden barriers]. Frankfurt am Main: Frankfurter Allgemeine Buch.

Bredella, L. (Ed.). (1999). *Interkultureller Fremdsprachenunterricht* [Intercultural foreign language teaching]. Tübingen: Narr.

Bredella, L., & Christ, H. (1995). *Didaktik des Fremdverstehens* [Didactics of the understanding of the other]. Tübingen: Narr.

Brislin, R., Cushner, K., Craig, C., & Young, M. (1986). *Intercultural interactions: A practical guide.* Beverly Hills, CA: Sage.

Chakkarath, P. (2003). *Kultur und Psychologie* [Culture and psychology]. Hamburg: Dr. Kovac.

Dadder, R. (1987). *Interkulturelle Orientierung* [Intercultural orientation]. Saarbrücken: Breidenbach.

Dahlén, T. (1997). *Among the interculturalists: An emergent profession and its packaging of knowledge.* Stockholm: Coronet Books.

Danckwortt, D. (1985). Anmerkungen zur theoretischen Fundierung der Analyse interkultureller Begegnungen [Analyzing the intercultural encounter: Theoretical foundations]. In A. Thomas (Ed.), *Interkultureller Austausch als interkulturelles Handeln* (pp. 193–206). Saarbrücken: Breitenbach.

Dathe, M. (2007). Wirtschaftskommunikation [Business communication]. In J. Straub, A. Wiedemann, & D. Wiedemann (Eds.), *Handbuch Interkulturelle Kommunikation und Kompetenz* (pp. 586–594). Stuttgart: J. B. Meztler.

Deller, J. (2000). *Interkulturelle Eignungsdiagnostik* [Intercultural aptitude diagnostics]. Grimma: Heidrun Popp Verlag.

Deller, J., & Kusch, R. I. (2007). Internationale Personal- und Organisationsentwicklung [International human resource and organizational development]. In J. Straub, A. Weidemann, & D. Weidemann (Eds.), *Handbuch Interkulturelle Kommunikation und Kompetenz* (pp. 565–576). Stuttgart: J. B. Metzler.

Eckensberger, L. H. (1996). Auf der Suche nach den (verlorenen?) Universalien hinter den Kulturstandards [Searching for the (lost?) Universals behind cultural standards]. In A. Thomas (Ed.), *Psychologie interkulturellen Handelns* (pp. 165–197). Saarbrücken: Breitenbach.

Esser, H. (1980). *Aspekte der Wanderungssoziologie. Assimilation und Integration von Wanderern, ethnischen Gruppen und Minderheiten; eine handlungstheoretische Analyse* [Aspects of a sociology of migration: Assimilation and integration of migrants, ethnic groups and minorities: An analysis based on action theory]. Darmstadt: Luchterhand.

Ettling, S. (2007). Interkulturelle Kompetenz im Gesundheitswesen aus der Perspektive der Medizinethnologie [Intercultural competence in health care: A medical anthropological perspective]. In M. Otten, A. Scheitza, & A. Cnyrim (Eds.), *Interkulturelle Kompetenz im Wandel* (Vol. 2, pp. 129–146). Frankfurt am Main: IKO–Verl.f. Interkult. Kommunikation.

Europarat. (2001). *Gemeinsamer Europäischer Referenzrahmen für Sprachen: Lernen, lehren, beurteilen* [Common European frame of reference for languages: Learning, teaching, judging]. Berlin: Langenscheidt.

Faschingeder, G., Kolland, F., & Wimmer, F. (Eds.). (2003). *Kultur als umkämpftes Terrain. Paradigmenwechsel in der Entwicklungspolitik* [Culture as a contested terrain: Change of paradigm in development policy]. Wien: ProMedia/Südwind.

Fischer, V. (2005). *Interkulturelle Kompetenz. Fortbildung, Transfer, Organisationsentwicklung* [Intercultural competence: Retraining, transfer, organizational development]. Schwalbach/Ts.: Verlag.

Friedlmeier, W. (2007). Kulturvergleichende Psychologie [Cross-cultural psychology]. In J. Straub, A. Weidemann, & D. Weidemann (Eds.), *Handbuch Interkulturelle Kommunikation und Kompetenz* (pp. 225–237). Stuttgart: J. B. Metzler.

Galtung, J. (1981). Structure, culture and intellectual style: A comparison of Saxonic, Teutonic, Gallic and Nipponic approaches. *Social Science Information, 20*, 816–856.

Geenen, E. (2002). *Die Soziologie des Fremden vor dem Hintergrund der Herausbildung unterschiedlicher Gesellschaftsformationen* [The sociology of the stranger against the background of the development of different social systems]. Opladen: Leske + Budrich.

Gerighausen, J., & Seel, P. (1982). Regionale Lehrwerke [Regional textbooks]. In H.-J. Krumm (Ed.), *Lehrwerkforschung—Lehrwerkkritik Deutsch als Fremdsprache* (pp. 23–35). München: Goethe-Institut Werkheft.

Göhring, H. (1980). Deutsch als Fremdsprache und interkulturelle Kommunikation [German as a foreign language and intercultural communication]. In A. Wierlacher (Ed.), *Fremdsprache Deutsch Bd. I* (pp. 71–91). München: Wilhelm Fink Verlag.

Goodenough, W. H. (1964). Introduction. In W. H. Goodenough (Ed.), *Explorations in cultural anthropology* (pp. 1–24). New York: McGraw-Hill.

Graf, A. (2004). *Interkulturelle Kompetenzen im Human Resource Management* [Intercultural competences in human resource management]. Wiesbaden: Gabler.

Hall, E. T. (1989). *Understanding cultural differences: Germans, French and Americans.* Yarmouth, ME: Intercultural Press.

Hammer, M. R. (1998). A measure of intercultural sensitivity: The Intercultural Development Inventory. In S. M. Fowler & M. G. Mumford (Eds.), *Intercultural sourcebook: Cross-cultural training methods* (Vol. 2, pp. 61–72). Yarmouth, ME: Intercultural Press.

Hammer, M. R., Gudykunst, W. B., & Wiseman, R. L. (1978). Dimensions of intercultural effectiveness. *International Journal of Intercultural Relations, 2*, 382–393.

Han, P. (2005). *Soziologie der Migration* [Sociology of migration]. Stuttgart: Lucius & Lucius.

Hannerz, U. (1992). *Cultural complexity: Studies in the social organization of meaning.* New York: Columbia University Press.

Hannigan, T. P. (1990). Traits, attitudes, and skills that are related to intercultural effectiveness and their implications for cross-cultural training: A review of the literature. *International Journal of Intercultural Relations, 14*, 89–111.

Hauser, R. (2003). *Aspekte interkulturelle Kompetenz. Lernen im Kontext von Länder- und Organisationskulturen Wirtschaftswissenschaft* [Aspects of intercultural competence: Learning in the context of national and organizational cultures]. Wiesbaden: Deutscher Universitätsverlag.

Heckmann, F. (2003). From ethnic nation to universalistic immigrant integration. In F. Heckmann & D. Schnapper (Eds.), *The integration of immigrants in European societies: National differences and trends of convergence* (pp. 45–78). Stuttgart: Lucius & Lucius.

Henze, J. (2007). Interkulturelle Kommunikation und Kompetenz—Nicht-westliche Perspektiven [Intercultural communication and competence: Non-Western perspectives]. In J. Straub, A. Weidenfeld, & D. Weidenfeld (Eds.), *Handbuch Interkultureller Kommunikation und Kompetenz* (pp. 304–314). Stuttgart: J. B. Metzler.

Hess-Lüttich, E. (1985). *Integration u. Identität. Sprachunterricht mit Ausländern* [Integration and identity: Foreign language teaching with foreigners]. Tübingen: Narr.

Hinz-Rommel, W. (1994). *Interkulturelle Kompetenz. Ein neues Anforderungsprofil für die soziale Arbeit* [Intercultural competence: A new requirement profile for social work]. Münster: Waxmann Verlag.

Hoffmann-Nowotny, H.-J. (1997). World society and the future of international migration: A theoretical perspective. In E. M. Uçarer & D. J. Puchala (Eds.), *Immigration into Western societies: Problems and policies* (pp. 95–117). London: Pinter.

Hüsken, T. (2006). *Der Stamm der Experten, Rhetorik und Praxis des interkulturellen Managements in der deutschen staatlichen Entwicklungszusammenarbeit* [The tribe of experts: Rhetoric and practice of intercultural management in German official development cooperation]. Bielefeld: Transcript Publishing House.

Jahoda, G. (1993). *Crossroads between culture and mind: Continuities and change in theories of human nature.* Newbury Park, CA: Sage.

Karkoschka, O., & Wölte, S. (2003). Interkultureller Dialog in der deutschen EZ. Evaluierungsbericht [Intercultural dialogue in German development cooperation: Evaluation report]. In Gutachten im Auftrag des BMZ, Referat 120, Bonn. Bonn und Offenbach.

Kiesel, D., & Volz, F. R. (2002). Anerkennung und Intervention: Moral und Ethik als komplementäre Dimensionen interkultureller Kompetenz [Recognition and intervention: Moral and ethics as a complementary dimension of intercultural competence]. In G. Auernheimer (Ed.), *Interkulturelle Kompetenz und Professionalität* (pp. 49–62). Opladen: Leske + Budrich.

Kieser, A. (1981). Die Bedeutung internationaler Forschung auf dem Gebiet der Organisationstheorie [The relevance of international research in organization theory]. *Zeitschrift für Betriebswirtschaft, Ergänzungsheft, 1,* 107–117.

Kinast, E.-U. (1998). *Evaluation interkultureller Trainings* [Evaluation of intercultural trainings]. Lengerich: Pabst.

Kinast, E.-U. (2003). Interkulturelles Coaching [Intercultural coaching]. In A. Thomas (Ed.), *Handbuch Interkulturelle Kommunikation und Kooperation Bd. 1* (pp. 217–226). Göttingen: Vandenhoeck & Ruprecht.

Knapp-Potthoff, A., & Liedke, M. (Eds.). (1997). *Aspekte interkultureller Kommunikationsfähigkeit* [Aspects of intercultural communication capability]. München: Iudicium.

Köppel, P. (2007). *Konflikte und Synergien in multikulturellen Arbeitsgruppen unter der Berücksichtigung virtueller Kooperation* [Conflicts and synergies in multicultural working groups in consideration of virtual cooperation]. Wiesbaden: Gabler.

Koptelzewa, G. (2004). *Interkulturelle Kompetenz in der Beratung. Strukturelle Voraussetzungen und Strategien der Sozialarbeit mit Migranten* [Intercultural competence in counseling: Structural preconditions and strategies of social work with migrants]. Münster: Waxmann.

Kühlmann, T. (Ed.). (1995). *Mitarbeiterentsendung ins Ausland: Auswahl, Vorbereitung, Betreuung und Wiedereingliederung* [International personnel transfer: Selection, training, support and reintegration]. Göttingen: Verlag für Angewandte Psychologie.

Kühlmann, T., & Stahl, G. (2001). Problemfelder des internationalen Personaleinsatzes [Problem areas in international personnel assignment]. In H. Schuler (Ed.), *Lehrbuch der Personalpsychologie* (pp. 533–557). Göttingen: Hogrefe.

Kühlmann, T., Stahl, G. K., & Mayrhofer, W. (Eds.). (2004). *Auslandseinsatz von Mitarbeitern* [Foreign assigment of personnel]. Stuttgart: Hogrefe.

Kulturpolitische Gesellschaft. (2007). *Culture and art for sustainable development: Declaration for a close co-operation between foreign cultural policy and development policy.* Retrieved August 8, 2008, from http://www.kulturbewegt.org/download/Manifest%20english.pdf

Kumbruck, C., & Derboven, W. (2005). *Interkulturelles Training* [Intercultural training]. Berlin: Springer.

Leenen, W. R., Groß, A., & Grosch, H. (2002a). Interkulturelle Kompetenz in der Polizei: Qualifizierungsstrategien [Intercultural competence in the police: Qualification strategies]. *Gruppendynamik und Organisationsberatung, 1,* 97–120.

Leenen, W. R., Groß, A., & Grosch, H. (2002b). Interkulturelle Kompetenz in der Sozialen Arbeit [Intercultural competence in social work]. In G. Auernheimer (Ed.), *Interkulturelle Kompetenz* (pp. 81–102). Opladen.

Lévy-Bruhl, L. (1923). *Primitive mentality.* London: Allen & Unwin.

Luchtenberg, S. (1999). *Interkulturelle Kommunikative Kompetenz. Kommunikationsfelder in Schule und Gesellschaft* [Intercultural communicative competence in school and society]. Wiesbaden: Westdeutscher Verlag.

Mandl, H., Dreher, M., & Kornadt, H.-J. (1993). *Entwicklung und Denken im kulturellen Kontext* [Growth/development and thinking in cultural context]. Göttingen: Hogrefe.

Mecheril, P. (2002). Kompetenzlosigkeitskompetenz. Pädagogisches Handeln unter Einwanderungsbedingungen [The competence of missing competence: Pedagogical action under immigration conditions]. In G. Auernheimer (Ed.), *Interkulturelle Kompetenz und pädagogische Professionalität* (pp. 15–34). Opladen: Leske + Budrich.

Menzel, U. (1992). *Das Ende der Dritten Welt und das Scheitern der großen Theorie* [The end of the Third World and the stranding of the grand theories]. Frankfurt/M.: Suhrkamp.

Mertens, D. (1974). Schlüsselqualifikationen. Thesen zur Schulung für eine moderne Gesellschaft [Key qualifications: Proposals for educating modern society]. *Mitteilungen aus der Arbeitsmarkt- und Berufsforschung, 7,* 36–43.

Moosmüller, A. (1997). *Kulturen in Interaktion. Deutsche und US-amerikanische Firmenentsandte in Japan* [Cultures in interaction: German and U.S.-American expatriates in Japan]. Münster: Waxmann.

Moosmüller, A. (2000). Die Schwierigkeit mit dem Kulturbegriff in der interkulturellen Kommunikation [The problem of "culture" in intercultural communication]. In R. Alsheimer, A. Moosmüller, & K. Klaus (Eds.), *Lokale Kulturen in einer globalisierten Welt* (pp. 15–31). Münster: Waxmann.

Moosmüller, A. (with Spieß, E., & Podsiadlowski, A.) (2001). International team building: Issues in developing multinational work groups. In M. Mendenhall, J. S. Black, T. Kühlmann, & G. Stahl (Eds.), *Developing global leadership skills: The challenge of HRM in the next millennium* (pp. 211–224). Westport, CT: Quorum.

Moosmüller, A. (Ed.). (2002). *Interkulturelle Kommunikation in der Diaspora* [Intercultural communication in the Diaspora]. Münster: Waxmann.

Moosmüller, A. (2004). Coping with cultural differences: A comparison of American and German companies. In J. Lears & J. van Scherpenberg (Eds.), *Cultures of economy— Economics of cultures* (pp. 135–145). Heidelberg: Bavarian American Academy.

Moosmüller, A. (2007). Interkulturelle Kommunikation aus ethnologischer Sicht [Intercultural communication from an anthropological perspective]. In A. Moosmüller (Ed.), *Interkulturelle Kommunikation. Konturen einer wissenschaftlichen Disziplin* (pp. 13–49). Münster: Waxmann.

Moosmüller, A., & Scheuring, G. (2008). Stammhausaufenthalte japanischer Fach- und Führungskräfte in Deutschland: Der Aufbau von interpersonalen Netzwerken [Assigments of Japanese specialists and managers in the German headquarters: The erection of interpersonal networks]. In T. Kühlmann, & H.-D. Haas (Eds.), *Internationales Risikomanagement: Auslandserfolg durch Netzwerke* (pp. 185–211). München: Oldenbourg.

Müller, B.-D. (1993). Interkulturelle Kompetenz. Annäherung an einen Begriff [Intercultural competence: Approximating the term]. *Jahrbuch Deutsch als Fremdsprache, 19,* 63–76.

Nauck, B. (2007). Bi-kulturelle Ehen, Familien und Partnerschaften [Bicultural marriages, families and partnerships]. In J. Straub, A. Weidenfeld, & D. Weidenfeld (Eds.), *Handbuch Interkultureller Kommunikation und Kompetenz* (pp. 729–737). Stuttgart: J. B. Metzler.

Nees, G. (2000). *Germany: Unraveling an enigma.* Yarmouth, ME: Intercultural Press.

Nieke, W. (1995). *Interkulturelle Bildung und Erziehung. Wertorientierungen im Alltag* [Intercultural education: Value orientation in everyday life]. Opladen: Leske + Budrich.

Nisbett, R. E. (2003). *The geography of thought: How Asians and Westerners think differently . . . and why.* New York: Free Press.

Nyírí, P., & Breidenbach, J. (2004). *China inside out: Contemporary Chinese nationalism and transnationalism.* Budapest: Central European University Press.

Oksaar, E. (1989). Problematik im interkulturellen Verstehen [Problems in intercultural understanding]. In P. Matusche (Ed.), *Wie verstehen wir Fremdes? Aspekte zur Klärung von Verstehensprozessen* (pp. 7–19). München: Goethe Institut.

Otten, M., Scheitza, A., & Cnyrim, A. (Eds.). (2007). *Interkulturelle Kompetenz im Wandel* [Intercultural competence in the state of flux] (Vols. 1–2). Frankfurt: IKO.

Parekh, B. (2000). *Rethinking multiculturalism: Cultural diversity and political theory.* Cambridge, MA: Harvard University Press.

Podsiadlowski, A. (2002). *Multikulturelle Arbeitsgruppen in Unternehmen. Bedingungen für erfolgreiche Zusammenarbeit am Beispiel deutscher Unternehmen in Südostasien* [Multicultural working groups in enterprises: Preconditions for a successful cooperation: The example of German enterprises in Southeast Asia]. Münster: Waxmann.

Podsiadlowski, A., & Spieß, E. (1996). Zur Evaluation eines interkulturellen Trainings in einem deutschen Großunternehmen [On the evaluation of an intercultural training in a German large-scale enterprise]. *Zeitschrift für Personalforschung, 1,* 48–66.

Rathje, S. (2006). Interkulturelle Kompetenz—Zustand und Zukunft eines umstrittenen Konzepts [Intercultural competence: State and future of a debated concept]. *Zeitschrift für interkulturellen Fremdsprachenunterricht.* Retrieved August 8, 2008, from http://www2.unijena.de/philosophie/iwk/publikationen/interkulturelle_kompetenz_rathje.pdf, pp 1–17.

Reckwitz, A. (2007). Kultursoziologie [Sociology of culture]. In J. Straub, A. Weidenfeld, & D. Weidenfeld (Eds.), *Handbuch Interkultureller Kommunikation und Kompetenz* (pp. 201–211). Stuttgart: J. B. Metzler.

Rehbein, J. (Ed.). (1985). *Interkulturelle Kommunikation* [Intercultural communication]. Tübingen: Narr.

Reuter, J. (2002). *Ordnungen des Anderen. Zum Problem des Eigenen in der Soziologie des Fremden* [Orders of the other: The problem of the self and the sociology of the stranger]. Bielefeld: Transcript Verlag.

Rost-Roth, M. (1994). Verständigungsprobleme in der interkulturellen Kommunikation [Communication problems in intercultural communication]. *Zeitschrift für Literaturwissenschaft und Linguistik, 24,* 9–45.

Roth, J., & Roth, K. (2001). Interkulturelle Kommunikation [Intercultural communication]. In R. Brednich (Ed.), *Grundriss der Volkskunde* (pp. 391–422) Berlin: Reimer.

Roth, J., & Köck, C. (Eds.).(2004). *Culture communication skills.* München: Bayerischer Volkshochschulverband.

Schmidt-Lauber, B. (Ed.). (2007). *Ethnizität und Migration. Einführung in Wissenschaft und Arbeitsfelder* [Ethnicity and migration: Introduction into the science and fields of work]. Berlin: Reimer.

Schönherr, T. (2003). *Deutungs- und Handlungsmuster interkulturellen Kontext* [Interpretative models and patterns of action in the intercultural context]. Frankfurt: IKO.

Schönhuth, M. (Ed.). (1991). *The socio-cultural dimension in development: The contribution of sociologists and social-anthropologists to the work of development agencies.* Eschborn: GTZ.

Schönhuth, M. (2005). *Glossar Kultur und Entwicklung* [The culture and development glossary]. Eschborn: GTZ, DEZA and Universität Trier.

Schönhuth, M. (2007). Plädoyer für eine Plattform [Plea for a platform]. In Auswärtiges Amt (Ed.), *Menschen bewegen—Kultur und Bildung in der deutschen Außenpolitik Berlin, Auswärtiges Amt 25.—26. Oktober 2006 Konferenzdokumentation* (pp. 105–108). Berlin: Foreign Office/Auswärtiges Amt.

Schugk, M. (2007). Marketing. In J. Straub, A. Weidenfeld, & D. Weidenfeld (Eds.), *Handbuch Interkultureller Kommunikation und Kompetenz* (pp. 595–604). Stuttgart: J. B. Metzler.

Shore, B. (1996). *Culture in mind: Cognition, culture, and the problem of meaning.* New York: Oxford University Press.

Simmel, G. (1971). The stranger. In D. Levine (Ed.), *Georg Simmel on individuality and social forms* (pp. 143–149). Chicago: University of Chicago Press.

Soekefeld, M., & Laviziano, A. (Eds.) (2005). *Ethnologie und interkulturelle Kommunikation* [Cultural anthropology and intercultural communication]. Hamburg: Institut für Ethnologie.

Straub, J. (2007). Kultur [Culture]. In J. Straub, A. Weidenfeld, & D. Weidenfeld (Eds.), *Handbuch Interkultureller Kommunikation und Kompetenz* (pp. 7–24). Stuttgart: J. B. Metzler.

Straub, J., Weidemann, A., & Weidemann, D. (Eds.). (2007). *Handbuch Interkultureller Kommunikation und Kompetenz* [Handbook of intercultural communication and competence]. Stuttgart: J. B. Metzler.

Straub, J., & Zielke, B. (2007). Gesundheitsversorgung [Health care]. In J. Straub, A. Weidenfeld, & D. Weidenfeld (Eds.), *Handbuch Interkultureller Kommunikation und Kompetenz* (pp. 716–728). Stuttgart: J. B. Metzler.

ten Thije, J. D., & Porila, A. (2007). Ämter und Behörden [Bureaus and public authorities]. In J. Straub, A. Weidenfeld, & D. Weidenfeld (Eds.), *Handbuch Interkultureller Kommunikation und Kompetenz* (pp. 687–699). Stuttgart: J. B. Metzler.

Thomas, A. (Ed.). (1985). *Interkultureller Austausch als interkulturelles Handeln—Theoretische Grundlagen der Austauschforschung* [Intercultural exchange as intercultural action: Theoretical foundations of research on (youth) exchange]. Saarbrücken: Breitenbach.

Thomas, A. (Ed.). (1991). *Kulturstandards in der internationalen Begegnung* [Cultural standards in the international encounter]. Saarbrücken: Breidenbach.

Thomas, A. (1993). *Kulturvergleichende Psychologie* [Cross-cultural psychology]. Göttingen: Hogrefe.

Thomas, A. (2003). Interkulturelle Kompetenz: Grundlagen, Probleme und Konzepte [Intercutural competence: Foundations, problems and concepts]. *Erwägen Wissen Ethik, 14,* 137–150.

Thomas, A. (2007). Jugendaustausch [Youth exchange]. In J. Straub, A. Weidenfeld, & D. Weidenfeld (Eds.), *Handbuch Interkultureller Kommunikation und Kompetenz* (pp. 657–666). Stuttgart: J. B. Metzler.

Trommsdorff, G. (1986). German cross-cultural psychology. *German Journal of Psychology, 10,* 240–266.

Trommsdorff, G. (Ed.). (1989). *Sozialisation im Kulturvergleich* [Cross-cultural study of socialization]. Stuttgart: Enke Verlag.

Uzarewicz, C. (2007). Ethnologische Gesundheitsarbeit und transkulturelle Pflege [Anthropological health care and transcultural nursing]. In B. Schmidt-Lauber (Ed.), *Ethnizität und Migration. Einführung in Wissenschaft und Arbeitsfelder* (pp. 293–301). Berlin: Reimer.

von Keller, E. (1982). *Management in fremden Kulturen* [Management in foreign cultures]. Bern: Haupt.

Weber, M. (1993). *The sociology of religion.* Boston: Beacon. (Original work published 1922)

Weber, W. (1991). *Defizite internationalen Management Trainings* [Deficits in international management trainings]. Chur/Zürich: Verlag Rüegger.

Wierlacher, A. (Ed.). (1987). *Perspektiven und Verfahren interkultureller Germanistik* [Perspectives and methods of intercultural German studies]. München: Iudicium.

CHAPTER 12

India

A Cross-Cultural Overview of Intercultural Competence

Ranjini Manian and Shobha Naidu

> *India is the cradle of the human race, the birthplace of human speech, the mother of history, the grandmother of legend, and the great grandmother of tradition. Our most valuable materials in the history of man are treasured up in India only!*
>
> Mark Twain

This chapter suggests that intercultural "cooperation" is written into the DNA of Indians.

According to the Indian worldview, society is conceived as a cooperative but nonegalitarian structure, and the unity of all things big and small, material and spiritual is at the core. The caste structure reinforced interdependence and regulated the nature of relationships between the higher and the lower occupational castes since certain social functions were only carried out by certain castes.[1] It was the prescribed do's and don'ts between different castes that traditionally determined the nature of the interaction, communication, and competence. Marriage stipulations of endogamy further reinforced and reproduced social distinction.

This "social capital" that has originated in caste has enabled Indians to succeed economically, politically, and socially wherever they have gone—witness the 20 million-plus Indian Diasporaand the exceptional caliber of Indian students in Western universities, their capacity and competence to make the most of available opportunities and transform their lives. Here we would like to refer to Milton Bennett's (1993) developmental model of intercultural sensitivity in which he proposes a framework to explain the reactions of people to cultural difference. Indian successes in a predominantly Western culture can be illustrated by what he calls the "acceptance" stage of being "ethnorelative" as opposed to ethnocentric. Acceptance of cultural difference, he writes, does not necessarily mean agreement. "I can maintain my values and also behave in culturally appropriate ways."[2] Indians live their lives adapting to one another and setting and managing expectations. (Naidu & Chandrashekhar, 2008).

The topic of cross-cultural competence in India is vast and would necessarily have to go back almost 2,500 years to the birth of Hinduism. For the sake of clarity the caveats that have influenced the topic are:

Caveat 1: There is not just one India—but several Indias, which intersect constantly.

The Indian intercultural model reflects diversity and polyculturality. Of course, this assertion holds true for many countries and cultures, but more so for India. Commonly referred to as a subcontinent, India displays all the characteristics of a continent and more: extreme topographical diversity, ancient cultural traditions and philosophies, regional identities marked by linguistic and cultural specificities, diverse religious beliefs and practices, rich and vibrant cultural art forms that range from the classical to folk, various historical influences, and a baffling diversity and interpretation of customs and practices. The intercultural model that we propose is like concentric circles that overlap with more or less intensity, depending on the nature of the social interaction (see also Shashi Tharoor, 1997, 2007, on different identities; Figure 12.1). Technology and modernization have, seemingly, in big cities, sandpapered the differences between the "symbolic capital" that is caste related and the "economic capital" that is class, especially in the modern work environment; however, these continue to remain, and areas of intersection are often areas of negotiation and conflict. All these come together and are reinvented as the country grapples with modernity.

The concept of different Indias can be puzzling for a globalized world tending toward the homogeneous. This chapter is an attempt to explore through juxtaposing intercultural models the complexity of social interactions in India. We can speak of the pragmatism and syncretism of the Indian intercultural models, which are simultaneously exclusive (distinctiveness of caste) and inclusive (interdependence between these).

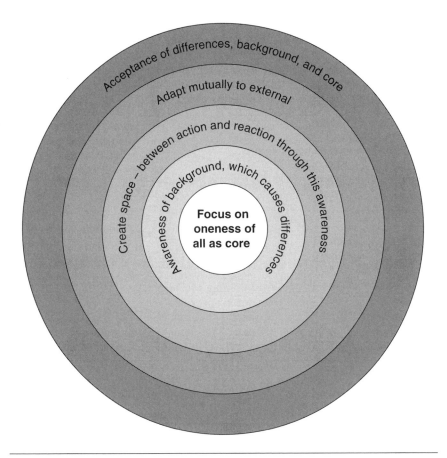

Figure 12.1   Cross-Cultural Competency Model—India

Conciliatory Intercultural Competence Model or the "Push" and "Pull" Cultural Model

With India being in full transition, professionals are required to "reconcile" their traditional practices and beliefs with Western "secular" behavioral norms, especially at the workplace (see Figure 12.2).

The professional and the personal in India intersect constantly. The whole colors the persons that we are, especially when we return home to our families—the food we eat, the rituals we follow, the books we read, the way we pray, and so on. This influences all interactions. It is the immersion in this "larger" intercultural model that enables Indians to survive. A unique competence that we, the authors, call "conciliatory" is required for us Indians to navigate the traditional and the modern, the sacred and the secular.

India has 28 states that are linguistically divided, with close to 300 languages and dialects. India has racial features ranging from Mongol to Dravidian, which means we display stark differences in the way we look, speak, live, and eat. However, we are united by the strong concept of one nation.

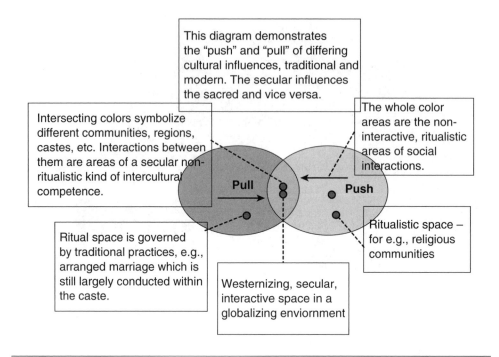

Figure 12.2 The Push-Pull Model

The notion of Indian identity is recent and was fueled by India's struggle for independence. It has given the country a new political identity.

Having an intimate knowledge of both Indian culture and Western ones, along with the added advantage of a combined half-century of experience in explaining India and its way of life to the West and vice versa, we present influences, theories, and perspectives that are uniquely Indian and govern an Indian's competence in handling other cultures both within and outside the country's borders. We have illustrated our positions with examples drawn from our experience.

Caveat 2: When we speak of India, we largely mean Hindu, although this does not exclude other communities, as they show strong cultural traits derived from Hinduism.

India is largely a Hindu-dominated country, with more than 80% of the population adhering to some form of Hindu custom and practice. It is commonly observed that Hinduism is not a religion but a way of life. It propounds the theory of one God or Divine Consciousness Principle as the inner core of all beings but worships His many forms based on personal preferences and allows a variety of choices. Even dynamic and vibrant minority religions such as Islam, Christianity, and Sikhism in India have been influenced, in different ways, by prevailing Hindu customs and have adapted/integrated certain practices within their own theological frameworks. For instance, it can be observed that idols of the Virgin Mary in most shrines in the state of Tamil Nadu are draped in traditional gold-bordered sarees.

The Muslim community, which constitutes more than 13% of the Indian population, it has been pointed out by Zarine Bhatty (1996, p. 249), has been influenced by the way caste in Hinduism traditionally functions. She writes, in the villages of Kasauli, her area of study, that the term *zat,* which is equivalent to the term *jati* in the Hindu caste system, is used to refer to caste, and the Ashrafs and non-Ashrafs are collectively referred to as *oonchi zat* (high caste) and *neechi zat* (low caste), respectively. For example, the Ashrafs consider themselves superior because of their foreign ancestry (as seen in Persianized Urdu names) to the non-Ashrafs, who are thought to be converts from Hinduism and drawn from the indigenous population. Bhatty shows that the practice of endogamy, or marriage within the subgroup and one of the basic attributes of the Hindu caste system, is also practiced in the two categories of Muslims—Ashrafs not marrying non-Ashrafs.

Thus, any study of cross-cultural competence in the Indian context would necessarily focus on Hindu beliefs and practices, for it is these that have molded the subcontinent's specific cultural traits and character for more than 2,500 years. But Hindu custom and practice have always remained porous and absorbed from other cultures and practices to reinvent their own.

Caveat 3: Our study is largely urban and middle class in nature, although many urban locations in India might show strong rural characteristics.

Given the authors' background and their familiarity with the urban milieu in India, the focus here is on urban India. However, massive rural exodus and the urban consumerist reach into rural hinterlands are altering rural India as never before.

The Urban-Rural Divide and Regional Identity

We need to keep in mind the fact that the divide between urban and rural India is drastic and perhaps more so than it would be in Western cultures. About 72% (Census of India 2001)[3] of the population continues to live in rural areas, which, until quite recently, were fairly isolated in terms of communication, infrastructure, and access to modern knowledge and technology. These rural areas continue to be far behind urban ones, taking human development indicators such as literacy and income into account. The Census of India 2001 puts rural literacy at 59.40% and urban literacy at 80.30%. While the male rural literacy is 59%, it is 39% for rural women. It is important to remember that there is no uniform literacy distribution in the country. Some regions are more advanced than others and some communities more "literate" than others. Income disparities between urban and rural India are more disturbing (Naik, 2003).

The urban-rural divide covers regional identities. These factors play an important part in a country that is in transition. It can be observed that rural traditions find new forms of expression in modern, "alien" spaces. *Pongal,* a harvest celebration in South India, an essentially rural ritualistic festival involving bonfires, is also celebrated in the cities. The strong attachment of Indian Diaspora across the world to certain customs and practices has often been perceived as archaic by modern India, which has no inhibitions to discard a ritual considered unnecessary.

Regional identities tussle for space with more urbanized, Westernized ones. This has given rise to a more politicized Hinduism, with certain political parties claiming to be the "protectors" of the faith. A fiercely Hindu political body has been known to resist Valentine's Day celebrations in an urban metropolis, seeing it as an invasion of a non-Hindu belief. The at times violent and vociferous rejection of perceived Western values by some highlights the tension and conflict inherent in India today.

Areas of interaction (could be perceived as forced sometimes) are areas of acceptance of the other but should also be viewed as rejection of the other. We think it is important to see it in the context of an emerging, more activist Hindu identity, for it is generally the young Indians who are more vociferous about such questions. An increasing number of voices are being raised against the concept of secularism, in the name of which many Hindus feel they have been misrepresented. Secular in India does not mean no religion; on the contrary it refers to respect for all religions.

Caveat 4: Regional identities: intracultural and cross-cultural: the outsider, insider dilemma.

Last, for the coherence of this study, it is important to mention that we look at cross-cultural competence in the Indian context at two levels. One level highlights internal, intracultural regional differences with the urban/rural variable thrown in. The second level would for us more explicitly refer to cultural differences between India and another country and culture. Obviously, we will be looking at issues of the outsider and the insider and how these are manifested at the modern workplace and social sphere.

The Scope of the Study

The information technology (IT) and business processing outsourcing (BPO) environment epitomizes the intercultural model in all its complexity. The electronic hubs in the southern cities especially are job magnets that attract young, educated men and women from all over India. Many of them work virtually with colleagues from across the world. Regional affinities (linguistic comfort) are a major reason for group connections at the workplace. India is a "young" country, with the average age of the Indian pegged at 24 years. It is supposedly 36 for the United States and about 50 for Europe. To a large extent, then, our exposé would need to address how intercultural competence is articulated by the youth in India. The youth today have an ambivalent attitude toward other cultures. The modern socioeconomic structure is compelling urban Indians to "participate in networks which include persons of several castes" on a competitive rather than on the traditionally cooperative basis (Kolenda, 1978). This increasingly determines the capacity for intercultural competence in a global environment.

This dichotomy is best illustrated by the IT-BPO segment, which is singularly young (average age 25 to 30). Acceptance and rejection, notably of perceived Western values, are evident in their interactions with other cultures.

As the subject of intercultural competence is vast and complex, we will limit our views to a sector and an age group that are at the forefront of global interaction today, that of 25- to 30-year-old upwardly mobile, urban Indian professionals. They work in electronic enclaves in the sphere of IT-BPO. Their interaction with world cultures is largely virtual, and cross-cultural competence is necessary for both sides to succeed.

Understanding the Indian Context

Having presented the caveats, what is unique to India, and influences on its intercultural competence perspectives, we come now to what is uniquely Indian that needs to be kept in mind to understand the positions that we take. In this section, we discuss such concepts as diversity, caste, family, and destiny.

Diversity and Multiple Identities

Pluralism is intrinsic to India. The Hindu pantheon boasts of thousands of gods and goddesses, each a different manifestation of the same consciousness. India presents greater complexity and diversity than the whole of Europe put together. Hindi, spoken by around 30% of the population, is the national language. However, English, along with Hindi and the vernacular language of the concerned region, is the preferred language of communication for both political and commercial purposes and more or less the administrative lingua franca 60 years and more after the British finally conceded the Indians' right to rule themselves.

Racially, its people can be classified this way: Indo-Aryan 72%, Dravidian 25%, and Mongoloid and other 3%. Categorized according to religion, the 2001 census breaks up the population in this manner: Hindu 80.5%, Muslim 13.4%, Christian 2.3%, Sikh 1.9%, other 1.8%, and unspecified 0.1%. Geographically, historically, and politically, it is a land of many parts. The very fabric of India is polycultural.

Put simply, a single Indian can hold many simultaneous identities and understands that a compatriot may be similarly composed of multi-identities. This understanding comes with the in-built competency to coexist not only peacefully but also productively.

Despite differences, there are some patterns that emerge that can be considered generalizations about India, which will be discussed later in the chapter.

This is what Shashi Tharoor (2007), former Under Secretary General of the UN and leading political journalist, writes in "Mapping a Nation: Pluralism at 60": "The simple fact is we are all minorities in India. There has never been an archetypal Indian to stand alongside the archetypal Englishman or Frenchman." He goes on to add that "many Indians have more in common with foreigners than with other Indians":

Affinities between Indians span one set of identities and cross into another. I am simultaneously Keralite (my state of origin), Malayali (my linguistic affiliation), Hindu (my religious faith), Nair (my caste), Calcuttan (by marriage), Stephanian (because of my education at Delhi's St. Stephen's College) and so on, and in my interactions with other Indians, each or several of these identities may play a part. Each, while affiliating me to a group with the same label, sets me apart from others; but even within each group, few would share the other identities I also claim, and so I find myself again in a minority within each minority.

Tharoor explained in an interview with the Indian Web site Rediff.com, "And so the Indian identity that I believe in celebrates diversity: if America is a melting-pot, then to me India is a 'thali,' a selection of sumptuous dishes in different bowls. Each tastes different, and does not necessarily mix with the next, but they belong together on the same plate, and they complement each other in making the meal a satisfying repast" (http://www.rediff.com/freedom/08tha2.htm).

On the other hand, underlying the regional differences, there is a certain commonality of approach, a knowledge of which will make it easier for the outsider to interact with Indians professionally. These commonalities are basically a preference for relationship building, informality, and a generally nonconfrontationist attitude.

Caste

Any study related to India would have to deal with the controversial topic of caste. Broadly speaking, caste is a system of social stratification, with different castes coexisting in a hierarchy. M. N. Srinivas (1996), social anthropologist and one of the foremost authorities on caste, says that for nearly three millennia, caste has dominated the lives of the people in the Indian subcontinent, influencing, if not determining, diverse aspects of their life, including their occupation, diet, and selection of a spouse. Education and access to "secular" jobs in modern industry have fueled social mobility among castes, with class considerations gaining importance. Endogamy is, in urban areas, slowly giving way to intercaste marriages.

Caste in India is a layered classification of society: *Brahmins* (teachers), *Vaishyas* (businessmen), *Kshatriyas* (administrators), and *Shudras* (unskilled laborers). This classification was profession, birth, or personality based. It had no hierarchy intended except in the personality-based division, where a person living an exemplary life was said to be the highest Brahmin. In later years, the distortion of the caste system, skewing it to birth alone, resulted in the "lower" castes being exploited by the "higher" castes. In the traditional Indian context of a caste-defined society, competence was the specific occupational skill that a boy (generally) acquired and learnt from his father or male members of his family. For example, a weaver's son learnt the art and craft of weaving and became a good weaver. Linked to his craft were customs and practices, as well as value systems that ensured the "correct" social interactions with higher ups and others below that the weaver and his family had with the immediate society. Work and social relationships mirrored each other in the weaver's occupational and social interactions.

Family

Family is the smallest unit of caste, and in many parts of India, a family continues to be an extended family with several patrilineal generations living together. It is important to note that although extended families are slowly becoming nuclear, especially in urban areas, often for want of space and not always because of individual considerations, the family continues to be governed by joint family sentiment. The kind of closeness observed/exhibited between professionals in the modern workplace is reminiscent of an extended family environment—being able to depend on each other is crucial for the project work to get done. Outsourced work is potentially disruptive; the differences in the communication and the managerial style between the home and the host country need constant vigilance on the part of project leaders, who are required to "protect" and "interpret" their team members from or for the "hostile outsider." These are important points when considering relationships in a corporate setup. This takes precedence even over work, and it is not uncommon for an employee to take leave to attend a cousin's wedding or nephew's naming ceremony. It appears that corporate entities that "nurture" and "mentor" their assets, especially in the fast-moving IT-BPO sectors, have a lower rate of attrition than those for whom it is not a priority.

The "allegiance" to the family is important from the perspective of intercultural competence. Trainees at a large garment manufacturing firm were asked about the corporate values that defined their work. Several mentioned the "sense of belonging to a family" and of "being looked after." The sense of belonging to a corporate family, in our opinion, seems to wane when it comes to embracing a global network. When confronted with having to make global allegiance, Indian professionals tend to assert their Indian identity before the corporate. During a visit to the Bangalore office of a large Web-based service provider, we were surprised to see a five-foot Indian flag hanging (very much in the manner of football clubs) in the section where young programmers were working. This would normally be seen in government institutions, not in the IT-BPO sectors. In changed circumstances of the world economic order, the family and caste system act as a buffer against the shock of recession. Youngsters who had moved out of their parental homes, buoyed by financial plenty, are moving back, and marriage is no longer as experimental a process, breaking fences of caste and religion. Returning to roots is a classic Indian phenomenon.

Professional Versus Personal

The importance Indians place on family may well affect their willingness to work. For instance, an employee might prefer to resign if he is transferred to a place where his family cannot be shifted for one reason or another. Relations within the family peer group are characterized by familiarity, affection, playfulness, and a sense of obligation to help when needed. This gets easily reflected at the workplace. The informality and lack of reserve that one can observe among similar peer groups contrast vividly with the formal, deferential attitude adopted by younger and more junior people when they address their seniors.

The corporate structure is often considered as a family structure. Spending long hours at work is not uncommon at all in India, and the chatting that accompanies family relationships, especially those with peers, easily gets extended into the corporate world. The boss is looked on as a patriarch, and a good boss is seen as one who looks after you (and your family) and gives you generous money, a good job title, and regular guidance on work you do. A good employee/subordinate is one who doesn't take too much vacation, is always ready to comply with the boss's request, and is honest. A good colleague is one who will gladly help you in your tasks, one who shares his space and personal as well as professional time with you.

Often, employee loyalty can be ensured by simple interventions in personal life, such as using the employer's social clout to secure school admissions (often an arbitrary process in India) for his or her child. This comes as a big surprise to Western cultures, where the personal is kept completely separate from professional. One wouldn't dream of asking, and if one did, one wouldn't be offended if a personal request was turned down. Turning down a personal request in an Indian workplace could be risky and may even result in losing an employee.

An Indian official would also think nothing of a colleague invading his private time to discuss official matters. This is another example of how the personal and the professional are inextricably intertwined.

What we would like to retain from this discussion is the fact that work and personal space are not separate in India. Both were traditionally governed by similar rules of hierarchy and responsibility. This implied an acceptance of hierarchic relations with those higher up in the caste structure and of obligation and responsibility toward those below. Negotiating relationships becomes crucial in large extended families, and it is an art that Indians generally bring to and continue to focus on in the work environment.

Time, Rules, and the Supernatural

Apart from what has been discussed thus far, a Westerner would do well to remember that Indians are in general not as "go-getting" as people of other nationalities. Deadlines are not always sacrosanct, and it may be difficult to get across the concept of punctuality. Time is elastic.

Then there is the rather fuzzy way of following rules, particularly those of the road. Queues are very often jumped, and the concept of privacy of time and space isn't understood in the same way as it is in the West.

Some other characteristics that may be "generalized" when it comes to understanding Indian culture include the emphasis on the supernatural or what, to a Western mind, may appear irrational. The importance given to astrology, numerology, and the principles of *Vaastu* (roughly the Indian equivalent of feng shui) are examples of this. The concept of good time and bad time is rigorously followed, especially in matters like signing contracts or starting new ventures.

Fatalism

Indians in general are instilled with the concept that this life is just one in a long cycle of births and deaths, not necessarily all human. The concept of reincarnation is therefore an inherent part of the Indian psyche, and it indirectly influences a lot of other beliefs and, consequently, cultural behavior. The belief in the life cycle lends itself to the corollary that whatever actions have been done in earlier human lives could have their consequences in this life, and actions performed in this lifetime may have repercussions in not only this but also future lifetimes. The timing of such manifestation of consequences is believed to be beyond the individual's control since it is governed by a cosmic law or theory of karma. This is the basis of the widespread Indian belief in fatalism, or destiny. There are two ways this belief translates to overt behavior:

- Fatalism, or destiny, could lull a person to apathy and inaction because he or she sees futility in all action and exercise of free will. This, however, is the view of only a small minority in India.

- The more prevalent effect of the belief in destiny is the ability to take life as it comes and not be buffeted by its ups and downs. Understanding the law of karma enables the Indian to change what can be changed, accept what cannot, and have the wisdom to know the difference. The Indian is thus able to put in the best effort possible and take the results of such efforts in stride, without getting unduly euphoric or disappointed. Prayer, meditation, and yoga provide the balance between doing and being.

For instance, an employee complaining to a senior adviser that he had been overlooked for promotion despite good performance and a colleague preferred over him could be told that it was all in the stars and might be advised to "keep on working; it'll all come right." In all probability, he would accept the explanation and advice.

Face

Duties and obligations rule over rights and responsibilities in Indian cross-cultural situations. Skirting the issue, saving face, hesitation, and indirectness are all part of communication in this context in India. The relationship has to be preserved at all costs—simply exchanging information is not the goal of communication, as it is "heartless." Indians are very careful about protecting people's reputation or "face" and put it above all else even in professional interactions.

For example, an Indian team leader might hesitate to take the drastic step of firing a subordinate even if his boss gives him the authority to do so. He will be swayed by subjective considerations such as the length of time the employee has been with the company and the comfortable personal relationship they enjoy, instead of going by a purely objective assessment of his value on the team.

By extension, an Indian employee will be apt to take professional criticism personally. For instance, if he is told that a report he prepared is "bad," he will read it as a comment that he himself is bad. This aspect sets up a potential minefield for intercultural relationships.

A little bit of thought toward saving face will go a long way toward employee loyalty, particularly if a reprimand has to be issued in public. Take the case of an employee who has been thoughtless in the matter of expenses and was not proactive about disconnecting an unnecessary telephone line. If he has to be pulled up in the presence of others, it would be better to let him down lightly by also praising another cost-cutting step he has taken.

Conflict

Conflict is the opposite of harmony, and Indians, especially in a family or community setup, would generally try to avoid this. On the other hand, conflict in what we term as "open" contexts where people are not concerned about saving family or community face, is quite frequent and vociferously expressed. It is not unusual to see people fighting in the street and arguing loudly. Very often, they would have little or no "connection" to each other. Any family member present would hasten to break up the fight. Anger is one of the emotions that Indian teachers and gurus warn against, for it symbolizes more than anything else loss of control over the self. Impatience, haste, anger, and raising one's voice are considered super detrimental to relationships. This is the reason that Indian professionals often say that they are surprised by the "tone" used by some of their foreign colleagues and consultants or clients. A "deferential" body language too is considered more becoming of the subordinate.

Modern India and Intercultural Competence

Vivek Saxena and Kendra Carpenter (2008), in their presentation at a conference in Chennai, India, on traditional Indian philosophy and a new model of cross-cultural competency, seem to suggest that several Indian philosophical concepts are very similar to Western notions of intercultural competence. "Denial" and "defense" (found in Bennett's [1993] developmental model of intercultural competence) are akin to *maya* (as suggested by Saxena & Carpenter, 2008) and can impede one's successful interactions and growth; likewise, the practice of *asanas* in yoga implies the movement both physical and intuitive from the egocentric to the ethnorelative ("stretching from and stretching to").

It has been mentioned earlier that information technology cities of Bangalore, Hyderabad, and Chennai are miniature Indias united by modern technology. The intracultural mix is intense, with the young from different locations in India coming to these cities for work. Information technology migration is characterized by big and better opportunities in terms of technical competence and salaries. The young move on fairly quickly in search of better pastures. Intermixing and marriages are on the rise but not dramatically so.

Adaptation is slowly beginning, though it needs acceleration. IT-BPO employees are learning about other cultures through training, which is a big investment at such major firms. They are invaded by and open to receiving modern messages via television, Internet, and mobile phone communication to keep up with and learn about the other parts of the world. Lunch cafeterias at all major information technology companies have Kentucky Fried Chicken and Pizza Hut alongside the Indian curry meals. The call center employee who goes back to his desk after lunch can actually relate to the cross-cultural food he has just eaten!

What Is Intercultural Competence From India's Standpoint?

Now that we have provided some understanding of the Indian context, we turn our attention to intercultural competence itself from an Indian perspective (see Figure 12.3). Before we begin to explore intercultural competence from an Indian perspective, though, it is important to define what we understand by *competence*. Competence is the ability or capacity to quickly adapt (but not convert), which in this case leads to appropriate social behavior. Cooperation and collaboration get heightened in such a cultural framework without the essence being diluted.

What do our traditions teach us about other cultures and cooperating with them? Intercultural competence from an Indian perspective is centered on the concept of oneness or *Vishwa Roopa Darshanam: Vishwa* = Universe, *Roopa* = the forms, *Darshanam* = vision. The entire universe and all its forms are seen as one, and at the core of all beings is one divine consciousness. This is the cross-cultural competence model on which the Indian is raised and, to use the Hofstede analogy, the software program that is written into his mind through unsaid words. There are five compulsory practices prescribed to an Indian in the daily way of life that deeply ingrain respect of man, plant and animal kingdom, ancestors, divinity, and scriptures:

Man: The daily greeting employed commonly between individuals is one example of how importance is given to treating others with respect. The gesture— joint hands—is used to greet all people, irrespective of social standing, to acknowledge the nonseparateness of all beings. The word that accompanies the gesture is *Namaste*—a composite word, with *Nama* meaning I bow and *te* meaning to you— Seeing divinity in you, I bow.

Animals and plants: All animals and plants are considered holy even though the Indian cow has become the most ubiquitous symbol of this. Animals are held sacred with this vision of the common divinity as their core, too. This is the basis of vegetarianism practiced by the majority in the country. The snake, monkey, elephant, and myriad other animals form part of mythology and folklore. Multiple forms of God adorn Indian temples, and each idol has an animal as the vehicle or preferred companion. These are as diverse as the eagle, the parrot, the crow, and even the python, symbolizing, in a large sense, the need to preserve the ecological balance. Watering a holy basil plant as a daily ritual, deifying trees like the peepul, reverentially going around them uttering silent prayers, placing a spoonful of the rice for the crows on your windowsill before taking it to the table—these are all common acts that portray reverence of plants and animals in India.

Ancestors or elders are given much respect; divinity is worshipped in nature as the sun or moon and also takes many forms in the shape of idols as symbols of values to be practiced. Scriptural study can be seen as an instruction manual on how to live life so that you reduce emotional turmoil and is an essential part of daily life in India.

Seeking self-improvement to get rid of negative tendencies such as jealousy or greed and acceptance of others are milestones along the way of spiritual progress in the Indian psyche. The whole way of life involves constant acknowledgment of the oneness and divinity in all.

The *Bhagwad Gita,* a holy book for the Hindus, with wisdom encapsulated in 700 verses, was Gandhi's spiritual reference book. Eknath Easwaran, former professor at Berkeley and founder of the Blue Mountain Centre of Meditation, explains the essence this way:

It is helpful to keep each of these three aspects in mind—attention, detachment, and the job at hand. With complete attention, everything in life becomes fresh. If we can forget ourselves and give full attention to the job at hand, we cannot help but excel. That's what detachment means: you need nothing from anything or anyone outside you; you are complete. They are three elements of a single skill. When you dedicate yourself to the task at hand with complete concentration and without any trace of egotistic involvement, you are learning to live completely in the present. You are making yourself whole, undivided, work done in this spirit as an offering to him who pervades the universe, who is in my heart and yours. (www.easwaran.org)

If we grasp this great truth—we will never be discourteous to others, we will never be unkind, we will never try to avoid people, and we will always be glad to work in harmony with those around us—then it becomes impossible to quarrel, to be angry, to hurt others, to move away.

This doesn't mean weakening one's convictions or diluting one's principles. Disagreeing without being disagreeable is one of the arts of civilized living and is the basis of the cross-cultural competence model in India.

The *Gita*'s universal teachings apply to events in our own lives and times. Oneness of the universe, born of food, is seen as the basis of all life.

One of the most ancient scriptural texts, *Taitreya Upanishad*, talks of our connection in the universal web of life, with food being the essence of that web.

Beings are born from food, food is produced by rain, rain comes from sacrifice (worshipping nature and making offerings so it may rain adequately), and sacrifice comes from good actions (offerings or good actions have as a basis steps to preserve eco-balance). So in other words, man lives in balance with nature, global warming–like phenomena are avoided, and timely copious rain comes. When there is enough rain, food grows, and new humans are conceived and are born. Once born, they live because of food (mental, physical nutrition); on dying, they enter into food (earth to earth). Again the cycle starts, and beings are born from food.

The cross-cultural competence model in Figure 12.3 is therefore based on this essential belief on which Indians are raised, whether in rural or urban India.

At the core is the oneness of all life, called the consciousness principle, which is the real and all-time focus of all human interaction (see Figure 12.1). Focus on that oneness and look beyond external differences. Unequivocally, be aware that there is the background from which external differences and observable behavior come. The background is made up of two parts. One is the upbringing and life experiences of this life, which you could explain if you delved deep enough. The other part of the background is a result of actions of past lives, which leave traces based on both good and bad merits earned through actions done in past lives. This cannot be explained or seen. It is an invisible background.

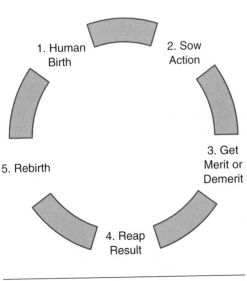

Figure 12.3   The Chain/Cycle

1. Human Birth
2. Sow Action
3. Get Merit or Demerit
4. Reap Result
5. Rebirth

Create space between action and reaction in that acceptance—so that your actions are well thought through (see Figure 12.1). When a situation of confrontation between cultures comes up, don't respond to someone else's comment immediately. Take the time to think through.

Acceptance and Adaptation

Amartya Sen, Nobel laureate, economist, professor, and author, has justly pointed out that Indian acceptance is not necessarily an acknowledgment of equality (live and let live is the way we are). Engaging with someone implies greater equality. This explains the relative stability and continuity of a cultural tradition that has not been disrupted since 2500 B.C.

In an astonishingly comprehensive reading of Indian culture, Sen (2005), the economist makes a subtle distinction between acceptance and equality. Talking about the coexistence of different cultures in India, he writes, "I will use the Sanskrit word 'swikriti' in the sense of 'acceptance,' in particular the acknowledgement that the people involved (different cultures) are entitled to lead their own lives. The idea of 'swikriti' need not of course, convey any affirmation of equality of the standing of one 'accepted' group compared with another" (p. 34). According to Sen, the denial of *swikriti* by the dominant group is crucial in present-day multicultural societies for it denies the other the right to lead his or her own life. "Tolerate" involves some amount of grumbling, but "accept" involves a wholehearted, positive regard.

So, acceptance leads to adaptation, creating space and better intercultural understanding. Indian culture is dominantly Hindu but pronouncedly plural. The Indian brand of cultural syncretism has enabled diverse cultures to coexist and thrive in the subcontinent for centuries. Caste, together with family, has been the bedrock on which Indian society has structured itself and is the fault line that separates Indian culture from another. Careful hierarchic relations of patronage, obligation, allegiance, and deference are maintained for different caste groups to cooperate with each other as a functional whole, but as identifiable and "significant" parts, and to enable interaction with other cultures. Globalization, to a large extent, has accentuated the push and pull factors between the traditional and modern at the workplace and in society. Access to education, technology, and newer jobs are resulting in the birth of a new caste: the global Indian.

There is a humorous comparison that Eknath Easwaran makes in one of his talks about the essential unity of cultures. He says that the habit we have of comparing our religions, behaviors, or ways of life is like speaking of mathematics as "German geometry," "French algebra," and "English arithmetic" when in fact all are one.

To quote partially from an essay from his book *The Compassionate Universe*:

Where I used to identify people on the basis of how they differed from me in language, or politics, or personality, now those differences seem superficial . . . our differences are only one percent of who we are. The other 99% is common to all . . . (we) realize that the life we know and love is the same as the life others know and love, and the powerful current flowing through us also flows through the hearts of those around us. (www.easwaran.org)

Conclusion

To summarize, Indians value relationships over time and responsibility, but they are faced with more direct cultures that do some plain speaking in today's global world and whose worldviews differ from that of seeing oneness as core to existence. Indians are attempting to adapt and learn more efficient ways. We Indians have always been teachers and traders, monks and merchants. While we are essential for the growth and success of the rest of the world, our contribution of the philosophy of life pronouncing oneness is equally important for spiritual well-being. As Mahatma Gandhi said, "I do not want my house to be walled in on all sides and my windows to be stuffed. I want the cultures of all the lands to be blown about my house as freely as possible. But I refuse to be blown off my feet by any."

The reason we end with his quote, apart from the fact that it is, like the Mahatma, simple yet deep in meaning and philosophy, is because somewhere, no matter how young or old we are, all of us in India but also worldwide are intrinsically influenced by Gandhi's teachings, his principles, and his passion for India. Gandhi is Indian, and his thoughts belong to the world.

Put succinctly, India's contribution to intercultural competence is in the core principle of "oneness," of recognizing differences while focusing on commonality.

Notes

1. Certain social functions considered as polluting were carried out by the lower castes; the disposal of the dead was one such "cooperative" relation where "higher castes" required the assistance of the "lower castes."

2. At the SIETAR international congress on culture and globalization in Granada, Bennett and Paige (2008) point out that being in the vicinity of culture does not mean you are having the cultural experience.

3. The Census of India is a gigantic process of population enumeration that is carried out every decade. It was last conducted in 2001. The first census was done in 1860.

References

Bennett, M. (1993). Towards a developmental model of intercultural sensitivity. In R. M. Paige (Ed.), *Education for the interculturual experience.* Yarmouth, ME: Intercultural Press.

Bennett, M., & Paige, M. (2008, October). *Making cross-cultural intercultural: Conceptual history and current research of intercultural learning in study abroad.* Paper presented at the SIETAR Global International Congress, Granada.

Bhatty, Z. (1996). Social stratification among Muslims in India. In M. N. Srinivas (Ed.), *Caste: It's twentieth century avatar.* Delhi: Penguin.

Kakar, S., & Kakar, K. (2007). *The Indians.* New Delhi: Penguin/Viking.

Kolenda, P. (1978). *Caste in contemporary India.* San Francisco: Benjamin/Cummings.

Naidu, S., & Chandrasekhar, P. (2008, October). *Globalization and the transformation in mate selection in urban India.* Paper presented at SIETAR, Granada, Spain.

Naik, S. D. (2003, August). Correct regional disparities, rural-urban divide. *The Hindu Business Line.*

Saxena, V., & Carpenter, K. (2008, January). *Traditional Indian philosophy: A new model of cross-cultural competency.* Paper presented at the SIETAR INDIA conference, Chennai, India.

Sen, A. (2005). *The argumentative Indian.* Delhi: Penguin.

Srinivas, M. N. (1996). *Village, caste, gender & method: Essays in Indian social anthropology.* Delhi: Oxford University Press.

Tharoor, S. (1997). *India: From midnight to the millennium.* Delhi: Viking Penguin.

Tharoor, S. (2007, August). Mapping a nation: Pluralism at 60. *Business Outlook Magazine.*

CHAPTER 13

Interculturality Versus Intercultural Competencies in Latin America

Adriana Medina-López-Portillo and John H. Sinnigen

W̶e are currently living in the midst of a maelstrom of crises that requires a fresh examination of the norms and practices that have been dominant in the modern world system—namely, the "Western" (Euro-U.S.) paradigm of an individualistic, militarist, consumerist culture; capitalist economics; and elite-dominated electoral politics. The worldwide economic meltdown has aggravated the already existing state of crisis evident in a severely degraded environment, ceaseless wars, and increasing social polarization of poor and rich within individual nations and throughout the world system (Wallerstein, 1990). Although progressive analysts have been discussing the decline of the American empire since the Vietnam War, in November 2008, even U.S. intelligence agencies explained a decline in U.S. world dominance in the face of emerging powers such as India and China (Shane, 2008). Indeed, at the November 14–15, 2008, economic summit in Washington, the exclusive club of the Western powers plus Japan, known as the G7, was compelled to open its doors to the wider group of the G20, which included China and India, as well as other countries from Asia and Latin America and Saudi Arabia, and clearly the United States was a follower in the search for solutions to the crisis, while China, India, and Brazil were among the leaders (Nayar, 2008). It would seem that the Washington Consensus, in which neo-conservative economic structural adjustment policies, promoted by the United States and imposed across the underdeveloped world by the International Monetary Fund and the World Bank, is coming to an end. The urgency of this maelstrom of crises requires that scholars and practitioners of intercultural communication seek ways to participate in new solutions. Our contribution is to examine interculturality in Latin America, and this will necessarily draw us out of academia since intercultural concepts are embedded in indigenous-led social movements in different parts of the continent whose concept of interculturality is communitarian and egalitarian and recognizes the need for decisive political action.

In the United States, there is a developing consensus around the idea that intercultural competency refers to the individual skills, knowledge, attributes, behaviors, and attitudes needed to interact successfully with people from different cultures (Deardorff, 2006). According to this largely academic consensus, individuals need to focus on their personal intercultural exchanges and receive training to improve their skills and knowledge. The result of this learning process should be an enhanced quality of the effectiveness and appropriateness of such exchanges and an ever increasing capacity for getting along with individuals from different cultural backgrounds. Such an approach is appropriate for training professionals in the growing number of areas that require interculturally competent workers. In Latin America, although there are approaches similar to this U.S. concept of intercultural competence,[1] the preferred term is *interculturality*, and the difference between the two terms is conceptual. Intercultural competence refers to an individual set of skills that can be acquired and learned; interculturality refers to a historic condition. Intercultural competence is primarily an academic matter and produces valuable scholarship and training programs and methodologies. Interculturality points to the radical restructuring of the historically pronounced uneven relations of wealth and power that have existed between Europeans and their descendants and indigenous and other subordinated groups during the last half millennium. This history has been characterized by an ongoing process of conquest, exploitation, *and resistance*. In Latin America, interculturality is used to describe the necessary conditions for a new social configuration that allows historically marginalized indigenous groups and others, primarily Blacks, to pursue cultural, political, and economic equality.

This chapter examines the relationships between Latin America's indigenous populations and the dominant groups in their respective countries, as well as implications for effective and equitable intercultural exchange.[2] In other words, the discussion leads to an examination of power and equity among the groups and strategies for social change. These intercultural issues are matters of extreme urgency in all those countries with large indigenous populations and at this moment, particularly in Bolivia and Ecuador; we will highlight these two national cases in this chapter. Both countries have been immersed recently in intense struggles around the formulation of new constitutions that promote intercultural economic and political equality.[3] In both countries, the central struggle has been between recently empowered indigenous social movements and the entrenched White/*mestizo* oligarchies and their foreign allies that have traditionally held power. The recently elected governments of both countries play different sorts of mediating roles; their policies are challenged by both the oligarchs and the social movements, and they both are responses to extreme political instabilities exemplified by the continual toppling of presidents. The 49-year-old Aymara leader, Evo Morales, elected in December 2005 with 53% of the vote, is the first indigenous president of Bolivia, where native peoples make up 63% of the population. Not a professional politician, he became the general secretary of the coca growers union in 1985 and came to the presidency as the leader of an indigenous social movement. In a recent recall referendum, he received the support of 67% of voters. The 45-year-old Rafael Correa, elected president of Ecuador in December 2006 with the support of 57% of the voters in a second-round ballot, is a *mestizo* politician trained as an economist and a former finance minister of this country with a 40% indigenous population. He has received the critical support of the largest movement of native peoples, the Confederation of Indigenous Nationalities of Ecuador (CONAIE, its acronym in Spanish). Morales and Correa have both overseen the drafting of new constitutions for their countries, and both propose a "re-founding" of their respective nations. The Ecuadorian constitution was approved with a 65% yes vote in September 2008, and the new Bolivian constitution was approved in January 2009 with a 61% yes vote. Thus, these intercultural issues are of immediate political importance (for the full texts of both constitutions, see Asamblea Constituyente de Bolivia, 2007; Asamblea Constituyente de Ecuador, 2008).

John Stolle-McAllister (2007), who studies the Ecuadorian CONAIE, points out that the movement's recent successes are based on 20 years of theorizing and living interculturality through dialogues and political practices aimed at the decolonization of institutions and the sociocultural fabric of the country. He argues that "one of the indigenous movement's goals has been to create an intercultural society in Ecuador that is based on mutual respect and equitable distribution of resources and power. Intercultural policies go beyond recognizing the fact that many different cultural groups share the same territory and history, instead proposing that those different groups construct meaningful ways to interrelate" (p. 165). This concept of interculturality has been initiated by the historically marginalized indigenous peoples and has as its goal a society in which there would no longer be any marginalized groups and requires a national effort to bring about cultural, economic, and political equality. A central pillar of this interculturality is the Andean philosophical concept *alli kawsay* (good living), a concept that stresses reciprocal, complementary, and cooperative relations and that puts into question the European/U.S. civilizational web of individualism, colonialism, and modernity. Thus, this Ecuadorian concept of interculturality points to a serious need to interrogate the philosophical basis of intercultural competency, especially in the current conjuncture in which the Western individualistic, capitalist paradigm is showing severe signs of weakness in dealing with urgent ecological, social, and economic crises, crises that will be with us for quite some time.

In the Bolivian case, the social movement led by Morales generated a new political party, the Movimiento al Socialismo (MAS, Movement to Socialism). Morales has stated that he reluctantly became a politician only when he realized that politics could become genuine public service, rather than a road to personal wealth and prestige. In this declaration, Morales was echoing the words of another leader of an indigenous movement, Subcomandante Marcos of the Mexican neo-Zapatistas, who declared that the new politics they practice and support is based on the concept of *mandar obedeciendo*, governance through obedience to the popular will (Holloway, 1996). We recognize that such declarations of deference to the popular are uttered by many political leaders who then pursue personal wealth and prestige. The difference is that these still-being-tested principles of Morales and Marcos are consonant with the communitarian principles of indigenous cultures, and their practice thus far indicates an adherence to them. The Bolivians have a philosophy similar to that of CONAIE Article 1 of the proposed constitution, a product of more than 25 years of debate, which reads, "Bolivia is constituted as a Unified Social, Plurinational, Communitarian, free, independent, democratic, intercultural, and decentralized State with autonomies. Bolivia is founded on plurality and political, economic, juridical, cultural and linguistic pluralism in the process of integrating the country" (Asamblea Constituyente de Bolivia, 2007).[4] It also stresses Andean philosophical principles, including *suma qamaña* (good living) and *ñandereko* (harmonious living) and the need to decolonize the country. That is, their proposal to re-found the nation invokes the traditional communitarian values of the majority population that includes respect for "Pachamama," Mother Nature, the earth, the supreme goddess of the Aymara and Quechua religions, which is being destroyed by industrialization and neoconservative economic policies (Rebick, 2006). The Bolivian MAS combines cultural identitarian politics with an egalitarian communitarian intercultural economic and political agenda. They advocate what Bolivian Vice President Álvaro García has called "Andean/Amazonian capitalism" (Cockcroft, 2008) and call for a mixed economy with private, state, and communitarian property based on the pre-Columbian *ayllu*. Their international vision is anti-imperialist, and their commitment to interculturality extends to all the peoples of the world. Such a daring policy has been actively opposed by the traditional elites, who see their traditional privileges threatened, and by the U.S. government, which has historically relied on local elites to assert its imperial power and has no assurances of success.[5]

The Need for History

A popular saying throughout Latin America goes something like "U.S. Americans never remember, and we never forget," and indigenous social movements are steeped in history. Their call for re-founding the nation through decolonization points to the fact that nominal political independence obtained in the 19th century led to neocolonialism rather than effective economic and political sovereignty.

To understand the different attitudes toward history and interculturality in the economically hyper-developed United States and the economically underdeveloped Latin American nations, we need to look at the incorporation of both areas into the expanding European capitalist system in the 16th century, and there we come to the tale of the silver and the rock. In Latin America, most notably in the areas of the Aztec and Inca empires, large quantities of silver were found, and these areas were rapidly turned into major exporters of valuable minerals and other raw materials, through what the Uruguayan writer Eduardo Galeano (1971) has called the open veins of Latin America. Thus, silver, a synecdoche of rich natural resources, condemned Latin America to a path of what Andre Gunder Frank (1969) called "the development of underdevelopment." Those veins are still open; Latin American economies have always been organized around the needs of the international markets, and Latin American rulers frequently have more interests in common with metropolitan elites than with the majority of their fellow citizens, especially the indigenous and Black citizens. The conquest of the Americas involved genocide of the indigenous populations north and south, but in Latin America, especially in the areas of the Aztec and Inca empires, those populations had developed a high level of civilization. The Spaniards and Portuguese then turned the peasants and artisans into miners and workers in other sorts of slave-like occupations, and a new ethnic/cultural group emerged, the mixed-blood *mestizos*. The cultures of the area have been a hybrid ever since. Thus, interculturality has been a condition of life in Latin America for over 500 years. Of course, it has been a sort of interculturality with no equality. The original mixed-blood *mestizos* were first produced by the rape of Indian women by the conquistadors, and the continued hegemony of the Europeans and their descendents was guaranteed by arms and by laws. The indigenous communities, along with the African slaves who joined them during the colonial period, were always treated as less than human by their White rulers, and numerous epithets are used to refer to them, epithets emphasizing their ignorance that are similar to those used by racist Whites in the United States to refer to Blacks—for example, right-wing Bolivians refer to Evo Morales as an "Indian monkey" (Cockcroft, 2008). Even the 19th-century liberals sought a European-based society that would require the acculturation of the indigenous populations. Of course, there were always defenders of the rights of the Indians, like Fray Bartolomé de las Casas, the first bishop of Chiapas, but the assertion of the autonomy of indigenous cultures and communities is a relatively new phenomenon (see de las Casas, 2003).

In recent Latin American history, while Europeans and their descendents have composed the dominant elites, *mestizos* have gained some economic and political power (especially in Mexico after the 1910–1921 Revolution), and the marginalized Indians have continually resisted European rule. Thus, current movements are but the most recent and advanced version of a 500-year struggle, and in fact, 1992, the quincentenary of Columbus's maiden voyage, was an important moment of reflection and consolidation for native peoples with the award of the Nobel Peace Prize to Rigoberta Menchú and the first Continental Indigenous Summit held in Teotihuacan, Mexico. In fact, Morales says that it was at that moment that his movement decided to "move from resistance to the taking of power" (Rebick, 2006).

Unlike the rich mineral resources found by the Spaniards and Portuguese in Latin America, a major source of wealth for the development of European capitalism, the English Mayflower Pilgrims who arrived on the coast of Massachusetts in 1620 found only Plymouth Rock (so the tradition goes) and no evident natural resources of great value. Thus, the United States had the good fortune to be born unimportant to the world economy—*La importancia de no nacer importante* (Galeano, 1971, p. 170). The colonists and the newly independent country developed primarily on the basis of small farms and manufacturing, and they formed a strong internal market and infrastructure that were a sound basis for subsequent economic development. Native peoples in the area of the United States were primarily nomadic and never effectively incorporated into this developing economy. There was little miscegenation of Europeans and Indians, and many Indians were killed and pushed off their lands, with many still living on reservations today (Zinn, 1980, especially chap. 1). On the other hand, Latin American countries such as Mexico celebrate their indigenous heritage as part of their national identity, even though Indians are continually subjected to repression and discrimination; in the United States, the indigenous heritage is almost never celebrated, except perhaps fleetingly at Thanksgiving. The native basis of interculturality in Latin America and the aggressive role of their social movements in asserting the rights of their marginalized communities in the framework of a new foundation of the nation provide the historical basis for understanding the strong social communitarian anti-imperialist force of interculturality in countries such as Bolivia and Ecuador.

All objects of study need to be treated as moments in a world historical process, and that is true of the differences between intercultural competencies in the United States and interculturality in Latin America. As a hegemonic world power, the United States is (in)famous for its monolingualism and ethnocentricity, and most intercultural communication programs in the country do not require advanced study of a language other than English. Thus, this U.S. perspective treats language, an essential human trait, as incidental to intercultural studies. The Latin American social movements we have analyzed briefly have developed through over 500 years of struggle against hegemonic world powers, from Spain in the 16th century to the United States in the 21st, and these movements are all multilingual and intercultural by definition, a function of the linguistic richness of their cultures. The world has much to learn from their counterhegemonic intercultural politics and discourse that, starting from the needs of marginalized cultures, advocate mutual respect and economic and political equality of all cultures rather than the acculturation of the oppressed.

The Formation of Nation-States in Latin America and the Impact on Interculturality

The development of the rich and diverse indigenous cultures in the region suffered a near fatal blow with the arrival of the Europeans. Five hundred years of genocide, exploitation, rape, submission, appropriation of territories and natural resources, and cultural imperialism ensued. The indigenous populations were dehumanized by the Europeans, who treated the indigenous groups as soulless savages, which—in their eyes—legitimized their right to destroying their customs, traditions, religion, and culture by determining that such cultural eradication was the indigenous people's only way to salvation and to "civilization" (De la Torre, 2006). This "civilizing idea," alive to this date, has permeated all sectors of society, from the *criollos* and *mestizos* to significant sections of the indigenous populations who, as a result of the pervasiveness of the attack, have developed a paradoxical state of internalized prejudice and discrimination, on one hand, and of cultural pride and resistance, on the other.

The 19th century witnessed the independence of the different regions in the continent, and "Latin America," as we know it, was born. Nation-states were created, and an attempt to develop national identities began. Subercaseaux (2002) distinguishes four periods of national identity creation: the foundational period of Independence (the most intense period, which was in effect between 1810 and 1840), an Integrative period from 1890 to 1920, the Revolutionary period (1950–1975), and the

Globalized period that started in the 1980s.[6] He explains how the concept of the nation-states and their mythologies evolved and were expanded through time. In the Independence period, the purpose was to build, educate, and civilize nation-states led by the elites and the state. During the Integrative period, the goals of the Independence period were expanded to add the integration of new social and ethnic sectors. The state services were expanded, and the concept of nation was linked to the idea of *mestizaje*. The Revolutionary period's goal was to transform the socioeconomic structures to benefit workers and the poorest in society. The concept of nation was linked to the concept of social class and anti-imperialism. Finally, the goal of the Globalized period, in which we are now, is for the nation-states to enter the globalization stage while keeping their identity in a context of cultural diversity.

The Latin American scholar who has theorized globalization the most extensively is the Argentine-Mexican philosopher-anthropologist Nestor García Canclini. García Canclini's best-known work in the United States is his interdisciplinary 2005 *Hybrid Cultures: Strategies for Entering and Leaving Modernity* (published originally in Spanish in 1989). Here he seriously interrogates the trope of tradition/modernity typically used in the analysis of Latin America and argues for a process of political and cultural democratization in which traditional cultural symbols and practices, although necessarily "impure," need to resist being trampled by modernity. García Canclini focuses on interactions and argues against essentialisms of all sorts, asserting instead that culture is a process and that identities are always in flux. He states that contemporary conditions of commerce and communication produce cultural hybrids as the globalization of economic and cultural processes allows, for example, indigenous communities in places such as Mexico and Perú to produce and export their crafts to a global market, rather than just selling them to tourists, as the satellite dish and the computer meet the loom and pottery wheel. Through such exchanges, traditional production processes are at once maintained and transformed; the modern is articulated with the traditional. Subcomandante Marcos and the neo-Zapatista movement that appeared on the world scene on January 1, 1994, the day the modernizing project of North American Free Trade Agreement (NAFTA) went into effect, would be a prime example of such hybridization, as they express throughout the world through an extremely astute use of the Internet their demands based in indigenous traditions. In his 1999 *La globalización imaginada* (*Imagined Globalization*, not yet available in English), García Canclini analyzes the relations between globalization and interculturality, and he maintains that contemporary globalization is modifying the meaning of culture. He points out that from the 1960s to the 1980s, sociosemiotic, anthropological, sociological, and other studies were establishing culture as "the process of production, circulation, and consumption of meanings in social life," a concept that was intended for each individual society (García Canclini, 1999, pp. 61–62). Then in the 1990s, however, there was a push for a reconceptualization of culture in the direction of interculturality, such that the study of culture would necessarily be intercultural, that is, a relational study of culture (Sinnigen & Medina, 2002).

Demographics and Interculturality

Subercaseaux (2002) observes that it is difficult to determine an exact current indigenous population size in Latin America and asserts that conservative numbers indicate that out of 515 million Latin Americans, there are between 33 and 41 million indigenous people, that is, between 6.4% and 8% of the total population. According to the scholar, only five countries are home to approximately 90% of this population: Perú with 27%, Mexico with 26%, Guatemala with 15%, Bolivia with 12%, and Ecuador with 8%. The roughly 41 million indigenous people form 400 different ethnic groups. Each of these groups is a complex cultural system, with its own symbols—language being a fundamental one—cosmovisions, traditions, and socioeconomic and political organization. The only Latin American country without an indigenous population is Uruguay, followed by Brazil, with only an approximate .2%.

We conclude this section by recapitulating the examples we have offered so far that illustrate the expressions of interculturality as implemented in Latin America: (a) additions and changes to the constitutions or other state documents in at least 15 countries that acknowledge the multicultural character of the population and explicitly state the rights of the diverse groups, including the recognition of linguistic pluralism; (b) diverse indigenous movements throughout the region—we mentioned the cases of Chiapas, Mexico, Bolivia, and Ecuador; (c) the elected governments of Ecuador and Bolivia—with the previous creation of a new political party in the latter country; (d) dialogues and political and intercultural practices; (e) self-governance of indigenous communities—Chiapas, Mexico, is a good example; (f) respect for Pachamama and encouragement for *good living;* (g) communitarian practices; and (h) the dissemination of intercultural bilingual education, to which we now turn our attention.

Interculturality and Intercultural Bilingual Education

As mentioned in this chapter, one mechanism for implementing interculturality in some Latin American countries has been through intercultural bilingual education. The historic background of interculturality and intercultural bilingual education is one and the same, with interculturality being the condition that allowed intercultural bilingual education to flourish, and we can trace their origins back to the Colonization Era.

The approach of the Europeans to indigenous cultures was one of acculturation, that is, the suppression of indigenous cultures and the assimilation of the native peoples into the European model. In their thorough article on intercultural bilingual education, "La Educación Intercultural Bilingüe en América Latina: Balance y Perspectivas" ("The Intercultural Bilingual Education in Latin America: Balances and Perspectives"), López and Küper (1999) indicate that at the beginning of the Conquest, the indigenous languages were used in education along with Castilian and Latin, a practice soon to be changed when the Spanish Crown banned the use of native languages. During the Independence and Integrative periods of nation building, the emphasis was placed on creating monolingual and monocultural states, which accelerated the assimilation process by the indigenous groups. As a result of this ideology, acquiring education became a major challenge for the indigenous students, who had to learn the curriculum in Spanish, a foreign language to them. This practice slowed down their learning, with many of them having to repeat each grade for 2 or 3 years. In response to this incongruence, starting in the 1930s, teachers around Latin America began to teach in the students' languages to create a bridge to the Spanish language. Although the emphasis of this method was placed on the learning of Spanish, it was by far a gentler pedagogy than the previous one. By the 1940s, this idea of teaching in native languages with the goal of assimilation was pervasive and became institutionalized, supported by the Evangelists who came from the United States. This was the beginning of the bilingual education model.

In 1940, the Cuban sociologist Fernando Ortiz used the term *transculturation* rather than *acculturation* to describe Cuban society. According to this concept, the different cultural communities in Cuban history, Taino Indians, Spaniards, Africans, and others, all contributed to the economic, cultural, and political development of the nation, thus arguing against the prevalent concept of acculturation according to which the descendants of African slaves needed (the Tainos were eradicated) to acculturate into the dominant culture of the descendants of the slave owners. In his *Contrapunteo cubano del tabaco y el azúcar* (*Cuban Counterpoint*), Ortiz wove a fascinating cultural, economic, and political tale of the two principal products of the island, tobacco and sugar, the former native to Cuba, the latter imported, in the transcultural process of the formation of the Cuban nation and the development of the world capitalist system. Regarding tobacco, he states, "What among the Indians had been a social institution of a magic-religious character became among the whites an institution of economic character, a characteristic phenomenon of complete transculturation" (Oritz, 1963, pp. 219–220).[7] This sort of transcultural study, grounded in the intersection of the cultural, the economic, and the political, is an important precursor of the contemporary use of interculturality as a strategy for cultural, economic, and political social transformation.

In the 1960s and 1970s, new experimental models developed apart from the neo-Evangelist and assimilationist models (López & Küper, 1999). According to López and Küper (1999), the indigenous groups were now supported in learning their own native language in the schools, along with a second language. This practice was based on the understanding that the learning of the first language would help the learning of the second language. Simultaneously, a need surfaced to modify the curriculum so that it corresponded to the reality and context of the students.

In his article "La Praxis de la Interculturalidad en los Estados Nacionales Latinoamericanos" ("The Praxis of Interculturality in the Latin American Nation-States"), Tubino (2005) asserts that in the 1970s, the aim was to offer an intercultural and bilingual education. The term *bicultural* was dropped due to the conceptual problems that arose. In this context, biculturalism was understood as the ability to function equally and simultaneously in two different cultural environments. This framework ignored the uneven existing power relations between the indigenous groups and the dominant group, as well as the prestige differential between the indigenous languages and the national languages. The culture and language of the dominant group were the acceptable ways of being, knowing, and communicating. According to Tubino, the concept of bicultural education meant to place both languages and cultures together, as if they were parallel. "On the contrary, the concept of interculturality places emphasis on communication, contact, the interrelation between both languages, but, above all, the cultures" (p. 87). The term *bicultural* was replaced by the term *intercultural*, which has as its backdrop the notion of interculturality, the cultural platform espoused by the indigenous groups.

Guerrero Arias (in Stolle-McAllister, 2007) introduces the concept of interculturality and describes its different elements and implications:

> Interculturality is not the simple coexistence of different cultures, but rather the sharing of these cultures in their difference, and sharing is only possible from living of everyday life among culturally differentiated communities, each with its own and distinct meanings of existence. It implies dialogical meetings and a continuous relation of alterity between concrete subjects, among human beings endowed with distinct visions of the world, among those that produce symbolic exchanges of senses and meanings. (p. 165)[8]

Interculturality in this sense implies the sharing of experiences and physical and imaginary spaces among peoples who are culturally different. This exchange and coexistence can only be successful if equal participation in all decision-making processes is guaranteed. At the level of a nation-state, an example would be the representation of the diverse groups in the Ecuadorian Congress. At an international level, such interculturality would require the full and equal participation of the native people's organizations in all decisions made by foreign agencies and non-governmental organizations that affect them.

In turn, De la Torre (2006) defines interculturality as "the dynamic articulation between ethnic groups (internally) and with the hegemonic society, in a search of a permanent harmonic space of social interrelation that promotes into the future important processes of decentralization and social participation in more equitable conditions." The model of interculturality he proposes (informed by the intercultural project in Ecuador) is that of knowledge exchange, respect for the characteristics and interests of each group, and identity reaffirmation in the dynamic context of the contemporary world.[9]

An important aspect of the concept of interculturality is the idea that the indigenous cultures are not stagnant and frozen in time but that they evolve and hybridize with intercultural contact (Tubino, 2005). Cultures and identities are diachronic, and there is no need to isolate them from external influences. "Cultural conservationism presupposes atemporal inexistent essences. Intercultural education, in contrast, instead of suggesting a forced return to an idealized past or to the essence of an abstract culture, will have as its goal to better the quality and symmetry of the exchanges" (Tubino, 2005, p. 88). That is to say that the interculturality paradigm is not an attempt to preserve indigenous cultures intact but to make them active participants in and contributors to the cultural, political, and social life of their respective countries. By the organic nature of the exchange, it is to be expected that the indigenous and hegemonic cultures will both be influenced and transformed in subtle and not so subtle ways.

Tubino (2005) summarizes his discussion by underlying the two key notions regarding interculturality discussed above. First, the strengthening of the ethnic-cultural identities of the indigenous groups has to occur simultaneously to the intercultural dialogue as identities are created in relation to the "other." Ways of making the ethnic-cultural identities stronger are the reappropriation of cultural traditions, the revival of native tongues, and the banishment of internalized racism. He continues by stating, "From this point of view, interculturality is a way of understanding and rebuilding the socialization processes that are produced in asymmetrical multicultural contexts" (p. 89). Second, there is a need to redefine the power relationship between the official national culture and the indigenous cultures.

Interculturality, understood this way, promotes the relationship and an active coexistence among the different cultural groups (De la Torre, 2006; Tubino, 2005). Isolation and encapsulation in one's own cultural traditions and understandings of the world go against the dynamic process of culture and represent a stagnant and unrealistic view of what culture is.

López and Küper (1999) argue that since the early 1980s, some Latin American policy makers have offered intercultural bilingual education, which entails a curriculum based on the students' cultural frame of reference and introduces elements of other cultures at the same time, including the hegemonic culture. It is imparted in the native language and another language of European origin. They explain the intercultural dimension in education as follows:

> The intercultural dimension in education refers to the curricular relationship between the practical and theoretical knowledge and the native or adopted values of the indigenous societies and those unknown and other, as much as the search for dialogue and a permanent complementarity between the traditional culture and the Occidental one, in order to satisfy the needs of the indigenous populations and to contribute to the quest of better life conditions. (p. 22)

Intercultural bilingual education contains paradoxes and challenges; a significant pitfall is that this education is targeted to the indigenous populations only. Thus, the task of achieving mutual understanding is not shared by hegemonic groups. It is a lopsided system that places the burden (and the gains) on the indigenous groups, as if only those groups needed the intercultural education. It seems to us that until the hegemonic groups enter the dialogue and accompany it with meaningful actions, interculturality will not be fully achieved. These meaningful actions may be participation in the intercultural bilingual education, where the members of the hegemonic groups have to learn about, with, and from indigenous groups. At a political level, it may mean that the indigenous groups share the power, as has been already suggested, as in having political representation in Congress.

In addition, Tubino (2005) is concerned about the emphasis that teachers place on the "promotion and reinvindication of the 'original culture' of the users" (p. 88). This goal implies a focus on the past, on the culture of the ancestors, and goes against the natural evolution of cultures that occurs when they are in contact with each other. Finally, Salmerón (1998) acknowledges the difficulties of attempting to oper-ate within an intercultural frame of reference: "The recognition of egalitarianism is the golden rule of democratic societies for the public sphere, but it bears a difficulty: the demand to give a space to some differences, that is, to something that, by defini-tion, is not universally shared" (p. 55). In other words, as cultures come together, they bring along a set of unique characteristics that may clash with the unique char-acteristics of the other cultures with which they interact. Thus, the challenge of implementing interculturality is this lack of knowledge in understanding the values, cosmovision, and ways of living and knowing of the particular groups. These ele-ments have to be negotiated but at a table where all groups have equal value.

At a nation-state level, there are also important matters to be considered. Several Latin American countries have appropriated the interculturality discourse and have inserted it in their constitutions and other major legal documents. This move is contrary to the 19th-century goal of homogenizing the population to create and develop national identities that would bring cohesiveness to the diverse popula-tions. It also challenges the hegemonic group's desire to retain its wealth and power. Therefore, there is a concern that, once interculturality becomes part of official dis-course, interculturality may be turned into a slogan with no real applications (Tubino, 2005; Walsh, 2002) unless the indigenous groups continue to advance their agenda, something that is currently occurring in Ecuador and Bolivia.

Conclusion

In this chapter, we have situated a comparison of intercultural competencies in the United States and the theory and practice of interculturality in parts of Latin America in the context of the maelstrom of economic, ecological, and social crises in which we are currently immersed and in the disparate histories of the United States and Latin America. In a search for alternatives to the individualistic, capitalist, and militarist social and cultural models that underlie the current crises, we have looked to the com-munitarian theories and practices of indigenous social movements in Latin America, especially in Ecuador and Bolivia. These movements are steeped in over 500 years of resistance to colonial and neocolonial rule in the area and seek a re-founding of their nations through a process of decolonization based on intercultural principles of mutual human respect, equality, and respect for nature. We have looked at examples such as the draft of the new Bolivian constitution in which the term *intercultural* is used frequently in referring to mutual respect of all peoples and cultures (Afro-Bolivians are expressly included). As illustrated in this chapter through the examples of Bolivia and Ecuador, interculturality is incorporated into an antihegemonic socio-cultural-political movement that is operating on severely contested terrain.

This study would suggest that to be truly effective, intercultural communication should move beyond the limits of individualistic and interpersonal concerns. Although by and large, there is not an equivalent in the United States to the traditions of communitarian egalitarian practices in countries such as Bolivia and Ecuador, there is a long and too often ignored ideal of equality, and that ideal can become a force for achieving greater economic and political equality among groups and not just a supposed equality of opportunity for primarily middle-class individuals. It would require that the hegemonic White upper- and middle-class groups listen to the less privileged Black and Latino minorities instead of insisting on their assimilation and that all Americans address the negative impacts of U.S. imperialism throughout the world. Those negative impacts and the reactions to them are particularly evident in the midst of the current crises in which the United States is engaging in wars in Afghanistan and Iraq, the U.S. government and finance capitalists are responsible for the financial meltdown, and the government persists in efforts to destabilize governments in Latin America, specifically in Bolivia. The realization of the ideal of equality would obviously include an end to poverty in the richest country in the history of the world, a realization of the "freedom from want" espoused by President Franklin D. Roosevelt and largely ignored by his successors. U.S. interculturalists can benefit from a reflection on the civil rights movement, perhaps the greatest example of successful intercultural communication in U.S. history, a great social movement initiated by African Americans that gained considerable support among other groups and became a source of inspiration for social movements throughout the world. Although this movement's initial demands were an end to legal segregation and disenfranchisement, it later incorporated economic equality and anti-imperialism.

We would conclude by posing Stolle-McAllister's (2007) challenge to the readers of this chapter: "In our studies of the humanities [and social sciences], how can our work contribute to understanding diversity as a way of contributing to the much needed cultural, political, social, environmental and economic changes that our societies and our global civilization need to prosper and to find a sustainable *alli kawsay,* or good living? How does our work contribute to improving the human condition that we purport to be studying?" That, after all, is a goal shared by all interculturalists.

Notes

1. An example of scholarship that follows this trend is Cantú-Licón's (2001) work in which she measures intercultural competencies in college students at the Instituto Tecnológico y de Estudios Superiores de Monterrey (ITESM) in Monterrey, Mexico, for which she used the Cross-Cultural Adaptability Inventory (CCAI). The scholar frames her study using the framework of globalization and the imperatives of effective and appropriate communication that it brings. As with most intercultural competencies discourses in the United States, this study and other similar works speak to affluent sectors of society that focus their approach on national cultures to enhance business and communication practices. This is not to say that this trend and its worldview is not legitimate and that it does not have its place, but they only speak to the reality of a fraction of the population in a hegemonic position.

2. For reasons of space, this chapter focuses only on the indigenous populations of Latin America.

3. Eleven countries have included in their constitution articles and wording that underline the multicultural and/or multilingual nature of the nations, and four others have recognized the indigenous rights in various state legal documents. The countries whose constitutions have been modified are Argentina, Bolivia, Brazil, Colombia, Ecuador, Guatemala, Mexico, Nicaragua, Paraguay, Perú, and Venezuela. The countries that have included it in other legal documents besides the constitution are Chile, El Salvador, Honduras, and Panama (López & Küper, 1999).

4. Unless otherwise stated, all translations are ours.

5. As scholars in the fields of intercultural communication and Latin American studies, we have gone outside the academy in our study of interculturality because the most compelling and urgent intercultural visions are those of the indigenous social movements and not those of scholars. We are inspired by those movements that are putting their visions into practice on a massive scale in ways that provide hope for a continent where the military dictatorships of the 1960s, 1970s, and 1980s were followed by the disastrous application of neoconservative economic policies that are still in effect. Regarding these policies, there is a vernacular Latin American expression to the effect that, at a macroeconomic level, the economy is doing fine, but the people are in terrible shape. Maybe that situation is changing, although there are no guarantees. Latin American history is filled with stories of dashed hopes, and this compelling story could become another one of them. We do not idealize these movements or the individuals involved in them. We have not dealt with the many polemics around them because this chapter did not seem to be the appropriate place to do so (Cockcroft, 2008).

6. The dates are approximations.

7. Citation from the English translation by Harriet de Onís.

8. Translation is Stolle-McAllister's.

9. The intercultural project in Ecuador stems from the indigenous resistance to the racist attitudes and practices inherited from colonial times (Stolle-McAllister, 2007). The scholar reports that the Confederation of Indigenous Nationalities of Ecuador (CONAIE) was founded in1986. Starting in 1990, CONAIE organized uprisings that advanced significantly the cause of the indigenous population, such as "the recognition of indigenous communities as important and culturally different than the rest of Ecuador, the granting of land title to Amazonian peoples, regularization of land titles in the highlands, and the foundation of bilingual/intercultural education for indigenous children" (p. 164). By 1996, CONAIE's political party was winning seats in Congress and regional offices, and in 2007, CONAIE participated in the constitution's rewrite. At the heart of these initiatives is the push toward an intercultural society that will decolonize "public institutions and individual minds, [find] new forms of representation and eliminat[e] the structural economic and social inequalities" (p. 165).

References

Asamblea Constituyente de Bolivia. (2007, December). *Nueva Constitución del Estado.* Retrieved November 23, 2008, from http://www.presidencia.gob.bo/asamblea/nueva_cpe_aprobada_en_grande_en_detalle_y_en_revision.pdf

Asamblea Constituyente de Ecuador. (2008, October). Retrieved March 27, 2009. http://www.asambleaconstituyente.gov.ec/documentos/definitiva_constitucion.pdf

Cantú-Licón, L. (2001). *Medición de habilidades interculturales en estudios universitarios* [Intercultural skills assessment in university studies]. Unpublished master's thesis, Instituto Tecnológico y de Estudios Superiores de Monterrey, Campus Monterrey, Monterrey, Mexico.

Cockcroft, J. (2008, November 28–30). Indigenous people rising. *Counterpunch.* Retrieved November 29, 2008, from http://www.counterpunch.org/cockcroft11282008.html

De la Torre, L. (2006). La interculturalidad desde la perspectiva del desarrollo social y cultural [Interculturality from a perspective of social and cultural development]. *Revista Sarance, Instituto Otavaleño de Antropología—Universidad de Otavalo, 25,* 62–87.

de las Casas, B. (2003). *An account, much abbreviated, of the destruction of the Indies, with related texts* (F. W. Knight, Ed., & Andrew Hurley, Trans.). Indianapolis, IN: Hackett.

Deardorff, D. K. (2006). Identification and assessment of intercultural competence as a student outcome of internationalization. *Journal of Studies in International Education, 10,* 241–267.

Frank, A. G. (1969). *Latin America: Underdevelopment or revolution; essays on the development of underdevelopment and the immediate enemy.* New York: Monthly Review Press.

Galeano, E. (1971). *Las venas abiertas de América Latina* [The open veins of Latin America]. Mexico: Siglo XXI.

García Canclini, N. (1999). *La globalización imaginada [Imagined globalization].* Buenos Aires: Paidós.

García Canclini, N. (2005). *Hybrid cultures: Strategies for entering and leaving modernity* (C. L. Chiappari & S. L. López, Trans.). Minneapolis: University of Minnesota Press.

Holloway, J. (1996). *The concept of power in the Zapatistas.* Retrieved November 26, 2008, from http://www.korotonomedya.net/chiapas/power.html

López, L. E., & Küper, W. (1999). La educación intercultural bilingüe en América Latina: Balance y perspectivas [The intercultural bilingual education in Latin America: Balances and perspectives]. *Revista Ibero Americana de Educación, 20.* Retrieved October 8, 2008, from http://www.rieoei.org/rie20a02.htm

Nayar, K. P. (2008, November 17). Global table changeth: New faces make their presence felt at rich man's club. *The Telegraph.* Retrieved November 26, 2008, http://www.telegraphindia.com/1081117/jsp/frontpage/story_10121960.jsp

Ortiz, F. (1940). *Cuban counterpoint: Tobacco and sugar.* Harriet de Onís, trans. New York: Alfred Knopf.

Ortiz, F. (1963). *Contrapunteo cubano del tabaco y el azúcar* [Cuban counterpoint]. Havana: Consejo Nacional de la Cultura.

Rebick, J. (2006, September 9). *Peaceful revolution is taking place.* Retrieved November 22, 2008, from http://www.zmag.org/znet/viewArticle/3238

Salmerón, F. (1998). *Diversidad cultural y tolerancia* [Cultural diversity and tolerance]. Mexico: Paidós.

Shane, S. (2008, November 20). Global forecast by American intelligence expects Al Qaeda's appeal to falter. *New York Times.* Retrieved November 22, 2008, from http://www.nytimes.com/2008/11/21/world/21intel.html?_r=1&scp=1&sq=intelligence%20decline&st=cse

Sinnigen, J., & Medina, A. (2002). Modern language class struggles. *Bulletin of the Association of Departments of Foreign Languages, 33,* 50–56.

Stolle-McAllister, J. (2007). Constructing interculturality in Ecuador: Challenges to the humanities. *International Journal of the Humanities, 5*(6), 163–169.

Subercaseaux, B. (2002). *Nación y cultura en América Latina: Diversidad cultural y globalización* [Nation and culture in Latin America: Cultural diversity and globalization]. Santiago, Chile: Editorial LOM.

Tubino, F. (2005). La praxis de la interculturalidad en los estados nacionales latinoamericanos [The praxis of interculturality in the Latin American nation-states]. *Cuadernos Internacionales, 3*(5), 83–96.

Wallerstein, I. (1990). Culture as the ideological battleground of the modern world-system. In M. Featherstone (Ed.), *Global culture* (pp. 31–55). London: Sage.

Walsh, C. (2002). (De) Construir la interculturalidad. Consideraciones críticas desde la política, la colonialidad y los movimientos indígenas y negros en el Ecuador [(De)constructing interculturality: Critical considerations from politics, coloniality and indigenous and Black movements in Ecuador]. In N. Fuller (Ed.), *Interculturalidad y Política: Desafíos y Posibilidades* (pp. 116–142). Lima: Red para el Desarrollo de las Ciencias Sociales en el Perú.

Zinn, H. (1980). *People's history of the United States.* Retrieved November 26, 2008, from http://www.historyisaweapon.com/zinnapeopleshistory.html

Synthesizing Conceptualizations of Intercultural Competence

A Summary and Emerging Themes

Darla K. Deardorff

W hat is necessary for people from different cultural backgrounds to get along with each other? What is intercultural competence? How is intercultural competence defined from a variety of cultural perspectives? How does intercultural competence intersect with other concepts such as identity, leadership, conflict resolution, and global citizenship? These are some of the questions addressed by the chapters in this first section of *The SAGE Handbook of Intercultural Competence,* with the first section of the handbook focusing specifically on conceptualizations of intercultural competence, including from a variety of different cultural perspectives. (The second section of this handbook focuses on specific applications of intercultural competence in different professional fields, while the third and final section of the handbook addresses research and assessment in intercultural competence.) So what common themes emerge from these chapters in regard to intercultural competence? This chapter provides a brief reflection, from a U.S. perspective, on the discussions that have transpired in these chapters. Readers are also invited to reflect on these discussions by identifying for themselves the different themes that have emerged, looking for the intersections between these different perspectives, and interpreting these discussions from those different perspectives.

An initial read of these chapters brings to the fore several themes regarding intercultural competence that will be highlighted here, including the importance of relationship development and of identity, the importance of context and interconnectedness in intercultural competence, the need for transcendence of boundaries, the transformation of differences, and the need for genuine respect—and humility—toward each other.

Importance of Relationships

As discussed in Chapter 1 in this volume, much scholarly effort has been invested, particularly among Western cultures, in defining intercultural competence. As noted in that chapter, three common themes can be found in most Western models of intercultural competence—empathy, perspective taking, and adaptability. The chapter ends by calling for more of a focus on relational aspects in developing future models of intercultural competence, which means focusing on the relationships and on all interactants involved, beyond the individual (who is the primary focus of Western models and definitions), since this was a noted gap in the existing Western definitions of intercultural competence. Other chapters in this section reinforce this call for a focus on the relational, in particular the chapters on Arab, African, and Latin American perspectives of intercultural competence. Zaharna, in her chapter on Arab perspectives on intercultural competence (Chapter 9), discusses the importance of relationship building within intercultural competence, noting that "the significance, meaning, and purpose of communication are derived from relationships among the parties" (pp. 183–184). Nwosu (Chapter 8) illustrates how Africans' very identity is found in who they are in relation to others. And Medina-López-Portillo and Sinnigen's chapter (Chapter 13) highlights the Andean concept of "*alli kawsay* (good living), a concept that stresses reciprocal, complementary, and cooperative relations" and the implications of such relationships, including the role and importance of equality in such relationships (p. 251). Other chapters in this section also highlight in some way the importance of relationship in intercultural competence. For example, in the chapter on a Chinese perspective of global leadership, Chen and An (Chapter 10) even go so far as to note that "the degree of a leader's ability to achieve harmonious relationships can be used to represent the degree of the leader's competence" (p. 199). Ting-Toomey in Chapter 5 discusses the dichotomy of individualistic versus collectivist cultures in which those in more collectivist cultures "think of themselves as individuals with interlocking connections with others" (p. 108), which in turn has implications for conflict resolution across cultures, including a possible communal approach to conflict resolution in which there is a "recognition of authentic interdependent connection to others and genuine interpersonal equality" (p. 108). And in Ashwill and Du'o'ng's chapter (Chapter 7), which includes a Vietnamese perspective, the authors note the importance of intercultural competence in providing "the necessary skills to make those real, interpersonal connections—to forge deep, mutually beneficial, and lasting cross-cultural personal bonds" (p. 156). As part of those necessary skills,

Bennett (Chapter 6) notes that two "core intercultural competencies—empathy and anxiety management—contribute importantly to enhancing the impact of intercultural contact" and thus relationship development (pp. 132–133). These various perspectives on the relational aspects of intercultural competence raise several questions for further discussion, investigation, and research: How can future definitions of intercultural competence better integrate this relational aspect, given its prominence within non-Western conceptualizations of intercultural competence? What are the implications of this relational focus for those who have been culturally conditioned in cultures oriented toward the individual? How do holistic views of interconnectedness affect intercultural competence development? As raised in Chapter 1, where is competence situated—within the individual or within all individuals involved in the interaction? How do intercultural competence models account for relationships over time? And what are the ramifications for assessment if the focus of intercultural competence is placed more on the relational aspects rather than on the knowledge, skills, and attitudes of an individual, especially given the plethora of individual-focused assessment tools that exist?

Identity in Intercultural Competence

Identity, as well as understanding the lens through which we each view the world, becomes a foundational point for exploring intercultural competence. As Kim discusses in her chapter (Chapter 2), research has shown that an inclusive identity orientation and a strong identity security (the degree to which an individual feels secure in his or her identity) are both important in successful intercultural engagement, leading to greater degrees of adaptability, flexibility, and cultural empathy, all elements of intercultural competence. Indeed, Kim sees this inclusive identity orientation and identity security as "a necessity for anyone striving to develop meaningful and fruitful intercultural relationships" (p. 62). Other contributors to this volume note that identity is often defined in juxtaposition with another cultural group. Kim concurs by noting that the human tendency is to identify oneself through in-group or out-group categorizations. Ting-Toomey (Chapter 5) further elaborates on the role of in-group/out-group identities in intercultural conflicts. And Hofstede (Chapter 4) elaborates on the role of trust in intercultural competence as it emphasizes the in-group/out-group distinctions.

Numerous cultural perspectives abound regarding the conceptualization of identity in intercultural competence. Nwosu (Chapter 8) discusses how in many African cultures, one's identity is through the community and not based in the Western conceptualizations of the individual. He cites several African sayings to this end, including the Xhosa saying "a person is a person through persons" and the expressions of *ubuntu*, "I am, because we are; and since we are, therefore I am" (p. 167). And Zaharna (Chapter 9) notes that individuality (which is different from individualism) can be found within Arab cultures, where individuality is viewed within the larger social context of the group. She notes that individuals "must learn to straddle the dichotomy of individuality and collective conformity" (p. 192). This placement of the individual within the context of the larger community is echoed in other chapters such as Manian and Naidu's chapter (Chapter 12) on an Indian perspective of intercultural competence and Medina-López-Portillo and Sinnigen's chapter (Chapter 13) on understanding Latin American perspectives on intercultural competence, which places the emphasis on the relational as well as contextual aspects of intercultural competence, and defining identity in relation to "the other." Ashwill and Du'o'ng (Chapter 7) discuss identity within the larger national identity, including the impact of the Vietnamese insecurity around identity, which relates back to Kim's key points in her chapter. Based on the discussions in these chapters regarding the pivotal role of identity in intercultural competence, it seems that transcending boundaries in regard to one's identity is crucial in developing intercultural competence. In this age of globalization that often leads to politicized cultural identities, this transcendence of one's identity seeks to defy simplistic categorizations of cultural groups, addresses the adaptive and fluid nature of multicultural identities, and strives to instead understand the fullness of who one is, moving beyond the traditional dichotomous in-group/out-group mentality to one that embraces and respects others' differences as well as commonalities and, in so doing, keeps the focus on the relational goals of engagement.

Context and Intercultural Competence

Numerous chapters in Part I of this volume emphasize the importance of context in intercultural competence, and while most Western definitions and models of this concept tend to view this construct in a vacuum devoid of context (although understanding of contexts was one aspect agreed upon by intercultural experts in Deardorff's models of intercultural competence found in Chapter 1), the chapters in this volume on Latin American, Arab, and German perspectives of intercultural competence, as well as the chapter on American and Vietnamese conceptualizations around global citizenship (Chapter 7), note to some degree how crucial it is to consider the political, historical, and social contexts of intercultural competence. For example, Moosmüller and Schönhuth (Chapter 11) note that "there is a widespread conviction that it is impossible to discuss intercultural competence without reference to equality of power" (p. 210) and that common German conceptions of intercultural competence emphasize "context boundedness" (p. 211). Likewise, Medina-López-Portillo and Sinnigen (Chapter 13), in their chapter on Latin American perspectives on intercultural competence, raise key questions about the role of equality and power in intercultural competence, as well as the impact of such historical contexts as colonialism and its subsequent effect on indigenous cultures. The chapters on Indian and Chinese perspectives discuss the more holistic context, with the Manian and Naidu chapter (Chapter 12) highlighting the core principle of "oneness" and the Chen and An chapter (Chapter 10) noting the harmony that can be achieved through balance within a constant state of change. Ashwill and Du'o'ng (Chapter 7), discussing the U.S. and Vietnamese conceptualizations of intercultural competence within global citizenship, point out the interconnectedness of multidimensional global citizens:

"Global citizens think and feel themselves as part of something much grander and all-inclusive than one culture or nationality" (p.). Situating intercultural competence within these contexts becomes fundamental in understanding the true complexity of intercultural competence. Thus, how can future research and modeling of intercultural competence provide a more holistic and contextualized juxtaposition of intercultural competence within larger societal and global issues?

Other Key Points and Research Areas in Intercultural Competence

In reviewing other discussions around conceptualizations of intercultural competence, several additional key points can be found. Two chapters (Chapters 3 and 10) address interculturally competent leadership, one from a Chinese perspective and one from a U.S. perspective (concepts of interculturally competent leadership will be applied through a discussion in Chapter 16 within the specific context of leading global teams). Common themes in both global leadership chapters in Part I, though from different cultural perspectives, include the need for leaders to have a multicultural mind-set and empathy and to be able to manage change, which according to Chen and An (Chapter 10), is a "fundamental principle of the universe that dictates human interaction" (p. 198) in Chinese philosophy. In Chapter 6, Bennett discusses the importance of intentionally cultivating one's intercultural competence, in which "identifying our own cultural patterns, acknowledging the patterns of others, and, eventually, learning to adapt across cultures" play a key role in such development (p. 122). Intercultural competence usually does not naturally occur, and thus it becomes crucial to address the intentional development of intercultural competence.

Several areas of research emerge from these discussions. One key area for further research includes what appropriate behaviors "look like" in different cultures and in different contexts, such as professional fields (this will be discussed some in Part II of this volume). Another key question that often arises in regard to intercultural competence is the degree to which one should adapt to "the other," which provides fertile ground for further debate. As Spitzberg and Changnon point out in Chapter 1, the question is to what extent must one adapt to another? "If both are adapting, it seems possible that both interactants become chameleons without a clear target pattern to which to adapt" (p. 35). This question certainly deserves further discussion and research. (For further discussion on adaptation, see Bennett's Chapter 6 in this volume.) One solution to consider is that of finding "common ground" or a "third way" where both parties must adapt to a certain extent to the other and, in some cases, even creating a "third culture" to which both can subscribe.

One final set of questions raised after reading the discussions in these chapters: First of all, what is missing in these discussions? For example, Moosmüller and Schönhuth raise the question of what intercultural competence looks like at the organizational level, given the current Western preoccupation with intercultural competence primarily at the individual level. Second, given this diversity of perspectives around intercultural competence, is it possible to develop a global definition of intercultural competence, of developing an intercultural competence model that can be applied across many cultures and contexts? What are the many different cultural conceptualizations of this concept, and is it possible to find enough overlapping themes and common values within these and other perspectives that would give rise to a more universal model of intercultural competence? Or are models and definitions too simplistic in capturing the essential realities of human interaction? There are currently few answers to these questions, and further research is certainly welcome and needed on this.

Conclusion

As we continually search for ways to get along together as human beings sharing this one planet, the need to transcend boundaries, to bridge and transform our differences, to be in relationship with one another, to join in the oneness of our humanity while accepting our differences—these needs will continue to drive us as we seek to overcome misunderstandings and conflicts (Chapter 5) arising from differences that may divide us, which in some cases lead us to the point of war and unimaginable atrocities. This search for intercultural competence underscores the need for genuine respect and humility as we relate to one another, meaning that we arrive at the point of truly valuing each other and, in so doing, bridge those differences through relationship building. In the end, intercultural competence is about our relationships with each other and, ultimately, our very survival as the human race, as we work together to address the global challenges that confront us.

PART II

Applying Intercultural Competence

CHAPTER 15

Intercultural Competence in Human Resources

Passing It On

Intercultural Competence in the Training Arena

Craig Storti

This chapter will examine how to create—or at least how to lay the foundation for—intercultural competence through face-to-face training. There are many other routes to developing intercultural competence, of course, including first-hand experience in another culture, reading about another culture, spending time with people from another culture, and, in the past few years, learning about other cultures through various kinds of online or Web-based training. The author's experience, principally in the United States, has been in face-to-face or classroom training, with groups or in one-on-one tutoring sessions, and that will be the primary focus of this chapter.

No two trainings are alike, of course, with a number of variables affecting the content, design, and delivery of the training. These include

- The number of participants
- The knowledge/previous cultural experience of the participants
- The context(s) in which the participants will have contact with people from other cultures (in short, the needs of the trainees)
- The objectives of the organization or division sponsoring the training
- The target country or countries of the training
- The length of the training

While these variables will certainly affect the design, delivery, and certain content specifics, most trainers usually try to address a few key concepts no matter the audience, the venue, or even length of the training (for any training of half a day or longer). These concepts, what we might call the fundamentals of good cross-cultural training, will be the main focus of this chapter.

What Cross-Cultural Training Is *Not*

Before we get to those fundamentals, however, we might briefly discuss what cross-cultural training does *not* typically include. While there would be nothing wrong with addressing some or all of these topics in such training, the topics discussed in this section do not of themselves constitute effective cross-cultural training because they do not touch on the aforementioned fundamentals.

The first topic is what is commonly referred to as cultural "do's and don'ts" of the details of business and social etiquette. These are very often what the audience or what the client is expecting, incidentally--what they think they need--and thus what they ask for. And while there is no reason not to include these in the training, they are not as important as people sometimes think they are, and if the training is of limited duration, they should be dropped in favor of more essential content. Or, better yet, they can be included in the form of handouts that do not need to be discussed.

So why could the do's and don'ts be skipped? First of all, because the locals in a particular culture are typically quite forgiving of the faux pas or cultural mistakes that result from not knowing business and social etiquette. They often realize that the hapless foreigners don't know any better—that they are not trying to be offensive or impolite—and they tend to give them the benefit of the doubt and assume they mean well, probably because they hope to be given the same free pass when they make mistakes in the foreigner's culture.

Another reason do's and don'ts are not essential content is that the bad impressions they might lead to are not usually so significant that they cause a breakdown in relations with people from another culture. If you don't know you're supposed to greet the chairman of the delegation first, that you're not supposed to lay your used chopsticks on the table, or that it's improper for a woman not to touch a Buddhist monk, you may come across as boorish or even impolite, but you probably still convey your good will and good intentions by numerous other behaviors. Cultural faux pas, in other words, are usually not deal breakers, not something that seriously undermines the possibility of successful interactions.

Another body of knowledge that is not essential cross-cultural content is "country" information, facts about the history, geography, religion, arts, politics, and so on of the target country. This is very useful information and can certainly add to and help explain the cross-cultural fundamentals, but it would not on its own be enough to prepare a person to interact successfully with a native of that country. Like do's and don'ts, country information ultimately falls into the category of nice to know rather than need to know. And, perhaps more to the point, information of this type can be found easily in hundreds of books and on thousands of Web sites, so covering it is not usually a very efficient use of classroom training time.

Four Fundamentals of Cross-Cultural Training

So what is this elusive, need-to-know content that makes up effective cross-cultural training? To be truly *cross*-cultural—truly *inter*cultural—training should do the following:

1. Define culture and explain how it will manifest in interactions with people from a different culture.

2. Identify the key values and assumptions of the participants' own culture.

3. Identify the key values and assumptions of the target culture(s).

4. Identify the key differences between one's own and the target culture, the most common issues—challenges, surprises, problems—these differences cause, and offer strategies for dealing successfully with these issues.

When training expatriates and those going to live in a different culture, there should be a fifth item included in this list: content dealing with culture shock and cultural adjustment.

The First Fundamental: Defining Culture

Different trainers may define culture somewhat differently, but almost all practitioners agree on the basics. Indeed, they even agree on the metaphor for describing culture: the "iceberg." The essence of the iceberg concept is that there is a visible dimension of culture that one can see and that people are aware of—the tip of the iceberg—and an invisible, largely subconscious dimension that one can't see: the submerged part of the iceberg.

Trainers may use different words to describe what they place above and below the water line, but even here there is basic agreement. In its simplest form, the iceberg looks something like Figure 15.1.

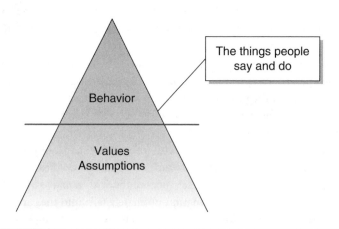

Figure 15.1   The Elements of Culture

The essential points to make about the iceberg are these:

Culture includes both the visible and invisible parts of the iceberg.

You're not going to encounter someone's culture; you're going to encounter their behavior, the things they say and do. Or, to put it another way, you're going to encounter their culture *in the form* of their behavior. And it's other people's behavior you're going to have to understand, interpret correctly, and ideally be able to anticipate (and vice versa for the people who are interacting with you).

But people's behavior is not arbitrary or accidental; it is a result (at least in part) of the things below the line in the iceberg, hence invisible and unconscious.

So to understand, interpret correctly, and be able to anticipate behavior, you need to have a general understanding of values and assumptions.

When I train, I then present Figure 15.2 to illustrate what happens when a person from one culture interacts with someone from a different culture.
And I then make the following points in the following order:

1. When you (left iceberg/triangle) interact with someone from another culture (right iceberg/triangle), you go into this interaction with the values and assumptions (below the line) you have been raised with which have given you a set of typical, normal, natural, and logical behaviors (above the line).

2. Now you're interacting with someone from another culture (right triangle) who will have some values and assumptions (below the line) different from yours. To the extent that any of those values and assumptions are different from yours, that person is bound to have a different set of typical, normal, natural, and logical behaviors (above the line) from yours.

3. And just like your behavior (I point to the left triangle above the line) is perfectly logical to you (I point to the left triangle below the line), that other

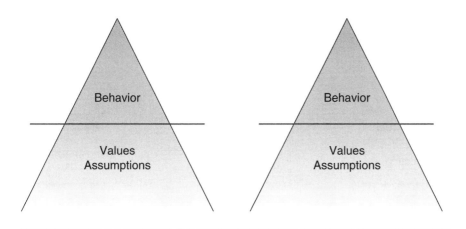

Figure 15.2   Making Cultural Comparisons

person's behavior (right triangle above the line)—which could be very different from yours—is nevertheless perfectly logical (right triangle below the line) to him or her.

4. However it is done, an explanation along these lines makes the essential point that as people from different cultures are bound to have some different values and assumptions, then they are bound to have behaviors that are also different *but nevertheless normal and logical within their respective cultures.* In other words, when people do something that makes absolutely no sense to you, that may even be offensive or very frustrating to you, it's almost guaranteed it makes perfect sense to them. And vice versa.

Putting Culture in Context

Once these points have been made, the groundwork has been laid for the next two fundamentals of intercultural training: identifying the basic values and assumptions of the participants' culture (Item 2 in the list above) and those of the target culture (Item 3). Once participants understand where behavior comes from, in short, then they will appreciate the need to explore the origins of behavior. But before going on to those origins, it's important to do one more thing early on in any kind of intercultural training: to put cultural behavior into context, to remind participants that cultural behavior, important as it is, is not the only show in town.

There are two key points that need to be made here, which I often illustrate with a drawing found in Figure 15.3.

Participants should not think that *everything* is different about someone from another culture; they need to know that there are ways we are all alike, certain universal assumptions and values, hence behaviors, that we sometimes call human nature. In other words, there are lot of things you already know about someone from another culture and a lot of things people from other cultures already know about you. I usually say at this point that we're not going to spend any time talking about these things because they do not cause any problems when you interact with someone from another culture.

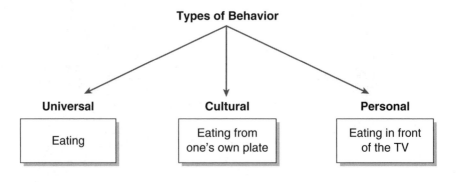

Figure 15.3 Putting Culture Into Context

And participants should also not think that cultural information will apply equally and always to every *individual* from a particular culture. While we are all the same in some ways (the universal box) and like the people from our culture in some ways (the cultural box), each of us is also unique in some ways (the personal box). The personal box means that you can't take information you have learned about a particular culture and assume it applies to all individuals from that culture. Such information *may* be true of individuals raised in that culture, but it also may not. Cultural information is true in general, but you will never meet a general person and you will never be in a general situation.

This three-box paradigm allows the trainer to make the very important point that to talk about culture, we have to generalize. And the even more important point that when we generalize, we may be accurate about a group, but we would only be coincidentally accurate about any single person from that group. It's important to make this point about generalizing because it usually curtails concerns about stereotyping.

The Second Fundamental: Identifying Key Values and Assumptions of the Participants' Culture

The next step of the training, then, is to focus on the trainees' home culture (or cultures if trainees come from more than one country). Participants may initially wonder why they need to look at their own culture, assuming (a) they already know it and (b) that it's the foreign culture they need to learn about. It *is* the foreign culture they need to learn about, of course, and the training will eventually get to that, but what they need to know about the foreign culture is what exactly makes that culture foreign—what makes it different. After all, foreign cultures aren't foreign to the people who come from them; they are only foreign to the people who come from outside them. What people need to learn about a foreign culture is how it is different *from their own* because it is those differences that are going to surprise, confuse, annoy, and in some cases offend the person who is not from that culture. Identifying differences is the name of the game, then, and that must begin with describing the participants' own culture, which then becomes the inevitable point of departure—the reference point—against which the target culture can be compared.

As for the other objection people might make to analyzing their own culture, that they already know it, that is not usually the case. They typify their culture in all their beliefs and actions, but people who grow up in a culture, who are conditioned at an early age by their culture's norms and values, internalize their culture without ever consciously reflecting on it or thinking about it. They *are* their culture, but they can't necessarily see it and don't necessarily know it.

Different trainers will teach values and assumptions in different ways, but most will have participants examine their own culture via a number of well-established cultural concepts that have stood the test of time and in many cases rest on a substantial body of research.[1] These concepts correspond to certain dimensions of the human experience that all people in all cultures must face. The most common of these dimensions are listed as follows:

Locus of control (internal/external)

Concept of self or identity (individual/collective)

Attitude toward risk (risk taking/risk averse)

Attitude toward uncertainty (high tolerance/low tolerance)

Concepts of right and fairness (universalism/particularism)

Sense of limits (limited/unlimited possibilities)

Concept of status (egalitarian/hierarchical)

View of human nature (benign/skeptical)

Attitude toward time (monochromic/polychromic)

Management style (decentralized/centralized)

Manager-subordinate relations (equals/superiors and subordinates)

Degree of supervision (hands off/hands on)

Basis for decision making (heart/head)

Communication style (direct/indirect)

Task versus relationship orientation

As in the list provided here in this chapter, these concepts are almost always presented in the form of a dichotomy, which identifies the extremes between which most cultures function. Indeed, many trainers introduce these concepts via a series of continuums (such as the following, illustrating the dimension we have called locus of control) and ask participants to locate their culture along the continuum:

Locus of Control	
Internal	*External*
What you accomplish in life is up to you. Fate or other external forces exert minimal influence. There's nothing you can't do or get if you want it bad enough/are willing to try hard enough. The only limits to achievements/results/success are internal (those you impose on yourself). Failure means you didn't try hard enough. You make your own "luck." Life is what I do.	Fate plays a major role in how much you achieve. Some things in life are just not meant to be and you must accept this. Success is in part a result of personal effort and in part a result of good or bad fortune (which you cannot do anything about). Sometimes failure is unavoidable no matter how hard you try. Some limits are "real" (not self-imposed). Life is in part what happens to me.

Whether it's via a continuum or any of a number of other techniques, participants are asked to reflect on their own society through the lens of these dimensions, thereby creating a general picture of their culture.

The Third Fundamental: Identifying Key Values and Assumptions of the Target Culture

The next task of cross-cultural training is to create a picture of the target culture against which participants can then compare their own. The same cultural concepts or dimensions would be used here, of course, to ensure that participants are comparing apples to apples. In the case of the target culture, the trainer may have to supply the information vis-à-vis the dimensions, unless there are people from the target culture participating in the training.

Regarding this fundamental and the preceding one, trainers should distinguish between values and assumptions, the unconscious, invisible dimensions of culture (below the water line in the iceberg analogy) and behavior and the things people say and do (the tip of the iceberg). Trainers should give examples of how the former lead directly to the latter, thereby establishing the essential relationship between assumptions and behavior. When participants can see how assumptions lead to behavior, they are a short step away from accepting that *different* cultural assumptions must lead to different behaviors.

The Fourth Fundamental: Identifying Differences Between One's Own and the Target Culture and Strategies for Dealing With the Differences

Whatever mechanisms or techniques have been used to identify the norms of the target culture with respect to the cultural dimensions being analyzed, those norms should now be set against and compared to those of the participants' culture. In the culmination of all that has gone before, participants are now in a position to carry out the final and most important task in developing cultural competence: identifying all the ways—assumptions, values, and behaviors—they are different from the people of the target culture.

If we use the continuum approach that was just discussed and select the United States and Egypt as the two cultures being compared, the locus of control continuum might look like this:

USA	*Egypt*
INTERNAL	EXTERNAL

The trainer and participants would now identify and discuss examples of how differences in this and all the other cultural dimensions being analyzed would affect interactions between U.S. Americans and Egyptians. These differences are at the heart of all the challenges a person will encounter—and have to overcome—to deal effectively with someone from another culture (or living in another culture in the case of expatriates). Identifying cultural differences and helping participants develop strategies to address those differences are the ultimate goals of cross-cultural training, and the four fundamentals are the means to this end.

Common Challenges in Cross-Cultural Training

Stereotyping

With respect to the content of cross-cultural training (as opposed to the logistics), trainers tend to face a number of common challenges. One of the foremost is the charge of stereotyping. It is indeed very difficult to talk about entire nationalities—Brazilians, Canadians, Indians, Chinese—without incurring accusations of stereotyping. The only effective way I know to rebut this charge (which, after all, contains more than a kernel of truth) is to explain that it is not possible to talk about culture *without* generalizing. And then add words to the effect of "everything we say today should be taken with a grain of salt." Remind participants that they will never meet a general person and never be in a general situation, and then close with the observation that generalizations are only accurate for groups and may or may not be true of individuals. In making this point, some trainers draw a bell curve and note that for any particular cultural trait, some people (20%, let's say) will always demonstrate this trait, another 20% never will, and a lot of people (60%) usually will.

Uncooperative Participants

Another inevitable challenge is when trainees in the room who come from a given culture openly disagree with something the presenter says about their culture. If the presenter is not from the local culture, who is the rest of the audience going to believe: the trainer or the local? This is not as serious a problem as it sounds, but it can present challenges to novice trainers. The fix for this problem is to refer back to what you (should have) said earlier in your setup: that we have to generalize today, and not everything will be true for everyone from a particular culture. If the trainer can, he or she should then add that many people from the culture in question have agreed with the particular characterization or trait being discussed and that the trainer has observed this behavior on a number of occasions in _____ (name of country). The main point in this instance is not to get into an argument with the locals; you can't win.

Another form this challenge can take is when there is someone in the workshop who has spent time in the culture in question and who disputes what the trainer says. This is easier to deal with than the previous example and can be resolved in more or less the same way, by pointing out that the trait in question has been found to be true of many people in a given culture.

Assessment

Another challenge trainers face, outside the classroom in this case, is questions from the client about how they will know if the training was effective. It is notoriously difficult to assess the impact of any training, intercultural or otherwise, whose primary goals are to raise awareness, change attitudes, or somehow make people more sensitive. The best approach here in my experience is to reorient the conversation: I ask clients if the people coming to the workshop interact with people from other cultures. When they say yes, I then ask them if the participants are aware of the main differences between themselves and people from other cultures. When they say no, I ask the clients if they think ignorance of cultural differences could cause problems in such cross-cultural interactions. When they say yes, I ask if it's likely that raising awareness will mitigate or avoid some of those problems. And when they say yes. . . . For the most part, anyone who has gone far enough to call a cross-cultural trainer and inquire about a workshop has probably been convinced that training is needed, regardless of whether the outcomes can be measured.

There are some tools for measuring whether anything has been learned in a training, but to be able to tie that learning to the typical behavioral indicators of training effectiveness is very tricky. In my opinion, it's better not to start down the assessment road if you don't have to. (For a more in-depth discussion on assessment, see Chapters 27 and 28 in this volume.)

Meeting Client Needs

This paragraph offers advice rather than describes a challenge, but if the advice given here is ignored, the result will be a challenge. The advice is to be wary of getting your information about the training audience from those in human resources. While human resources is the point of contact for most training and the liaison between the trainer and his or her audience, human resources will not necessarily have a good grasp of what the audience needs. A general rule to follow, consequently, is to always talk to several of the "end users," the people who will be in the classroom, before designing and delivering any training event. Even when human resources has a general understanding of what the participants do, hence what they need, a general understanding can be very dangerous. Most trainers learn this lesson the hard way, preparing a workshop on U.S. and Asian cultural differences, for example, because that's the word from human resources as to what is needed, only to learn—standing in front of the trainees—that what the audience actually needs is a workshop on India and Indian cultural differences.

What Makes a Good Cross-Cultural Trainer?

A competent cross-cultural trainer needs to have expertise in three key areas:

Thorough knowledge of the basic concepts of intercultural communications

Overseas experience

Training design and platform skills

For classroom training, these are still the big three, and we will briefly discuss each one below; for desktop training, however, platform skills are clearly irrelevant, replaced by expertise in designing engaging computer-based content (which we also discuss in the following section).

Content Expertise

Whether for classroom or desktop training, trainers have to "know their stuff"—to be thoroughly familiar with the core technical content of the intercultural field. Some trainers come by this content formally, through university degree programs, and others informally, through personal experience; by attending training programs, seminars, and workshops; and through extensive reading in the field. The means by which the trainer comes by his or her content expertise is less important than the fact of having it.

Some practitioners, incidentally, may believe themselves to possess this subject matter expertise merely by virtue of having lived abroad, but this is not necessarily true. An extended stay overseas certainly offers numerous opportunities for *encountering* cultural differences, but it does not by itself guarantee that the individual will learn from or understand those experiences. Indeed, many people who have lived abroad have said that they did not understand what happened to them until they began reading about the different theories in the intercultural field. While most interculturalists, then, would agree that overseas experience is a necessary condition of being an effective trainer (see the next section for further discussion on this), it is not sufficient.

Overseas Experience

Overseas experience is probably the least critical of the three areas of expertise needed by a good intercultural trainer, but all other things being equal, a trainer who has overseas experience is clearly preferable to one who has not. The operative phrase here is "all things being equal"; a trainer who is a former expatriate but who is not grounded in the core content and theories of the intercultural field would not necessarily do a better job than one who knows the content but has never lived abroad.

There's no doubt, however, that someone with overseas experience, someone who has lived what he or she is talking about, is automatically more credible to an audience and to potential clients (deservedly or not) than someone who has not had that experience. Moreover, expatriates tend to have a rich vein of stories and anecdotes they can use to make abstract, theoretical content more vivid and practical. Finally, experienced expatriates, unlike those who have not lived overseas, have had the invaluable experience of actually *being* a foreigner, a perspective that is indispensable for this kind of work.

Training Design and Platform Skills

Content knowledge and overseas experience are a potent combination, but at the end of the day, if the person standing at the front of the room can't keep the attention of the audience, then whatever he or she is doing, it's not training. Call it talking, lecturing, reminiscing, or ego-tripping—it's not doing the audience any good. Any good trainer (in any field) has to be able to take the subject matter of the training program and turn it into various training activities—role-plays, quizzes, critical incidents, simulations, case studies—that engage and involve the participants. In other words, the trainer has to be able to do more than simply lecture. (See the reference section of this chapter for a list of training resources.) And, finally, the trainer should have good platform skills; he or she should be what is usually referred to as dynamic or interesting, which typically means that the person has a strong and interesting voice, a good pace, good audience rapport, a sense of humor, and a keen sense of the audience.

Of the three criteria for a good trainer, this is the one that is most often lacking or, if not actually lacking, then not fully developed. The best way to determine if a trainer has this expertise is either to observe him or her in action or to talk to people who have; design and platform skills should never be taken for granted. Indeed, it's surprising how often an otherwise knowledgeable, experienced intercultural professional is not a very good presenter.

Expertise for E-learning

In the brave new world of computer-based training (see the next section), intercultural trainers are really acting in the capacity of content experts. As such, they must still have the first two qualifications discussed above (especially knowledge of the subject matter) and training design skills, but clearly they do not need to be good in front of an audience. Design skills, the ability to present content in interactive formats, are probably the most important criteria of all for computer-based training because lecture is not an option.

Trends in Cross-Cultural Training

The field of cross-cultural training has changed significantly in recent years and is even now in the midst of another change. The biggest change that most practitioners will recognize (at least those of a certain age) is that cross-cultural training has "gone domestic." Not so long ago, the only people who got cross-cultural training were expatriates, people who were going to live and work overseas—corporate types, members of the military, exchange students, missionaries, development workers, and so on—and, sometimes, people who regularly traveled abroad as part of their job. These were the only folks who were likely to have regular and sustained contact with foreigners, after all, and therefore be in need of cross-cultural training.

The Multicultural Revolution

In recent years, however, with the rise of multiculturalism and the field of diversity, it has become increasingly common to deliver cross-cultural training to people in their own culture who are not going anywhere but who nevertheless interact on a regular basis with people *from* different cultures, in the form of immigrants and their families, refugees, international visitors, colleagues from overseas branches or subsidiaries of a multinational corporation . . . the list goes on. This audience is different from the "classic" audience because their contact with foreigners is relatively limited, and more important, this contact takes place in the participants' home country. It's one matter to train people who are going to *be* foreigners and quite another to train people who are encountering foreigners in the comfort of their own country.

One of the biggest differences of this "domestic" training is the audience's depth of exposure to and understanding of people from other cultures. In many cases (although not always), participants in the domestic audience may not have traveled extensively abroad or otherwise had much experience interacting with people outside their own country, and the training content, as a consequence, may have to be adjusted to some extent. Another related difference is the common perception of a domestic audience that it's the "foreigners" who need this training, but not the locals; that the "foreigners" are the ones who need to adapt.

Virtual Teams

Another new audience for domestic intercultural training is people who work on virtual global teams. This is a domestic audience in the sense that the training is usually delivered in the participant's home country, but it is different from the preceding audience in the sense that the people who work on such teams may never meet face-to-face with their team members in other countries. While these people do not have direct contact with each other, their interactions are no less significant for being virtual, and the opportunities for cross-cultural confusion are, if anything, even greater than in the case of face-to-face contact. Once again, the content of such training has to be adjusted to meet the special needs of people engaged in this virtual intercultural contact.

Desktop Training

Another major shift in intercultural training has to do with the delivery mechanism. Most observers would agree that the future of cross-cultural training, like the future of most other training, is computer-based e-learning. Face-to-face classroom training featuring personal, real-time interaction between trainer and trainees is probably going to become less common. Whatever one may think of the effectiveness of computer-based desktop training, its sheer convenience makes it irresistibly attractive. It can be done wherever and whenever the subject wants, for as long as he or she wants, as often as he or she likes, with no need for a trainer, a classroom, or any type of logistics beyond a computer. As this becomes the delivery mechanism of choice for an increasingly wide variety of content, especially for the millennial generation, computer-based training will soon make significant inroads into the intercultural field.

While such training may not supplant classroom training altogether, intercultural trainers of the future will be increasingly called on to deliver training packages via laptops and desktops to "participants" they will never meet. The content of intercultural training will probably not change much in this brave new desktop world—participants will still need to know the same frameworks for understanding people from different cultures—but the delivery of this kind of training, as discussed here, will require a somewhat different skill set of its practitioners.

Conclusion

This chapter has outlined key points cross-cultural trainers should keep in mind as they work to build intercultural competence. Regardless of how intercultural training may evolve in the years ahead, of the various new ways content may be packaged and delivered, the need for interculturally competent individuals in today's global economy is only going to grow.

Note

1. This research on cross-cultural values is derived from work that primarily reflects a Western orientation such as Hofstede and Kluckhorn.

Training Resources

Bennett, J. M. (2008). Transformative training: Designing programs for culture learning. In M. A. Moodian (Ed.), *Contemporary leadership and intercultural competence: Understanding and utilizing cultural diversity to build successful organizations* (pp. 95–110). Thousand Oaks, CA: Sage.

Boyacilgiller, N. A., Goodman, R. A., & Phillips, M. E. (Eds.). (2003). *Crossing cultures: Insights from master teachers.* New York: Taylor & Francis.

Brussow, H. L. & Kohls, L. R. (1995). *Training know-how for cross-cultural and diversity trainers.* Duncanville, TX: Adult Learning Systems, Inc.

Fowler, S. M., & Mumford, M. G. (Eds.). (1995). *Intercultural sourcebook: Cross-cultural training methods* (Vol. 1). Yarmouth, ME: Intercultural Press.

Fowler, S. M., & Mumford, M. G. (Eds.). (1999). *Intercultural sourcebook: Cross-cultural training methods* (Vol. 2). Yarmouth, ME: Intercultural Press.

Gardenswartz, L., & Rowe, A. (1998). *Managing diversity: A complete desk reference and planning guide* (Rev. ed.). New York: McGraw-Hill.

Hofstede, G. J., Pedersen, P. B., & Hofstede, G. (2002). *Exploring culture: Exercises, stories, and synthetic cultures.* Yarmouth, ME: Intercultural Press.

Kohls, L. R., & Knight, J. M.(1994). *Developing intercultural awareness: A cross-cultural training handbook.* Yarmouth, ME: Intercultural Press, Inc.

Kolb, D. A. (1984). *Experiential learning: Experience as the source of learning and development.* Englewood Cliffs, NJ: Prentice Hall.

Lambert, J., Myers, S., & Simons, G. (Eds.). (2000). *Global competence: 50 training activities for succeeding in international business.* Amherst, MA: HRD Press.

Landis, D. L. Bennett, J. M., & Bennett, M. J. (2004). *Handbook of intercultural training* (3rd ed.). Thousand Oaks, CA: Sage.

Osland, J. S., Kolb, D. A., Rubin, I. M., & Turner, M. E. (2007). *Organizational behavior: An experiential approach* (8th ed.). Englewood Cliffs, NJ: Prentice Hall.

Paige, R. M. (Ed.). (1993). *Education for the intercultural experience* (2nd ed.). Yarmouth, ME: Intercultural Press.

Saphiere, D. H., Mikk, B. K., & DeVries, B. I. (2005). *Communication highwire: Leveraging the power of diverse communication styles.* Yarmouth, ME: Intercultural Press.

Seelye, H. N. (1996). *Experiential activities for intercultural learning.* Yarmouth, ME: Intercultural Press, Inc.

Singelis, T. M. (Ed.). (1998). *Teaching about culture, ethnicity, and diversity: Exercises and planned activities.* Thousand Oaks, CA: Sage.

Storti, C. (1998). *Figuring foreigners out: A practical guide.* Yarmouth, ME: Intercultural Press.

Storti, C. (1994). *Cross-cultural dialogues: 74 brief encounters with cultural difference.* Yarmouth, ME: Intercultural Press, Inc.

Stringer, D. M., & Cassiday, P. A. (2003). *52 activities for exploring values differences.* Yarmouth, ME: Intercultural Press.

Thiagarajan, S. (2000). *Facilitator's toolkit.* Bloomington, IN: Workshops by Thiagi.

CHAPTER 16

Intercultural Competence in Business

Leading Global Projects

Bridging the Cultural and Functional Divide

Robert T. Moran, William E. Youngdahl, and Sarah V. Moran

M uch of the work of individuals working for global organizations at this time, whether for profit or not for profit, is project work (Moran & Youngdahl, 2008). In this chapter, we attend to key competencies required for successfully leading global projects. Sophisticated skills are necessary for the purposes of leading global projects, and while some theory is addressed, our emphasis is on application. It is our conviction that these competencies are situated at the intersection of project management, leadership, and cross-cultural competence, or effectiveness. Effective leaders of global projects must understand and apply the fundamentals of project management if they are to be successful at making the most of their leadership potential to influence project members across the cultural divides of functions and countries.

These indispensable competencies that separate effective leaders of global projects from less effective project leaders have been derived from direct interaction with hundreds of project leaders from over 30 countries. Through many in-depth interviews with project leaders and individuals responsible for corporate learning within many large corporations, we have developed programs to help both intentional project leaders and accidental project leaders to become more effective in leading complex global projects.

The "flattening" of the globe though transportation, the Internet, telecommunications, and other factors (Friedman, 2005) has led to multitudes of projects from global branding and global sourcing to offshoring of both manufacturing (Quinn, 1999) and service work (Youngdahl & Ramaswamy, 2007). Global projects that are considerably large deal with complexity in the technical and organizational areas, requiring complex coordination between the project members involved. As such, these complexities also involve other macro-level factors such as political, economic, and environmental uncertainties that can create ambiguity between project participants and setbacks (Mahalingam & Levitt, 2007). In essence, projects are the manifestation of global strategy. Through projects, global organizations implement strategy, and in the private sector, the globalization of manufacturing, marketing, research, and development is facilitating the spread of strategic alliances (Shore & Cross, 2005).

We define a project as a set of interrelated activities aimed toward achieving a unique arrangement of outcomes within a predefined time frame and budget. The uniqueness of the outcome separates project work from more repetitive work within the area of manufacturing and service. We are finding that the majority of work in most organizations is now project work. If the majority of leaders and organizations are leading or contributing to projects and initiatives, then a clear need exists for identifying the skills and knowledge required to lead in a project-based world. Global projects are unique in that they are a combination of individual and organizational exchanges and work efforts from divergent backgrounds and national/cultural circumstances.

In our work with more than 1,000 global project leaders, we have found that three interdependent themes are essential for effective global project leadership: (1) strategic project management, (2) cross-cultural leadership effectiveness, and (3) project leadership (Moran & Youngdahl, 2008). We believe that the ability to succeed in a project-based world depends on our skills to lead multicultural teams with a clear understanding of the language, contexts, and cultures that surround the projects that invariably influence team dynamics. Given the nature of global projects, the ability to lead from a position of cross-cultural effectiveness represents an additional essential skill set for effective of global project leaders.

Our approach in developing these competencies has been decisively practical, and therefore our presentation of these aptitudes will be based primarily on what we have observed to be effective in application. We begin by presenting a brief summary of project management fundamentals as a foundational set of competencies and knowledge required of all global project leaders. We then present a model for influencing, without formal authority, a key competency for leaders who need to influence across functions and companies with limited or no formal authority. Finally, we suggest many of the key cross-cultural competencies required for global project leadership effectiveness.

Strategic Project Management

Projects represent strategy in action. Therefore, global project leaders must view projects through a strategic lens (Johnson, 2004). Research (Mahalingam & Levitt, 2007) that has compared institutions in various countries has found that organizations that have an institutional environment in which their procedures and activities are more entrenched are strategically advantageous. This creates a tone of legitimacy and competitive advantage as compared to those firms whose procedures actually deviate from the entrenched institutional practices and tend to encounter an increase in transactional cost (Mahalingam & Levitt, 2007).

Entrenching the project within the strategic parameters of the organization enables project leaders to communicate how their projects contribute various forms of value to the organization, ranging from financial value to broader measures of values such as organizational effectiveness. Thus, the leader who positions the project with the organizational strategy at the forefront is more likely to find success than one who simply focuses on the individual project itself. In essence, effective global project leaders have portfolio management mind-sets as discussed in the next section.

Project Portfolio Management and Value Contribution

An organization's portfolio of projects provides a glimpse of where the organization is heading. Ideally, projects are selected that support the strategy of the organization. Project portfolio management provides a structured opportunity for ensuring alignment of projects and organizational objectives (Archer & Ghasemzadeh, 1999). Any project portfolio management effort should begin with a clear understanding of the organization's strategy, often expressed as long-term goals and intended actions. If part of the job of a project leader is to ensure that projects achieve strategic objectives, then understanding those strategic objectives is paramount.

Once the strategy is clear, a census of all significant projects can be taken to identify how strategy is currently being implemented and what resources are being consumed. The overall goal of project portfolio management is to screen all significant projects against a set of attractiveness criteria developed by leaders within the organization. In addition, projects are screened against relative risk factors. Ideally, functional heads sit on a portfolio management committee and make decisions about the priority of projects and the allocation of resources.

Projects are rank ordered and budget is allocated to the highest priority projects first until there is no additional budget to complete the lower priority projects. This overall process of prioritizing projects and allocating resources according to priority depends on different functional groups having a strong voice in the process. If significant differences exist among functional groups in terms of power-distance and other cultural dimensions, the ranking of projects and ultimately the effective implementation of strategy will not be realized. Byosiere and Luethge (2007) studied how project activities fluctuate in the corporate subsidiaries located in the United States and Europe of a multinational company. In essence, they found that the results "suggest that within this global technology-oriented company, a clear definition of the roles of stakeholders is important, and in particular, having an upper-level sponsor for a project that crosses national boundaries is critical to success" (Byosiere & Luethge, 2007, p. 27).

Not all organizations will choose to adopt a formal portfolio management strategy. Our recommendation is to ensure that project leaders possess project portfolio management mind-sets. They need to understand how their project contributes to the overall strategy of the organization and be able to communicate that message clearly to the project members. In our seminars, we use a simple approach called the project value elevator speech. Project leaders need to be able to communicate the value of their project in no more than 15 seconds, the time it takes to ride up or down a couple floors in an elevator. How would you communicate the value of your project, adapting your communication style to fit the recipient, in just 15 seconds? For developing the elevator speech and global project leadership in general, project leaders need to communicate in both the language of project management and a style that best fits the recipient.

Scope Clarity

Project leaders must be exceedingly clear about the scope of a project or what has to be achieved. In the language of project management, we speak of scope in terms of project deliverables and success criteria for the deliverables. What has to be done, and how will we know that we have successfully completed our project objectives? Scope creep represents the seemingly natural tendency for organizations to allow project scope to increase over time. Causes for scope creep include customer input, new technological innovations, and a rather natural organizational tendency to want to deliver something of even greater value. A problem introduced by scope creep is that the budget for the original project has been sent based on the original scope. Scope creep necessitates additional budget, or additional time, or both.

Project scope tends to involve very low-context communication when it comes to communicating specific project deliverables. The process of achieving buy-in from diverse and geographically distributed stakeholders requires significant shifting in communication approaches. For example, we speak with marketing managers in the language of marketing, and we communicate in a higher context with Japanese stakeholders than we would with their German counterparts. Once we have agreed on the overall scope of what has to be achieved, we need to communicate this agreement in very low-context language, to ensure complete understanding among all members.

A project leader at a global pharmaceutical company shared with us the concept of "life-saving slides" as a method of protecting the project from arbitrary scope changes. Every time steering committee members or other stakeholders asked for changes in project scope, the project leader would refer to a set of four PowerPoint slides that clearly outlined the agreed-upon project scope. This technique proved to be culturally robust in terms of its effectiveness in reducing potential scope creep. The clarity of the agreed-upon project scope and the budget and schedule implications for increasing the scope improved understanding across culturally diverse stakeholders represented on the project team. Quite simply, the slides reduced the potential for misunderstanding.

Schedule, Budget, and Resource Clarity

Other potential opportunities for misunderstanding stemming from cross-cultural communication include the allocation of resources, budget, and schedule. The schedule depends on the availability of resources, and more often than not, project leaders and global organizations are navigating matrix organizations in which they have to borrow resources from functional areas. In addition, they are competing with other project leaders for the same resources. While the direct use of resources represents a majority of most project budgets, the lack of availability of resources when they are truly needed represents a hidden cost of most projects. Mahalingam and Levitt (2007) found that "such interactions, even on technologically routine global projects, often lead to additional misunderstandings, increased transaction costs, friction between project participants, and coordination and communication difficulties" (p. 517). If project resources are not available, project leaders may have to hire contract employees and suffer schedule impacts and revenue loss. In the case of contractual obligations, schedule slippages could result in significant financial penalties and can substantially increase the costs that can range from 30% to 700% of the estimated costs at the onset of the project (Mahalingam & Levitt, 2007).

A "speak-up" culture is important within project-based organizations to avoid surprises related to scope, schedule, and budget and the types of previously discussed costly misunderstandings. By speak-up culture, we refer to a culture in which individuals are encouraged to raise concerns so they can be addressed before they become costly problems. A speak-up culture requires clear understanding of project objectives and an expectation that anything that might put the project at risk will be addressed in clear language that is understood by relevant stakeholders.

Clarity is also paramount in achieving alignment among the strategy of the organization, the scope of the project, and the resources and schedule required to achieve project objectives. Strategic project management requires clear definition of the strategy for which the project is being pursued and the scope of the project that defines successful completion of project deliverables. In this brief chapter, we cannot cover all aspects of strategic project management, but being clear on the strategy and the scope are the fundamental underpinnings of strategic project management.

In addition, having a project portfolio management mind-set ensures that leaders help organizations maintain the proper mix of projects to achieve strategic objectives. Thus, global project leaders must use their best influencing skills to mobilize stakeholders to work on their projects given all of the potential distractions in most work environments. In this next section, we discuss some basic influencing approaches that can be used by global project leaders to achieve stakeholder alignment.

Influencing Without Formal Authority

We have adapted the exchange-based influencing framework of Cohen and Bradford (2005) in our development of an influencing approach for global project leaders. The work of Patterson, Grenny, Maxfield, McMillan, and Switzler (2008) is also valuable and relevant, for a fundamental challenge facing most project leaders is that they must influence stakeholders over whom they have no direct formal authority. We have found that project leaders who have established reputations for fair exchanges tend to be the best influencers. They are able to understand the world of those whom they are trying to influence and answer the "What's in it for me?" question from the stakeholders' perspectives. They understand the needs and wants of the people whom they are trying to influence and offer these people something of value. Fortune and White (2006) did a review of 63 published articles that focused on critical success factors, and they recognized the following: "support from senior management, clear realistic objectives, a strong/detailed plan kept up to date, good communications/feedback, and user/client involvement as the top five success factors across all of these studies . . . which show that these success factors relate not so much to the deliverables but to the process of project management."

Since most project leaders do not lead with formal authority or even have direct reports, offering financial incentives of any significance is generally not an option. They must turn to what Cohen and Bradford (2005) refer to as currencies. Currencies can include sources of inspiration, help in achieving tasks, improved relationships, enhanced stature, or a myriad of other offerings that might be personal wants and needs of individuals.

Developing an Influencing Strategy

Developing an influencing strategy requires clear focus on the goals of the project. Influencing must be grounded in the realities of what needs to be done to achieve the goals of the project. Then we can identify what we need as project leaders and match our needs with what stakeholders can offer. It is also important to identify the extent to which stakeholders support or block the project and their level of power in terms of the potential impact that they might have on the project. The approach that we have adapted from Cohen and Bradford (2005) for developing an influencing strategy has been field-tested with over 1,000 practicing global project leaders in executive development courses for a major pharmaceutical company as well as a financial services organization (see Moran & Youngdahl, 2008, chap. 5).

Understand the Strategy That the Project Supports. Once the influencing strategy is decided upon, it needs to be clearly linked to the project management process. We must be clear on the strategy that we are supporting through the selection and implementation of the project. Unless we are clear on both the strategy and the scope of the project, we may misdirect our influencing efforts. Influencing is about getting others to do something that they might not otherwise do without our guiding influence. Before we begin identifying those whom we might influence, our efforts to clarify strategy set us on a path of developing a project plan that will both deliver organizational value and provide direction in terms of whom we need to influence to achieve specific project results.

Challenges in global projects can easily be due to institutional strategic differences and the expectations among participants representing different organizations.

These challenges arise when the strategies incorporated and valued in one organization come into contact with a different organizational strategy through the global project participants. Often these divergent behaviors and practices are reflections of each institutional environment and require not only sensitivity to these divergent practices but also sophisticated skills and often excess cost to manage them when conflicts arise (Mahalingam & Levitt, 2007).

Identify and Clearly Communicate What Needs to Be Done. As previously described, clearly defining the scope of the project allows us to determine which resources will be required to complete the project work. We cannot determine whether an individual possesses the requisite skills to complete project work unless we are very clear on what project work needs to be completed. Although project leaders do not always have complete control over who might be on the project team, these leaders do need to match individual contributors with project work.

One tool that that can be used for clearly communicating project scope is the work breakdown structure (WBS). A work breakdown structure provides a low-context map of the actual work that needs to be performed. The starting point for a work breakdown structure is the highest level deliverable, the project itself. Further project detail is displayed in tabular or graphical format to depict a progressively detailed set of deliverables and project work. Having a map of the work that needs to be done provides an invaluable starting point for matching individual contributors to project tasks. Figure 16.1 shows a work breakdown structure for a consulting project.

Identify and Clearly Communicate Why We Are Working on the Project. We have yet to identify any project leader or individual contributor who is truly inspired by

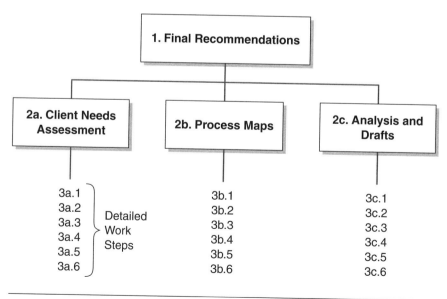

Figure 16.1 An Example of a WBS for a Consulting Project

scope and work breakdown structures. While clear description of project scope provides clarity and opportunities for matching individual contributors with project tasks, the development of a project vision provides an opportunity to create a sense of shared purpose for pursuing any given project. Moran and Youngdahl (2008) have developed a straightforward process for developing a project vision: "A project vision is a snapshot of the preferred future. Quite simply, a project vision statement is a snapshot of the preferred future that will result from (1) achieving our project's deliverables and (2) being involved with the project as a contributor. The vision describes what's in it for those who receive the benefits of the project deliverables and what's in it for those doing the project work" (p. 71). This project visioning process is outlined in Table 16.1.

Map the Stakeholder Terrain. Each stakeholder, whether the stakeholder is an individual or a group, can be identified along an intention and power continuum. It is important to understand each stakeholder's power to affect the project and his or her intentions with respect to supporting the project. This knowledge helps project leaders direct their influencing energy to stakeholders who have the power to positively affect the project but are not inclined to help. These relationships between intention and power are outlined in Figure 16.2. Although the relationships are depicted as discrete quadrants, power and intention are actually best thought of as continuous scales.

High-powered blockers require the greatest influencing attention. They have the power to help, but their inclination is to use the power to block the project, possibly leading to early termination. Clearly, it is important to listen to these

Table 16.1 Developing a Project Vision Statement

Visioning Step	Key Points
Introduce the overall purpose of the exercise.	The purpose is to identify why we are pursuing the project and to keep the team energized.
Identify the small-group team members.	Make the small groups diverse (function and country) and limit to about six members.
Brainstorm individually key words that describe the reasons to be excited about the actual project work as well as the outcomes of the project after successfully achieving the deliverables.	Limit to 15 minutes. Write words on separate sticky notes or pieces of paper.
Sort words into conceptual themes.	Group exercise. Separate aspirational vision words from low-context objective words.
Create a vision statement and set of objectives from the themes.	Group exercise. Assign a facilitator to ensure that each group member's input is heard.

SOURCE: Adapted from a project visioning exercise by Moran and Youngdahl (2008, pp. 75–76).

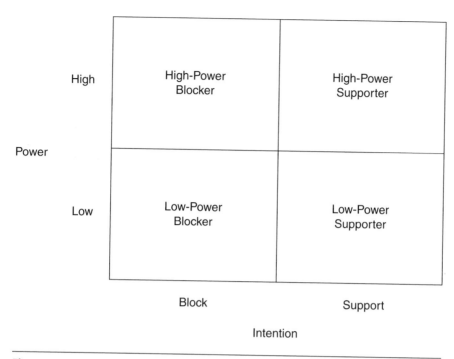

Figure 16.2 Mapping the Stakeholder Terrain

blockers to learn about any legitimate reasons they might have for not supporting the project. This information could be used to make adjustments to the project that might reduce the impacts of certain risks. Similarly, low-power blockers should be listened to in order to identify and avoid or mitigate potential project risks. However, project leaders should not expend as much energy trying to influence low-power blockers as they would in their efforts to sway high-power blockers given relative potential impacts.

Low-power supporters lack status, knowledge, and/or abilities to affect projects. Project leaders are advised to help these stakeholders make meaningful contributions to the project while they learn and acquire new skills and abilities. There is no need to influence the stakeholders since they are already inclined to support the project. Thus, the key challenge is to maximize their contribution. High-power supporters should be fully supported by project leaders as they have the greatest potential for adding significant value.

Look Through the Lens of the Individual Whom You Are Trying to Influence and Seek Favorable Exchanges. This prescription is a critical component to linking influential leadership to the importance of cross-cultural understanding:

> Spend the time to diagnose the world of others. This diagnosis could be from a cross-cultural perspective, looking through another's lens, or simply from the perspective of finding out if there are any big changes in the professional and personal lives of project contributors. We're not suggesting that you get overly personal, just

that you show enough compassion as a project leader to understand that there's more to the lives of others than contributing to your project. That little bit of understanding goes a long way toward finding favorable exchanges, and even in some cases determining who should be on the project team. (Moran & Youngdahl, 2008, p. 131)

In developing a favorable exchange, project leaders must understand the currencies of the stakeholders whom they are trying to influence (Cohen & Bradford, 2005). This process of seeking clarity about what needs to be done and why it needs to be done and then setting about influencing based on an understanding of the stakeholder terrain provides a process that project leaders can follow to develop effective influencing strategies.

If designed and implemented properly with mutually agreed-upon, well-defined goals, project management not only can help firms neutralize the frequent intradepartmental rivalries between functional "silos," but it also can help forge linkages between product group or divisional "fiefdoms" and even help bridge strategic alliance or joint venture partners, enhancing the creation and dissemination of knowledge and the exchange of other critical resources in the process. (Byosiere & Luethge, 2007, p. 19)

Understanding how to influence and communicate across functional and geographical divides separates project leaders from global project leaders. In the remaining sections, we focus on this critical cultural dimension of global project leadership.

Bridging the Cultural Divide

Verité en-deça des Pyrénées, erreur au delà (There are truths on this side of the Pyrenees that are falsehoods on the other.)

Pascal, 1670

In our work with many project leaders from a significant number of different countries, we have never met a person who believes that people are the same everywhere and that culture does not count or matter. All have experienced the challenge of working across cultures and have experienced both successes and failures, as observable in the subsequent cited research.

Barczak, McDonough, and Athanassiou (2006), after 10 years of research within the European Union (including England), the United States, and Mexico in more than 300 global teams within 230 different companies whose products include consumer-oriented products, consumer packaged goods, and industrial products, found four overarching main challenges that are faced by global leaders and teams. These four challenges are exposed when the following interact:

1. Team members who are working together and speak dissimilar native languages, and thus communication and understanding often become difficult.

2. Project members who are working together and are not of the same cultural backgrounds and thus exhibit different norms, values, customs, communication styles, and behavior that can create disputes among members.

3. Members who are not living in the same location as each other and who live and work in numerous nations, and thus the opportunities to really get to know each other are a challenge, resulting in less trust and significant informational gaps.

4. Project members who are working together who are beholden to different companies, and thus the challenge behind merging different corporate strategies involves a much larger network of expectations and knowledge than that of the members of the project team.

Barczak et al. (2006) established that the process of developing and introducing new goods in today's marketplace has become even more multifaceted as corporations work to merge their strategy and their process in an effort to satisfy global and local customers needs and integrate design and development scattered around the world. Mahalingam and Levitt's (2007) case study evaluated global construction projects and revealed that "institutional values produced a certain type of regular behavior among the Europeans (they all preferred, and took it for granted, that high-rise buildings would have operable windows) and a different type of regular behavior among the Americans (who all preferred to have non-operable windows). These opposing views clashed and neither party was willing to relent, as each party was used to working in ways dictated by their own institutional environments" (p. 524).

As is evident in these studies, conflicts are inevitable in global endeavors. Mintzberg (1983) identified three different tactics that we believe project leaders should assimilate into their strategies to build effective coordination among multicultural and multilingual team members and thus be efficient in preventing or managing conflict due to global disparities. Global project leaders will be more effective if they incorporate, sometimes during dissimilar instances, the following three strategies (Mintzberg, 1983) while leading their projects: stipulating that project members should mutually adjust to each other, at times applying direct supervision, and creating a standardized work process and output while reinforcing interdependence among tasks and objects. Superior global project management is process focused and thus also requires knowledge of cultural specifics, how cultures vary across nations along with political dynamics, and how these differences affect the people working within the projects and the institutions to which they are beholden.

The following is a brief description of culture and its impact upon behavior. Project leaders who recognize the many ways that culture affects behavior understand culture-specific behavioral tendencies can apply a cross-culturally competent leadership style that is adaptable, and are more likely to lead a successful project process that results in a positive outcome. Thus, developing and exhibiting cross-cultural competencies as a global project leader is essential to one's success.

Culture—What Is It?

There are many definitions of culture in the published works of anthropologists, sociologists, psychologists, and others. Our definition of culture is this: "the way we do things here," which includes *values, assumptions,* and the subsequent *behaviors that are influenced by cultural values and assumptions.* Cultural *values* are fundamental beliefs that are learned very early and are the basis of many behaviors such as the value of punctuality. For example, Germans, Scandinavians, and others are more likely to be very punctual. They usually arrive on time to attend a meeting. Latin Americans may not have the same value of punctuality. Cultural *assumptions* are expectations about preferred and expected ways of being that influence values, beliefs, behavior, and communication. Assumptions such as "people are basically good" versus "people are fundamentally evil" (and therefore cannot be trusted) is an example of an assumption.

Culture Is Learned

Culture is learned, and individuals from the same culture have similar but not the same learning experiences. These learning experiences shape values, beliefs, and ultimately behavior.

Scholars (Kardiner & Linton, 1939; Linton, 1945; Sapir, 1949; Wallace, 1970) have learned that

- An individual's early childhood experiences exert a strong effect on one's personality.
- Similar early experiences tend to produce similar personality types in children who experience them.
- The child-rearing and socialization practices of any culture are patterned and tend to be similar for families in the same culture.
- Finally, child-rearing practices vary from culture to culture.

The most fundamental aspects of a person's nature—their values, beliefs, assumptions, and thus behavior—are learned through the socialization process children experience and thus are resistant to change. Project managers who seek to understand first and then adjust their approaches to work with different and even perhaps unfamiliar cultural values, assumptions, and beliefs are more likely to experience success.

Culture Is Complex

Culture is like an iceberg. In this analogy, one tenth of culture is visible and above the surface, and about nine tenths is below the surface and invisible. For leaders of global projects, it is not being aware of, or understanding, the below-the-surface component of culture that causes the most challenges in leading global projects. Through recognizing the value of the following 10 aspects of culture (Moran, Harris, & Moran, 2007), project leaders can conduct a "cultural due diligence" to anticipate similarities and differences that most likely will affect the process of the project and, if not managed successfully, the ultimate success of a project. For the competent project leader, this cultural due diligence should use these 10 aspects not only in the context of the project itself but also with careful attention to the many different cultures that are participating in the project.

1. *Sense of Self:* An individual's sense of self can be manifested, for example, by humble bearing in one culture and by macho behavior in another. Each culture validates self in a unique way. Some cultures are very structured and formal, while others are more flexible and formal. Some cultures are very close and precisely determine an individual's place, while others are more open and changing.

2. *Communication and Language:* The communication system, both verbal and nonverbal, distinguishes one group from another.

3. *Dress and Appearance:* This includes the outward garments and adornments that tend to be culturally distinctive.

4. *Food and Feeding Habits:* The manner in which food is selected, prepared, presented, and eaten often differs by culture.

5. *Time and Time Consciousness:* One's sense of time differs by culture.

6. *Relationships:* Cultures determine human and organizational relationships by age, gender, status, wealth, power, and wisdom.

7. *Values and Norms:* From a culture's value system, norms of behavior are determined for that society.

8. *Beliefs and Attitudes:* People in all cultures have concerns for the supernatural that is evident in their religions and religious practices.

9. *Mental Process and Learning:* The mind is internalized culture, and people's internal mental process involves how information is organized and processed.

10. *Work Habits and Practices:* In some cultures, the worthiness of the activity is narrowly measured in terms of the income produced.

In addition, it is in the interaction of these 10 components *cross-culturally* that conflict within projects can materialize and thus jeopardize its overall success. The competent global project leader becomes skilled at recognizing where in the 10 components conflict can arise within their respective projects and then, through encouraging and reinforcing adaptive behaviors, either manages or prevent conflicts while simultaneously demonstrating that all project members are valued.

Communication Skills

As the previous 10 aspects of culture are not always obvious and often found below the visible "iceberg" of culture, so are the communication styles that send the messages project managers need to learn to hear. For it is oftentimes within the messages themselves that values and assumptions about the 10 aspects of culture are communicated. Edward T. Hall (1959), an American anthropologist, made a distinction between high- and low-context cultures and how the *context* affects communications. "A high context culture uses high context communication: information is either in the physical context or internalized in the person with less communicated in the explicit words or message. Japan, Saudi Arabia, Spain, and China are cultures engaged in high context communications. On the other hand, a low context culture employs low context communication: most information is contained in explicit codes, such as words. Germany, Sweden, and the United States are cultures that engage in low context communication" (Moran & Youngdahl, 2008, p. 26). Successful project managers learn to "read" between the lines and change their communication style to suit the listener, through being adaptive in their communicative styles.

A Cross-Cultural Communication Example

The following example (Moran & Youngdahl, 2008, p. 26) provides a vivid illustration in communicated meaning:

Question: "Do you think Mr. Sim will be able to come to the course next week as I would like to make hotel reservations for him and the hotel is quite full?"

Answer: "It is possible he may have to attend a meeting in Shanghai."

Follow-up question 2 days later and before the course begins:

Question sent by e-mail: "I am following up on my earlier conversation and am wondering if Mr. Sim will be attending the course?"

Answer by e-mail: "As I told you previously, he will NOT attend."

Result: A significant misunderstanding between the Chinese human resources (HR) director and the Westerner. The HR director then proceeded to ignore the Westerner at work for several days.

Figure 16.3 is a way for project leaders to understand the role of culture.

Figure 16.3 Cultural Iceberg and the Continuum of Cultural Variables

Leaders of Global Projects

"We all have the capacity to inspire others. But we must first be willing to devote ourselves to our personal growth and development as leaders" (George, Sins, Mclean, & Mayer, 2007). The challenge today is for business and political leaders to build their own competencies to be competent global leaders. Leaders of global projects, in our experience, must develop many of these same leadership skills. We choose to refer to only one leadership book, *Shackelton's Way: Leadership Lessons From the Great Antarctic Explorer* (Morrel & Chapparell, 2001), to illustrate our point.

An Example of a Great Leader of a Global Project

We believe that Ernest Shackleton, the late Antarctic explorer, had superior leadership skills (Morrel & Chapparell, 2001). The Imperial Trans-Antarctic Expedition between 1914 and 1916 in which he was in charge of leading originally had the goal of sailing into the Antarctic and then crossing on foot. This goal was cut short when their ship, *Endurance,* became confined in ice, severely damaged to the point where it was no longer seaworthy, and subsequently sank. To help save his multinational crew, Shackleton guided them to a place where they found a safe haven on Elephant Island and then traveled in an open boat with five of his men, 800 miles into the Southern Ocean, to South Georgia. After reaching the remote island, he and two others crossed a mountainous land to reach a whaling station. Their ordeal lasted almost 2 years, and Shackleton was able to save the lives of all 27 crew members.

This is an extreme example of superior project leadership skills of a multinational group. The forces challenging these explorers were not only global cultural differences or global institutional forces that pulled the project in different directions; instead, it was unpredictable weather patterns and survival needs that threatened the undertaking. The factors that endangered the success of this team were having to live without shelter with severely cold weather in an extremely remote location, with no vegetation and diminutive animal life, and their objective was to enable a team process that ensured their project goal—survival. The following behavioral traits reflected in Shackleton's leadership behavior are an excellent "real-life" illustration of the successful global project leader.

A Shortened Synopsis of Morrel and Chapparell's (2001) Analysis of the Journals of Crew Members Concerning Shackleton's Leadership Behavior

Shackleton's Way of Developing Leadership Skills

- Find a way to turn setbacks and failures into advantages.
- Be bold in vision and careful in planning.
- Never insist on reaching a goal at any cost.

Shackleton's Way of Selecting and Organizing a Crew

- Start with a solid core of talent you know from past experience.
- Your second in command is your most important person.
- Hire those with talents and expertise you lack.

Shackleton's Way of Forging a United and Loyal Team

- Whenever possible, have people work together on tasks.
- Be fair and impartial.
- Lead by example.

Shackleton's Way of Developing Individual Talent

- Make sure each person has challenging and important work.
- Match the person to the position.
- Give consistent feedback on performance.

Shackleton's Way of Getting the Group Through a Crisis

- Plan several options in detail.
- Keep your malcontents close to you.

Shackleton's Way of Forming Groups for the Toughest Tasks

- Empower the team leaders so that they have the authority to handle their own team.
- Do not be afraid to change your mind when you see your plan is not working.
- Celebrate small and large accomplishments.

Conclusion

Leading global projects successfully is challenging and requires the best skills of all the individuals involved. We focused on introducing some foundation concepts in project management and some ways of analyzing culture, and we concluded with the leadership story of Ernest Shackleton in an effort to provide a real-life story that validates the global project leadership theory we discussed.

References

Archer, N., & Ghasemzadeh, F. (1999). An integrated framework for project portfolio selection. *International Journal of Project Management, 17,* 207–216.

Barczak, G., McDonough, E., & Athanassiou, N. (2006). So you want to be a global project leader. *Research Technology Management, 49*(3), 28–35.

Byosiere, P., & Luethge, D. (2007). Project management processes across borders: A comparison of EU-US corporate subsidiary project activities. *Project Management Journal, 38*(2), 18–29.

Cohen, A., & Bradford, R. (2005). *Influence without authority.* New York: John Wiley.

Fortune, J., & White, D. (2006). Framing of project critical success factors by a systems model. *International Journal of Project Management, 24,* 53–65.

Friedman, T. L. (2005). *The world is flat.* New York: Farrar, Straus & Giroux.

George, W., Sins, P., Mclean, N., & Mayer, D. (2007, February). Developing your authentic leadership. *Harvard Business Review.*

Hall, E. (1959). *The silent language.* New York: Doubleday.

Johnson, L. (2004, June). Close the gap between projects and strategy. *Harvard Management Update,* pp. 3–5.

Kardiner, A., & Linton, R. (1939). *The individual and his society.* New York: Columbia University Press.

Linton, R. (1945). *The cultural background of personality.* New York: Appleton-Century-Crofts.

Mahalingam, A., & Levitt, R. E. (2007). Institutional theory as a framework for analyzing conflicts on global projects. *Journal of Construction Engineering and Management, 133,* 517–528.

Mintzberg, H. (1983). *Structures in fives: Designing effective organizations.* Englewood Cliffs, NJ: Prentice Hall.

Moran, R., Harris, P., & Moran, S. (2007). *Managing cultural differences: Global leadership strategies for the 21st century* (7th ed.). Oxford, UK: Elsevier/Butterworth-Heinemann.

Moran, R. T., & Youngdahl, W. E. (2008). *Leading global projects: For professional and accidental project leaders.* Oxford, UK: Butterworth-Heinemann.

Morrel, M., & Chapparell, S. (2001). *Shackleton's way: Leadership lessons from the great Antarctic explorer.* New York: Penguin.

Patterson, K., Grenny, J., Maxfield, D., McMillan, R., & Switzler, A. (2008). *Influences: The power to change anything.* New York: McGraw-Hill.

Quinn, J. B. (1999). Strategic outsourcing: Leveraging knowledge capabilities. *Sloan Management Review, 40*(4), 9–21.

Sapir, E. (1949). *Culture, common language and personality.* Berkeley, CA: Language Behavior Research Laboratory.

Shore, B., & Cross, B. (2005). Exploring the role of national culture in the management of large-scale international science projects. *International Journal of Project Management, 23,* 55–64.

Wallace, A. (1970). *Culture and personality.* New York: Random House.

Youngdahl, W., & Ramaswamy, K. (2007). Offshoring knowledge and service work: A conceptual model and research agenda. *Journal of Operations Management, 21*(6), 212–221.

CHAPTER 17

Intercultural Competence in Teacher Education

Developing the Intercultural Competence of Educators and Their Students

Creating the Blueprints

Kenneth Cushner and Jennifer Mahon

eveloping the intercultural competence of young people, both in the domestic context as well as in the international sphere, requires a core of teachers and teacher educators who have not only attained this sensitivity and skill themselves but are also able to transmit this to the young people in their charge. While education has attempted to address the needs of a changing society with varying degrees of success for decades, concepts related to intercultural understanding and competence remain on the margins, rather than central to the institutional mission.

There is no exact blueprint for building intercultural competence. Despite the ironic fact that concepts of culture and intercultural interaction naturally exist in and permeate all aspects of education, introducing the concept of intercultural education in schools in most nations is a particularly slow and complex process. Unlike the discipline-centered approach that underlies most of the educational curricula encountered in school, intercultural education has no readily identifiable or discipline-based core. In addition, because most teacher education programs in the United States also lack such interdisciplinary or multidisciplinary structure, teachers are often ill-prepared to adequately address intercultural concepts. Large-scale or institution-wide goal setting and programming designed to address intercultural competence thus becomes difficult, especially in the ever-increasing high-stakes, test-crazed environment in which most educators in the United States, and increasingly in other nations, find themselves. Finally, an attempt to address intercultural competence must consider aspects associated with psychosocial development of young people, entrenched value systems that underlie such actions as racism and homophobia, and the cognitive and affective readiness of both teachers and teacher educators. In this chapter, we attempt to locate the place of "intercultural" in both the historical as well as current state of affairs in the broad field of education, to analyze the intercultural competence of teachers and students, and propose the direction we believe the field of education should move.

Situating "Intercultural" in the Field of Education

The concept "intercultural" is not new to the field of education. In the 1600s, Comenius proposed a pansophic college based on ideas of pedagogical universalism, or the belief that a multiplicity of perspectives not only was foundational to knowledge acquisition but also encouraged mutual understanding between people of differing backgrounds (Piaget, 1957; Sadler, 1969). Piaget (1957), who deemed Comenius "the apostle of international collaboration in education itself" (p. 2), explained,

> Education, according to Comenius, was not merely the training of the child at school or in the home; it is a process affecting man's whole life and the countless social adjustments he must make. The great principles of peace and the international organization of education that make him a forerunner of so many modern institutions and trends of thought likewise stem, in his work, from this unique synthesis between nature and man. (p. 2)

Today, aspects of Comenius's ideas are conceptualized within terms such as *intercultural education,* which gained attention in the first half of the 20th century, with *intercultural competence* appearing only recently. A plethora of terminology now exists that makes reference to culture in education, including multicultural education (J. A. Banks & Banks, 2004), global or international education (Hanvey, 1975; Merryfield, 1996), peace education (Stomfay-Stitz, 1993), and culturally relevant or responsive education (Gay, 2000; Ladson-Billings, 1994). Multicultural education is by far the most prevalent, as indicated by the existence of synoptic texts such as the *Handbook of Research on Multicultural Education* (J. A. Banks & Banks, 2004) and organizations such as the National Association of Multicultural Education (NAME), both of which are devoted entirely to this field. Because the *Handbook of Research on Multicultural Education* is the only large review of research with a sole focus on culture in relation to the preparation and development of teachers, it potentially holds considerable sway in the development of individual understanding in this area. Thus, we begin our discussion with the history of intercultural education as discussed in this text.

Four chapters of the *Handbook of Research on Multicultural Education* (C. A. M. Banks, 2004; J. A. Banks, 2004a, 2004b, 2004c) discuss intercultural education, but at times, the authors appear to differ in their conclusions. J. A. Banks (2004c) attributes the development of the field to educators' needs to respond to increased anti-Semitism and racial rioting in the 1930s in the United States and describes intercultural education as a movement dedicated to "help immigrant students adapt to American life, maintain aspects of their ethnic identity, and become effective citizens of the commonwealth" (p. 231). In a subsequent chapter, Cherry A. M. Banks (2004) delves further into the genesis of the movement, detailing the Progressive Education Association's creation of the Commission on Intercultural Education, which "officially coined" the term in 1935 to describe the work of educators "seeking to help students reduce their prejudice and increase their understanding and appreciation of ethnic, racial and religious diversity" (p. 754).

Intermittently, both authors equate intercultural education with intergroup education. J. A. Banks (2004b) explains, "A prominent vision within the intergroup education ideology was interracial harmony and desegregation; another name for the movement was *intercultural education*" (p. 11). What becomes less clear, however, is why at other times the movements are not seen as identical. For instance, citing work by Taba, Brady, and Robinson (1952), J. A. Banks (2004c) states, "*Like intercultural education,* the aims of intergroup education were to minimize ethnic cultures and affiliations, help students become mainstream Americans and effective citizens, and teach racial and ethnic tolerance" (p. 231, emphasis added).

C. A. M. Banks (2004) offers substantial evidence to suggest that points of tension clearly existed between different factions of intercultural/intergroup educators that may explain this confusing interchanging of the terms. One issue involved the degree of maintenance of cultural identity by immigrants in relationship to assimilation to cultural norms of the United States. In addition, educators disagreed on whether the audience for their programs should be the immigrants themselves or members of the host culture. Curriculum was also debated, with one side advocating a culture-specific approach—that is, giving specific information on individual groups—whereas the other side emphasized the need for teachers to learn prejudice reduction skills and improve relationships between different groups.

The Bankses appear to disagree slightly on the state of intercultural education today. C. A. M. Banks (2004), whose analysis of intercultural education stops with references in 1959, describes the influence of intercultural/intergroup education as "waning" (p. 766). J. A. Banks (2004b), however, unequivocally claims, "The intergroup education movement had quietly died without a requiem" with the advent of the civil rights movement (p. 11) and ideas "antithetical" to the intergroup movement such as the ethnic and racial separatism of the 1960s and 1970s. "America envisioned by most intergroup educators was a nation in which ethnic and racial differences were minimized and all people were treated fairly and lived in harmony" (J. A. Banks, 2004b, p. 11). C. A. M. Banks surmised that intercultural educators "did not seem to recognize or were not prepared to address the enormous problem of minority discrimination." Rather, she contends, "Today multicultural educators are addressing these and other related issues" (p. 766).

The intercultural/intergroup movement is discussed along with the ethnic studies movement in regard to the historical development of multicultural education, "a field of study designed to increase educational equity for all students that incorporates for this purpose content, concepts, principles, theories, and paradigms from history, the social and behavioral sciences and ethnic studies and women's studies" (J. A. Banks, 2004a, p. xi). It is the early ethnic studies movement's focus on individual group empowerment, as opposed to the intercultural education focus on intergroup harmony, that is specified as the historical antecedent of multicultural education.

The *Handbook of Research on Multicultural Education* (*HRME*; J. A. Banks & Banks, 2004) gives a valuable interpretation of intercultural education's historical legacy in the United States. We recognize that extensive reviews of research must take a position on terminology, just as we are doing within this handbook. However, we believe that intercultural education is more alive and more dynamic than the *HRME* would have us believe. Its modern conceptualizations have a great deal to offer us in pursuit of answers to the crucial educational questions. As John Dewey (1902) wrote, "Thus sects arise: schools of opinion. Each selects that set of conditions that appeals to it; and then erects them into a complete and independent truth, instead of treating them as a factor in a problem, needing adjustment" (p. 4).

Regardless of the terminology used, in our opinion the problem needing adjustment is that many teachers continue to graduate from preparatory institutions and settle into careers without the requisite competencies to ensure the educational equity that enables all students to attain their personal and professional goals in this global, postmodern world.

Getting the Lay of the Land: Competencies, Standards, and Culture in the Field of Education

Lonner and Hayes (2004) argue, "Implicit in the notion of competence is the ability to intelligently select one's behavior or course of action in response to the various opportunities and challenges of daily living, including managing social and work-focused relationships as well as conceptualizing and executing solutions to an array of human problems" (p. 91). If one is to accept this definition, it seems logical that intercultural competency should be a central dimension of teacher preparation. Intelligent selection of culturally competent teacher behaviors would enable educators to facilitate the learning of students from multiple cultural backgrounds while providing them with the skills to succeed in an increasingly culturally diverse world. Competency, as well as its assessment, has become a central focus in the United States as elsewhere. Competent teachers, or what has come to be called "highly qualified teachers" through the federal legislation known as No Child Left Behind (NCLB) in the United States, ostensibly lead students to competence in the current content and performance standards set by state and local educational bodies.

To ensure teacher competence, U.S. schools of education look to the standards guiding teacher education and programming for professional development created by three national organizations. These include the Interstate New Teachers Assessment and Support Consortium (INTASC, 2007), the Association for Teacher Educators (ATE), and the National Council for Accreditation of Teacher Education (NCATE). Of these, the latter organization, as the chief accrediting body, is the one most commonly consulted, and its Standard 4 addresses the essential requirements regarding diversity:

> The unit designs, implements, and evaluates curriculum and experiences for candidates to acquire and apply the knowledge, skills, and dispositions necessary to help all students learn. These experiences include working with diverse higher education and school faculty, diverse candidates, and diverse students in P–12 schools. (NCATE, 2008b, p. 12)

NCATE (2001) further discusses performance targets under each standard and lists the following for diversity:

> Curriculum, field experiences, and clinical practice help candidates to demonstrate knowledge, skills, and dispositions related to diversity. They are based on well-developed knowledge bases for, and conceptualizations of, diversity and inclusion so that candidates can apply them effectively in schools. Candidates learn to contextualize teaching and to draw upon representations from the students' own experiences and knowledge. They learn how to challenge students toward cognitive complexity and engage all students, including students with exceptionalities, through instructional conversation. Candidates and faculty review assessment data that provide information about candidates' ability to work with all students and develop a plan for improving their practice in this area. One of the goals of this standard is the development of educators who can help all students learn and who can teach from multicultural and global perspectives that draw on the histories, experiences, and representations of students from diverse cultural backgrounds. Therefore, the unit provides opportunities for candidates to understand the role of diversity and equity in the teaching and learning process. Coursework, field experiences, and clinical practice are designed to help candidates understand the influence of culture on education and acquire the ability to develop meaningful learning experiences for all students. (p. 34)

Perhaps in reflection of these standards, 41% of U.S. states require teacher education programs to have a diversity component (Evans, Torrey, & Newton, 1997). However, fewer than one-third of states in the United States had teacher certification requirements necessitating training in diversity (Miller, Strosnider, & Dooley, 2000). The states seem to recognize the importance of intercultural competency, but the lack of knowledge in this area is evidently not *enough* to keep a teacher out of the classroom. Currently, only Alaska and North Dakota offer "specific certification in areas related to multicultural education for all teachers" (Morrier, Irving, Dandy, Dmitriyev, & Ukeje, 2007, p. 33). Eleven states (Arizona, California, Colorado, Florida, Massachusetts, Minnesota, New Jersey, New York, North Dakota, Rhode

Island, and Vermont) required competency for licensure when an individual was pursing certification or endorsement in bilingual education or English as a second language (ESL). The remaining 39 states have no specific certification requirements (Morrier et al., 2007).

The standards clearly point to the necessity for interculturally skilled teachers, yet researchers have argued that none of these standards is extensive enough to ensure that teachers will, in fact, be competent to meet the needs of students from culturally diverse backgrounds (Peterman, 2005; Zeichner, 2003). Beginning in the fall of 2007, NCATE modified its standards. Linguistic diversity was added for the first time, and *diversity* is now defined according to the U.S. census categories. Perhaps most significant is the addition of the following statement: "Candidates are helped to understand the potential impact of discrimination based on race, class, gender, disability, sexual orientation, and language on students and their learning" (NCATE, 2008a, p. 2). To put it another way, since the inception of compulsory schooling in the mid-1800s, no U.S. institutions have been accountable regarding the preparation of teachers in regard to the impact of discrimination on the teaching and learning process.

Educational benefits of teacher cultural competence and communicative competence have been well documented (Au & Kawakami, 1994; Ladson-Billings, 1994). Substantial research-based evidence indicates the effects of this lack of knowledge on interactions between teachers and students—especially in regard to discipline (Davis & Jordan, 1994; Gordon, Della Pinna, & Keleher, 2000). For instance, Gordon et al. (2000) found racism in particular to be an undeniably pervasive factor affecting outcomes such as dropout and discipline rates across districts examined in 11 of 12 states. Using extensive data collected from numerous school districts across grade levels, class levels, and urban, rural, and suburban school types, Wu, Pink, Crain, and Moles (1982) explained that educators most often used the logic that students of color had higher levels of school suspensions because they committed more infractions. Multiple regression analyses, however, clearly indicated that the best predictors of suspension were not numbers of misbehaviors but rather teacher referrals, school characteristics, academic bias, racial inequalities, and teacher disinterest. Gay (2006) notes that Wu's data were so incontrovertible, the author suggested,

> Students would have a better chance of reducing their suspension rates by transferring to schools with fewer suspensions than improving their attitudes, or reducing their misbehavior. Teachers could help to reduce disproportionality in suspension rates by eliminating apathy and indifference, and cultivating better attitudes towards students of color. (pp. 350–351)

Examining the Foundation: Profiles of U.S. Teachers in the 21st Century

The teacher is obviously a vital link to the development of intercultural competence in young people, but given what we know about the demographics and experiences of most U.S. teachers, there is cause for primary concern. While a diversified teaching force by itself does not guarantee intercultural sensitivity or competence, the demographics of the teaching force in the United States remains rather constant, despite increasing cultural and ethnic diversity of students and increased efforts to recruit underrepresented groups into the teaching field (Cushner, McClelland, & Safford, 2009; Sleeter, 2007).

Across the United States, teaching is still a rather homogeneous profession, the majority of teachers being European American, with fewer than 16% being teachers of color (National Center for Education Statistics, 2002). Newly licensed teachers in urban schools show a bit more variation with 22% being teachers of color (Shen, Wegenke, & Cooley, 2003). Women continue to dominate the field (65%–70%) and are by far the majority in elementary or primary schools (80%+). Most teachers are middle class and live in small- to medium-sized suburban communities. This is in contrast to the increasing percentage of students of color in American public schools (who now represent upwards to 40% of the school population nationwide and higher in many urban areas) and the fact that an increasing number of students live in poverty. The picture is not much different in other nations, except that the predominant ethnic background of teachers may vary from nation to nation (Cushner, 1998).

Today's teacher education students, at least in the United States, do not promise to bring much change to these demographics. They tend to be relatively cross-culturally inexperienced, with most living within 100 miles of where they were born. Fewer than 10% report an eagerness to teach in urban or multicultural environments; rather, they desire to teach in schools similar to the ones they attended. Fewer than 5% of American teachers are fluent and able to teach in any second language. Add to this the fact that the majority of teacher education students spend all or most of their time with people of their own ethnic and racial group and that most believe minority and low-income children are not capable of learning the higher level concepts in the subject areas they are preparing to teach, and the situation becomes increasingly dire. Teachers and teachers in training, it appears, live in vastly different worlds from the students in their charge (Cushner et al., 2009).

Assessing Educator Intercultural Sensitivity: Recent Studies Using the Intercultural Development Inventory (IDI)

The Intercultural Development Inventory (IDI; Hammer & Bennett, 2003) has been increasingly used to assess the level of intercultural sensitivity of teachers. The IDI is a valid and reliable instrument based on Bennett's developmental model of intercultural sensitivity that identifies where an individual falls along a continuum from highly ethnocentric to highly ethnorelative (Hammer & Bennett, 2003). Three stages lie on the ethnocentric side of the continuum (denial, defense, and minimization), and three stages reflect increasingly ethnorelative perspectives and skills (acceptance, adaptation, and integration). Research from these studies suggests that today's teachers may not have the requisite disposition to be effective intercultural educators or the skills to guide young people to develop intercultural competence.

Mahon's (2006) study of 155 teachers from the American Midwest placed all of them at minimization or below—all on the ethnocentric side of the scale. Similarly, Grossman and Yuen's (2006) survey of 107 teachers in schools in Hong Kong found 55% of this group in denial or defense and 43% in minimization, with only 2% in the acceptance or adaptation stages. Complicating the situation is the fact that teachers tend to overestimate their intercultural sensitivity as reported by their perceived means. Teachers report treating all children alike, not seeing color or difference, and not discriminating, which according to Mahon (2006) is exactly the skill teachers need to develop. Believing they are doing well, this makes it all the more difficult to advance to a more ethnorelative stage.

A study by Pappamihiel (2004) found that even after taking one class in multicultural education and another one specific to the needs of English-language learners, early childhood teacher education students still exhibited a low level of intercultural sensitivity. Basing her study on the developmental model of intercultural sensitivity but not using the IDI, Pappamihiel asked respondents to compare how they would express caring behaviors to children in an ESL (English as a second language) class compared to similar-aged children in a general education class. Very few of the 28 respondents reported that they would behave any differently in their interactions or demonstrated any indication that they understood, accepted, and valued cultural differences between these groups of students. Like others in minimization, they reported that they would treat all children alike by offering "hugs and smiles" as the predominant way to express caring to all.

There appears to be a surprising disparity between teachers, teacher education students, and the children they are preparing to teach, with young people demonstrating higher levels of intercultural sensitivity than their teachers. Pedersen (1997) administered a modified version of the IDI to 145 seventh-grade students in six social studies classrooms from three schools (one each from urban, rural, and suburban settings). Contrary to the findings among the teacher cohorts, more than 70% of these middle school students were found to be in high minimization or acceptance (53 in minimization and 52 in acceptance). The number of intercultural relationships one reported, along with interest in talking with people from different cultures, were statistically significant predictors of levels of intercultural sensitivity. Those with higher IDI scores reported having more intercultural friendships and interactions with people from different cultural or ethnic groups than did those with low IDI scores.

Geography played a role in the quality and orientation of the intercultural experience as well, with urban and suburban students having more frequent and regular interactions across cultural, racial, and ethnic boundaries than did their rural counterparts. Rural students, who generally do not have the same opportunity for frequent intercultural interaction but who scored high on the IDI in Pedersen's (1997) study, generally expressed curiosity as well as a desire to have more of such experiences. Unlike their urban and suburban counterparts, however, rural students tended to view intercultural exchanges as exotic or as "adventures" with non-Americans. Those with low IDI scores were more hesitant and suspicious of intercultural contact.

In addition to the IDI, the students in the Pedersen (1997) study completed Bem's Sex Role Inventory, Bryant's Empathy Index, and Altemeyer's Adapted Authoritarian Scale. An interesting finding in this study was that those who were categorized as androgynous—that is, girls and boys who identified strongly with both feminine and masculine traits—had significantly higher scores on the IDI. The androgynous children (4 of the 19 who were interviewed) had more flexible and curious attitudes about learning and interacting and those with are culturally different. There was also a statistically significant negative relationship between authoritarianism and intercultural sensitivity, and those with lower IDI scores have reflecting inflexible and conventional attitudes. Likewise, there was a statistically significant negative relationship between empathy and authoritarianism, with those with high IDI scores having developed the skill of perspective taking to a higher degree than those scoring low.

A more recent and related study by Straffon (2003) found even greater disparity between students' levels of intercultural sensitivity and that of the teachers reported in the studies above. Assessing the levels of intercultural sensitivity of 336 high school students attending an international school in Southeast Asia, he found only 3% on the ethnocentric side of the IDI. In this study, the longer students were in attendance in the school (mean length of time in this school was 5.7 years), the higher their IDI score, with 71% in acceptance and 26% in cognitive adaptation. The author suggests that attendance in an international school does promote intercultural sensitivity.

Gathering the Raw Materials: Understanding What Interculturally Competent Educators Must Know and Do

Intercultural competence can be conceived as one of the long-term goals of intercultural education, if not its primary objective. Lonner and Hayes (2004) explain that intercultural competence is a multifaceted concept involving aspects of emotional (Goleman, 1995), contextual (Sternberg, 1988), and interpersonal intelligence (Gardner, 1993) to combine to form "a person who is emotionally caring yet controlled, sensitive to interpersonal dynamics, and genuinely perceptive when in complex and highly interactive situations" (p. 92).

While no single study can be cited that lists all of the essential qualities of intercultural competence, Deardorff (2006) was able to document consensus among leading intercultural experts on 22 dimensions of intercultural competence. Certain constructs that repeatedly emerge throughout the literature include an understanding of both cultural general and cultural specific knowledge (Triandis, 1972), psychological differentiation (Witkin, Dyk, Faterson, Goodenough, & Karp, 1962), categorization width or the ability to expand or broaden how information is construed (Detweiler, 1978), openness (McCrae, Costa, del Pilar, Rolland, & Parker, 1998), and respect in the form of transcultural ethnic validity (Tyler, 2001).

Brislin (2000) identifies four criteria for intercultural success: positive feelings about intercultural relationships, reciprocity of those feelings from others in the culture, task achievement, and stress minimization. Kealey (1996) offers three main areas to consider in intercultural success, including adaptation skills such as positive attitude and flexibility; cross-cultural skills such as realism, cultural involvement, and political astuteness; and partnership skills, including openness, perseverance, and problem solving. Below we discuss some of these essential components of intercultural competency as they relate to education.

Perception, Perspective, and Relationship Building

Within the field of education, many studies point to the power of teacher perception, especially as it relates to student behavior (McCarthy & Benally, 2003; Sheets, 1996). Wu et al. (1982) found students were more likely to be punished with suspension from school when educators perceived the students were of low ability, not because of any data considered on their actual abilities. Sheets (1995, 1996) interviewed both students and teachers about discipline and found that students of color reported feeling frequently victimized through accusations of guilt by association with peers or family members.

Another issue involves perception of culturally determined patterns of thinking, communicating, and behaving rooted in different value systems. McDermott (1987) suggests that "because behavioral competence is differently defined by different social groups, many children and teachers fail in their attempts to establish rational, trusting, and rewarding relationships across ethnic, racial and class boundaries in the classroom" (p. 173). Differences in perceptions of appropriate communicative behaviors, especially in regard to personal disclosure, discourse, and display (Gay, 2006), have been shown to lead to misunderstanding and conflict, which serves as a barrier to maintaining an efficient and effective learning environment (McCarthy & Benally, 2003) According to Powell and Caseau (2004), poor relationships lead to awkward, perfunctory, and difficult communication. Such relationships affect the academic sphere as well, notes Gay (2006), and "the students then assume teachers do not care about what they have to say or whether they learn, and are determined to assault their personal integrity. Some of them stop participating in instructional discourse and learning activities entirely" (p. 355).

Cognition, Complexity, and Conflict

Sheets (1995) reports that classroom discipline issues sometimes arose from teachers' own "lack of interpersonal skills, knowledge of cultural diversity and competence in classroom management for preventing or minimizing confrontations with ethnically and racially different students" (as cited in Gay, 2006, p. 353). Students in this study reported frustration with not being able to share their side of issues or give a context to situations that occurred. When students did speak out, teachers often viewed this as insubordinate, disrespectful, or defiant behavior. Many students of color, it was reported, are simply "not willing to passively submit to the demands of teachers for immediate and unquestioning compliance in conflict situations, especially if they feel they are treated unfairly and denied the opportunity to defend themselves" (Gay, 2006, p. 353). It appears that teachers feel the need to correct what they see as inappropriate actions while students may feel confused or wrongly accused. From their cultural perspective, they believe they have made an appropriate behavioral choice in the situation (Gay, 2006; Powell & Caseau, 2004).

Coulby (2006) argues that educators need more complex understandings of culture to competently handle the difficult and tenuous aspects of intercultural interaction. He believes that intercultural education should be "an education able to negotiate between cultures rather than to show that there is more than one culture" (p. 247). Furthermore, he believes that "in order to make an academic contribution that goes beyond the parochial," educators must engage in debates around the central issues inherent in intercultural education, including "identity and identity politics, government and governance, transitional economies and societies; nationalism and nation construction; globalization" (p. 254).

In a study of the development of intercultural sensitivity over the life span, Mahon (2003) found that teachers with higher levels of sensitivity engaged in complex internal and external conversations. They did not shy away from reflecting on challenges to their own taken-for-granted assumptions regarding complex cultural issues or from engaging in conversations where those assumptions were challenged. Rather, they recognized the importance of engagement to understanding the other person's perspective.

Cultural Knowledge, Attitude, and Efficacy

Hilliard (1998) has argued for the demonstration of cultural competence in education through the performance standards used in teacher education programs. However, others (Parajes, 2003; Siwatu, 2007) question whether such performance will be sustained into the teachers' careers unless issues of self-efficacy and outcome expectancy are addressed. That is, unless they believe in the results possible through their own efforts, teachers are less likely to retain such practice. Research has shown evidence of this discrepancy. Whitfield, Klug, and Whitney (2007) reported preservice teachers had positive attitudes toward cultural differences and culturally relevant teaching techniques but lacked confidence in their knowledge of these differences and their abilities to address students' individual needs.

International Worldview

Coulby (2006) argues that an important component of nearly all intercultural education includes demographic movement and its creative forces such as economic or political events. Related to this movement is intergroup differentiation, which includes aspects of inequality such as ethnic cleansing and neocolonialism that must be examined through a global lens. Notes the author, "To the extent to which the context of globalization is overlooked, intercultural education will have de-politicized its subject matter, and, despite its progressive normative position it will ill-serve both its subjects and wider social understanding" (p. 249). Intercultural educators must be taught to understand wider contexts, "a more complex conceptualization" with "an insistence that the complexity of the social context be explored and clarified as a precursor to meaningful research; and an awareness that education is an international activity and neither its pupils nor its subject matter can be constrained by familiar boundaries" (p. 254).

In our view, the importance of an international worldview is a critical component of intercultural competence for educators that must not be overlooked. This, too, was the only aspect of intercultural competence that the leading intercultural experts in the Deardorff (2006) study were in total agreement upon. This aspect is certainly lacking in the accounts of the intercultural education movement of the early 20th century, as described in the *Handbook of Research on Multicultural Education* (J. A. Banks & Banks, 2004). Unfortunately, teacher education in the 21st century has not come nearly as far as one might hope. For example, in the current edition of the AERA Report on Research and Teacher Education, the editors (Cochran-Smith & Zeichner, 2005) state that the review of research was intended to examine what is known about how preservice teachers are prepared to work with diverse students. Unfortunately, this report makes absolutely no mention of intercultural education or intercultural competency, and international topics are referenced only twice. Rather, much attention is given to diversity.

To us, both the words *diversity* and *multicultural education* have a particularly Western, U.S.-based connotation. While one may argue that U.S. educators should certainly concern themselves with the populations within their own borders, this should not be at the risk of marginalizing the international context. One very dangerous outcome of such a stance is a normalization of U.S. educational approaches, ignoring the valuable curricular and pedagogical practices that may occur in teacher preparation and development efforts in other regions of the world.

Pouring a New Foundation: Ensuring the Development of Intercultural Competence

Socialization refers to the process by which people acquire the necessary attitudes, values, and behaviors needed to be a successful member of any group. Young people today are entering an increasingly interconnected society, which demands they acquire intercultural competence so they not only understand the complexity of global problems but also develop the ability to collaborate with others in their resolution. Schooling as we know it today is not socializing students sufficiently for a global context, in part because many say it is beyond the scope of U.S. educational standards. This is especially ironic given that as a nation, the United States continues to be criticized that lackluster educational results in many areas limit our global economic competitiveness. Given this, attention to the intercultural dimension of learning should become the essential fourth "R" in education—Reading, 'Riting, 'Rithmetic, and, we might propose, Relations.

Sleeter (2007) identifies changes she believes are needed to prepare teachers to be more culturally competent. Recruiting and retaining more diverse teachers, especially teachers of color and older adults from urban contexts, she suggests, is a step in the right direction. However, she warns that "it may be that the greatest redesign barrier is not a lack of potential teachers of color but rather the institutionalized ways of higher education, as well as faculty who do not see compelling reasons for change" (p. 189).

This supports the notion that if we are truly serious about preparing teachers and, subsequently, the pupils in their charge to be more interculturally competent, then we must understand the process of culture learning. Developing intercultural sensitivity and competence is not achieved in the cognitive-only approach to learning that is common in most classrooms today, be it with children or preservice teachers. Culture learning develops only with attention to experience and the affective domain that is then linked to cognition. It is through impactful experiences, where people are challenged to make sense of their new environment and accommodate to the difference, where they ultimately gain more sophisticated knowledge about other people and a feeling of being at home in a new context.

Sleeter (2007) goes on to suggest that teachers should engage in immersion experiences in a cultural context other than their own as an essential step in the development of intercultural competence. Merryfield's (2000) analysis of 80 teacher educators recognized by their peers for their success in preparing teachers in both multicultural and global education supports this notion. Merryfield discovered significant differences between the experiences of people of color and European Americans that reflect the importance of impactful, experiential learning. Most American teachers of color have a double consciousness (DuBois, 1903/1989). That is, many have grown up conscious of both their own primary culture as well as having experienced discrimination and the status of being an outsider by encountering a society characterized by White privilege and racism. Middle-class White teacher educators who are effective at teaching for diversity had their most profound and impactful experiences while living outside their own country. These teachers had thus encountered discrimination and exclusion by being an outsider within another cultural context, and they had found ways to bring this to their teaching.

As Merryfield's (2000) study suggests, those who leave the comfort of their home society for an extended period of time come to understand what it is like to live outside the mainstream and to be perceived as "the Other." It is the impactful international experience that has facilitated these mainstream European American teachers to become more ethnorelative in their understanding of others, more skilled at crossing cultures, and committed to bringing about change through their work. A significant international experience thus leads to new, firsthand understandings of what it means to be marginalized, to be a victim of stereotypes and prejudice, and how this might affect people. Immersion experiences enable prospective teachers to learn from adults in those communities and then to shape curriculum, pedagogy, and interactions in ways that build on cultural assets.

While it has always been difficult to integrate significant international and intercultural experiences in the preparation of teachers due to tightly controlled state-mandated teacher education curricula, a number of international and intercultural networks and bilateral relationships have been designed to enable teacher education students to complete their student teaching requirements immersed in other cultural settings (Cushner & Brennan, 2007). A series of ongoing studies have documented the profound personal and professional impact such an experience can have on increasing self-efficacy, challenging ideas about self and others, and on global mindedness—all essential to the development of intercultural competence (Cushner & Mahon, 2002; Quezada & Alfaro, 2007; Stachowski, 2007).

Likewise, effective school/community partnerships have long been viewed as critical for the success of students from diverse cultural or linguistic backgrounds (Ford, 2002). This is supported by studies designed to determine what teachers see as their biggest challenges. Hoover-Dempsey, Walker, Jones, and Reed (2002) report that 20% of new teachers identify classroom discipline, and 31% admitted that parent communication and involvement to be among their greatest challenges. Teachers also report that uncertainty regarding communication with families of diverse backgrounds was a significant barrier to effective involvement. Further compounding the issue is the perception on the part of parents from diverse backgrounds of the school as unwelcoming, especially when "the cultural/linguistic/ethnic/class makeup of school personnel does not mimic that of the student body" (National School Public Relations Association, 2006, p. 13). Finally, as the research on school discipline referenced previously in this chapter has shown, there are serious issues with institutional approaches to understanding the behaviors of students of color.

Conclusion

In conclusion, it would appear that future directions for teacher education and development should place intercultural competence at the foundation of this work, both in terms of its process and content dimensions in both the domestic as well as international domains. Broadening teachers' understanding and ability to think, communicate, and interact in culturally different ways and from multiple perspectives, as discussed throughout this chapter, will be no easy task, especially given what we know both about culture learning as well as personal and institutional resistance to change. Nevertheless, this is an aspect of all people's education which can no longer be ignored.

References

Au, K., & Kawakami, A. (1994). Cultural congruence in instruction. In E. Hollins & W. Hayman (Eds.), *Teaching diverse populations: Formulating a knowledge base* (pp. 5–24). Albany: State University of New York Press.

Banks, C. A. M. (2004). Intercultural and intergroup education, 1929–1959: Linking schools and communities. In J. A. Banks & C. A. McGee Banks (Eds.), *Handbook of research on multicultural education* (2nd ed., pp. 753–769). San Francisco: Jossey-Bass.

Banks, J. A. (2004a). Introduction. In J. A. Banks & C. A. McGee Banks (Eds.), *Handbook of research on multicultural education* (2nd ed., pp. xi–xiv). San Francisco: Jossey-Bass.

Banks, J. A. (2004b). Multicultural education: Historical development, dimensions, and practice. In J. A. Banks & C. A. McGee Banks (Eds.), *Handbook of research on multicultural education* (2nd ed., pp. 3–29). San Francisco: Jossey-Bass.

Banks, J. A. (2004c). Race, knowledge construction, and education in the United States: Lessons from history. In J. A. Banks & C. A. McGee Banks (Eds.), *Handbook of research on multicultural education* (2nd ed., pp. 228–239). San Francisco: Jossey-Bass.

Banks, J. A., & Banks, C. A. M. (2004). *Handbook of research on multicultural education* (2nd ed.). San Francisco: Jossey-Bass.

Brislin, R. W. (2000). *Understanding culture's influence on behavior.* Fort Worth, TX: Harcourt Brace.

Cochran-Smith, M., & Zeichner, K. M. (Eds.). (2005). *Studying teacher education: The report of the AERA panel on research and teacher education.* Mahwah, NJ: Lawrence Erlbaum.

Coulby, D. (2006). Intercultural education: Theory and practice. *Intercultural Education, 17*(3), 245–257.

Cushner, K. (1998). *International perspectives on intercultural education.* Lanham, MD: Lawrence Erlbaum.

Cushner, K., & Brennan, S. (Eds.). (2007). *Intercultural student teaching: A bridge to global competence.* Lanham, MD: Rowman & Littlefield.

Cushner, K., & Mahon, J. (2002). Overseas student teaching: Affecting personal, professional and global competencies in an age of globalization. *Journal of International Studies in Education, 6*(2), 44–58.

Cushner, K., McClelland, A., & Safford, P. (2009). *Human diversity in education: An integrative approach* (6th ed.). Boston: McGraw-Hill.

Davis, J. E., & Jordan, W. J. (1994). The experience of school context, structure, and experiences on African American males in middle and high schools. *Journal of Negro Education, 63*, 570–587.

Deardorff, D. K. (2006). Identification and assessment of intercultural competence as a student outcome of internationalization. *Journal of Studies in International Education, 10*, 241–266.

Detweiler, R. A. (1978). Culture, category width and attributions: A model-building approach to the reasons of cultural effects. *Journal of Cross-Cultural Psychology, 9*, 259–284.

Dewey, J. (1902). *The child and the curriculum.* Boston: Heath.

Dubois, W. E. B. (1989). *The souls of Black folks.* New York: Bantam. (Originally published in 1903)

Evans, E. D., Torrey, C. C., & Newton, S. D. (1997). Multicultural education requirements in teacher certification: A national survey. *Multicultural Education, 4*(3), 9–11.

Ford, B. A. (2002). African American community resources: Essential educational enhancers for African American children and youth. In F. E. Obikar & B. A. Ford (Eds.), *Creating successful learning environments for African American exceptional learners* (pp. 159–174). Thousand Oaks, CA: Corwin.

Gardner, H. (1993). *Multiple intelligence: The theory in practice.* New York: Basic Books.

Gay, G. (2000). *Culturally responsive teaching: Theory, research, and practice.* New York: Teachers College Press.

Gay, G. (2006). Connections between classroom management and culturally responsive teaching. In C. M. Evertson & C. S. Weinstein (Eds.), *The handbook of classroom management: Research, practice, and contemporary issues* (pp. 343–370). Mahwah, NJ: Lawrence Erlbaum.

Goleman, D. (1995). *Emotional intelligence.* New York: Bantam/Doubleday/Dell.

Gordon, R., Della Pinna, L., & Keleher, T. (2000). *Facing the consequences: An examination of racial discrimination in U.S. public schools.* Oakland, CA: Applied Research Center.

Grossman, D., & Yuen, C. (2006). Beyond the rhetoric: A study of the intercultural sensitivity of Hong Kong Secondary School Teachers. *Pacific Asian Education, 18*(1), 70–87.

Hammer, M., & Bennett, M. J. (2003). Measuring intercultural sensitivity: The Intercultural Development Inventory. *International Journal of Intercultural Relations, 27*, 403–419.

Hanvey, R. G. (1975). *An attainable global perspective.* New York: New York Center for War/Peace Studies.

Hilliard, A. G. (1998). *The reawakening of the African American mind.* Gainesville, FL: Makare.

Hoover-Dempsey, K. V., Walker, J. M., Jones, K. P., & Reed, R. P. (2002). Teachers involving parents: An in-service teacher education program for enhancing parental involvement. *Teaching and Teacher Education, 18*, 843–867.

Interstate New Teachers Association Support Consortium. (2007). *Standards*. Washington, DC: Author.

Kealey, D. J. (1996). The challenge of international personnel selection. In D. Landis & R. S. Bhagat (Eds.), *Handbook of intercultural training* (2nd ed., pp. 81–105). Thousand Oaks, CA: Sage.

Ladson-Billings, G. (1994). *Dreamkeepers: Successful teachers of African-American children*. San Francisco: Jossey-Bass.

Lonner, W. J., & Hayes, S. A. (2004). Understanding the cognitive and social aspects of intercultural competence. In R. J. Sternberg & E. L. Grigorenko (Eds.), *Culture and competence: Contexts of life success* (pp. 89–110). Washington, DC: American Psychological Association.

Mahon, J. (2003). *Intercultural sensitivity development among practicing teachers: Life history perspectives*. Doctoral dissertation, Kent State University.

Mahon, J. (2006). Under the invisibility cloak: Teacher understanding of cultural difference. *Intercultural Education, 17,* 391–405.

McCarthy, J., & Benally, J. (2003). Classroom management in a Navajo middle school. *Theory Into Practice, 42,* 296–304.

McCrae, R. M., Costa, P. T., del Pilar, G. H., Rolland, J. P., & Parker, W. D. (1998). Cross-cultural assessment and the five-factor model: The Revised NEO Personality Inventory. *Journal of Cross-Cultural Psychology, 29,* 171–188.

McDermott, R. (1987). Achieving school failure: An anthropological approach to illiteracy and social stratification. In G. D. Spindler (Ed.), *Education and cultural process: Anthropological approaches* (2nd ed., pp. 173–209). Prospect Heights, IL: Waveland.

Merryfield, M. M. (1996). *Making connections between multicultural and global education: Educators and teacher education programs*. Washington, DC: American Association of Colleges of Teacher Education.

Merryfield, M. M. (2000). Why aren't teachers being prepared to teach for diversity, equity, and global interconnectedness? A study of lived experiences in the making of multicultural and global educators. *Teaching and Teacher Education, 16,* 429–443.

Miller, M., Strosnider, R., & Dooley, E. (2000). States' requirements for teachers' preparation for diversity. *Multicultural Education, 8*(2), 15–18.

Morrier, M., Irving, M. A., Dandy, E., Dmitriyev, G., & Ukeje, I. C. (2007). Teaching and learning within and across cultures: Educators' requirements across the United States. *Multicultural Education, 14*(3), 32–40.

National Center for Education Statistics. (2002). *Selected characteristics of students, teachers, parent participation, and programs and services in traditional public and public charter elementary and secondary schools: 1999–2002*. Retrieved January 21, 2008, from http://www.nces.gov

National Council for the Accreditation of Teacher Education. (2001). *Standards, procedures, policies for the accreditation of professional education units*. Washington, DC: Author.

National Council for the Accreditation of Teacher Education. (2008a). *NCATE unit standards revisions*. Washington, DC: Author. Retrieved February 2, 2008, from http://www.ncate.org/documents/standards/SummaryMajorChangesUnitStd.pdf

National Council for the Accreditation of Teacher Education. (2008b). *Standards, procedures, policies for the accreditation of professional education units*. Washington, DC: Author.

National School Public Relations Association. (2006). *How strong communication contributes to student and school success: Parent and family involvement*. Retrieved March 30, 2008, from http://www.nspra.org/files/docs/Strong_Communication_Students_School_Success.pdf

Pappamihiel, N. E. (2004). Hugs and smiles: Demonstrating caring in a multicultural early childhood classroom. *Early Child Development & Care, 174,* 539–548.

Parajes, F. (2003). Self-efficacy beliefs, motivation, and achievement in writing: A review of the literature. *Reading and Writing Quarterly, 19,* 139–158.

Pedersen, P. (1997, November). *Intercultural sensitivity and the early adolescent*. Paper presented at the meeting of the 77th Conference of the National Council for the Social Studies, Cincinnati, OH.

Peterman, F. P. (Ed.). (2005). *Designing performance assessment systems for urban teacher preparation*. Mahwah, NJ: Lawrence Erlbaum.

Piaget, J. (1957). John Amos Comenius. *Prospects, 23*(1–2), 173–196. Retrieved January 21, 2008, from http://www.ibe.unesco.org/publications/ThinkersPdf/comeniuse.PDF

Powell, R. G., & Caseau, D. (2004). *Classroom communication and diversity: Enhancing instructional practice*. Mahwah, NJ: Lawrence Erlbaum.

Quezada, R. L., & Alfaro, C. (2007). Developing biliteracy teachers: Moving toward cultural and linguistic global competence in teacher education. In K. Cushner & S. Brennan (Eds.), *Intercultural student teaching: A bridge to global competence* (pp. 123–158). Lanham, MD: Rowman & Littlefield.

Sadler, J. E. (1969). *Comenius*. London: Collier-MacMillian.

Sheets, R. A. (1995). *Students and teacher perception of disciplinary conflicts in culturally pluralistic classrooms*. Unpublished doctoral dissertation, University of Washington, Seattle.

Sheets, R. A. (1996). Urban classroom conflict: Student-teacher perception: Ethnic integrity, solidarity, and resistance. *The Urban Review, 28*(2), 165–183.

Shen, J., Wegenke, G. L., & Cooley, V. E. (2003). Has the public teaching force become more diversified? *Educational Horizons, 81*(3), 112–118.

Siwatu, K. O. (2007). Preservice teachers' culturally responsive teaching self-efficacy and outcome expectancy beliefs. *Teaching and Teacher Education, 23*, 1086–1011.

Sleeter, C. (2007). Preparing teachers for multiracial and underserved schools. In E. Frankenberg & G. Orfield (Eds.), *Lessons in integration: Realizing the promise of racial diversity in American schools* (pp. 171–190). Charlottesville: University of Virginia Press.

Stachowski, L. L. (2007). A world of possibilities within the United States: Integrating meaningful domestic intercultural teaching experiences into teacher education. In K. Cushner & S. Brennan (Eds.), *Intercultural student teaching: A bridge to global competence* (pp. 88–122). Lanham, MD: Rowman & Littlefield.

Sternberg, R. J. (1988). A triarchic view of intelligence in cross-cultural perspective. In S. H. Irvine & J. W. Berry (Eds.), *Human abilities in cultural context* (pp. 60–85). Cambridge, England: Cambridge University Press.

Stomfay-Stitz, A. M. (1993). *Peace education in America, 1928–1990: Sourcebook for education and research*. Metuchen, NJ: Scarecrow Press.

Straffon, D. A. (2003). Assessing the intercultural sensitivity of high school students attending an international school. *International Journal of Intercultural Relations, 27*, 487–501.

Taba, H., Brady, E., & Robinson, J. (1952). *Intergroup education in public schools*. Washington, DC: American Council on Education.

Triandis, H. C. (1972). *The analysis of subjective culture*. New York: John Wiley.

Tyler, F. B. (2001). *Cultures, communities, competence, and change*. New York: Kluwer Academic/Plenum.

Whitfield, P., Klug, B. J., & Whitney, P. (2007). 'Situative cognition': Barrier to teaching across cultures. *Intercultural Education, 18*, 259–264.

Witkin, H. A., Dyk, R. B., Faterson, H. F., Goodenough, D. R., & Karp, S. A. (1962). *Psychological differentiation*. New York: John Wiley.

Wu, S. C., Pink, W. T., Crain, R. L., & Moles, O. (1982). Student suspensions: A critical reappraisal. *The Urban Review, 14*, 245–303.

Zeichner, K. (2003). The adequacies and inadequacies of three current strategies to recruit, prepare, and retain the best teachers for all students. *Teachers College Record, 105*, 490–519.

CHAPTER 18

Intercultural Competence in Foreign Languages

The Intercultural Speaker and the Pedagogy of Foreign Language Education

Michael Byram

The purpose of this chapter is to explain the notion of the intercultural speaker, its origins and applications within foreign language education and beyond. It is a concept that has been developed in the field of foreign language education, where there is a substantial history of linking the teaching of language per se with knowledge about one or more countries where the language is spoken. The focus on "knowing that" widened to include "knowing how" (Ryle, 1949)—knowing about a country and knowing how to interact with people with different ways of thinking, believing, and behaving—more or less in parallel with the introduction of the aims of communicative language teaching. The challenge to imitating the native speaker as a basis for teaching linguistic competence is also paralleled by the introduction of the concept of the intercultural speaker.

The phrase *intercultural speaker* was coined by Byram and Zarate in a working paper written for a group preparing what eventually became the *Common European Framework of Reference for Languages* of the Council of Europe (2001). In that same paper, Byram and Zarate (1994, 1997) attempted to refine what in Council of Europe papers (e.g., van Ek, 1986) was called *sociocultural competence* by defining four *savoirs,* four dimensions of knowledge, skills, and attitudes. In 1997, Byram published a monograph that built on but modified substantially the Council of Europe paper, and his book, *Teaching and Assessing Intercultural Communicative Competence,* is the main starting point for this chapter. During this process, the coining of the phrase *intercultural speaker* was accompanied by the introduction of the phrase *intercultural competence* within the field of foreign language education and then, in the monograph, *intercultural communicative competence.*

In parallel with this work, there were publications by Kramsch (1993) in the United States, Bredella (1992) in Germany, and Risager (1993) in Denmark—all interested in foreign languages—and, under the label *British (cultural) studies,* further work in several European countries on relating English-language teaching to teaching about Britain. A much fuller and more detailed account of the evolution of a cultural dimension in language teaching has now been presented in authoritative form by Risager (2006, 2007). In the past decade or more, what is often referred to as a model of intercultural competence presented by Byram in 1997 has been widely cited and, less widely, critically evaluated.

This chapter describes and explains that model of intercultural (communicative) competence, the uses it has served, and the critiques it has attracted.

Intercultural Competence in Foreign Language Teaching

The model in question is firmly based in foreign language teaching, as the title of the monograph indicates, and as is stated at the beginning of the first chapter. It attempts to build on what had, by the mid-1990s, become accepted theory of "the communicative approach" in North America and in Western Europe (Savignon, 1997, 2000), even if classroom practice did not always reflect the theory. It deliberately referred to the Council of Europe, whose work was already influential and became even more so when the *Common European Framework of Reference for Languages* was published in 2001.

The model developed by Byram attempted to include nonverbal communication while recognizing that many teachers would not see the need or feel qualified to teach nonverbal communication. It drew on theory other than applied linguistics and sociolinguistics, which had hitherto dominated theorizing about language teaching and had interpreted Hymes's definition of communicative competence in a way that underplayed the cultural situatedness of communicative competence (Byram, 1997, p. 8). Those other theories included social identity theory (Tajfel, 1981); cross-cultural communication (Gudykunst, 1994), which referred rarely, if at all, to language competence; and Bourdieu's theory of social and cultural capital (Bourdieu, 1990).

The model is based on the explicit assumption that language teaching needs to focus on one or more countries where the language is spoken. It has been criticized for this, as we will discuss later in the chapter.

The main development in the 1997 model from the work of Byram and Zarate (1994) is an emphasis on the pedagogical purposes of foreign language teaching in obligatory education. This is the "fifth *savoir,*" referred to in English as *critical cultural awareness* and in French as *savoir s'engager.* It is compared to the purposes of *politische Bildung* in the (West) German educational tradition, with its aim of encouraging learners to reflect critically on the values, beliefs, and behaviors of their own society. In foreign language education, this is done through a comparative study of other societies. Furthermore, substantial changes were made to definitions of other *savoirs;* only *savoir être* and *savoir apprendre* remained unchanged. The two models are different.

The definition of *savoir s'engager* is "an ability to evaluate critically and, on the basis of explicit criteria, perspectives, practices and products in one's own and other cultures and countries." This definition involves a number of assumptions, but its main focus on "ability" to realize some activity is part of defining intercultural competence as abilities, knowledge, and dispositions. The choice of the phrase *savoir s'engager,* with connotations of political engagement, was deliberate, and in more

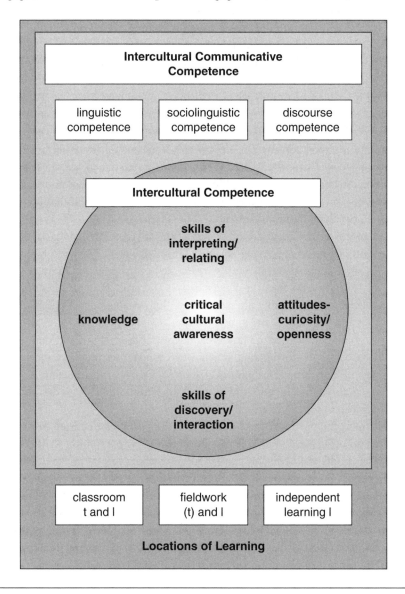

Figure 18.1 A Model of Intercultural Communicative Competence

recent writings, the relationship of intercultural competence to "education for intercultural citizenship" has been developed further (Byram, 2008).

In the explanation of "explicit criteria," it is made clear that the intercultural speaker has a "rational and explicit standpoint" from which to evaluate. This implies that the intercultural speaker has a morality that is consciously brought to bear on the perspectives, practices, and products and that the morality is founded in rationality in the Kantian tradition. It is also argued that a human rights morality is one which teachers might comfortably adopt, for both are related, as Wringe (2007, p. 56) shows. The position taken implicitly excludes other options for a moral basis, including religion. Wringe's exposition of moral education explains other options, although he too argues against an exclusively religious basis as a defensible option. He argues that moral education should not lead to learners adopting one option only but that the outcomes of moral education should be an ability to deal with moral dilemmas through reasoning, which draws on all of the possible options presented by moral philosophers (Wringe, 2007, pp. 105–106). This argument shows that the reference to an explicit rational standpoint in *savoir s'engager* is too narrow. Reasoning may lead a person to make an evaluation not according to criteria of rationality but of "maximizing happiness" or "communitarianism" or "caring," to use Wringe's keywords—and to acting accordingly.

There is a further problem in consistency in the definition of *savoir s'engager*. In a more detailed exposition (Byram, 1997, p. 64), some possible standpoints or "ideological perspectives" are listed. Here there is again reference to human rights but also to religious bases for morality; Moslem and Christian are mentioned. Wringe (2007, pp. 19–24) has demonstrated convincingly that religious standpoints are not adequate for making moral judgments.

In the more detailed formulation of the *savoirs* (Byram, 1997, chap. 3), particular attention is paid to specifying an intercultural speaker's behavior, knowledge, and skills: attitudes (*savoir être*), with phrases such as "is interested in other's experience" or "actively seeks the other's perspectives and evaluations of phenomenon," and knowledge (*savoirs*), using phrases such as "knows about conventions of communication and interaction" or "knows the events and their emblems . . . which are markers of national identity" or "knows about social distinctions and their principal markers." Skills are formulated largely with "can-do" terminology such as "can use a range of questioning techniques" (skills of discover and interaction—*savoir apprendre/faire*) or "can identify causes of misunderstanding . . . and dysfunctions" (skills of interpreting and relating—*savoir comprendre*).

In all cases, the purpose is to specify "objectives" that can be used in planning teaching and assessment, and it is this purpose that is paramount in the monograph. The model shall help foreign language teachers to plan more deliberately than they often do, to include intercultural competence in their pedagogical aims. This focus on planning originated in research showing that teachers intend to include a cultural dimension but do so only intermittently and in unplanned ways (Byram, Esarte-Sarries, & Taylor, 1991). As was confirmed later (Byram & Risager, 1999), this can be attributed to lack of attention to the cultural dimension in teacher training, and the close specification of objectives, which is part of the model, provides a basis for training teachers to plan and to develop an integrated didactics of intercultural linguistic competences. Such integration is implied in the term *intercultural communicative competence* and in the model that presents linguistic and intercultural competences together.

The disposition of the competences within the whole image represents their relationships: critical cultural awareness/*savoir s'engager* in the center symbolizes its significance as the element, which ensures that language teaching has an educational function. The model does not, however, represent links of dependency or interdependency among the competences; it is a "list model," not a "structural model" (Bolten, in Rathje, 2007).

A Prescriptive "Model" of Intercultural Competence and Its Uses

Models can represent ideals toward which we strive—to be a "model pupil," for example. They can also represent reality in a schematized and simplified way, which helps us to see the essence of what is being proposed. By proposing the "intercultural speaker" as a substitute for the native speaker, the model implies a prescription of what a learner needs to strive toward. However, by recognizing that only some characteristics of an intercultural speaker are included—omitting any discussion of personality types, for example—it is a simplification of the complexity of acting as an intercultural person; it identifies, from a conceptual analysis, some of the competences needed in multicultural and international encounters. The model is presented descriptively; the abilities of intercultural speakers and what they can do in intercultural interaction are listed and specified in detail. However, the focus on teaching and assessing, as well as on the use of these descriptions in the formulation of teaching objectives, makes the model prescriptive. It prescribes what teachers should attempt to develop in their learners and, with reference to *savoir s'engager* or *critical cultural awareness,* prescribes a moral position on evaluation and judgment.

Because the model is a schematization and does not specify in every detail an intercultural speaker, the prescription of how learners should develop is limited. The specifications of what an intercultural speaker can do and what attitudes and knowledge they need are detailed, but they are not exhaustive. This means that the ideal is not defined, the perfect exemplar, and there is no definition of levels or degrees of ability, knowledge, and attitudes, of stages on the way to perfection. Only a minimal "threshold" can be determined for a given context, and no general statement of a threshold level makes sense.

The model does not describe or prescribe relations among the subcompetences, neither within intercultural competence nor within the more complex model of intercultural communicative competence. It is not a psychological model of the interaction of subcompetences within or among individuals. Nor does it suggest a didactic ordering of which aspects of which competences should be taught prior to others.

In short, the model describes the main characteristics of intercultural competence in some detail. It places these within a more complex model of intercultural communicative competence. It is then proposed as a prescriptive model for the guidance of teaching and assessment. It includes a view of the moral position teachers might teach, based on a combination of "rights" and "rationality," and does so because it is a model to be used in compulsory schooling whose purpose is the liberal education of (young) people.

The model can also be used analytically, to determine the presence or absence of subcompetences, and thence to predict the success or failure of individuals in intercultural interaction. Such prediction, however, is likely to be limited in accuracy since the model does not (claim to) include all the characteristics of intercultural speakers. Other models, also partial in their reach, can be used to complement description and prediction—or, indeed, prescription—for situations that are more complex than can be handled in the ordinary classroom (Guo, 2007).

The Intercultural Speaker/Mediator and "Intercultural Citizenship"

The original coining of the phrase *intercultural speaker* was a deliberate attempt to distance the notion of intercultural competence from the cultural competences of a native speaker. It does not have any implications for or against the native speaker as a model for linguistic competences. The phrase *intercultural speaker* was not taken into the *Common European Framework of Reference* (*CEFR*), although there are many references to intercultural skills, awareness, and competence and one reference to "intercultural personality." The original model, proposed by Byram and Zarate (1994), was much amended in the *Common European Framework of Reference,* even though the terminology of four *savoirs* was adopted. Furthermore, although Byram (1997) is cited in the references of the *CEFR,* there is no discernible influence. In particular, there is no reference to *savoir s'engager,* which is the crucial educational dimension of intercultural competence. This is perhaps because the *CEFR* does not relate only to obligatory schooling, and the introduction of an educational aim into other situations of language teaching and learning is less self-evident, although equally important. The *CEFR* thus presents a third "list" model substantially different from Byram and Zarate (1994) and from Byram (1997). Nonetheless, one element of the concept of "intercultural speaker"—namely, that of "mediation"—is present in the *CEFR* and is described as the ability to "act as an intermediary between interlocutors who are unable to understand each other directly—normally (but not exclusively) speakers of different languages" (Council of Europe, 2001, p. 87). Cultural intermediary roles would include "the ability to bring the culture of origin and the foreign culture into relation with each other" and, inter alia, "the capacity . . . to deal effectively with intercultural misunderstanding and conflict situations" (Council of Europe, 2001, pp. 104–105).

This emphasis on the role of mediator, including reference to conflict resolution, is not developed further in the *CEFR,* but Zarate's (2003) work has focused more on the language learner as someone "between"/*entre deux,* emblematic of the conditions of many people in postmodernity, whose identities and identifications are far less simple than those promoted by identification with nation-states (Zarate, 2003). This has sometimes led to the substitution of *intercultural mediator* for *intercultural speaker,* but *intercultural speaker* has the advantage of not reducing the planning, teaching, and assessing of objectives to only those that are necessary in mediation. Learners can use their competences in many other contexts—for example, in periods of residence in another country, in interactions with people of other social groups in their own country, and in their daily experience of hybridity of cultures, which are not simply a product of postmodernity, as Le Page and Tabouret-Keller (1985) have shown.

Intercultural speaker can thus be used in a minimalist way simply to refer to someone who has some or all of the five *savoirs* of intercultural competence to some degree. It emphasizes the differences from the cultural competences of a native speaker. It reminds teachers and learners of the educational aims and objectives of foreign language teaching. It does not have any implications for the psychology of the individual or his or her identification with any specific roles or social groups. It can also be interpreted in a more complex way and linked to the concept of intercultural citizenship. This is a further development of the central concept of critical cultural awareness or *savoir s'engager.*

Education for citizenship is a recent formulation of what, in some countries, has long existed as *politische Bildung, éducation civique,* civics, and so on (for accounts of different traditions, see Alred, Byram, & Fleming, 2006). In this recent formulation, there is particular emphasis on *active citizenship*—a phrase used in the promotion of Education for Democratic Citizenship in Europe—or, in a phrase used in the United States, *civic participation* (Center for Civic Education, 1994–2003). Knowledge should be accompanied by action, and the competences described, to be used as objectives for teaching and learning, include skills of communication, mediation, and conflict resolution, which echo the description of the competences of the intercultural speaker.

The weakness in education for citizenship is the assumption that the focus of attention should be local and national, that political literacy means knowledge about processes and institutions within one's own school, neighborhood, and state/country, and activity should be focused at one or more of these levels. There is nothing surprising in this since education systems are usually national and were formed with the intention of creating identification with nation-states (Hobsbawm, 1992). But this is now a weakness in the contemporary world of global economies and international organizations, both civic and political.

The notion of intercultural citizenship and a description of the competences involved address this weakness and introduce into education for citizenship an international or supranational dimension. Combining a definition of intercultural competence with a definition of the competences of citizenship provides a set of teaching objectives that can guide cooperation across the curriculum and particularly allow foreign language teachers to include in their teaching aims the encouragement of international political activity among their learners (Byram, 2008).

Political activity does not necessarily lie in the narrowly political sphere but, more often, in action in civil society. Such action involves cooperation with others to pursue agreed purposes and presupposes the creation of a community of communication and action, permanent or temporary. Such communities of action may form within a state/country, bringing together people of different languages, ethnicities, and cultures, and this requires intercultural competence. Intercultural citizenship encouraged by foreign language teachers goes further and promotes the formation of communities of action beyond the boundaries of the state/country.

Such communities bring new perspectives—international groups for human rights, for environmental issues, for example—that do not exist within their national or subnational equivalents, but they also bring misunderstanding and conflicting traditions. Intercultural competence is a crucial consideration, as well as the competences required for political activity.

The notion of intercultural citizenship is thus not confined to foreign language teaching, but it does introduce into foreign language teaching a political education dimension in a more complex and specific way than is present in the notion of intercultural competence and *savoir s'engager*. It remains to be seen if this will awaken interest in or reflect the commitments of language teachers in practice in the way that intercultural competence has done.

Intercultural Competence in Practice

As Belz (2007), citing Bredella, points out, "Byram is one of the very few scholars . . . who extensively operationalizes the notion of intercultural competence in instructed foreign language learning" (p. 136). The application of the concept of the intercultural speaker is one way of meeting the demands now made of language teaching. As Davis, Cho, and Hagenson (2005) say,

> Achieving intercultural competence through intercultural learning is a major goal that complements the development of students' language competence. Many modern foreign language experts claim there are working definitions of intercultural learning, and related research has identified ongoing challenges in assessing learners' intercultural competence. Byram's model, which is widely used in foreign language classrooms, requires the development of the following. (p. 2)

Davis et al. (2005) are writing an introduction to articles on teacher training, where the requirement put on trainee teachers to make their objectives explicit should include intercultural competence objectives.

The requirement might be for each lesson planned and also for a course of study, as illustrated in Byram (1997, pp. 81–86). This is more likely to be within the reach of experienced teachers in in-service training, as illustrated by chapters in Byram, Nichols, and Stevens (2001). In one case, a teacher of English in Bulgaria planned a lesson on "Christmas and Christmas cards," which introduced students to the importance of investigating the habits of people in their own environment, analyzing two sets of Christmas cards—first Bulgarian, then British—and drawing conclusions about the way Christmas as a social phenomenon had changed after the fall of communism. They noticed that British cards are often sold to collect money for charities, that the need for public charities had not existed in communist times, and that charities are beginning to appear in Bulgaria with the appearance of poverty and the withdrawal of the state from financial support for the poor. From a simple lesson on Christmas cards—a common topic but addressed with specific objectives in mind—the lesson became an intellectually and emotionally challenging discussion of contemporary Bulgarian society, stimulated by comparison with British artifacts but focused on issues nearer to their own lives.

This example demonstrates the importance of explicit objectives concerning learning, which is more complex than acquisition of knowledge. Objectives allow the teacher to evaluate if she or he has achieved her or his intentions. Objectives should also provide the basis for assessment of the competences of learners, as is explained in Byram (1997, chap. 5), but this remains unexplored in the Bulgarian lessons, which is not surprising since the need to introduce assessment of intercultural competences into the assessment systems of educational systems is still under investigation. However, when educational planning turns to the definition of outcomes as the mode of evaluating and financing teaching (Hu, 2007), it is crucial to ensure that assessment includes objectives in intercultural competence, or teachers will not be able to justify spending time on the kinds of lesson just described.

Critiques and Developments

In a review of the concept of intercultural competence and its future, which deals with the current debate in the German-speaking world, Rathje (2007) speaks of a "dizzying amount of material" due to a lack of unity in definition of the term. On a broader front, Kramsch (personal communication, 2008) also sees a diversity and confusion in different uses of the term in different countries. Both may be hoping for the impossible—an agreed and definitive definition—because of the evolution of theories and because of the constant social changes that none but the most general theories can capture. Specific theories or models have the advantage of helping teachers to teach but also have the disadvantage that they must change to meet new societal circumstances and the new demands made of teaching as a consequence.

Rathje (2007) suggests four dimensions for evaluation of models:

> Goal: What is intercultural competence good for?
> Scope: is intercultural competence universal or culture-specific?
> Application: when is intercultural competence required?
> Foundation: what understanding of culture informs intercultural competence?
> (p. 255)

It is the fourth criterion, which, when applied to the model of intercultural (communicative) competence and the intercultural speaker, has led to most criticisms.

These criticisms have two aspects: that the concept of culture, which informs the model, implies a homogeneity and rigidity that do not exist; they have the limitations of structuralist approaches:

- They see the boundaries between cultures, between Self and Other, Native and Foreign, as much more *rigid* than they really are.

- They see cultures as much more homogeneous than they really are, especially in national terms (Kramsch, 1999, p. 43).

The emphasis on the critique of national culture is echoed, for example, by Belz (2007), who says it "does not adequately recognise or value national-internal diversity . . . or the evidence of ideologically or ethnically bound groups that span national borders . . . or who have no national borders" (p. 137). However, as Risager (2007, p. 124) points out, the focus on national cultures is a conscious strategy, not an effect of banal nationalism (Billig, 1995). It is a consequence of writing for a particular audience of language teachers working within a tradition that focuses on national cultures. The point is that *foreign* language teachers and their learners engage with one kind of otherness, expressed in the notion of national identity; other teachers may focus on interactions with other identities and identifications with the multitude of other groups that any individual forms.

The criticism of a national perspective can also include the claim that any account of a national culture essentializes and, by reduction, misrepresents the complexity of the phenomenon (Holliday, Hyde, & Kullman, 2004). This can be countered in three ways. First, the model of the intercultural speaker does not refer only to the elements that make up a national culture but, above all, to the ways in which its boundaries are marked (Barth, 1969) through notions of a national memory, a concept of the national space, and the interactions between the nation-state of the learner and the one or ones where the language they are learning is a national language. Second, the demonstration of the processes of "banal nationalism" (Billig, 1995) and the impact these have, as evident in young people's identification with their nation (Barrett, 2007), strongly suggests that national identity is a reality through which people interact with others. Third, anthropologists have provided convincing accounts of national cultures (Barley, 1989; Fox, 2004) or of dominant groups in a nation-state (Le Wita, 1994). Fox (2004) presents, after much fieldwork, a grammar of English behavior, a description of the rules, "the unofficial codes of conduct that cut across class, age, sex, region, sub-cultures and other social boundaries . . . rules that define our national identity and character" (p. 2).

The problem with taking a national culture and identity as the basis for teaching intercultural competences is not, therefore, the problem of essentializing or reductionism. The problem lies in the exclusive focus on one identity and the assumption that, in interaction in a foreign language, it is the only identity present. For it is evident that, although a national identity may be never forgotten, other identities are also present: professional, age, sex, ethnic, and so on. The exclusive focus is a didactic necessity, a need for simplification, particularly in the early stages of learning, a simplification common to all didactics. This is complemented by the focus on skills, which raise awareness of other groups and identities and the means to "discover" and "understand" them. The model thus has both specific and generic elements and a generative character that prepares learners for interaction with any social groups, not only national ones.

Conclusion

As indicated in the introduction, the aims and purposes of foreign language education have changed in the past few decades, with the much stronger emphasis on communication. Initially, this was conceived as the exchange of messages and information, but it was gradually realized that even in minimal exchanges of information, the presence of the people and their identities cannot and should not be ignored. The purpose of defining the competences of the intercultural speaker is, above all, to ensure that those teaching foreign languages can take this into consideration in a systematically planned approach to teaching and learning.

In short, this means that language teachers should plan their teaching to include objectives, materials, and methods that develop the specific elements of intercultural competence. The specification of competences encapsulated in the notion of the intercultural speaker provides a framework for doing this. Teachers of language need to become teachers of language and culture.

References

Alred, G., Byram, M., & Fleming, M. (2006). *Education for intercultural citizenship: Concepts and comparisons.* Clevedon, UK: Multilingual Matters.

Barley, N. (1989). *Native land.* Harmondsworth, UK: Penguin.

Barrett, M. (2007). *Children's knowledge, beliefs and feelings about nations and national groups.* Hove, UK: Psychology Press.

Barth, F. (1969). Introduction. In F. Barth (Ed.), *Ethnic groups and boundaries.* London: Allen & Unwin.

Belz, J. A. (2007). The development of intercultural communicative competence in telecollaborative partnerships. In R. O'Dowd (Ed.), *Online intercultural exchange: An introduction for foreign language teachers* (pp. 127–166). Clevedon, UK: Multilingual Matters.

Billig, M. (1995). *Banal nationalism.* London: Sage.

Bourdieu, P. (1990). *In other words: Essays towards a reflexive sociology.* Cambridge, UK: Polity.

Bredella, L. (1992). Towards a pedagogy of intercultural understanding. *Amerikastudien, 37,* 559–594.

Byram, M. (1997). *Teaching and assessing intercultural communicative competence.* Clevedon, UK: Multilingual Matters.

Byram, M. (2008). *From foreign language education to education for intercultural citizenship.* Clevedon, UK: Multilingual Matters.

Byram, M., Esarte-Sarries, V., & Taylor, S. (1991). *Cultural studies and language learning: A research report.* Clevedon, UK: Multilingual Matters.

Byram, M., Nichols, A., & Stevens, D. (2001). *Developing intercultural competence in practice.* Clevedon, UK: Multilingual Matters.

Byram, M., & Risager, K. (1999). *Language teachers, politics and cultures.* Clevedon, UK: Multilingual Matters.

Byram, M., & Zarate, G. (1994). *Definitions, objectives and assessment of socio-cultural competence* (CC-LANG (94) 1). Strasbourg, France: Council of Europe.

Byram, M., & Zarate, G. (1997). Defining and assessing intercultural competence: Some principles and proposals for the European context. *Language Teaching, 29,* 14–18.

Center for Civic Education. (1994–2003). *National standards for civics and government.* Calabasas, CA: Author.

Council of Europe. (2001). *Common European framework of reference for languages: Learning, teaching, assessment.* Cambridge, UK: Cambridge University Press.

Davis, N., Cho, M. O., & Hagenson, L. (2005). Editorial: Intercultural competence and the role of technology in teacher education. *Contemporary Issues in Technology and Teacher Education, 4*(4), 1–9.

Fox, K. (2004). *Watching the English.* London: Hodder.

Gudykunst, W. B. (1994). *Bridging differences: Effective intergroup communication* (2nd ed.) London: Sage.

Guo, Y. (2007). *Assessing the development of cultural sensitivity and intercultural competence: A case study of British university students in China.* Unpublished doctoral dissertation, University of Durham, England.

Hobsbawm, E. J. (1992). *Nations and nationalism since 1780.* Cambridge, UK: Cambridge University Press.

Holliday, A., Hyde, M., & Kullman, J. (2004). *Intercultural communication: An advanced resource book.* London: Routledge.

Hu, A. (2007, October). *Interkulturelle Kompetenz. Zum Problem der Dimensionierung und Evaluation einer Schlüsselkompetenz fremdsprachlichen Lernens* [Intercultural competence. On the problem of measurement and assessment of a key competence of foreign language learning]. Paper at the conference of the Deutsche Gesellschaft für Fremdsprachenforschung, Giessen, Germany.

Kramsch, C. (1993). *Context and culture in language teaching.* Oxford, UK: Oxford University Press.

Kramsch, C. (1999). Thirdness: The intercultural stance. In T. Vestergaard (Ed.), *Language, culture and identity* (pp. 53–89). Aalborg, Denmark: Aalborg University Press.

Le Page, R. B., & Tabouret-Keller, A. (1985). *Acts of identity: Creole-based approaches to language and ethnicity.* Cambridge, UK: Cambridge University Press.

Le Wita, B. (1994). *French bourgeois culture.* Cambridge, UK: Cambridge University Press.

Rathje, S. (2007). Intercultural competence: The status and future of a controversial concept. *Language and Intercultural Communication, 7,* 254–266.

Risager, K. (1993). Buy some petit souvenir aus Dänemark! Viden og bevidsthed om sprogmødet. In K. Risager, A. Holmen, & A. Trosborg (Eds.), *Sproglig mangfoldighed— on sproglig viden og bevidsthed* (pp. 30–42). Roskilde, Denmark: ADLA, RUC.

Risager, K. (2006). *Language and culture: Global flows and local complexity.* Clevedon, UK: Multilingual Matters.

Risager, K. (2007). *Language and culture pedagogy: From a national to a transnational paradigm.* Clevedon, UK: Multilingual Matters.

Ryle, G. (1949). *The concept of mind.* London: Hutchinson.

Savignon, S. J. (1997). *Communicative competence: Theory and classroom practice.* New York: McGraw-Hill.

Savignon, S. J. (2000). Communicative language teaching. In M. Byram (Ed.), *Routledge encyclopedia of language teaching and learning* (pp. 124–129). London: Routledge.

Tajfel, H. (1981). *Human groups and social categories.* Cambridge, UK: Cambridge University Press.

van Ek, J. (1986). *Objectives for foreign language learning: Vol. 1. Scope.* Strasbourg, France: Council of Europe.

Wringe, C. (2007). *Moral education: Beyond the teaching of right and wrong.* Dordrecht, The Netherlands: Springer.

Zarate, G. (2003). Identities and plurilingualism: Preconditions for the recognition of intercultural competences. In M. Byram (Ed.), *Intercultural competence* (pp. 85–118). Strasbourg, France: Council of Europe.

CHAPTER 19

Intercultural Competence in International Education Administration

Cultural Mentoring

International Education Professionals and the Development of Intercultural Competence

R. Michael Paige and Matthew L. Goode

This chapter examines the role of international education professionals in facilitating the development of intercultural competence among their students, a process we refer to as cultural mentoring. These professionals include study abroad advisers, language instructors, international student advisers, faculty members, and others who work closely with students involved in international educational exchange programs. We are particularly interested in the knowledge and skills international education professionals themselves need to serve as cultural mentors.

This topic has gained considerable currency at this time because there is a worldwide demand for the graduates of our education institutions to be "global citizens," "world minded," "globally engaged," and "interculturally competent." The response at the secondary and tertiary levels of education in many countries has been a noticeable increase in programs that provide students with intercultural learning opportunities (i.e., programs that introduce them to cultural diversity and cultures other than their own). Through exposure to cultural differences, it is hoped that these learners will acquire the skills, knowledge, attitudes, and more sophisticated worldviews regarding cultural difference that will enable them to communicate and interact effectively, in a mutually understood and supportive manner, with persons from other cultures.

The development of student intercultural competence is increasingly being viewed as an important role for international education professionals (J. M. Bennett, 2008, p. 13; Sunnygard, 2007, p. 168; Ziegler, 2006, p. 51). Savicki and Selby (2008) wrote, "As practitioner-educators, it is our responsibility to ensure that students derive as much benefit as possible from time abroad" (p. 349). O'Donovan and Mikelonis (2005, pp. 91–95) observed that higher education institutions are focusing efforts on internationalizing the curriculum on and off campus with the goal of increasing students' intercultural competence, a process that calls for interculturally competent faculty and staff to carry out these initiatives.

Recent research has shed light on these issues in two important ways. First, there is important new evidence from the Georgetown Consortium and *Maximizing Study Abroad* studies demonstrating that intercultural learning is significantly enhanced when it is facilitated (Paige, Cohen, & Shively, 2004; Vande Berg, 2007; Vande Berg, Balkcum, Scheid, & Whalen, 2004; Vande Berg & Paige, Chapter 25, this volume). The second set of studies, however, indicates that this type of cultural mentoring by international education professionals is uneven at best and often nonexistent (Cohen, Paige, Shively, Emert, & Hoff, 2005; Goode, 2008; Paige et al., 2004; Ziegler, 2006). These findings regarding both the importance and scarcity of cultural mentoring set the stage for our discussion of the international education professionals' role in the development of intercultural competence.

This chapter seeks to familiarize international education professionals with the concepts of intercultural learning, intercultural development, and intercultural competence. Our fundamental goal is to provide frames of reference that will lead eventually to more systematic and deliberate efforts to facilitate intercultural competence in the programs that we are offering our students. We examine the research literature, summarize relevant findings, and draw lessons from those studies as they pertain to intercultural development. The chapter then identifies and describes resources that are available to help international education professionals support intercultural learning. It concludes with a set of recommendations and practical suggestions for international education professionals.

Theoretical Framework

We draw on four conceptual models relevant to the development of intercultural competence: Paige's (1993a) model of intensity factors in intercultural experiences, Paige's (2006) model of culture learning, Deardorff's (2008; Chapters 1 & 28, this volume) model of intercultural competence, and M. J. Bennett's (1986, 1993) developmental model of intercultural sensitivity. Each of these has an important contribution to make regarding intercultural experiences, culture learning, and intercultural development. Each has implications for how cultural mentoring can be facilitated.

The Nature of Intercultural Experiences

In his analysis of intercultural experiences, Paige (1993a) identifies 10 situational variables and personal factors that can cause intense emotions and psychological stress. It is useful to examine these factors because cultural mentoring requires support for our students, especially at times when they are feeling strongly challenged by cultural differences. International education professionals are not only leading students in the quest for new subject matter knowledge, but are also being called to assist their students in adapting to and understanding the new culture.

The 10 factors are as follows:

1. *Cultural Differences.* Psychological stress is increased as the degree of cultural difference increases between the person's own and the other culture. Moreover, the more negatively the individual evaluates those cultural differences, the more stressful the intercultural experience will be. Predeparture exploration and regular on-site reflection of key cultural differences are a very important part of cultural mentoring.

2. *Ethnocentrism.* Ethnocentrism is a stress factor that expresses itself in two ways. First, ethnocentric persons, particularly those in denial and defense stages of intercultural sensitivity (M. J. Bennett, 1993), find intercultural experiences more threatening. Second, some cultural communities are themselves less accepting of outsiders. Sojourners in those more ethnocentric cultures can experience greater stress.

3. *Cultural Immersion.* The more immersed the person is in another culture, the greater the amount of stress. "Culture fatigue" is a common problem for persons who are deeply immersed in another culture, living and working with host culture persons, and speaking a language other than their own. Cultural mentoring can include opportunities for students to periodically take "time out" so as to regain their sense of cultural equilibrium, cultural reaffirmation, and renewal.

4. *Cultural Isolation.* When persons are isolated by geography and other circumstances from members of their own culture group, their intercultural experiences are far more stressful. It is even more important for them to have the chance to occasionally have contact, in person or via technology, with their culture group. Arranging these is part of the role of the cultural mentor.

5. *Language.* Persons unable to speak the language of the host culture will find the intercultural experience more stressful. Furthermore, the more essential language ability is to functioning in the target culture, the greater will be the stress of the experience. Lack of language skills can lead to social isolation and frustration.

6. *Prior Intercultural Experience.* Prior intercultural experience provides the opportunity to acquire generalizable culture learning, adaptation, and intercultural communication skills. Lacking these, persons with a limited intercultural background will likely experience more stress when exposed to cultural difference. The role of the cultural mentor here is to give students ideas and opportunities to experience and learn more about the host culture.

7. Expectations. There are two major expectation issues in intercultural work. One is that persons who have positive but unrealistic expectations about the new culture will feel a psychological letdown after a time. The other is that persons who have high expectations of themselves may feel that they are failing and hence will experience stress when they have the normal cultural adjustment problems. One aspect of cultural mentoring is exploring student expectations in advance so that the students have at least thought about their hopes and expectations of the sojourn.

8. Visibility and Invisibility. Persons who are physically different from members of the host culture may become the object of curiosity, unwanted attention, or discrimination. Stress can also occur when an important aspect of one's identity is invisible to members of the host culture (e.g., political views) or is concealed because it is not accepted in the host culture (e.g., sexual orientation). This is an important matter to discuss in advance when it is predictably the case that students will have these experiences.

9. Status. Status dislocations can take several forms. Students may feel they are not getting the respect they deserve or, alternatively, may feel they are receiving unearned recognition. In addition, they may not recognize the status markers and their importance in the host society. All of these issues can challenge learners and should be discussed before and during the program.

10. Power and Control. One of the most consistent research findings is that persons in cultures other than their own feel a loss of power and control over events compared to what they possessed at home. Psychological stress is associated with this loss of personal efficacy. One way to attenuate this phenomenon is to give learners lots of advice about how to get things done in the host culture. Knowing the simple things such as how to make an international phone call or use public transportation can be very helpful.

Understanding Paige's (1993a) stress factors provides international education professionals with insights relevant to the facilitation of culture learning before, during, and after intercultural programs. This information can also help with the matching of prospective international sojourners to programs that fit best with their intercultural readiness. Paige's intensity factors represent an important foundation for planning and designing intercultural programs, as well as for cultural mentoring itself.

The Dimensions of Intercultural Learning

Paige (2006, pp. 40–41) contributes another building block to our understanding of intercultural development with his conceptual map of five culture learning dimensions.

1. Learning About the Self as a Cultural Being. This refers to becoming aware of how the culture(s) we are raised in contribute to our individual identities, our preferred patterns of behavior, our values, and our ways of thinking. Cultural self-awareness is the foundation for intercultural competence because understanding one's own culture makes it easier to recognize other cultural practices, anticipate where cultural differences are greater, and thus be better prepared for those cultural challenges. Cultural mentoring can include engaging students in dialogues about their own cultures.

2. Learning About the Elements of Culture. To be effective culture learners, people must understand culture. M. J. Bennett (1998) distinguishes between *objective culture,* the institutions and products of a culture group, and *subjective culture,* "the learned and shared patterns of beliefs, behaviors, and values of groups of interacting people" (p. 3). For the purpose of this chapter, our focus is on the latter—that is, those patterns of everyday life that identify a group of people and organize their communication and interaction. One aspect of cultural mentoring is to prepare students to begin to see culture by knowing what it is and what to look for.

3. Culture-Specific Learning. One of the most common ways to think about culture is to consider the cultural elements of the host culture you will be visiting. Culture-specific learning thus refers to becoming knowledgeable about the elements of culture—both subjective and objective—in your specific cultural setting. This is the dimension of culture learning most commonly supported by international education professionals.

4. Culture-General Learning. Culture-general learning refers more broadly to the intercultural experiences that are common to all who visit another culture. The key concepts here are intercultural development, adjustment, adaptation, culture shock, acculturation, and assimilation. These are phenomena that occur whenever individuals move across cultural boundaries and interact with people from other cultures. Culture-general learning is central to the mentoring process because students predictably will be struggling with adaptation issues during their international programs. Helping them recognize cultural adaptation for what it is, a normal part of the intercultural experience, is very important.

5. Learning About Learning. The premise here is that more effective culture learners become more interculturally competent. By knowing and using specific strategies, such as learning from the media and interacting with host culture persons, learners become more familiar with the host culture. Effective culture learning includes testing and refining one's understanding of the culture (Crawford-Lange & Lange, 1984), participating in the culture, and reflecting on one's intercultural experiences (Kolb, 1984). Cultural mentors can integrate guided reflection into the overall learning process.

Paige's (2006) dimensions of culture learning provide us with the template for an intercultural curriculum that can be embedded in the experiences made available to our learners, the intercultural content associated with them, and the pedagogical processes of reflection that bring meaning to those experiences.

Process Model of Intercultural Competence

Based on the consensus of leading intercultural experts, Deardorff (2008) proposes a dynamic model of intercultural competence that identifies three key sets of elements: knowledge and comprehension, skills, and attitudes. Knowledge and comprehension consist of "cultural self-awareness, deep cultural knowledge, [and] sociolinguistic awareness" (p. 36). The skills relevant to intercultural competence include the ability "to listen, observe, evaluate. To analyze, interpret, and relate" (p. 36). The requisite attitudes include "Respect (valuing other cultures); Openness (withholding judgment); [and] Curiosity and Discovery (tolerating ambiguity and uncertainty)" (p. 36).

These interact in such a way as to support what Deardorff (2008) refers to as the "desired internal and external outcomes." The central internal outcome is having "a frame of reference shift, in which adaptability and flexibility play a central role" (p. 38). The external outcome of intercultural competence is "effective and appropriate communication and behavior in intercultural situations" (p. 39).

Deardorff (2008, pp. 42–46) specifies the cultural mentoring implications of her model for international education professionals in terms of preparation and support, skills development, reflection, meaningful intercultural interactions, and assessment. Her work suggests content areas and learning processes for international education professionals to incorporate into their programs.

Developmental Model of Intercultural Sensitivity

Milton Bennett (1986, 1993) has made a substantial contribution to the literature by conceptualizing intercultural competence as a developmental phenomenon. His core concept is intercultural sensitivity, which Bennett (1993) defines as "the way people construe cultural difference and . . . the varying kinds of experience that accompany these constructions" (p. 24).

These subjective, social constructions of reality constitute the foundation for intercultural competence. As M. J. Bennett (1993) states, "It is the construction of reality as increasingly capable of accommodating cultural difference that constitutes development" (p. 24).

The six stages of his developmental continuum are organized into two clusters: the ethnocentric stages, where the experience of one's own culture is central to reality, and the ethnorelative stages, where other cultures are viewed as viable in their own right and best understood in their own context. In ethnorelativism, the experience of one's own beliefs and behaviors comes to be seen as just one way in which reality can be organized among many other possibilities.

1. Denial. Denial is a stage of such limited understanding of cultural difference that other cultures do not really matter and one's own culture is experienced as the only authentic one. The beliefs, behaviors, and values that constitute one's culture are thus seen as unquestionably true and real. In denial, people tend to avoid cultural difference.

2a. Defense. Defense is characterized by polarization, where one's culture is viewed as being superior, others are inferior, and cultural difference is experienced as a threat. While there is clearly recognition of difference in the defense stage, it is accompanied by a negative evaluation and stereotyping of other cultures.

2b. Reversal. In reversal, an adopted culture is experienced as superior to one's primary socialization culture, and the adopted culture is idealized and viewed uncritically. Persons in reversal are overly critical of their primary culture.

3. Minimization. A shift to minimization occurs when the elements of one's own culture are experienced as universal. In this stage, there is the discovery of cultural similarities and common humanity. In minimization, cultural differences are seen as less important than similarities. Interaction with other cultures is possible by being anchored in the belief that our similarities are the most important aspect of our relationships.

4. Acceptance. Movement to acceptance is a major worldview shift away from ethnocentrism to ethnorelativism. Now, one's own culture is experienced as one of many equally complex and viable cultures. There is an understanding of what constitutes culture, a positive attitude toward cultural difference, and a growing curiosity about different cultural communities. Here, we see persons seeking out intercultural experiences such as study abroad.

5. Adaptation. Persons in adaptation can incorporate the relevant constructs from the other culture into their understanding of it; that is, they can cognitively shift their cultural frame of reference. They can also adapt their behavior to the cultural context in which they find themselves. Cognitive and behavioral adaptation are central to intercultural competence.

6. Integration. Integration means incorporating alternative cultures into one's worldview, moving fluently back and forth across cultures, and seeing culture as both a social and individual construction. Persons in integration often work in positions that require cultural mediating skills.

M. J. Bennett's (1986, 1993) model has been enormously influential for educators since it was first published. It can assist international education professionals in thinking about how very different the needs of learners are as a function of their intercultural sensitivity levels, what the most appropriate learning content and process might be at different stages of their intercultural development, when different types of learning experiences can be introduced, and how an overall program can be sequenced with respect to intercultural learning. In her discussion of study abroad programs, J. M. Bennett (2008) summarizes with the observation that "the Developmental Model of Intercultural Sensitivity . . . provides particularly useful grounding for the intentional balancing of optimal learning in stressful contexts" (p. 24). M. J. Bennett's developmental model is an especially important cultural mentoring tool for international education professionals.

Literature Review

In reviewing the literature around intercultural competence and international education professionals, we discovered a limited amount of research that investigated the role that intercultural competence does or should play in the work of international educators. One challenge is to make the link between the international dimension of education and intercultural competence, which some scholars have begun to explore. Cornwell and Stoddard (1999, pp. 35–41) called for a greater integration of international and intercultural education, and James (2005, pp. 324–326) presented the argument that intercultural education is actually a more accurate description of the work in which international educators should be engaged.

While intercultural competence is often listed as among the most important goals of international education programs, it may not be the case that all international education professionals share this mission. From the literature, three key themes emerge that help us map the somewhat complex relationship between international educators and intercultural competence: (a) intercultural concepts and theory, (b) intercultural training of international education professionals, and (c) a pedagogy for developing the intercultural competence of students.

Intercultural Concepts and Theory

If the pursuit of intercultural competence is to be a primary goal of international education, a broad understanding among international education professionals of the key intercultural concepts and theories is necessary. Deardorff (2008) wrote that "helping students acquire intercultural competence presumes that we know what the concept is" (p. 50). In the context of systems theory, Mestenhauser (2006) stated that "international education professionals . . . should have, like other professionals, a recognizable and codified body of knowledge" (p. 74).

The research literature suggests that such knowledge cannot be assumed. Savicki (2008), for example, reported that international education programs today are "taught by a variety of educators with a variety of experience in international education" (p. xiii). Ziegler (2006) found that international education professionals have varying degrees of knowledge regarding intercultural learning and competence and concluded that "the continued development of study abroad as a profession requires that workers in the field share a common knowledge base around culture learning, intercultural communication, and intercultural competence development that can be articulated, implemented, assessed, and subjected to outside scrutiny" (p. 170). Goode (2008), in his study of faculty members leading study abroad programs, found that there was a limited understanding of intercultural learning and how to facilitate it.

We are in agreement with Savicki (2008), who advocated for "a balance of theory, research, and application" in building the intercultural knowledge of international educators (p. xiv). Extending this logic, we feel it is incumbent upon international education professionals to become familiar with the concept of intercultural competence and to think of study abroad and related intercultural experiences as opportunities for intercultural development.

Intercultural Training of International Education Professionals

The literature acknowledges the importance of intercultural understanding and competence development for international education professionals, and the solution most commonly offered is a targeted intercultural training intervention. Paige (1993b) reported that "the training of trainers" (e.g., international educators) "requires learners to make a quantum leap from a basic understanding of intercultural experience and grasp of intercultural skills to a point where they can apply that foundation of knowledge and skills as intercultural educators" (p. 194).

One of the first steps toward development of intercultural competence in international education professionals is the cultivation of cultural self-awareness during the training process (Sunnygard, 2007; Ziegler, 2006). As mentioned earlier, Paige (2006) listed "Cultural Self-awareness" as one of five culture learning dimensions, and he states further (Paige, 1993b) that it is one of the key personal characteristics of a "competent" trainer (p. 192). In terms of study abroad program professionals, Ziegler (2006) determined that these international educators "should . . . be aware of their own developmental issues so that they can transparently meet the students' needs rather than let their own issues cloud their work with students" (p. 172). Regarding faculty directors of study abroad programs, Sunnygard (2007, p. 168) stated that these key international educators need to assess their own comfort level in other cultures to be most effective in their role.

Studies by Goode (2008) and Sunnygard (2007) have found that international education professionals sometimes do not receive adequate preparation to help foster cultural self-awareness and intercultural competence among their students. Rasch (2001, p. 13) reported that faculty preparation of any type for serving as study abroad directors was sorely lacking. Sunnygard (2007) stated that "less than half of faculty directors who direct short-term programs have had some preparation for teaching off-campus programs" (p. 167). Goode (2008, p. 166) found in his study of faculty director training at a U.S. liberal arts institution that even when this training does occur, it does not always include sufficient intercultural content. Ziegler (2006) stated that the international education professionals in her study had "level[s] of formal intercultural training [that] varie[d] considerably" (p. iv).

If intercultural training for international educators is being called for, how should these preparatory experiences be most successfully designed? Savicki (2008) argued for the importance of intercultural training for "teach-abroad faculty" before their first overseas assignment, to assist them with their own intercultural development as preparation for instructing students in an intercultural context. As a complement to this predeparture training, Deardorff (2008) reported that universities "are also beginning to move beyond solely pre-experience preparation and are building in ways to support . . . faculty learning during the time abroad and after their return" (p. 43). One of the challenges to the effective intercultural preparation of international educators is that this training agenda must compete with the more traditional emphasis on policies, finances, and liability issues (Sunnygard, 2007, p. 167). Goode (2008, p. 157) found that formal preparation focused more on the "logistical" and "Dean of Students" dimensions than on the intercultural dimension. In considering the literature on the intercultural preparation of international education professionals, there is clearly more that needs to be done to provide successful intercultural training for this specific population.

What would the content of intercultural training for international education professionals include? Paige (1993b) discusses "specific cognitive understandings, behavioral skills, and personal qualities" that will be relevant to the international education professional (p. 170). These include 32 distinct knowledge and skill areas related to (a) "Intercultural Phenomena," (b) "Intercultural Training," (c) "Trainer-Learner Issues," (d) "Ethical Issues," (e) "Culture-Specific Content," (f) "Trainer Issues," (g) "International Issues," and (h) "Multicultural Issues" (pp. 178–190).

To bolster the case for intercultural preparation of international education professionals, Ziegler (2006) discovered that the study abroad program professionals in her research who had received "intercultural training showed more expertise and confidence when discussing intercultural development issues and were able to discuss their struggles in a more sophisticated manner than those who had little to no conceptual framework on which to draw" (p. 162).

A Pedagogy for Developing the Intercultural Competence of Students

The most recent literature emphasizes that the design of international education programs, with regard to student intercultural learning and development, should be intentional rather than by "trial-and-error" (Savicki, 2008, p. xiii). One key to the development of intercultural competence in students is the effective design of orientation sessions before students go abroad (Deardorff, 2008, p. 43; Ziegler, 2006, p. 51). Deardorff (2008), however, noted that "predeparture orientations tend to give short shrift to the intercultural piece, focusing more on logistics" (p. 43). In addition to orientation design, international education professionals also need to integrate intercultural learning into students' experiences while abroad and after they return to their home culture (J. M. Bennett, 2008, p. 23).

There is a literature that addresses the importance of approaching student intercultural competence (and language acquisition) through a culture-learning lens (J. M. Bennett, M. J. Bennett, & Allen, 2003; Engle & Engle, 2004; Paige et al., 2004; Paige & Kippa, 2006). Paige et al. (2004) found that "students who go on study abroad programs frequently leave without any formal preparation for language and culture learning in the field and without materials specifically intended to assist them" (p. 254), and thus the expected gains in language acquisition and intercultural competence are not being realized. The *Maximizing Study Abroad* series (Mikk, Cohen, & Paige, 2009; Paige, Cohen, Kappler, Chi, & Lassegard, 2006) is a useful source of information on designing education-abroad programs for student language learning and intercultural competence. In addition, scholars have analyzed the development of intercultural competence in the home-campus language classroom. J. M. Bennett et al. (2003, pp. 237–270) explored the process by which instructors can assist their students in the language classroom toward developing greater intercultural competence. In the same volume, Damen (2003) argued that "culture learning as a process should be included as an ongoing element in the language classroom" (p. 81).

Along with impactful program design, international education professionals must also play a direct role in the facilitation of their students' intercultural competence (J. M. Bennett, 2008, p. 13; Goode, 2008, pp. 166–167; Ziegler, 2006, p. 51). Ziegler (2006) discovered that the in-country study abroad professionals in her study "identified different culture learning goals for students, from developing cultural self-awareness, to learning about the host culture, to experiencing and being open to social 'otherness,' to cross-cultural bonding, to creating global community" (p. 163). There was little consistency in their understandings of culture learning or how to facilitate intercultural development. Goode (2008, pp. 163–164) found that his study abroad faculty were aware of the intercultural learning outcomes they wanted for their students but had not actively supported their students in the development of intercultural competence. Indeed, not all international education professionals recognize the need to facilitate the process of intercultural learning for their students. J. M. Bennett (2008) "recall[ed] a study abroad advisor who, when asked what he was doing to prepare students joining him on a program in Hong Kong, noted that intercultural preparation was not necessary, since they were going to study geology, and English is commonly spoken" (p. 16).

Researchers have explored a range of frameworks useful to international education professionals for supporting the development of students' intercultural competence. In a case study of Eastern Michigan University (Krajewski-Jaime, Brown, & Ziefert, 1993), faculty directors explained their own intercultural learning process to their study abroad students to model "the different ethnocentric and ethnorelative stages" for them (p. 8). Sunnygard (2007) offered that "it is helpful for the faculty director to know the general and, as well as possible, the specific baselines of program participants to intercultural situations" (p. 169). This knowledge would then allow the faculty directors, as well as other international education professionals, to better support students in their individual journeys toward greater intercultural competence.

Literature Review Summary

In summary, the literature advises international education professionals to (a) learn about the key intercultural concepts and theories, (b) obtain the appropriate intercultural training to become self-aware and more interculturally competent, and (c) pay attention to the design of international education programs and the role international education professionals play in the development of intercultural competence in students. At the same time, there is certainly significant room for further research into the importance of intercultural competence in the work of international education professionals.

Intercultural Resources for International Education Professionals

In this section, we introduce resources that are specifically related to the development of intercultural competence and can provide practical guidance for international education professionals. The materials being described have been developed by professional international education associations and international/intercultural educators. In addition to these written materials, readers are encouraged to participate in intercultural workshops offered by professional associations such as NAFSA: Association of International Educators; the Society for Intercultural

Education, Training, and Research (SIETAR); the Forum on Education Abroad; and the Council on International Educational Exchange. SIETAR (www.sietar.org), with a presence in the United States, Canada, Europe, the Middle East, India, and Japan, functions as a global network for those interested in the field of intercultural relations. SIETAR also offers a variety of intercultural resources for international education professionals and others, including conferences and a variety of special interest groups. The Intercultural Communication Institute offers numerous intercultural workshops at its Summer Institute for Intercultural Communication. In the past 20 years, we have also seen the emergence of graduate programs at the MA and PhD levels in Intercultural Relations, Intercultural Communication, and Intercultural Education that are very relevant for those seeking to become professional international educators. In addition, the Intercultural Communication Institute provides "foundations," "practitioner," and "professional" certificate programs, as well as Intercultural Development Inventory Qualifying Seminars in the United States and abroad.

Maximizing Study Abroad Guides

The *Maximizing Study Abroad* guides (Mikk et al., 2009; Paige et al., 2006) for instructors and students are designed "to assist students who will be studying abroad, as well as the study abroad program professionals and language instructors who are facilitating their language and culture learning" (Paige & Kippa, 2006, p. 79). The students' guide has sections on culture learning and language learning and provides specific activities and strategies to help facilitate student intercultural learning and competence. For example, Bennett's Developmental Model of Intercultural Sensitivity is explained to students in a way that they can apply the concepts of the model to their own intercultural experiences (Paige, 2006).

The instructors' guide offers insights to international education professionals for using the students' guide most effectively to increase student intercultural competence. The *Instructional Guide,* for instance, includes a chapter on "instructional strategies for facilitating langage and culture learning" (Mikk et al., 2009, pp. 95–125).

The Guide to Successful Short-Term Programs Abroad

Published by NAFSA: Association of International Educators, this resource includes a chapter, "If You Cross over the Sea . . . Program Leadership for Intercultural Development," about student intercultural learning and competence in the context of short-term study abroad programs. This chapter is especially useful for study abroad faculty directors and the program professionals who work with them in designing international education programs and discusses three intercultural models that can assist international education professionals in understanding, acquiring, and teaching intercultural competence (Sunnygard, 2007, pp. 168–171). In general, this section of the volume "seeks to provide a development-based foundation for any 'international educator' leader" (Sunnygard, 2007, p. 167).

NAFSA's Guide to Education Abroad for Advisers and Administrators

The third edition of this comprehensive guide for international education professionals provides a wealth of information on a variety of topics. Among the most helpful chapters regarding intercultural development is "Integrating Intercultural Learning Into Education Abroad Programming" (Hoff & Kappler, 2005). This chapter serves as a primer for international education professionals on the topic of intercultural learning and competence, including sections on frequently asked questions, learning styles, intercultural communication, and intercultural tools (Hoff & Kappler, 2005, pp. 195–206).

Finding Your Way: Navigational Tools for International Student and Scholar Advisers

This resource targets those international education professionals who work with international students and scholars. In the context of career planning, this small volume highlights "Mindsets" and "Skill Sets" that are important in the work that these international education professionals do. Along with competencies such as "Curiosity" and "Taking the Perspective of Others," the editors explore the "Cross-Cultural Skills" required for success in this profession by sharing a case study that illustrates the complexities of intercultural understanding and competence (Gooding & Wood, 2006, pp. 95–97).

Learning Interdependence: A Case Study of the International/Intercultural Education of First-Year College Students

A profile of the "First-Year Intercultural Experience" at Hartwick College (New York), this book is instructive for both international education faculty and administrators (Bachner, Malone, & Snider, 2001). Two particularly compelling essays, by an economics professor and foreign language professor respectively, describe their own intercultural experiences and the rewards and challenges of guiding students on their intercultural journeys. There is also a chapter that presents excerpts from Hartwick College students' study abroad journals that demonstrate the dynamics of the students' experiences on the path to greater intercultural competence.

Recommendations for International Education Professionals

As a preface to our recommendations, we wish to make several points. First, in the international education field, in the United States and abroad, the development of intercultural competence has emerged as a major goal. Second, the research is showing that intercultural development is enhanced by the facilitation and guidance of international education professionals (Paige et al., 2004; Vande Berg & Paige, Chapter 25, this volume). The research also suggests that international education professionals are not necessarily knowledgeable about or comfortable in this culture-learning role (Goode, 2008; Zeigler, 2006). International education professionals in the field are role models, intentionally or not, of intercultural competence for their students. Our recommendations below flow from these observations:

1. Providing opportunities for international education professionals to gain more knowledge of intercultural concepts and theory is essential if their role in facilitating intercultural competence is to be realized.

2. The intercultural dimension needs to be integrated throughout the student learning process, from predeparture orientation through reentry and beyond, both for domestic students studying abroad as well as for international students studying in a host country. This necessarily involves international education professionals who will be interacting with students at different phases of the process. Predeparture programs can establish the intercultural learning frame of reference. On-site provision of culture-learning opportunities combined with systematic reflection regarding intercultural experiences can support students in developing intercultural competence. Reentry programs can integrate intercultural knowledge and skills into life decisions related to further education and careers.

3. International education professionals can benefit from knowledge regarding intercultural development. With that knowledge, they can provide support for students consistent with their particular needs as intercultural learners, experiencing the world through different developmental lenses. Students in the defense stage of Bennett's Developmental Model of Intercultural Sensitivity, for example, will experience the host culture quite differently than students in the adaptation stage.

4. The design of intercultural experiences in study abroad should be sequenced such that more challenging culture-learning activities come later and build on prior knowledge. Throughout, students should be given the chance to reflect on and make sense of their intercultural experiences.

5. International education professionals do not need to be intercultural specialists to successfully promote and facilitate culture learning. They do need to have a grasp of the core concepts we have presented in this chapter, which, combined with their expertise as educators, can support intercultural learning among their students.

Conclusion

In this chapter, we have sought to make several major points. First, the development of intercultural competence is an emergent learning outcome that is receiving considerable attention in the United States and abroad. Second, international education professionals have an important cultural mentoring role to play, particularly before and during students' international programs. Third, international education professionals generally do not have an intercultural theoretical background and thus lack an understanding of the cultural variables that are central to the intercultural experience of their students. Accordingly, the cultural mentoring role is not well understood, and intercultural learning and development are often left up to the students themselves. Fourth, when cultural mentoring does occur—on site, in person, online, and also via texts such as *Maximizing Study Abroad*—students gain greater intercultural competence.

With these conclusions in mind, we have presented information about intercultural competence and made suggestions about how to use this information in a cultural mentoring process. It is our hope that this chapter will contribute to the ongoing professional development of those working most closely with students on international education programs and will support more systematic, deliberate, and effective cultural mentoring.

References

Bachner, D. J., Malone, L. J., & Snider, M. C. (Eds.). (2001). *Learning interdependence: A case study of the international/intercultural education of first-year college students.* Columbia: University of South Carolina, National Resource Center for the First-Year Experience and Students in Transition.

Bennett, J. M. (2008). On becoming a global soul: A path to engagement during study abroad. In V. Savicki (Ed.), *Developing intercultural competence and transformation: Theory, research, and application in international education* (pp. 13–31). Sterling, VA: Stylus Publishing LLC.

Bennett, J. M., Bennett, M. J., & Allen, W. (2003). Developing intercultural competence in the language classroom. In D. L. Lange & R. M. Paige (Eds.), *Culture as the core: Perspectives on culture in second language learning* (pp. 237–270). Greenwich, CT: Information Age Publishing.

Bennett, M. J. (1986). Towards ethnorelativism: A developmental model of intercultural sensitivity. In R. M. Paige (Ed.), *Cross-cultural orientation: New conceptualizations and applications* (pp. 27–69). Lanham, MD: University Press of America.

Bennett, M. J. (1993). Towards ethnorelativism: A developmental model of intercultural sensitivity. In R. M. Paige (Ed.), *Education for the intercultural experience* (pp. 21–71). Yarmouth, ME: Intercultural Press.

Bennett, M. J. (1998). Intercultural communication: A current perspective. In M. J. Bennett (Ed.), *Basic concepts of intercultural communication: Selected readings* (pp. 1–34). Yarmouth, ME: Intercultural Press.

Cohen, A. D., Paige, R. M., Shively, R. L., Emert, H. A., & Hoff, J. G. (2005). *Maximizing study abroad through language and culture strategies: Research on students, study abroad program professionals, and language instructors.* Minneapolis: Center for Advanced Research on Language Acquisition, Office of International Programs, University of Minnesota.

Cornwell, G. H., & Stoddard, E. W. (1999). *Globalizing knowledge: Connecting international & intercultural studies.* Washington, DC: Association of American Colleges and Universities.

Crawford-Lange, L., & Lange, D. (1984). Doing the unthinkable in the second-language classroom. In T. Higgs (Ed.), *Teaching for proficiency: The organizing principle* (pp. 139–177). Lincolnwood, IL: National Textbook Company.

Damen, L. (2003). Closing the language and culture gap: An intercultural communication perspective. In D. L. Lange & R. M. Paige (Eds.), *Culture as the core: Perspectives on culture in second language learning* (pp. 71–88). Greenwich, CT: Information Age Publishing.

Deardorff, D. K. (2008). Intercultural competence: A definition, model, and implications for education abroad. In V. Savicki (Ed.), *Developing intercultural competence and transformation: Theory, research, and application in international education* (pp. 32–52). Sterling, VA: Stylus Publishing LLC.

Engle, L., & Engle, J. (2004). Assessing language acquisition and intercultural sensitivity development in relation to study abroad program design. *Frontiers: The Interdisciplinary Journal of Study Abroad, 10,* 219–236.

Goode, M. L. (2008). The role of faculty study abroad directors: A case study. *Frontiers: The Interdisciplinary Journal of Study Abroad, 15,* 149–172.

Gooding, M., & Wood, M. (Eds.). (2006). *Finding your way: Navigational tools for international student and scholar advisers.* Washington, DC: NAFSA: Association of International Educators.

Hoff, J. G., & Kappler, B. (2005). Integrating intercultural learning into education abroad programming. In J. L. Brockington, W. W. Hoffa, & P. C. Martin (Eds.), *NAFSA's guide to education abroad for advisers and administrators* (3rd ed., pp. 193–206). Washington, DC: NAFSA: Association of International Educators.

James, K. (2005). International education: The concept, and its relationship to intercultural education. *Journal of Research in International Education, 4,* 313–332.

Kolb, D. A. (1984). *Experiential learning: Experience as the source of learning and development.* Upper Saddle River, NJ: Prentice Hall.

Krajewski-Jaime, E. R., Brown, K. S., & Ziefert, M. (1993, March–April). *Developing cultural competence in human service providers.* Paper presented at the Eastern Michigan University Conference on Languages and Communications for World Business and the Professions, Ypsilanti, MI.

Mestenhauser, J. A. (2006). Internationalization at home: Systems challenge to a fragmented field. In H. Teekens (Ed.), *Internationalization at home: A global perspective* (pp. 61–77). The Hague: Netherlands Organization for International Cooperation in Higher Education.

Mikk, B. K., Cohen, A. D., & Paige, R. M. (with Chi, J. C., Lassegard, J. P., Meagher, M., & Weaver, S.). (2009). *Maximizing study abroad: An instructional guide to strategies for language and culture learning and use.* Minneapolis: Center for Advanced Research on Language Acquisition, University of Minnesota.

O'Donovan, K. F., & Mikelonis, V. M. (2005). Internationalizing on-campus courses: A faculty development program to integrate global perspectives into undergraduate course syllabi. In L. C. Anderson (Ed.), *Internationalizing undergraduate education: Integrating study abroad into the curriculum* (pp. 91–95). Minneapolis: Learning Abroad Center, University of Minnesota.

Paige, R. M. (1993a). On the nature of intercultural experiences and intercultural education. In R. M. Paige (Ed.), *Education for the intercultural experience* (pp. 1–19). Yarmouth, ME: Intercultural Press.

Paige, R. M. (1993b). Trainer competencies for international and intercultural programs. In R. M Paige (Ed.), *Education for the intercultural experience* (pp. 169–199). Yarmouth, ME: Intercultural Press.

Paige, R. M. (2006). Dimensions of intercultural learning. In R. M. Paige, A. D. Cohen, B. Kappler, J. C. Chi, & J. P. Lassegard (Eds.), *Maximizing study abroad: A students' guide to strategies for language and culture learning and use* (2nd ed., pp. 40–41). Minneapolis: Center for Advanced Research on Language Acquisition, University of Minnesota.

Paige, R. M., Cohen, A. D., Kappler, B., Chi, J. C., & Lassegard, J. P. (2006). *Maximizing study abroad: A student's guide to strategies for language and culture learning and use* (2nd ed.). Minneapolis: Center for Advanced Research on Language Acquisition, University of Minnesota.

Paige, R. M., Cohen, A. D., & Shively, R. L. (2004). Assessing the impact of a strategies-based curriculum on language and culture learning abroad. *Frontiers: The Interdisciplinary Journal of Study Abroad, 10,* 253–276.

Paige, R. M., & Kippa, S. (2006). Curriculum transformation in study abroad: The Maximizing Study Abroad guides. In H. Teekens (Ed.), *Internationalization at home: A global perspective* (pp. 79–89). The Hague: Netherlands Organization for International Cooperation in Higher Education.

Rasch, D. C. (2001). *Faculty voices from the field: Perceptions and implications of study abroad.* Unpublished doctoral dissertation, Peabody College of Vanderbilt University, Nashville, TN.

Savicki, V. (2008). Preface. In V. (Ed.), *Developing intercultural competence and transformation: Theory, research, and application in international education* (pp. xiii–xiv). Sterling, VA: Stylus Publishing LLC.

Savicki, V., & Selby, R. (2008). Synthesis and conclusions. In V. Savicki (Ed.), *Developing intercultural competence and transformation: Theory, research, and application in international education* (p. 349). Sterling, VA: Stylus Publishing LLC.

Sunnygard, J. (2007). If you cross over the sea . . . program leadership for intercultural development. In S. E. Spencer & K. Tuma (Eds.), *The guide to successful short-term programs abroad* (2nd ed., pp. 167–174). Washington, DC: NAFSA: Association of International Educators.

Vande Berg, M. (2007). Intervening in the learning of U.S. students abroad. *Journal of Studies in International Education, 11,* 392–399.

Vande Berg, M., Balkcum, A., Scheid, M., & Whalen, B. (2004). A report at the half-way mark: The Georgetown Consortium project. *Frontiers: The Interdisciplinary Journal of Study Abroad, 10,* 101–116.

Ziegler, N. J. (2006). *Culture learning in study abroad from the perspective of on-site staff in France and Senegal.* Unpublished doctoral dissertation, University of Minnesota, Minneapolis.

CHAPTER 20

Intercultural Competence in Social Work

Culturally Competent Practice in Social Work

Rowena Fong

The United States is a country of diverse and growing populations of immigrants and refugees. In 1970, less than 5% of the population was foreign born, but by 2006, the foreign-born population had increased to 12.5% (37.5 million), numbers projected to reach 13% and 40 million in 2010 (Capps, 2008). Two thirds of these immigrants live in the six states of California, Texas, Illinois, Florida, New York, and New Jersey (Capps, 2008). Social workers serving these immigrants and refugees need to understand the different ethnic backgrounds, contexts, and social environments upon which culturally competent practice is founded.

While the profession of social work is committed to working with all members of society, culturally competent practice typically has focused on working with persons of color and ethnic minority community members. It is not surprising, therefore, if private and public agency social workers have clients in their caseloads as different as a separated family from Somalia, a poor mother from Central America, an underemployed Spanish-speaking father from Mexico, a neglected "lost boy" from Sudan, a severely depressed Asian woman, or an elderly Tongan grandmother in poor health who adopted her grandchild.

These types of clients usually suffer from familiar problems, but not every social worker understands the clients' ethnic contexts and situations. Many social workers are unaware of or uncomfortable with the demands of culturally competent practice

(Earner, 2007; Fong, McRoy, & Hendricks, 2006). In social work, *culturally competent practice,* the term more commonly known rather than *intercultural competence,* is the acquisition of knowledge, values, and skills needed by social workers to work with persons from different ethnic cultural backgrounds. In this kind of practice, social workers are also examining their own values to determine if there might be culture clashes in which the social worker would not be or feel competent to work with the client from another cultural background. Social workers are to examine their values and belief systems to ensure that personal racism, ageism, or homophobia are not going to be barriers to objectively and effectively serve clients.

This chapter discusses what it means to be culturally competent in the social work setting. It addresses what cultural competence looks like in the discipline, offering distinct theories, definitions, assessment principles, and methods for working with individuals, families, groups, communities, and organizations. The chapter also addresses implications for practice and recommendations for future research.

Introduction

In social work, culturally competent practice is similar to intercultural competence in that it examines cross sections of cultures normally guided by variables such as values, beliefs, and actions and defined by variables such as race, ethnicity, gender, sexual orientation, social class, religion, and political persuasion (Lum, 2007). Skilled social workers will seek to understand how cross sections of these variables intersect to affect the individual's functioning in his or her family or community environment. While all the variables mentioned affect a person's life, this chapter will focus primarily on the race and ethnicity variables as they relate to clients in contexts of families, groups, communities, and organizations. However, it is useful to acknowledge that all variables are important because of their intersectionality as they affect the individual's functioning and well-being.

Terminology

Culturally competent practice is the process by which the social worker, engaged with persons from a specific race or ethnic background, gathers knowledge about his or her ethnic clients' cultural values and traditions and is able to assess, provide, and evaluate interventions that are culturally appropriate for the ethnically diverse client caseload (Fong & Furuto, 2001). The culturally competent social worker learns theories and treatment practices that include both Western interventions and indigenous treatments (Fong, Boyd, & Browne, 1999). The social worker is examining cultural similarities and differences between and within cultures so appropriate assessments and interventions can be made. For example, in the East Asian culture, there is quite a bit of variation within the Chinese population depending on the client's homeland origins (China vs. Hong Kong vs. Taiwan), and the culturally competent social worker would use this knowledge in his or her assessment skills of the Chinese client.

Intersectionality, a term used in social work because of the emphasis of focusing on both intra- and interdifferences within an individual, family, or community, is the process of assessing, selecting, and putting together two or more variables such as race and ethnicity or gender and relevant cultural values to discern not only what intersects or overlaps but also what is different when these variables interact. Intersectionality also involves identifying cultural values and finding a way to integrate them into treatment planning. A social worker assessing a depressed Asian woman, for example, may focus on the fact that the client is female and her culture does not value her as highly as a male. This Asian value may intersect with the Asian cultural variable of respect due to an elder, contributing to the client's depression because in her Chinese nursing home, she receives less care and respect than her Chinese male counterpart.

Culturally competent practice also entails understanding the acculturation process to determine what attitudes, values, beliefs, and behaviors immigrants and refugees retain from their countries of origin and what new attitudes, values, and beliefs clients choose to acculturate to in their new homelands (Delgado, Jones, & Rohani, 2005; Webb, 2001). Effective practice then requires identifying interventions or treatments compatible with the client's unique blend of cultural values.

Because in social work, generalist practice typically means serving an individual in the context of families, groups, communities, and organizations, a culturally competent social worker will also have to understand the individual ethnic client in these contexts (Armour, Bain, & Rubio, 2007). It also means social workers are trained to operate in all five of these social systems. When an ethnic group is having difficulty in acculturating or finding adequate resources or finding culturally relevant interventions, a community-based social worker will work with the ethnic community to help solve the problem and find acceptable solutions to the problem.

Culturally Competent Practice With Ethnic Minority Clients

Social workers serve American-born and foreign-born clients. Understanding definitions and terminology facilitates work with both populations. American-born clients are born in the United States, whether they have ethnic backgrounds among European Americans, African Americans, Mexican Americans or Latinos, Native Americans or First Nations Peoples, Asian Americans, Pacific Islander Americans, or a combination of these. *Foreign born* refers to residents born outside the United States. They are typically trying to adapt to ways that are alien to the ethnic traditions, values, beliefs, and material, social, physical, and political conditions of their lands of origin. For example, a single mother from Liberia will have myriad adjustments to make when she arrives in the United States from a refugee camp.

Diversity Within Foreign-Born Populations

While 1 out of 10 persons in the United States is foreign born (Fong, 2004), they arrive under a variety of different immigration statuses. This influences how well they are received and how they adjust to their new environment. Social workers need to discern the differences among clients who are refugees, asylees, victims of human trafficking, unaccompanied refugee minors, immigrants, and undocumented immigrants (Fong, 2007). This discernment plays a critical role in culturally competent practice with these various foreign-born populations. Culturally competent social workers need to have knowledge about the different immigration statuses of the clients and the political environments of the clients' home countries that have contributed to their trauma. Some examples of different immigration statuses are as follows:

- Refugees have fled their country of origin and are seeking protection from political or religious persecution. They cannot return to their countries of origin for fear of death or torture.

- Asylees have sought refuge after entering the United States from persecution and life-threatening situations in homelands.

- Unaccompanied children arrive without an adult or parent who is responsible for their well-being. They can be either unaccompanied alien children (UAC) or unaccompanied refugee minors (URM). Immigrants have voluntarily left their countries of origin to settle in another country in pursuit of better economic or other opportunities.

- Undocumented persons are immigrants who have left their countries of origin without legal documentation at the time of departure or persons living in a host country that allow their visas to expire and consequently are reclassified as undocumented illegal immigrants.

- Victims of human trafficking are also categorized as undocumented immigrants. These individuals, usually women in sex trafficking or men in labor trafficking, are deceived and forced into slavery. Social workers involved with this population have to deal with life-threatening situations for the individual person who is trafficked as well as that person's family members, who may also be at risk.

All of these immigrant and refugee populations share new and maybe frustrating experiences of coming and acculturating to the United States, but most will have endured very different migration journeys and varying degrees of trauma and persecutions. American-born ethnic minority populations may not share these kinds of experiences that the foreign-born populations have had to endure.

Theories Frameworks for Cultural Competence

Culturally competent practice in social work is based on three theoretical frameworks: the ecological approach, strengths perspective, and empowerment theory.

The ecological approach is based on the human behavior and social environment philosophy that behavior is shaped by one's living conditions and contexts at the individual, family, community, and societal levels (Zastrow & Kirst-Ashman, 2006). This approach stresses the importance of social environments and their impact on human functioning.

When assessing an individual's overall functioning, a culturally competent social worker will consider how an individual behaves in social environments when alone, interacting with family members, engaged in ethnic communities, and responding to societal norms and expectations. Social environments will typically reflect norms and expectations based on cultural values. So, the ecological approach is a framework that supports the generalist practice of working with individuals, families, groups, communities, and organizations in cultural contexts. Since cultural expectations are dictating all these five systems, the ecological approach forces the social worker to formulate problem-solving steps through a systems approach and a cultural lens.

The strengths perspective is a theoretical way of approaching the client and purposefully collecting information about the client's positive attributes and behaviors (Saleeby, 2002). The social worker assesses the client's strengths and integrates them into the treatment plan, which affects how the social worker views, approaches, and assists the client. The strengths perspective is particularly important for the culturally competent social worker because the ethnic client's worldview may be so different from mainstream culture that strengths are neglected, minimized, or even misinterpreted as malfunctioning behaviors (Fong, 2004; Weaver, 2004).

Social workers need to be careful that for clients who lived in cultures whose ways were and still are foreign to the American lifestyle that the strengths of these clients are not ignored. For example, many refugees occupy professional positions in their homelands but because of language barriers, their status and sometimes respect are reduced because of the label they bear. Determining the client's strengths needs to be a routine and ongoing part of assessments with foreign-born populations.

The empowerment approach maintains that each person has strengths, skills, and talents that can enable the client to function positively and enhance his or her own well-being (Gutierrez, Parsons, & Cox, 1998). Sometimes a client is unable to achieve this potential because he or she is culturally, psychologically, socially, or physically blocked. The culturally competent social worker helps the client find ways to overcome these barriers and become fully functioning again.

Empowerment theory is manifested when the culturally competent social worker is able to include and intersect the cultural values of clients with strong ethnic ties into assessments and intervention planning (Fong, 2004). Fong et al. (1999) have developed a framework of intersecting and incorporating cultural values and indigenous interventions with Western interventions to encompass a "biculturalization of interventions" approach to culturally competent practice. This approach empowers ethnic clients by honoring and valuing their cultural values and by using familiar indigenous interventions that clients have confidence in and that inspire intercultural competence.

Culturally Competent Practice and Social Work

Social work as a profession endorses culturally competent social work practice.

The National Association of Social Work (NASW) in 2001 approved Standards for Cultural Competence in Social Work Practice, dictating how social workers are to behave and how they are to offer services to ethnically diverse populations. As stated in the standards, "Cultural competence in social work practice implies a heightened consciousness of how clients experience their uniqueness and deal with their differences and similarities within a larger social context" (p. 8). To understand the social contexts and environments of ethnically diverse clients, social workers are required in their professional education to learn about human behaviors and social environments. The standards assume that social environments significantly affect the behaviors of individuals, families, groups, and communities. Consequently, in the assessment and intervention implementation phases of culturally competent social work practice, this knowledge is critical.

In 2001, the NASW established 10 standards for cultural competence in social work practice: Ethics and Values, Self-Awareness, Cross-Cultural Knowledge, Cross-Cultural Skills, Service Delivery, Empowerment and Advocacy, Diverse Workforce, Professional Education, Language Diversity, and Cross-Cultural Leadership. These standards are typically enforced in schools of social work that adopt them in their field practicum curriculum and in social work agencies that use them for performance measures. The different schools of social work or social service agencies develop measurement tools and means to enforce them. Individualized consequences of not upholding the standards would be determined between teacher and student and employer and worker.

The standards address the social worker's understanding of the client's social environments and the impact on the client's behavior. The standards also challenge the social worker to personally examine how upbringing and social environments have shaped his or her own behaviors and attitudes.

A culturally competent social worker must confront his or her own racism and assess whether he or she has attitudes and behaviors that consciously or unconsciously oppress and discriminate against a client on the basis of race or ethnicity. Okayama, Furuto, and Edmondson (2001) warn, "A culturally sensitive social work practitioner acknowledges and understands how our learned prejudices and stereotypes, including racist attitudes and beliefs, have a direct effect on interactions with others" (p. 90).

This discrimination may become evident during the interviewing process when the social worker is assessing the client's problem. Racism may arise when the treatment planned or given to the client reflects negative stereotypes of the client's ethnicity. A culturally competent social worker needs to be aware of his or her own biases; take steps to control them, such as suspending habitual negative and critical judgments; and not allow them to infer with assessments and interventions. Instead, "culturally competent attitudes evolve out of having an open mind and heart and a willingness to increase awareness about one's own cultural identity and the cultures of others" (Okayama et al., 2001, p. 89).

Culturally Competent Practice Skills

Culturally competent practice is based on knowledge and skills. Knowledge of the client's cultural values, ethnic customs, and behaviors inform and guide good assessment. Cross-cultural knowledge helps identify culturally appropriate treatments or interventions for clients systems composed of individuals, families, groups, and communities.

Assessment. Culturally competent social workers have to do thorough assessments to learn about the client's background and factors that, from the client's perspective, perpetuate the problem. Principles, methods, and tools help ensure culturally competent assessments. Principles guide the ways social workers conduct their assessments in practice and ensure that cultural protocols have been respected and abided by. Methods are the means by which social workers obtain information to reflect cultural values and beliefs in the data collection stage of assessments. Tools, such as culturagrams, help determine the appropriateness of interventions to be selected after the assessment of the problem is completed.

Mindful that the individual client intersects with the other systems of families, groups, and communities, the culturally competent social worker may direct assessment probing at all levels of questioning. For example, at the microlevel of working with the individual, the culturally competent social worker will have assessment questions targeted about gender, roles, or birth order since in some cultures, females are the nonpreferred child or adult. A culturally competent social worker would know which ethnic cultures followed that viewpoint and would assess the female client's problem from that cultural context lens.

Working With Individuals. It is important for the social worker working with individuals to assess the usual information about the client's functioning and his or her perspective about the problem. Gender, ethnicity, and sexual orientation may intersect, and these variables would make a difference in reflecting the client's perspective.

When working with individuals, the social worker should also assess the client in the context of his or her family functioning. In many cultures, the self is defined by one's role in the family, so that factor must be assessed. It is important to assess for cultural values and strengths because each client's ethnic background entails cultural values that are strengths to the client. For example, in Hawaiian culture, an elderly woman can be a *kupuna,* which is a position of a wise elder in the community, a position normally thought to be attributed to males only.

Social workers need to also assess for gender roles and expectations. The gender of the client might allow the social worker to understand the lens through which the client sees the world and experiences problems. In other words, the social worker needs to assess what the client thinks and account for what might be contributing to the problem from an ethnic cultural perspective. If language is a barrier, it might be prudent to employ an interpreter proficient in the client's language or dialect, with the caveat that children and youths should be avoided as interpreters because of the stress it imposes on them and their relationships with their parents.

When language is an obstacle between the client and social worker, stories or narratives might be used. Even with adults hindered by language barriers, assessment may be possible through art or artistic expression of the problem. Assessment might also be done through the use of an elder informant, as in Hawaiian cultures, where a *kapuna* or elder might be asked about his or her perspectives on a societal issue to give the context of the individual's frustrations related to his or her problem. For example, a Hawaiian *kupuna* may be working with a substance-abusing mother to help the woman understand the mother's frustration with her own lack of sufficient connectedness to her ethnic identity and the connection to the *'aina*

(Hawaiian term for land). Without the connection to the land, the woman's ethnic identity is floundering, and she is using substances to medicate herself.

Working With Families. Working with families involves a different set of assessment principles. The social worker needs to identify and assess the family's social networks—is the family isolated or supported? It is also helpful to determine whether the family is first, second, or third generation since in immigrant and refugee families, the cohort factor influences accessibility to resources. Families who arrive earlier than the most recent arrivals may be less sympathetic to the plight of the newcomers if they perceive that resources are scarce. Families from the same home countries may not always be willing to help with adjustment and acculturation, as a social worker might assume, because families fighting to survive may not believe they have the resources to be so generous.

Family assessments benefit from understanding how families communicate and make decisions. In many ethnic families, nonverbals communicate more than their verbal interactions. In families from patriarchal cultures, for example, the roles of males, particularly an elder male like the grandfather or elder uncle, should be noted, so that their voice is not excluded in the assessment process.

The culturagram is another tool available for the assessment of culturally diverse families (Congress, 2002). The purpose of the culturagram is to individualize culturally diverse families rather than assume that families from the same culture always share common characteristics. As Congress (2002) states, "Completing a culturagram on a family can help a clinician develop a better understanding of the family" (p. 57). The culturagram covers 10 areas: (1) reasons for relocation, (2) legal status, (3) time in community, (4) language spoken at home and community, (5) health beliefs, (6) crisis events, (7) holidays and special events, (8) contact with cultural and religious institutions, (9) values about education and work, and (10) values about family—structure, power, myths, and rules. Knowing the information described in these 10 areas can help the culturally competent social worker differentiate and capture the uniqueness of each immigrant and refugee family's migration journey.

For example, a social worker in a refugee service provider agency may be working with a family from Iraq, and the culturagram helps the social worker to understand the extent of connectedness, family support, and community involvement the Iraqi couple had in their homeland. This information would help the social worker assess the degree of losses experienced by this couple and family members.

Working With Groups. Those who work with ethnic groups need to assess the purpose of the group and its connection to the ethnic community both in the United States and in their countries of origin. This is important because ethnic groups themselves are internally diverse. For example, the Chinese population may seem monolithic to an outsider, but within a single Chinese church, there can be an English-speaking group for American-born Chinese, a Cantonese-speaking group for immigrants from Hong Kong, and two different Mandarin-speaking groups, one for members from Taiwan and the other for members from mainland China. A culturally competent social worker would have the background knowledge of the different social and political environments of the Chinese populations to know that mixing groups from Taiwan and China can cause trouble.

While people seek ethnic group affiliations for support, affirmation, and familiarity of language, food, and customs, conflicts may arise amid racial dynamics internal and external to the group. Davis, Galinski, and Schopler (1995) have a RAP (recognize, anticipate, and problem solve) framework that is both a method and a tool to assess and guide the leadership skills needed to do group work and address the concerns of persons of color. Group leaders need to recognize the racial and ethnic differences among group members and understand that racial tensions within ethnic groups might be personality differences but might also be due to institutional racism and frustrations aimed at the group and ethnic community that grow from feelings of powerlessness. Leaders need to anticipate how racial issues and problems might affect members. Leaders' problem-solving skills and solutions ought to include culturally appropriate interventions and goals. For example, in working with a group of Korean wives who have been identified as having limited English-speaking skills and tend to be isolated as spouses of foreign students at the university, it would be important for the culturally competent social worker to set goals in the context of the expected role of the wife in the traditional Korean culture. Promoting strong feminist practices may cause more internal tensions for the Korean women whose external tension (social environment related) is pushing toward a potential clash in Eastern and Western cultural values.

Working With Communities. In working with ethnic communities, it is important to assess how old and viable the community is as well as its resources. Principles to guide this assessment are based on the following questions:

1. How old and resourceful is the community?

2. How welcoming is the community toward new immigrant and refugee newcomers?

3. How well is the ethnic community integrated into the larger U.S. community?

4. What are the ethnic community's strengths?

5. What is the leadership structure of the ethnic community?

6. What indigenous resources does the community have?

7. How does the community use its indigenous resources?

When assessing ethnic communities, it is helpful to have cultural informants who are members of the community to guide the assessment, ask the right questions, and get information from community members. It is also important to understand structure and leadership style in the community. Key questions to ask are as follows:

1. What are the structure and leadership style of the ethnic community?

2. How does the ethnic community fit in with other communities?

3. What is the priority of the ethnic community?

4. What are the needs of this ethnic community?

Chow (2001) writes about using tools such as "The User Profile," "The Service Profile," and "The Agency Profile" to identify community and organization practices in Asian and Pacific Islander communities. The profiles pose questions to determine if services are accessible, available, and appropriate for the respective communities. These profiles could also be used in other ethnic communities. For example, child welfare workers in Black communities are working on addressing the issue of disproportionality, which is the overrepresentation of African American children in the child welfare system. These workers are creating agency profiles and partnering with public and private foster care agencies to invite Black community participation and leadership in addressing this issue.

Practice and Research Implications

Culturally competent practice in social work has evolved from a time when the profession recognized little or no distinction within or between ethnic groups. For example, Asians were not differentiated from Pacific Islanders, and the Asian American "model minority" stereotypes prevailed without the acknowledement of the degree of diversity in this population. In 1994, Fong and Mokuau wrote of the need to distinguish group differences within an ethnic population and forewarned of the dangers of treating immigrants and refugees as a single category. Because migration is a growing phenomenon around the world, the gaps about the distinctions among and between the various immigrant and refugee groups remain in social work practice and research.

More education and training is needed in institutions of higher education, in public and private agencies, and in communities where these populations reside. Lacking is continuous and updated information about who the current refugees are, what the conditions are in their homelands, why they are coming to the United States, and what they had to endure in refugee camps. Information about federal regulations and state subsidies is often sketchy and confusing. Clearer information about federal and state regulations and immigration laws is needed.

Child welfare agencies, mental health clinics, school settings, and health care facilities need to promote knowledge of the ethnic groups in their client populations. Assessments need to always include strengths, cultural values, and knowledge of clients' migration journeys. When refugees are victims of human trafficking, professionals dealing with this population need to be educated about aspects of the migration journey that may have coerced and the deceit involved, resulting in indentured service and slavery (Busch, Fong, Heffron, Faulkner, & Mahapatra, 2007).

Future researchers and scholars need to refine the culturally competent assessments that clinicians and agencies are developing, working with ethnic communities to implement more "biculturalization of interventions" (Fong et al., 1999). These steps would include indigenous interventions as a more regular part of treatment planning and implementation. Faith healers, informal support systems, and community cultural resources would also be added to these interventions.

Finally, evidenced-based practices for ethnic individuals, families, groups, communities, and organizations need to be grounded in their cultural values. When interventions are set up for ethnic families to verbally communicate their conflicts, they often lack theoretical frameworks that match or respect the ethnic families' cultural practices. For example, where cultural values strongly advocate respecting elders and not speaking against adults, children and youth in family therapy are unlikely to respond well to a therapist who insists that the child tell the grandparent how angry he or she feels about living with the grandparent in a kinship care adoption case. This intervention causes more tension for the child and grandparent, is disrespectful of cultural values, and will not bring about good outcomes. In this case, the social worker needs to pay more attention to structural family therapy principles, which support the cultural value of paying attention to the structure of the family. In this family structure, the role of the elder is very important, and giving the elderly grandparent respect is critical. This choice of theory grounds the social work practice in the family's cultural value of respecting the elders.

Future scholars and researchers need to continue to conduct research and offer education about the needs of immigrants and refugees and ethnic minority populations in the United States. Culturally competent social workers need to continue to focus on the strengths of the ethnic clients and use cultural values more in the assessments, planning of treatments, and selection of interventions. They should promote more interventions that combine Western and indigenous treatments. Matching interventions that fit family-centered practices that are actually happening in the ethnic families and communities so culturally appropriate outcomes can be achieved is also necessary for current and future work.

References

Armour, M., Bain, B., & Rubio, R. (2007). *Educating for cultural competence: Tools for training field instructors.* Alexandria, VA: Council on Social Work Education.

Busch, N., Fong, R., Heffron, L., Faulkner, M., & Mahapatra, N. (2007). *Assessing the needs of human trafficking victims: An evaluation of the Central Texas Coalition against human trafficking.* Austin: Center for Social Work Research, University of Texas at Austin.

Capps, R. (2008, April). *Paying the price: The impact of immigration raids on America's children.* Paper presented at the Intersection of Immigration and Child Welfare: Emerging Issues and Implications Second National Forum, Chicago.

Chow, J. (2001). Assessment of Asian American/Pacific Islander organizations and communities. In R. Fong & S. Furuto (Eds.), *Culturally competent practice: Skills, interventions, and evaluations* (pp. 211–224). Boston: Allyn & Bacon.

Congress, E. (2002). Using the culturagram with culturally diverse families. In A. Roberts & G. Greene (Eds.), *Social work desk reference* (pp. 57–64). New York: Oxford University Press.

Davis, L., Galinsky, M., & Schopler, J. (1995). RAP: A framework for leadership of multiracial groups. *Social Work, 40*(2), 155–165.

Delgado, M., Jones, K., & Rohani, M. (2005). *Social work practice with refugee and immigrant youth in the United States.* Boston: Allyn & Bacon.

Earner, I. (2007). Immigrant families and child welfare: Barriers to services and approaches to change. *Child Welfare, 83*(3), 63–91.

Fong, R. (Ed.). (2004). *Culturally competent practice with immigrant and refugee children and families.* New York: Guilford.

Fong, R. (2007). Immigrant and refugee youth: Migration journeys and cultural values. *Prevention Researcher, 14*(4), 3–6.

Fong, R., Boyd, T., & Browne, C. (1999). The Gandhi technique: A biculturalization approach for empowering Asian and Pacific Islander families. *Journal of Multicultural Social Work, 7*(1–2), 95–110.

Fong, R., & Furuto, S. (Eds.). (2001). *Culturally competent practice: Skills, interventions, and evaluations.* Boston, MA: Allyn & Bacon.

Fong, R., & Mokuau, N. (1994). Social work periodical literature review of Asians and Pacific Islanders. *Social Work, 39*(3), 298–312.

Fong, R., McRoy, R., & Hendricks, C. (2006). *Intersecting child welfare, substance abuse, and family violence: Culturally competent approaches.* Alexandria, VA: Council on Social Work Education.

Gutierrez, L., Parsons, R., & Cox, E. (Eds.). (1998). *Empowerment in social work practice: A sourcebook.* Pacific Grove, CA: Brooks/Cole.

Lum, D. (2007). *Culturally competent practice: A framework for understanding diverse groups and justice issues.* Pacific Grove, CA: Brooks/Cole.

National Association of Social Work. (2001). *NASW standards for cultural competence in social work practice.* Washington, DC: Author.

Okayama, C., Furuto, S., & Edmondson, E. (2001). Components of cultural competence: Attitudes, knowledge, and skills. In R. Fong & S. Furuto (Eds.), *Culturally competent practice: Skills, interventions, and evaluations* (pp. 89–100). Boston: Allyn & Bacon.

Saleeby, D. (2002). *The strengths perspective in social work practice* (3rd ed.). Boston: Allyn & Bacon.

Weaver, H. (2004). *Explorations in cultural competence.* Belmont, CA: Wadsworth.

Webb, N. (Ed.). (2001). *Culturally diverse parent-child and family relationships: A guide for social workers and other practitioners.* New York: Guilford.

Zastrow, C., & Kirst-Ashman, K. (2006). *Understanding human behavior and the social environment* (7th ed.). Pacific Grove, CA: Brooks/Cole.

CHAPTER 21

Intercultural Competence in Engineering

Global Competence for Engineers

John M. Grandin and Norbert Hedderich

Whether from the perspective of business leaders, politicians, educators, or the populace in general, the United States has become concerned about global competitiveness, trade, innovation, and technological advantage, especially as they relate to the nation's economic future. Among those alert to these issues are engineering educators, who are painfully aware of the fact that technological superiority, once enjoyed by a small number of nations, is now no longer geographically privileged. As Thomas Friedman (2005) has written, the world of information and knowledge has become "flat," open without prejudice to all who are connected to the Internet, educated, and motivated to claim their share of global wealth. Though, as Friedman observes, a young genius in the developing world might have been outflanked in the past by the privileged "average American in Poughkeepsie," that is no longer the case (p. 194). The playing field has been leveled, and those in Poughkeepsie, or even in Silicon Valley, must recognize that innovative ideas and the newest technology may evolve anywhere across the globe.

Twenty years ago, American engineering educators could smile with confidence at the emergence of China, India, and other Third World nations as players in the realms of business and technology. After all, their best students were clamoring for admission to our graduate programs, recognized as the best in the world, and often then remaining in the United States, helping to keep the United States at the cutting edge. But now that India and China have embraced the free market and have built universities and scientific research centers comparable to the best in our country, that picture has changed. The startling numbers of highly competent engineering graduates in these countries are compounded by the fact that many of their older compatriots, educated in the United States, are now returning to their homelands with knowledge, experience, ideas, and financial resources strong enough to found new companies and research centers, many of which have already become major competitors for U.S. business and industry (Saxenian, 2006).

Business Week (July 31, 2006) describes the changes in the way business is done, especially where business is done, as nothing less than a "seismic shift," which will require major adjustments on the part of Americans, including engineers and engineering educators. Given the fact, for example, that very competent engineers and engineering services are now available in other global locations at less cost, questions arise about the very demand for engineering in the United States. Do we need to maintain strong engineering and science programs at our universities when programs abroad are of high quality and at a lower price? Do we really need as many computer engineers or computer scientists, for example, if we can purchase the services of that field abroad for a fraction of the expense? But even more important, if we downsize our own capacity for technical education, how can we maintain a grip on the emergence of new ideas and new technologies? In short, what engineering education changes do we need to undergo in this rapidly evolving global environment?

Fortunately, American business leaders and entrepreneurs are finding ways to adapt to this new "flattened" world. Global sourcing, for example, determines where things are developed, how and by whom, and who ultimately controls them. When Boeing developed its new Dreamliner, it could theoretically have designed and manufactured all components in the United States, with total assembly in Washington state. In reality, however, Boeing searched the globe for the best talent, the best engineers, the best ideas, the best practices, and the best prices, eventually employing more than 5,000 engineers in many different countries to design, develop, and produce its new airliner.

As Lynn and Salzman (2006) point out, the technical advantage in the global marketplace is no longer in the hands of one or a few national groups or geographical areas by virtue of their knowledge base and wealth but rather in the hands of those who, like Boeing, can best learn to collaborate across borders and cultures on a global scale. The new Boeing Dreamliner is a brilliant example of how companies are learning to scout for talent across the globe and to work together harmoniously for a common goal. But, one can well imagine the potential for misunderstandings when engineering teams from so many cultural perspectives decide to collaborate. At the same time, one can well imagine the potential for a high-level product when entrepreneurs can actually pull the best global talent together on their behalf. Lynn and Salzman describe this as the "collaborative advantage," pointing out that the future belongs to those who can learn to work or team together with other groups without regard to location, heritage, and national and cultural difference.

Given this "seismic shift" in the way business is done, educators must ask what changes need to be undertaken at the university level to better prepare engineers for a drastically different workplace. The Accreditation Board for Engineering and

Technology (ABET), the American Society for Engineering Education, the National Academy of Engineering (2005a, 2005b), and others are, therefore, seeking to redefine the engineer for the coming decades, based on what he or she must know, what skills he or she should acquire, and which so-called soft skills should be in the mix and what role they should play. While one group might weigh one skill set more than another, there nevertheless is growing agreement on several issues:

- It goes without saying that an engineer must have a solid *technical understanding* and that his or her knowledge base must be competitive with that of peers from any other part of the world.

- It is likewise broadly accepted that engineers today need to be able to look beyond the classical departmental perspectives (i.e., engineers must be able to *work interdisciplinarily*). Automotive engineers, for example, who once came largely from mechanical engineering, now need to be equally savvy in the electrical and computer areas. We thus see new cross-disciplinary technical fields emerging such as mechatronics, pharmaceutical engineering, and biotechnical engineering.

- Given the rapid pace of change and the concomitant fact that the state of engineering knowledge on graduation day will be inadequate in a few very short years, engineers must learn how to stay current and how to become effective *lifelong learners.*

- Given the global presence of companies today and the multilocational nature of research, development, manufacturing, marketing, and distribution, engineers must be trained to work effectively in *global teams*. Indeed, many companies now speak of research and development as a 24/7 phenomenon, where work is performed in one part of the world and then passed on to the next time zone for continuation.

- Engineers today must have an array of skills to enter and compete in the global workplace. Engineers, like most professionals today, must be skilled at *cross-cultural communication* as a major step toward becoming *globally competent*. Based on personal interaction with dozens of engineers and human resource professionals in global companies over the past two decades, engineers today are asked to be

  - mobile, open, flexible, and tolerant;
  - knowledgeable about other places in the world;
  - culturally aware and attuned to and accepting of difference;
  - multilingual;
  - perceptive of difference in terms of engineering cultures.

The globally competent engineer must be cross-culturally savvy and interculturally competent in the broadest sense but also specifically sensitive to the differences in the daily practice of engineering from nation to nation. The latter involves the extent to which issues such as quality, design, aesthetics, sustainability, greenness, neatness, and thoroughness play a role but also the way engineers work on a day-to-day basis. Is value placed on teamwork over individual contribution? Does the engineer work as a specialist, doing his or her portion and then passing it "over the wall"? Or does he or she function as part of a group, fully cognizant of the larger picture? Many of these questions transcend the issues one generally considers to be associated with cross-cultural sensitivity, and yet they determine engineering priorities and drive engineering practice.

Among this list of qualifications, the call for global competence is being heard with greater frequency from the private sector, and yet it is perhaps the one component that Americans, due to their insularity and traditional self-sufficiency, lack the most. As early as the 1990s, a RAND Corporation survey of business and educational leaders confirmed the emerging importance of this issue for the global marketplace (RAND Corporation, 1994). The study found that "cross-cultural competence is considered by members of both the academic and corporate communities to be the most important new attribute for an individual's effective performance in the global marketplace. However, they also believe it is a skill that is severely lacking among American college graduates" (p. 64).

One of the most comprehensive recent analyses of the need for global competence among engineers is the report "In Search of Global Engineering Excellence: Educating the Next Generation of Engineers for the Global Workplace," commissioned by the German manufacturer Continental AG (Continental, 2006). The report portrays current trends in engineering and engineering education in major economies of the world: Brazil, China, Germany, Japan, Switzerland, and the United States. It concludes that "many engineers will find themselves working and living in foreign environments during much of their career" and states that engineering curricula must "instill a global mindset" (Continental, 2006, p. 31). The report lists the following three key elements needed to produce globally competent graduates: coursework in international studies, second language proficiency, and international experience. It furthermore cites four factors that typically impede the worldwide capacity to better prepare global engineers:

1. Unfortunately, most engineering educators do not view engineering as it is practiced in other countries as central to the education of their students.

2. Despite the pace of change in the world and its shrinking size, international mobility remains a challenge for many U.S. students because it is not customary and due to financial constraints.

3. Globalization and collaboration go hand-in-hand with partnerships with universities and industry, of which there are too few.

4. There is a significant lack of knowledge about proven theories and effective practices for instilling global competence (Continental, 2006, p. 41).

These four conditions summarize the reasons why it has proven difficult to implement internationalization in engineering education on a wider scale. They also explain why internationalization is often done in the form of "add-ons," such as a short summer study abroad program conducted in English, and why full-fledged international engineering programs integrating engineering and language/culture study with an internship in the target culture are still the exception. Finally, "In Search of Global Engineering Excellence" summarizes the desired attributes of globally competent engineers as "technically adept, culturally aware, broadly knowledgeable, innovative, entrepreneurial, flexible and mobile" (p. 33).

The Accreditation Board for Engineering and Technology (ABET), the recognized accreditor for college and university programs in applied science, computing, engineering, and technology, also acknowledges the international dimension of engineering today. The criteria for accrediting engineering programs for the 2008–2009 accreditation cycle list 11 program outcomes, one of which states that engineering programs must demonstrate that their students attain "the broad education necessary to understand the impact of engineering solutions in a global, economic, environmental and societal context (ABET, 2008, p. 2). With this statement, ABET recognizes that U.S.-based engineering can no longer ignore the implications of globalization on the design, manufacturing, and sale of goods.

Definition of Global Competence

How to define global competence and how it relates to intercultural communication has been a major challenge for all parties involved in international education, and this is certainly true for engineering educators as well. Definitions have important ramifications for the planning, execution, and evaluation of international efforts in higher education. In the engineering field, there seems to be no one preferred term to describe this international competence, with the most commonly used terms being *global, international,* and *cross-cultural.* If anything, there is a gradual dawning of awareness that engineering students are likely to have to work internationally in the coming years and that they should be prepared for this fact.

Looking more generally at definitions of global competence, Olson and Kroeger (2001, p. 117) list the term *intercultural communication or competence* as a part of global competence. Their definition of global competence includes the following three components:

- Substantive knowledge (knowledge of cultures, languages, world issues, global dynamics)

- Perceptual understanding (open-mindedness, resistance to stereotyping, recognition that one's worldview is not a universal perspective)

- Intercultural communication (skills used to effectively engage with others, including adaptability, empathy, and cross-cultural awareness

Thus, *global competence* can be seen as an umbrella term describing human ability to effectively interact with substantive knowledge, perceptual understanding, and intercultural communication skills across national borders. With respect to a definition of intercultural competence, Deardorff's (2006) study reports experts' consensus on broad rather than specific definitions of the concept as well as the overarching importance of attitudes, especially openness and tolerating ambiguity.

Hunter, White, and Godbey (2006) see no clear consensus on a definition for the term *global competence.* The authors suggest it may be an "essentially contested concept." They conclude that a final definition for this and other contested terms is "impossible because virtually every person or organization that might be a party to the definitional process approaches that process with philosophical values or a programmatic agenda very much in mind" (Hunter et al., 2006, p. 267). Having surveyed the literature on global competence, this wide array of constituents becomes clear. They come from different scholarly traditions—the "tribes of academic international specialists" (Lambert, 1996, p. 9) work in academic and nonacademic environments, have separate professional organizations, disseminate findings in certain publications, and—unfortunately—often appear to work in isolation from each other. Within academia, these "players" in the intercultural/global competence field for the professions include cultural anthropologists (e.g., Hofstede & Hofstede, 2005), engineering educators (e.g., Downey et al., 2006; Lohmann, Rollins, & Hoey, 2006), foreign language educators (e.g., Grandin, 2006), and study abroad professionals (see Carlson, 2007). Outside of academia, intercultural trainers and industry representatives disseminate information on global competence issues (see Caspersen, 2002). A major effort to bring these constituents together for engineering education has been the University of Rhode Island's Annual Colloquium for International Engineering Education (www.uri.edu/iep).

So, how do we best define the elusive concept of global competence? Hunter et al. (2006) brought together representatives from multinational companies, human resource managers of transnational corporations, senior international educators, United Nations (UN) and embassy officials, and intercultural specialists. These experts agreed on the following working definition for the term *global competence:* "Having an open mind while actively seeking to understand cultural norms and expectations of others, leveraging this gained knowledge to interact, communicate and work effectively outside one's environment" (Hunter et al., 2006, p. 270). Lambert identified a globally competent person as "one who has knowledge (of current events), can empathize with others, demonstrates approval (maintains a positive attitude), and has an unspecified degree of foreign language competence and task performance (ability to understand the value in something foreign)" (qtd. in Hunter et al., 2006, p. 273).

The American Council on Education (ACE) has created learning outcome statements for a globally competent student graduating from college. These competencies are divided into knowledge, skills, and attitudes. The knowledge portion focuses on understanding one's own culture in a global and comparative context, knowledge of global issues and trends, and knowledge of other cultures. The skills portion suggests culturally competent students use diverse cultural frames of reference to think critically and use foreign language skills and/or knowledge of other cultures to extend access to information, experiences, and understanding. Finally, the attitudes portion states the globally competent student tolerates cultural ambiguity and shows ongoing willingness to seek out intercultural opportunities (ACE, 2008).

In sum, an interculturally competent person understands that all individuals' views of the world have been unknowingly shaped by one's own culture. This person also has sufficient knowledge of the target culture, including history, geography, customs, and so on, to put observations into a meaningful perspective. He or she also understands the importance of clear communication. Also, given the fact that culturally important and unique words often do not have a direct equivalent in the English language, the culturally competent persons understands the limitations presented by a lack of proficiency in the other culture's language.

Developing Global
Competence in Engineering Students

Successful development of intercultural or global competence depends on a whole host of variables, such as nature of the academic preparation, degree of language proficiency, and nature and type of the international experience. Other variables, such as a student's personality, are also important factors. Most important, intercultural learning also takes time and, in fact, is a lifelong journey. Those in the engineering field who describe themselves as "comfortable" in two cultures, both in terms of everyday life and professionally, generally have multiyear experiences in both countries and almost always have advanced proficiency in the language of the host country.

Hunter et al.'s (2006) study offers a three-step path to developing global competence. The first and most critical step is for a person to "develop a keen understanding of his or her own cultural norms and expectations: A person should attempt to understand his or her own cultural box before stepping into someone else's" (p. 279). The intercultural training community deserves credit for bringing this critical point to the forefront. It can be taught in many ways, through traditional academic methods but probably more effectively through simulation and gaming activities where participants experience a sense of "otherness." A student who at least has been sensitized to his or her own cultural norms before the beginning of the overseas stay is less likely to place negative value judgments on the target culture when inevitable puzzling cultural encounters occur.

The second step in developing global competence is the actual international experience. Here it is important that the students go out of their comfort zone and seek authentic experiences. Hunter et al. (2006) stress the importance of "directly experiencing cultures outside of one's own box . . . and by extensive foreign language training" (p. 279). In this phase, the student should learn to observe differences in a nonjudgmental way and to appreciate the cultural differences with an attitude of openness.

In the third stage, a globally competent person has a strong sense of the major social, political, economic, and cultural aspects of both the home and the host country. In Hunter et al.'s (2006) words, "To become globally competent one must establish a firm understanding of the concept of globalization and world history. It is here that the recognition of the interconnectedness of society, politics, history, economics, the environment, and related topics becomes important" (p. 279).

Global competence in engineering is a multifaceted concept. At a basic level, the important driving forces are (a) having positive attitudes toward ideas, issues, and people outside one's realm, including openness and a willingness to tolerate ambiguity; (b) showing a serious interest in another country, as demonstrated by gaining knowledge of important aspects of geography, history, and culture as well as some proficiency in a foreign language; and (c) interacting with host country nationals at a professional or academic level. Furthermore, for engineers specifically, global competence includes the ability to work with people who define problems differently and use different engineering and managerial approaches to solve those problems (Downey et al., 2006). Defining and solving problems always takes place in a country-specific context, which may involve factors such as availability of resources, climate, workforce, and cultural preferences. Finally, as Deardorff (2006) states, there is no magical point at which one becomes globally competent—it is indeed a lifelong process subject to development and refinement over time.

Key Program Elements Needed to Produce Globally Competent Engineers

The most comprehensive view of key program elements needed to produce globally competent students and a listing of higher education programs for international engineering have been offered by Lohmann et al. (2006). According to this study, four program types or options have emerged in the United States:

1. Dual majors or degree programs (e.g., Pennsylvania State University, Iowa State University, and University of Rhode Island)

2. Minors or certificates (e.g., Georgia Tech, Iowa State University, Purdue University, University of Illinois, University of Michigan, University of Pittsburgh)

3. International internships or projects (e.g., Worcester Polytechnic Institute and Pennsylvania State University)

4. Study abroad (e.g., University of Minnesota)

For the development of global competence, Lohmann et al. (2006) find agreement in the international education community on three key elements: (1) coursework in international studies, (2) second language proficiency, and (3) international experience. The authors amend this list with two additional statements. They believe that "the type of international knowledge and the nature of the international experience are important and the international knowledge and experience should be integrated and relevant to a student's field of study; i.e., global competence should include an understanding of the relevance of international cultures to a student's major" (p. 121).

The first item, coursework in international studies, draws on a wide range of disciplines, including economics, political science, history, and geography. The International Plan at Georgia Tech, for example, requires three international studies courses and a capstone experience where students choose from courses such as international relations, international trade, the European Union, sustainability, society and culture of world regions/countries, and so on.

Second language proficiency, the second item, receives various degrees of attention, from no foreign language requirement in some short-term project-based programs to a full bachelor's degree in a foreign language with extensive time spent abroad. At the University of Rhode Island's International Engineering Program, students earn a BA in German, French, and Spanish or a minor in Chinese in addition to their BS degree in their chosen engineering discipline. In the case of the

German program, students in this 5-year program spend their entire fourth year abroad. This includes a 1-month intensive language course at the advanced intermediate level, a full semester of engineering coursework, and advanced German courses at the Technical University of Braunschweig and a 6-month professional internship in the student's chosen engineering discipline at a company or research institute in Germany.

The international experience requirement varies in length from summer overseas experiences to the full-year study abroad/internship combination at the University of Rhode Island described previously. The Global Perspectives Program at Worcester Polytechnic Institute sends large numbers of engineering students on 7-week overseas design course projects abroad, where students, accompanied by a faculty member, immerse themselves in a host country, designing solutions to local problems. They complete predeparture cultural orientation sessions and work with host nationals while at the project site (Lohmann et al., 2006).

In addition to the length, the nature of an engineering student's overseas stay is critical for the development of intercultural competence. A U.S. student going to a university overseas with a group of peers, accompanied by a faculty member from the home institution, taking discipline-specific courses taught by the U.S. faculty member, and living with other U.S. students is likely to return with less intercultural knowledge and awareness than a student who is completing a 6-month internship by himself or herself in a foreign country. The latter student will not only see the foreign country through the eyes of the work world but also will gain valuable insight into the mind-set of engineering in the foreign country (i.e., the culture of engineering in Germany as it is practiced on a day-to-day basis). The supervised professional internship abroad is a highly prized opportunity for American engineering students.

Lohmann et al.'s (2006) final point, the relevance of the international experience to a student's field of study, is also significant. Preparatory coursework, such as Virginia Tech's course on engineering cultures (Downey et al., 2006), can provide the background knowledge for understanding how engineers in different countries approach engineering issues differently, define problems differently, and use different, culturally conditioned teamwork dynamics to arrive at solutions to engineering problems. While overseas, it is critical that the student has the opportunity to have discipline-specific experiences. While studying abroad, engineering students generally make this important connection when they take a carefully chosen engineering course for host country students taught in the target language. The student in a supervised professional internship is directly experiencing the relevance of the target culture to his or her field of study.

Yet another model for global engineering experience is Purdue University's GEARE Program—Global Engineering Alliance for Research and Education, which is a strategic alliance of global universities (Purdue, Shanghai Jiao Tong, IIT Bombay, U. Karlsruhe, and Monterrey Tech) with focus on collaborative student research. The GEARE curriculum includes language and culture preparation, one domestic internship, one subsequent international internship/practicum at the same company, one semester enrolled abroad with fully transferable engineering course credits, and a two-semester multinational design team project (one semester at home university, one abroad) with students from international partner universities. Here the focus is on preparation for work in global teams, which is very much the profile for engineering careers in today's global workplace. The multinational design team project is a key component of the GEARE program. During their semester abroad, the U.S. students are teamed with students of the foreign partner university. They collaborate in planning and designing a chosen project. The following semester, the same international student teams conduct the fabrication and testing phase of the project in the United States.

How Do We Assess Global Competence?

The need for reliable evaluation instruments in international engineering education is clearly recognized. Returning students frequently respond enthusiastically to study abroad and internship experiences, industry clamors for more graduates with an international background, and, as we have seen above, higher education is beginning to offer more overseas opportunities to engineering students. But how do we best assess the outcome of an international engineering education experience? How do we know what they have gained from their experiences abroad? To what extent have they become globally competent? Developing reliable assessment instruments for this complex construct is challenging because there are so many variables. The outcome may be influenced by the student's general social competence, foreign language proficiency, the degree of cultural preparation, length of stay, type of program attended, the nature and the degree of interaction with host country nationals, housing arrangements, and many more.

Traditional means of education-abroad evaluation in engineering have focused on the reliability, cost-effectiveness, safety, and student satisfaction of international student experiences. As Bettez and Lineberry (2004) and Lohmann et al. (2006) state, more recently, several higher education institutions have started using some assessment instruments and methods to assess specifically the learning outcomes connected with global competence. The International Plan at Georgia Tech has developed an elaborate assessment plan, designed to assess participation goals, second language proficiency, comparative global knowledge, intercultural assimilation, global disciplinary practice, and intercultural sensitivity. This evaluation is accomplished through a considerable array of assessment methods. To assess second language proficiency, for example, the program uses pre/postexperience competency tests and postinternational experience reflective essays. To assess global disciplinary practice, the program uses a survey of employers of interns and evaluates the senior design projects using appropriate rubrics.

Considering the individual nature of many international engineering education programs, institutions of higher learning will most likely customize their evaluation procedures and use several methods of assessment, based on their specific learning outcomes related to global competence. Deardorff (2005) indicates the importance of aligning outcomes with assessment tools. Furthermore, her study concluded that when measuring intercultural competence specifically, it is important that a multimethod, multiperspective approach is used, one that is ideally integrated into the curriculum and program as a whole. Some institutions may use standardized instruments as part of the assessment process—in which case cost becomes a factor for many institutions of higher learning, and again those instruments must be aligned with the learning outcomes when and if they are used. Most assessment instruments will be "home grown." An example is the University of Kentucky's program (Bettez & Lineberry, 2004), where—for returning students—the institution developed a survey, administered it electronically, followed up with a structured interview with the students, and reported the results to department and college personnel for advising students about to go abroad. In conclusion, it is fair to say that as of the writing of this chapter, assessment of global competence in engineering is lagging behind the development of global engineering programs. Existing efforts at assessment appear to be U.S. based. (For further discussion on intercultural competence assessment, see Fantini [Chapter 27] and Deardorff [Chapter 28], this volume.)

Conclusion

The authors of this chapter take comfort in the fact that growing numbers of engineering educators across the United States are actively developing international experiences for their students. In Europe, engineering majors traditionally have had more opportunities for exchange through the intra–European Union mobility programs, such as ERASMUS (Heitmann, 2005).

While engineering students have traditionally been among the least likely to incorporate international experiences into their undergraduate programs, it is clear that this trend is being reversed. It is particularly noteworthy that international educator organizations have identified the internationalization of engineering education as a priority, as noted, for example, in the November 2007 edition of NAFSA's[1] quarterly publication, *International Educator* (Bremer, 2007). Funding organizations are likewise identifying the need to prepare engineers and scientists for careers in an increasingly competitive global environment. The National Science Foundation in the United States, for example, has set the tone with its well-funded Program in International Research and Education (PIRE) and its International Research and Education in Engineering (IREE) initiative. Though there is much to be learned about this complex concept and how best to develop and assess global competence in engineering students, we can be confident that engineering educators are rapidly reaching agreement that global skills belong to the core competencies of an engineer for the 21st century.

Note

1. NAFSA is an association of international educators. It promotes international education and provides professional development. Formerly known as National Association of Foreign Student Advisers.

References

Accreditation Board for Engineering and Technology (ABET). (2008). *Criteria for accrediting engineering programs.* Retrieved March 31, 2009, from www.abet.org

ABET (2008). *Criteria for Accrediting Engineering Programs.* Baltimore, MD: ABET. www.abet.org

American Council on Education. (2008). *Assessing international learning outcomes.* Retrieved May 21, 2008, from http://www.acenet.edu/Content/NavigationMenu/ProgramsServices/International/Campus/GoodPractice/fipse/index.htm

Bettez, D. J., & Lineberry, G. T. (2004, June). *Assessing engineering students' study abroad experiences.* Paper presented at the 2004 American Society for Engineering Education Annual Conference & Exposition, Salt Lake City, UT.

Bremer, D. (2007, November). Engineering the world. *International Educator,* pp. 30–37.

Carlson, S. (2007). A global approach to engineering: Universities push their future engineers to study abroad, with limited success. *Chronicle of Higher Education, 53*(39), 33–36.

Caspersen, R. (2002). Encouraging engineers to learn cross-cultural skills. *Global Journal of Engineering Education, 6,* 135–137.

Continental. (2006). *In search of global engineering excellence.* Retrieved May 21, 2008, from http://www.global-engineering-excellence.org/

Deardorff, D. K. (2005, May/June) A matter of logic? *International Educator,* pp. 26–31.

Deardorff, D. K. (2006). Identification and assessment of intercultural competence as a student outcome of internationalization. *Journal of Studies in International Education, 10,* 241–266.

Downey, G. L., Lucena, J. C., Moskal, B. M., Parkhurst, R., Bigley, T., Hays, C., et al. (2006, April). The globally competent engineer: Working effectively with people who define problems differently. *Journal of Engineering Education,* pp. 107–122.

Friedman, T. (2005). *The world is flat: A brief history of the twenty-first century.* New York: Farrar, Straus, & Giroux.

Grandin, J. M. (2006). Preparing engineers for the global workplace. *The Online Journal for Global Engineering Education, 1*(1). http://digitalcommons.uri.edu/ojgee/

Heitmann, G. (2005). Challenges of engineering education and the curriculum development in the context of the Bologna Process. *European Journal of Engineering Education. 30,* 447–458.

Hofstede, G., & Hofstede, G. J. (2005). *Cultures and organizations: Software of the mind: Intercultural cooperation and its importance for survival.* New York: McGraw-Hill.

Hunter, B., White, G. P., & Godbey, G. C. (2006). What does it mean to be globally competent? *Journal of Studies in International Education, 10,* 267–284.

Lambert, R. D. (1996). *Educational exchange and global competence.* New York: CIEE.

Lohmann, J. R., Rollins, H. A., Jr., & Hoey, J. J. (2006). Defining, developing and assessing global competence in engineers. *European Journal of Engineering Education, 31,* 119–131.

Lynn, L. H., & Salzman, H. (2006, Winter). Collaborative advantage: Globalization of innovation and engineering. *Issues in Science and Technology,* pp. 74–82.

National Academy of Engineering. (2005a). *Educating the engineer of 2020: Adapting engineering education to the new century.* Washington, DC: National Academies Press.

National Academy of Engineering. (2005b). *The engineer of 2020: Visions of engineering in the new century.* Washington, DC: National Academies Press.

Olson, C. L., & Kroeger, K. R. (2001). Global competency and intercultural sensitivity. *Journal of Studies in International Education, 5,* 116–137.

RAND Corporation. (1994). *Developing the global work force: Insights for colleges and corporations.* Santa Monica, CA: Author.

Saxenian, A. (2006). *The new Argonauts: Regional advantage in a global economy.* Cambridge, MA: Harvard University Press.

CHAPTER 22

Intercultural Competence in Religious Organizations

Neither Jew nor Gentile

*Lessons About Intercultural
Competence in Religious Organizations*

George Yancey

eligion serves the critical function of addressing questions of meaning, or
ultimate concern, for members in a given society. Religious beliefs equip
individuals for dealing with dilemmas surrounding meaning, purpose, and
identity. It is in religious organizations that we find like-minded individuals who
provide the support and counsel we often need to address such concerns. Thus,
healthy religious organizations, or some possible substitute thereof, are important
to the health of a vibrant society.

Yet, except for our families, religious organizations are the most racially segre-
gated institution in the United States. Less than 8% of all religious congregations
have a numerical racial group that is less than 80% of the group (Emerson, 2006).
The overwhelming racially homogeneous nature of these religious organizations is
in contrast to the increasing racial diversity of our larger society. For religious organizations to continue to meet important human needs, it is essential for them to
adapt to changing multiracial societal norms. Modern religious organizations have
an increasing need to interact with racialized out-group members.

An important aspect of the transition many religious organizations have to
make is the development of intercultural competency skills that allow those

organizations to deal more easily with individuals who are not members of the numerical majority racial group.[1] Religious organizations will discover new challenges as they become comfortable addressing the cultural concerns of the numerical majority group. This focus of this chapter is how religious organizations, their leaders, and their members can develop the intercultural competency necessary for our changing society.[2]

Culture as Feature of Religion and Race

Our culture affects all aspects of our social lives, and so there are important cultural aspects to the religious and racial dimensions in our society. For example, although many individuals perceive racial differences as linked to biological distinctions, in reality, racial differences are socially constructed. We perceive each other as being racially different because of rules set up by society. One of the best illustrations is the social rules determining whether one is labeled Black by having any African heritage. In U.S. society, we have the development of what has been called the one-drop rule for African Americans (Davis, 1991). Other racial groups are not so automatically defined by their racial heritage, and the one-drop rule has traditionally only applied to African Americans, indicating the arbitrary nature of this rule. The rule is not determined by any biological necessity, but it is the result of cultural preferences.

There are definite consequences to the racial rules embedded in the United States. For African Americans, the one-drop rule sets up a social barrier that alienated them from the mainstream of society (Yancey, 2003b). As a result of this process, an oppositional culture (Ogbu, 1990; Waters, 1999) has been developed by African Americans, which leads to their rejection of mainstream societal values. Thus, notions of biological distinctions lead to cultural differences between African Americans and majority group members.

Racial distinctions also serve as markers for newcomers into the United States. Hispanic and Asian Americans are racial groups that have immigrated into the United States. As a result of this immigration, they have encountered a culture different from their native lands. But they also possess phenotypical markers that designate them as "outsiders." Thus, second- and third-generation immigrant racial groups maintain a culture shaped both by their immigrant status and their rejection from the larger culture. In this way, we can see that most, if not all, minority racial groups have experienced historical and social dynamics that influence the cultural values of individuals in those groups.

There are important cultural aspects within religious institutions as well. While a variety of definitions of religion are available, I have always tended to favor the ones that focused upon religion as a way to answer questions of meaning (Niebuhr, 1960; Tillich, 1957; Yinger, 1970). Questions of meaning deal with issues such as purpose and direction, how to make sense of tragedy, the meaning of good and evil, and so on. The drive to deal with such questions is overwhelming, and different religious systems enable individuals to find answers that comfort and sustain them in an uncertain social world. It is not just individuals who need such answers. Societies and communities also need to provide answers about the purpose of their group, what is desirable about the group's culture, how to handle the unique challenges of the group, and so forth. Religious beliefs within a group help to provide such answers. Rituals imbed those answers among the group members and remind them of how questions of meaning should be addressed.[3]

Answers to these questions of meaning are often linked to the racial group(s) in which the religion has developed. This is true even within a single religion. For example, Emerson and Smith (2000) document different ways Black and White evangelicals in the United States interpret social conditions through their theological beliefs. White evangelicals tend to construct theological beliefs that focus on freewill individualism as the way to explain social inequality, while Black evangelicals use their religion to support structuralism, or the belief that social structures are important, to explain this inequality. This tendency is true even though both groups tend to agree on the major Christian theological tenets. Their different social positions have created cultural distinctions that must be taken into account as we attempt to understand cultural diversity within religious institutions. Religious organizations that incorporate different racial groups must also find ways to deal with multiple cultural presuppositions and assertions that come with those groups.

In the United States, religious organizations have a powerful tendency to be dominated by a given racial group. Thus, religious sites have been places where cultural aspects of different racial groups are intensified in a setting that reflects concepts of meaning within those racial groups. It is not an accident that predominately White Christian congregations tend to reinforce individualism (Emerson & Smith, 2000), while predominately Black congregations tend to reinforce demands for social justice (Cavendish, 2000; Chaves & Higgins, 1992) as these concepts are linked to racialized meaning mechanisms dominant in those racial communities. For White Christians, the acceptance of individualism is indicative of the general White racial identity embedded within majority group society. For Black Christians, the emphasis on racial justice comports well with their desire to resist the dominant culture that has placed them lower in the racial hierarchy. In both cases, how a racial group develops answers to concerns of ultimate meaning helps promote the goals of that group, reinforcing the values and norms promoted by that racial group.

While reinforcement of meaning systems provides a utilitarian purpose for religious institutions, this reinforcement also provides a powerful barrier for the development of intercultural competence within these organizations. Naturally racialized individuals in religious groups become comfortable in the culture of the numerical majority. They find a culture that meets many of their spiritual and social-psychological concerns. They do not always have an incentive to alter this cultural atmosphere so that they can respect and welcome racial groups with other cultural presuppositions. As a result, individuals who may have developed a high level of intercultural competence in other arenas of their lives (educational, occupational, political) may not have put forth the time and energy necessary for developing intercultural competency within the religious dimensions of their lives. Within voluntary religious organizations, they may develop a powerful barrier that stymies meaningful intercultural interaction. There is a critical need to motivate members in a religious organization about the need to develop intercultural competency skills.

Developing the Vision for Intercultural Competence

Christians often use the phrase "neither Jew nor Gentile" to indicate the idea that God does not favor one racial/ethnic group over another. However, this passage was provided as the early New Testament evangelist Paul criticized Jewish Christians who attempted to force non-Jewish Christians into accepting their Jewish culture. Paul argues that instead of requiring other Christians to assimilate into Jewish culture, they should be encouraged to develop a faith based on their own culture. Christians generally view this passage as a measure of individual acceptance when in fact it is a statement about cultural acceptance. It can even be argued that this passage is a call to develop intercultural competence.

For my purposes, I define intercultural competence as the ability to work and develop primary relationships with individuals from distinct cultures. Such ability is vital if religious organizations are to become sites of intercultural primary relationships. Because of the natural tendency to defend one's own subculture and the importance of religious organizations in addressing the ultimate concerns of that subculture, there is going to be resistance to the intrusion of other cultural norms into an established religious setting. It is critical that leaders of religious institutions who desire a higher level of intercultural competence prepare and train members of their organizations for the introduction of individuals from different racial groups. Failure to make such preparations will almost guarantee disaster when individuals from different racial subcultures come to the religious group.

An example of the failure to make such preparations can be illustrated from my previous research. Before making a trip to a city, I and the other researchers were told a particular church was racially mixed. However, upon arrival at that church, we found it to be all White. The pastor hired an African American minister before preparing the congregation for the changes to come. As this minister brought Blacks into the church, the White congregates refused to make any cultural accommodations and were even hostile to the visitors. The Black visitors did not return, and the Black minister moved on. The pastor attempted to do the same thing again, only this time with a Hispanic minister. The same results ensued, and soon that Hispanic minister had to move on. The Blacks and Hispanics in the neighborhood have now been warned about the chilly reception they will receive and will not come back to that church. Since there is not a large group of non-Whites in the city who are neither Black nor Hispanic, the pastor now has no option but to maintain a Eurocentric church.

This is an example of the consequences of not preparing the congregation for an influx of those who are racially and culturally different. Fortunately, other religious leaders have made such preparations and serve as positive examples. In one particular church, the pastor was inspired several years ago to reach out to those of different races. The pastor began by convincing the elders and staff members that it was important to attempt to minister to those of different races. The pastor was a biracial individual and already had some intercultural skills.[4] The pastor trained the leaders in cultural self-awareness, empathy for other cultures, and adaptability.

Once the leaders of the church were sufficiently enlightened and motivated, they became the pastor's allies. Their influence was soon felt throughout the congregation, and over time, that church became ready for a multiracial outreach. After this preparation and training, the pastor hired an African American minister to further develop an atmosphere of racial acceptance and to prepare the congregation for the cultural differences new African American members would bring. With the African American pastor's ministry in the congregation, there became a small but growing group of African Americans who joined the church; plans were being implemented to attract even more African Americans.[5]

It took years for that pastor to get the congregation to a point in which members were ready to develop a multicultural atmosphere, but by investing that time, the pastor greatly increased the chances of success. Notice how the pastor first worked with the clergy and lay leaders of the church before attempting to convince the entire congregation about the value of intercultural outreach. I have found this to be a common pattern for religious organizations that want to move toward intercultural competence. Preparation of the current leadership is vital if one expects to move the entire congregation in such a challenging direction.

However, some individuals in a religious organization may not be willing to move in the direction of becoming culturally flexible or to conduct an honest assessment of their own ethnocentrism. Given the cultural ramifications of becoming an interculturally competent organization, this is not surprising. Those who want to move their religious congregations toward an atmosphere of racial and cultural acceptance may have to do something quite difficult. They may have to either remove some of these individuals from their group or be willing to have such individuals remove themselves. My discussion with pastors who have taken a racially homogeneous church and transformed it into a multiracial congregation often found that such individuals came to the point where they had to stop fighting to retain every member who wanted to leave. In fact, some of them commented that their religious group benefited from the departure of members who resisted any meaningful changes. After such individuals left, the congregation generally grew in diversity and in numbers. Religious leaders are generally taught to attempt to keep all of their current members while adding others when possible. However, when it comes to creating an atmosphere whereby intercultural competency is the norm, sometimes the old saying "less is more" is quite applicable.

Respecting Culturally Based Differences

Of course, an important part of any process toward intercultural competence is the development of an empathic and ethnorelative view so that individuals can help those from other cultures to be comfortable. The values of adaptability and flexibility are critical as members of the group deal with the new values and perspectives brought by those in other cultures. However, this process takes on a whole new challenge as it concerns religious organizations. Because these organizations address issues of ultimate concern, there are likely to be concepts and principles where flexibility is difficult. Such flexibility can be seen as an indication that the values and norms emphasized by the organization are not important, and thus the organization's reason for existence can be questioned.[6]

For this reason, it is not as simple as instructing members of religious groups to learn to accept whatever cultural distinctions individuals of different races and cultures may bring. Potential cultural alterations that challenge the basic core principles of a religious congregation may threaten the basis for a particular religious orientation. Congregations that base their notions of pacifism or premarital sexual abstinence within their interpretation of meaning should not feel compelled to support arguments for just war theory or sexual freedom to accommodate needs for intercultural competence. Religious organizations must set some standards as to what cultural alterations they will and will not accept.[7] A careful examination of how a religious organization attempts to deal with issues of ultimate concern and what sort of cultural norms and practices can violate the values is necessary before a decision can be made about the cultural differences that emerge from distinct racial/ethnic groups. This type of cultural self-awareness must be done openly and deliberately. Business meetings, special speakers, or lay leader assemblies are ways in which these issues can be hammered out. These gatherings can help to define core values and how those values may be expressed in distinct cultures, as well as the limits those core values may place within contrasting cultural expressions. For religious organizations, such conceptualizing is essential for the possibility of intercultural competency to be realized.

While it is acceptable for a religious organization to reject certain practices or cultural norms as out of the range of acceptability for members of its group, it is quite important to struggle with what is immutable and what is negotiable for a particular group. This effort seems to suggest a more narrow-minded perspective, but it actually can lead to less rejection of possibly objectionable alternate cultural practices. Once a religious organization has decided upon what is acceptable, then the members of that organization will be in a position to be flexible with all that does not violate its way of addressing questions of meaning. This will allow such individuals to find different cultural ways to express the religious organization's questions of meaning. The members of the congregation can be free to have an attitude of acceptance without having a fear of "selling out" that can come if the difficult work of evaluating one's own answers to ultimate meaning has not been done.

A practical example may suffice to illustrate how this can work. One of the churches in our study had begun to attract a larger Hispanic population. To help serve this population, the church hired a Hispanic minister. Generally, the church required all of its ministers to attend both the Sunday morning and evening service, but the new hire soon began to skip the evening service. This created some degree of consternation among other ministers. When asked about this absence, the minister pointed out that Sunday evening was an important family time in Hispanic culture. For the minister to serve this population, it was important to respect this cultural value. The leaders of the congregation soon realized that the ultimate purpose of the church was the promotion of its monotheistic beliefs and not attending all the functions of the church. These leaders came to the conclusion that if family time on Sunday evening was the best way this minister could promote these beliefs to the Hispanic community, then making this cultural accommodation for the minister was worth the effort. In making such an accommodation, the congregation also signaled to the Hispanics in the congregation that they would not be stigmatized for missing the Sunday night service. Needless to say, such a signal was important for helping to maintain positive relations between the European and Hispanic members of the church.

So much of what we think is a critical difference between those of other cultural groups and ourselves is not as important as we may think. Until we recognize what is of vital concern to us, there is a tendency to focus on superficial differences to maintain our distinctiveness from other groups. Such a focus inhibits our ability to create a welcoming atmosphere for those of other racial and cultural groups. Furthermore, focusing on whether cultural practices and/or norms violate a religious group's answers to questions of ultimate concern also limits the degree to which a group's own social, political, and economic interest can be used to exclude those of other racial groups. In fact, this focus enables individuals of different groups to challenge the egocentric basis of their own cultural values. For example, White Christians may want to reconsider their reliance upon the values of individualism, and Black Christians may want to do the same as it concerns their adherence of oppositional culture (Ogbu, 1990), if they cannot directly connect these values to how they address questions of meaning. This reconsideration may create an atmosphere of intercultural acceptance whereby White and Black Christians listen to each other's concerns rather than worship in separate churches and reify their differences with each other.[8]

As we consider the cultural differences that those of distinct racial groups bring into a church, there is an important principle that must be taken into account. While members of all groups must make accommodations for those of other cultures, the individuals who are in the numerical majority will often have to make the greatest accommodations. Those who are in the numerical minority are already making a high level of adjustment in their willingness to attend a religious group where they are greatly outnumbered. Thus, all other things being equal, it is important that those in the numerical majority show a willingness to make cultural adaptations that make the experiences of those in the numerical minority more enjoyable. There should be communications between the numerical majority and minority as these accommodations are made so that chances of misunderstanding are minimized, but preference, when possible, should generally be given to the numerical minority.

Those of us who work with religious organizations should also take into consideration our own biases and be careful not to promote those biases as we aid these groups. I have often worked with religious groups that have theological presuppositions quite different than mine own. When this happens, I strive to remember that my purpose is not to impose my own religious values into these groups but rather to help them to identify the core of their own beliefs and how to become flexible in accommodating others of different racial/ethnic groups as they adhere to that core. I do not try to convince them to accept what they state as "heretical," but rather I help them to be certain that what they reject is not merely cultural and indeed violates their core religious values.

Finding Commonalities Between Different Racial/Ethnic Groups in Religion

An important part of intercultural competence is the ability to have empathy and adaptability for cultural distinctions that differ from one's own culture. Learning what to accept as inconsequential and what to hold on to as vital to one's meaning system is one of the skills that members of religious organizations have to develop to enhance their intercultural competency abilities. However, it is not enough to understand the cultural contrasts between different racial/ethnic groups. There is also value in focusing on the similar drives and desires found within most of us. This is particularity important as we use our religious system to address our ultimate concerns.

I have no desire to paper over the differences between religious and racial groups. Those who too easily dismiss these differences are not taking seriously the values and perspectives of individuals in those groups. What I do argue is that sometimes perceptions of these differences are greater than they actually are. Finding out what core values we have in common can serve as a way to connect with each other and make the cultural differences we do possess more palatable. Once we have identified these commonalities, then it is important to use them to bring together those from distinct racial/ethnic groups.

For example, a multiracial church in the North Central region of the United States was able to attract roughly equal numbers of European, African, and Hispanic Americans. The neighborhood in which the church was located was plagued with a high crime rate. As noted earlier in this chapter, majority group Christians in the United States generally use an individualistic rubric to understand social problems and place the responsibility of this high crime rate on the actions of the criminals. African American Christians are more likely to look at the structuralist determinants of crime and make attributions about the responsibility upon social systems. Yet both majority and minority group members shared a fear of the crime in this community. This fear was forced to the surface by a particularly brutal murder that took place in the neighborhood of the church.

The church had to become a place that could address the concerns and fears of individuals of different race and ethnic groups. To only call for individual responsibility or systematic change would have served some individuals at the expense of others in their multiracial religious community. Yet members of all groups had fears of crime that had to be dealt with. Thus, the leadership of the church decided to conduct a "prayer march" from their church building to the site of the murder. Doing so enabled the members of the church to feel empowered that they could take their street back again. It also produced a sight for the community of a multiracial group that was no longer afraid. Outsiders could look at this march as a call for individuals to take responsibility for their actions and thus put an end to crime. Or outsiders could take a look at this march as a call to alter the social systems that encourage such a brutal murder. This ambiguous definition helped the march to represent what the members of a particular group needed it to mean, while still allowing the members of all racial/ethnic groups to confront the fears they had because of the crime. In this way, the church leaders found creative ways they could address the common needs of members of different groups and still provide some level of cultural-specific help. Religious leaders of multiracial organizations will, at times, have to use a similar level of creativity if they are going to provide support for those in several different racial groups.

A Practical Example of What Intercultural Competency Looks Like in Religious Settings

I have drawn upon my research of multiracial churches, as well as relationships with leaders/members of multiracial churches, to address some issues of intercultural competence. Within these religious organizations, valuable lessons can be drawn. To build on this methodology, I take one church that I have worked with in the past and explore more fully how intercultural competence can create a religious environment inclusive of individuals of different racial/ethnic groups.

Eastern Christian Church[9] is located in a medium-size town close to the East Coast of the United States. Until a few years ago, it was a predominately White church. At that time, the pastor was inspired to attracted members of different racial groups into the congregation. But the pastor seemed to be the only person so inspired. The pastor began to talk about this vision with other staff members. Slowly they begin to see the value of a racially diverse congregation. Eastern Christian Church is built around small groups, many of them led by staff members. These staff members started to influence other church members through these small groups. Then the church reinforced its intentions by hiring an African American clergy member. That staff member was well known among other Blacks and developed community ministries that drew in not just African Americans but other individuals of color as well. It is at this point that Eastern Christian Church had to deal with the different racial cultures that have now entered the church.

These different racial cultures have to submit to the vital internal values of Eastern Christian Church. It is an evangelical church that also focuses on meeting the social needs of their community. The evangelical focus of the church indicates a priority of proselytizing and traditional moral values. New members of the church are encouraged to give up habits and norms that violate those values. The desire to meet the social needs of the community directs members of the church to put time and effort into serving less fortunate members of the lower-class community. Individuals coming into the church are expected to find ways to provide support for the local neighborhood. Concerns of traditional morality, evangelism, and social community are expected of all members of the church, regardless of the racial culture they come from. However, this does not mean that this congregation ignores cultural differences. In fact, the congregation makes intentional efforts to confront directly the cultural issues that arise in the congregation.

One of the cultural issues the church confronted was worship. The worship in the main service had been based on the type of traditional hymns found in many European American churches. This music is led by a team adept at performing traditional music. Abruptly stopping the performance of traditional music would cause much conflict within the church. Yet the leadership of the church quickly recognized that alteration of the worship style did not violate the internal values that contributed to the answers the church provides for questions of ultimate concern. As a result of this realization, a compromise was struck where two other music teams were formed. One of the music teams is based on a Black gospel style of music, and the other is a mixture of ethnic and traditional music. The teams rotate on different Sundays, allowing members of different racial groups to gain a taste of their culture at various times of the month.

Another cultural issue that members of the church were forced to confront was how to address church leaders. Majority group Christians generally call pastors and staff members by their first name. This denotes a level of equality that European Americans like to emphasize. But some, although not all, people of color have a history in which they have felt deprived of titles they rightly earned. Some cultures also embrace an underlying cultural value in which greater "power distance" is given to those in positions of perceived higher status positions, denoted by the use of titles. They tend to address church leaders as "pastor" instead of their first name. The tendency of some to ignore the titles of those in leadership was a source of cultural tension within the church. The head pastor helped to ease the tension by instructing the members of the church to use "pastor" when addressing the staff. The pastor reasoned that since Whites were the numerical majority, they would have to make accommodations to help the numerical minorities feel more at ease.

The way ministries are conducted is also an issue that emerges as an important cultural difference between majority and minority group members in religious organizations. European Americans tend to emphasize the importance of organizational structures in accomplishing the ministerial goals of the church, having been influenced by a results-oriented culture. Individuals of color tend to emphasize the need to develop meaningful relationships as a way to facilitate ministry, having been influenced by cultural backgrounds influenced by group-oriented values. The goals of the ministry are the same for both groups—evangelism, community service—but there are cultural differences in how these goals can be reached. Even today, members of the church are struggling with how to alter their organizational structure to meet the needs of both groups. They are doing this with a committee that is intentionally multiracial so that the needs and desires of individuals from several different racial groups can be heard. In this way, Eastern Christian Church illustrates that even after a church has achieved a degree of diversity success, it is still important to create avenues by which the perspectives of those from the numerical minority groups can be heard and addressed. The struggle to develop intercultural competence does not end with early success; rather, it is an ongoing process. Religious organizations are wise to continue intentional efforts at managing diversity for a long period of time and to be aware of becoming overconfident.

The church has since added another Black minister. This minister was younger than the other Black minister and thus brings in issues of youth, as well as racial, culture for the church. Even as the struggles within this church continue, it is vital to note that Eastern Christian Church has become known in its denomination for its multiracial makeup and has developed a positive reputation within its city. The efforts it made to develop a more positive atmosphere for intercultural communication has led to more than increased numbers of new members. It has led to a vibrant environment that foreshadows the direction that future religious groups need to follow if they are going to survive in an increasingly diverse society.

Conclusion

This brief chapter has pointed to several themes that can aid a religious organization in developing intercultural competence. In summary, here are the major steps that must be considered. First, a group has to invest in preparation before making any major alterations. It is vital for the leaders of the group to cast a powerful vision even at the cost of some current church members. Second, the group needs to consider what are an essential core vision and a cultural option. Such consideration is vital for providing members the freedom to accept cultural variations. Third, group members have to search for commonalities without dismissing the differences of their culture. An acknowledgment of both is important for creating a healthy intercultural environment. Finally, the group must attend to needed institutional alterations (i.e., racially diverse leadership, worship styles). Once again, space does not permit me to fully explore all of these alterations, but previous work of mine (Yancey, 2003a) can provide much-needed guidance for those who desire to make institutional changes.

The assertions of this chapter are based on my work with multiracial congregations. This may provide the impression that I perceive intercultural competence as only relevant in dealing with racial and ethnic differences. Of course, cultural differences are not solely based on race and ethnicity. There are also differences based on gender, social-economic status, education, lifestyle, age, and a variety of other dimensions. A "multicultural" church has to account for more than racial and ethnic differences. However, the concepts outlined in this chapter can help religious organizations deal with differences that have emerged from other social dimensions. In this way, I hope that this chapter possesses a higher level of generalizability than a mere discussion of racial differences.

As our society becomes more culturally diverse, there is a need for religious organizations to handle this diversity successfully. It is in these organizations that we can develop answers to our ultimate concerns that go beyond the perceptions of a single racial or ethnic group. Previous religious institutions have been built amid the racial separation that has dominated American society, and they are unlikely be able to serve the United States's developing multiracial environment.[10] Since providing pathways in which individuals can address those questions of meaning is important, we must look toward religious organizations willing to create these multiracial communities.

In conclusion, intercultural competence is a necessary but not sufficient component that religious groups will need address in regard to racial diversity. Religious organizations will also need to make institutional adjustments in their leadership structure. This often includes making alterations to the physical structure of their buildings and surroundings to communicate racial and ethnic acceptance and welcome. They may have to explore what their organization's central purpose is and how that purpose is served in a multiracial community. It is a mistake to rely exclusively on developing individuals' skills of intercultural competency if religious organizations want to attract a multiracial clientele. Addressing institutional and organizational barriers, such as language or physical location of congregation, will also be important in creating a multiracial religious experience.

Notes

1. I will use the term *numerical majority* when I do not want to be confused with the majority group in the larger society. Within a religious organization, it is the numerical

majority that has the dominant power. Thus, within a predominately African or Hispanic American church, European American congregates possess less power, even if they continue to possess disproportionate power in the rest of society.

2. The information that I will draw upon will be from data collected from the Lilly Congregational Study (1999–2001) and my experience working with multiracial congregations.

3. As a side note, it should be observed that religious answers do not have to be based on supernaturalist expressions of faith. Certain social groups may address questions of meaning without reliance on the supernatural. For example, it is well established that belief in traditional religious expressions is low within the humanities and social scientists (Ladd & Lipset, 1975). Supernatural expressions may be a competitor for expression of morality to the scientific assertions of such individuals (Dynes, 1974; Glock & Stark, 1965; Waldo, 1961), and secular ideologies such as Marxism and feminism may replace supernatural religion as answers to questions of meaning among academics.

4. Research (Field, 1996; Hall, 1992) has suggested that biracial individuals are also more likely to be bicultural as well.

5. Space does not allow me to address the need to influence the pastors through seminary training or religious socialization. Obviously waiting for individual clergy to become inspired is insufficient to create an atmosphere of intercultural competence among most individuals of faith. Ideally, future work will determine how best to create the leadership necessary to facilitate intercultural competence among communities of faith.

6. Kelley (1972) points out in his classic work on conservative churches that strictness is actually an asset for religious congregation since it helps to clarify the purpose of such organizations. He contends that more liberal religious congregations that de-emphasize strictness tend to lose members over time. While his theory has been updated by Smith's (1998) subcultural theory of congregational vitality, the basic need for some standards within religious groups is still evident.

7. There is a temptation to only perceive more conservative religious organizations as ones that have preconceived cultural expectations. This would be a mistake. Cultural expectations may differ in more progressive religious organizations, but they are present nonetheless. For example, members of a racial/ethnic subculture that emphasizes very traditional gender roles (i.e., women not working outside home, girls but not boys can live away from parents) can develop cultural conflict when they come into a progressive religious organization. I suspect that this cultural difference would quickly raise the ire of members in that progressive religious organization. I do not suggest that such organizations must accept these traditional cultural norms, but they must recognize that they, like conservative religious organizations, have cultural expectations that are often imposed on those from other racial/ethnic groups.

8. Indeed, I have conducted research suggesting that within multiracial churches, majority group members are more likely to alter their racial attitudes than minority group members (Yancey, 1999, 2001). I contend that this difference may have arisen because people of color are more likely to have had to deal with racial issues than majority group members and thus are less likely to alter their racial attitudes due to interracial contact (Yancey, 2007). This suggests that although it is theoretically possible, for example, that both Black and White Christians will alter their racial attitudes due to an intercultural atmosphere, it is more likely that the individualistic attitudes of Whites will change rather than the structuralist preferences of Blacks.

9. A pseudonym.

10. Emerson (2006) discusses what he terms "Sixth Americans." He argues that these individuals do not easily fit into the existing racial categories. Rather, they have a high degree of multiracial social networks and move easily between communities of different racial groups. Such individuals are likely to increase in number over time, and Emerson argues that they are particularly drawn toward multiracial religious groups.

References

Cavendish, J. C. (2000). Church-based community activism: A comparison of Black and White Catholic congregations. *Journal for the Scientific Study of Religion, 39,* 371–384.

Chaves, M., & Higgins, L. M. (1992). Comparing the community involvement of Black and White congregations. *Journal for the Scientific Study of Religion, 31,* 425–440.

Davis, J. F. (1991). *Who is Black? One nation's definition.* Philadelphia: Pennsylvania State University Press.

Dynes, R. R. (1974). Sociology as a religious movement. *The American Sociologist, 9*(4), 169–176.

Emerson, M. (2006). *People of the dream: Multiracial congregations in the United States.* Princeton, NJ: Princeton University Press.

Emerson, M. O., & Smith, C. (2000). *Divided by faith: Evangelical religion and the problem of race in America.* Oxford, UK: Oxford University Press.

Field, L. D. (1996). Piecing together the puzzle: Self concept and group identity in biracial Black/White youth. In M. P. P. Root (Ed.), *The multiracial experience: Racial borders as the new frontier* (pp. 114–126). Thousand Oaks, CA: Sage.

Glock, C. Y., & Stark, R. (1965). *Religion and society in tension.* Chicago: Rand McNally.

Hall, C. C. I. (1992). Please choose one: Ethnic identity choices for biracial individuals. In M. P. P. Root (Ed.), *Racially mixed people in America* (pp. 250–264). Newbury Park, CA: Sage.

Kelley, D. (1972). *Why conservative churches are growing.* New York: Harper & Row.

Ladd, E. C., & Lipset, S. M. (1975). *The divided academy: Professors and politics.* New York: McGraw-Hill.

Niebuhr, H. R. (1960). Faith in God and in gods. In H. R. Neibuhr (Ed.), *Radical monotheism and Western culture* (pp. 211–226). New York: Harper & Row.

Ogbu, J. (1990). Minority status and literacy in comparative perspective. *Daedalus, 119*(2), 141–168.

Smith, C. (1998). *American evangelicalism: Embattled and thriving.* Chicago: University of Chicago Press.

Tillich, P. (1957). *Dynamics of faith.* New York: Harper & Row.

Waldo, D. (1961). *Research for public policy.* Washington, DC: Brookings Institute.

Waters, M. C. (1999). *Black identities: West Indian immigrant dreams and American realities.* Cambridge, MA: Harvard University Press.

Yancey, G. (1999). An examination of effects of residential and church integration upon racial attitudes of Whites. *Sociological Perspectives, 42,* 279–304.

Yancey, G. (2001). Racial attitudes: Differences in racial attitudes of people attending multiracial and uniracial congregations. *Research in the Social Scientific Study of Religion, 12,* 185–206.

Yancey, G. (2003a). *One body, one spirit: Principles of successful multiracial churches.* Downers Grove, IL: InterVarsity Press.

Yancey, G. (2003b). *Who is White? Latinos, Asians, and the new Black/nonblack divide.* Boulder, CO: Lynne Rienner.

Yancey, G. (2007). *Interracial contact and social change.* Boulder, CO: Lynne Rienner.

Yinger, J. M. (1970). *The scientific study of religion.* New York: Macmillan.

CHAPTER 23

Intercultural Competence in Health Care

Developing Skills for Interculturally Competent Care

Rohini Anand and Indra Lahiri

A major challenge for today's health care providers around most of the world is that culturally diverse groups comprise the largest growing segment of the patient population. Individual health care choices and outcomes must be understandable to patients in terms of their own culture and experience. Thus, health care workers are faced with the need to develop intercultural competencies that allow them to recognize their own cultural norms, understand the patient's unique viewpoint, and effectively adjust their behaviors to maximize care.

While understanding the client's unique perspective is a challenge shared across industries, in health care, intercultural competence can be argued to be even more complex and challenging, primarily due to the intensely personal nature of the services offered, which often touch the core of patients' and providers' culturally influenced values, beliefs, and attitudes. Intercultural competence, also commonly referred to as cultural competence, may in the context of health care be briefly

AUTHOR'S NOTE: Much of this chapter is based on the work of Rohini Anand, PhD, in *Cultural Competency in Healthcare: A Guide for Trainers* (3rd ed.), 2004, published by National MultiCultural Institute and used with permission.

defined as the ability to deliver "effective, understandable, and respectful care that is provided in a manner compatible with [patients'] cultural health beliefs and practices and preferred language" (Office of Minority Services, 2000, p. 80865).

With global culture a reality in today's health care systems and a clear mandate that interculturally competent care is a necessity for successful patient outcomes, how is it possible to learn about all the specific variations with regard to illness, health, care, communication, and other issues related to the delivery of health services? No one has a formula explaining all the variables for every culture. Attempting to provide training on specific cultures may be helpful, yet it is likely to backfire if the information is offered in a one-dimensional manner or if it is used to stereotype individuals.

The key to providing quality care to patients of all cultural backgrounds lies in developing skills to learn about cultural and personal beliefs in a respectful fashion. What are the questions that providers should be asking? What are the cues that a cultural clash may be occurring? How can care providers overcome cultural clashes? This chapter examines these issues and offers models and ideas for developing skills for interculturally competent care.

The field of medical anthropology is credited with shaping the discipline of intercultural competence in health care. Using ethnographic methods, medical anthropologists have studied relationships and interactions between care providers and patients, often with special emphasis on the physician-patient relationship. Medical anthropologists have often "described the traditional culture of Western medicine as being disease-oriented, focusing on biological concepts and processes, and largely discounting the importance of cultural and psychosocial factors to health" (American Institutes for Research, 2002, p. 6). This disease orientation is itself merely a cultural norm. By approaching medicine through only this norm and often discounting other cultural beliefs and approaches to health and illness, Western medicine has evolved into a service that inadvertently provides unequal treatment to patients whose cultural backgrounds differ from those of the majority of providers.

As the demographics of our world shift, with many countries experiencing global culture on a domestic level, intercultural competence is becomingly an increasingly critical skill, both to ensure quality care for all patients and to ensure the continuing economic viability of the industry. Indeed, Reynolds (2004) puts it succinctly when he says, "Cultural and linguistic barriers are posing a problem for an industry that is already financially strained. If strategies to provide more culturally appropriate care are not implemented, financial pressures will continue to rise, and quality of care will suffer" (p. 237).

Overview of Business Case for Interculturally Competent Care

Intercultural competence is a necessary component of any health care provider's general competence. Not only are interculturally competent services being increasingly mandated at the federal and local levels, but cultural diversity among patient and patient populations is an ever-growing reality. Patient satisfaction, community support, patients' willingness to seek treatment, and patient outcomes are all dependent on culturally appropriate care and communication. The increasingly broad mix of cultures represented among health care patients and providers is evident with a simple review of recent statistics and projections:

In the United States alone:

- In 2006, not including people who identify as more than one race (who comprised 2% of the total U.S. population), African Americans constituted 12.4% of the total U.S. population, Latinos/Hispanics (who can be of any race) 14.8%, Asian Americans 4.4%, and American Indians or Alaskan Natives .8% (U.S. Census Bureau, 2006).

- From 2000 to 2050, White non-Hispanics will decrease from 69.4% of the total U.S. population to just over half (50.1%), while African Americans will increase from 12.7% to 14.6%, Hispanics (of any race) will increase from 12.6% to 24.4%, and Asians from 3.8% to 8% (no projections for American Indians and Alaskan Natives were provided) (U.S. Census Bureau, 2004).

- Nearly 55 million individuals, or 19.7%, speak over 30 languages other than English at home—an increase of nearly 23 million from 10 years before (U.S. Census Bureau, 2006).

Around the world:

- The world's population is aging: Between 2005 and 2050, the median age of the global population is expected to increase from 28 to 39, although developed countries across the globe have a significantly higher median age than do developing countries (United Nations Population Division, 2006).

- In developed countries, the current annual rate of population growth (excluding immigration) is less than 0.3%, while in the rest of the world, the population is increasing almost six times as fast. Because developed countries often have stronger economies and more job opportunities, an ever increasing number of young people from developing countries are migrating to developed countries, thus increasing cultural and ethnic diversity (McCarthy, 2000).

Given that people of color are often disproportionately affected by disease and health care problems, these statistics are significant. In fact, the impact of these demographic trends on health care quality is well documented. The *2004 National Healthcare Disparities Report* reveals that disparities associated with race, ethnicity, and socioeconomic status continue, especially with regard to patient outcomes and safety, timeliness, and patient centeredness (Agency for Healthcare Research and Quality, 2005). In 2001, the Commonwealth Fund also uncovered disparities, by race and ethnicity: "African Americans, Asian Americans, and Hispanics are more likely than whites to experience difficulty communicating with their physician, to feel that they are treated with disrespect when receiving healthcare services, and to experience barriers to care, including lack of insurance or a regular doctor. Moreover, a substantial proportion of minorities feel they would receive better care if they were of a different race or ethnicity" (Collins, 2002, p. v).

While health systems work to respond to the shifting populations among communities they serve, the public is becoming more involved in their own health decisions and therefore more demanding of individualized approaches to care. To compound matters, today's health care organizations participate in an extremely competitive market environment. Contrary to the economic model of most industries, wherein management decisions control the destiny of the organization within the marketplace, health care systems not only must satisfy their customers but also must adhere to guidelines set by third parties such as insurance companies and Medicaid, which apply pressure to keep costs down, in order to be paid for their services (Lahiri & Sedicum, 2000a, 2000b).

Thus, to meet the challenges of countless cultures merging into one health care arena in many parts of the world, health care systems must increase relationship-driven, individualized, and interculturally competent care while decreasing costs.

Importance of Cultural Competence for Health Care Providers

Prejudice can have a profound impact on the delivery of health care. If a provider is ethnocentric, his or her interactions, diagnosis, and treatment will be skewed by his or her biases. Intercultural competence is central to equalizing power dynamics in medicine that often lead to those with less power (such as those in a cultural, ethnic, linguistic, or economic minority) receiving a lower quality of care. As the American Institutes for Research (2002) point out,

> Social issues such as stereotyping, institutionalized racism, and dominant-group privilege are as real in the examining room as they are in society at large. Therefore, the goal of cultural competence training in healthcare should be to guide physicians in bringing these power imbalances into check. This process, consisting of ongoing self-reflection and self-critique, requires humility. In fact, the concept of "cultural competence" may be better described as "cultural humility" (Tervalon & Murray-Garcia, 1998). (p. 22)

Often, when learning about cultural influences on approaches to health and illness, health care providers implicitly believe that they have a superior value system and the correct, most accurate approach to health care. For example, in some cultures, it is believed that when one talks about a death, it accelerates the loss of life. Many Western health care practitioners would view this as an erroneous belief. Similarly, in some cultures, the notion of affixing metal to a child's teeth and forcing the teeth to move would be considered cruel. Yet in the United States, this is a common treatment (braces) and viewed as standard practice.

Illustrative here may be an excerpt from an interview with a traditional healer of a Native American tribe (Lahiri, 2000):

> Ogema, an Anishinaabe (Native American) healer and spiritual teacher explains his perspective on [the debate on integrating traditional and Western forms of

medicine], "Western science is trying to somehow legitimate traditional medicine when they do not even speak the same language as we do. The things that we consider proven beyond a shadow a doubt (just as much as they are convinced through their scientific procedures) are the same things they are saying need to be studied. Most Western physicians are not equipped to deal with our different reality, just as they have a reality we have difficulty with. (p. 1)

Medical ethnocentrism is a barrier to accessing health care because it inhibits a practitioner's understanding of the patient's beliefs and behaviors. This is especially true when these conflict with a provider's diagnosis or treatment plan. Possible results of medical ethnocentrism are as serious as they are varied and can include exacerbation of a patient's condition or even a patient's death. For example, some patients may believe that to heal, they must show complete faith in God. For some, taking medication would be an indication of a lack of faith and therefore would actually cause them not to heal. If a provider does not know about or understand this belief, the patient's noncompliance could lead to her or his death. If, on the other hand, the provider is aware of this belief, she or he can work with the patient to find a resolution that respects the patient's belief system and also addresses her or his health issues.

Medical ethnocentrism on the part of the health care provider may cause patients to refuse to communicate beliefs or behaviors that they feel will cause a negative reaction in the provider, thus causing significant data to be lost. Providers may interpret situations using their own beliefs as a barometer and may be totally incorrect, or they may unknowingly prejudge based on their own implicitly held stereotypes and assumptions about a cultural group.

Impact of Culture on Provider-Patient Relationships

Disparate treatment as a result of medical ethnocentrism has been shown to have a significant impact on quality of care (Institute of Medicine, 2002), specifically:

- Inaccurate diagnosis and treatment
- Exacerbated illnesses
- Noncompliance

In all of these cases, the quality of communication and the relationship between patient and provider is the key predictor of positive or negative outcomes. In fact, a great deal of attention has been paid to the lack of trust, understanding, and loyalty in the patient-physician relationship (Fredericks, Miller, Odiet, & Fredericks, 2006). Many times, these can be traced back to cultural differences between the health care provider and patient.

Case Study[1]

Roberto, a terminally ill Latino, is referred to a hospice program. When the nurses visit his home, they are met by nine adults who appear to have come from all over the country. The adults all have various pieces of advice for the nurses. They do not want the nurses to wear their hospice badges in the house. They also ask the nurse not to talk about death with Roberto but instead tell him that "he will be fine." Roberto's children are constantly asking him who he'd like to see and what he'd like to eat. The family members spend much of their time cooking his favorite foods and showing him pictures of family members who are unable to visit him.

Discussion

Roberto's hospice nurses may come from a cultural background that views full disclosure of their role as hospice care provider, as well as Roberto's condition as terminal, as the morally appropriate behavior. They may feel that Roberto needs to know of his impending death in order to prepare for it and may be uncomfortable with what they perceive as dishonest and possibly disrespectful behavior.

Roberto's family is likely to view talking about Roberto's terminal condition as either unnecessary or unsupportive. They are likely to view their presence and behavior as providing Roberto with the information that he is not expected to live much longer. They may also feel that the kindest way to care for Roberto is by focusing only on the good: family, friends, loved ones, favorite foods, and perhaps music, flowers, and laughter.

Disclosure, then, is an example of an area where culture affects provider-patient relationships in both profound and challenging ways. To the provider socialized in a Western biomedical context, patient autonomy and self-determination are important. Telling the truth about the disease is seen as essential for patients to challenge the disease, be in control of the situation, and plan for the future. This is in sharp contrast with the cultures of others, where the patient is protected from bad news by the family. Patient autonomy is not seen as empowering but as burdensome. The provider, however, often feels that disclosure is necessary to allow the patient to make decisions about and to obtain consent for the treatment.

Cultural Barriers in Patient Care

Cultural barriers between provider and patient may take a variety of forms. Some additional examples include the following:

- The patient's level of comfort with the practitioner and fear of what he or she may find upon examination (e.g., the concern that the patient's lifestyle and habits may not meet with the provider's approval)

- A different understanding, on the part of the patient, regarding the role and function of the health care system and health care providers, which may vary greatly based on cultural context

- A fear of rejection of personal health beliefs. Patients may face providers who do not respect their beliefs and who may even challenge those beliefs. Given that many of these beliefs are rooted in the patient's spiritual traditions as well as his or her cultural orientation, this is an extremely sensitive issue

- Differing expectations regarding the patient's ability to choose treatments. For example, the provider may feel that he or she has to lay out choices for the patient. If the patient sees the provider as an authority, having choices presented may be strange or unsettling for him or her

Understanding how powerfully cultural differences can affect the quality of patient care, with so many ways that cultural differences may arise, it becomes clear that understanding the patient's frame of reference is critical to providing quality health care services.

Understanding the Patient's Frame of Reference

To meet the patient's expectations and to raise the chances of successful treatment, the provider must understand the patient's frame of reference. Different values to which the patient might subscribe are at the basis of the differing approaches to and expectation from health care providers.

Case Study[2]

Thally, a 14-year-old Haitian immigrant who speaks a smattering of English, is referred to a mental health care provider, Donna. Her case report states that Thally was repeatedly scaring her ninth-grade classmates by telling them that she was possessed by a spirit and asking them to help her get rid of the spirit. Hospital authorities note that Thally refuses to eat or sleep. She sits on her bed, clutching her knees to her chest, and rocks back and forth. Although her parents have been informed of their daughter's illness and whereabouts, they do not come to see her in the hospital. They tell Donna on the phone that there is nothing wrong with their daughter. How might Donna familiarize herself with Thally and her parents' frames of reference, so that she can adequately evaluate the situation and develop a treatment plan?

Discussion

Many Western-socialized health care providers, when faced with this situation, would fall into a trap of medical ethnocentricity, believing that there is no such thing as possession by spirits, and therefore Thally must be mentally ill. A useful approach for Donna might be to learn more about Thally's concerns. It would be most helpful if Donna could secure the help of an interpreter and ask Thally to explain what she is experiencing and what would help her. If Thally does not open up to Donna, she would do well to secure the advice of a person with expertise in Thally's belief systems. Perhaps a respected member of the Haitian community would be an appropriate intermediary in this case. Once Thally's experience and frame of reference are thoroughly understood, Donna will be in a position to develop a treatment plan that is appropriate within Thally's frame of reference. In many cultures, being possessed by a spirit may not be a cause for alarm or constitute abnormal behavior. Or, there may be simple remedies that could help Thally to banish the spirit.

Similarly, Donna must also learn about Thally's parents' frame of reference, including their refusal to come to the hospital and their belief that there is nothing wrong with their daughter. Donna may have more success with Thally's parents by visiting them, along with an interpreter. Another option would be for Donna to ask the same trusted intermediary mentioned above to discuss the situation with Thally's parents.

We do not know whether Thally's family is in the country legally, and in some cases, illegal immigrants are fearful to talk with "officials" for fear of deportation. In some countries, mental institutions may be viewed as places of torture. There are many plausible reasons that Thally's parents may have for their behavior, based on their frame of reference and culturally based values.

Different Approaches to Health and Their Impact on Treatment

People have different "illness belief systems" or "a relatively coherent set of ideas regarding what causes illness and its course and treatment" (Chrisman, 1991). Chrisman (1991) organizes the range of illness causalities into four illness belief systems. This, he suggests, can be used as a starting point for understanding the patient's point of view. The four illness belief systems are germ theory, equilibrium, god- and spirit-caused illness, and sorcery and witchcraft.

It is critical that these belief systems be approached not just with respect but as truth. In other words, we cannot just acknowledge the belief and then try to make the treatment we want to use fit into the patient's belief structure. This only demonstrates our lack of understanding and will not help the patient. Instead, we must approach our treatment from the perspective of the patient, assuming the patient's belief is in fact the correct belief and working from that truth toward an optimal outcome.

Germ theory is the basis of Western medicine. It holds that tumors, abnormal cells, and chemicals are the causes of illness and disease. Germ theory is prevalent among most cultural groups across the United States and Canada, as well as many groups in Western Europe.

Equilibrium is a theory based on balance and holds that illness results when things are unbalanced. Chrisman (1991) advises Western clinicians to address this non-Western belief by suggesting that patients engage in activities or eat certain foods in moderation. The most common equilibrium beliefs are humoral pathology and harmony. The humoral pathology belief system maintains that the four humors—blood, phlegm, black bile, and yellow bile—must regain balance within one's body. When the humors are out of balance, illness is the result. The hot-cold system is one of the humoral pathology belief systems. According to this system, the body requires a balance of hot and cold. Medical conditions themselves are classified as either hot or cold and balanced by food and fluids (which are also classified as hot or cold) to restore balance. For example, a cold is treated with hot fluids but never with cold fluids, such as orange juice. Cancer, which is hot, should be treated with cold remedies, while chemotherapy and radiation are heat producing and therefore compound the problem. Patients may therefore counter the treatment with fresh fruits and vegetables, which are cold.

Another equilibrium belief is harmony. In this belief system, health is brought about by harmony in a person's life, whereas being out of harmony causes illness. To become healthy, patients must first reestablish harmony and then treat the health condition specifically. Reestablishing harmony can be done through personal work, meditation and reflection, spiritual ceremony, or, in some instances, by visiting a medicine woman or man.

God- and spirit-caused illness theory attributes illness to divine causes. Sometimes in this belief system, dead ancestors are punishing or testing descendants for not honoring the family. In other situations, spirits may cause sickness and may need to be appeased before the patient can be cured.

Chrisman (1991) describes a fourth theory of sorcery and witchcraft as the cause of illness. Hexes, or evil eyes, may cause illnesses, in which case shamans or ceremonies can restore health by removing the hex.

These illness belief systems can have significant implications for health care. Sometimes a patient may believe that a physician can treat symptoms, but a traditional healer may be needed to eradicate the root problem before the sickness is cured.

Case Study[3]

Alisa is a health care provider working with Yen, a Chinese woman who has recently been diagnosed with cancer. Yen speaks little English, and her husband translates for her. When her husband is present, Yen denies pain. When he leaves the room, she admits to having pain. Yen's husband indicates that he has very little faith in the U.S. medical community. Because he believes that pain medications interfere with the body's "natural healing process," he keeps her pain pills out of Yen's reach. Instead, he provides his wife with curative herbal teas. He also refuses to let Alisa tell his wife that she has advanced stages of cancer.

Discussion

It is easy to see how this scenario presents challenges and perhaps some confusion or frustration for the health care provider. Is Yen in pain, or not? Is her husband preventing Yen from receiving the best possible treatment and causing her to endure pain because of his beliefs? Does Yen agree with the decision to replace pain pills with herbal teas? Should not Yen be told the truth about her cancer?

It is important that Alisa, the health care provider, does not make judgments hastily. It would be easy to assume that Yen is telling the truth about her pain when her husband leaves the room and that perhaps her husband is not translating accurately. However, we do know that Yen speaks very little English. She may be agreeing with Alisa that she is in pain because she does not understand. Yen may also hold the cultural belief that it is impolite to disagree and be trying to please Alisa by saying that she is in pain. Yen may also be agreeing with her husband out of a similar desire to please.

In many cultural belief systems, our thoughts and feelings play a crucial part in our healing. Therefore, Yen's husband's preference not to tell Yen about how advanced her cancer is may be a desire to support her in continuing to think positively about healing. Taking pain medications could also depress Yen and cloud her thoughts, so these, too, would interfere with healing.

The most helpful thing that Alisa could do would be to bring in an interpreter who is not related to Yen. Through the interpreter, Alisa could respectfully learn more about Yen's and her husband's belief systems. Together, they could then build a treatment plan that provides the best possible care and is comfortable within the framework of the patient's culture.

It is important that the provider listen and understand the patient's belief system to avoid stereotypically assigning beliefs to members of certain ethnic groups.

Frequently, "alternative" health beliefs may be subscribed to when biomedicine is not successful, when the treatment is too long or expensive, or when the problems are psychological. Often, "alternative" medicines are used simultaneously with Western medicine for the terminally ill.

Providers should think through how they will respond if there is a conflict between what they believe and what their patients believe. In some cases, the provider's and patient's beliefs may complement each other, yet in many cases, they may seem to contradict one another. Developing strategies for addressing these situations is critical for a culturally competent provider.

The provider who does not take the patient's beliefs into consideration when developing a treatment plan is likely to wind up with a noncompliant patient or to be dismissed. Listening to the patient's explanation of the cause of the illness without judgment might suggest whether the treatment will be successful or if an alternative treatment should be suggested (Harwood, 1981).

Different values systems may affect a variety of aspects of health care, such as the degree to which the family is involved in the patient's treatment. In collectivist cultures, for example, decisions are made by a family unit or other group, and the patient is not expected to decide on the treatment independent of the family's involvement. There might also be a preference for addressing important news to the family rather than to the patient alone.

It may be necessary for providers to work within the family hierarchy to ensure success of the treatment plan. Often a family member, perhaps the oldest male, might make decisions for the patient.

The gender of the provider might become an issue in the success of treatment. Patients from some cultures may value male opinions above those of female clinicians, while women from some cultures may be uncomfortable with a male health care provider.

There are often differing expectations of the provider's role and scope of responsibilities. The potential discrepancy between the provider's and patient's expectations can be compounded when the interaction takes place across cultures. While some may expect that the health care provider will offer holistic assistance, others will expect that the service will be more narrow and targeted. Yet others may not be satisfied with a visit to the doctor unless they receive an injection or a prescription. These differing expectations can result in misunderstanding and a breakdown of trust.

Personal history sharing may be an alien concept to patients from some cultures, and thus providers may not get the information they need for successful treatment. Many patients feel that certain health problems, particularly mental health concerns, should be dealt with within the family or community. Hence, if a provider is not seen as a part of the community, additional challenges may arise.

Attitudes toward seeking help from the health care system may vary, and as a result, providers may see a higher representation of chronically ill patients from some cultural groups. Some groups may mistrust the health care system, while others may rely on the family and turn to an outsider as a last resort. This is particularly true of mental health patients, where there may be a stigma associated with mental illness.

Patients may have different experiences around pain and what they label as a symptom based on their cultural framework. For some individuals, the tolerance for pain may be higher because of cultural norms. Hence, some patients may wait longer before they label pain as a symptom or communicate it to the provider. Similarly, what is labeled as a symptom in some cultures may be the norm in others.

Conflicts Between Provider and Patient

Conflicts between a provider's and patient's worldviews can result in a misdiagnosis of the problem, an inadequate treatment plan, or noncompliance to essential treatment. Such a conflict can be resolved in many ways. Leinenger (1988) describes these interventions as different "modes of care."

One option might be cultural preservation, or maintenance of the patient's perspective. Often, traditional treatments can complement the Western medical treatment plan, and in such situations, it is important to collaborate. For example, drinking herbal teas is not in conflict with biomedical treatment. The provider will get better results by acknowledging the tea and recommending it in conjunction with her or his preferred approach.

Compromise and accommodation are also options for the provider to consider. In such situations, the provider can make changes to the treatment plan to accommodate the patient. When the patient's requests are not harmful to him or her, the provider should promote their use (Leinenger, 1988).

In some situations, the patient's worldviews may be in direct conflict with the provider's preferred treatment plan. In these situations, it is useful for the provider to educate himself or herself about the patient's frame of reference and reasoning. This could be as simple as reading about specific cultural beliefs online, although we strongly recommend that any reading or independent research be supplemented by respectful conversations with diverse members of the patient's cultural group, as well as the patient, Once the health care provider has truly understood the patient's position, she or he can introduce alternative treatments as necessary. Before the provider makes recommendations, however, it is necessary to evaluate the consequences for the patient and his or her family and balance that against the provider's illness theory, with the ultimate goal of the well-being of the patient.

Underlying all of these options is the importance of the provider listening to the patient's explanation of the cause of illness without judgment. Listening to the cause and understanding the preferred mode of treatment suggests whether the treatment will be successful and whether an alternative will be followed.

Models for Interculturally Competent Care

There are several models for developing intercultural competence, three of which we will refer to in this chapter because we find them to be the most useful. These include Campinha-Bacote's (2002) culturally competent model of care, Milton Bennett's (1993) developmental model of intercultural sensitivity, and Darla Deardorff's (2006) process model of intercultural competence.

The culturally competent model of care, developed by Josepha Campinha-Bacote (2002), was developed specifically for the health care industry. In this model, cultural competence consists of several critical elements, including cultural awareness, cultural knowledge, cultural skills, and cultural encounters. In combination, these have the "potential to yield culturally responsive assessments which will in turn yield culturally relevant interventions" (Campinha-Bacote & Padgett, 1995, p. 33).

Cultural competence, in Campinha-Bacote's (2002) view, is a process, not an event, "in which the healthcare provider continuously strives to achieve the ability to effectively work within the cultural context of an individual or community from a diverse cultural/ethnic background" (p. 181).

Cultural awareness requires recognition of and sensitivity to the patient's perspectives, especially when the patients are from a different culture than the provider is. Exploring our own biases and prejudices, as well as developing a clear understanding of how these affect our interactions with culturally diverse patients, is the first step in developing cultural awareness. Campinha-Bacote (2001) makes a clear distinction between a "culturally sensitive" approach and a "culturally responsive" approach. She explains that "a culturally sensitive approach requires only an awareness of the values, beliefs, life ways, and practices of an individual, while a culturally responsive approach incorporates the individual's values, beliefs, life ways, and practices into a mutually acceptable treatment plan" (p. 11).

Cultural knowledge refers to the health care provider obtaining information about the other cultures' perspectives and beliefs about health and illness, whether this knowledge is gained through reading, academic pursuits, conferences, workshops, or talking with members of specific cultural groups. Campinha-Bacote (2002) cautions against stereotyping, pointing out that not all people from a given cultural background hold the same belief systems. Instead, she suggests that cultural knowledge can be used by health care professionals as a starting point in developing relationships with individuals from specific cultural groups and that through those relationships, relevant points about a patient's personal and cultural orientations will emerge.

Of course, each patient is an individual, with experiences, perceptions, and beliefs that may not be shared by his or her cultural group. It is therefore critical that health care providers learn how to gather information directly from patients through respectful and sensitive questions and conversation. These skills prevent cultural knowledge from being applied stereotypically to all members of a cultural group. Campinha-Bacote (2002) refers to cultural skill as the process of learning how to gather information about a patient's culture. Campinha-Bacote suggests that conducting a cultural assessment (which is how she refers to the process of gathering information about the patient's individual beliefs, values, practices, and life ways) requires much more than a list of assessment questions, as some other theorists have suggested. She argues, instead, that the best way to elicit the needed information is through gaining trust and developing relationship, which is done through each provider's unique personal style. This style, of course, can and should be flexible to accommodate patients' cultural norms. The cultural assessment phase requires both awareness and knowledge to sensitively elicit information directly from the patient.

Cultural encounters, another component in Campinha-Bacote's (2002) model of cultural competence, refer to activities that allow the practitioner to experience a given culture firsthand. These may include spending time in an ethnic community, maintaining relationships with several members of a cultural group, or other similar firsthand activities. The purpose of cultural encounters is for health care providers to engage directly in cross-cultural interactions with diverse patients. It allows health care providers to check their own understanding of specific cultures and prevent stereotyping.

The developmental model of intercultural sensitivity, developed by Milton Bennett (1993), described also in Chapter 1 of this handbook and consisting of a continuum of six stages moving from ethnocentrism to ethnorelativism, is also particularly useful in the health care arena. The ethnocentric stages in Bennett's model are denial, defense, and minimization. As one develops intercultural sensitivity, he or she moves from ethnocentrism to ethnorelativism. The ethnorelative stages are acceptance, adaptation, and integration.

In the first stage, denial, an individual denies that cultural differences exist. For example, a provider in this stage is likely to presume that the patient shares the provider's illness belief system and therefore will not notice any cues that the patient is viewing her or his condition and treatment differently. This position may be more common among individuals who do not interact routinely with culturally diverse groups. In the second stage, defense, an individual recognizes that cultural differences exist but constructs defenses against the differences because they are threatening to her or his own reality and sense of self (e.g., a provider in this stage may have the point of view that "they are in the United States now; they must know that we don't have the evil eye here").

The third stage in Bennett's (1993) model is minimization. An individual in this stage acknowledges cultural differences but minimizes them, reasoning that human similarities far outweigh any differences. For example, a provider may concede that a patient views the cause of her or his illness differently yet concludes that, since the patient and provider both want the patient to get well, the cause of illness is irrelevant, and the course of treatment will be agreed on. The danger of this stage is that similarity is assumed rather than known, so that the provider may not check for agreement on the course of treatment and never find out that the patient has no intention of complying. In the fourth stage, acceptance, an individual recognizes and values cultural differences without evaluating those differences as positive or negative. This stage moves an individual from ethnocentrism to ethnorelativism. First comes a respect for cultural differences in behavior and then a deeper respect for cultural differences in values.

In the fifth stage, adaptation, individuals develop and improve skills for interacting and communicating with people of other cultures. The key skill at this stage is perspective shifting, the ability to look at the world "through different eyes."

The final stage of Bennett's (1993) model is integration. Individuals in this stage not only value a variety of cultures but are constantly defining their own identity and evaluating behavior and values in contrast to and in concert with a multitude of cultures. Rising above the limitations of living in one cultural context, these individuals integrate aspects of their own original cultural perspectives with those of other cultures.

The major theme that emerges when studying intercultural competence in health care is understanding the patient's worldview and perspective, which is addressed in Deardorff's (2006) process model of intercultural competence (also discussed in Chapters 1, 3, 19, and 28, this volume). In fact, Deardorff created her model based on input from leading intercultural communication experts and scholars, and the only element of intercultural competence that 100% of the experts agreed on was understanding others' worldviews and perspectives.

Deardorff (2006) organizes her model by four major components, each of which includes specific attributes, skills, and behaviors that comprise intercultural competence. The categories are as follows:

Attitudes

Knowledge and Comprehension and Skills

Desired Internal Outcome

Desired External Outcome

Attitudes include respect, which is defined as "valuing other cultures" (p. 256); openness, which refers to "withholding judgment" (p. 256); and curiosity and discovery, clarified as including tolerance of ambiguity. Thus, for a health care provider, these attitudes would allow one to appreciate and accept different illness belief systems, an integral first step to providing culturally competent treatment.

Knowledge and comprehension in this model include cultural self-awareness, deep cultural knowledge, and sociolinguistic awareness. The skills in this stage of the model include listening, observing, and evaluating, as well as analyzing, interpreting, and relating. Hence, in the realm of health care, a person with these skill sets would be adept at learning about patients' cultures and would therefore be more agile in her or his ability to provide appropriate care.

The desired internal outcome is an "informed frame of reference shift," which requires adaptability, flexibility, an ethnorelative view, and empathy. This would mean that a health care provider would have the requisite litheness to provide whatever the patient needs.

The desired external outcome refers to "effective and appropriate communication and behavior in an intercultural situation" (Deardorff, 2006, p. 256), which is the ultimate goal in the health care arena, providing interculturally competent care.

Deardorff's (2006) model is useful for a variety of reasons. It reflects the most current thinking of today's leading intercultural competence scholars versus being the theory of only one or two experts, as is usually the case. Her model also remains flexible so that, as the world and our view of it changes, the model can be adapted as well. It emphasizes that developing intercultural competence is an ongoing process that one never finishes completely and also encompasses more than just behaviors or skills, pointing out that our attitudes and even emotional responses play critical roles in intercultural competence.

Conclusion

Intercultural competence in health care, defined as the ability to deliver "effective, understandable, and respectful care that is provided in a manner compatible with patients' cultural health beliefs and practices and preferred language" (Office of Minority Services, 2000), is indispensable in today's health care industry. Not only does the provider's level of intercultural competence directly affect patient outcomes, but the health care organization's level of intercultural competence is directly related to its continuing financial viability as an organization.

For providers, the key to providing quality care to patients of all cultural backgrounds lies in developing skills to learn about cultural and personal beliefs in a respectful fashion. Through case studies and discussion, we have provided examples of the kinds of questions that providers should be asking, as well as some cues that a cultural clash may be occurring and ideas on how care providers can overcome cultural clashes.

For health care systems, the key to remaining financially viable and providing interculturally competent care lies in developing and implementing long-term strategies and systems that support both providers and patients. For example, health care professionals would do well to examine their policies and practices, forms, meals, and so on to ensure that patients from all walks of life will feel welcomed and nurtured. They must also examine the ways that they recruit, select, manage, develop, and support their staff to ensure that staff is given the skills and tools they need to provide interculturally competent care and that they are held accountable for doing so.

Together, providers and patients co-create interculturally competent health care that is respectful and effective. Only through these partnerships can we ensure optimal patient outcomes.

Notes

1. From Anand (2001, p. 33). Used with permission.
2. From Anand (2001, p. 123). Used with permission.
3. From Anand (2001, p. 111). Used with permission.

References

Agency for Healthcare Research and Quality. (2005). *2004 national healthcare disparities report.* Rockville, MD: Author.

American Institutes for Research. (2002). *Teaching cultural competence in health care: A review of current concepts, policies and practices.* Washington, DC: Author.

Anand, R. (2004). *Cultural competency in healthcare: A guide for trainers.* Washington, DC: National MultiCultural Institute.

Anand, R. (with Hart, S. H.). (2001). *Customizing diversity training using case vignettes.* Washington, DC: National MultiCultural Institute.

Bennett, M. (1993). Towards ethnorelativism: A developmental model of intercultural sensitivity. In R. M. Paige (Ed.), *Education for the intercultural experience.* Yarmouth, ME: Intercultural Press.

Campinha-Bacote, J. (2001). A model of practice to address cultural competence in rehabilitation nursing. *Rehabilitation Nursing, 26*(1), 8–11.

Campinha-Bacote, J. (2002). The process of cultural competence in the delivery of healthcare services: A model of care. *Journal of Transcultural Nursing, 13,* 181–184.

Campinha-Bacote, J., & Padgett, J. (1995). Cultural competence: A critical factor in nursing research. *Journal of Cultural Diversity, 2*(1), 31–34.

Chrisman, N. J. (1991). Cultural systems. In R. M. S. Baird (Ed.), *Cancer nursing: A comprehensive textbook.* Philadelphia: W. B. Saunders.

Collins, K. S. (2002). *Diverse communities' common concerns: Assessing health care quality for minority American.* New York: The Commonwealth Fund.

Deardorff, D. K. (2006). Identification and assessment of intercultural competence as a student outcome of internationalization. *Journal of Studies in International Education, 10,* 241–266.

Fredericks, J., Miller, S. I., Odiet, J. A., & Fredericks, M. (2006). Toward a conceptual reexamination of the patient-physician relationship in the healthcare institution for the new millennium. *Journal of the National Medical Association, 98,* 378–385.

Harwood, A. (1981). Guidelines for culturally appropriate care. In A. Harwood (Ed.), *Ethnicity and medical care* (pp. 482–509). Cambridge, MA: Harvard University Press.

Institute of Medicine. (2002). *Unequal treatment: What healthcare providers need to know about racial and ethnic disparities in healthcare.* Washington, DC: Author.

Lahiri, I. (2000, February 15). Integrating cultures in medicine. *Cultural Diversity at Work.* Retrieved from DiversityCentral.com

Lahiri, I., & Sedicum, A. (2000a, March 15). The issues are critical: Diversity in healthcare. *Cultural Diversity at Work.* Retrieved from DiversityCentral.com

Lahiri, I., & Sedicum, A. (2000b, October 15). Providing interculturally competent healthcare. *Cultural Diversity at Work.* Retrieved from DiversityCentral.com

Leinenger, M. (1988). Leinenger's theory of nursing: Cultural care, diversity, and universality. *Nursing Science Quarterly , 4,* 152–160.

McCarthy, K. (2000). *World population shifts: Boom or doom? Population matters.* Santa Monica, CA: RAND.

Office of Minority Services. (2000). National standards for culturally and linguistically appropriate services (CLAS) in health care. *Federal Register, 65,* 80865–80879.

Reynolds, D. (2004). Improving care and interactions with racially and ethnically diverse populations in health care organizations. *Journal of Healthcare Management, 49,* 237–249.

United Nations Population Division. (2006). *World population prospects.* New York: Author.

U.S. Census Bureau. (2004). *U.S. interim projections by age, sex, race, and Hispanic origin.* Washington, DC: Author.

U.S. Census Bureau. (2006). *2006 American Community Survey.* Washington, DC: Author.

PART III

Research and Assessment in Intercultural Competence

CHAPTER 24

Methodological Issues in Researching Intercultural Competence

Fons J. R. Van de Vijver and Kwok Leung

S ome 40 years ago, the study of intercultural communication started from a problem that triggered the interest of communication experts. The internationalization of business and migration streams led to an increase in cross-cultural encounters. However, not all encounters were successful; expatriates sometimes returned before the end of their assignment because they could not cope with their new colleagues or the business culture or because of homesickness of their family members. Intercultural competence plays an important role in the lives of expatriates, sojourners, and permanent settlers. Moreover, it is a competence that is also relevant for all employees of a multicultural team. In the past decade, new forms of multicultural teams are emerging; for example, it is more common nowadays to find project teams that never meet, such as international teams in which the expertise needed for developing some product or service comes from different countries, and the functioning of such virtual teams is based on computer-aided communication. Practical problems in intercultural communication have boosted the development of the field. The question of what science can offer to increase the success of intercultural encounters is addressed in a rapidly expanding collection of training procedures. The commercial success of these training procedures has been a mixed blessing. This market continues to provide work for many trainers. However, the downside of the success has been conceptual sluggishness of the field and the dearth of well-designed research that can further the understanding of intercultural competence. There has never been a pressing need to engage in more fundamental research studies on this complex concept, including the testing of coherent frameworks that specify the components of intercultural competence, which of these components can be modified by training/interventions, which can be assessed, the best ways to develop intercultural competence, and which intercultural competence assessment methodologies are most effective (Van de Vijver & Breugelmans, in press).

We argue that the increase in interest in intercultural competence witnessed during the past decades has not led to a much better understanding of intercultural competency or to an adequate handling of methodological issues of such studies. The literature has produced a large number of frameworks, definitions, and approaches of intercultural competence (e.g., Byram, 1997; Collier, 1989; Deardorff, 2004; Gudykunst, 2005; Imahori & Lanigan, 1989; Mol, Born, & Van der Molen, 2005; Redmond & Bunyi, 1993), as discussed by Spitzberg and Changnon in Chapter 1 of this volume. The next step would be to put these to the test and to engage in more fundamental research on this complex construct. We are now in the stage where we are unable to decide which theories are well supported by empirical data, which frameworks should be modified, and which ones should be abandoned altogether. It is also important for research studies to indicate which interventions are most effective in developing intercultural competence as well as which assessment instruments and methodologies are most effective in measuring this complex construct.

The present chapter gives an overview of methodological issues that are relevant in researching intercultural competence and in testing models of intercultural competence, assessment methodologies, and so on. Because of space constraints, we do not deal with discourse analysis and other kinds of content analysis of cross-cultural encounters, but we discuss conceptual and research issues of intercultural competence (including its training). In our view, intercultural competence research faces three types of challenges that are discussed in the next three sections of the chapter. First, we present *conceptual challenges and their methodological ramifications*, such as the lack of using research-based definitions of intercultural competence. Second, intercultural competence research often takes place in field settings such as multinational companies, which introduces various *sampling and design challenges* to meet the requirements of proper research. Third, much intercultural competence research takes place in cross-cultural settings; as a consequence, *cross-cultural assessment challenges* are fairly common in the studies. Conclusions are drawn in the final section.

Conceptual Challenges and Their Methodological Ramifications

The most important challenge in the field of intercultural competence is not methodological but conceptual. In our view, we do not yet have a comprehensive theory of intercultural competence that adequately addresses three questions:

1. Components of intercultural competence: What are its core elements?

2. Structure and nomological network of intercultural competence: What is the relation of these elements? How is intercultural competence structured? What are the antecedents and consequents of intercultural competence?

3. Intercultural competence in actual intercultural encounters: How do the elements of intercultural competence manifest themselves in actual intercultural encounters? As indicated previously, this aspect is not discussed extensively in the present chapter.

Components of Intercultural Competence

Various authors have proposed overviews of attitudes and skills that are supposed to be part of intercultural competence (e.g., Gudykunst, 1998, 2005; see also Spitzberg & Changnon, Chapter 1, this volume). Examples are cultural empathy, accommodation of cross-cultural differences, flexibility in dealing with new cultural situations, communication effectiveness, and language competence. There is no agreement about similarities and differences of intercultural competence with related concepts such as social intelligence and negotiation skills. It could be argued that intercultural competence is no exception to the rule that there are no widely shared definitions of crucial concepts in psychology. The field of intelligence illustrates convincingly that a field can be successful and generate numerous theories and interesting data sets without a proper definition of its core concept (Sternberg, 2000). The field of intelligence evolved quickly a century ago because tests measuring the concept predicted important real-life behavior (school performance). However, it is unlikely that intercultural competence will ever approach the immense level of interest intelligence tests have enjoyed; tests of intercultural competence are not as predictive of success in intercultural encounters as are IQ tests in the prediction of school performance. More work on the conceptualization of intercultural competence is needed to advance the field.

There is almost no empirical work in which the various models that have been proposed are compared and tested. As a consequence, a leading theory of intercultural competence is missing. We are still in this stage of conceptual development in which overlapping, complementary, and incompatible models coexist. However, it should be noted that a recent study (Deardorff, 2004) is the first to document consensus among leading intercultural experts, primarily in the United States, on a research-based definition of intercultural competence, which resulted in two models using the consensual aspects of this concept. (See Chapter 1 for Deardorff models.) We argue that the use of proper designs and analytic methods can greatly enhance the level of theorizing about intercultural competence. One of these issues that would benefit from the use of advanced designs and analytic methods is what could be called the componential definition of intercultural competence. These definitions provide a list of the components that together constitute the concept of intercultural competence. The numerous components that have been proposed as constituent elements of intercultural competence can be reduced to four types (cf. Ruben, 1989). The first could be labeled attitudes or orientations, such as attitudes toward other cultures and diversity in an organization or country. The second type involves personality traits such as cultural empathy and emotional intelligence. The third type is more cognitive and refers to skills presumably relevant in cross-cultural encounters such as negotiation skills and mastery of relevant languages. The fourth type refers to actual behavior in intercultural encounters; in particular, this latter aspect has not received the empirical attention it deserves (Gudykunst & Shapiro, 1996; Mol et al., 2005).

Most progress in the conceptualization of intercultural competence in the past decade comes from studies of personality aspects. Studies that tried to predict intercultural adjustment on the basis of global personality traits have met with limited success (Matsumoto, LeRoux, Bernhard, & Gray, 2004), but specific measures of personality seem to have more predictive power than global measures (Matsumoto, Le Roux, Robles, & Campos, 2007; Van der Zee & Van Oudenhoven, 2000, 2001). For instance, Matsumoto and colleagues (2001) have developed the Intercultural Adjustment Potential Scale (ICAPS), which includes traits such as emotion regulation, openness, flexibility, and critical thinking that are more relevant to intercultural competency than are general traits such as the Big Five. The Multicultural Personality Questionnaire (MPQ) is another instrument that has been specifically developed to measure traits that are relevant to people working in international and multicultural environments (Van der Zee & Van Oudenhoven, 2000, 2001). The MPQ measures cultural empathy, open-mindedness, social initiative, emotional stability, and flexibility, a number of traits that are related to the Big Five, but are more specifically geared toward predicting intercultural effectiveness. There is some evidence that the traits measured by the MPQ are related to psychological and social well-being in a foreign environment (Van Oudenhoven & Van der Zee, 2002). The considerable overlap in traits measured by the two instruments, such as flexibility, empathy, and openness, points to convergence as to which personality characteristics are crucial in intercultural competence.

Recently, the notion of cultural intelligence has been proposed for predicting intercultural success (Earley & Ang, 2003). Cultural intelligence or CQ refers to the capability to function effectively in culturally diverse settings, with four major factors. Metacognitive CQ refers to the mental capability to acquire and understand cultural knowledge. Cognitive CQ refers to the general knowledge and knowledge structures about culture. Motivational CQ refers to the capability for an individual to direct energy toward learning about and functioning in intercultural situations. Finally, behavioral CQ refers to the capability of an individual to exhibit appropriate verbal and nonverbal actions in culturally diverse settings. Cultural intelligence has been shown to be predictive of intercultural adjustment and performance in intercultural settings (e.g., Ang et al., 2007).

Structure of Intercultural Competence

After having established the components that comprise intercultural competence, the next question to consider when researching this construct is the relations of the components. Suppose that we have administered a questionnaire to assess intercultural competence and that we observed positive correlations between the subscales. If we examine the structure of intercultural competence, we look for statistical models that provide summaries of such positive correlations. There is no agreement on how the relations should be conceptualized. Methodological tools can go a long way to compare these conceptualizations and to provide statistically compelling evidence for selecting the model that best describes our data.

We present three kinds of relations between the components. The first is what could be called a *black box* or *input-output* model. Studies using these models do not deal with the theoretical background or conceptualization of intercultural competence but focus on the establishment of significant associations between antecedent variables (among which is intercultural competence) and outcome measures. This model is exemplified in the numerous studies in which intercorrelations are reported between components of intercultural competence or in which they are used to predict real-life outcomes in a group of immigrants, sojourners, or expatriates or to predict training outcomes in a group of students (Mol et al., 2005). The studies provide useful ideas of contingencies in the field of intercultural competence. However, their conceptual value is limited because the relations between the different aspects of intercultural competence are not examined further.

The second model views intercultural competence as a *hierarchical* concept. This model, implicitly undergirding much research, holds that intercultural competence is a superordinate construct with various interrelated components. Statistically speaking, the model specifies that correlations between the components, such as positive correlations between communication competence and cultural empathy, are due to their common dependence on a single latent factor, called intercultural competence. Conceptually speaking, the model indicates that intercultural competence manifests itself in various aspects of psychological functioning, but intercultural competence may be more influential in some domains than others (e.g., communication skills may have a stronger intellectual component than cultural empathy). This conceptualization can be statistically captured in a two-tier factor structure with the domains constituting the lower level and intercultural competence in the apex. We expect higher within- and lower cross-domain correlations. As an example, Cui and Van den Berg (1991) used confirmatory factor analysis to support their model, which holds that intercultural effectiveness consists of three interrelated components—namely, communication competence, cultural empathy, and communication behavior.

The third model places intercultural competence in a *mediation or moderation* framework. What is common in these frameworks is their focus on how the components of intercultural competence influence outcome variables, such as adjustment or expected performance, or how they are influenced by antecedent factors, such as cultural distance, discrimination, and ethnocentrism of the mainstream population (Fox, 1997; Mamman & Richards, 1996). Compared to the input-output models, the mediation/moderation framework starts from a model about how intercultural competence is related to intercultural outcomes. As an example of a mediation model, suppose that a certain personality type of a prospective expatriate makes a person a better negotiator, which leads to a better performance as an expatriate. The negotiation skills mediate the link between personality and expatriate performance. The situation in which the relation between personality and expatriate performance is (statistically) completely explained by negotiation skills is called complete mediation. Partial mediation refers to the situation in which all relations between the three constructs are significant. A moderation variable, on the other hand, has an influence on the relation of two other variables. For example, suppose that negotiation skills are more strongly related to expatriate performance for males than for females. Gender is then said to moderate the relation between negotiation skills and expatriate performance.

An example of the mediation model can be found in the work by Bush and Ingram (1996), who developed a model for intercultural communication skills in buyer-seller relationships. They argue that intercultural dispositions, such as empathy and cultural knowledge, influence intercultural skills, which in turn have an influence on success in intercultural buyer-seller relationships. From the perspective of the current chapter, this model is very different from the hierarchical model by Cui and Van den Berg (1991) described before in that the former implies a causal order between different aspects of intercultural competence, whereas the latter does not imply any causal order. Redmond's (2000) work among international students in the United States illustrates a moderation approach. He used scores on the Hofstede (1980, 2001) dimensions on the students' country of origin as a measure of cultural distance. Intercultural communication competence included language competence, adaptation, social decentering, communication effectiveness, social integration, and knowledge of the host culture. These competencies were used to predict the experience and handling of stress in a multiple regression equation. The author found different regression weights for the intercultural competencies between respondents from cultures closest to the United States in cultural values and those furthest.

Methodological Ramifications

Can methodological tools help to clarify the conceptual issues in intercultural competence research? In our view, adequate methods can go a long way. Key to the appropriate use of research methods is a good appreciation of their strengths and weaknesses and of the need to establish a firm link between theory and methods (Bhawuk, 1998, 2001). Good theorizing, adequate designs, and adequate methods are complementary and indispensable for advancing the field. The conceptual fuzziness of the intercultural competence field is much related to a lack of clear insight in the components of intercultural competence and their relations (Leung & Van de Vijver, 2008). Causal techniques can help to test specific theories about these relations. Furthermore, both experimental and nonexperimental techniques can be used to establish a causal order between variables.

Causality: Strengths and Weaknesses of Experimental Techniques. Experimental designs are powerful tools to eliminate unwanted group influences by randomizing participants across treatment groups (Christensen, 2003). Randomization of participants across treatment procedures, which should ideally also include a control condition, is an effective tool in intercultural competence research to control for confounding participant differences that may have a bearing on training outcomes. As a consequence, random allocation reduces the number of alternative interpretations of study outcomes considerably and increases the internal validity of the evaluation study (Shadish, Cook, & Campbell, 2002).

On the other hand, randomization has its limitations. Intercultural competence research often takes place in very specific cultural settings, involving a group of students or (potential or actual) expatriates or sojourners that may show a limited cultural variability. Randomization may help to control for various participant-related variables, such as personality and intelligence. However, randomization does not do away with the problem of the specifics of the sample, cultural context, or training procedure (such as personal characteristics of the training administrator). The generalization of findings to new groups of participants, treatment procedures, or cultural contexts for which the training was designed may be problematic and difficult to determine without gathering new evidence on the influence of potentially confounding variables.

Causality: Strengths and Weaknesses of Nonexperimental Techniques. The first nonexperimental procedure to establish causality involves the use of longitudinal designs (often used in intervention studies that are based on a pretest-training-posttest design). The main strength of these designs is that the temporal order of changes can be determined. For example, by systematically observing participants engaged in intercultural encounters before and after training, it becomes possible to identify which aspects of intercultural competency are affected by training. From a methodological perspective, these designs have attractive properties (mainly related to their high internal validity) and relatively few weaknesses (such as the potential loss of motivation or memory effects at the posttest). The many practical problems associated with longitudinal designs (expensive to conduct and often cumbersome to implement) have precluded their widespread usage; most training studies of intercultural competence use cross-sectional designs in which all variables of interest are measured at the same point in time (Shaughnessy & Zechmeister, 1997).

The second type of nonexperimental techniques in establishing causality can be found in the numerous so-called causal techniques. Good examples are stepwise regression analysis, path analysis, and confirmatory factor analysis (e.g., Kline, 2005). Within the context of intercultural competence, these techniques are able to model the relations between various competency-related constructs, such as skills, personality, and attitudinal aspects of intercultural competence. Much literature on intercultural competence and intercultural competence-related aspects is based on models that are not easy or even impossible to reconcile. Is self-esteem a resource for sojourners to deal with acculturative stress (Al-Sharideh & Goe, 1998), is it influenced by this type of stress (Nesdale & Mak, 2003), or is it a mediator that links discrimination to stress (Corning, 2002)? Is perceived cultural distance mainly a function of more or less objective country-level characteristics (Ward, Bochner, & Furnham, 2001), or is it influenced by acculturation experiences (Galchenko & Van de Vijver, 2007)? Is perceived discrimination an antecedent of acculturative stress (Vedder, Van de Vijver, & Liebkind, 2006) or an outcome of acculturation (Ward, 2006)? It is an attractive feature of these causal models that they provide a statistical test of the goodness of fit, which indicates to what extent the theoretically presumed state of affairs that led to the model being tested is corroborated by the data. Differences between different hierarchical models of intercultural competence components (such as different mediation or moderation models) can be compared in causal models; these models allow for empirical tests of the extent to which different models provide an accurate description of the empirical data.

Psychological acculturation studies provide relevant examples of mediation and moderation models. Psychological acculturation refers to the psychological consequences of prolonged contact with other cultural groups (Graves, 1967). It is surprising that the literature on intercultural competence does not make more reference to acculturation studies, despite the relevance of acculturation in overseas assignments. Acculturation research has studied extensively the relations between input, intervening, and psychological outcomes of migration (Sam & Berry, 2006). For example, Ait Ouarasse and Van de Vijver (2004) studied acculturation outcomes (psychological and sociocultural) among 155 Moroccan-Dutch young adults as a function of both input variables (perceived characteristics of the mainstream and immigrants' culture) and mediating variables (acculturation orientations, which refer to the preference to adopt the mainstream culture and/or maintaining the ethnic culture). The perceived mainstream context consisted of a tolerance factor and an integration factor, while the perceived minority context consisted of a permissiveness to adjust factor and an ethnic vitality factor. A path model in which both the perceived mainstream and minority contexts predicted acculturation outcomes showed a good fit. The effects, flowing from perceived context to outcomes (stress and success at school and work), were both direct and indirect (through acculturation orientations). The mainstream context was crucial for work success, and the minority context was especially important in leading to school success and good mental health.

The immense flexibility of causal models, combined with their detailed analysis of model fit and procedures to improve this fit, holds great potential for intercultural competence and intercultural research in general. However, this flexibility can easily become a weakness. It is often tempting to change a hypothesized model of relations among variables with the aim of maximizing the fit of the model, thereby challenging the replicability of the results. Progress in the field is hampered by the imbalance between the low level of theorizing about intercultural competency and the sophisticated statistical tools that are available to test our theories.

Strengthening the Validity of Cross-Cultural Causal Inferences: The Consilience Approach. Dealing with causality in nonexperimental research is a thorny issue. In our view, multiple strategies can be adopted to increase the validity of causal inferences. We coined the term *consilience approach* to describe all efforts to strengthen casual inferences by means of providing diverse evidence based on a sound theoretical basis, multiple sources of data, different research methods, and explicit refutation of alternative interpretations (Leung & Van de Vijver, 2008). Causal inferences are taken to be stronger in this approach when independent lines of evidence support the inferences and/or alternative explanations are refuted. Causal inferences can be supported by four types of consilience. First, *contextual consilience* requires that diverse evidence is collected from a wide range of cultural contexts and cultural groups (e.g., an intercultural competence training procedure with a claimed global efficacy is found to yield the predicted improvement in communications skills in various countries). Second, *methodological consilience* requires the demonstration of a causal relationship with diverse methods, such as surveys, experimentation, and longitudinal studies (e.g., the training shows improved skills across a wide variety of outcome measures). This notion is consistent with the practice of triangulation (i.e., the verification of a finding with different methods; Crano & Brewer, 2002; Saris,

2003). Third, the notion of *predictive consilience* means that diverse predictions based on a causal theory are evaluated, and the confirmation of these predictions provides strong evidence for this theory (e.g., suppose that the training is predicted to differentially influence various components of intercultural communication; confirmation of a complex pattern of null, small, and large effects provides a test of the causal effects of the training). Finally, *exclusive consilience* requires that no alternative explanation is able to explain the evidence for a given causal explanation. A working assumption underlying exclusive consilience is that we may take a causal relationship as valid, but a wide range of alternative explanations should be evaluated. The emergence of conflicting evidence will lead to the revision of the causal relationship. For example, the effect of an intercultural competence training should not be a consequence of increased scores at the posttest due to repeated exposure to the test instrument.

Caveat. The field of intercultural competence uses both individual- and culture-level concepts. The distinction between these two is not always taken into account. It is all too common to see that culture-level concepts are applied at the individual level. Many examples of this so-called ecological fallacy (Hofstede, 1980, 2001; Robinson, 1950) can be found in the literature on individualism-collectivism. This dimension is a culture-level characteristic, but the concept is often applied at the individual level. For example, convenience samples of Japanese adults are all supposed to be collectivistic, whereas similar samples of American adults are supposed to be individualistic. Now, it may well be that, if measured properly, a random sample of Japanese would score higher on collectivism than a random sample of Americans, but the difference in means does not justify the indiscriminate application of culture-level characteristics to individuals. For example, education level is known to have a strong, positive relation with individualism. As a consequence, a Japanese sample with a high level of education could well be more individualistic than a sample of less educated Americans. It is only in multilevel models that individual- and culture-level variables can be jointly assessed in a statistically adequate manner (Raudenbush & Bryk, 2002). However, such analyses require a large number of cultures. In the absence of prior evidence, we have to be careful not to mix individual- and culture-level characteristics and to ensure that ascriptions of culture-level characteristics to individuals can be validated or at least defended.

External Validity: Sampling and Design Challenges

The main challenge for intercultural competence studies is presumably the enhancement of their external validity. Threats to this validity come from two sources: The first is the small samples in field studies and the inadequacy of student samples for many types of intercultural competence research. Results obtained with students may not apply to expatriates. Second, intercultural competence research takes place in various settings, both in laboratories and the field. Both contexts create their own challenges. In laboratory settings, it is often relatively easy to recruit large samples and to implement complicated designs, such as training studies with multiple conditions. Obtaining large samples and implementing complex designs are much more difficult to achieve in field settings. Studies of expatriates with sample sizes larger than, say, 100 participants are hard to find. Similarly, there are only a few studies with complicated training designs. There is an important trade-off to consider in choosing samples and research sites. Studies involving students, assessed in the laboratory, may have high internal validity but low external validity. The instruments may show good psychometric qualities, and the training procedure may have been implemented in an adequate manner so that differences in scores by control and experimental groups can be interpreted in a straightforward manner. However, these favorable findings regarding internal validity do not provide much information as to their applicability in groups of professionals who work in an intercultural context. Studies in field settings may have low internal validity and their sample sizes may be limited, but the generalizability of their findings to other contexts with similar employees may be more readily assumed (if samples are sufficiently large).

The question arises as to how the low external validity of many intercultural competence studies can be improved. In addition to the obvious solution of using larger and more representative samples, other possibilities may be easier to implement. The first is to assess more aspects of intercultural competence than usually done. Classifications of the elements of intercultural competence tend to be fairly broad and include various components ranging from personality characteristics to skills, but actual measures of intercultural competence are often a poor rendering of this variety. The second is to measure other aspects of the participants and their cultural and organizational context more extensively to establish their associations with intercultural competence. Using broader measures of intercultural competence, combined with measures of relevant personal and contextual aspects, will lead to a better generalizability of research findings.

Cross-Cultural Assessment Challenges

Studies of intercultural competence require adequate treatment of assessment issues. Without proper measures of intercultural competency before and after training, it is impossible to establish the value of training procedures. Most often, the assessment instruments that are used in intercultural competence research are based on self-reports, which have well-documented limitations. Given the complexity of assessing intercultural competence research, Deardorff (2004) has shown that it is important to use a multimethod, multiperspective approach when assessing intercultural competence. This kind of approach has been rarely used to date. Nonetheless, when selecting instruments to use in research studies of intercultural competence, the instruments should meet two methodological criteria. First, there are the usual requirements of good psychometric properties, such as adequate internal consistency of all measures that should be above a minimum threshold of .70 or .80 (Cicchetti, 1994). Second, the instruments should be adequate from a cross-cultural perspective.

We provide a short summary here, and interested readers can consult Van de Vijver and Leung (1997) for a detailed treatment. A judicious use of instruments in intercultural competence research requires knowledge of multicultural assessment and awareness of the issues that threaten such assessment. Assessment problems in intercultural competence are related to those in multicultural testing (Hambleton, Merenda, & Spielberger, 2005; Suzuki, Ponterotto, & Meller, 2001), which come from three sources: the underlying construct, sample characteristics or mode of administration, and specific items. In cross-cultural assessment, these problems are labeled construct bias, method bias, and item bias, respectively (Van de Vijver & Leung, 1997). A measure of intercultural competency shows construct bias if the items inadequately cover the construct in the sample or target culture (e.g., specific aspects of this competency are much more important in some target cultures than in others) or if a measure does not show the same factorial structure across groups of sojourners coming from or living in different countries. There is tentative evidence for the factorial stability of some instruments such as the Intercultural Adjustment Potential Scale of Matsumoto and colleagues (2001) and the Multicultural Personality Questionnaire (Van der Zee & Van Oudenhoven, 2000), yet the implicitly assumed universal applicability of measures of intercultural competency has never been addressed systematically in a wide range of cultures. (For discussion of other instruments, see Fantini [Chapter 27], this volume.)

Method bias is a major challenge for intercultural competence-related assessment. This kind of bias can come from different sources. Samples may differ on relevant background characteristics such as education; educational differences may then lead to an underestimation or overestimation of cross-cultural differences in intercultural competence scale scores. Because English is the lingua franca in most intercultural competence research, it may seem obvious to use test norms established in an English-speaking country. However, such norms are usually based on American or British (monocultural) samples and cannot be used until new, pertinent validity data for the target cultural groups have been presented. In addition, people from different cultures may have different response styles. For example, some cultural groups may avoid the use of extreme scores on a scale, and cultural differences may reflect this bias rather than cultural differences in the construct that was intended to be measured by the items (Harzing, 2006; Van Hemert, Van de Vijver, Poortinga, & Georgas, 2002). Acquiescence and social desirability are stronger in less affluent countries. Finally, the administration procedure of an assessment instrument or the implementation of an intervention may differ in subtle ways across cultures, which may be a source of confounding influence that threatens a cross-cultural comparison.

A last source of bias resides in items. There may be cultural differences in the extent to which an item is indicative of its underlying construct. In other words, the same score on an item may reflect different levels of the underlying construct that it measures across cultural groups. A simple cross-cultural comparison may be misleading because a culture that has a higher scale score than another culture does not guarantee that this culture is indeed higher in the construct that the scale is supposed to tap. A well-known example is that cultural differences in IQ test scores may not reflect genuine cultural differences in intelligence because some items may be biased.

Another common source of item bias comes from translation when imported scales are used, and inaccurate translation can be a source of confounding influence.

Even if a translation seems accurate, differences in nuances may cause some unnoticed shift in meaning. Various linguistic problems such as American or British colloquialisms can reduce the adequacy of an instrument. When English is not the mother tongue of the target group, test scores may, unintentionally, be influenced by the knowledge of the testing language and culture.

Conclusion

Intercultural competence research enjoys a well-deserved wide interest, yet from a methodological perspective, such studies face various challenges. The present chapter describes the most salient issues in designing and analyzing such studies. These issues can be classified as intrinsic problems that are due to the state of the field or the nature of the study topic, such as poor theorizing that complicates the choice of good indicators of intercultural competence and the specification of relations between the indicators, as well as the often difficult field conditions in which these studies take place. Other problems, however, do not reflect intrinsic characteristics of the field but are the consequences of inadequate research methodologies commonly adopted in the field, such as poor sampling or the use of small samples and the infrequent usage of sophisticated statistical analyses. A judicious use of good designs and methods can boost the quality and impact of intercultural competence research. The use of advanced designs and statistical analyses cannot compensate for poor theorizing, but it can help to test competing models of intercultural competence, differentiate the central and peripheral aspects of intercultural competence, decipher which aspects of intercultural competence are influenced by training, and determine to what extent intercultural competence influences expatriate performance and expatriate functioning influences intercultural competence. In short, advanced designs and tools can help to break potential deadlocks and to guide researchers to be precise in conceptualization and measurement.

Let us give a few concrete examples of how advanced designs and analyses can help to advance the field. Longitudinal studies can be used to identify which aspects of intercultural competence remain invariant during a sojourn and which aspects are altered by intercultural encounters. Adequately designed intervention studies can help to identify which training design is more (or less) effective in preparing expatriates for an overseas assignment. Structural equation modeling can help to evaluate the role of intercultural competence as an antecedent variable or mediator of expatriate performance and adjustment (in addition to predictors such as cultural distance and ethnic vitality). Confirmatory factor analysis can help to identify the structure (hierarchical or otherwise) of multicomponent measures of intercultural competence. Finally, bias and equivalence analyses can determine whether an intercultural competence measure is appropriate for use in a multicultural group of sojourners.

The time is ripe for a new wave of intercultural competence studies that are guided by sound and rigorous research designs and methods. The first wave of publications was mainly conceptual (see Chapter 1 for Deardorff models); this wave has led to a rich database of conceptualizations and empirical results. However, past efforts should be integrated in more comprehensive, in-depth research on the various issues related to intercultural competence. In the past two decades, numerous relevant statistical techniques have been developed, and many examples of sophisticated intervention studies in various psychological domains can be found in the literature. The combination of these techniques and designs can help to boost the development of intercultural competence research and eventually a more thorough our understanding of intercultural competence.

References

Ait Ouarasse, O., & Van de Vijver, F. J. R. (2004). Structure and function of the perceived acculturation context of young Moroccans in the Netherlands. *International Journal of Psychology, 39,* 190–204.

Al-Sharideh, K. A., & Goe, W. R. (1998). Ethnic communities within the university: An examination of factors influencing the personal adjustment of international students. *Research in Higher Education, 39,* 699–725.

Ang, S., Van Dyne, L., Koh, C., Ng, K. Y., Templer, K. J., Tay, C., et al. (2007). Cultural intelligence: Its measurement and effects on cultural judgment and decision making, cultural adaptation, and task performance. *Management and Organization Review, 3,* 335–371.

Bhawuk, D. P. S. (1998). The role of culture-theory in cross-cultural training: A multimethod study of culture-specific, culture general, and culture theory-based assimilators. *Journal of Cross-Cultural Psychology, 29,* 630–655.

Bhawuk, D. P. S. (2001). Evolution of culture assimilators: Toward theory-based assimilators. *International Journal of Intercultural Relations, 25,* 141–163.

Byram, M. (1997). *Teaching and assessing intercultural communicative competence.* Clevedon, UK: Multilingual Matters.

Bush, V. D., & Ingram, T. (1996). Adapting to diverse customers: A training matrix for international marketers. *Industrial Marketing Management, 25,* 373–383.

Christensen, L. B. (2003). *Experimental methodology* (9th ed.). Boston: Allyn & Bacon.

Cicchetti, D. (1994). Guidelines, criteria and rules of thumbs for evaluating normed and standardized assessment instruments in psychology. *Psychological Assessment, 6,* 284–290.

Collier, M. J. (1989). Cultural and intercultural communication competence: Current approaches and directions for future research. *International Journal of Intercultural Relations, 13,* 287–302.

Corning, A. F. (2002). Self-esteem as a moderator between perceived discrimination and psychological distress among women. *Journal of Counseling Psychology, 49,* 117–126.

Crano, W. D., & Brewer, M. B. (2002). *Principles and methods of social research* (2nd ed.). Mahwah, NJ: Lawrence Erlbaum.

Cui, G., & Van den Berg, S. (1991). Testing the construct validity of intercultural effectiveness. *International Journal of Intercultural Relations, 15,* 227–241.

Deardorff, D. K. (2004). *The identification and assessment of intercultural competence as a student outcome of internationalization at institutions of higher education in the United States.* Doctoral dissertation, North Carolina State University, Raleigh.

Earley, P. C., & Ang, S. (2003). *Cultural intelligence: Individual interactions across cultures.* Palo Alto, CA: Stanford University Press.

Fox, C. (1997). The authenticity of intercultural communication. *International Journal of Intercultural Relations, 21,* 85–103.

Galchenko, I. V., & Van de Vijver, F. J. R. (2007). The role of perceived cultural distance in the acculturation of exchange students in Russia. *International Journal of Intercultural Relations, 31,* 181–197.

Graves, P. L. (1967). Psychological acculturation in tri-ethnic community. *South-Western Journal of Anthropology, 23,* 337–350.

Gudykunst, W. B. (1998). *Bridging differences: Effective intergroup communication* (3rd ed.). Thousand Oaks, CA: Sage.

Gudykunst, W. B. (Ed.). (2005). *Theorizing about intercultural communication.* Thousand Oaks, CA: Sage.

Gudykunst, W. B., & Shapiro, R. B. (1996). Communication in everyday interpersonal and intergroup encounters. *International Journal of Intercultural Relations, 20,* 19–45.

Hambleton, R. K., Merenda, P. F., & Spielberger C. D. (Eds.). (2005). *Adapting educational and psychological tests for cross-cultural assessment.* Mahwah, NJ: Lawrence Erlbaum.

Harzing, A.-W. (2006). Response styles in cross-national survey research: A 26-country study. *International Journal of Cross-Cultural Management, 6,* 243–266.

Hofstede, G. (1980). *Culture's consequences.* Beverly Hills, CA: Sage.

Hofstede, G. (2001). *Culture's consequences: Comparing values, behaviors, institutions, and organizations across nations* (2nd ed.). Thousand Oaks, CA: Sage.

Imahori, T. T., & Lanigan, M. L. (1989). Relational model of intercultural communication competence. *International Journal of Intercultural Relations, 13,* 269–286.

Kline, R. B. (2005). *Principles and practice of structural equation modeling* (2nd ed.). New York: Guilford.

Leung, K., & Van de Vijver, F. J. R. (2008). Strategies for strengthening causal inferences in cross-cultural research: The consilience approach. *International Journal of Crosscultural Management, 8,* 145–169.

Mamman, A., & Richards, D. (1996). Perceptions and possibilities of intercultural adjustment: Some neglected characteristics of expatriates. *International Business Review, 5,* 283–301.

Matsumoto, D., LeRoux, J. A., Bernhard, R., & Gray, H. (2004). Unraveling the psychological correlates of intercultural adjustment potential. *International Journal of Intercultural Relations, 28,* 281–309.

Matsumoto, D., LeRoux, J. A., Ratzlaff, C., Tatani, H., Uchida, H., Kim, C., et al. (2001). Development and validation of a measure of intercultural adjustment potential in Japanese sojourners: The Intercultural Adjustment Potential Scale (ICAPS). *International Journal of Intercultural Relations, 25,* 483–510.

Matsumoto, D., LeRoux, J. A., Robles, Y., & Campos, G. (2007). The Intercultural Adjustment Potential Scale (ICAPS) predicts adjustment above and beyond personality and general intelligence. *International Journal of Intercultural Relations, 31,* 747–759.

Mol, S. T., Born, M. Ph., & Van der Molen, H. T. (2005). Developing criteria for expatriate effectiveness: Time to jump off the adjustment bandwagon. *International Journal of Intercultural Relations, 29,* 339–353.

Nesdale, D., & Mak, A. (2003). Ethnic identification, self-esteem and immigrant psychological health. *International Journal of Intercultural Relations, 27,* 23–40.

Raudenbush, S. W., & Bryk, A. S. (2002). *Hierarchical linear models* (2nd ed.). London: Sage.

Redmond, M. V. (2000). Cultural distance as a mediating factor between stress and intercultural communication competence. *International Journal of Intercultural Relations, 24,* 151–159.

Redmond, M. V., & Bunyi, J. M. (1993). The relationship of intercultural communication competence with stress and the handling of stress as reported by international students. *International Journal of Intercultural Relations, 17,* 235–247.

Robinson, W. S. (1950). Ecological correlations and the behavior of individuals. *American Sociological Review, 15,* 351–357.

Ruben, B. D. (1989). The study of cross-cultural competence: Traditions and contemporary issues. *International Journal of Intercultural Relations, 13,* 229–240.

Sam, D. L., & Berry, J. W. (Eds.). (2006). *The Cambridge handbook of acculturation psychology.* Cambridge, UK: Cambridge University Press.

Saris, W. E. (2003). Multitrait-multimethod studies. In J. A. Harkness, F. J. R. Van de Vijver, & P. Ph. Mohler (Eds.), *Cross-cultural survey methods* (pp. 265–274). New York: John Wiley.

Shadish, W. R., Cook, T. D., & Campbell, D. T. (2002). *Experimental and quasi-experimental designs for generalized causal inference.* Boston: Houghton-Mifflin.

Shaughnessy, J. J., & Zechmeister, E. B. (1997). *Research methods in psychology* (4th ed.). New York: McGraw-Hill.

Sternberg, R. J. (Ed.). (2000). *Handbook of intelligence.* Cambridge, UK: Cambridge University Press.

Suzuki, L. A., Ponterotto, J. G., & Meller, P. J. (Eds.). (2001). *Handbook of multicultural assessment: Clinical, psychological, and educational applications* (2nd ed.). San Francisco: Jossey-Bass.

Van de Vijver, F. J. R., & Breugelmans, S. M. (in press). Research foundations of cultural competency training. In R. Dana & J. Allen (Eds.), *Professional training for practicing psychology in a global society.* New York: Springer.

Van de Vijver, F. J. R., & Leung, K. (1997). *Methods and data analysis for cross-cultural research.* Thousand Oaks, CA: Sage.

Van der Zee, K. I., & Van Oudenhoven, J. P. (2000). The multicultural personality questionnaire: A multidimensional instrument of multicultural effectiveness. *European Journal of Personality, 14,* 291–309.

Van der Zee, K. I., & Van Oudenhoven, J. P. (2001). The multicultural personality questionnaire: Reliability and validity of self- and other ratings of multicultural effectiveness. *Journal of Research in Personality, 35,* 278–288.

Van Hemert, D. A., Van de Vijver, F. J. R., Poortinga, Y. H., & Georgas, J. (2002). Structural and functional equivalence of the Eysenck Personality Questionnaire within and between countries. *Personality and Individual Differences, 33,* 1229–1249.

Van Oudenhoven, J. P., & Van der Zee, K. I. (2002). Predicting multicultural effectiveness of international students: The multicultural personality questionnaire. *Asian Journal of Social Psychology, 6,* 159–170.

Vedder, P., Van de Vijver, F. J. R., & Liebkind, K. (2006). Predicting immigrant youth's adaptation across countries and ethnocultural groups. In J. W. Berry, J. S. Phinney, D. L. Sam, & P. Vedder (Eds.), *Immigrant youth in cultural transition: Acculturation, identity and adaptation across national contexts* (pp. 143–166). Mahwah, NJ: Lawrence Erlbaum.

Ward, C. (2006). Acculturation, identity and adaptation in dual heritage adolescents, *International Journal of Intercultural Relations, 30,* 243–259.

Ward, C., Bochner, S., & Furnham, A. (2001). *The psychology of culture shock.* London: Routledge.

CHAPTER 25

Applying Theory and Research

The Evolution of Intercultural Competence in U.S. Study Abroad

Michael Vande Berg and R. Michael Paige

This chapter examines how intercultural theory and research have been applied to the development of intercultural competence in six different study abroad program contexts. For each program, we trace back to the conceptual foundations and research origins that have led to the intercultural education approaches being used. These projects provide us with unique contributions to our understanding of how intercultural competence can be facilitated. There are also important intersections and complementarities across programs. We attempt to identify these wherever possible.

We consider these six projects to be study abroad exemplars of important, yet different, approaches to the development of their students' intercultural competence. We are not claiming that they are the only programs interested in intercultural development, but we do consider them to be among "the best" that have emerged over the past several decades. Each has made a unique, innovative contribution to the development of an effective intercultural pedagogy in the project's particular historical moment, and each has built upon the work of its predecessors. There is also a remarkable synergy across these programs that informs the study abroad field today in important ways.

We begin with the observation that our understanding about what intercultural competence is and how it develops has changed dramatically over the past half century. Thus, in addition to examining the six programs, we provide a brief look at the early history of the concept. Then the chapter proceeds to explore how intercultural competence has been defined and applied, implicitly or explicitly, in these various study abroad projects, each of which was designed to enhance the global learning of U.S. students studying abroad. As our approach is historical, we present these projects chronologically.

These six programs have addressed the three principal research questions at the core of our inquiry in this chapter. They are as follows:

1. What is the *nature* of intercultural competence?

2. What is the process by which intercultural competence *develops?*

3. How can individuals be *taught, trained, and/or mentored* regarding the development of intercultural competence?

Tracing the genesis of these projects will allow us to better understand how intercultural training and education is evolving in U.S. study abroad.

Foundations of Intercultural Learning: The Anthropological and Sociological Legacy

We open our historical overview of intercultural competence in U.S. study abroad by reviewing *When Americans Live Abroad,* a pamphlet published by the U.S. State Department in 1955 that aimed to improve the intercultural adaptation of foreign service officers and other U.S. citizens who were planning to work abroad (Foreign Service Institute, 1955). Authored by Glen Fisher, a sociologist and anthropologist serving as a foreign service officer,[1] this 35-page pamphlet provides a fascinating introduction to several assumptions and popular beliefs about U.S. study abroad that are still with us today.

Influenced by the earlier writings of anthropologists such as Margaret Mead and Clyde Kluckhohn,[2] Fisher treats intercultural competence as a largely cognitive phenomenon and anticipates several themes still relevant to the intercultural perspective. First, he notes that individuals who will be working abroad need "culture-specific" knowledge and understanding. As Fisher advises, "Know as much as you can about your area of assignment, its significant geography, history, current events and problems, economics, and relationships with other ideas and nations" and the "major value systems we hold" (Foreign Service Institute, 1955, pp. 33, 35). Second, Fisher discusses the importance of "culture-general" knowledge when he states that "human interaction is complicated by cultural differences" (p. 1) and "ethnocentrism is natural" (p. 3), ideas that are applicable to all intercultural immersion experiences. Third, Fisher addresses intercultural pedagogy with the now well-known culture contrast method, stating that sojourners need to recognize that "the qualities of normal American behavior . . . may be in contrast to local practices abroad" (pp. 3, 5, 15). Interestingly, Fisher seeks to reduce the potential challenges of international living with his comforting observation that sojourners need "to realize that basically foreign behavior is not so different from ours, as all humans are of one species and have fundamentally the same needs and potentialities" (p. 19)—what J. Bennett (1993, p. 41) will later refer to as a minimization strategy.

Fisher explains that individuals become competent in another culture in two ways: through spending enough time in it to be able to acquire the necessary culture-specific information and through learning the local language. The assertion that contact with difference will lead to intercultural competence is a core assumption of the "traditional learning paradigm" (Vande Berg, 2003, 2007; Vande Berg, Connor-Linton, & Paige, in press).[3] It has led generations of faculty and study abroad professionals to focus on "immersion" in designing study abroad programs, including such strategies as directly enrolling students in host universities abroad, housing them in the venerable home stay, and organizing cultural excursions.

New voices from anthropology, sociology, social psychology, and communications would quickly come to refine or redefine many of the anthropological and sociological concepts and methods that Fisher presents.[4] The training programs for foreign service officers that Edward Hall and his Foreign Service Institute colleagues began developing in 1955 would provide a fuller theoretical understanding about the nature of culture, particularly about the ways that culture is socially constructed, and they would introduce the use of experiential techniques as a way of teaching learners about other cultures. These evolving intercultural concepts and training approaches, grounded in the work of sociologists and anthropologists such as Fisher and Hall, would play an important part in the evolution of U.S. faculty and study abroad attitudes about study abroad, as discussed in the remainder of this chapter.

"A Nearly Perfect Laboratory": The University of the Pacific's Intercultural Training Program (1975–2008)

When Bruce La Brack joined the faculty of the University of the Pacific in the fall of 1975 as the resident anthropologist of Callison College,[5] he almost immediately began developing the activities, materials, and theoretical perspectives that would evolve into the intercultural training program that the university continues to offer its students today. Responding to problems that University of the Pacific students were experiencing as they returned to campus after a year spent studying abroad, La Brack created a program that sought to improve student learning through the strategic linking of the predeparture, in-country, and reentry phases of study abroad. It is an approach that differs significantly, in intention and in design, from the conventional approaches to intercultural learning that U.S. institutions typically follow in organizing study abroad for their students.

Rather than focusing almost exclusively on the study abroad site as the locus of learning, La Brack designed a program to support intercultural development through a "continuum of experiential learning" (La Brack, 1993, p. 245). He developed two academic, credit-bearing courses—Cross-Cultural Training I and II—that he offered before and after the study abroad program. The reentry course "uses the actual overseas experience as a behavioral/social text to be deciphered, analyzed, and finally melded with the student's ongoing academic pursuits and personal development" (p. 245). Through the pairing of orientation and reentry, "Topics of culture shock and reentry adjustment are thus psychologically, theoretically, and pragmatically interrelated through an examination of the students' own earlier work, an analysis of present feelings and behaviors, and a discussion of relevant conceptual research on these topics" (p. 255).

Intercultural competence is facilitated by (a) introducing students to key intercultural concepts and skills prior to departure, (b) asking them to apply the concepts and skills while living and studying in the new culture, and (c) asking them, following reentry, to reflect upon how they applied these concepts and skills while abroad. The students are then asked to reapply these to make sense of what is occurring to them now that they are back on campus. As La Brack (1993) puts it, "What was abstract theory in orientation would have been transformed by the overseas study into direct (and even painful) experience in reentry" (p. 247). The orientation and reentry courses are loci of intercultural learning and development that are at least as important as the study abroad experience itself.

La Brack's own training as a cultural anthropologist and his experience as a Language Fellow at the Institute of Indian Studies had given him insights into the reentry problems students were experiencing. He recognized the nature of the "frustrated expectations, various degrees of alienation, and mutual misunderstandings between returnees and their friends and family" (La Brack, 1993, p. 253). He offers the term *bricolage,* in the sense that Lévi-Strauss (1962/1966) gave it, to explain how he searched for useful texts and techniques, learning as he went and pulling together disparate elements to create practical teaching materials (B. La Brack, personal communication, October 2008).[6] Over time, he incorporated a variety of texts, including Edward Stewart's (1972) *American Cultural Patterns;*[7] Edward Hall's (1959) *Silent Language;* the *Transcultural Study Guide* (1987), developed by the Volunteers in Asia Program at Stanford University; Robert Kohls's (1979) *Survival Kit for Overseas Living;* and Milton Bennett's (1993) developmental model of intercultural sensitivity. Eventually, La Brack developed the handbook that his university continues to use in the orientation and reentry courses. The University of the Pacific, he reflects, "provided a nearly perfect laboratory within which to experiment with training techniques, linkages between phases, and the application of theory to practice" (La Brack, 1993, p. 247).

La Brack came to develop a rich, holistic understanding of intercultural competence, one that accounts for its cognitive, affective, and behavioral dimensions. Through the three phases of study abroad, students acquire "increased linguistic competency and sensitivity to nuance, understanding and appreciation of the arts, awareness of mutual cultural boundaries, recognition of value conflicts and ethical dilemmas, ability to 'read' proxemic/kinesic gestures, and a myriad of additional insights which form the substance of intercultural knowledge" (La Brack, 1993, p. 248). His training program represents a clear departure from Fisher's position in espousing a strategically designed training program that "consciously builds [intercultural learning] into linked orientation and reentry exercises" (La Brack, 1993, p. 250).

Placed in the historical context of U.S. study abroad, La Brack is an early and persistent skeptic regarding the traditional learning paradigm—that is, that students learn effectively when left to their own devices. His work is based on the recognition that intervening in student learning abroad can indeed enhance their learning. His training program offered a response to those questions at a period when few U.S. faculty and study abroad professionals were focusing intentionally on, and thinking strategically about, the development of their students' intercultural competence.

A Testing Ground: The AHA Train-the-Trainer Program (1977–1993)

In 1977, Janet Bennett and Milton Bennett developed and launched an intercultural training program for the American Heritage Association (known now as AHA International and an academic program at the University of Oregon[8]). The project offered train-the-trainer workshops to high school teachers who would be leading groups of their students on short-term study programs at sites in Europe, Asia, Mexico, and elsewhere.[9] This year-long AHA course[10] was designed to meet three goals: to train teachers to develop group cohesion and mutual responsibility for learning in the student groups, to facilitate the students' subjective intercultural experience, and to promote both objective and subjective cultural learning at the sites abroad. The project's goals and design responded to two concerns: first, that students were not taking advantage of opportunities abroad for cultural-specific learning and, second, that too many of them were misbehaving abroad to an unacceptable degree.

The program was organized into three weekend courses that participating teachers were required to attend. The first focused on the teaching and learning of area studies information, the second provided the teachers with training in leadership and group dynamics,[11] and the third trained them to facilitate the intercultural learning of their students. Prior to departure, teachers and students attended a "culture camp" on the Oregon coast, with the teachers leading orientations using activities learned during the earlier train-the-trainer sessions. While abroad, the teachers used such activities to facilitate their students' learning, and when the students returned to the United States, teachers and students both attended two reentry sessions.

The defining assumption of the Bennett and Bennett training paradigm is that individuals need some form of education, training, and mentoring to become interculturally competent. This view was consistent with La Brack's (1993) conclusion that intercultural competence could be "more effectively and predictably fostered within intercultural programs" (p. 250; La Brack, 1996). Milton Bennett (1993) took a very strong position on this matter, stating that "intercultural sensitivity is not natural. . . . Education and training in intercultural communication is an approach to changing our 'natural' behavior. With the concepts and skills developed in this field, we ask learners to transcend traditional ethnocentrism and to explore new relationships across cultural boundaries" (pp. 21, 26).

M. Bennett's (1993) developmental model of intercultural sensitivity (DMIS) can be traced in part to the years of experience working with AHA students and teachers regarding their encounters with difference. It appeared that these students were making sense of cultural difference in ways that were predictable; moreover, their understandings of difference changed notably as they became more competent intercultural communicators (J. Bennett & Bennett, 2004b). Bennett and Bennett, as well as others (e.g., Paige, 1986; Paige & Martin, 1983, 1996), also realized that intercultural training pedagogy needed to be more responsive to the developmental levels of the students. One idea that emerged was the importance of sequencing learning activities that would gradually incorporate more challenging activates, such as intercultural simulations, after first establishing a trusting environment for learning.

M. Bennett (1993) and J. Bennett and Bennett (2004b) define intercultural competence in "radical constructivist" terms, citing George Kelly's dictum that "it is the successive construing and reconstruing of what happens, as it happens, that enriches the experience of this life" (p. 153). Or as Janet Bennett puts it, "Learning from experience requires more than being in the vicinity of events as they occur. . . . In the study abroad context, learners may be in the vicinity of Asian events when they occur but be having an American experience" (personal communication, October 4, 2008).

In terms of developmental theory, intercultural sensitivity—increasing sophistication in dealing with cultural difference—is the cognitive foundation that is generative of intercultural competence, the ability to shift behavioral, attitudinal, and mental frames of reference to a given cultural context (M. Bennett, 1993, p. 22). J. Bennett, for example, discusses the cognitive ("mind-set"), behavioral ("skill set") and affective ("heart set") dimensions of intercultural competence and elaborates on how these apply to intercultural training (personal communication, October 4, 2008).

J. Bennett's incorporation of Nevitt Sanford's (1966) challenge/support hypothesis into intercultural training can also be traced back to the AHA training project (M. Bennett, personal communication, October 13, 2008). She explains the importance of appropriately incorporating both challenge and support: "For each learner, depending on his/her development stage, educators need to examine what aspects of the learning context can provide needed supports and what aspects present challenges. . . . The educator needs to assess the needs of the participants and carefully balance challenge and support to maximize learning" (J. Bennett, 1993, p. 122).

As we will see in the rest of this chapter, M. Bennett's (1993) developmental model of intercultural sensitivity and the challenge/support hypothesis will play important roles in the design and delivery of intercultural training projects for U.S. students abroad.

Identifying Program Learning Goals: The American University Center of Provence (1994 to the Present)

Lilli Engle and John Engle opened the American University Center of Provence in January 1994.[12] A small, independent study abroad program located in Aix-en-Provence, France, this center very intentionally focuses on intercultural and second language learning. Students from the United States who enroll in the program take, among other courses, a 3-credit French-language course and "French Cultural Patterns," a 2-credit course designed to develop their intercultural competence. "French Cultural Patterns" systematically exposes students to aspects of life in Aix-en-Provence and provides a space for group reflection, thereby reinforcing their cultural integration. Students sign a language pledge and are required to use French at all times. They live individually with local families; meet regularly with a language partner; participate actively in a sport, a club, or lessons of their choosing; and devote a minimum of 2 hours a week to community service.

The genesis of the center was Engle and Engle's observation that students were not developing the French language and intercultural skills that they had presumably wanted to learn in deciding to come to France in the first place. Instead, most were behaving as if they were still living and studying at their home campuses. Engle and Engle came to believe that U.S. students in Aix were unlikely to recognize the existence of French culture when left to their own devices. Too many of them were spending most of their time with other U.S. students, and as a result, they were having little meaningful contact either with events in Aix or the French who lived there.

Recognizing that "interaction with the host culture is finally what separates study abroad from study at home" (Engle & Engle, 2003, p. 4), this program would focus on optimizing "cross-cultural competence" by means of intense experience and reflection and by significantly increasing the students' French-language proficiency (Engle & Engle, 2004, p. 219). The resulting program linked "the classroom and the street, direct experience and abstract understanding" (Engle & Engle, 2004, pp. 221–222) through eight specific program features and requirements:

1. *duration* of at least one semester;

2. *entry target language competence* of at least a high intermediate/advanced low proficiency level on the American Council on the Teaching of Foreign Languages (ACTFL) scale;

3. *target language use:* required use of French in and outside of class;

4. *instruction* by local professors;

5. *coursework* that includes advanced language study, current social issues, and courses like French literature, art history, and so on;

6. *cultural mentoring* that includes an intensive 1-week arrival orientation program, followed by a required semester-long, credit-bearing course in cross-cultural communication;

7. *experiential learning* that consists of required community service, a personal interest activity (a club, a team, lessons), and so on;

8. *housing* in an individual, integrated home stay.

Engle and Engle launched their program in the midst of a longstanding debate in the United States about which was the better of two broad "types" of study abroad: the so-called direct enrollment or the U.S. island approaches, both of which had ardent supporters (Vande Berg et al., in press). Engle and Engle set up a program that aimed to change the terms of the debate by focusing on what students were learning and on how particular program and learner characteristics could be brought together to predict learning gains. They believed that "the presiding goal of study abroad, its raison d'être, distinguishing it from study on the home campus, should be to present participants with a challenge—the emotional and intellectual challenge of direct, authentic cultural encounters and guided reflection upon those encounters" (Engle & Engle, 2003, pp. 6–7).

They thus developed their program so that students would move outside of the "comfort zone" of U.S. culture. They did this by placing students in social situations— in homestays, service agencies, sports teams, and so on—where they would be required to develop their communication skills. They also created a program architecture that was interculturally rigorous, such as enrolling students only in courses taught by local instructors, signing a language pledge to speak French at all times, living individually with host families, and strictly limiting the amount of time they could spend (communicating in English) on the Internet or on e-mail.

Engle and Engle took the particularly important step of introducing students to key intercultural concepts, a decision based on their observation that students simply were not "seeing" culture. Like La Brack's training project, the American University Center in Provence trains students by focusing intentionally on the cognitive, affective, and behavioral dimensions of intercultural learning. The required French Cultural Patterns course is designed to develop student intercultural development by helping them understand local culture—which they are exposed to through required participation in homestays, service agencies, sports teams, language partnerships, and so on—by framing that experience within culture-general concepts. In 2001, Engle and Engle began to rely on the Intercultural Development Inventory to assess student intercultural development and to use the results to guide ongoing adjustments in the course and, more broadly, in the intercultural training techniques that are manifest in virtually all aspects of the program. In its holistic approach to intercultural learning, the program challenges the notion, popular in some U.S. study abroad circles, that an "immersion" experience necessarily means enrolling students in courses at host universities.

Training Intercultural Competence at a Distance: Bellarmine University and Willamette University Intercultural Learning Courses (1995 to the Present)

In 1995, Gabriele Bosley began to teach an online course, now called "Trans-Cultural Experience Through Cultural Immersion," to some Bellarmine University students who were studying abroad.[13] In 2000, Kris Lou began to teach his "Intercultural Study Within Cultural Immersion" course in an online format for Aquinas College juniors and seniors studying abroad and, since 2003, for students at Willamette University. When Bosley and Lou met at a conference in 2000, they discovered that their online courses were strikingly similar in intercultural aims and approaches, and they began a professional collaboration that continues to this day. They describe the type of course they are teaching as follows:

The overall intent of this writing-centered course is for students to develop inter-cultural skills while immersed in another culture and thereby capitalize on the transformative experiential learning potential of study abroad. (Lou & Bosley, 2008, p. 277)

Taught via e-mail and computer-based Blackboard software, the course links study abroad participants who are enrolling in the same course at different locations in the United States and abroad.

This peer mentoring approach allows students to reflect on and write about their individual experiences, wherever they may be studying, and then interact with and respond to each other about those experiences. According to Lou and Bosley (2008), "Advancing discussion of intercultural concepts with peers in other countries . . . avoids the common pitfall of soothing one another's discomfort with judgmental references. It forces each student to focus on the essence of each situa-tion because they cannot fall back on supposed common misunderstandings. The next step—the interculturalist-constructivist approach—raises the intercultural learning to a meta-level, that is, above the specific host culture and its idiosyn-crasies" (p. 280). Thus, a student studying in Spain cannot offer stereotypical expla-nations, grounded in the cultural specifics of Spain, about puzzling or disturbing local events or behaviors since students at other locations, in the United States or abroad, will in reading his or her comments only be able to process them at the "meta-level"—that is, in cultural-general terms.

Like Engle and Engle, Bosley and Lou questioned the assumption that students learn most effectively when left to their own devices. At the time she was studying German philology in Germany, Bosley learned to integrate the study of local culture in language courses. When Willamette University asked her in 1975 to establish both a Foreign Language Department and an International Programs Office, she decided to introduce a similar integration of second language and culture learning at the new study abroad programs she and her colleagues were establishing. Lou's experience with U.S. undergraduates had led him to conclude that students did not become effective culture learners when left to their own devices. Trained in political theory and influ-enced by Berger and Luckman's (1966) constructivist classic, *The Social Construction of Reality*, he convinced his Aquinas College colleagues that the "Global Explorations and Meanings" course taught on campus would be better taught abroad, where students would be able to learn experientially through encounters with real, rather than abstract, cultural differences and through reflection on those encounters.

Lou and Bosley (2008) have designed an online writing course that, taught by Bellarmine and Willamette faculty via Blackboard and e-mail, facilitates intercul-tural learning on site using an approach that balances "effective, multifaceted immersion [that] provides the space and time for reflection and guided discussion *with one's home culture peers and/or instructors*" (p. 276). In this account of inter-cultural learning, "immersing" students in another culture is a necessary, though not sufficient, condition for achieving what Lou and Bosley call "the transformative experiential learning potential of study abroad" (p. 277). Intervening in student learning, what Paige and Goode (Chapter 19, this volume) refer to as "cultural men-toring," is the sufficient condition.

In many respects, this is a largely cognitive account of intercultural competence, one that takes in both cultural-specific and cultural-general learning. However, their description of the course's "learning process" suggests a more holistic understanding of intercultural competence as well: "The intercultural learning process requires a framework within which students reflect on their experiences, analyze behaviors and values, suggest tentative conclusions or generalizations, and apply such to the next set of experiences." The course guides student intercultural development through a "repetition of this learning cycle," with students progressing as they experience "a blend of ethnographic and interculturalist-constructivist methods, focusing on a progression of critical analysis, moving from the examination of the self to the other and then to the synthesis or integration of the two" (Lou & Bosley, 2008, pp. 279–280). Lou and Bosley's completion of an Intercultural Development Inventory (IDI) Qualifying Seminar in 2004 served to sharpen their understanding of the constructivist perspective that underpins the DMIS and has allowed them to strengthen their course by incorporating the IDI as a teaching tool (Bosley, personal communication, October 13, 2008; Lou, personal communication, October 13, 2008; Lou & Bosley, 2008, pp. 288–289).

Lou and Bosley's approach to teaching and training their students is creative and varied. We cannot summarize all of their training methods in this chapter, but we do want to call attention to two. First, during a required predeparture workshop, Lou and Bosley introduce their students to key intercultural concepts that they will use in processing their experiences at the study abroad sites. During the "postimmersion" workshop, they ask the students to apply the insights and knowledge they have gained while abroad: "Primarily because of the meta-level cultural analysis resulting from working all semester with their peers around the world, the course participants easily recognize the transferability of the lessons to the reentry conundrums" (Lou & Bosley, 2008, p. 293). This linking of predeparture, study abroad, and reentry—including their statement that "the importance of the post-immersion workshop cannot be overstated" (p. 292)—immediately recalls La Brack's training project. We especially want to call attention to a technique that Lou and Bosley use in linking the three learning stages, one that we believe holds real promise for intercultural competence development: their reliance on peer mentoring to facilitate intercultural learning, at home and abroad. Following their students' completion of the preassessment IDI, Lou and Bosley pair students whose scores fall into adjacent development orientations: A student in the low minimization stage may be paired with a student in the high defense stage, a student in the high minimization stage with a student in the low acceptance stage, and so on.

Program Development Through Research: The University of Minnesota's Maximizing Study Abroad Project (1999 to the Present)

In 1999, Michael Paige, Andrew Cohen, and colleagues began a project to develop a set of easily accessible materials that would enhance student intercultural and second language learning during study abroad.[14] That project, known as Maximizing Study Abroad, has evolved through several stages, including an original curriculum development phase that culminated in the publication of three *Maximizing Study Abroad* guides, a 3-year research phase, and the current online, in-country course phase.

During the first phase (1998–2001), Paige, Cohen, and their colleagues produced three guides written respectively for students, study abroad professionals, and second language teachers.[15] During the writing of the guides, coauthor Barbara Kappler coordinated an intensive field-testing process of draft materials that involved the three stakeholder groups: University of Minnesota students who were or had been enrolled in study abroad programs, study abroad program professionals in the Learning Abroad Center (LAC) at the University of Minnesota and at other selected U.S.-based study abroad offices, and second language instructors. The feedback they received from these groups was incorporated into the final revisions of the guides.

The project's second phase, the 3-year research program (2002–2005), involved a rigorous empirical assessment of the guides that addressed the following central question: Would students using the guide while abroad show greater intercultural and linguistic gains than students who were not? An experimental research design was used whereby some participating students were randomly assigned to the Maximizing Study Abroad treatment group and others to the control group. While abroad, the language and culture learning of the treatment students was facilitated by the use of the guide; students had specific reading and activity assignments from the guide and, at 2-week intervals, completed reflective writing tasks. The controls did not experience the intervention. The IDI (Hammer & Bennett, 1998) was used to measure the intercultural learning, and the new Speech Act Measure of Language Gain (Cohen & Shively, 2002–2003) assessed language development. The results of this study (Paige, Cohen, & Shively, 2004; Cohen, Paige, Shively, Emert, & Hoff, 2005) demonstrated that the student guide provided an effective method for intervening in and supporting the intercultural and language learning of students while they were abroad.

The third phase of the project (2005–present) has been the development of an online culture and language learning course for in-country students, patterned on the model originally developed for the research study. Since 2005, the University of Minnesota's Learning Abroad Center, in cooperation with the Department of Educational Policy and Administration, has offered this one-credit course to students. The course has evolved into its current form, "Global Identity: Connecting Your International Experiences to Your Future," and is available to all students participating in LAC programs.[16]

Cohen and Paige brought unique skills as well as shared experiences to the project. Both were Peace Corps volunteers, had years of international living experience, and had their formal academic training in International Development Education at Stanford University. Cohen had long been involved in strategies-based language teaching and learning and brought his special expertise in language education to the project. Paige had decades of intercultural teaching, training, and research behind him and brought his unique strengths as an interculturalist to the project. For years, he had worked closely with Janet Bennett, Milton Bennett, Bruce La Brack, Mitchell Hammer, and other leading interculturalists in the United States and abroad. He had played an important role in the development and testing of the IDI (cf. Paige, 2003; Paige, Jacobs-Cassuto, Yershova, & DeJaeghere, 2003). And he had extensive intercultural experience, having served as a Peace Corps volunteer in Turkey from 1965–1967 and having lived and worked in Indonesia, Thailand, the Philippines, Kenya, Hong Kong, Japan, and Australia. His experiences, representative of a grounded research approach, led him to conclude that intervening in the learning of students abroad was not merely desirable but necessary. Paige had been theorizing about the nature of intercultural education and training for over 20 years, most notably in his edited volume, *Education for the Intercultural Experience* (1993); he and other authors in that volume, such as M. Bennett, J. Bennett, Brislin, Grove and Torbiörn, LaBrack, and Weaver, had suggested that learners without guidance can be overwhelmed by the intensity of intercultural experiences and, in such circumstances, will likely apply ethnocentric understandings of difference to the new culture. The strong anecdotal evidence combined with these theoretical ideas led to the learning strategies approach of the *Maximizing Study Abroad* guides.

The Maximizing Study Abroad project represents an important milestone in the evolution of intercultural education in U.S. study abroad. In a focused and intentional way, the project began with a theoretical understanding about what constitutes intercultural competence, proceeded to develop hypotheses about how that competence could best be facilitated through the specific learning interventions introduced in the guide, and culminated in a systematic assessment of the effectiveness of those interventions. To the best of our knowledge, no other language and culture learning materials have ever been developed that were theory driven and empirically tested.

The student guide shows the extent to which Paige's training and experience had led him to treat intercultural competence holistically, taking account of its behavioral, affective, cognitive, and developmental dimensions. These four approaches to intercultural learning are present throughout the "Culture Learning Strategies" section of the student guide. In the sections titled "Strategies for Social Relations—Interacting With Hosts," "Strategies for Intercultural Communication," and "Nonverbal Communication," for example, Paige is focusing on the behavioral dimension, working to develop students' abilities to develop appropriate and effective behaviors in the specific culture where they find themselves. Sections titled "You're a Culturally Diverse Person," "Understanding the Ways Cultures Can Differ in Values," and "Strategies for Developing Intercultural Competence" approach intercultural competence cognitively and developmentally: Here the guide asks students to learn and internalize concepts that can help them interpret the new culture. It also introduces them to the concept of intercultural development and encourages them to think about their own understandings of difference as necessarily changing and fundamentally being constructions of reality. With the "Adjusting," parts of the "Preparing to Return Home," and "Continue the Learning" sections, the guide shifts the focus to the affective domain. Here, Paige's earlier conceptual work on intensity and risk factors is clearly evident.

The developmental nature of intercultural learning is central to the guide. Students learn, for example, that

> intercultural competence is not considered a naturally occurring phenomenon— human beings over the centuries have tended to prefer contact with those with whom they are culturally similar, and societies as a whole are largely ethnocentric. It is only through the process of awareness and understanding of cultural differences that comes through education and experience that people begin to view cultural differences as being positive, interesting, desirable, and having their own internal logic within a certain culture. (Paige, Cohen, Kappler, Chi, & Lassegard, 2002b, p. 101)

From Theory and Research to Program Design: The CIEE Student Learning Project (Fall 2006 to the Present)

Our final training project is notable for the ways that it has applied intercultural theory and research in the design of its training program. In the fall of 2006, the Council on International Educational Exchange (CIEE) launched a multiphase Student Learning Project whose broad goal is to improve the intercultural, second language, and disciplinary learning of students enrolled abroad at CIEE Study Centers. CIEE had long been intervening actively in the learning of students. For years, each of the centers has been led by a resident director, who is responsible for managing the program at the site and for taking steps to ensure the quality of student learning. Over the years, CIEE had come to embrace the philosophy that if students are to learn effectively abroad, qualified educators need to intervene in their learning. When Michael Vande Berg came to CIEE in 2005, his own experiences living and working abroad (he had studied abroad in Mexico as a high school student, had lived and taught in France and Spain for 5 years, and had extensive experience developing and evaluating programs), as well as his experiences as a faculty member, study abroad administrator, international education researcher, and trainer in the United States, had led him to the same conclusion.

Beginning in the fall of 2006, Vande Berg and several CIEE colleagues[17] guided the resident directors of CIEE semester and academic year programs through a process of developing measurable learning goals for their individual programs: intercultural, second language (at sites with a local language other than English), intellectual/academic, global/local awareness, and ethical learning goals. Thirteen resident directors were selected to teach a pilot course during the 2008–2009 academic year, now known as the Seminar on Living and Learning Abroad. This seminar is designed to facilitate the intercultural learning of students prior to, during, and after study abroad. In the spring of 2007, Vande Berg initiated an intensive training program for the thirteen pilot resident directors.

In 2007–2008, Vande Berg and Meghan Quinn[18] designed and developed the "Tool Kit for Living and Learning Abroad." This online tool kit provides a structured curriculum for the seminar and serves as a training tool for the pilot resident directors, providing them with, among other things, a common set of intercultural goals, key intercultural concepts, and a series of activities designed to allow the students to work with those concepts and to develop skills for interacting effectively and appropriately with host country people. During the fall of 2008, ten of the pilot resident directors began to teach the seminar to some or all of the students at their sites.[19]

The decision, in the fall of 2006, to pilot an intercultural learning course was based on two insights about student learning abroad. First, research was confirming that many if not most U.S. students were not in fact learning effectively abroad when left to their own devices. The multiyear Georgetown Consortium study, which Vande Berg directed, provided a large-scale assessment of student learning at 61 U.S. study abroad programs. The researchers found that U.S. students clearly benefit when their learning is facilitated (Vande Berg et al., in press), a conclusion consistent with the findings of Engle and Engle's (2004, pp. 225–231) own research. Second, these findings also confirmed that improving student performance in second language acquisition and in their disciplinary coursework would require that students come to understand that all of their learning at the sites abroad is intercultural in nature. Students who were having a difficult time adapting, for example, to host university courses that featured a professor delivering lectures at a lectern, with little or no time given to student questions or discussion, would benefit from coming to understand that teachers at host universities teach the way they do for cultural reasons. The students would need to understand that the visible culture they were perceiving at the university and elsewhere at the study site was being informed by the culture's invisible beliefs, attitudes, and values. The decision to focus the course on intercultural learning was, in short, based on Vande Berg and his colleagues' understanding that intercultural learning is fundamental, in the etymological sense of the term—that if they wanted to improve student academic and language learning at the study centers, they were going to have to start building at the foundation. They were going to have to start by intervening in the students' intercultural learning and development.[20]

The Seminar on Living and Learning Abroad begins, prior to the students' departure for their programs abroad, through their participation in an On-Line Pre-Departure Orientation (OPDO) that allows them to meet with their resident directors and with other students in the program.[21] The orientation sets the tone for intercultural learning abroad, preparing students to learn in ways that they have not experienced at home and to participate at their sites in a seminar that will teach them concepts and skills that allow them to learn effectively in the new culture. These include understanding the nature of culture, stereotypes and cultural generalizations, objective and subjective culture, and some culture-general patterns. The resident directors continue to facilitate student learning during meetings that continue throughout the semester.

As a part of their assessment of student needs, resident directors have students complete the IDI, Kolb's Learning Style Inventory, and an additional questionnaire that CIEE has developed. By the end of the course (which meets weekly from weeks 1 through 5 and every other week for the rest of the semester), the students have practiced articulating what they have experienced and learned in ways that home school faculty, family, and future employers will understand and value. CIEE will also be developing an online reentry seminar designed to help students apply what insights they have learned abroad to their lives back home.

The tool kit draws upon several intercultural frames of reference: Deardorff's (2008) intercultural competence model, the constructivist and developmental perspectives that inform the developmental model of intercultural sensitivity (M. Bennett, 1993), and Kolb's (1984) learning cycle each play important roles. Deardorff's work has contributed conceptually to the identification of specific learning goals for the seminar. Bennett's development model, especially Bennett and Bennett's identification of the cognitive, affective, and behavioral manifestations of each intercultural stage, inform different types of culture learning activities and different approaches to teaching these for each intercultural stage (Hammer & Bennett, 1998; J. Bennett & Bennett, 2004a). Kolb's learning cycle provides an important organizing framework for the tool kit, which offers resident directors sequences of activities that offer the students a holistic learning program by engaging them in each of the four learning styles (Kolb, 1984).

Conclusion

The six study abroad intercultural training projects, considered historically, allow us to trace the emergence of the new learner-centered study abroad paradigm we have discussed. In addition to converging around the view that intercultural learning is enhanced through cultural mentoring, five of the six projects are also in the process of assessing their effectiveness in guiding the intercultural development of their students, most notably through their common reliance on the IDI—evidence of the growing importance of the constructivist perspective. It is notable as well that three of the projects are now relying on technology to support their students' intercultural learning. Together, these six projects underline the fact that in the face of research findings and the sorts of integrated predeparture, in-country, and reentry culture learning approaches we have described, the traditional noninterventionist study abroad paradigm is waning. As the intercultural training programs we have discussed in this chapter illustrate, a new paradigm is emerging, one based in the understanding that students learn more effectively abroad when we intervene in their learning. Application of research and theory continues to play a key role in expanding this understanding.

Notes

1. Fisher would spend 22 years in the U.S. Foreign Service. Information retrieved on November 4, 2008, at http://www.interculturalpress.com/store/pc/viewPrd.asp?idproduct=169& IDCategory=70.

2. Fisher cites and briefly annotates works by the first two in the pamphlet's list of "Suggested Readings." It is worth noting as well that Edward Hall joined the Foreign Service

Institute in 1955 (the same year that Fisher published this pamphlet) as director of the State Department's Point IV training program (Pusch, 2004, p. 15).

3. Vande Berg in 2004 and 2007 referred to the "Junior Year Abroad paradigm"; Vande Berg et al. (in press) refer to it as the "traditional learning paradigm."

4. Fisher's later work shows how his own thinking about intercultural competence and training continued to evolve as well: see *Across Different Cultures: Public Diplomacy and the Behavioral Sciences* (1977), *International Negotiation: A Cross-Cultural Perspective* (1980), and *Mindsets: The Role of Culture and Perception in International Relations* (1997).

5. Callison College was one of three "cluster colleges" at UOP at that time. Its curriculum focused on non-Western/Asia studies, and it sent all of its sophomores to study abroad. In the year preceding La Brack's arrival, all of the members of the sophomore class had studied for a year in Japan (La Brack, personal communication, October 2008).

6. Lévi-Strauss (1962/1966) gave this sense to the term in *The Savage Mind:* "The rules of [the bricoleur's] game are always to make do with 'whatever is at hand,' that is to say with a set of tools and materials which is always finite and also heterogeneous. . . . The elements are collected and returned on the principle that 'they may always come in handy'" (English translation, 1996, p. 19).

7. He would later have students read Stewart and Bennett's (1991) revised edition.

8. Retrieved on November 5, 2008, from the AHA International Web site: http://aha-intl.org/.

9. The information about the AHA program, except where otherwise noted, is from personal communication that Vande Berg had with Janet Bennett on October 4, 2008, and with Milton Bennett on October 13, 2008.

10. Graduate course credit was offered through Portland State University extension services: M. Bennett, personal communication, October 13, 2008.

11. A key part of the program focused on training the teachers to help their students learn to learn together—the theory being that students who actively learned together would learn more effectively at the study abroad sites and would be less likely to behave, while there, in objectionable ways. Among other things, Bennett and Bennett trained the teachers to give the students a task that would require them to focus on and assume significant responsibility for their own learning: to form themselves into "city committees" that corresponded to each of the sites abroad. These student committees were responsible, prior to departure, for obtaining logistical information, maps, and background about the places they would stay at or visit and about the events that they would attend.

12. Details about the AUCP program, except where otherwise noted, are from personal communications that Vande Berg had with Lilli Engle on numerous occasions, the last on September 21, 2008.

13. Except where otherwise noted, details about the online writing course described here are from personal communications that Vande Berg had with Gabriele Bosley and Kris Lou on October 13, 2008.

14. Except where otherwise noted, details about the development of the *Maximizing Study Abroad* guides are from numerous personal communications that Vande Berg had with Michael Paige about this project, the latest on October 13, 2008.

15. See Cohen et al. (2003) and Paige, Cohen, Kappler, Chi, and Lassegard (2002a, 2002b).

16. Students going abroad were required to take the one-credit "Maximizing Study Abroad" course from spring 2005 until fall 2008, when its name changed to "Global Identity: Connecting Your International Experience to Your Future" and became a one-credit optional course.

17. Five individuals have collaborated in important ways since the project's beginning: Martin Hogan, vice president for Program Development and Operation, and four program

directors who together supervise all CIEE study abroad programs—Catharine Scruggs, Christine Wintersteen, Daniel Olds, and Adam Rubin.

18. Meghan Quinn joined the project in September 2007 after coming to CIEE that month as manager of instructional development. She continues to play important roles in designing and coordinating the Student Learning Project, including the co-creation of the online Tool Kit for Living and Learning and the supervision of the On-Line Pre-Departure Orientations.

19. Student groups in the fall of 2008 varied in size from 10 to 25 students.

20. A striking finding from the Georgetown Consortium study underscores this point: Students who were enrolled in host university students alongside host country students showed significantly smaller gains in their intercultural learning than students enrolled in courses with other U.S. students, in courses with other international students, or in courses with mixed populations (Vande Berg et al., in press).

21. The Student Learning Project relies on Microsoft Live Meeting for the OPDO sessions.

References

Bennett, J. (1993). Cultural marginality: Identity issues in intercultural training. In R. M. Paige (Ed.), *Education for the intercultural experience* (pp. 109–135). Yarmouth, ME: Intercultural Press.

Bennett, J., & Bennett, M. (2004a). *Developing intercultural competence: A reader*. Portland, OR: The Intercultural Communication Institute.

Bennett, J., & Bennett, M. (2004b). Developing intercultural sensitivity: An integrative approach to global and domestic diversity. In D. Landis, J. Bennett, & M. Bennett (Eds.), *Handbook of intercultural training* (3rd ed., pp. 147–165). Thousand Oaks, CA: Sage.

Bennett, M. (1993). Towards ethnorelativism: A developmental model of intercultural sensitivity. In R. M. Paige (Ed.), *Education for the intercultural experience* (pp. 21–72). Yarmouth, ME: Intercultural Press.

Berger, P., & Luckman, T. (1966). *The social construction of reality: A treatise in the sociology of knowledge*. Garden City, NY: Anchor.

Cohen, A. D., & Shively, R. L. (2002–2003). Measuring speech acts with multiple rejoinder DCTs. *Language Testing Update, 32*, 39–42.

Cohen, A. D., Paige, R. M., Kappler, B., Demmessie, M., Weaver, S. J., Chi, J. C., et al. (2003). *Maximizing study abroad: A language instructors' guide to strategies for language and culture learning and use*. Minneapolis: Center for Advanced Research on Language Acquisition, University of Minnesota.

Cohen, A. D., Paige, R. M., Shively, R. L., Emert, H. A., & Hoff, J. G. (2005). *Maximizing study abroad through language and culture strategies: Research on students, study abroad program professionals, and language instructors*. Minneapolis: Center for Advanced Research on Language Acquisition, Office of International Programs, University of Minnesota.

Deardorff, D. K. (2008). Intercultural competence: A definition, model, and implications for education abroad. In V. Savicki (Ed.), *Developing intercultural competence and transformation* (pp. 32–52). Sterling, VA: Stylus.

Engle, L., & Engle, J. (2003). Study abroad levels: Toward a classification of program types. *Frontiers: The Interdisciplinary Journal of Study Abroad, 9*, 1–20.

Engle, L., & Engle, J. (2004). Assessing language acquisition and intercultural sensitivity development in relation to study abroad program design. *Frontiers: The Interdisciplinary Journal of Study Abroad, 10*, 219–236.

Fisher, G. (1977). *Across different cultures: Public diplomacy and the behavioral sciences.* Bloomington: Indiana University Press.

Fisher, G. (1980). *International negotiation: A cross-cultural perspective.* Yarmouth, ME: Intercultural Press.

Fisher, G. (1997). *Mindsets: The role of culture and perception in international relations* (2nd ed.). Yarmouth, ME: Intercultural Press.

Foreign Service Institute. (1955). *When Americans live abroad* (Department and Foreign Service Series 54). Washington, DC: Department of State Publication.

Hall, E. (1959). *Silent language.* Garden City, NY: Doubleday.

Hammer, M., & Bennett, M. (1998). *The intercultural development inventory (IDI) manual.* Portland, OR: Intercultural Communication Institute.

Kohls, R. (1979). *Survival kit for overseas learning.* Yarmouth, ME: Intercultural Press.

Kolb, D. (1984). *Experiential learning: Experience as the source of learning and development.* Englewood Cliffs, NJ: Prentice Hall.

La Brack, B. (1993). The missing linkage: The process of integrating orientation and reentry. In M. Paige (Ed.), *Education for the intercultural experience* (pp. 241–279). Yarmouth, ME: Intercultural Press.

La Brack, B. (1996, November). *Dual ethnocentrism: When study abroad may not lead to intercultural development.* Paper presented at the 49th International Conference of the Council on International Educational Exchange, Monterey, CA.

Lévi-Strauss, C. (1966). *The savage mind.* Chicago: University of Chicago Press. (Original work published 1962)

Lou, K., & Bosley, G. (2008). Dynamics of cultural contexts: Meta-level intervention in the study abroad experience. In V. Savicki (Ed.), *Developing intercultural competence and transformation* (pp. 276–296). Sterling, VA: Stylus.

Paige, R. M. (1986). Introduction to new directions in the theory and practice of cross-cultural orientation. In R. M. Paige (Ed.), *Cross-cultural orientation: New conceptualizations and applications* (pp. 1–25). Lanham, MD: University Press of America.

Paige, R. M. (1993). On the nature of intercultural experiences and intercultural education. In R. M. Paige (Ed.), *Education for the intercultural experience* (pp. 1–19). Yarmouth, ME: Intercultural Press.

Paige, R. M. (2003). The intercultural development inventory: A critical review of the research literature. *Journal of Intercultural Communication, 6,* 53–61.

Paige, R. M., & Martin, J. N. (1983). Ethical issues and ethics in cross-cultural training. In D. Landis & R. W. Brislin (Eds.), *Handbook of intercultural training* (Vol. 1, pp. 36–60). New York: Pergamon.

Paige, R. M., & Martin, J. N. (1996). Ethics in intercultural training. In D. Landis & R. Bhagat (Eds.), *Handbook of intercultural training* (pp. 35–60). Thousand Oaks, CA: Sage.

Paige, R. M., Cohen, A. D., Kappler, B., Chi, J., & Lassegard, J. (2002a). *Maximizing study abroad: A program professional's guide to strategies for language and culture learning and use.* Minneapolis: Center for Advanced Research on Language Acquisition, University of Minnesota.

Paige, R. M., Cohen, A. D., Kappler, B., Chi, J., & Lassegard, J. (2002b). *Maximizing study abroad: A student's guide to strategies for language and culture learning and use.* Minneapolis: University of Minnesota.

Paige, R. M., Cohen, A. D., & Shively, R. (2004). Assessing the impact of a strategies-based curriculum on language and culture learning abroad. *Frontiers: The Interdisciplinary Journal of Study Abroad, 10,* 253–276.

Paige, R. M., Jacobs-Cassuto, M., Yershova, Y. A., & DeJaeghere, J. (2003). Assessing intercultural sensitivity: A psychometric analysis of the Hammer and Bennett Intercultural Development Inventory. *International Journal of Intercultural Relations, 27,* 467–486.

Pusch, M. (2004). Intercultural training in historical perspective. In D. Landis, J. Bennett, & M. Bennett (Eds.), *Handbook of intercultural training* (3rd ed., pp. 13–36). Thousand Oaks, CA: Sage.

Sanford, N. (1966). *Self and society: Social change and individual development.* New York: Atherton Press.

Stewart, E. (1972). *American cultural patterns: A cross-cultural perspective.* Yarmouth, ME: Intercultural Press.

Stewart, E., & Bennett, M. (1991). *American cultural patterns: A cross-cultural perspective.* Yarmouth, ME: Intercultural Press.

Transcultural Study Guide. (1987). Stanford, CA: Volunteers in Asia Program. (Available through the program at Box 4543, Stanford, CA 94309)

Vande Berg, M. (2003). The case for assessing educational outcomes in study abroad. In G. T. Hult & E. Lashbrooke (Eds.), *Study abroad perspectives and experiences from business schools* (pp. 23–36). Stamford, CT: JAI Press.

Vande Berg, M. (2007). Intervening in the learning of U.S. students abroad. *Journal of Studies in International Education, 11,* 392–399.

Vande Berg, M., Connor-Linton, J., & Paige, R. M. (in press). The Georgetown Consortium project: Intervening in student learning abroad. *Frontiers: The Interdisciplinary Journal of Study Abroad.*

CHAPTER 26

Research Application

*Toward a General Framework
of Competence for Today's Global Village*

Fons Trompenaars and Peter Woolliams

he commercial world is changing ever more rapidly due to the internationalization of business and migration of people from their homelands. Yet we still observe that the major instruments and methods used for selecting, recruiting, evaluating, and assessing staff and the performance of their business units owe their origin to conceptual philosophies that are still dominated by an Anglo-Saxon or U.S. signature. One might conjecture that there is already a bountiful supply of diagnostic instruments to determine individual or company-based cross-cultural profiles and competence. Not surprisingly, we can all observe how each is promulgated by their originators and claiming their own is the best. These varying authors usually claim degrees of (statistical) "reliability," but this is not the same as them being "valid." Critical examination of established models reveals a plethora of deficiencies.

Problems arise because in the past decade, we have witnessed the development of the autonomous and reflective individual. It is an individual who has a full set of needs, internal and external to the organization. Power is diffused and shared. In contrast with traditional management, where structures and systems are derived from a predefined strategy, the new workplace will seek to balance what matters for the company (its strategy) and what matters for the individuals (their life strategies). In fact, management and employees decide and execute interactively. In this New World of the customized workplace (Bouchiki & Kimberly, 2001) in which priority for sustained personal development goes hand-in-hand with the employer's business performance and growth, the reconciliation of dilemmas is the new source of authority.

So what should we be seeking to define and thereby measure to inform the human resource function and corporate strategy to improve business performance in 2009 and future sustainability? This chapter discusses different aspects of competence and challenges for their assessment when cultural factors are included. A framework that seeks to integrate the important components that overcomes limitations of existing models is proposed.

Critical appraisal of existing frameworks shows that most are not free of cultural bias and are stuck in the time warp of focusing on cultural differences—and not how to assess (and thereby develop) the competence to deal with cultural differences. We had developed our own series of instruments over the past 20 years that sought to assess different aspects of cultural competence. These have included assessing fundamental awareness, determining cultural orientation, having the propensity to reconcile differences, and having the competence to realize the business benefits of cultural differences—and in the context of both country and corporate cultural frameworks. As individual instruments, they have served their purpose well. However, we have recognized limitations in (earlier versions of) some of our own cross-cultural frameworks and have been searching for solutions that overcome common problems faced by all consultants, researchers, and human resource practitioners in the quest for such.

We have observed many Western organizations that have sought to impose Western (or rather Anglo-Saxon) human resource competence systems on organizational cultures that were based on entirely different assumptions. The result was either "corporate rain dancing" or complete ineffectiveness of the intended outcome. What do we do include and define as relevant competencies consistent with a pay-for-performance scheme in the power dominant culture, or what about a formal job evaluation session in an unstructured, people-oriented (incubator) culture?

The process of attracting and retaining talent is one of the key tasks of human resource professionals. Competence frameworks deemed to be predictors of high and effective performance are claimed. However, hardly any attention has been given to a very much underresearched issue, which is the interdependence of the image and corporate climate of the organization to the job seeker. The values with which organizations entice scarce human resources are very different today.

Mining our database generates evidence that supports the proposition that the younger generation—from 20 to 30 years old—has become more increasingly inner directed in the past few years. They dare to express their emotions more, and they feel better working in teams. Moreover, it appears that these younger Generation X, high-potential employees have a shorter time horizon and have greater self-confidence in their own individual abilities. Their preference has shifted away from the task-oriented "guided-missile" corporates to the person-oriented "incubator" work environment. Their rationale for career security is based on maintaining a set of personal and transferable competencies. It is their "employability" rating based on their contemporaneous skills profile that drives them, not the old notion of corporate security from an employer of high longstanding regard or protection by their trades union. The old adage that working for a major corporate will ensure you a job for life is no longer true or an attractor.

Global companies are looking for people whose competencies are transferable to multiple locations and who are innovative team players—people who think in terms of diversity, who want to learn and value freedom of choice (to continuously maintain their employability profile). This global corporate mind-set thinking appears to be bland ("it's all the same everywhere") and static and does not offer the freedom to develop one's own persona. As a consequence, it is not attractive to the young Generation X people. Young, talented, recently graduated candidates prefer to work locally and have fun. We might conjecture that the definition of effective behaviors in a given competence set might have to be generation specific rather than universal.

Paradigms of Competences and Competencies?

Even without the complexity of the cultural context, confusion begins over the use of the term *competence*. It is applied variously to denote the capacity in an individual but also as an element of a job role. The term *competence* has its origins in the research of the McBer Consultancy in the late 1970s in the United States as part of the initiative by the American Management Association to identify the characteristics that distinguish superior from average managerial performance. The work was encapsulated in the seminal book *The Competent Manager* (Boyatzis, 1982). This has spawned a mass of literature and initiatives in organizational attempts to identify and construct the "competent" manager.

However, the term and its related concepts have become problematic as they have been taken and adapted to different environments. Some practitioners prefer to define the term as an underlying characteristic of a person. It could be a motive, trait, skill, aspect of one's self-image or social role, or a body of knowledge that one uses. Others would define competency as a set of behavior patterns that the incumbent needs to bring to a position to perform its tasks and functions with competence. Furthermore, the terms *skill* and *competence* are often used interchangeably. As a basis for management training needs analysis or organizational review and development, most authors fail to clarify which of these meanings they are ascribing to competence. Such differences are more than just American versus European spelling.

Table 26.1   Extreme Definitions

Singular	Plural	Definition
Competency	Competencies	Are the skills and knowledge that employees must have or must acquire to *input* into a situation to achieve high levels of performance
		(*what you know*—skills and knowledge)
		[Definition more commonly used in the United States]
Competence	Competences	A system of minimum standards and effective behaviors demonstrated by performance and *outputs*
		(*what you do*—how you apply your knowledge in practice)
		[Definition more commonly used in Europe]

Another consideration is to review what paradigm of conceptual framework might be appropriate for defining an approach to competence. And is it a single category, or should it embrace more than one domain?

In addition, and before we can resolve the issue of paradigms, we have the further challenge of how to design a framework and associated instrument that covers the spectrum of cultural effects that is itself free of cultural bias!

When we begin to incorporate non-Western types of logic, such as yin-yang or Taoism, we soon realize that we have all been restrictive in basing any profiling on bimodal dimensions. For example, earlier we had been trying to place respondents along a scale with individualism at one end and communitarianism (collectivism) at the other. But in a multicultural environment, a highly individualized leader will agonize over the fact that many subordinates prefer to work with their team. Conversely, the group-oriented leader will fail because of an apparent lack of not recognizing the efforts of individuals. Thus, we have a dilemma between the seemingly opposing

Table 26.2 Varying Paradigms of Assessments

Paradigm	Domain	Nature or Nurture	Human Resources Application
A	Cognitive—measuring capacity (knowledge and intelligence)	Rarely changes as one grows older	Checks that candidate has basic capacity to do the job
B	Motivational—measuring purpose; what a person wants	Shifts over time; when aligned with the organization's goals, performance and effectiveness increase	Hire or promote people who "fit"
			Help development and career path of existing staff
C	Personality—measuring tendencies and approaches to life (especially for unfamiliar situations)	Set in formative years (i.e., when young) but can change a little through life changes (dramatic events)	Match traits with job requirements, understand strengths of an employee/ candidate
D	Values—determining value and belief systems	The measurement of meaning, mainly set in formative years from the collective programming of one's culture	Only one aspect of cross-cultural differences
E	Behavioral—measuring actions (what people do)	Can be learned and modified at any time of career	Identify strengths and gaps in skills/ knowledge
F	Organizational culture—measuring corporate climate	The context that affects the ways things are done around the organization	Enhance commitment and engagement of employees

orientations of individualism or communitarianism. Similarly, do we find undue criticisms of staff in a business unit or an excess of support? Someone criticized by authorities feels attacked where support is absent or indulged where criticism is withheld. Any instrument that seeks to be free of cultural bias needs to avoid being based on this type of Western Cartesian logic that forces us to say if it is "either/or."

Current Practices

Recruitment and selection for assignments over many years have left many organizations staffed by people comfortable with the old ways of working, or old paradigms. The greater the need for global change, the greater the likelihood that new blood will be required, not simply to replace wastage and retirement but to bring in new key skills. Selecting the right person for a post is a key decision for human resources, and various tools and systems have been developed to support the decision-making process. There is considerable pressure on human resources to make good decisions in recruitment: to get the right person but to avoid discrimination and to create a position so that the appointee can do the current job well yet grow the job in the future. Human resources faces a whole series of such dilemmas.

We have been surprised to find in our many interactions with the human resources community and professionals that few or no conceptual frameworks and corresponding instruments serve these needs. Instead, we frequently have observed the continued use of established models such as the Myers-Briggs Type Indicator (MBTI), Sixteen Personality Factor Questionnaire (16PF), or the Dominance, Influence, Steadiness, Compliance (DISC) framework that describe personality preference being applied without any adaptation or regard to cultural factors, either within the instrument itself or even in the interpretation or application of any data generated. We also have observed the use of poorly constructed tools, often (literally) made up, that had not been subject to any critical development or evaluation, purely because the practitioner was desperate for something to use. In many cases, the latter were the worst possible (because they don't measure competence or predictors of performance) and were often based on questions about do's and don'ts in specific cultural situations. For example, when in Dubai, should you give your business card at the start or end of a meeting? And when making a list of delegates to a multicultural meeting, should you sort and print their names by surname or given name, remembering that some cultures (e.g., China) normally may show their family name followed by a given name?

Towards Hypercultural Competence

With the previous discussion in mind, we have recently assembled our HCP (Hypercultural Competence Profiler). We describe this new conceptual idea and its origins, not simply to raise awareness of this particular instrument but to provide a forum so that other practitioners and researchers may develop and/or adapt these ideas for their own situations and circumstances. We have not found parallel or competitive models with which we could have made comparisons and certainly not any that have been published to lay their frameworks open to such critique.

Our HCP model is an attempt to describe and measure certain modes of thought, sensitivities, intellectual skills, and explanatory capacities that might contribute to the formation of hypercultural competence. We offer the term *hypercultural competence* because our research reveals the need to embrace several of the paradigms listed in Table 26.2.

Bringing together our evidence from our formal academic research (from our cohorts of doctoral candidates) and our practitioner-led client-based consulting suggests that we should differentiate between and include different layers. Table 26.3 illustrates how we would thus separate and define the components of hypercultural competence, with hypercultural competence being the total of all subunits.

Table 26.3 Sublevels of Hypercultural Competence

Hypercultural Competence		Outcomes
Cross-cultural competence	The capability to function according to the cultural rules of more than one cultural system; ability to respond in culturally sensitive and appropriate ways according to the cultural demands of a given situation	Avoid blunders Avoid embarrassment Not exhibiting ethnocentricity
Intercultural competence	The capability of successful communication and effective collaboration with people of other cultures through recognition of differences and respect for other points of view	Communicate and work with other cultures
Transcultural competence	The capability to connect different points of view through the elicitation of dilemmas and their reconciliation	Reconcile differences
Transcultural competence	The capability to deliver the business benefits of cultural reconciliation through servant leadership	Leverage business benefits
Intracultural competence (aka servant leader)	The capability to leverage cultural and/or ethnic diversity and differences within teams	Managing and leveraging business benefits of diverse teams and employees

In trying to develop our new integrative framework, we used a range of methods to determine what paradigms and components of competence should comprise this new model. They include

- A critical review of extant knowledge of competence frameworks
- Observations of best practice of high-performing leaders (see Trompenaars & Hampden-Turner, 2002)
- Inductive analysis of our own cultural and competence databases
- Job analysis of global leaders and senior managers that shows how they have to deal with dilemmas
- Our own academy (including some 15 doctoral student completions)
- Best practice from our client organizations that face the challenges of multi-cultures and/or diversity

Our multifunctional instrument enables a participant to assess his or her current cultural competence that embraces the more important components of hyperculture. Unlike other competence tools, this does not focus on a single basic area of cultural knowledge or behavior but addresses the complete spectrum from cross-cultural awareness to the business benefits deriving from effective action in multicultural situations. It has been developed by combining our earlier frameworks based on our extensive research and intellectual property that originally addressed each area separately. Each component has been subject to rigorous research and testing with many doctoral projects plus extensive application in many client situations across the world. Recently, we have confirmed the reliability[1] of the combined integrated instrument with many samples that has included MBA students as well as senior managers and business leaders from our client base and triangulated with our own databases of separate components.

Our instrument is normally completed online. After completing their set of responses, participants download and save their own personal profile report as a PDF file for archiving and/or printing. Additional basic biographical data of the respondent provide more extensive benchmark comparisons across our rapidly evolving database and provide for researching how profiles may (or may not) vary by the functional discipline of a respondent's job role, for example.

Extensive feedback, extended interpretations, and theoretical background to the model are available in a series of interactive pages from the Web-based support center. Participants can explore their own personal profile through these online tutorials that offer further insights, "coaching" advice, and suggestions for competence development.

Rather than follow the incremental levels of Table 26.3, we approached the problem of hypercultural competence holistically and concluded by distinguishing 12 components in four clusters (see Figure 26.1):

1. Recognition: How competent is a person to recognize cultural differences around him or her?

2. Respect: How respectful is a person about those differences?

3. Reconciliation: How competent is a person to reconcile cultural differences?

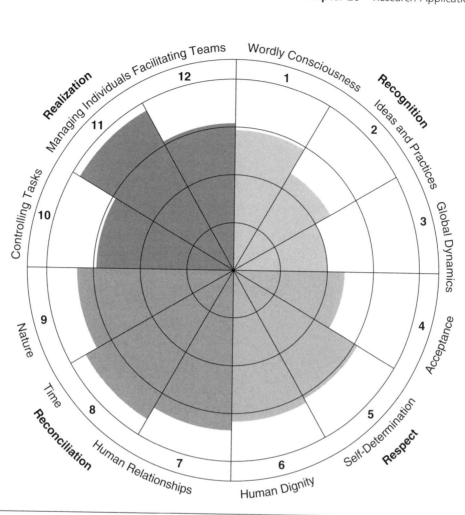

Figure 26.1   Toward a General Framework of Competence for Today's Global Village

4. Realization: How competent is a person to realize the necessary actions to implement the reconciliation of cultural differences?

Recognition

The first cluster is concerned with the individual's capacity to understand his or her condition in the community and the world and thereby make effective judgments. It includes the respondents' awareness of nations, cultures, and civilizations, including their own society and the societies of other peoples. The focus is on how these are all interconnected and how they change, as well as the individual's responsibility in this process. It defines some key elements of what we call a global consciousness—to flesh out some of the relevant constructs if we are to cope with the challenges of an increasingly interdependent world.

Operationally, it consists partly of the modes of thought, skills, and so on. But as conceived here, a recognition competence is not a quantum, something you either have or don't have. It is a blend of many things, and any given individual may be

rich in certain elements and relatively lacking in others. A very crucial part of intercultural awareness, as Eileen Sheridan (2005) found in her Delphi-based research,
is self-awareness.

In this cluster of recognition, we distinguish three main competence areas that
take account of the conceptualization developed by Robert G. Hanvey (2004):

1. Worldly consciousness that comprises perspective consciousness and "state
   of the planet" awareness

2. Fundamental cross-cultural awareness

3. Global dynamics that comprise knowledge of global dynamics and awareness
   of human choices

The diagnostic questions we have assembled and developed to measure this first
cluster have been based on many sources such as the ideas developed by Van der Zee
and Brinkmann (2004), Rew (2003), and in particular Hanvey (2004) in *An
Attainable Global Perspective*.

In summary, this quadrant of "recognition" covers the subcomponent of hypercultural competence that we described as cross-cultural competence in Table 26.3—
avoiding blunders and embarrassment.

Respect

How respectful is a person about those differences? Respect serves as the basis
for our attitudinal, cognitive, and behavioral orientation toward people who hold a
diversity of values.

In our professional practice, we have focused a significant part of our work on helping people to recognize cultural differences and structure their international experiences.
The risk of stopping at the level of awareness and recognition without progressing further is that one might be supported in one's (negative) stereotypes. But respect of these
differences is crucial for one's competence to deal with cultural differences.

According to the *Webster's Unabridged Dictionary* (Gove, 1981), the noun *respect*
is defined as the giving of particular attention, high or special regard, and expressions
of deference. As a verb, *to respect* is to consider another worthy of esteem, to refrain
from obtruding or interfering, to be concerned, and to show deference. A composite
definition of respect that reflects these characteristics can be presented as follows:

> Respect is a basic moral principle and human right that is accountable to the val-
> ues of human dignity, worthiness, uniqueness of persons, and self-determination.
> As a guiding principle for actions toward others, respect is conveyed through the
> unconditional acceptance, recognition, and acknowledgment of the above values
> in all persons. Respect is the basis for our attitudinal, cognitive, and behavioral ori-
> entation toward all persons with different values.

In our model, we have based the three components of respect on the research by
Kelly (1987) as they are appropriate for organizing the measurement of respect as
an attitude.

These components that form the cluster of respect comprise the following:

a. Respect for human dignity and uniqueness of a person from another culture
b. Respect for the person's rights to self-determination
c. Acceptance of other cultures' values

In summary, this quadrant of "respect" covers the subcomponent of hypercultural competence that we described as intercultural competence in Table 26.3, which is essential a priori for effective communication with others.

Reconciliation

This third cluster is the cornerstone of our research and consulting and addresses the propensity of a person to deal with the differences of which one is both aware and that one respects. This is close to the creativity a person displays in combining values that are at first sight contradictory (Trompenaars & Hampden-Turner, 2000). As a competent reconciler, you have to inspire as well as listen. You have to make decisions yourself but also delegate, and you need to centralize your organization around local responsibilities. As a competent professional, you need to master your materials and at the same time be passionately at one with the mission of the whole organization. You need to apply your brilliant analytic skills to place these contributions in a larger context. You are supposed to have priorities and put them in a meticulous sequence, while parallel processing is in vogue. You have to develop a brilliant strategy and at the same time have all the answers to questions in case your strategy misses its goals.

Because of these different views of the world, we have tensions deriving from these different value systems and/or current practice versus idealized behaviors. The task of the competent professional is to facilitate the reconciliation between these opposing differences in the area of their own function and to help build the wider reconciling organization.

Thus, this competence is not simply about compliance with legislation that demands positive discrimination to support minorities. First, we must recognize differences, whether from ethnic, gender, or age/generation origins. Then we must respect these contrasting orientations and consider that differing views from each group are equally valid. Then, and importantly, we must seize the opportunities that derive from these differences and integrate them, so that we can benefit from the variety of new ideas, new ways of working, and new insights that a multivariate workforce can offer.

We have identified three levels of reconciliation that are linked to the main constructs that we have used to organize the seven dimensions of culture.

Reconciling Aspects of Human Relationships

Standard and Adaptation. Do we have to globalize our approach, or do we just have to localize? Is it more beneficial for our organization to choose mass production than just focus on specialized products? High performers find the solution in the "transnational organization," where the best local practices are being globalized on a continuous basis. *Mass customization* is the keyword for reconciling standardized production and specialized adaptations.

Individual Creativity and Team Spirit. This demands the integration of team spirit with individual creativity and a competitive mind-set. High performers are able to make an excellent team out of creative individuals. The team is stimulated to support brilliant individuals, while these individuals deploy themselves for the greater whole. This has been called co-opetition.

Passion and Control. Is a competent person an emotional and passionate person, or does he or she control the display of emotions? Here there are two clear types. Passionate people without reasons are neurotics, and neutral individuals without emotions are robots. An effective performer regularly checks passion with reason, and if we look at the more neutral people, we see an individual who gives controlled reason by showing passion once in a while.

Analysis and Synthesis. Is the competent person a detached, analytical person who is able to divide the big picture into ready-to-eat pieces, always selecting for shareholder value? Or is it somebody whose behavior puts issues in the big picture and gives priority to the rather vague statement "stakeholder value"? The "helicopter view" was introduced as a significant characteristic of a modern leader—the capability to ascend and keep the overview while being able to zoom in on certain aspects of the matter. This is another significant attribute of the competent reconciler—namely, to know when and where to go in deep. Pure analysis leads to paralysis, and the overuse of synthesis leads to an infinite holism and a lack of action.

Doing and Being. "Getting things done" is an important characteristic of a manager. However, shouldn't we keep the rather vulgar "doing" in balance with "being," as in our private lives? As a reconciler, you have to be yourself as well. From our research, we found that successful reconcilers act the way they really are. They seem to be one with the business they are undertaking. One of the important causes of stress is that "doing" and "being" are not integrated. Excessive compulsion to perform, when not matching someone's true personality, leads to ineffective behavior.

Reconciling Aspects of Time

Sequential and Parallel. Notably, effective reconcilers are able to plan in a rigorous sequential way but at the same time have the ability to stimulate parallel processes. This reconciliation, which we know as "synchronize processes to increase the sequential speed"—or "just-in-time" management—is also very effective in integrating the long and short term.

Reconciling the Inner and the Outer Worlds

Push and Pull. This final component is the competence to connect the voice of the market with the technology the company has developed and vice versa. This is not simply about technology push or market pull. The competent reconciler knows that the push of technology finally leads to the ultimate niche market, that part without any clients. If you only choose for the market, the client will be unsatisfied.

Realization

After one has recognized, respected, and reconciled cultural differences, the emphasis shifts to processes in which the resolutions are implemented and rooted in the organization.

Components of this competence are captured in John Adair's (2005, 2006) action-centered leadership model. Competent managers and leaders should have full command of three main areas and should be able to use each of the elements contingent upon the situation. Being competent in each component delivers results, builds morale, improves quality, develops the productivity of teams, and is the mark of a successful manager and leader.

The key to nurturing leaders is to ensure your company recognizes excellence at three levels: strategic, operational, and team. "It is a common fallacy that all an organization needs is a good strategic leader at the helm," writes Adair (2005, p. 106).

This fourth cluster comprises the following:

a. Achieving the task
b. Developing the team or group to complete the project
c. Managing individuals

In summary, the third and fourth quadrants of reconciliation and realization cover the subcomponent of hypercultural competence that we described as transcultural competence in Table 26.3, which integrates cultural differences to a higher level and delivers the business benefits from synergies.

Based on the above clusters, the full instrument comprises some 100 questions that are used in different combinations to contribute to the total profile. Ratings are not simply added and averaged for the different scales. In many cases, the sectors are computed from the root mean square (RMS) quadrature[2] of competing questions to assess their mutual interaction. This is especially important for assessing the competence to reconcile in Cluster 3.

To accommodate different client/participant needs, we have developed several versions. Thus, in the 360 version, a participant's own self-assessment scores can be triangulated with peer feedback. This can even be based on additional input from clients, customers, or suppliers. The organization version is oriented to an analysis of the "competence" of the business unit and/or wider organization rather than the individual. In the diversity version, the focus is on diversity and ethnicity rather than country-derived cultures.

Intracultural Competence

Most competence frameworks include a descriptor to cover the issue of teamwork (being able to contribute effectively to a team). Such prescriptions are usually deficient in that they don't give sufficient attention to working in and with other cultures to synergize such differences.

It is part of received wisdom that groups of executives or managers should learn to operate as effective teams. Getting everyone to think the same way is a tempting strategy, but our research reveals that real teamwork comes when opposites are integrated to work with each other.

We believe the importance of reconciling these opposites has been largely ignored in competence models. There is too much one-dimensional thinking across too many competence frameworks and claimed solutions. Too many personality tests mark out people as either judging or perceiving. But why if you are a "judging" person can you not act as a "perceiving" person? And if you are "individualistic," can you not also be "collectivistic" and therefore work with others as a good team player?

Competence metrics for teams tend to pigeon-hole people as being able to offer their contribution through mainly what is their primary natural team role orientation. Traditional logic then purports that by combining several of such individuals, selected so that all required team roles are present as well as their individual competencies, this becomes the winning formula for the assembled group to be able to work as an effective team.

But is team building that simple? If members of a team play different roles and have different competencies, then the team is full of potential conflict and misunderstanding. Globally, we have found that the Anglo-Saxon world of the United States and United Kingdom tends to be more individualistic, while Asians take to a more communal teamwork approach. So as long as the Americans remain in the United States managing all-American teams, while, for example, the Chinese stay in China doing the same, then conflict and misunderstanding are at least on the local level. But in today's multicultural world, an American leader could be running a team of Thai, Chinese, French, and English members. And furthermore, what if the senior management group already in place comes with an imbalance of team roles?

We have taken the well-known model developed by Meredith Belbin (2003), in which he describes nine primary team roles for successful teams, as one example simply because it is recognized as the most widely used team inventory in the world, given that it is well researched, has been thoroughly validated, and has made a significant contribution to management development for over a decade. Each Belbin role contributes to the team in a different way. For example, he describes the Shaper, who is dynamic and provocative; the Plant, who is creative and unorthodox; and the (contrasting) Implementer, who is efficient and detailed. Of course, we know that the Belbin team role model is not intended for use simplistically as a model for team selection, recruitment, or team building but as an aid to analysis, reflection, and constructive debate. We should also remember that facilitators who have been trained and licensed to use such original models are well able to apply them creatively and effectively; but sadly, such models are sometimes used by other trainers in less sophisticated ways and often inappropriately. We have no wish to criticize the Belbin model or any other such inventory—just to discuss the usefulness of extending it in light of our own experiences.

The Belbin model was not intended as a device for comparing country-specific team role cultures, which can produce problems in a cross-cultural context. Even when the team role distributions of two cultures are quite similar, the cultures themselves are not necessarily similar. So it is not surprising that effective team behavior may not look the same in different cultures, let alone in multicultural teams.

Britain and the United States offer good examples. The team role distributions of both populations are similar, but the behavior that British resource investigators[3] enact to undertake this team role is quite different from the behavior that U.S. resource investigators perform to provide their contribution to their team. The differences in behavior do not necessarily indicate differences in team roles but differences in ways the preferences can be expressed and enacted within those cultures. There are cultural differences in behavior, but not in the team role.

Our concern is that, too often, consultants who often abuse such models assume that simply having all team roles present will make an effective team. They ignore the whole issue of how people with different team competencies should work together to combine their contributions. So our quest is to ask how can we extend orthodox models and thereby make them jewels that go far beyond any cultural preference.

We have sought to challenge respondents about what dilemmas they face in working in their team. Thus, with Pepsico, Stream, and other organizations, we asked members of their senior team what tensions they face when working with other members of their team who had opposite team roles to themselves as a means of exploring intracultural competence. Note that the focus was on the dilemmas they

Table 26.4 Working With Opposite Team Roles

Respondent		Other team member
Shaper Challenging, dynamic, thrives on pressure. The drive and courage to overcome obstacles but prone to provocation. Offends people's feelings.	Working with a contrasting team role	Finisher Painstaking, conscientious, anxious. Searches out errors and omissions. Delivers on time but inclined to worry unduly. Reluctant to delegate.
This is what he said about himself: "Difficult for me to take on and develop ideas I have not had an original input to."		And about his colleague: "May not appear interested in alternative viewpoints as focus is on detail and delivery."
This is what he proposed as a reconciliation:		
Request the finisher to structure meeting time to evaluate my new ideas and then to identify and discuss his or her concerns and how they could be overcome if my idea might be implemented.		

faced when working with other team members by virtue of the team roles, not aspects of interpersonal relationships. For many participants, simply posing these questions instantly generated new insights to how they were working with others and how well they were able to be creative about reconciling their own team role with opposite team roles. Consider a team member who is a Shaper.[4] What dilemma did he identify in working with the Finisher[5] role in a team, and how could he work better in the future by reconciling this dilemma?

Similarly, consider a team member who is naturally a Monitor-Evaluator.[6] What dilemmas did she say she faces when working with a Plant,[7] and how could she integrate her role with her opposites?

We have repeated this extended team role model with other client companies using an interactive Web-based system that captures strategies that enable participants to work better with others such that we are now able to build a team role dilemma database to explore all combinations.

While we have illustrated the need to reconcile opposites with team roles, it applies to all of such differences whether the origin of the differences is personality, generations, or national or ethnic cultures. It is this propensity to reconcile dilemmas across roles and functional disciplines that we offer as the new source of competence for working with other cultures.

Our growing database of these tensions are manifestations at the team level of the more generic dilemmas faced by organizations today. We also know from our work where we measure the impact of these reconciliations that this intracultural competence improves business performance at the bottom line exposed by this analysis.

Given the importance of reconciling opposites as a fundamental component of competence, we are surprised that no instrument that measures this has been

Table 26.5 Working With Opposite Team Roles: Second Example

Respondent		Other team member
Monitor-evaluator	Working with a contrasting team role	Plant
Sober, strategic, and discerning. Sees all options. Judges accurately but lacks drive and ability to inspire others.		Creative, imaginative, unorthodox, and solves difficult problems but ignores incidentals. Too preoccupied to communicate effectively.
"I want to influence others to take action."		"Idea generation conflicts with need to meet deadlines and work with team."
This is what she proposed as a reconciliation:		
Create action plans with key deliverables with clear roles and responsibilities but that include specific tasks for the review of new ideas, their evaluation, and assessment of their implications.		

devised—not in published form, at any rate. Our concern about applying any linear model for competence frameworks across international boundaries might be explained by our own overdeveloped reconciliation profiles. But we insist that with the combination of seemingly opposed orientations, a team can flourish in diversity. Yes, all team roles need to be present and played out, but it is the reconciliation between them that makes the team surpass. And no one has ever measured anything like that.

In Application

Data we have collected have already demonstrated that this composite hypercultural profile provides an objective measure for the individual and/or organization.

Significantly, it reveals identification of the stage "maturity" of the life cycle phase: Thus, does the client need cross-cultural awareness, leadership development, or the realization of business benefits, for example? Thus, one can identify the relative imperatives for cross-cultural awareness training, the requirement to develop mind-set changes and corresponding behavior development for performance, and the achievement of global business benefits by integrating cultural differences. And of course, "before" and "after" measurements provide evidence of the impact of any intervention that can be correlated with improved business performance.

It can be seen that cultural competencies need to embrace several of the different categories or paradigms of psychometric measurements we assembled in Table 26.3. The competence of an employee or job applicant might be initially set earlier but can be further developed. This new model can be used to assess existing value systems and the "lower levels" of cultural competence (Quadrants 1 and 2) and even provide an input to an assessment center for recruitment and selection. But feedback from our client workshops demonstrates over and over that basic cultural awareness training can change people's values and develop their competence readily. More important is Quadrant 3 (reconciliation). Again, we find from our workshops and executive coaching that getting leaders and managers to elicit and frame their business problems as a series of dilemmas, as well as working through our structured methodology that expands and reconciles the dilemmas, produces a quantum shift in their transcultural competence.

Initially, they develop their capability with particular dilemmas more mechanistically, but as they progress and practice, then it becomes a mind-set change with automatic subconscious capability (like when we first learn to drive an automobile but then drive automatically when proficient).

Global (one world) thinking creates tensions compared to a contrasting framework, which recognizes and values diversity (many realities). Multinational corporations now invite people who believe in the equal treatment of men and women and ask people from different ethnic backgrounds to develop into honorable citizens of the world. While apparently laudable, you can imagine the dilemmas that arise between being oriented toward teamwork (stability/tradition) versus innovation. The Japanese experience demonstrates that this is not easy to reconcile. Apart from these dilemmas, there is also the dilemma adhering to the image of a large organization and doubt whether these orientations can actually be put into practice.

Many of our clients achieve productivity improvement through reconciling the different orientations between their researchers (who want to do brilliant research) and their committed marketers (who want to satisfy their customer base). The traditional approach, based on competence models that embrace productivity incentives, goal setting (productivity goals), increased automation, and quality improvement initiatives, has mainly failed human resources departments. We help them use our hypercultural competence ideas to create the "reconciling organization" in which a strong sense of core values supports an environment in which managers are better able to manage change, overcome crises, focus on corporate longevity, achieve the retention of key/effective personnel, develop motivation, and identify and thereby realize (deliver) higher productivity through the alignment and integration of opposite orientations.

Conclusion: Rational Competence Behaviors

The discussion in this chapter and most authors writing on competence assume that the actor is rational. That is, employees and/or job applicants make rational decisions about their professional work and career and training needs, and they all want to improve and do better by extending their competence profile. But recent research by Ariely (2008) and Lunn (2008) shows that we are all not so rational—otherwise, why would we borrow on our credit cards when cheaper credit is available or smoke tobacco to endanger our health?

Ludwig von Bertalanffy (1950), considered to be one of the founders of the interdisciplinary general systems theory, would probably challenge this by saying that we are rational, but the total system is more complex and that we just don't understand how they (or ourselves) are being rational. And this might be the real value of competence research across cultures, not just to understand and manage differences in the short term but to get a better understanding of different points of view and how they can be connected for the benefit of society as a whole.

Notes

1. Based on Cronbach alpha studies of component scales.

2. For example: A contributing component score might be the square root (Question A score × Question B score).

3. Who is enterprising and develops contacts but is overly optimistic.

4. Challenging and dynamic but provocative.

5. Conscientious and painstaking but reluctant to delegate.

6. Discerning and judges accurately but is slow moving.

7. Creative and unorthodox but ignores incidentals.

References

Adair, J. (2005). *Effective leadership development.* London: Chartered Institute of Personnel and Development.

Adair, J. (2006). *How to grow leaders: The seven key principles of effective leadership development.* London: Kogan Page.

Ariely, D. (2008). *Predictably irrational: The hidden forces that shape our decisions.* New York: HarperCollins e-books.

Belbin, M. (2003). *Management teams: Why they succeed or fail.* London: Butterworth-Heinemann.

Bertalanffy, L. (1950). An outline of general system theory. *British Journal for the Philosophy of Science, 1,* 139–164.

Bouchiki, H., & Kimberly, J. (2001, October 22). All change in the customised workplace. *Financial Times,* pp. 4–5.

Boyatzis, R. E. (1982). *The competent manager: A model for effective performance.* New York: John Wiley.

Gove, P. B. (Ed.). (1981). *Webster's unabridged dictionary.* Springfield, MA: Merriam-Webster.

Hanvey, R. G. (2004). *An attainable global perspective.* New York: American Forum for Global Education. www.globaled.org/An.AttGlob_Persp_04_11_29.pdf

Kelly, B. O. (1987). *Perception of professional ethics among senior baccalaureate nursing students.* Unpublished doctoral dissertation, The Ohio State University, Columbus.

Lunn, P. (2008). *Basic instincts: Human nature and the new economics.* London: Marshall Cavendish.

Rew, L. (2003). Construct validity evidence for the intercultural evidence check. *International Journal of Selection and Assessment, 12,* 285–290.

Sheridan, E. (2005). *Intercultural leadership competencies for U.S. business leaders in the new millennium.* Unpublished doctoral dissertation, University of Phoenix, Phoenix, Arizona.

Trompenaars, F., & Hampden-Turner, C. (2000). *Building cross-cultural competence.* New Haven, CT: Yale University Press.

Trompenaars, F., & Hampden-Turner, C. (2002). *21 leaders for the 21st century: How innovative leaders manage in the digital age.* New York: McGraw-Hill.

Van der Zee, K. I., & Brinkmann, U. (2004). Construct validity evidence for the Intercultural Readiness Check against the Multicultural Personality Questionnaire. *International Journal of Selection and Assessment, 12,* 285–290.

CHAPTER 27

Assessing Intercultural Competence

Issues and Tools

Alvino E. Fantini

n today's world, globalizing trends and new technologies have had dramatic effects on people around the globe. More people than ever before in the history of the world now have both direct and indirect contact with each other, and increasingly, this contact includes people from a variety of diverse language and cultural backgrounds. This phenomenon has produced not only new communicative opportunities for everyone involved but significant new challenges as well.

As a result, many people are finding that they need to develop new abilities to be able to communicate across their language-culture differences. This means not only making themselves understood—in their own tongue, the interlocutor's tongue, or a third language not native to either party—but, perhaps more important, also learning new behaviors and interactional styles that go beyond those of their native systems. The expansion of one's communicative repertoire is important, especially since acceptance is not usually achieved on one's own terms but rather on the terms of one's interlocutors or hosts. Moreover, communication and acceptance are more likely to be strained by offending behaviors and less so by the use of incorrect grammar. These insights, recognized some 50 years ago, in fact stimulated the development of the field of intercultural communication (Wight, 1999, p. 11).

Despite the many years that have passed, however, many intercultural educators, while intensely concerned with perceptions, behaviors, and interactional strategies, continue to ignore the role that proficiency in the host language plays during an intercultural encounter, leaving this as the task of language teachers. And language teachers, conversely (culture notes aside), while intensely concerned with language, generally ignore behavioral and interactional aspects of communication, viewing themselves as "language" teachers, not teachers of "intercultural competence" (Sercu, 2006; Sercu et al., 2005). Yet, all three—language, behaviors, and interactional strategies—together form speech acts when dealing interculturally just as they do within one's own culture, and all three are needed for intercultural communication.

Whereas language educators have defined and redefined their field over the years, the intercultural field is still evolving. For this reason, many important issues remain unresolved, including the most fundamental question of all: What abilities are needed, in addition to language, for successful intercultural interaction? The answer to this question is key to the assessment process. Any lack of clarity on this point means that the focus of assessment is likewise unclear, notwithstanding an array of recently developed instruments that purport to predict intercultural success, monitor intercultural processes, or measure the outcomes of an intercultural experience. This chapter discusses the focus of intercultural assessment and the basics of assessing intercultural competence, and it also provides a list of tools to help in the assessment process.

The Focus of Intercultural Assessment

What, in fact, should be the focus of intercultural assessment? Anyone engaged in the intercultural field for any time has surely pondered the vagaries of intercultural abilities. Despite a number of important efforts (e.g., Byram, 1997; Byram, Nichols, & Stevens, 2001; Deardorff, 2004; Fantini, Arias-Galicia, & Guay, 2000; Humphrey, 2007; Martin, 1989; Wiseman & Koester, 1993), a search of the literature quickly reveals the dilemma. The wide array of terms in use confirms the lack of consensus among writers and researchers, to wit: biculturalism, multiculturalism, bilingualism, multilingualism, plurilingualism, communicative competence, cross-cultural adaptation, cross-cultural awareness, cross-cultural communication, cultural competence, cultural or intercultural sensitivity, effective intergroup communication, ethnorelativity, intercultural cooperation, global competitive intelligence, global competence, international competence, international communication, intercultural interaction, metaphoric competence, transcultural communication, and so forth. A review of assessment tools reveals the same. While some instruments bear superordinate titles that designate composites of abilities, others address varying subcomponents of intercultural competence. Some instruments focus on lingual rather than cultural aspects; some do the opposite. Other instruments stress international rather than intercultural and thereby exclude differences within national boundaries; still others are simply ambiguous and their intent is unclear.

Given this persistent situation, numerous workshops were organized over the years at professional gatherings of the Society for Intercultural Education, Training, and Research (SIETAR) to encourage members to examine and share their thoughts. The intent was to identify the most common and most comprehensive labels in use. Needless to say, no single term emerged, leaving important questions unresolved and with no clear consensus: What are the relevant abilities to assess within intercultural competence? Are they properly addressed in education and training efforts? Is there a clear relationship between instruction and evaluation? Are we assessing what really matters? Is there alignment between instructional objectives, course design and implementation, and assessment?

Happily, contributors to the present work are obviously comfortable with the term *intercultural (communicative) competence*. This label, in fact, has gained increasing ground, building nicely on a concept already widely used over many years by language educators—*communicative competence* (CC; cf. Byram, 1997, p. 3). In this view, each individual possesses a native communicative competence (CC_1) and, during intercultural contact, encounters that of one's interlocutor (CC_2). Those who choose to acquire a second communicative competence, CC_2, develop intercultural competence. Intercultural competence, then, acknowledges the presence of CC_1 and the development of CC_2 and, in addition, the insights that derive from now being in a position to compare and contrast both. This unique vantage point is an important aspect of intercultural competence and something that a monolingual, monocultural native of either system cannot possibly access (see Figure 27.1).

Stated another way, intercultural competence may be defined as complex abilities that are required to perform *effectively* and *appropriately* when interacting with others who are linguistically and culturally different from oneself. Whereas *effective* reflects the view of one's own performance in the target language-culture (LC_2; i.e., an outsider's or "etic" view), *appropriate* reflects how natives perceive such performance (i.e., an insider's or "emic" view). The challenge for language and intercultural educators and trainers, then, is to help learners recognize their etic stance while attempting to uncover the emic viewpoint of their hosts, assuming adequate motivation, interest, willingness, and contact.

Whereas scholars have researched and written about intercultural competence for many years (discussed by Spitzberg & Changnon in Chapter 1, this volume), its assessment depends on the clarity of both its definition and conceptualization. For this reason, an initial and extensive search of the literature was conducted to identify commonalities that were then used to build the construct of intercultural competence used here. This construct was later further substantiated through a research effort that investigated the intercultural abilities required of participants from three cultures (Ecuador, Great Britain, and Switzerland) during and after intercultural contact (Fantini, 2006). The data obtained confirmed the initial construct of intercultural competence with its multiple and interrelated components. These components included various attributes, three areas, four dimensions, target language proficiency, and developmental levels, together forming a framework for a holistic view of intercultural competence.

Communicative Competence₁ + Communicative Competence₂ (+ CC₃, ₄, etc.) ⇒

Intercultural Communicative Competence

Figure 27.1   Intercultural Communicative Competence

A brief explanation of each component follows: First, the *attributes* most commonly cited in the literature (and substantiated by the research) are flexibility, humor, patience, openness, interest, curiosity, empathy, tolerance for ambiguity, and suspending judgments. The *three interrelated areas* are the ability to establish and maintain relationships, the ability to communicate with minimal loss or distortion, and the ability to cooperate to accomplish tasks of mutual interest or need. The *four dimensions* are knowledge, (positive) attitudes (or affect), skills, and awareness. These are configured in Figure 27.2 in a sort of pinwheel (Fantini, 1999, p 184) to illustrate that the first three dimensions promote enhanced awareness—fostered through introspection and reflection—while enhanced awareness, in turn, stimulates development of the other three dimensions.

Figure 27.2 Intercultural Competency Dimensions

Evaluating these four dimensions presents special challenges to assessors. Whereas educators are accustomed to assessing knowledge and perhaps even skills, the assessment of attitudes and awareness is uncommon. Moreover, attitudes and awareness are not easily subjected to quantification and documentation. To help with this challenge, explicit objectives for each dimension may be found in various assessment instruments (cf. Byram, 1997, pp. 49–54, and the AIC, cited in Fantini, 2006, Appendix G). Since all four dimensions are important components of intercultural competence, all four must be addressed and assessed.

It is interesting to note that target language proficiency is frequently ignored in many models of intercultural competence. In the construct presented here, however, target language proficiency is considered central to the development of intercultural competence, although clearly not equal to it. Proficiency in a second language at any level enhances all other aspects of intercultural competence in quantitative and qualitative ways: For example, grappling with a second language causes us to confront how we perceive, conceptualize, express, behave, and interact. It promotes alternative communication strategies—and *on someone else's terms*. And it helps expand and transform our habitual view of the world. Conversely, the lack of second language proficiency, even minimally, constrains us to think about the world and act within it entirely in our native system, a decidedly ethnocentric approach.

Finally, intercultural competence is commonly a longitudinal and ongoing developmental process. Intercultural competence evolves over time, although occasionally with periods of stagnation or even regression. Attaining varying competence levels, of course, is contingent on degrees of contact as well as on one's motivation—whether instrumental or integrative—toward the target language-culture. Devising benchmarks can help to monitor development; for example, the use of numbers or descriptors such as educational traveler, sojourner, professional, and specialist (cf. Fantini, 2000–2001, 2006) or levels such as basic, intermediate, advanced, and native-like (cf. ACTFL Materials Center, 1985). In the end, all components of intercultural competence—from attributes to developmental levels—are important to monitor in a comprehensive and quality assessment process.

Some Basic Notions Regarding Assessment

When thinking about assessment, Mager's (1997, pp. v–vi) seahorse story comes to mind and is worth repeating here:

> Once upon a time, a Sea Horse gathered up his seven pieces of eight and cantered out to find his fortune. Before he had traveled very far he met an Eel, who said:
> "Psst, hey bud. Where 'ya goin'?"
> "I'm going out to find my fortune," replied the Sea Horse, proudly.
> "You're in luck," said the Eel. "For four pieces of eight you can have this speedy flipper, and then you'll be able to get there a lot faster."
> "Gee, that's swell," said the Sea Horse, and paid the money and put on the flipper and slithered off at twice the speed. Soon he came upon a Sponge, who said:
> "Psst. Hey, bud. Where 'ya goin'?"
> "I'm going out to find my fortune," replied the Sea Horse.
> "You're in luck," said the Sponge. "For a small fee I will let you have this jet-propelled scooter so that you will be able to travel a lot faster."
> So the Sea Horse bought the scooter with his remaining money and went zooming through the sea five times as fast. Soon he came upon a Shark, who said:
> "Psst, Hey, bud. Where 'ya goin'?"
> "I'm going out to find my fortune," replied the Sea Horse.
> "You're in luck. If you'll take this short cut," said the Shark, pointing to his open mouth, "you'll save yourself a lot of time."
> "Gee, thanks," said the Sea Horse, and zoomed off into the interior of the Shark and was never heard from again.

The moral of the fable, as Mager (1997) points out, is that if you're not sure where you're going, like the Sea Horse, you're liable to end up someplace else and not even know it.

In fact, the story is a perfect metaphor for the conundrum that exists within educational processes in which instructional objectives, course design and implementation, and assessment are not aligned. Although alignment seems absolutely basic, educators with inadequate preparation in assessment sometimes face just such a situation. This became obvious in a survey of intercultural communication course designs used at 50 universities, which revealed varying degrees of congruence among these three aspects (Fantini, 1997, pp. 125–148). Stated another way, instructional objectives, course design and implementation, and assessment must be inextricably linked; otherwise, the educational process is compromised.

Quality assessment, then, rests on this fundamental principle—that assessment is not separate from but integral to every other aspect of the educational process. This notion is reinforced graphically in the model depicted in Figure 27.3 (Fantini, 2000–2001, p. 101).

In this model, all of the components around the circle are connected—from needs assessment all the way around to evaluative assessment (including long-term assessment sometimes conducted after the formal experience is over). The intersecting lines show that each component is linked with all of the others. The model

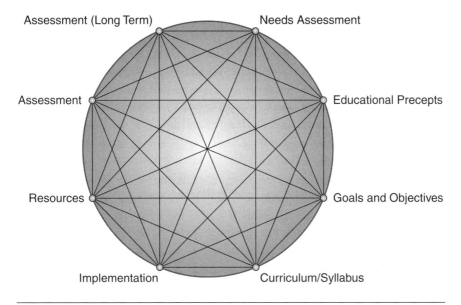

Figure 27.3   The Gemstone Model

graphically illustrates how assessment is related directly to explicitly articulated goals and objectives and that assessment measures their attainment by the learner. What is to be learned and what is to be measured are related; they are, in fact, the same. And since the goals and objectives are about developing components of intercultural competence, clear understanding of intercultural competence and these components again emerges as critical to the process. To be sure, educators and trainers must be competent in all of the areas cited around the circle—competent to establish instructional objectives and competent to assess these same objectives.

Assessment quality is also aided by reviewing several additional factors (adapted from Deardorff, 2004, p. 324):

- First of all, the purpose—that is, why assess?

- The target audience—that is, who is to be tested?

- Clarity about successful outcomes—that is, what outcomes are being assessed?

- The use of proper assessment tools and strategies that are aligned with the learning objectives

- The assessment procedure—that is, how the test is administered, evaluated, and scored

- Aspects of the tests used—that is, their scope, efficiency, and length as well as their validity and reliability

- Representative and varied samples of student achievement—that is, ongoing and not just end-testing)

- Avoiding bias—that is, extraneous interference that may affect obtaining adequate and appropriate samples

Fortunately, quality assessment is facilitated today owing to the development of many new approaches—outcomes assessment, mastery learning, and performance assessment, among others. Their purpose, however, always remains the same: to find out how well students attain established objectives. Newer test formats and strategies help to obtain this information in better and more varied ways, permitting a shift away from traditional paper-and-pencil tests that, taken alone, are never effective measures of intercultural competence. Approaches that incorporate portfolios, logs, observation, interviews, performative tasks, and the like are generally more valuable for assessing intercultural competence. These options permit multidimensional assessment approaches that are essential for monitoring and measuring a complex phenomenon such as intercultural competence.

Aspects of Assessment

Given the imperative of a multidimensional approach, then, it may be useful to review basic aspects of assessment in general. These include the areas to assess, test types, assessment formats, and assessment techniques and strategies, discussed in the section that follows.

Areas to Assess

To begin with, one needs to determine which areas of intercultural competence are being addressed. Of course, this is ascertained by returning to the instructional objectives and may include any of the intercultural competence components cited earlier: attributes, the three areas (building relationships, communicating, collaborating), the four dimensions (awareness, attitudes, skills, knowledge), host language proficiency, developmental indicators over time, or a combination of the above.

Test Types

After determining which components of intercultural competence are being addressed, we next consider which test types are best suited for the task. Since there are many test types, each with a specific purpose, you will want to choose the types that best serve your needs. These include, for example, the following:

Readiness tests—used to determine preparedness for an intercultural experience

Placement tests—which, unlike culture-general tests, may be used to ascertain compatibility with specific cultural contexts

Diagnostic tests—used to determine which areas of competency are strong as well as which may require further training or strengthening

Aptitude tests—used to ascertain one's potential for learning a specific set of skills or knowledge; these tests are commonly used in advance of language training but may apply to cultural areas as well

Attitude tests—used to investigate one's disposition toward a specific culture or group of people

Proficiency, communicative, or competency-based tests—used to measure performance within a given aspect of competency

Criterion-referenced and norm-referenced tests—used to examine one's mastery of a given aspect as compared with a specific set of criteria or a given population or group

Bilingual or culture-language dominance tests—used to determine one's relative ability with two languages and/or cultures

Formative tests—used to measure one's developmental progress at given moments over time

Achievement or standardized tests—used to measure one's attainment with regards to a given set of criteria and/or a given population or group that serves as the norm

Examples of many of these tests may be seen in Figure 27.5.

Assessment Formats

Varied formats are also recommended when assessing intercultural competence. The options are illustrated in chart form in Figure 27.4.

As always, it is important to choose the format or, better yet, the combination of formats that best aligns with your assessment objectives. To explain each option further, *direct* assessment is conducted at specified moments in time, usually announced, and directly documents actual learning. Traditional tests and quizzes measuring acquired knowledge are examples of direct assessment. Other direct examples include portfolios, capstone projects, and other variations of embedded course assessments.

Indirect assessment formats, in contrast, are normally ongoing and sporadic and not always obvious to the learner when being conducted. A teacher observes students during a class session, for example, and later makes notes about their performance

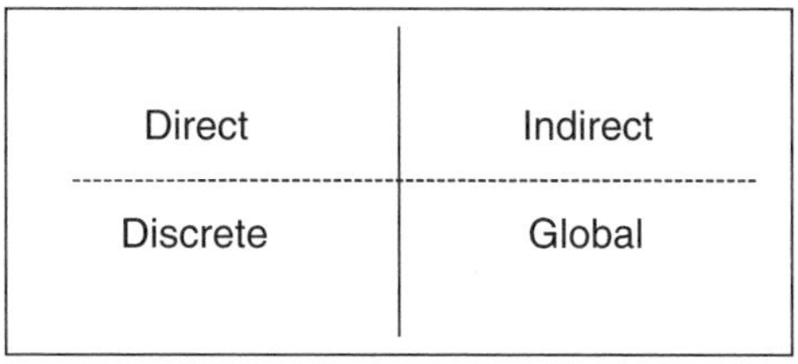

Direct	Indirect
Discrete	Global

Figure 27.4 Quadrant of Assessment Formats

based on criteria she or he has previously established. She or he might focus on how students interact or participate and whether they are experiencing problems, are asking questions, appear motivated, are on target, or are unengaged. Periodic notes about student performance help the teacher to follow up on specific issues, as needed, in subsequent sessions. Other indirect formats include self-report surveys, interviews, and focus groups in which students report impressions of their own learning.

Discrete assessment focuses on a very specific aspect of learning—for example, did the student grasp the point at hand, demonstrate a particular skill, or reveal a particular insight? Its focus is narrow and specific in contrast with *global* assessment, which considers abilities that require synthesis and applications in other contexts. Normally, however, several or all of these formats are used together. For example, true or false questions on a test are at once both direct and discrete, while a case study uses both indirect and global formats. In general, ongoing use of varied formats in combination produces the best indicators of learning over time.

Assessment Techniques and Strategies

Assessing intercultural competence also requires using a variety of different techniques and strategies. Some examples include the following:

- Closed and open-ended questions
- Objective strategies that involve scoring (e.g., matching items, true/false questions, multiple-choice questions, cloze or gap-filling items)
- Oral and written activities (e.g., paraphrasing, translation, essay)
- Active and passive activities
- Individual and interactive activities in pairs or groups
- Dialogue, interviews, debate, and discussion
- Demonstrations, poster sessions, role-plays, and simulations
- Structured and unstructured field tasks and experiences
- Questionnaires that require self-evaluation, peer evaluation, group evaluation, and/or teacher evaluation

In short, recent developments both in the field of assessment in general and in assessing intercultural competence in particular facilitate the use of multiple combinations of assessment types, formats, and strategies. These developments, coupled with processes that now include the learner in the evaluative process (through self-evaluation, reflection, and feedback), result in better and more varied indicators of progress and of attainment of the learning objectives. Portfolio assessments are one approach, for example, that has gained wide acceptance and improves not only the information obtained but enhances the learning process itself. And portfolio and proficiency approaches, taken together, provide an even better base for monitoring and assessing intercultural competence. Moreover, the increasing availability of a wide choice of external instruments that may be used in combination with teacher-devised assessment further enhances assessment possibilities. These instruments are described in the section that follows.

External Assessment Tools

Despite varied constructs of intercultural competence, a study by Deardorff (2006, p. 241) found that experts agree that intercultural competence can indeed be measured. The important thing to remember, however, as stated repeatedly, is that intercultural competence assessment be multidimensional as well as multiperspective, ongoing, integrated, aligned, and intentional. It should also include a " mix of quantitative and qualitative methods . . . including interviews, observation, and judgment by self and others" (Deardorff, 2006, p. 241). To aid in this approach, then, let us now consider a variety of external instruments.

Numerous external instruments now exist that purport to assess intercultural competence or at least differing aspects of it. These instruments are available from multiple sources—some appear in journal publications, others can be accessed online, and still others are available commercially or are administrated for a fee by specialized agencies or organizations. Figure 27.5 provides a selective, revised, and updated list containing 44 such instruments (Fantini, 2006, pp. 87–94). In each case, what each instrument purports to measure is cited, followed by descriptive comments and the source or location where the instrument may be found. From the titles alone, it is often obvious that the instruments represent varying conceptualizations of intercultural competence or otherwise address specific components. Often, this is also reflected in what they purport to measure and in their measurement approach as well.

Some of the instruments in Figure 27.5 are predictive; others are formative, normative, and/or summative. Most address intercultural competence without regard to language; a few address language without regard to other aspects of intercultural competence. In several cases, both language and culture areas are addressed. When selecting an instrument, therefore, it is important to understand exactly what each instrument measures and to be sure that its purpose is compatible with the goals and objectives being assessed. There is no point to using an external instrument if it does not provide the information you want. And in all cases, it is important to remember that a single instrument alone is usually inadequate for measuring all aspects of intercultural competence.

To aid in selecting an appropriate test instrument for your needs, ask yourself the following questions (adapted in part from Deardorff, 2004, p. 203):

- First of all, is the tool compatible with your goals and objectives?

- Does it improve your overall assessment plan?

- Is it based on a theoretical foundation?

- Does it have a cultural bias, or can it be used for any ethnic or national group?

- Is it appropriate for the age level and developmental level of those involved?

- What logistical aspects are involved in administering the tool, including cost, time, and other resources needed?

- Who are the results intended for—that is, are the results for the students, used to inform the teaching/learning process, or are they mainly for researchers, teachers, administrators, or supervisors?

ACTFL Proficiency Scale & Guidelines

Measures: Foreign language proficiency

Description: This instrument provides detailed descriptions of levels of language proficiency based on five levels originally established by the U.S. Foreign Service Institute. The scale lists various levels of communication functions, range of vocabulary, degree of accuracy, and flexibility that language learners are able to control in four skill areas (listening, speaking, reading, and writing). These descriptions help in setting learning goals, planning learning activities, and evaluating proficiency.

SOURCE: Online from the American Council for the Teaching of Foreign Languages (ACTFL), 1982, revised 1985.

Assessment of Intercultural Competence (AIC)

Measures: Intercultural competence, including language proficiency

Description: This questionnaire, designed in a YOGA Format ("Your Objectives, Guidelines, and Assessment"), is used for self-assessment and assessment by peers and teachers. The tool monitors the development of the intercultural competence of sojourners (and hosts) over time, providing valid and reliable indicators that are normative, formative, and summative. Shorter and longer versions exist, as well as versions in English, British English, Swiss German, and Spanish. For the underlying research and the tool, go to http://www.experiment.org/resources.html (click on Final Report, then Appendix G.); for a shorter version, see: http://www.world learning.org/7803.htm (click on Occasional Papers Series Issue No. 1 and scroll down to pp. 25–42).

SOURCE: For permission to use, contact alvino.fantini@sit.edu.

Assessment of Language Development (ALD)

Measures: Foreign language development

Description: This questionnaire, designed in a YOGA Format ("Your Objectives, Guidelines, and Assessment"), is used for self-assessment and assessment by peers and teachers. This tool charts the development of language proficiency over time, providing normative, formative, and summative indicators.

SOURCE: For permission to use, contact alvino.fantini@sit.edu.

Australian Second Language Proficiency Ratings (ASLPR)

Measures: Second language proficiency

Description: This tool rates second language proficiency on a scale from zero to native-like, providing performance descriptions in terms of practical tasks. Developed initially for English second language teaching, it was adapted for English dialects in Australia and several other languages. The ASLPR is the standard means for stating language proficiency in Australia.

SOURCE: Developed by D. E. Ingram, 1996.

Behavioral Assessment Scale for Intercultural Communication (BASIC)

Measures: Cross-cultural behavior

Description: This tool explores the cross-cultural equivalence of the Behavioral Assessment Scale for Intercultural Communication. Containing eight scales, it is based on an empirical study identifying significant skill profiles and validated with 263 university students.

SOURCE: Olebe, M., & Koester, J. (1989). Exploring the cross-cultural equivalence of the behavioral assessment scale for intercultural communication. *International Journal of Intercultural Relations, 13,* 333–347.

Beliefs, Events, and Values Inventory (BEVI)

Measures: Personal disposition toward transformational experiences

Description: Designed to identify and predict a variety of developmental, affective, and attributional processes and outcomes that are integral to equilintegration theory, which seeks to explain the processes by which beliefs, values, and worldviews are acquired and maintained; why their alteration is typically resisted; and how and under what circumstances their modification occurs. The BEVI is proposed for assessing international learning and determines whether, how, and to what degree people are, or are likely to be, "open" to transformational experiences such as international education.

SOURCE: Craig N. Shealy, PhD, James Madison University. shealycn@jmu.edu

http://www.acenet.edu/programs/international/fipse/PDF/BEVI_Abstract.pdf

Cross-Cultural Adaptability Inventory (CCAI)

Measures: Individual potential for cross-cultural adaptability

Description: A culture-general instrument designed to assess individual potential for cross-cultural adaptability based on the assumption that individuals adapting to other cultures share common feelings, perceptions, and experiences that occur regardless of their own cultural background or target culture characteristics. The inventory contains 50 items, resulting in individual profile scores along four dimensions.

SOURCE: Kelley, C., & Meyers, J. Intercultural Press. Tel: 1-800-370-2665.

Cross-Cultural Assessor (CCA)

Measures: Individual understanding of self and others

Description: This tool is designed to improve people's understanding of themselves and others as well as to promote positive attitudes to cultural difference. The tool also provides a personal navigator system that allows individuals to conduct a self-assessment to aid in successful communication across cultures through a multimedia program that measures, builds, and manages cross-cultural skills and characteristics through exercises and questionnaires.

SOURCE: Richard Lewis Communications. www.crossculture.com

Cross-Cultural Counseling Inventory

Measures: Cross-cultural counseling aspects

Description: Developed primarily for the counseling milieu, this tool provides an inventory of cross-cultural counseling factors.

SOURCE: LaFromboise, T. D., Coleman, H. L., & Hernandez, A. (1991). Development and factor structure of the Cross-Cultural Counseling Inventory–Revised. *Professional Psychology: Research and Practice, 22,* 380–388.

(Continued)

(Continued)

Cross-Cultural Sensitivity Scale (CCSS)

Measures: Cross-cultural sensitivity

Description: A scale designed to measure cross-cultural sensitivity in the Canadian context, normed on undergraduate students.

SOURCE: Pruegger, V. J., & Rogers, T. B. (1993). Development of a scale to measure cross-cultural sensitivity in the Canadian context. *Canadian Journal of Behavioural Science, 25,* 615–621.

Cultural Competence Self-Assessment Questionnaire (CCSAQ)

Measures: Cross-cultural competence

Description: Designed to assist service agencies working with children with disabilities and their families in a self-evaluation of their cross-cultural competence. Intended for U.S. domestic use.

SOURCE: Mason, J. L. (1995). Portland State University.

Cultural Orientations Indicator® (COI®)

Measures: Cultural preferences

Description: A Web-based cross-cultural assessment tool that allows individuals to assess their personal cultural preferences and compare them with generalized profiles of other cultures. Cultural profiles are based on 10 dimensions particularly applicable in doing business in multicultural situations. A validated report is also available upon request.

SOURCE: http://www.tmcorp.com

Culture in the Workplace Questionnaire™

Measures: Personal cultural profile

Description: This questionnaire provides insights about yourself and a better understanding of how your cultural preferences and the cultural preferences of others affect working relationships. It also provides a framework for understanding diverse approaches to workplace interactions such as problem solving, working in teams, and managing projects.

SOURCE: http://www.itapintl.com/ITAPCWQuestionnaire.htm

Development Communication Index

Measures: Communication quality and accuracy of perception

Description: This field instrument, developed as a result of the Kealey study, is designed to assess the quality of communication and the accuracy of perception between Canadian advisers and their national counterparts working in development projects abroad. The index presents 30 scenarios related to issues such as project progress and adaptation skills and may also be used as a problem-solving tool.

SOURCE: http://www.tamas.com/samples/source-docs/ROI-Briefings.pdf

European Language Portfolio (ELP)

Measures: Foreign language proficiency

Description: This tool, devised by the Council of Europe's Modern Languages Division and piloted in 15 member states between 1998 and 2000, was launched throughout Europe in 2001. The portfolio has three components: a language passport, a language biography, and a dossier, designed to help partners describe proficiency levels required by existing standards, tests, and examinations to facilitate comparisons among differing systems of qualifications.

SOURCE: The Council of Europe's Modern Languages Division.

Expatriate Profile (EP)

Measures: Self assessment of cross-cultural competence

Description: A computer-based cross-cultural competence self-assessment instrument for international professionals that results in an expatriate profile.

SOURCE: Park Li Group. (1996). (2nd edition). New York.

Foreign Assignment Success Test (FAST)

Measures: Cross-cultural workplace adaptation

Description: An instrument designed to measure the ability of American expatriate managers to make successful work role transitions in Japan. The instrument employs six scales, validated on 67 American managers in Japan.

SOURCE: Black, J. S. (1988). Work role transitions: A study of American expatriate managers in Japan. *Journal of International Business Studies, 19*, 277–294.

GAP Test: Global Awareness Profile

Measures: World knowledge in specific areas

Description: This tool measures how much world knowledge a person has concerning selected items of international politics, economics, geography, culture, and so on.

SOURCE: J. Nathan Corbitt. Intercultural Press, ISBN 1-877-864-55-2 P.O. Box 700 Yarmouth, ME 04096 USA. Tel: 866-372-2665

Global Literacy Survey

Measures: World knowledge

Description: A self-test used to measure the degree of knowledge young Americans have about the world.

SOURCE: Available online. National Geographic Survey: www.nationalgeographic.com/roper2006/

Global Mindedness Scale (GMS)

Measures: Effects of study abroad on student global mindedness

Description: Pre- and post-surveys designed to determine how study abroad influences the development of global mindedness among university students.

(Continued)

(Continued)

The tool measures five dimensions: cultural pluralism, responsibility, efficacy, globalcentrism, and interconnectedness.

SOURCE: E. Jane Hett (1993). Florida State University.

Global Perspectives Inventory (GPI)

Measures: Individual global perspective

Description: This tool consists of a survey of 46 items designed for self-reports of student perspectives in three domains of global learning: cognitive, interpersonal, and intrapersonal. Interested parties can take the GPI online, identifying their home institution, since results are provided to institutions that request reports to assist in creating an environment that promotes a global perspective among their student body.

SOURCE: Survey available online at www.gpi.central.edu. Institutions interested in obtaining reports for a fee, should click on "Ordering the GPI."

Global Team Process Questionnaire™ (GTPQ)

Measures: Effectiveness of global teams

Description: A proprietary instrument designed to help global teams improve their effectiveness and productivity. Developed in the form of a questionnaire, this diagnostic tool enables team leaders and other decision makers to develop and support global teams by helping to identify barriers to success on global teams.

SOURCE: http://www.itapintl.com/gtpq.htm

GlobeSmart

Measures: Effectiveness of global teams

Description: A Web-based tool that investigates how to conduct business effectively in 35 countries. The tool examines information on communicating effectively, managing employees, transferring technology and skills, and improving relationships with international customers and suppliers.

SOURCE: Meridian Resources Associates http://www.meridianglobal.com/demoregistration.html

Intercultural Competence Assessment (INCA) Project

Measures: Intercultural competence

Description: A 3-year project designed to develop a framework, diagnostic tool, and record of achievement for the assessment of intercultural competence. The tool links both language competence and subject knowledge competence.

SOURCE: Available online. http://www.incaproject.org/index.htm

Intercultural Competence Questionnaire

Measures: Global literacy

Description: A brief questionnaire that provides a self-test of intercultural competence described as global literacy.

SOURCE: Available online. www.7d-culture.nl/Content/cont053b.htm

---

Intercultural Competency Scale

Measures: Intercultural effectiveness

Description: A competency scale designed to measure intercultural effectiveness. The tool is especially oriented to missionaries and foreign students.

SOURCE: Elmer, M. I. (1987). *Intercultural effectiveness: Development of an intercultural competency scale.* Unpublished doctoral dissertation, Michigan State University.

Intercultural Development Inventory (IDI)

Measures: Orientation to cultural differences

Description: A 50-item assessment instrument designed to measure individual and group intercultural competence along a developmental continuum regarding the respondents' orientation toward cultural differences and their readiness for intercultural training. A statistically reliable and valid measure of intercultural sensitivity, translated into 12 languages and applicable to people from various cultural backgrounds. Users must take a qualifying seminar to use this instrument.

SOURCE: Hammer Consulting, LLC, Tel. 410-208-1120.

Intercultural Living and Working Inventory (ILWI)

Measures: Intercultural skills

Description: A living and working overseas predeparture questionnaire, intended as a professional development tool to help individuals identify intercultural skills that need improvement prior to undertaking an international assignment. The tool is also used in personnel selection to help interviewers do targeted selection by focusing on areas of weakness and risk identified in the test results.

SOURCE: Kealey, D. J. http://www.dfait-maeci.gc.ca/cfsi-icse/cil-cai/ilwi-ici-en.asp

---

Intercultural Orientation Resources (IOR)

Measures: Personality analysis

Description: This tool is used as a predictive index and personality analysis, using a voluntary checklist.

SOURCE: Administered by IOR Global Services. http:/www.iorworld.com

---

Intercultural Readiness Check (IRC)

Measures: Intercultural skills

Description: A tool designed to assess participants' intercultural skills in areas of sensitivity, communication, leadership, and management of uncertainty. Clients preparing for an assignment, a project, or training complete an online questionnaire, and IRC licensees provide online support and client management tools.

SOURCE: Intercultural Business Improvement, The Netherlands. http://www.ibinet.nl

---

Intercultural Sensitivity Inventory (ICSI)

Measures: Intercultural sensitivity

(Continued)

(Continued)

Description: This tool measures intercultural sensitivity using the contrastive concepts of individualism and collectivism. The tool has been validated with 46 undergraduate and 93 graduate students.

SOURCE: Bhawuk, D. P. S., & Brislin, R. W. (1992). The measurement of intercultural sensitivity using the concepts of individualism and collectivism. *International Journal of Intercultural Relations, 16,* 413–436.

International Assignment Profile (IAP)

Measures: Potential success for an international assignment

Description: This tool is designed to increase the human and business success of international assignments by spotting key issues and pinpointing weak links or problems that could compromise an international relocation.

SOURCE: Neill M. Carson & Donald R. Young. Tel: 713-842-2087

International Candidate Evaluation (ICE)

Measures: Personality analysis

Description: This validated assessment instrument provides a personality analysis completed by supervisors of candidates for overseas assignments or assignments at home that require working with other nationalities. The ICE serves as a companion tool for the Overseas Assignment Inventory (see below) and focuses on motivation, expectations, and attributes.

SOURCE: Administered by Tucker International. http://www.tuckerintl.com

International Mobility Assessment (IMA)

Measures: Readiness for international work

Description: An interactive, self-assessment tool designed to help employees assess their readiness to take on the challenges of living and working in another country. Available in two interactive booklets designed for "Family IMA" for the employee candidate and his or her family and the "Single IMA" for the unaccompanied employee. Interactive exercises guide the user through three critical areas—the family or personal issues (for the unaccompanied employee), a new country and culture, and a different workplace—and concludes with a decision-making exercise.

SOURCE: Available online. http://www.tuckerintl.com

Living and Working Overseas Inventory

Measures: Readiness for cross-cultural adjustment

Description: This instrument is in the form of a questionnaire completed by Canadian technical advisers and their spouses who are candidates for overseas development assignments. The tool is used to predict overseas outcomes by measuring interpersonal and other related skills associated with intercultural effectiveness and predicts their potential for success in their cross-cultural adjustment.

SOURCE: Kealey, Daniel J. (1990). Canadian International Development Agency. Hull, Quebec, Canada.

MAXSA Instruments

Measures: Foreign language strategies, culture learning strategies, and speech acts

Description: Three instruments designed for use in assessing strategies that learners use for language acquisition, intercultural development, and language gain. The first two, known as the Language Strategy Use Inventory and the Culture-Learning Strategies Inventory, were created for students pre- and post-study abroad, both analyzed for validity and reliability. The third is the Speech Act Measure available in English, Spanish, and French.

   All three instruments can be used as independent measures or in the context of a broader study or program.

SOURCE: Web site for the final report containing all three instruments (pp. 325–355) is http://www.carla.umn.edu/maxsa/documents/MAXSAResearchReport.pdf

Multicultural Counseling Inventory (MCI)

Measures: Multicultural counseling competencies

Description: A self-report instrument designed to measure multicultural counseling competencies. The results identify four factors within a multicultural context: awareness, counseling skills, counseling relationship, and counseling knowledge. The instrument has been administered to 604 psychology students, psychologists, and counselors and to 320 university counselors.

SOURCE: Sodowsky, G. R., Taffe, R. C., Gutkin, T., & Wise, S. L. (1994). Development of the Multicultural Counseling Inventory: A self-report measure of multicultural competencies. *Journal of Counseling Psychology, 41,* 137–148.

Objective Job Quotient System (OJQ)

Measures: Cross-cultural employee performance

Description: A computer-assisted tool that provides cross-culturally appropriate feedback to evaluate and rank employee performance. The OJQ uses multiple raters and "scaled direct comparisons," ensuring reliability and validity.

SOURCE: http://www.globalinterface.com.au/how_we_do_it.html

Overseas Assignment Inventory (OAI)

Measures: Readiness for international work

Description: A self-response questionnaire designed for employees and their spouses considering or preparing for international assignments or assignments that require working with other nationalities at home. The questionnaire is based on empirical research and examines three areas (motivations, expectations, and attributes) and 14 attributes correlated with successful cross-cultural adjustment and performance. Individual profiles are compared to a database of other respondents representing 40 nationalities.

SOURCE: Administered by Tucker International. http://www.tuckerintl.com

Personal Orientation Inventory (POI)

Measures: Readiness for overseas volunteer work

(Continued)

(Continued)

Description: This tool is used to predict the success of Peace Corps trainees undergoing preparation for an overseas assignment. The tool was validated with 92 Peace Corps trainees.

SOURCE: Uhes, M. J., & Shybut, J. (1971). Personal orientation inventory as a predictor of success in Peace Corps training. *Journal of Applied Psychology, 55,* 498–499.

Peterson Cultural Awareness Test (PCAT) & Peterson Cultural Style Indicator (PCSI)

Measures: Cross-cultural awareness and effectiveness

Description: Two assessment tools designed to measure cross-cultural effectiveness and awareness of cultural differences. These reliable and valid tools provide pre- and post-indicators of intercultural learning before/after training and also promote global business success.

SOURCE: Accessible online. Brooks Peterson, Across Cultures, Inc. www.acrosscultures.com

Schwartz Value Survey (SVS)

Measures: Compatible cross-cultural values orientation

Description: This survey, based on more than 60,000 individuals in 64 nations, explores the compatibility of a candidate's cultural orientations and the expected dominant cultural orientations of the region or country of assignment. The tool also provides information about different value orientations within a multicultural team and their effects on the team's work.

SOURCE: http://www.imo-international.de/englltisch/html/svs_info_en.htm

Team Management Systems (TMS)

Measures: International competencies

Description: This tool evaluates individuals in 10 competency areas required by highly effective professional operators to transfer skills from a domestic to an international context: openness, flexibility, personal autonomy, emotional resilience, perceptiveness, listening, orientation, transparency, cultural knowledge, and influencing synergy.

SOURCE: TCO International, Australia. http://www.tco-international.com/competencies.asp

Tests for Hidden Bias

Measures: Unconscious prejudices

Description: A series of online tests, each about 10 minutes, known as Implicit Association Tests or IATs addressing a variety of topics. The tests are designed to examine unconscious hidden bias, hidden negative prejudices, and stereotypes that influence one's perceptions and actions. Results and interpretations are reported instantly followed by access upon completion of the tests to studies on more than 100 topics regarding social groups, personality, and culture.

SOURCE: http://www.tolerance.org/hidden_bias/index.html

Figure 27.5 Chart of Intercultural Competence Assessment Instruments

NOTE: All URLs were confirmed at the time of this writing; however, URLs and Web sites may change over time. Also, several other promising instruments are under development but unpublished and could not be included at this time. For an expanded list of over 90 instruments, see Fantini (2006).

One final note: Inclusion of the instruments in this chart should not be construed as an endorsement. Interested users will need to investigate each instrument more thoroughly. The questions cited in this section will help in selection, but beyond that, one should also investigate test validity and reliability since this tells something about the instrument's quality. Validity indicates whether the test measures what it says it does and relates directly to the test's purpose. Reliability tells how well the instrument produces consistent results each time it is used. Tests with high validity and reliability factors are obviously desirable.

Conclusion

As educators and trainers, we need to be absolutely clear and explicit about what we do. This is especially challenging in a field still in the process of defining the fundamental concept so central to our work—intercultural competence. How we conceptualize our subject matter affects how we define goals and objectives, design and implement courses, and monitor and assess outcomes. Testing and evaluation are an integral part of the educational process, not only at the end of a course but also at the beginning and throughout as well. Assessment seeks to ascertain whether and to what extent our students attain the objectives set forth. While we often also make intuitive judgments about this, sound assessment, based on a conscious, purposeful, multiple, and explicit approach, provides objective indicators to balance our subjective views.

Today, increasing assessment options are available that can help in conducting effective and reliable evaluation. In addition to assessment activities devised by teachers, external tests can also help; however, it is important to ensure that the information they provide aligns with the outcomes we intend to measure. Quality assessment requires a thoughtful approach that takes into account much of what was discussed in this chapter. Properly executed, good assessment not only provides solid information that can guide our educational practices from start to finish but can also enrich and transform the teaching and learning processes for both teachers and students.

References

ACTFL Materials Center. (1985). *ACTFL proficiency guidelines.* Hastings-on-Hudson, NY: Author.

Byram, M. (1997). *Teaching and assessing intercultural competence.* Clevedon, England: Multilingual Matters.

Byram, M., Nichols, A., & Stevens, D. (2001). *Developing intercultural competence in practice.* Clevedon, England: Multilingual Matters.

Deardorff, D. K. (2004). *The identification and assessment of intercultural competence as a student outcome of internationalization at universities of higher education in the United States.* Unpublished doctoral dissertation, North Carolina State University, Raleigh.

Deardorff, D. K. (2006). Identification and assessment of intercultural competence as a student outcome of internationalization. *Journal of Studies in International Education, 10*, 241–266.

Fantini, A. E. (1997). A survey of intercultural communication courses. *International Journal of Intercultural Relations, 21,* 125–148.

Fantini, A. E. (1999). *Foreign language standards: Linking research, theories, and practices* (J. K. Phillips, Ed.). Lincolnwood, IL: National Textbook Co.

Fantini, A. E. (2000–2001). Designing quality intercultural programs: A model and a process. *Interspectives: A Journal on Transcultural Education, 18,* 100–105.

Fantini, A. E. (2006). *Exploring and assessing intercultural competence.* Brattleboro, VT: Federation of the Experiment in International Living. http://www.worldlearning.org/ 7803.htm or http://www.experiment.org/resources.html (Click on Publications & Resources)

Fantini, A. E., Arias-Galicia, F., & Guay, D. (2000). *Globalization and 21st century competencies* (Paper N0.11). Tucson, AZ: CONAHEC (Consortium for North American Higher Education Collaboration).

Humphrey, D. (2007). *Intercultural communication competence: The state of knowledge.* London: CILT, The National Centre for Languages.

Mager, R. F. (1997). *Preparing instructional objectives* (3rd ed.). Atlanta, GA: CEP Press.

Martin, J. N. (Ed.). (1989). Intercultural communication competence [Special issue]. *International Journal of Intercultural Relations, 13.*

Sercu, L. (2006). The foreign language and intercultural competence teacher: The acquisition of a new professional identity. *Intercultural Education, 17,* 55–72.

Sercu, L., Bandura, E., Castro, P., Davcheva, L., Laskaridou, C., Lundgren, U., et al. (Eds.). (2005). *Foreign language teachers and intercultural competence: An international investigation.* Clevedon, England: Multilingual Matters.

Wight, A. (1999). SIETAR's past, present, and future. *The SIETAR International Journal, 1.*

Wiseman, R. L., & Koester, J. (Eds.). (1993). *Intercultural communication competence.* Newbury Park, CA: Sage.

CHAPTER 28

Implementing Intercultural Competence Assessment

Darla K. Deardorff

C an intercultural competence be assessed? This question generates a variety of responses, including from those who feel it is simply not possible to assess intercultural competence. A group of leading intercultural experts, however, was asked this question and not only agreed that it could be assessed but also agreed on methods for assessing intercultural competence (see Figure 28.1).

Fantini, in his chapter in this volume (Chapter 27), discusses numerous methodologies and tools for assessing intercultural competence. The starting point for assessment of intercultural competence, as he notes, is not with methods or tools but rather in defining what it is we are measuring and ensuring that the goals are aligned with overall mission and purpose of the course, program, or organization.

In the United States, there is an increasing focus on assessing learning outcomes, particularly within higher education, meaning that the focus is on assessing the learning of individuals (Banta, 2002; Bolen, 2007; Driscoll, 2008; Driscoll & Wood, 2007; Fennes & Hapgood, 1997; Huba & Freed, 2000; Maki, 2004; Marzano, Pickering, & McTighe, 1993; Musil, 2006; Palomba & Banta, 2001; Salvia & Ysseldyke, 1998; Serban & Friedlander, 2004; Sims, 1992, Suskie, 2004). Such learning outcomes can also be used in the aggregate on the programmatic and organizational levels by mapping individual learning outcome statements (and assessment results) to the broader curricular or programmatic educational practices, as well as to those found at the institutional/organizational level.

One of the frequently cited learning outcomes in postsecondary education in the United States is to graduate "interculturally competent" students. Yet, there is often much confusion and anxiety as to how to implement actual assessment of intercultural competence. Frequent responses of those undertaking such assessment include avoidance, uncertainty, ignoring it, complaining about it, or feeling overwhelmed

WAYS TO ASSESS INTERCULTURAL COMPETENCE INCLUDE:				
Accepted	Rejected	Mean	*SD*	ITEM
18	2	3.2	0.9	Case studies
18	2	2.9	1.0	Interviews
17	3	3.7	0.8	Mix of quantitative and qualitative measures
17	3	3.4	0.7	Qualitative measures
17	3	3.2	0.9	Analysis of narrative diaries
17	3	3.2	0.9	Self-report instruments
17	3	3.2	0.9	Observation by others/host culture
17	3	3.1	1.0	Judgment by self and others
16	4	3.1	1.1	Developing specific indicators for each component/dimension of ICC and evidence of each indicator
16	4	3.0	1.2	Triangulation (use of multiple data collection efforts as corroborative evidence for the validity of qualitative research findings)

Figure 28.1   Assessment Items With 80% to 100% Agreement Among Top Intercultural Experts

with even knowing where or how to start with assessment. Having a clear understanding of definitions, processes, pitfalls, and resources related to assessment can help alleviate some of the uncertainty surrounding assessment. This chapter discusses practical steps for implementing assessment of intercultural competence at the individual level, as well as some pitfalls and challenges to such assessment, some possible responses, and a guide to evaluating the effectiveness of assessment efforts. For the purposes of this chapter, assessment is defined as a process—"the systematic collection, review, and use of information about educational programs undertaken for the purpose of improving . . . learning and development" (Palomba & Banta, 1999, p. 4).

Defining Intercultural Competence

One of the first steps in assessing intercultural competence is in knowing exactly what it is that is to be assessed—in this case, in defining the actual concept of intercultural competence. Too often, this term (or other similar terms) is used without a concrete definition. As discussed in Fantini's chapter (Chapter 27, this volume), it is essential to arrive at a definition of intercultural competence before proceeding with any further assessment steps. Spitzberg and Changnon, in Chapter 1 of this volume, discuss in detail numerous models and definitions of intercultural competence primarily from a Western perspective, while other chapters in this volume discuss non-Western perspectives on this concept. It is important to recognize that much scholarly effort has been invested in defining this concept, and thus such work should be considered when developing a definition of intercultural competence. One study (Deardorff, 2006) showed that in the case of postsecondary institutions, such definitions and work were often not used, and instead, definitions relied primarily on faculty discussions without any consultation of the literature.

Most definitions and models tend to be somewhat general in terminology, so once a definition has been determined, it is important to then develop a process that generates very specific measurable outcomes and indicators within the context to be assessed. As illustrated by the chapters in Part II of this volume, intercultural competence manifests itself somewhat differently in a variety of contexts so, for example, specific measurable outcomes for interculturally competent engineers may vary from those for interculturally competent health care workers. For the purposes of this chapter, we will use a definition that is derived from the first study to document consensus among leading intercultural experts, primarily from the United States, on aspects of intercultural competence (Deardorff, 2006), as determined through a research methodology called the Delphi technique, an iterative process used to achieve consensus among a panel of experts. The aspects upon which these experts reached consensus were categorized and placed into a model, found in Figure 28.2, that lends itself to assessment and to the further development of detailed measurable outcomes. Specifically, this model was derived from the need to assess this nebulous concept and hence its focus on internal and external outcomes of intercultural competence, based on the development of specific attitudes, knowledge, and skills inherent in intercultural competence. Given that the aspects within each of these areas in the model are still broad, each aspect can be developed into more specific measurable outcomes and corresponding indicators, depending on the context. The overall external outcome of intercultural competence is defined as the *effective* and *appropriate* behavior and communication in intercultural situations, which again can be further detailed in terms of *appropriate* behavior in specific contexts (appropriate behavior being assessed by the other involved in the interaction).

There are several key points to consider in this grounded theory-based model that have implications for the assessment of intercultural competence. According to this research study, intercultural competence development is an ongoing process, and thus it becomes important for individuals to be provided with opportunities to reflect upon and assess the development of their own intercultural competence. Given the ongoing nature of intercultural competence development, it is also valuable to incorporate integrated assessments throughout a targeted intervention. Another point to note is that critical thinking skills play a crucial role (see the Skills module of the model in Figure 28.2) in an individual's ability to acquire and evaluate knowledge. This means that critical thinking assessment could also be an appropriate part of intercultural competence assessment. Attitudes—particularly respect (which is manifested differently in cultures), openness, and curiosity—serve as the basis of this model and affect all other aspects of intercultural competence. Addressing attitudinal assessment, then, becomes an important consideration. There was only one aspect agreed upon by all the intercultural experts in this study, and that was the ability to see from others' perspectives—thus, assessing global perspectives and the ability to understand other worldviews becomes an important consideration as well. One final note is that deep cultural knowledge entails a more holistic, contextual understanding of that culture, including the historical, political, and social contexts. Thus, any assessment of culture-specific knowledge needs to go beyond the conventional surface-level knowledge of foods, greetings, customs, facts and so on to understanding the intricacies of these deeper contexts. For further discussion of this process model of intercultural competence, along with a variation on the model, see Spitzberg and Changnon in Chapter 1 of this volume.

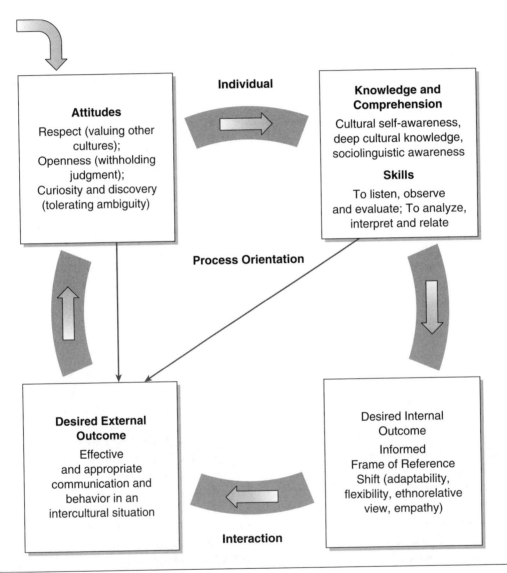

Figure 28.2 Process Model of Intercultural Competence

SOURCE: Deardorff (2006).

NOTES:

- Begin with attitudes; move from individual level (attitudes) to interaction level (outcomes)
- Degree of intercultural competence depends on degree of attitudes, knowledge/comprehension, and skills

Prioritizing Goals Related to Intercultural Competence

Since assessing the whole of intercultural competence can be a daunting task, it is recommended to prioritize specific aspects of intercultural competence, based on the overall mission and purpose of the course, program, or organization. The definition that is used for intercultural competence will determine both the aspects that will be assessed as well as the level of assessment (i.e., individual, program, organization). As in the case of learning outcomes, the level is usually that of the individual and the learning that occurs for each individual. For example, based on the overall mission of the program or organization, "understanding others' perspectives" may be an essential aspect of intercultural competence to assess and thus becomes a stated goal. From that point, one would engage other key persons in dialogue about the specific measurable outcomes related to this overall goal of "participants' ability to understand others' perspectives" as to the best ways to achieve this goal. These ways of achieving the stated goal become the specified objectives, which will be discussed in more detail shortly. It is important to note that simply stating the goal of "understanding others' perspectives" remains too broad to assess and thus the need for more specific measurable outcomes related to this goal.

The process of prioritizing various aspects of intercultural competence is an important one and should not be done too quickly or taken lightly. Often the process itself involves dialogue and discussion with key stakeholders, including learners themselves when possible, to determine which specific elements of intercultural competence should be the focus of programmatic efforts and assessment endeavors. It is important that prioritization is not a one-time discussion but rather an ongoing process since the priorities may change from program to program or from year to year. Generally, it is advisable to choose two to three specific aspects to assess at any given time due to the time, effort, and resources that are needed in the assessment efforts.

Stating Goals and Measurable Objectives

Once the specific aspects of intercultural competence have been prioritized, it is time to write goals and measurable objectives related to each of the prioritized aspects. First, let's look at what constitutes goals and objectives, or learning outcomes, as they are also called. Goals are generally defined as the "end destination." Objectives, on the other hand, are the means by which the goal, or destination, is reached. Objectives specify concrete learning expectations and how the learners will achieve the end goal. In stating goals, it is important to define success in that particular program or course. What will success look like for the participant in this course or program? By the end of the program or course, what will the participant be able to do as a result of the learning that occurred? What will be the evidence of this? For example, a goal may be broadly stated as "Participants will be able to understand others' perspectives" or "Learners will demonstrate the awareness, understanding, and skills necessary to live and work in a diverse world" or "Learners will become more interculturally competent." Specific, measurable objectives must then be articulated that state the learning expectations in achieving these goals. What will the learner need to be able to do in order to achieve the goal? The objectives become the "road map" for reaching the destination—the markers of important learning that ensure achievement of the goal.

What do measurable objectives or outcomes look like? In the assessment arena, a common way of thinking about measurable objectives is through the acronym SMART: Specific (what, why, how), Measurable, Action oriented, Realistic, and Time delineated. A key part of this statement is that the objective is realistic—it needs to fit what can realistically be accomplished with the parameters of the course or program. For example, it would not be realistic for a participant at a beginning language level to speak another language fluently after only 2 or 3 weeks in another country. For short-term study-abroad programs in postsecondary institutions, outcomes must realistically match the program length. For example, if the program exposes participants to another culture for 6 weeks, what can participants realistically be expected to achieve regarding intercultural competence development within that 6-week period, given the level and quality of cultural preparation, the program parameters, and the way in which the intercultural experience has been set up? This in turn relates back to the overall priorities and which aspects of intercultural competence are deemed to be most important to that program or course.

In writing an assessment objective, usually only one action verb is used per outcome statement. Outcome statements (objectives) are focused on learning itself, not on infrastructure, instructor, or activity. When appropriate, it is often helpful to work with participants in having them develop their own learning objectives related to the overall intercultural competence goals. This ensures a more effective and relevant learning process. In some cases, learning contracts are developed between the learner and instructor (see the work of Malcolm Knowles, 1975, for further details on learning contracts) in which learners take responsibility for their own learning. Examples of measurable outcomes under the general goal of "understanding others' perspectives" are "By the end of the program, learners can articulate two different cultural perspectives on global warming" or "By the end of this class, learners can define what a worldview is and three ways in which it impacts one's behavior." Writing specific outcomes statements (learning objectives) related to aspects of intercultural competence and developing indicators of the degree to which the statements can be assessed remains an area in need of further research and work, especially within specific fields such as engineering, policing, and health care.

Developing an Assessment Team and Plan

Once the goals and specific learning objectives related to intercultural competence have been determined, ideally through a dialogical process, the next step is to conduct a thorough review of resources already available for implementing the assessment. This includes documenting assessment history to date in regard to intercultural competence assessment, noting what data are already being collected (including in-class assignments that lend themselves to intercultural competence assessment such as journals/blogs, reflection papers, portfolios, etc.) and which data could be adapted as evidence of meeting the stated learning objectives, detailing who is available to aid in collecting assessment data, specifying financial resources available, and noting any assessment expertise available within the organization. Documenting assessment history to date is especially important since this can aid in reflecting on what has worked well in the past and what could be improved in terms of assessment efforts. This also highlights particular methods or tools that could be adapted in collecting the evidence needed to demonstrate achievement of the learning outcomes. For example, if a pre-post satisfaction survey has typically been used in the program or course, what questions could be added that could collect evidence of learning in regard to the stated intercultural competence objectives? If an instructor is already collecting various assignments from learners, how can those assignments be adapted to yield further evidence of learning in regard to the stated objectives?

It is important to remember that assessment of intercultural competence is too large of an undertaking to be implemented solely by one individual. In the initial review process just discussed, it is important to explore others in the organization who could aid in this assessment process. Those persons may include external and internal stakeholders (including the learners themselves), any persons with whom you collaborate on this program (including those you may have consulted in developing the initial goals and objectives), persons with particular expertise in technical, content, or assessment areas, and so on. Once those persons have been identified, then an assessment team can be formed (American Council on Education, 2008). This team may change and evolve over time, depending on the assessment needs.

The assessment team's first task is to develop an assessment plan, taking into account the results of the initial review of what's already being done in terms of assessment of intercultural competence and ways in which to adapt currently used assessment methods. Key components of the assessment plan begin with the overall mission, goals, and specific measurable learning objectives, which must be aligned with each other. This means that they need to match, with objectives flowing from goals, which in turn flow from the mission/purpose. The assessment team then explores which assessment tools and/or methods can best be used to collect evidence of learning that fits with the specific objectives. In other words, the learning objectives determine which tools and methods to use in collecting learning evidence. Fantini's chapter in this volume (Chapter 27) discusses in detail what needs to be considered when selecting tools and methods, as well as listing some specific tools used to assess various aspects of intercultural competence. To reiterate what Fantini discussed, it is important to know exactly what aspect(s) of intercultural competence is measured by the tool or method and to align those tools and methods with the specific learning objectives. Based on the Deardorff (2006) study, it was found that in measuring intercultural competence, a multimethod, multiperspective (beyond self-report instruments) assessment approach must be used to adequately assess intercultural competence. One tool or method alone is not sufficient to measure the complexity of intercultural competence. This means putting together a comprehensive assessment package of a variety of tools and methods to use in the assessment plan, which, at a minimum, triangulates the data collected, meaning that at least three different sources are used to ensure the validity and reliability of the data. As assessment expert Peggy Maki (2004) reiterates, "Relying on one method to assess the learning described in outcome statements restricts interpretations of . . . achievement within the parameters of that method" (p. 86). However, in using multiple measures/tools, it is important to make sure they are all actually measuring the same aspects of intercultural competence, in alignment with stated goals and learning outcomes.

Once the assessment team has determined which tools and methods best fit the learning objectives (outcome statements), the team can complete the assessment plan, which includes determining a timeline and then assigning responsibility for implementing the plan, which includes clearly articulating and assigning roles. The assessment plan can then be implemented with collection of data, which are then analyzed for trends, consistency over time, any anomalies or gaps, and so on. The data can be used in numerous ways: First and foremost, the data should be used to provide feedback to the learners in improving and honing their intercultural competence development. The data can also be used in aggregate to determine gaps in the learning program and to recommend program changes; ultimately, those recommendations would be implemented in actually making those changes that will continue to prove participants' learning. The data also need to be interpreted and communicated to other stakeholders who could benefit from the assessment results. Thus, the assessment plan includes details on how the data from each tool/method will be analyzed, interpreted, communicated, and used. For a template of the beginning of an assessment plan, see Figure 28.3.

Once the assessment plan has been fully implemented, it is also important to evaluate the effectiveness of the assessment plan itself. To evaluate this process, one can use the checklist in Figure 28.4.

MISSION:					
Goal	Objective(s)	Assessment Tool/Method and What It Measures	Planned Use of Data From Tool/ Method	Timeline	Shared Responsibility for Implementation (Including Analysis, Communication, etc.)

Figure 28.3 Starting an Assessment Plan

_____Aligned: Are goals, objectives, and assessment measures aligned?
_____Intentional: Is assessment intentionally addressed through an assessment plan?
_____Developed: Have assessment issues (including logistical implementation) been carefully analyzed before a plan is implemented?
_____Integrated: Is assessment integrated throughout the program and not viewed as an "add-on" (i.e., implemented only as a pre-post phenomenon)?
_____Focused: Is assessment realistic within the parameters of the program/course, with two to three outcomes being assessed per program/course?
_____Shared: Are assessment responsibilities shared with others (i.e., through an assessment team)?
_____Supported: Is the senior leadership supportive of assessment efforts?
_____Resourced: Is there adequate time and funding for assessment efforts, and have administrators received sufficient training and knowledge in assessment, with ongoing professional development?
_____Analyzed: Have the assessment tools, results, and process been analyzed and evaluated?
_____Communicated: Have the assessment results been communicated to all stakeholders?
_____Used: Have the results been used for program improvement as well as for learner feedback?
_____Reviewed: Has the assessment process and strategy been reviewed on a regular basis and improved upon?

Figure 28.4 Checklist for Evaluating Assessment Efforts

SOURCE: Deardorff (2008).

Pitfalls in Assessing Intercultural Competence

There are numerous pitfalls in any assessment efforts. Here is a list of pitfalls that the author has encountered when working with different programs and organizations in assessing various aspects of intercultural competence:

1. Not clearly defining or prioritizing what is being measured (and not consulting the intercultural competence literature when developing a working definition). The definition would ideally be based on theoretical principles and frameworks found in the literature. (See Chapter 1, this volume, for a discussion of some of the literature on intercultural competence.)

2. Not planning intentionally for intercultural competence assessment or simply not having an assessment plan. By not having a developed assessment plan, this means that implementation logistics have not been examined thoroughly.

Without a plan, intercultural competence assessment occurs randomly and may or may not actually measure the stated goals and learning objectives.

3. Blindly borrowing assessment plans, tools, and methods from others. Just because another organization is using a particular assessment tool doesn't mean that the tool will match your stated goals and learning objectives. As much as it may be desired, there are unfortunately no universal assessment plans and tools that can be widely used since each course or program has different parameters and intercultural competence aspects (based on mission and goals) that need to be uniquely assessed. The assessment plan needs to be tailored to your specific mission/goals/objectives and program parameters, which means others' plans/methods may not work in your particular assessment context.

4. Making assessment the responsibility of one individual and leaving assessment "to the end." Assessment involves teamwork, collaboration, and the support of many. To garner that needed support and expertise, more than one person must be involved in the assessment process. Thus, delegating assessment to one person or office is not encouraged. Furthermore, it is important that dialogue about learner success and learning outcomes takes place among all relevant persons in the beginning of the process. Too often, programs may bring in "an assessment person" toward the end of the process, when it becomes much too late to properly develop and implement an assessment plan and team, meaning it then becomes quite difficult if not impossible to backtrack. Assessment needs to be both formative and summative, meaning that it is woven into the entire process.

5. Not aligning assessment tools/methods with stated goals and objectives. As discussed previously, it is very important to understand the purpose(s) of each tool/method to make sure those fit in collecting the evidence needed to determine the achievement of the learning objectives.

6. Using only one tool or method to assess intercultural competence. As already discussed, intercultural competence is a very complex concept with a variety of components and aspects. One tool or method does not provide a comprehensive measurement of the complexity of this concept. Furthermore, it is important that tools/methods include a multiple-perspective approach since part of intercultural competence can only be determined by "the other" as to how appropriate the individual has been in the intercultural interaction. (See Ting-Toomey in Chapter 5, this volume, for a further discussion on appropriateness.) Thus, a multimethod, multiperspective assessment package needs to be developed as part of the assessment plan.

7. Trying to assess too much at once (i.e., the whole of intercultural competence). Given the amount of effort and resources needed in using a multimethod, multiperspective approach in assessing intercultural competence, it is important to prioritize aspects of intercultural competence in the assessment process, as discussed earlier in this chapter, and select just a few aspects of intercultural competence to assess for a period of time.

8. Collecting the data and then stopping. Too often, programs may engage in assessment by collecting the data, and then nothing is done with the data. Instead, the data may reside in a spreadsheet or on a shelf until eventually discarded. It is

incredibly important to use the data collected—in providing feedback to the learners, in improving the program, and in communicating results to stakeholders. Thus, one adage in the assessment process is to collect only what will be used. If it's not going to be used, then don't collect it. To ensure usage of assessment data, the assessment plan needs to include detailed points on how data from each tool/method will be used.

9. Not evaluating the assessment plan and process. One area that is easy to overlook is in evaluating how well the assessment plan worked and what could be improved in the future, including how well the tools/methods worked in collecting the evidence needed and whether the same set of priorities should be continued in the future or reset to include other priorities. It is also valuable for the learner to assess the learning process—to be able to reflect on the overall process of his or her intercultural competence development and learning. This reflection is key to a learner's development, as illustrated by Figure 28.1, and thus learners need to be made aware of their own role in this assessment process. (See also Janet Bennett's chapter [Chapter 6] in this volume for more on the process of intercultural competence development.)

10. Not using a control group or collecting baseline data. Depending on the purpose of assessment (beyond providing feedback to students), a control group and/or baseline data may be desired to ascertain whether a certain intervention or learning experience was successful in contributing to a learner's intercultural competence development. Control groups and baseline data are some of the best ways to demonstrate the success of such interventions.

Intercultural Competence Assessment: Challenges and Responses

We have already discussed the challenges inherent in clearly defining intercultural competence, in aligning goals/outcomes and tools/methods, and in ensuring that outcomes are realistic to the parameters of the intervention or learning experience. Several other challenges to intercultural competence assessment will be considered in this section.

Learner Articulation of Outcomes. Too often, without adequate preparation as well as a balance of intervention and support in the cultural learning processes, learners are not able to articulate clearly and specifically what they have learned. When asked to respond about a particular cultural learning experience, such as an overseas internship or education-abroad experience, learners may only be able to allude to a "life-changing experience." So, the question becomes, Have learners been prepared adequately for intercultural experiences and in interacting appropriately with those from different cultural backgrounds, thus intentionally developing learners' intercultural competence to at least some degree? This goes beyond "objective" cultural knowledge of literature, history, and so on to include "subjective" cultural knowledge such as communication styles and underlying cultural values so that learners better understand some of what is beneath the tip of the cultural iceberg, of what influences others' behaviors and communication patterns. Through adequate preparation and in-depth cultural learning, as well as ongoing intervention and support, learners are able to more sufficiently articulate the learning that occurs. (For examples of possible interventions, please see the following chapters in this volume: Cushner & Mahon [Chapter 17], Paige & Goode [Chapter 19], and Vande Berg & Paige [Chapter 25].)

Integration of Assessment Tools/Methods in an Ongoing Basis. Have the intercultural competence assessment tools and methods been integrated into the program or course on an ongoing basis instead of being proctored as a pre-post assessment only? Integration of such assessment and tools remains a challenge in some contexts when assessment is viewed as an "add-on," as something that is done only as a pre-post exercise. However, for intercultural competence assessment to be truly effective, such assessment—and thus learner feedback—must be integrated as much as possible throughout the duration of the course or program and ideally even beyond the end of the program. This allows for more guided feedback to be provided to the learner in the continual process of intercultural competence development. Examples of integrated assessment include more direct and qualitative measures such as journals or blogs and e-portfolio assessment. One implication of integrated intercultural competence assessment is that instructors/facilitators need to be knowledgeable about intercultural competence to guide participants through the developmental process and provide appropriate feedback. Intercultural competence training of instructors/facilitators often presents yet another challenge but can be accomplished through workshops, seminars, and facilitated discussions.

Synthesizing the Data From the Assessment Package. Given that a multimethod, multiperspective approach must be used in assessing intercultural competence, the question arises as to how to make sense of the data coming from a variety of sources. What do the data indicate about the learner's overall intercultural competence? One innovative tool under development is called the Intercultural Competency (ICC) Score (Deardorff & Deardorff, 2008), which uses a specially formulated algorithm to synthesize assessment data collected from a variety of qualitative and quantitative measures into several subscores and a total ICC Score that provides an overall measure of intercultural competence, along with an estimated range of certainty based on the reliability and validity of the assessment measures used. The ICC subscores are helpful in indicating which aspects of an individual's intercultural competence need further development. The ICC subscores can also be used to identify aspects of a program or course that need attention such as improvement of content areas/learning interventions related to intercultural competence or refinement of assessment measures. The ICC Score is similar to an Intelligence Quotient (IQ) score in that it provides a holistic measure of an individual's intercultural competence, which facilitates comparisons between individuals and groups. At the writing of this chapter, the ICC Score, which is based on the Deardorff model of intercultural competence, has been successfully pilot tested and is undergoing further testing and development.

Resources. Given that there is no "quick fix" or easy way to assess intercultural competence properly, resources can become quite a challenge to implementing such assessment. Not only does such assessment take time and money, but it also requires leadership support for efforts to be successful. In addition, those involved in the assessment need to be trained in both content and process. In some cases, someone may have assessment expertise but lack in-depth knowledge of intercultural competence, or conversely, someone may be an intercultural expert but lack assessment knowledge. This is where the importance of the assessment team can be highlighted—with those on the team leveraging needed resources, whether those be money, time, or expertise. Sometimes it becomes necessary for an organization to use a consultant who has expertise in both intercultural competence and assessment to guide a team through the intercultural competence assessment process.

There are other challenges, certainly, to assessing intercultural competence, including the specification of degrees of intercultural competence (i.e., what constitutes a low level of intercultural competence versus a higher level). These degrees of intercultural competence could vary by context and field, and more research is needed in this area. More research is also needed in what constitutes effective and appropriate behavior within specific professional fields, for example. To guide further thinking about intercultural competence, consider the following guide in Figure 28.5 that emerged from the results of the Deardorff (2004) study.

Questions to analyze when assessing intercultural competence:

1) Has the term *intercultural competence* been defined using existing definitions in the literature? From whose cultural perspective?

2) What are the cultural biases of the evaluator? Of the assessment tools and methods?

3) Who is the locus of the evaluation?

4) What is the context of the assessment?

5) What is the purpose of the assessment?

6) How will the assessment results be used? Who will benefit from the assessment?

7) What is the time frame and timeline of the assessment (i.e., one point, ongoing, etc.)?

8) Do the assessment methods match the working definition and stated objectives of intercultural competence?

9) Have specific indicators been developed for the intercultural competence assessment?

10) Is more than one method being used to assess? Do the methods involve more than one evaluator's perspective?

11) In regard to intercultural competence, are the degrees of intercultural competence being assessed? What is to be done with those not meeting the minimal level of intercultural competence?

12) Has the impact of situational, social, and historical contexts been analyzed in the assessment of intercultural competence?

13) How do the assessment methods affect the measurement outcomes? Have the limits and cultural biases of the instruments/measures been accounted for?

14) Have participant goals been considered when assessing intercultural competence?

Figure 28.5 Intercultural Competence Assessment Guide

SOURCE: Deardorff (2004).

Some Examples of Programs Assessing Intercultural Competence

Given the pitfalls and challenges to assessing intercultural competence, are there general examples of programs that are indeed engaged in such assessment? International education programs in postsecondary institutions provide some examples of this. On a broader scale, the American Council on Education has worked with numerous institutions within the United States in articulating global learning outcomes. Through this process, multiple assessments were used primarily through an e-portfolio method and through a custom-developed self-report instrument. Other postsecondary institutions have also engaged in assessing intercultural competence through multiple measures, including through the use of self-report measures, journals, host family observations, supervisor observations, embedded in-class assignments, participant interviews, focus groups, and portfolios. It was not unusual for these programs to spend months—and in one case up to 2 years—articulating the initial goals and objectives for developing and implementing an assessment plan on intercultural competence and cultural learning.

In the corporate world, there are examples of companies using a combination of self-report tools, 360-degree feedback instruments, and employee interviews to assess employees' intercultural competence development.

Conclusion

Assessing intercultural competence is hard work. There are pitfalls and challenges to be overcome through the intentional implementation of intercultural competence assessment plans. Such plans start with the overall mission, which is then implemented through a working definition of intercultural competence, stated goals, and measurable objectives related to prioritized aspects of intercultural competence. Involving others on an assessment team is crucial in the implementation process. Areas of further research include specification of degrees (levels) of intercultural competence, as well as the delineation of specific indicators of interculturally competent behavior within given contexts. Through all this, one fact persists: Assessment of intercultural competence remains an imperative in the development of intercultural competence given that assessment is ultimately about learning. As Palomba and Banta (2001) state, "The ultimate goal of assessment is to . . . improve . . . learning. Whether or not assessment will be successful in this regard is not determined at the time evidence is generated; it is determined early in the process when the groundwork for assessment is put in place" (p. 21). This chapter has outlined some key ways to ensure the groundwork is indeed in place for meaningful intercultural competence assessment. Given the growing importance of intercultural competence in the 21st century, assessment becomes an important tool in the development of individuals' intercultural competence.

References

American Council on Education. (2008). *Web guide: Assessing international learning outcomes.* http://www.acenet.edu/Content/NavigationMenu/ProgramsServices/cii/res/assess/index.htm

Banta, T. W. (2002). *Building a scholarship of assessment.* San Francisco: Jossey-Bass.

Bolen, M. (2007). *A guide to outcomes assessment in education abroad.* Carlisle, PA: Forum on Education Abroad.

Deardorff, D. K. (2004). *The identification and assessment of intercultural competence as a student outcome of internationalization at institutions of higher education in the United States.* Unpublished doctoral dissertation, North Carolina State University, Raleigh.

Deardorff, D. K. (2006). Identification and assessment of intercultural competence as a student outcome of internationalization. *Journal of Studies in Intercultural Education, 10,* 241–266.

Deardorff, D. K. (2007, April). *Assessment methods and tools in international education.* Presentation given at Undergraduate Assessment Symposium, North Carolina State University, Raleigh.

Deardorff, D. K. (2008). *Checklist for evaluating assessment efforts.* Unpublished paper.

Deardorff, D. K., & Deardorff, D. L. (2008, February). *Assessing intercultural competence in teacher education.* Presented at the Association of International Education Conference, Washington, DC.

Driscoll, A. (2008, April). *Aligning pedagogy, curriculum, and assessment: Support for student success.* Presented at North Carolina State University, Raleigh.

Driscoll, A., & Wood, S. (2007). *Developing outcomes-based assessment for learner-centered education: A faculty introduction.* Sterling, VA: Stylus.

Fennes, H., & Hapgood, K. (1997). *Intercultural learning in the classroom: Crossing borders.* London: Cassell.

Huba, M. E., & Freed, J. E. (2000). *Learner-centered assessment on college campuses: Shifting the focus from teaching to learning.* Boston: Allyn & Bacon.

Knowles, M. S. (1975). *Self-directed learning: A guide for learners and teachers.* Englewood Cliffs, NJ: Prentice Hall/Cambridge.

Maki, P. L. (2004). *Assessing for learning: Building a sustainable commitment across the institution.* Sterling, VA: Stylus.

Marzano, R. J., Pickering, D. J., & McTighe, J. (1993) *Assessing student outcomes: Performance assessment using the dimensions of learning model.* Alexandria, VA: Association for Supervion and Curriculum Development

Musil, C. M. (2006). *Assessing global learning: Matching good intentions with good practice.* Washington, DC: Association of American Colleges and Universities.

Palomba, C. A., & Banta, T. W. (1999). *Assessment essentials: Planning, implementing, and improving assessment in higher education.* San Francisco: Jossey-Bass.

Palomba, C. A., & Banta, T. W. (2001). *Assessing student competence in accredited disciplines: Pioneering approaches to assessment in higher education.* Sterling, VA: Stylus.

Salvia, J., & Ysseldyke, J. E. (1998). *Assessment* (7th ed.). Boston: Houghton Mifflin.

Serban, A. M., & Friedlander, J. (Eds.). (2004). *Developing and implementing assessment of student learning outcomes.* San Francisco: Jossey-Bass.

Sims, J. S. (1992). *Student outcomes assessment: A historical review and guide to program development.* New York: Greenwood.

Suskie, L. (2004). *Assessing student learning: A common sense guide.* Bolton, MA: Anker Publishing.

CHAPTER 29

The Real Cost of Intercultural Incompetence

An Epilogue

Joseph E. Trimble, Paul B. Pedersen, and Eduardo S. Rodela

B efore you opened *The SAGE Handbook of Intercultural Competence* and read your first chapter, perhaps you were wondering what you could do to promote intercultural competency and sensitivity; maybe the book's title stimulated your curiosity or you wanted to learn more about the topic. Perhaps you wanted to be stimulated to effect constructive and proactive change. If you read some of the chapters to this point, though, and accepted the promises, then you already made a bold step in a positive direction. Indeed, throughout the pages of this handbook, prominent attention has been given to intercultural competence and the various forms the concept and process take as we negotiate relationships with others, especially those who are culturally and ethnically different.

The handbook's content punctuates the finding that the field of interculturalism and diversity has rapidly grown to extraordinary proportions; a scan of the publications cited in *PsychINFO,* for example, shows an increase of considerable proportions in the specialized area of counseling, for example. Before 1976, close to 25 articles and chapters were written on the subject of culture and counseling. In 2008, about 15,000 books, book chapters, conference presentations, and journal articles were written expressing a variety of perspectives on the topic ranging from theory to research findings. The accelerated rate of interest and concern generated on the topic in the past 30 years or so is not surprising. (Refer to Chapter 1 for a review of some of the key literature on intercultural competence). The argument and justification for the increased interest rest on the contention that conventional human service delivery approaches are incompatible with the lifeways and thoughtways of some ethnocultural groups. Since all thoughts and behaviors are culturally biased, accurate assessment, meaningful understanding, and culturally appropriate interventions are required for the understanding of each context for communication to occur effectively and appropriately.

Culture and all that it implies is explicit and implicit to intercultural communication (Trimble, 2007). Instead of asking whether one is culturally competent, perhaps it would be better to ask if one is *interculturally competent* as this captures the direction of the field and the interest. Interest in the field has accelerated to the point where it is now influencing communication at all levels. Pedersen (1999; Pedersen, Carlson, & Crethar, 2008) emphasizes that *interculturalism* is a new perspective in human service communication complementing the three other major theoretical orientations in human service communication theory—psychodynamic, existential-humanistic theory, and cognitive-behavioral theory addressing the needs of culturally diverse client populations. Asking whether one is *interculturally competent* captures the direction of the field and the interest; conversely it may be just as important to explore what it means to be interculturally incompetent, especially in terms of research and in terms of leaders within an organization.

Achieving true intercultural competence and cultural sensitivity is complex and daunting. Putting the constructs into action in a research or clinical setting compounds their complexities. However, achieving a state of competence and sensitivity can be accomplished at some level of proficiency to the point where individuals and organizations are able to be successful within diversity.

There are a number of theoretical perspectives about intercultural communication. One definition that fits well is one offered by Orlandi (1992), who defines cultural competence as "a set of academic and interpersonal skills that allow individuals to increase their understanding and appreciation of cultural differences and similarities within, among, and between groups" (p. vi). He continues by drawing attention to one's "willingness and ability to draw on community-based values, traditions, and customs and to work with knowledgeable persons of and from the community in developing focused interventions, communications, and other supports" (p. vi). The key words in his definition are *skills, understanding, appreciation, willingness,* and *ability;* perhaps the most salient of these is *willingness,* for without a conscious intent and desire, the achievement and realization of *cultural competence* is not likely to occur.

While there is a great deal of discussion and even disagreement about definitions of *intercultural competency,* there is much more agreement about recognizing instances of *intercultural incompetence.* The fallout and the untoward consequences of intercultural incompetence, especially in regard to human services, are unprecedented in the annals of the history of our planet; the emotional, psychological, physical, ecological, and economic costs are extraordinary and often beyond comprehension. Advocating and encouraging intercultural competency in every aspect of life will reduce the sociological, psychological, organizational, and financial costs of intercultural incompetence.

This chapter suggests a new approach to defining competence through the "back door" of identifying examples of "incompetence" especially in terms of research on intercultural competence. It is much easier to find agreement on examples of incompetence than it is to agree on the criteria of competence. By agreeing that an example of behavior is indeed an example of "incompetence," we can establish common ground for discussing why a particular behavior or action is incompetent and from that point discussing how that behavior or action can usefully be changed. It is our hope that this chapter, while incomplete in examining the consequences of incompetence, will stimulate a discussion among readers about what can be learned by looking at our many mistakes as well as our very few successes in applying communication to the intercultural context.

Achieving true intercultural competence and intercultural sensitivity is complex and often overwhelming. Putting the constructs into action in a research or social setting compounds their complexities. However, achieving a state of competence and sensitivity can be accomplished at some level of proficiency to the point where it does not sap our courage and subdue our fears and anxieties. Each specific instance of intercultural incompetence can and usually does become extremely expensive.

In the following sections, we provide two descriptions of the effects of incompetence and outline ways it can be avoided. In the first section, attention is given to ethical decision making for research with ethnocultural populations that reflects the unique historical and sociocultural realities of ethnic and racial groups of people and their communities. The need and rationale for identifying intercultural incompetence about ethics is multifold. It emerges from the increasing distrust ethnocultural communities are expressing toward researchers. Countless community members are intolerant and unforgiving of past research efforts for a variety of valid reasons; much of their suspicion and concerns derives from the cultural incompetence and insensitivity of researchers. Researchers should be prepared to collaborate with the communities, share results that have practical value, and accept the conditions imposed by the community in gaining access to respondents.

In the second section of this chapter, attention is given to the finding that organizational leaders, managers, and employees are intolerant of intercultural incompetence for a variety of reasons. The outcomes most frequently associated with intercultural incompetence among managers range from a lack of employee and managerial commitment about the goals of an organization to the disregard for employees' attitudes and behaviors, low levels of motivation, and high levels of stress among all concerned—leading to an impact on the well-being of all employees.

The Costs of Irresponsible Conduct of Research With Ethnocultural Populations

Anyone who has conducted participatory community-based fieldwork with unique ethnocultural populations knows it is tough and sometimes dangerous for everyone involved. To gather the information necessary to frame an ethnocultural perspective of a human condition or phenomenon requires extraordinary patience accompanied with well-developed value orientations and research skills that are sensitive to the lifeways and thoughtways of the community (Trimble & Fisher, 2006). Access to the field to conduct research with ethnocultural populations is becoming more and more difficult and demanding; gaining trust becomes imperative. An intense concern about field-based research, whether it is with individuals or groups, is emerging from numerous communities that are becoming highly vocal about the problems many researchers create for them; the problems they have encountered came about because of cultural incompetence of the researchers and their violation of ethical professional guidelines (Trimble, 2008). In the following section, descriptions of research with two distinct ethnocultural groups—male African Americans from Macon, Georgia, and the Havasupai tribe of American Indians in Arizona—provide distressing examples of culturally incompetent and insensitive research approaches that have left indelible psychological scars on the participants and their ancestors.

Numerous researchers are acutely aware of the now infamous Tuskegee syphilis study carried out in Macon County, Alabama, from 1932 to 1972. Originally titled the "Tuskegee Study of Untreated Syphilis in the Negro Male," it was by every ethical standard and principle a shocking and scandalous example of medical research gone wrong. Moreover, it is a chilling example of unethical and immoral research practices as well as an example of cultural incompetence. Medical researchers from the U.S. Public Health Service, in trying to learn more about syphilis and justify treatment programs for Blacks, withheld adequate treatment from a group of poor Black men who had the disease, causing needless pain and suffering for the men and their loved ones. The study involved 600 Black men—399 with syphilis and 201 who did not have the disease. Researchers told the men they were being treated for "bad blood," a local term used to describe several ailments, including syphilis, anemia, and fatigue (Caplan, Edgar, & King, 1992; Jones, 1993). In truth, they did not receive the proper treatment needed to cure their illness. In exchange for taking part in the study, the men received free medical exams, free meals, and burial insurance. Although originally projected to last 6 months, the study actually went on for 40 years.

Knowledge of the study was first published on July 25, 1972, by Jean Heller and appeared in the *Washington Evening Star* and in the *New York Times;* the next day, the story was carried in numerous newspapers worldwide and in radio and television newscasts (Jones, 1993). In response to the allegations, the U.S. government swiftly established and convened an ad hoc review committee to carefully and closely examine the charges and allegations. At the end of the investigation, the committee overwhelmingly concluded that the study was "unethical" and that it must be stopped. The establishment of the National Commission soon followed the committee's recommendation for the Protection of Human Subjects of Biomedical and Behavioral Research and the first federal regulations establishing national institutional review boards and standards for the ethical conduct of research for U.S. based researchers.

The Tuskegee syphilis study is one of many instances where scientists have exploited historically oppressed groups, presumably to advance an understanding of the human condition (Ibrahim & Cameron, 2005). The outcomes of the Tuskegee study should serve as a warning to those who would abuse participants and deny them their rights; that does not appear to be the case. Consider the significance and importance of the headlines in a February 2004 Arizona newspaper that read, "Havasupai File $25M Suit vs. ASU" (Hendricks, 2004). In the story, the journalist summarizes the research circumstances that prompted Havasupai tribal members and the tribe to file a combined lawsuit and status report on the suit's developments. Between 1990 and 1994, researchers from Arizona State University collected blood samples from tribal members that were to be used to study diabetes. Tribal members eventually learned that the blood samples had been used for purposes other than those they agreed to when the respondents signed the human subjects consent forms. The ASU researchers ostensibly used the samples to study schizophrenia, inbreeding, and factors that could explain human migration patterns. In May 2007, a Maricopa Arizona County Superior Court judge dismissed the tribe's case because of a legal technicality; tribal officials said they plan to resubmit the suit and take the case to the Arizona Court of Appeals.

The financial costs for research irregularities, transgressions, and intercultural incompetence can be staggering. According to a consultant for the U.S. Office of Scientific Integrity, the cost of misconduct in the medical field alone "has been estimated to be as high as $1 million per case" (Langlais, 2006, p. B11). Consider that in 2006, the U.S. Office of Scientific Integrity (OSI) handled 266 misconduct allegations; the number of allegations received in 2006 closely matched the 2005 level of 265, but the levels for both years represent close to a 50% increase over the 2003 level (Office of Scientific Integrity, 2007). If it requires the Office of Scientific Integrity close to $1 million to process a single allegation, the total annual costs could well reach into millions of dollars. The costs for the research misconduct, cultural incompetence, and breaches of scientific ethics and principles in the Tuskegee syphilis experiment and the Havasupai tribe lawsuit with the researchers at ASU and the Arizona Board of Regents also run into the millions; combined, the lawsuits reach an astounding $35 million, factoring in the possibility that the Havasupai tribe will receive their full settlement. What has not been factored in the cost estimates are the personal costs to the participants as they strive to deal with anger, frustration, disbelief, trauma, and related hardships created by outside researchers who seemingly were more concerned about their professional welfare than they were for their participants.

No one is certain how many people from assorted ethnocultural communities participated in field-based research projects. Not every research participant has been harmed or negatively affected by the research experience and consequences, and if they were, they might not be willing to acknowledge the harm. Indeed, relatives and descendants of the participants in the infamous Tuskegee syphilis experiment were harmed in a most dreadful and scandalous manner; the untoward aftereffects continue to torment and influence the lives and memories of the descendants. The Havasupai "blood study" participants and their large extended families continue to experience distress, aggravation, mistrust, and torment from their experiences with outside researchers.

The costs for intercultural incompetence go far beyond the costs to the participants and their communities. The costs weigh in heavily on researchers who aspire to work closely and collaboratively with ethnocultural communities, as they will have to devote considerable time building trust and forging close long-term relationships with community leaders and members. Trickett and Espino (2004) summarized the extensive literature on participatory community research approaches and commented that "it is time to place the collaboration concept in the center of inquiry and work out its importance for community research and intervention. Although some would see it as merely a tool or strategy to getting the 'real' work of behavioral science done, our strong preference is to view the research relationship in community research and intervention as a critical part of the 'real' work itself" (p. 62). Without establishing and working through community partnerships, research ventures are doomed to failure at every stage of the process. Intercultural competence plays a crucial role in building trust and developing relationships in communities.

It is essential for the success of culturally sensitive researchers to foster and encourage ethical decision making with ethnocultural populations that reflects the unique historical and sociocultural realities of ethnic and racial groups of people and their communities. A secondary objective is to provide linkages between irresponsible research and intercultural incompetence. There are three ethical dimensions of interculturally sensitive research: (1) applying an intercultural perspective to the evaluation of research risk and benefits, (2) developing and implementing interculturally respectful informed consent procedures and culturally appropriate confidentiality and disclosure policies, which includes the necessity to build trust, and (3) engaging in community and participant consultation with a standard of "principled cultural sensitivity" (Trickett, Kelly, & Vincent, 1985). The need and justification for identifying intercultural incompetence about ethics is multifold, especially given multiple cultural perspectives on ethics. It emerges from the increasing distrust ethnocultural communities are expressing toward researchers. Consequently, it is imperative for researchers to prepare themselves to collaborate with the communities and individuals, share results that have practical value, and accept the conditions imposed by the community in gaining access to respondents. In addition, researchers must be aware of scientific, social, and political factors governing definitions of race, ethnicity, and culture; understand within-group differences; and become familiar with skills in constructing culturally valid and reliable assessment instruments (Trimble, 2003; Trimble & Fisher, 2006).

Case Study: The Cost of Intercultural Incompetence in an Organization

The purpose of this section of the chapter is to explore the impact of intercultural incompetence within an organization and to illustrate how such intercultural incompetence within an organizational culture is likely to affect employee well-being and work performance. In this case study, we are concerned about organizational cultures based on the principles of healthy work organizations, a concept which communicates the need to study and understand what organizational factors contribute to healthy employees and work performance (Murphy & Cooper, 2000; Sauter, Lim, & Murphy, 1996). From our understanding of the perspective of healthy work organizations' factors, misalignment of managerial behavior with organizational expectations results in intercultural incompetence and is associated with increased employee stress and reduced work performance.

The authors see healthy work organization factors as organizational values that will need to be disseminated throughout the organization. These values eventually will become embedded as organizational practices and can, at some point, be referred to as the organization's culture. We argue that managerial behavioral variations from the organizational culture can be viewed as intercultural incompetence. We will discuss how the healthy work organizations' scholars hypothesize relationships between organizational cultural and management practices (independent variables) and performance and employee well-being (dependent variables) in work organizations. Organization factors that do not adhere to healthy work organization principles may increase risk factors deleterious to the health, well-being, and work performance of an organization's employees.

One of the authors was involved as a consultant in a multisource feedback pilot (also known as 360-degree feedback assessment) for managers.[1] The agency, like other federal agencies, wanted to be proactive in dealing with the multitude of changes confronting the entire federal government (e.g., reduced budgets and retirement-eligible workforce). One crucial human resources element of the agency's change strategy was its managerial corps. The agency wanted to use the 360-degree (multisource) feedback pilot as a way to communicate to its managers the importance of the agency's changing workforce-related values. That is, the agency's upper leadership was highlighting the need for an organizational culture change by using the 360-degree feedback efforts. The multisource feedback literature supports the role of a 360-degree feedback for managers as a strategic organizational culture change intervention (Martineau, 1998). We will make the case that managers' behaviors need to be aligned with a healthy work organization culture to lessen the likelihood of a negative impact on the employees' well-being. The argument can also be made that work performance can also be affected with the implementation of a healthy work organization culture. Thus, this case study addresses intercultural incompetence within an organization and the way in which an assessment tool can be used to begin implementing positive change.

Healthy Work Organizations

The theoretical model and the existing empirical literature suggest that healthy work organizations have a healthy workforce and are financially successful. The National Institute of Occupational Safety and Health (NIOSH) proposed a holistic healthy work organizations model that describes relationships between organizational factors (leading indicators) and organization performance and employee health (lagging indicators) (Sauter et al., 1996). While there are few empirical studies using the healthy work organizations model, Sauter et al. (1996) offer empirical findings illustrating relationships between organizational factors predicting both organizational effectiveness and employees' stress. The organizational factors include the following:

- Continuous improvement, career development, strategic planning, human resources planning, and fair pay and rewards (*examples of management practices*)

- Innovation, cooperation, diversity, conflict resolution, and a sense of belonging (*examples of organizational climate/culture factors*)

- Commitment to technology, employee growth and development, and valuing the individual (*examples of organizational values*)

For a more detailed summary of the healthy work organizations empirical research literature, refer to Sainfort, Karsh, Booske, and Smith (2001). Healthy work organizations' researchers advocate an integrative approach to the type of organizational studies: They encourage research work, which simultaneously measures organizational factors work performance and employee well-being (Murphy & Cooper, 2000; Sainfort et al., 2001; Sauter et al., 1996). It can be argued that intercultural competence plays an important role in healthy work organizations, particularly through employee growth and development and in valuing individuals. Organizational factors such as cooperation and diversity are also part of intercultural competence.

Organizational Culture and Cultural (In)Competence

The focal federal agency piloted a 360-degree feedback project as part of a human resources strategy to change the organization's culture. Its purpose was to change the agency's managerial behavior so that such behavior could become more closely aligned with organizational expectations and culture. What is organizational culture? According to Schein (1992), organizational culture is "[a] pattern of shared basic assumptions that the group learned as it solved its problems of external adaptation and internal integration, which has worked well enough to be considered valid and, therefore, to be taught to new members as the correct way you perceive, think, and feel in relation to those problems" (p. 12). Schein is quick to point out that he does not include behavior in his definition because behavior is an outcome of organizational values and assumptions. We argue that when behavior is not aligned with the assumptions and related values espoused by the organization, there is some degree of cultural incompetence. Only through empirical studies will the degree of cultural incompetence be determined.

Assessment Intervention

In their effort at organizational culture change, the focal federal agency used the Manager and Executive Skills Assessment (MESA) instrument to communicate values and to gather information on the degree of a gap (intercultural incompetence). While creating a healthy work organization was not the intention of the agency's 360-degree feedback pilot, the authors felt we could frame the agency's experience in terms of healthy work organizations and employee outcomes. Many of the concepts associated with healthy work organizations are captured by the MESA instrument. A quick summary of the MESA survey concepts illustrates the similarities with healthy work organization concepts. The MESA concepts are career development, strategic planning, human resources planning, commitment to quality, fair pay and rewards, diversity, innovation, and employee growth and development.[2]

Agency organizational culture change advocates were composed of 30 agency senior executive service leaders representing both regional and headquarters organizations; they acted as the "governing board" for the agency's Human Resources Office (HRO). The Human Resources Association (HRA) met on a quarterly basis to address agency human resources issues. When the HRA directed the HRO to conduct a 360-degree feedback pilot, their objective was to communicate to all agency managers the importance of these values, contained in the MESA, and to communicate the importance of an organization-wide behavior change.

The emphasis on managerial behavior change has strong performance implications. For example, Edward Deming's work on organizational performance, cited in

Rummler and Brache (1995), stated that organizational performance problems are based on 85% managerial and systems factors and 15% employees. Logically, one can argue that if there is a misalignment between a healthy work organization's culture and managerial behavior (cultural incompetence), there is a likelihood that organizational problems will spread across and down the entire organization; as such, work performance and employee well-being will be affected negatively. Thus, the main purpose of the 360-degree feedback process was to bring managerial behavior more in line with the espoused values of the agency and thus reduce cultural incompetence.

Given organizational systems theory (Katz & Kahn, 1978), one of the authors understood, that using a 360-degree feedback for managers was not a sufficient intervention for a massive organizational culture change. That is, changing managerial behavior was necessary but not sufficient to secure organizational culture change. However, the leadership literature informs us of the need to include the organization's leaders to start any strategic change (Bennis, 2003; Kotter, 1996). Further, the leadership literature suggests that before any true organizational change can occur, leaders must approve, model, communicate, and support the change effort (Bennis, 2003; Kotter, 1996). After all, leadership support is truly essential. No organizational change will occur without leadership support.

Recommendations

What are the recommendations emerging from this assessment intervention? Foremost, leadership support is absolutely essential in moving from incompetence to competence. The potential organizational culture change rests on the premise that six related interventions are linked to maximize the 360-degree feedback process. The first is that top leadership/management must explicitly communicate that the behaviors embedded in the 360-degree feedback survey are the new values (manifesting in behaviors) expected in the organization; they are the new target culture. Second, top leadership/management should model the behaviors on a consistent basis, at meetings and other decision-making forums. Third, the 360-degree feedback assessment purpose and process must be clearly communicated well across the agency; the more details that are communicated across the managerial corps, the better. Fourth, individualized coaching must be made available to help focal managers commit to and implement appropriate plans to change the behaviors currently not aligned with new expectations. Fifth, the agency will need to modify its present reward system to tie it to the organizational culture change. While 360-degree feedback systems are initially used for development purposes (Tornow, London, & CCL Associates, 1998), management could eventually decide to use it as part of its performance management system; the agency would need to use a reward system that supports appropriate behavioral change. Finally, the organization must develop and implement a human resources development system that links all of the target behaviors to human resources programs such as training, coaching, mentoring, and other learning programs. Such interventions are key to further intercultural competence development. For example, the agency should have a strategic planning course or access to such a course for senior-level managers to help build the competency in those whose feedback suggests a need to do so. Such intervention is crucial in further developing managers' intercultural competence within the organization.

This case study has discussed one example of intercultural incompetence within an organization, incompetence initially resulting from misaligned managerial behavioral variations. Outcomes associated with this intercultural incompetence include employee stress, negative employee attitudes and behaviors, lower levels of performance, lower levels of employee motivation, and lower levels of commitment to the organization, all of which escalate the ultimate costs of intercultural incompetence within the organization.

Conclusion

This chapter has briefly explored the repercussions of intercultural incompetence, both in research and within an organizational culture. Key lessons learned that can be gleaned from interculturally incompetent research include the importance of building trust (see Chapter 4 in this Handbook for a more thorough discussion on this), the necessity of applying an intercultural perspective to the evaluation of research risk and benefits, developing and implementing interculturally respectful informed consent and disclosure procedures and engaging in community and participant consultation with intercultural sensitivity. In regard to organizational culture, lessons learned include garnering top leadership support in intercultural competence development, the importance of aligning managerial behavior with organizational expectations, ensuring that there is a clear communication process in place within an organization and making certain that human resources fully support employee development, once assessment is implemented. Such lessons are crucial so as to reduce the costs of intercultural incompetence that can be found in many different contexts.

Developing intercultural competence is extraordinarily complicated, especially if one aspires to work with people from seemingly countless cultural backgrounds and levels of acculturation. Becoming more interculturally competent can occur in a variety of ways though—through such activities as reading, participating in intensive training workshops and courses and attending conference presentations. However, the acquisition of competency and knowledge through didactic approaches is incomplete (see Chapter 6 in this Handbook for more on the process of intercultural competence development). One must experience a culture in all of its moods and settings to gain a deeper understanding of that culture and to more fully understand the potential applicability of skills and techniques within a cultural milieu. Indeed, intercultural competence development is a lifelong endeavor.

Becoming interculturally competent does not imply that one discard the contributions of past and present knowledge. In fact, it is in learning from past and present knowledge that we understand more about it means to be interculturally competent—and incompetent. The challenge for the reader is to recognize that we cannot fully understand the human condition without viewing it from an intercultural and ethnocultural perspective. What was learned about the human condition in the past can be reframed and tested with new approaches in contexts not previously considered. Thus, we leave the reader to determine new approaches in learning more deeply about the human condition and in understanding what it truly means to be interculturally competent in the 21st century.

Notes

1. The purpose of the 360-degree feedback program is to have managers receive work performance feedback from their employees, peers, and their supervisors. As a result of the feedback, managers are asked to change behavior to reflect the feedback and thus enhance their work performance.

2. Unfortunately, one of the authors was not able to use any of the collected 360-degree feedback data given our pledge to strict confidentiality. We did not have access to any data at the individual level. As a result, we were not able to aggregate the data to determine agency means or other descriptive analyses. Our information technology arrangements did not allow for the use of data beyond the feedback that each manager received at his or her desk.

References

Bennis, W. (2003). *On becoming a leader.* New York: Basic Books.

Caplan, A., Edgar, H., & King, P. (1992). Twenty years later: The legacy of the Tuskegee Syphilis Study. *Hastings Center Report, 22,* 29–38.

Helms, J., & Richardson, T. (1997). How 'multiculturalism' obscures race and culture as differential aspects of counseling competency. In D. Pope-Davis & H. Coleman (Eds.), *Multicultural counseling competencies: Assessment, education and training, and supervision* (pp. 60–79). Thousand Oaks, CA: Sage.

Hendricks, L. (2004, February 28). Havasupai file $25M suit vs. ASU. *Arizona Daily Sun,* p. A1.

Ibrahim, F. A., & Cameron, S. C. (2005). Racial-cultural ethical issues in research. In R. T. Carter (Ed.), *Racial-cultural psychology and counseling: Theory and research* (Vol. I, pp. 391–414). New York: John Wiley.

Jones, J. H. (1993). *Bad blood: The Tuskegee syphilis experiment* (Rev. ed.). New York: Free Press.

Katz, D., & Kahn R. L. (1978). *The social psychology of organizations.* New York: John Wiley.

Kotter, J. P. (1996). *Leading change.* Boston: Harvard Business School Press.

Langlais, P. (2006). Ethics for the next generation. *Chronicle of Higher Education, 52*(16), B11.

Martineau, J. W. (1998). Using 360-degree surveys to assess change. In W. W. Tornow, M. London, & CCL Associates (Eds.), *Maximizing the value of 360-degree feedback* (pp. 217–248). San Francisco: Jossey-Bass.

Murphy, L. R., & Cooper, C. L. (2000). *Healthy and productive work: An international perspective.* New York: Taylor & Francis.

Office of Scientific Integrity. (2007, May). *Annual report, 2006.* Rockville, MD: Department of Health and Human Services, Office of the Secretary, Office of Public Health and Science.

Orlandi, M. (Ed.). (1992). *Cultural competence for evaluators working with ethnic minority communities: A guide for alcohol and other drug abuse prevention practitioners.* Rockville, MD: Office for Substance Abuse Prevention, Cultural Competence Series 1.

Pedersen, P. (Ed.). (1999). *Multiculturalism as a fourth force.* Philadelphia: Brunner/Mazel.

Pedersen, P., Carlson, J., & Crethar H. (2008). *Inclusive cultural empathy.* Washington, DC: American Psychological Association.

Rummler, G. A., & Brache, A. P. (1995). *Improving performance: How to manage the white space on the organization chart* (2nd ed.). San Francisco: Jossey-Bass.

Sainfort, F., Karsh, B.-T., Booske, B. C., & Smith, M. J. (2001). Applying quality improvement principles to achieve healthy work organizations. *Journal of Quality Improvement, 27,* 469–483.

Sauter, S. L., Lim S. Y., & Murphy, L. R. (1996). Organizational health: A new paradigm for occupational stress research at NIOSH. *Japanese Journal of Occupational Mental Health, 4,* 248–254.

Schein, E. H. (1992). *Organizational culture and leadership* (2nd ed.). San Francisco: Jossey-Bass.

Tornow, W. W., London, M., & CCL Associates. (Eds.). (1998). *Maximizing the value of 360 degree feedback.* San Francisco: Jossey-Bass.

Trickett, E. J., & Espino, S. L. (2004). Collaboration and social inquiry: Multiple meanings of a construct and its role in creating useful and valid knowledge. *American Journal of Community Psychology, 34,* 1–71.

Trickett, E. J., Kelly, J. G., & Vincent, T. A. (1985). The spirit of ecological inquiry in community research. In E. Susskind & D. Klein (Eds.), *Community research: Methods, paradigms, and applications* (pp. 7–28). New York: Praeger.

Trimble, J. (2003). Cultural competence and cultural sensitivity. In M. Prinstein & M. Patterson (Eds.), *The portable mentor: Expert guide to a successful career in psychology* (pp. 13–32). New York: Kluwer Academic/Plenum.

Trimble, J. E. (2007). Prolegomena for the connotation of construct use in the measurement of ethnic and racial identity. *Journal of Counseling Psychology, 54,* 247–258.

Trimble, J. E. (2008). Commentary: No itinerant researchers tolerated: Principled and ethical perspectives and research with North American Indian communities. *Ethos, 36,* 380–383.

Trimble, J. E., & Fisher, C. (2006). *Handbook of ethical considerations in conducting research with ethnocultural populations and communities.* Thousand Oaks, CA: Sage.

Author Index

Subject Index

Note: Page references followed by *f* indicate illustration figures; those followed by *t* indicate tables.

About the Editor

Darla K. Deardorff is currently Executive Director of the Association of International Education Administrators, a national professional organization based at Duke University, where she also teaches cross-cultural courses. In addition, she is Adjunct Professor at North Carolina State University and the University of North Carolina–Chapel Hill and is on faculty of the Summer Institute for Intercultural Communication in Portland, Oregon. She has received numerous invitations from around the world to speak on her research on intercultural competence and assessment and is a noted expert on these topics. With nearly 20 years of experience in the international education field, she has published widely on topics in international education and serves as a consultant and trainer on intercultural competence development and assessment for universities, corporations, and nonprofit organizations. She is the recipient of numerous awards, including an outstanding alumnus award from her undergraduate alma mater as well as a distinguished alumnus award on the faculty of her graduate alma mater. Dr. Deardorff holds a master's and doctorate from North Carolina State University, where she specialized in international education. Her dissertation, on the definition and assessment of intercultural competence, has drawn national and international attention, and her intercultural competence models developed through the research are being used by organizations and postsecondary institutions worldwide. She was recently nominated as a "Rising Star in Academia" for the *Chronicle of Higher Education* and is a Member of the International Academy of Intercultural Research. Her research interests include intercultural competence, outcomes assessment, internationalization, and teacher education. She has lived and worked in Germany, Japan, and Switzerland.

About the Contributors

Ran An is currently Professor and Dean of the School of International Education at the South China University of Technology in Guangzhou, China. She received her doctoral degree at the University of Reading on the topic of "Learning in Two Languages and Cultures: The Experiences of Mainland Chinese Families in Britain" in 1999. Her main research interests are in multicultural education and intercultural communication. Currently, she is the principal investigator of several national research projects on the intercultural communication competence of international students and teaching staff in China. Her publications are in the areas of cultural awareness, educational marketing, teaching Chinese as a foreign language, and intercultural communication.

Rohini Anand is Senior Vice President and Global Chief Diversity Officer for Sodexo, a leading provider of food and facilities management services with $20 billion in annual revenue and 355,000 employees in 80 countries. Dr. Anand is responsible for the overall strategic direction, implementation, and alignment of Sodexo's integrated global diversity initiatives including sustainable development and corporate citizenship strategies. In North America, Dr. Anand was responsible for developing the organization's workforce diversity strategy, launching sustained culture change initiatives, implementing a comprehensive learning strategy, and introducing a "diversity scorecard" that links managers' diversity achievement with their annual compensation. Widely considered a leading expert on organizational change and diversity and inclusion, Dr. Anand has authored several manuals and has been published in numerous trade journals. In addition, she has been the recipient of many prestigious awards and honors including the 2009 Women's Foodservice Forum *Trailblazer Award*, the Maryland *International Business Leadership Award*, and the American Institute for Managing Diversity's *Individual Leader Award*.

Mark A. Ashwill is country director of the Institute of International Education (IIE) in Vietnam with offices in Hanoi and Ho Chi Minh City (HCMC). He earned his PhD in Comparative and Higher Education from the Department of Educational Leadership and Policy at the State University of New York at Buffalo (SUNY/Buffalo). In 2003, he became the first U.S. American to be awarded a Fulbright Senior Specialists Grant to Vietnam. He has written widely on issues related to Vietnam, U.S.-Vietnam relations, Vietnamese studying overseas, international student access and equity, and the development of intercultural competence. His most recent book, *Vietnam Today: A Guide to a Nation at a Crossroads* (with Thai Ngoc Diep), was published in 2005.

Prior to moving to Vietnam, he was an administrator, instructor, and Fulbright adviser at SUNY/Buffalo. He has studied, taught, and conducted research in Germany, the United States, and Vietnam.

Janet M. Bennett is Executive Director and cofounder of the Intercultural Communication Institute and Director of the Master of Arts in Intercultural Relations jointly sponsored by ICI and the University of the Pacific. Her PhD is from the University of Minnesota, where she specialized in intercultural communication and anthropology. For 12 years, she was Chair of the Liberal Arts Division at Marylhurst College, where she created innovative academic programs for adult degree students. As a trainer and consultant, she specializes in developing intercultural competence programs, both domestically and internationally, for colleges and universities, corporations, legal organizations, social service agencies, international relief nongovernmental organizations (NGOs), and professional associations. She teaches in the training and development program at Portland State University and publishes in the area of intercultural training and adjustment processes. She recently coedited *The Handbook of Intercultural Training,* 3rd edition (2004).

Derek Bok is the 300th Anniversary University Professor, University President Emeritus, and Faculty Chair of the Hauser Center for Nonprofit Organizations. He has been a lawyer and Professor of Law, Dean of the Law School, and President of Harvard University (1971–1991). After 15 years away from the Harvard presidency, Bok returned to lead the university as interim president on July 1, 2006. He was succeeded by Drew Gilpin Faust on July 1, 2007. He has written six books on higher education: *Beyond the Ivory Tower, Higher Learning, Universities and the Future of America, The Shape of the River, Universities in the Marketplace,* and *Our Underachieving Colleges.* He serves as Chair of the Board of the Spencer Foundation and was formerly Chair of Common Cause. His current research interests include the state of higher education and a project sponsored by several foundations on the adequacy of the U.S. government in coping with the nation's domestic problems. His two books on this subject are *The State of the Nation* and *The Trouble With Government.* He has served on the Board of Trustees of the World Resources Institute, the University of Massachusetts, and Chair of the Board of Overseers of the Curtis Institute of Music in Philadelphia. In 1999, he became the National Chair of Common Cause, a position he held until 2006. He is presently Chair of the Spencer Foundation and Faculty Chair of the Hauser Center for the study of nonprofit organizations and philanthropy at Harvard.

Michael Byram is Professor Emeritus, School of Education at the University of Durham, England. After reading modern and medieval languages at King's College Cambridge, he wrote a dissertation on Danish literature and then taught French and German at the secondary school level and in adult education in an English comprehensive community school. After being appointed to a post in teacher education at the University of Durham in 1980, he carried out research into the education of linguistic minorities and foreign language education. Publications include *Teaching and Assessing Intercultural Communicative Competence* and *From Foreign Language Education to Education for Intercultural Citizenship.* He is the editor of the *Routledge*

Encyclopedia of Language Teaching and Learning. He is an Adviser to the Council of Europe Language Policy Division and is currently interested in language education policy and the politics of language teaching.

Gabrielle Changnon received her MA in the School of Communication at San Diego State University in May 2008 and continues to pursue consulting and human resources applications of communication expertise in the private sector.

Guo-Ming Chen is Professor of Communication Studies at the University of Rhode Island. He was the recipient of the 1987 outstanding dissertation award presented by the SCA International and Intercultural Communication Division. He is the founding president of the Association for Chinese Communication Studies. He served as Chair of the ECA Intercultural Communication Interest Group and the coeditor of *International and Intercultural Communication Annual.* In addition to serving as an editorial board member of several professional journals, he is the Executive Director of the International Association for Intercultural Communication Studies and the coeditor of *China Media Research.* His primary research interests are in intercultural/organizational/global communication. He has published numerous articles, books, book chapters, and essays. Those books include *Foundations of Intercultural Communication, Introduction to Human Communication, Communication and Global Society, Chinese Conflict Management and Resolution,* and *Theories and Principles of Chinese Communication.*

Kenneth Cushner, Professor of Education at Kent State University, is author or editor of several publications in the field of intercultural education and training, including *Human Diversity in Education: An Integrative Approach,* 6th ed. (2009); *Intercultural Student Teaching: A Bridge to Global Competence* (2007); and *Intercultural Interactions: A Practical Guide,* 2nd ed. (with Richard Brislin, 1996). He is a Founding Fellow of the International Academy for Intercultural Research (IAIR), President of IAIR (2007–2009), and past Director of the Consortium for Overseas Student Teaching. He has developed and led intercultural programs on all seven continents and consults with school districts and social service agencies across the United States.

Alvino E. Fantini holds graduate degrees in anthropology and applied linguistics and has been involved in intercultural communication and language education (ESOL and Foreign Languages) for over 40 years. He has worked in the United States and abroad, in education and training, in field situations and in academia, and with a variety of languages and cultures. He has conducted significant research and published widely, including *Language Acquisition of a Bilingual Child* and *New Ways in Teaching Culture.* He served on a National Advisory Panel to develop National Foreign Language Standards for U.S. education. He is past president of the prestigious professional society, SIETAR International (the Society for Intercultural Education, Training, and Research), and recipient of its highest award. Currently, he is Professor Emeritus at World Learning's SIT Graduate Institute in Brattleboro, Vermont, on the graduate faculty at Matsuyama University in Japan, and serves as an international consultant.

Rowena Fong, graduate of Harvard University, University of Berkeley, and Wellesley College, is the Ruby Lee Piester Centennial Professor in Services to Children and Families at the University of Texas at Austin. Her research interests are immigrants and refugees, child welfare, international adoptions, Chinese American children and families, and culturally competent practice. Author of more than 100 publications, she has written *Culturally Competent Practice: Skills, Interventions, and Evaluations* (coauthor Sharlene Furuto, 2001); *Intersecting Child Welfare, Substance Abuse, and Family Violence: Culturally Competent Approaches* (coauthors Ruth McRoy and Carmen Ortiz Hendricks, 2006); and *Culturally Competent Practice With Immigrant and Refugee Children and Families* (2004). She is also the recipient of the Council on Social Work Education 2008 Award for Distinguished Recent Contributions in Social Work Education and the University of Texas at Austin 2007 Texas Exes Teaching Award.

Matthew L. Goode is a Program Director in the International Programs office at the Carlson School of Management, University of Minnesota. His master's research focused on the role of study abroad faculty directors and was published in *Frontiers: The Interdisciplinary Journal of Study Abroad* (Winter 2007–2008). His master's degree is from the University of Minnesota, where he is currently a doctoral student in Comparative and International Development Education.

John M. Grandin is Professor of German and Director of the International Engineering Program at the University of Rhode Island, an interdisciplinary curriculum, through which students complete simultaneous degrees (BA and BS) in German, French, Spanish, or Chinese and in an engineering discipline. He has received numerous awards for his work combining languages and engineering, including the Federal Cross of Honor from the Federal Republic of Germany, the Award for Educational Innovation from ABET, and the Michael P. Malone Award for Excellence in International Education from NASULGC, the National Association of State Universities and Land Grant Colleges. He has published widely on such cross-disciplinary initiatives and has been the principal investigator for several funded projects related to the development of the International Engineering Program. He also organizes and hosts an Annual Colloquium on International Engineering Education, bringing together university faculty and business representatives to develop a more global engineering education nationally (http://uri.edu/iep).

Norbert Hedderich teaches German at the University of Rhode Island, where he also serves as Director of the German Summer School of the Atlantic. He teaches all levels of courses in the undergraduate German curriculum from introductory German language to courses in German for the professions as well as seminars on Business German and Linguistic Variations of German. His areas of scholarly interests include Language for Special Purposes, Language Learning Methodology, Language Learning Technology, and Intercultural Communication. He has published articles in *Die Unterrichtspraxis/Teaching German, Global Business Languages, The NECTFL Review, Schatzkammer,* and the *Journal of Language for International Business.* He is a member of the editorial board of *Dimension,* the annual journal of the Southern Conference on Language Teaching (SCOLT), and is coeditor of the

Online Journal for Global Engineering Education (OJGEE). His doctorate is from Purdue University.

Gert Jan Hofstede is Associate Professor at Wageningen University, Social Science department, and Delft University, Man-Machine Interaction, both in the Netherlands. He is also a guest lecturer at universities in several countries. He holds an MSc in population biology and a doctorate in information modeling from Wageningen University. His interests can be summarized as the cultural biology of organization, with research interests including organizational behavior, cross-cultural management, information management, trust and transparency across organizations, and the evolution of culture. He is a well-known speaker for varied types of audiences and in several continents and languages. He is also a creator of simulation games that tease out basic elements of human behavior. He is one of the authors of *Exploring Culture* (2002), *Hide or Confide* (2004), *Cultures and Organizations* (2nd ed., 2005), and *Why Do Games Work?* (2008).

Young Yun Kim is a Professor of Communication at the University of Oklahoma in Norman and has her PhD from Northwestern University. Investigating theoretical issues of cross-cultural adaptation and of associative/dissociative interethnic communication, she has conducted original research among Asian and Hispanic immigrants as well as native-born Americans, including American Indians. Her published works consist of over 90 book chapters and journal articles, along with 12 books, including *Communication and Cross-Cultural Adaptation* (1988), *Becoming Intercultural* (2001), and *Communicating With Strangers* (4th ed., 2003, with W. B. Gudykunst). She has served on the editorial boards of 11 academic journals, including *Communication Research, Journal of Communication, Human Communication Research, International and Intercultural Communication Annual,* and *International Journal of Intercultural Relations.* She is a Fellow of the International Communication Association, a Founding Fellow of the International Academy for Intercultural Relations, and a recipient of Top Scholar Award for Lifetime Achievement in Intercultural Communication.

Indra Lahiri is the author of *Creating a Competency Model for Diversity and Inclusion Practitioners* (2008) and *Brown Eyes, Blue Eyes: Linking Perceptions and Performance* (2002). As the founder of Global Inclusion Strategies, she provides strategic diversity/inclusion consultation, coaching, and support to executive leadership of major global corporations. Success is evident in measurable results for client organizations, including reduced turnover and increased employee engagement. Clients have routinely received awards and recognition for their diversity and inclusion success. Combining personal multicultural experience and academic knowledge of cultural differences, Indra Lahiri provides realistic consultation and support for organizations wishing to shift from merely having an international presence to being truly global. She holds a doctorate in organizational psychology and graduate certificates in Human Resource Management from Cornell University and Women's Studies from the University of Pennsylvania.

Kwok Leung is a Chair Professor of Management at City University of Hong Kong. His research areas include justice and conflict, cross-cultural research methods, social axioms, and international business. He is a senior editor of *Management and Organization Review,* the president-elect of the International Association for Cross-Cultural Psychology, and a former chair of the Research Methods Division of Academy of Management. He is a fellow of Academy of International Business, Academy of Intercultural Research, and Association for Psychological Science. He received his PhD from the University of Illinois, Urbana-Champaign.

Jennifer Mahon is an Assistant Professor of Sociocultural Education at the University of Nevada, Reno. Her work focuses on the development of intercultural awareness among educators, especially how their notions of conflict affect that understanding. Growing out of the critical tradition, she examines the ways in which cross-cultural and cross-disciplinary experiences can affect change and how institutional norms and structures become barriers to growth. She holds her master's and doctoral degrees from Kent State University, with undergraduate study at the University of Dayton (United States) and the University of New England (Australia). She is a Junior Fellow with the International Academy of Intercultural Research and has lived and worked as an educator in Australia, England, and Costa Rica.

Ranjini Manian is Founder–CEO of Global Adjustments Services Pvt Ltd, India's premier relocation, realty, and cross-cultural services company. She holds a bachelor's degree from Elphinstone College, Mumbai, and a Diploma in French Literature from the University of Sorbonne, Paris. She has worked with thousands of clients from over 70 nationalities across six Indian cities. She has trained several thousands of Indian professionals to become global citizens as well. She has authored *Doing Business in India for Dummies,* writes regular columns in leading business dailies, and is a sought-after speaker. She has co-chaired the Worldwide Employee Relocation Council's Global Workforce Symposium and received its ERC Meritorious Service award. She is the only Indian on the Women's leadership Board at Harvard University.

Adriana Medina-López-Portillo is Assistant Professor of Intercultural Communication and Spanish in the Department of Modern Languages, Linguistics, and Intercultural Communication at the University of Maryland Baltimore County (UMBC). Her research focuses on intercultural competencies and intercultural sensitivity development, study abroad, and Latin American culture. She graduated with a master's degree in Intercultural Communication and a doctoral degree in Language, Literacy, and Culture with a concentration on Intercultural Communication, both from UMBC. In addition, she is Associate Faculty at the Summer Institute of Intercultural Communication (SIIC) in Portland, Oregon. As an intercultural and diversity trainer, she offers workshops to institutions, organizations, and corporations. The focus of the trainings ranges from intercultural competencies and sensitivity development to conflict and diversity management to staff training and team building.

Alois Moosmüller is a Full Professor of Intercultural Communication and Cultural Anthropology at Munich University, Germany. His current research is on transnational networks of business people sent abroad. He has done research on religious and social movements in Indonesia, on the German-Japanese and the

American-Japanese collaboration in multinational companies in Japan, and on expatriate communities in Japan, Indonesia, and Mexico. From 1992 to 1997, he was professor at the Keio University in Tokyo, Japan, where he taught intercultural communication. He received his PhD in cultural anthropology at Munich University and his Habilitation (postdoctoral qualification) in cultural anthropology and intercultural communication at the University Fribourg, Switzerland. He is also an intercultural trainer and consultant who works with international transferees and teams in multinational companies.

Robert T. Moran, PhD, is a Professor of Global Management, Emeritus, at the Thunderbird School of Global Management. He has designed and conducted executive seminars for Saudi Aramco, General Motors, Toyota, Intel, Motorola, Honeywell, Novartis, Bayer, and Singapore Airlines, among others. He has also been a faculty member in executive education programs at Babson, ESSEC (in Paris), Emory, Penn State, SMU, Stanford, MIT, and Wharton.

Sarah V. Moran is a PhD student of Organizational Behavior at McGill University, Desautels Faculty of Management. She has a background in Psychology (BS) and Organizational Communication (MA). Currently in Canada, she has also lived in the United States, France, Taiwan, and South Korea. While in Taipei, Taiwan, she worked as the education adviser for the Fulbright Foundation and as liaison between the American Institute in Taiwan and the Fulbright Office. An up-and-coming scholar, she has coauthored one book, *Managing Cultural Differences: Global Leadership Strategies for the 21st Century* (2004 and 2007), and an in-press article on active procrastination in the *Journal of Social Psychology*. Her current research interests include global leadership strategies, cross-cultural management, and stakeholder impact on project implementation, management, and completion in international nonprofit organizations.

Shobha Naidu is Senior Manager in Global Adjustments Cross-Cultural Services in Bengaluru, India. Her responsibilities include understanding customer needs in training, customization of content, and delivery with the help of her team of cross-cultural specialist trainers. She has an MPhil in development studies from Geneva and is proficient in French. She has worked as a cultural and language interpreter in France and in India, with university students, corporate houses, and foundations on the issues of corporate social responsibility. Having lived and worked in several countries, she appreciates the need for greater sensitivity toward other cultures in a globalized work environment.

Peter Ogom Nwosu is American Council on Education (ACE) Fellow in the Office of the President at Tennessee State University, Nashville (at the time of this writing). As ACE Fellow, he served on the President's senior leadership team as strategic planning fellow, and provided leadership and oversight in developing the university's 2010–2015 integrative strategic plan. At California State University, Northridge, where he is tenured full professor, he serves as special assistant to the provost and vice president for academic affairs on diversity initiatives. A communication studies professor and former chair of the Council of Chairs, a body (comprising of department heads) that advises the provost on academic planning and implementation, he has served as chair of the department of communication studies and the department of urban studies and planning respectively, and on numerous policy-making committees and advisory councils at the university. He received his PhD in Human Communication Studies from Howard University, and has authored more than 60 scholarly writings and presentations, including three books, book chapters, journal articles, trade publications, and conference presentations. His articles have appeared in the *International Journal of Intercultural Relations* and the *Howard Journal of Communications,* among others. He is also editor-in-chief of *Africa Media Review.* His most recent book, *Beyond Race: A New Vision of Community in America* (2009) looks at race, communication, and public policy in America. A nationally recognized expert on multicultural issues, communication training, and development, he has provided consultation and technical support to numerous agencies on strategies for managing workplace differences. He has directed and participated in sponsored research and programs of the U.S. Department of Education, the African Development Foundation, the World Bank, the U.S. Institute of Peace, and the Council for the Development of Social Science Research in Africa. His work has taken him to more than 25 countries.

Du'o'ng Thị Hoàng Oanh obtained her master's degree in TESOL at Canberra University, Australia and her PhD in Applied Linguistics at Victoria University of Wellington, New Zealand. She finished her Post Doctoral Fellowship in Higher Education Management at Yale University. She is a lecturer and Associate Director of the Office for International Cooperation of Hue University, Vietnam. Formerly, she was the Dean of the International Studies Department and also Dean of the English Department. Her interests include cross-cultural studies, educational reforms, curriculum design, learner autonomy, and classroom practices. She has won national and international grants and awards for research on educational reforms, higher education management, and assessment. She has chaired and presented papers at many international conferences. Her publications include chapters for books and articles on learner autonomy, needs assessment, community values and classroom dynamics, and images of Vietnamese women.

R. Michael Paige is a Professor of International and Intercultural Education in the Department of Educational Policy and Administration at the University of Minnesota, Minneapolis. A returned U.S. Peace Corps Volunteer (Turkey, 1965–1967), he has also lived and worked in Indonesia, Thailand, the Philippines, Kenya, and Hong Kong. In 2003–2004, he was a visiting professor at Nagoya University and at the University of South Australia. An active scholar, he has authored numerous books and articles, including *Maximizing Study Abroad: A Student's Guide to Strategies for Language and Culture Learning and Use* (Paige et al., 2006), *Culture as the Core: Perspectives on Culture in Second Language Learning* (Lange and Paige, 2003), and *Education for the Intercultural Experience* (Paige, 1993). He has served on the faculty of the Summer Institute for Intercultural Communication since 1979 and coedits the training section of the *International Journal of Intercultural Relations* (*IJIR*).

Paul B. Pedersen is a Visiting Professor in the Department of Psychology at the University of Hawaii and Professor Emeritus from Syracuse University. He has taught at the University of Minnesota, Syracuse University, University of Alabama at Birmingham, and for six years at universities in Taiwan, Malaysia, and Indonesia. He was also on the Summer School Faculty at Harvard University, 1984–1988, and the University of Pittsburgh—Semester at Sea voyage around the world, spring 1992. International experience includes numerous consulting experiences in Asia, Australia, Africa, South America, and Europe and a Senior Fulbright award teaching at National Taiwan University, 1999–2000. He has authored, coauthored, or edited 40 books, 99 articles, and 72 chapters on aspects of multicultural counseling and international communication. He holds a PhD from Claremont Graduate School.

Margaret (Peggy) Pusch is Executive Director of SIETAR-USA (Society for International Education, Training, and Research–USA); Associate Director of The Intercultural Communication Institute, Portland, Oregon; and an intercultural trainer. She cofounded and was President of The Intercultural Press, Inc. for over 15 years. She serves as Chair of the Board of Trustees of the International Partnership for Service Learning and Leadership, was President of NAFSA: Association of International Educators (1995–1996), and was President (2000–2003) of SIETAR and is on the faculty of the Summer Institute for Intercultural Communication. Her most recent publications include "Reflection, Reciprocity, Responsibility, and Committed Relativism" with Martha Merrill in *Developing Intercultural Competence and Transformation* (2008); "Dual Career Transitions," a response to an incident, in *Case Incidents in Counseling for International Transition* (2008); and "Intercultural Training in Historical Perspective" in *Handbook of Intercultural Training,* 3rd ed. (2004).

Eduardo S. Rodela has been an independent organizational development (OD) practitioner for over 25 years. He is interested in the relationship between organizational characteristics and employee well-being and has consulted in both the private and public sectors in his OD career. His publications address issues pertaining to workplace stress and individual outcomes. He has been an adjunct professor (over 17 years) with the School of Social Work, Virginia Commonwealth University, where he teaches research methodology. He holds a PhD from the University of Michigan.

Michael Schönhuth is an Associate Professor of Cultural Anthropology at the University of Trier, Germany. He is also an acting director in the Cluster of Excellence, "Societal Dependencies and Social Networks," and project leader in the German Science Foundation, Branch 600, "Foreignness and Poverty." He graduated with a doctoral thesis on witchcraft in Europe and Africa. He is cofounder of the journal *Entwicklungsethnologie,* the only German-language journal on the anthropology of development. His scientific work focuses on participatory methods, migration, social networks, diversity, culture and development, and intercultural issues, and since the 1990s, he has served as a consultant with governmental and nongovernmental agencies and foundations in these fields.

John H. Sinnigen is a Professor of Spanish and Intercultural Communication at the University of Maryland, Baltimore. A recipient of a PhD in Romance Languages from the Johns Hopkins University, in his research and teaching, he focuses on the intersections of cultural, economic, and political forces and the ways they unfold in a world historical process, particularly in Latin America and Spain. The author of four books and 50 articles, he is quite taken with the new opportunities in Latin

America that are related to the advances made by primarily indigenous social movements.

Brian H. Spitzberg is Professor in the School of Communication at San Diego State University. His areas of research include interpersonal communication competence, communication skills assessment, computer-mediated communication, conflict management, jealousy, infidelity, intimate violence, sexual coercion, and stalking. He is author or coauthor of three scholarly books, coeditor of three scholarly books, and author or coauthor of numerous scholarly articles and chapters. He holds a PhD from the University of Southern California.

Craig Storti has over 30 years of experience as an intercultural trainer and consultant, with wide experience in the government, business, and education sectors. His clients include numerous *Fortune* 500 companies, leading business schools, and international organizations such as the United Nations and the World Bank. He is the author of seven books in the intercultural field, including *The Art of Crossing Cultures, Cross-Cultural Dialogues, Americans at Work,* and his newest book, *Speaking of India* (2007). He can be reached at craig@craigstorti.com.

Stella Ting-Toomey is a Professor of Human Communication Studies at California State University, Fullerton. Her teaching passions include intercultural conflict management and intercultural communication training. Her research interests have focused on testing and fine-tuning the conflict face negotiation theory and the cultural/ethnic identity negotiation theory. She is the author and editor of 17 books. Her most recent book includes *The SAGE Handbook of Conflict Communication* (coedited with John Oetzel). She has published more than 90 journal articles and chapters in academic journals and monographs. She has delivered keynote speeches on the theme of transcultural communication competence in South Africa, Portugal, Germany, Norway, China, Japan, Canada, and different regions of the United States. She is also the 2008 recipient of the Cal State University Wang Family Excellence Award and the CSU-Fullerton Outstanding Professor Award in recognition for her contributions to teaching, research, and service. She holds a PhD from the University of Washington.

Joseph E. Trimble, formerly a Fellow at Harvard University's Radcliffe Institute for Advanced Study, is Professor of Psychology at Western Washington University and a Research Associate for the National Center for American Indian and Alaska Native Mental Health Research at the University of Colorado Health Sciences Center. He has generated over 130 publications on cross-cultural and ethnic topics in psychology, including 17 books. He has received 20 excellences in teaching, research, and service awards for his work in the field of ethnic and cultural psychology, including the Janet E. Helms Award for Mentoring and Scholarship in Professional Psychology at Teachers College, Columbia University. He holds a PhD from the University of Oklahoma.

Fons Trompenaars is the world's foremost authority and keynote speaker on cross-cultural management. He studied economics at the Free University of Amsterdam and later earned a PhD from Wharton School, University of Pennsylvania, with a dissertation on differences in conceptions of organizational structure in various cultures. He experienced cultural differences firsthand at home, where he grew up speaking both French and Dutch, and then later at work with Shell in nine countries. In 1989, he founded the Centre for International Business Studies (now Trompenaars Hampden-Turner Consulting), a global consulting and training organization for international management with partners Charles Hampden-Turner and later Peter Woolliams. Dr. Trompenaars's first book, *Riding the Waves of Culture: Understanding Cultural Diversity in Business,* sold over 150,000 copies and was translated into French, German, Dutch, Korean, Danish, Turkish, Chinese, Hungarian, and Portuguese. He has recently published *Riding the Whirlwind* and *Servant Leadership Across Cultures* as well as coauthoring other books with a focus on culture and business.

Michael Vande Berg is Vice President for Academic Affairs at the Council on International Educational Exchange (CIEE). He received his PhD in Comparative Literature from the University of Illinois at Urbana-Champaign. He has served on the Board of the Association of Academic Programs in Latin America and the Caribbean and is also a founding board member of the Forum on Education Abroad. He has authored numerous publications on international education topics and on literary movements and authors and has published English-language translations of two Spanish novels. He has served as principal investigator of a wide variety of study abroad research projects, including the "Georgetown Consortium" study; was Outside Consultant and evaluator of the University of Minnesota Curriculum Integration project; and was Guest Editor of a special assessment issue of *Frontiers: The Interdisciplinary Journal of Study Abroad.* He frequently speaks with faculty and staff or leads training workshops about international education topics and he has served on the faculty of the Summer Institute for Intercultural Communication since 2007.

Fons J. R. Van de Vijver has studied psychology at Tilburg University in the Netherlands. He holds a PhD from the same university (1991). He holds a chair in cross-cultural psychology at Tilburg University, the Netherlands; in addition, he is extraordinary professor at North-West University, South Africa. He is the past editor-in-chief of the *Journal of Cross-Cultural Psychology.* He is on the board of the *European Journal of Psychological Assessment,* the *International Journal of Testing,* and the *Asian Psychologist;* he has evaluated manuscripts for about 50 journals as ad hoc reviewer. He has published over 275 publications, mainly in the domain of cross-cultural psychology. An important theme in his work is the comparability of test scores obtained in different countries. Another important theme in his work involves psychological acculturation and multiculturalism. He has field experience in Southern Africa, Libya, and Turkey.

Peter Woolliams, PhD, is Emeritus Professor of International Management at Anglia Ruskin University (UK) and is an owner/partner in Trompenaars Hampden–Turner Consulting. His earlier work was on computer-based corporate models and simulation studies for business strategy development and formulation. His collaboration with Fons Trompenaars has been to support the development of the cross-culture and knowledge management databases and their reliability and consistency through extensive rigorous analysis and the development of associated diagnostic Web-based tools. He has collaborated and published jointly with Fons over some

19 years and is coauthor with Fons for *Business Across Cultures* (available in several languages) and *Marketing Across Cultures* (2004).

George Yancey is Professor of Sociology at the University of North Texas. He has a PhD from the University of Texas at Austin. He has published several research articles and books on the topics of interracial marriage and multiracial churches. He also wrote *Who Is White?*, a book that explores the effects of the alienation that African Americans have experienced in our society, and *One Body, One Spirit: Principles of Successful Multiracial Churches*, which is based on data from a landmark Lilly Endowment study. His current book is *Interracial Contact and Social Change*, which takes a comprehensive look at the potential of interracial contact to alter racial reality in the United States. He also has coauthored books entitled *Multiracial Families* and *United by Faith*. His current research projects include an investigation of the racial atmosphere on Protestant campuses and assessments into which colleges do a better job attracting and/or retaining disadvantaged students of color.

William E. Youngdahl is an Associate Professor of Project & Operations Management at the Thunderbird School of Global Management. He received his PhD in Business Administration and MS in Systems Management from the University of Southern California and a BS in Mechanical Engineering Technology from Cal Poly, Pomona. He is also a certified Project Management Professional (PMP) and has developed and delivered executive education programs in areas of global project leadership, leadership, and service excellence for clients around the globe. He is widely published in leading academic journals and coauthored (with Robert Moran) a trade book titled *Leading Global Projects: For Professional and Accidental Project Leaders*.

R. S. Zaharna is an Associate Professor of Public Communication at the School of Communication, American University in Washington, D.C. She specializes in strategic communication theory and intercultural public communication. In addition to 20 years of teaching strategic communication, she has advised on communication projects for multinational corporations, nongovernmental organizations, diplomatic missions, and international organizations. She holds an undergraduate degree in Foreign Service from Georgetown University and graduate degrees in Communication from Columbia University and is author of *Strategic US Public Diplomacy in a Global Communication Era*.

Supporting researchers for more than 40 years

Research methods have always been at the core of SAGE's publishing program. Founder Sara Miller McCune published SAGE's first methods book, *Public Policy Evaluation*, in 1970. Soon after, she launched the *Quantitative Applications in the Social Sciences* series—affectionately known as the "little green books."

Always at the forefront of developing and supporting new approaches in methods, SAGE published early groundbreaking texts and journals in the fields of qualitative methods and evaluation.

Today, more than 40 years and two million little green books later, SAGE continues to push the boundaries with a growing list of more than 1,200 research methods books, journals, and reference works across the social, behavioral, and health sciences. Its imprints—Pine Forge Press, home of innovative textbooks in sociology, and Corwin, publisher of PreK–12 resources for teachers and administrators—broaden SAGE's range of offerings in methods. SAGE further extended its impact in 2008 when it acquired CQ Press and its best-selling and highly respected political science research methods list.

From qualitative, quantitative, and mixed methods to evaluation, SAGE is the essential resource for academics and practitioners looking for the latest methods by leading scholars.

For more information, visit **www.sagepub.com**.